Plan de la Nouvelle Orleans, Ville Capitalle de la Province de la Louissianne, by Dumont de Montigny. Archives Nationales, Paris. Reproduced from the collection of the Library of Congress, Washington, D.C. The plan illustrates Chemin au Bayou St Jean as it appeared to Dumont about 1732. The large palisaded complex to the left of the Chemin is the brickyard of the Company of the Indies, sold to Charles de Morand in 1731 when the company reverted to the French Crown.

NEW ORLEANS ARCHITECTURE

VOLUME VI
Faubourg Tremé and the Bayou Road

2257 Bayou Road (Governor Nicholls)

NEW ORLEANS ARCHITECTURE

VOLUME VI

Faubourg Tremé and the Bayou Road

North Rampart Street to North Broad Street
Canal Street to St. Bernard Avenue

Authors:
ROULHAC TOLEDANO
MARY LOUISE CHRISTOVICH

Photographers:
BETSY SWANSON
ROBIN von BRETON DERBES

PELICAN PUBLISHING COMPANY
GRETNA 1980

Manufactured in the United States of America
Published by Pelican Publishing Company, Inc.
630 Burmaster Street, Gretna, Louisiana 70053
Designed by Barney McKee

Library of Congress Cataloging in Publication Data (Revised)

Friends of the Cabildo.
    New Orleans architecture.

    Includes bibliographies and indexes.
    CONTENTS: v. 1. The Lower Garden District.—v. 2. The
American sector (Faubourg St. Mary)—v. 3. The
cemeteries.—v. 4. The Creole Faubourgs. [etc.]
    1. Architecture—New Orleans. 2. New Orleans—
Buildings. I. Wilson, Samuel, 1911–
II. Christovich, Mary Louise, ed. III. Title
NA735.N4F74   1971   720'.9763'35   72–172272
ISBN 0–88289–166–9 (v. 6)

CONTENTS

1133 Bayou Road (Governor Nicholls)

FOREWORD

The Friends of the Cabildo and the Louisiana State Museum have been a team since 1954. The necessity of bringing professionalism to one of the nation's most important regional history museums catapulted the private, nonprofit Friends into a combative existence. Many stormy years are part of its history, as are efforts to communicate between boards, politicians, and citizens in order to establish a philosophy for the museum's progress. Success is the result when, twenty-six years later, a list of accomplishments by the volunteer group includes raising over six million dollars in state and federal funds for restoration of museum properties: the Presbytère (1964), the Cabildo (1970), the Creole House (1974), Madame John's Legacy (1975). The 1850 House, located in the lower Pontalba building, was redecorated and refurbished (having been opened to the public through the efforts of the Friends in 1955) in the fall of 1978. The Old U.S. Mint building, the Jackson House, and the Arsenal are scheduled for completion in 1980.

These eight buildings form the network of historic structures that are the Louisiana State Museum. Their dates range between 1795 and 1865. The collections housed within, including the French and Spanish records, are the nucleus of Louisiana history from the earliest days of the eighteenth century. The nineteenth century is chronicled with artifacts, costumes, and the largest portrait collection in the South. Recognizing the importance of the buildings and the collections to the city, state, and nation, the Friends have dedicated these past years to the protection and improvement of each. Thousands of Louisianians have been introduced to their past and have had their knowledge reinforced through the organization's educational programs, seminars, exhibitions, and tours.

Moving within the museum's scope but beyond its properties, the Friends in 1969 donned activist garb to record and inform the city of the importance of its architecture to its history. Surveys to identify and evaluate these historic resources were undertaken by a large group of volunteers under the direction of members of the board of directors. First, the neighborhoods were defined; then, buildings selected and photographed. Through present addresses, ownership titles were run; analysis of data and architectural elements were synthesized; and again through combined efforts, a text was written to register in an orderly fashion the true significance of each neighborhood.

This assessment of neighborhood building types revealed New Orleans' rich architectural diversity. The two- or three-story, side-hall, galleried, frame and brick houses are reflective of *The Lower Garden District*. Its story was revealed in a book by that name in 1971. Elegant, nineteenth-century, multileveled brick townhouses and four-level, brick commercial rows replaced French and Spanish creole cottages in *The American Sector*, Faubourg Ste Marie; this volume was published in 1973. The history of thirty-one *New Orleans Cemeteries* was released the following year. Their importance as integrated spaces throughout the city, each containing art and architecture exhibiting the preferences and tastes of eighteenth- and nineteenth-century New Orleanians, was emphasized.

The Creole Faubourgs (1975) revealed that house and building types and styles were all-inclusive and representative of New Orleans' vast architectural forum. *The Esplanade Ridge*, published in 1977, is the story of a street stretching 3.3 miles between the Mississippi River and Bayou St. John. The narrow avenue forms a luxurious boundary to thirty-six former plantations, all of nineteenth-century importance. After the unveiling of each volume, exhibitions and lectures provided the museum with current topics of interest to the city.

Volunteers, most associated with the Friends, participated in the educational programs and formation of new preservation organizations, such as the Lower Garden

District Association, the Central Business District Improvement Association, Save Our Cemeteries, Faubourg Marigny Association, and the Esplanade Improvement Association. The Preservation Resource Center quickly followed with the mandate to coordinate the many neighborhood groups and implement the Friends of the Cabildo's city-wide "Building Watchers" street tours.

It is with great pride that the organization which provides thousands of dollars each year to the museum for conservation and acquisitions continues to furnish, at no expense to the city, an inventory of its historic neighborhoods. Many civic-minded individuals have contributed to the expenses of these former publications, but for the present volume a federal grant from the National Endowment for the Arts was received. Congresswoman Lindy Boggs was a front-runner in assisting the Friends in obtaining the N.E.A. grant; she was assisted by Congressman David Treen and Louisiana's two senators, Russell B. Long and J. Bennett Johnston. The resulting book has taken five years and the efforts of many volunteers. The two dedicated authors, Roulhac Toledano and Mary Louise Christovich, both board members of the Friends and volunteers in this project, join with me in a heartfelt expression of appreciation. Special recognition for the early efforts goes to Emay Baird, who took windshield descriptions for the initial survey. Alison Kimball Hoagland's knowledge of French and superb organizational abilities enabled her to run over two hundred house titles, collating through existing addresses information gathered from theses, will books, newspapers, and census lists. Bobbie Sontheimer's organizational and research abilities were an integral part of the compilation of information. Ann Gunderson Conroy, having absorbed the *Chicago Manual of Style*, copyread and corrected the manuscript. The organization is also grateful to the following persons:

Richard B. Allen, director, William Ransom Hogan Jazz Archives, Tulane University
Eugenie Wilson Alsobrook, copy reading
Bonnie Baird, house analysis
Kathryn W. Barnett, typing, copy reading
William C. Belote, field research
Betty Bird, NEA grants assistance
Pam Bowen, typing
Marie Elise Christovich, title research
Michael Mossy Christovich, legal research
Ann Gunderson Conroy, editing
Ernest Crayton, New Orleans Notarial Archives
Irving Crayton, New Orleans Notarial Archives
Boyd Cruise, Historic New Orleans Collection
L. J. Dahlman, Dahlman-Junod Map and Manuscript Collection
Ron Domin, draftsman
Wayne M. Eberhard, New Orleans Public Library, research
Sally Evans, title research
Fenella Castanedo Farrington, Spanish colonial research
Judy Faust, photography
Rosemarie Fowler, editing
Marcus Fraser, photography
Stanton Frazar, director, Historic New Orleans Collection
Thelma Fricke, library research
Esmond Grosz, library research

Natalie Grosz, library research
William Markwith Grote, photography, New Orleans Notarial Archives
Collin Hamer, Louisiana Division, New Orleans Public Library
Clive Hardy, Rare Book Room, University of New Orleans
Alicia Moody Heard, research
Danny Hero, library research
Alison Kimball Hoagland, research, French manuscript translations, 250 property titles
Jack D. L. Holmes, Spanish colonial history
Stanley Hordes, Louisiana State Museum Archives
Robin Woody Ingram, title research
Hilary Irvin, title research
John Kemp, archivist, Louisiana Historical Center
Shirley Kern, typing
Henry Krotzer, consultant on architectural style
Rose Lambert, Louisiana Historical Center
Maria Landry, research
John H. Lawrence, Historic New Orleans Collection
Jodie A. Legendre, library research
Bernard Lemann, consulting architect
Joseph Logsden, research
Robert Macdonald, director, Louisiana State Museum
John Mahé, Historic New Orleans Collection
Anne Maylie, title research

Rosanne McCaffrey, map research

Margaret McCutchen, research

Elizabeth McDermott, Louis Armstrong Park research

Aline H. Morris, Louisiana Historical Center, library research

Joanne Platou, Historic New Orleans Collection

Ghislaine Pleasanton, archivist, Louisiana Historical Center, research, translations

Beatrice Pollock, photography

James Pontillo, Department of Spanish, Tulane University, Spanish manuscript translations

Adèle Pourcine, Duchamp family history

Patricia Rittiner, field research

Robin Riley, research

Beth Woodward Ryun, research

Dorothy Schlesinger, title research

Nancy Sherar, research

Lynes Sloss, photography

Helen Michele Smith, title research

William Smither, Department of Spanish, Newcomb College, Spanish manuscript translations

Bobbie Sontheimer, title research

Dale Stewart, typing

Jack Stewart, research

Joseph Swanson, draftsman

Martha Ann Swayze, executive secretary, Friends of the Cabildo

Ben C. Toledano, research

Peter Trapolin, draftsman

Janet Urian, photography, typing, research

Kenneth Urquhart, Historic New Orleans Collection

Gypsy Van Antwerp, title research

John Walker, Walker and Avery, surveyors

Samuel Wilson, Jr., historical research and consulting architect

Janet Winkler, typing

Jackie Winter, typing

Daniel Wogan, French and Spanish manuscript translations

Guy Wootan, New Orleans Notarial Archives

Thomas B. Favrot
President
The Friends of the Cabildo, 1978–79

1100 Block Bayou Road (Governor Nicholls)

x

INTRODUCTION

Faubourg Tremé is the history of the Road to Bayou St. John or, as the French called it, Le Chemin au Bayou St. Jean. The Spanish officially referred to it as El Camino al Gran Bayou llamado San Juan. The road, trace, or portage predated the city, following a narrow strip of high land that led from the Mississippi River past Bayou Sauvage, called Gentilly, to an intersection with Bayou St. John. The portage was part of the natural levee or highland contiguous with the bayou as it curved along its way to Lake Pontchartrain. The Road was of such importance that the French and Spanish land grants outside the limits of the city were measured parallel and perpendicular to it from 1708 until the prolongment of Esplanade Avenue between 1820 and 1850. One still finds an occasional house and property line with an ancient alignment, reflecting the early history of this section.

Bayou Road, on both its left and right sides, served as frontage for a series of concessions made first by the Company of the Indies, then by the kings of France, and later, the Spanish Crown. Simultaneously to the laying out of the city by Le Blond de la Tour and Adrien de Pauger, the king's engineers, these tracts of land to the rear of the city were developed into *habitations* (plantations) with houses and outbuildings facing each side of Bayou Road, having orchards behind and cultivated fields extending to the swamps. In spite of the luxurious depths of many of these early Bayou Road *habitations*, cultivation was limited in the eighteenth century to a three-*arpent* depth (one *arpent* equals 192 feet) on each side of the Road, with the undeveloped swamps beyond. By the time of the Louisiana Purchase, many of the larger French colonial tracts had been subdivided into smaller *habitations*, or country seats, measuring from one to two *arpents* fronting on the Road, by three to fourteen *arpents* in depth.

The land was surveyed in terms of *arpents*, one of which corresponds to approximately one-half of a present city block. Along the right side of Bayou Road, land often extended to a line that followed the route of modern St. Bernard Avenue, once the upper line of the plantation owned consecutively by the Dubreuils, Sigurs, St. Maxents, and Marignys. On the left side, grants or concessions and tracts stretched in depth to the plantation of the military governor, Jean Baptiste Bienville, the boundary of which is the present-day Common Street and Tulane Avenue. The Bienville Plantation passed into the possession of the Jesuits in 1726, and subsequently during the Spanish colonial period to Madame Marie Josephe Deslondes Pradel and her second husband, Bertrand Gravier. In 1788 the section was subdivided by Carlos Laveau Trudeau and named Faubourg Ste Marie.

As the city expanded, the area from N. Rampart to N. Broad and from Common and Tulane Avenue to St. Bernard Avenue was realigned to continue the street arrangement of the old city, as seen on the Charles Zimpel map of 1834. The project was initiated with the purchase of the Tremé land by the City Corporation in 1810. The development of these *habitations* and the life-style of the Bayou Road residents were recorded in thousands of notarial acts by French and Spanish notaries: by ancient surveys, plats, and maps drawn by surveyors to the king, as well as those produced by the local city government.

Proof of ownership, ordered by the Office of the Land Management, an agency of the United States government, served to establish title to lands within the Louisiana Purchase Territory and was required by law. The results were published in the American State Papers and are a major source of documentation of the activities of the citizens of this region during the eighteenth and nineteenth centuries. Into the records were placed the rich validation of French and Spanish colonial surveys, as well as eighteenth-century agreements by private signature. By such surveys, the expertise of Olivier de Vezin, "Keeper of the [French] King's Highways"; Carlos Trudeau, surveyor general of Spanish Louisiana; and his assistant Vincente Sebastian Pintado were important in the disposition of the boundaries of the land along the Road to the Bayou.

Among the notaries whose records have revealed the day-to-day life of Bayou Road residents is Jean Baptiste Garic, royal notary to both the French and Spanish Crowns. Contemporary notaries, who like Garic filled hundreds of books with their acts, include Fernando Rodriguez, Andrés Almonester y Rojas, Rafael Pérdomo, Carlos Ximenes, Esteban de Quinones, Pierre Pedesclaux, and Narcisse Broutin.

After the Louisiana Purchase and Transfer, Trudeau resigned as Spanish surveyor general and refused to turn over the land records that he had in his possession. In 1805 Trudeau and Pintado divided their documents; Trudeau retained those papers relating to Louisiana, and Pintado took those relating to Spanish West Florida with him to his new post as the Spanish surveyor general of Pensacola in 1805[1]. Barthélemy Lafon, Jacques Tanesse, Joseph Pilié, Allain d'Hémécourt, Charles Bourgerol, Louis Bringier, and Charles F. Zimpel—city surveyors after 1800—continued to be decisive figures in the land subdivision behind the city.

Notaries such as the Pedesclauxs, the de Armases, and de Quinones, who as Spanish subjects recorded their contracts in Spanish, continued in office after the Louisiana Transfer, but reverted to recordation in French. Among the most prolific real estate notaries during the early 1800s were Leonard de Mazange, Adolphe Mazureau, L. T. Caire, and Marc Lafitte.

From the earliest days of the founding of the city, land claim lawsuits were filed with the French Superior Council and later with the Spanish Judicial Cabildo. These proceedings also are an extremely important source of information. Frequent lawsuits arose over mundane matters during the French colonial period, and the persistent Spanish request for proof of purity of blood forced individuals to register their families officially. These documents are today preserved in the archives of the Louisiana State Museum, presently housed in the Louisiana Historical Collection. Many of the records were translated during a 1930s Works Progress Administration program; synopses of many were listed in the museum's "Black Books." The Louisiana Historical Society, in its superb set of *Quarterlies*, published many of the French Superior Council papers translated by Heloise H. Cruzat and those from the Spanish Cabildo by Laura L. Porteous. The authors have appreciated the value of both of these sources but have wherever possible studied and translated the original documents.

Throughout the colonial period, the services of the courts were available to all. Slaves, slaveowners, simple merchants, and large landowners are vividly recalled in thousands of handwritten legal documents. Then as now, time either inflamed or resolved many of the problems presented in court. The heirs of Chevalier Charles Antoine de Morand and those of the Marquis de Lafayette, the Baroness de Pontalba, and Myra Clark Gaines spent many years unraveling their land disputes. The Morands lost their claim in a boundary dispute, and the heirs of Lafayette settled for a miniscule portion of a huge tract; but the Baroness de Pontalba and Myra Clark Gaines simply outlived their adversaries, frustrating heirs and officials into profitable settlements.

These colorful transactions reveal much about the customs and life-styles of the inhabitants. The personalities and interactions among families, curators, tutors, and friends were richly defined and were markedly different during the French and Spanish colonial periods. During both eras the courts were burdened with routine legal necessities, as well as litigation between enraged neighbors. The system of curatorship and tutorship prevailed in a time when early deaths were the rule rather than the exception. Frequent widowhood and multiple marriages interlaced the matrix of most families, joining many and separating some by legal decisions.

French and Spanish law and the Civil Code of Louisiana, as well as the Code of Practice of 1825, provided that an estate could sell directly to a purchaser only by public auction. The need for a partition of property in an estate was also cause for a public auction. The property of a minor could be sold only after a notarized family meeting was instituted authorizing sale at public auction. Such auctions were preceded by exacting inventories taken by the Superior Council, Cabildo, or court; the property was then advertised three times to the public. Invaluable documentation of real property, buildings, furnishings, and slaves and their duties are the tangible results of this atypical inheritance system.

Among the early French colonists who emerge as important participants in life along the Bayou Road were: Marc-Antoine Hubert, *ordonnateur* for the Company of the Indies; Louis Césaire Lebreton, *Councillor Assessor* under Governor Vaudreuil; Vincent le Senéchal d'Auberville, interim governor of the province; and Joseph Delfau de Pontalba. Chevalier Charles de Morand, an unheralded colonist, was the first man to establish and maintain a plantation on the land that was to become Faubourg Tremé. Other colonists unrecognized in settling the Road to the Bayou include Joachim de Gauvrit, the Frenchman in charge of the first troops to arrive in the colony in 1714; Alexandre Latil, an *entrepreneur*; Joseph Delisle Duparc, a factor and trader to the Company of the Indies; Gabriel Peyroux de la Roche Molive, a speculator; Louis Gatien Lebreton Dorgenois, Charles Griffon, and Pierre Gueno, all owners of *habitations* absorbed into Faubourg Tremé.

During the Spanish colonial period, French settlers continued to develop property along Bayou Road; at the same time Spaniards like Andrés Almonester y Rojas, Antonio Ramis, and Ramis' son-in-law, José Castanedo, bought, sold, and cultivated much of this land behind the city. Juan Rodriguez, Carlos Ximenes, Spanish colonial intendant and attorney general Nicolas Maria Vidal, notary Pedro Pedesclaux, Juan Lugar, and Francisco X. Bermudez were vigorous bargainers in acquiring similar large tracts within the area. Carlos Guadioli, Joseph Suarez, and Domingo Fleitas obtained land grants and lived along Bayou Road just prior to the Louisiana Purchase.

Women, through good management of their property and inheritances, often held the balance of power along the Road. Many were shrewd businesswomen who actively bought, sold, and subdivided huge tracts. The names of Elizabeth de Gauvrit de Monléon; Anna Corbin, Widow Pierre Voisin; Micaela Almonester, the Baroness de Pontalba; Myra Clark Gaines; and Elizabeth Desruisseaux, wife of Joseph Chalon, constantly appear in the early-nineteenth-century land titles. Françoise Petit de Coulange (Widow d' Auberville) and Louis Césaire Lebreton's first wife, Marguerite Chauvin de la Frenière, were persons of financial consequence. It was Françoise Loubie, Pierre Gueno's widow, who subdivided the Faubourg Gueno. Marie Rose Ramis (Widow Castanedo) and Basilice Pedesclaux (Widow Duchamp) were responsible for the urbanization of their lands. Fanchon Montreuil, alias Carrière, a free Negress, was a significant property owner and slaveholder on the Road to the Bayou. Suzanna Caüe, Widow Peyroux, looms large as one of the earliest female property owners in lands that became Faubourg Tremé. Her father came to Louisiana from Calais, France; and her mother was the former Anne Gandolfo, whose family arrived in Louisiana before 1739.

Similarly, the land transactions in Tremé of free persons of color, both male and female, indicate that these citizens enjoyed far more influence, power, and economic participation in the affairs of the city during the French and Spanish colonial periods than has been acknowledged. *Gens de couleur libres*, as they are identified in legal documents, included builders, architects, land speculators and developers, planters, plantation owners, philanthropists, and military officers. They resided on Bayou Road as early as 1726 when one Jean Congo and his wife, both free persons of color, were listed there in the census. His occupation was the Keeper of the High Road. Free men of color owned property on the Bayou Road before the American Revolution. San Louis Lanuitte, "a free man of color of Louisiana," purchased in 1774 two large tracts of the high land on Bayou Road from early colonist Alexandre Latil. Formerly, Lanuitte had been the slave of Jean Pradel, whose plantation was situated across the river; however, he had been an important advisor to his master and a trusted companion while accompanying the Pradel daughters to France. Jean Baptiste Mayorquin, mulatto, bought a small *habitation* on the right side of Bayou Road near Le Petit Bayou about 1789. Another free man of color, known only as Jean Baptiste, with his wife Marguerite bought a portion of land from Lanuitte in 1777. In quick succession more *gens de couleur libres* became residents along the Bayou Road: Paul Cheval, Gabriel Bic (Montreuil), Carlos Montreuil, and Pedro Martina and his wife, Susanna. Carlos Montreuil, a member of the Spanish *pardo* (light skin) militia in New Orleans, bought land from Claude Tremé near the city and also a tract toward Le Petit Bayou in 1780.

Jean Baptiste's daughter, Françoise, alias Fanchon Montreuil (Carrière), owned a home near the Bridge of the Washerwomen, or la Puente de las Lavadoras, together with part of the former Lanuitte plantation inherited from her father. She expanded her Bayou Road holdings to three cultivated tracts, which were leased and worked in the late eighteenth century by Matthew Austin or Hostén, as the Spanish called this white man. She had a number of slaves who also lived on these properties, working the land.

Paul Cheval, married to Isabelle Dupart, joined the ranks of other eighteenth- and early-nineteenth-century free men of color who were landowners and slaveowners along Bayou Road. Jean Baptiste Derneville was sold a key Bayou Road lot by Charles Griffon, a white Creole. Marie Noyan Michel, along with Marthe Lebreton, free women of color, owned Bayou Road tracts in the early 1800s that were acquired in 1829 by the executor of their estates, Scotsman Alexander Milne. Caton Marc, a free woman of color, held a Bayou Road *habitation* in the first quarter of the nineteenth century, eventually selling it to entrepreneur Bernard Coquet.

Thomy Lafon, a resident of Faubourg Tremé, is the best known of the free colored persons because of his considerable acts of charity on behalf of the blacks of New Orleans. He was born in New Orleans in December of 1810 to Modeste Foucher, a free woman of color. After an education in France, Lafon taught school in New Orleans before going into real estate and becoming an outstanding financier. He led a frugal life and earned the respect of both the black and white communities. He resided with a widowed sister, Mme L. Baudin, at the corner of Robertson and Ursulines in Faubourg Tremé. The Thomy Lafon Home of the Holy Family was built by him in the 1860s and remains standing at 1125 N. Tonti in the old Marc-Coquet tract. Lafon left an estate of about $500,000 for the establishment and maintenance of several institutions for persons of color. He died in New Orleans on December 22, 1893, and his accomplishments were heralded the following day in all New Orleans newspapers.

By 1830 *gens de couleur libres* acting as speculators, investors, and developers were dealing heavily in real estate in the well-established faubourgs of Tremé and Nouvelle Marigny. From the year 1827 onward, François Montreuil was active in land dealings in the Guerlain section, a narrow strip that ran along the diagonal angle of St. Bernard Avenue between N. Rampart and N. Johnson streets; and in

Faubourg Nouvelle Marigny, Drausin Barthélémy Macarty, natural son of a prominent white man, bought entire blocks beyond Esplanade Avenue on which he erected rental units, creole cottages, and shotgun houses in the late 1840s, continuing his activity through the next decade. Macarty and his wife, Louise Courcelle, built and occupied the house that still stands at 1612 St. Philip Street. Pierre Colvis and Joseph Dumas, free men of color, builders and investors in the 1850s, built in the Duchamp, Pontalba, and Castanedo divisions.

Nelson Fouché, free colored émigré, was a real estate speculator and builder, who owned lots along the 1200 block of N. Claiborne Avenue and also in large sections of the City Commons, after establishing himself as a man of property in Faubourg Marigny. Rudolph Desdunes, famed colored poet, lived on Marais Street in a house demolished for the Cultural Center, now the site of Louis Armstrong Park.

The building trade had long been a traditional occupation among the free Negroes; major developers and builders in Faubourg Tremé between 1820 and 1855 included Myrtile Courcelle and the Soulié brothers, who resided both in France and in New Orleans. Norbert Soulié lived in the 200 block of N. Rampart Street and managed the properties of his well-to-do brothers, Albin and Bernard, who spent most of their time in Paris, although they owned homes in New Orleans as well. Pierre Edouard Courcelle, a builder living on St. Philip Street between N. Villere and N. Robertson streets in 1842, worked for Soulié and his brothers. Joseph Dolliole and his wife, Josepha Rodriguez, *gens de couleur*, lived in the 1500 block of Bayou Road (now Governor Nicholls Street). Jean Louis Dolliole purchased the site of the present 1502 Bayou Road in 1807 and built a *maison de maître* in which he lived while constructing scores of houses in the area. Pierre Olivier and François Muro, men of color, built the house at 1717 Kerlerec Street in which the Muro family lived. Hundreds of buildings, ranging from the simplest creole cottages to the finest brick double-level homes, were constructed by, leased from, or occupied by these significant people. Their names appear repeatedly in reference to title research throughout this volume.

Today the Bayou Road area is associated with the name Tremé. Claude Joseph Tremé, a native of Sauvigny in France, arrived in New Orleans by 1785 and was listed as a "hatter" by trade. Accused of murdering a slave, he was tried and found guilty and served a term in the prison on the Plaza de Armas (Cabildo). Within the trial documents and later his marriage and business contracts, his surname, Tremé, is recorded with an accent on the final é in the Spanish manner. Prior to that time, the name carried the traditional French *accents aigus*, Trémé. The Spanish form continues today, the accent signifying a two-syllable pronunciation. Only one-fourth of the property that the city named Faubourg Tremé was owned by Claude Tremé and sold by him to the city for $40,000 in 1810. The appellation Faubourg Tremé now refers to the entire area, including Esplanade Avenue between N. Rampart and N. Broad, the City Commons, and all the "back of town" *habitations* to St. Bernard Avenue. These boundaries form the perimeter for this book.

With the enlargement of the original Faubourg Tremé and the continuations of French Quarter streets, as well as those running in a north-south direction, properties were often realigned. The ancient Road to the Bayou was tolerated with its natural bend to the right. Too many houses would have been affected if the planners had attempted to have the old portage parallel to Canal Street. Indeed, Bayou Road held its own as a major artery and a desirable residential street. Important transit lines ran along it with horse cars. Continuing evidence of the street's popularity may be discerned by the construction of homes there by prominent and affluent citizens.

Alexander Milne built a fine residence on the right side of Bayou Road between

N. Robertson and N. Claiborne after 1800. Simon Meilleur demolished a *maison de maître* in the early 1830s for an important villa complex diagonally across from the Milne Plantation. St. Augustine's Church was built on Bayou Road adjacent to the old Tremé plantation house in 1840. The sons of Joseph Chalon and Elizabeth Desruisseaux, a distinguished family, built fine houses directly across from Milne's mansion. Some of these complexes were built on grounds large enough to be called *habitations* and were often referred to in the English newspapers by that French word, or by the name "country seats." "Manor house," or the French equivalent *maison principale*, was another term used in describing an estate.

Homes on smaller grounds, usually comprising about a quarter of a square, were called *maisons de maître* in period building contracts and auction notices. These were usually galleried, hall-less houses having two to four rooms. To the rear, a stairway within a *cabinet* (small room) led to usable rooms in the dormered attics. By 1830 brick *maisons de maître* were being built in increasing numbers. A separate structure parallel to the main house was the traditional two-story brick kitchen; in some cases this was a one-story, gable-sided replica of the residence. The immediate grounds were of parterres in the formal French manner, utilizing more distant spaces for orange groves, orchard bowers, and vegetable gardens.

Whereas the Bayou Roadway remained in place, its name was changed in the early nineteenth century to continue its French Quarter counterpart, Hospital Street.[2] The old French hospital had long disappeared when the city desired to honor one of its most distinguished Civil War heroes and post-Reconstruction governors, Francis Tillou Nicholls. Therefore, that section of Bayou Road between the river and N. Claiborne was rechristened Governor Nicholls in 1906. The original name, Bayou Road, is used within this book in an effort to recapture the historic importance of this ancient artery.

From N. Claiborne, however, Bayou Road retains its original route and name, crossing Esplanade at N. Galvez and continuing to N. Broad. A comparison of early and modern maps indicates that above N. Broad, St. John Street follows the original Bayou Roadway. Both St. John Street and Grand Route St. John were levees in the eighteenth century and portage routes because of the natural Bayou Fanchon, later called Bayou Clark. This small bayou meandered between the present two streets from Bayou St. John and Bayou Gentilly. Of these historic waterways, only Bayou St. John remains.

Within this volume, sixteen chapters of history and the "Architectural Inventory" with 500 entries relate the development of this large, fan-shaped section of New Orleans. The land and the houses documented in the eighteenth and nineteenth centuries have their histories superimposed on the maps of the twentieth century. For the purpose of the entire series of six volumes of *New Orleans Architecture*, most title work ends in the 1930s, the terminating date for architectural selections. The history section carefully outlines the first *habitations* with individual maps and includes the modern streets encompassed within the boundaries. Focusing on the lively individuals, their heirs and relatives, emphasis is placed on the interrelationships of the inhabitants. The chapter headings indicate these prominent personages whose decisions had impact on land transfers. Remaining buildings of significance are highlighted within the "History of Faubourg Tremé and the Commons," providing the reader with an indication of neighborhood or subdivision style and house-type. These houses and buildings are repeated in the "Architectural Inventory," with the disclosure of more title information and architectural analysis.

"Restoration by Analogy" is an exposition on the three Rs of nineteenth-century building renaissance: restoration, renovation, and rehabilitation. A full description of six major house-types is provided and illustrated with watercolor drawings from the Notarial Archives. In Faubourg Tremé the creole cottage is the *sine qua non*; they are today and always were the norm. Ten variations of the creole cottage are depicted. Many exemplify the developmental period from the former plantations to an incorporated city subdivision.

This section, above all others, should serve as a handbook for recycling these nineteenth-century neighborhoods. A framework for awareness is offered to all those who would, with twentieth-century ingenuity, incorporate the methods of analogous restoration. Each faubourg within the containing Faubourg Tremé has important similarities; their building types and styles are not disjointed but confluent architectural expressions ranging from the 1820s through the early twentieth century. The names of builders and architects responsible for the development of this huge area of New Orleans are attached, not as an addendum, but as an introduction to some individuals whose contributions have never before been recognized.

LIST OF ABBREVIATIONS

Friends of the Cabildo	F.O.C
Historic New Orleans Collection	H.N.O.C
Louisiana Historical Center (Archives and Library)	L.H.C. (A.), (L.)
Louisiana Historical Quarterly	*L.H.Q.*
Louisiana State Museum	L.S.M.
New Orleans Notarial Archives	N.O.N.A
New Orleans Public Library	N.O.P.L.

NEW ORLEANS ARCHITECTURE

VOLUME VI

Faubourg Tremé and the Bayou Road

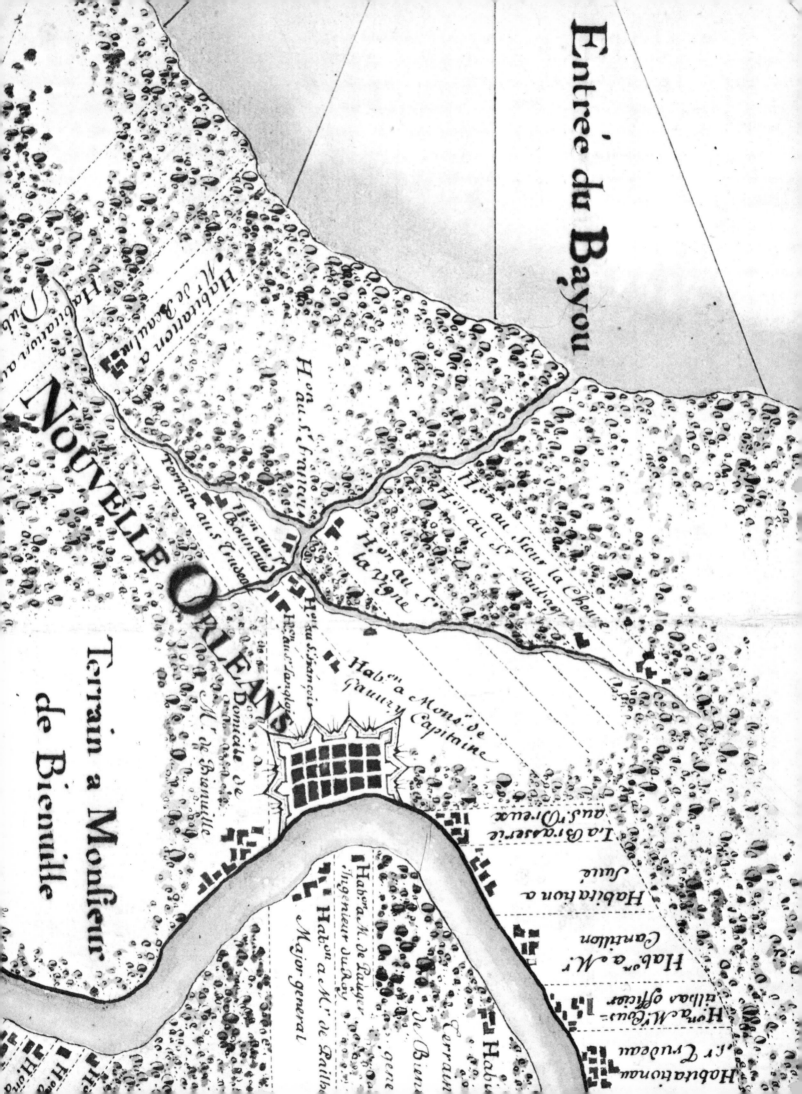

CHAPTER I

Early Settlement

One of the first settlers to gain a Bayou Road *habitation* was Marc-Antoine Hubert, Commissaire de la Marine for the new colony and later director of the Compagnie d'Occident.[1] He was a major figure in the beginning years of the Louisiana French colony. Having sailed from St. Malo, France, with Governor Jean Michel de L'Epinay and a group of colonists aboard two frigates, the *Ludlow* and *Le Paon*, he arrived at Dauphin Island in March of 1717.[2] Other future New Orleanians at Dauphin Island during Hubert's stay were Joachim de Gauvrit and Mandeville de Marigny. Hubert remained in the colony until September of 1722, when he returned to France. As a former Commissaire de la Marine whose father had occupied the same post in Dunkerque and Le Havre, Hubert was, after L'Epinay's departure, the company's highest local representative. Bienville's military government and Hubert's economic jurisdiction were to extend from the Gulf of Mexico through the Illinois country, and conflict between the men was to span their entire five-year relationship.

Earlier in his career, Hubert had been a head clerk and later a Commissaire in Toulon.[3] This experience served him well, for he was to find himself at Dauphin Island attempting to solve problems caused by differences in temperament and philosophy between natives, clergy, and the military commandant, Bienville. Despite the fact that Hubert was known to oppose Bienville's selection for the site of New Orleans, he accepted a concession there in the year of the city's founding, 1718, on the right side of Bayou Road, measuring eighteen *arpents* fronting along the Road and three *arpents* in depth.[4] He had, indeed, most of the high land on the right side, which would correspond today to land from N. Claiborne to N. Dorgenois, Bayou Road to Kerlerec or Columbus, following the contour of the Road.

According to his contemporary and confidant André Penicaut, with whom he later went to Natchez, Hubert "came also to New Orleans by way of Lake Pontchartrain, into which flows a little river that has since been named, to this place, about three-quarters of a league. A few days after his arrival, he chose a place two musket shots from the enceinte around New Orleans, in the direction of the little river of the same name and had a very pretty house built there."[5] Hubert was active in all the affairs of the new city and was, by necessity of his financial responsibilities, a member of the first Superior Council of New Orleans, joining the king's attorney general, Cartier de Baune, Chateaugué, and Pierre Dugué du Boisbriant. Madame Hubert—Elizabeth de Lesterier, daughter of Henri de Lesterier of Montpellier, France—joined her husband in New Orleans with the son who had been born to them on May 18, 1718, at Fort St. Louis, Mobile.[6]

A report to the directors of the Company of the Indies on the state of Louisiana, June, 1720, described the high ground leading to the bayou, which further documents Hubert's Bayou Road property.

> M. de Bienville . . . has a *habitation* called Belair with twenty slaves, blacks, and savages . . . [with a *maison principale* situated between the present Canal and Poydras streets and continuing upriver to Felicity Street]. The river, which overflows every year, is inconvenient and greatly damages the houses built too near the water. One ought naturally to place the city at the place where Sieur Hubert has chosen for his *habitation*. The land there is dry at all times and the citizens would be so much better in this place where one might be able there to approach by two sides, by the Mississippi and by the Bayou.[7]

That same year, Hubert abandoned, leased, or sold his New Orleans *habitation* and moved to Natchez where his daughter was born. His voyage there was recounted by the eighteenth-century historian, Penicaut:

> The Commissary General [in 1720] left New Orleans where he lived, to go up to the Natchez. At the same time he had eight boats taken there, loaded with merchandise and his belongings. . . . He had his whole family with him and sixty servants [concession workers] whom he had brought from France. . . . Upon reaching the Natchez, M. Hubert took his family to stay with M. de la Loire, the manager of the warehouses, and the next day he had all the merchandise belonging to the Company and his own personal belongings moved there.[8]

Hubert resigned "due to old age" and in 1721 sold his share of the St. Catherine Concession at Natchez with eighty slaves to M. Kollys, leaving it to be managed by M. Fauçon Dumanoir.[9] He left for France on March 30, 1722, on *L'Adair* which sank, forcing his return to Louisiana; his final departure was on *L'Aventure* in September of 1722. Mme Hubert had written a letter to the Company of the Indies in which she discussed the hatred that Bienville had for her husband, even accusing him of delaying Hubert's trip back to France.[10] Hubert's plan to lobby against the Bienville administration was known. Nevertheless, Hubert was unable to effect changes before his death the following year, in November of 1723. Despite his forty years of service to the French government, his widow died impoverished in 1724.

It is interesting to note that all cartographers, surveyors, and planners continued to delineate the original Hubert concession of eighteen by three *arpents*. It was important and oft-traded land from the eighteenth century until the twentieth. This long narrow strip of high land is the key upon which all the properties on the right side of Bayou Road from N. Claiborne to N. Dorgenois link to one another. Although there is a record of Hubert's sale of his Natchez plantation, none has surfaced for that of his New Orleans concession; and it may be assumed that the land retroceded to the French Crown. Eighteenth-century maps and surveys indicate that the bayou-ward six *arpents* of the original Hubert eighteen were absorbed into the plantation of Jean Baptist Brasilier *dit* Tourangeau. These extensive lands stretched over Bayou Road reaching from the farthest point, present St. Bernard Avenue, to the waters of Bayou St. John; the vast holdings were owned by Brasilier Tourangeau from the time of Hubert's departure until the sales in 1756 to Vincent d'Auberville and to Delisle Duparc in 1760.[11]

Between the Brasilier Tourangeau land and its lower ten *arpents* were two *arpents* that belonged to a free man of color, Jean Baptiste Mayorquin. He is one of the earliest recorded persons of color to own land on Bayou Road. This is noted in the 1780s by Carlos Trudeau in a retrospective map. The lower

Opposite page: Fig. 1. Carte Particuliere du Fleuve St Louis, c. 1723 (Courtesy of Ayer Collection, Newberry Library, Chicago)

ten *arpents* became part of the third parcel of the vast concession of Charles de Morand, another Frenchman, but one who, unlike Hubert, remained in the colony.

Joachim de Gauvrit, Hubert's contemporary and fellow Marine officer, was from Oleron, France. In 1714 he was appointed by Antoine Crozat to bring four military companies to Louisiana. He was known to have "one of the best built houses" at Dauphin Island, where he and his first wife, Catherine Pierre, lived with their daughter Catherine.[12] Gauvrit, in command of a company of soldiers, was transferred to the new garrison at New Orleans in 1722, establishing himself on the left side of Bayou Road behind the brickyard of the Company of the Indies. He lived there with his second wife, Marianne de Lesterie, and two daughters.[13] His house, *L*-shaped, is shown with an outbuilding on the "Carte Particulière du Fleuve St. Louis" (Mississippi River) circa 1723. The map marks the *habitation* as, *Hab..en à Monsr. de Gauvry Capitaine*. The huge plantation included most of the future Faubourgs Tremé and St. Jean (fig. 1).[14]

Gauvrit left New Orleans to become the commandant of the Natchez post, and by 1729, he had sold his Bayou Road holdings to M. Boissière.[15] The Superior Council recorded Boissière on October 13, 1731, at the Bayou Road site when "M. de Morand, resident at the brickyard on the way to Bayou St. Jean, lodged a complaint against him." Boissière "blustered and threatened the plaintiff with the accusation that he had killed the defendant's pig," whereas Morand countered "with the demand for restitution for the wounding of one of his Negroes."[16] Colonial records are spiced with such lawsuits, demanding restitution for grievances for anything from trampling cabbage patches and potato fields to stealing wood or enticing away slaves. The suits also leave evidence that the settlers conducted their private business transactions along with their governmental and military duties.

The next important proceeding concerning the Gauvrit-Boissière property was its acquisition by Louis Césaire Lebreton through a 1752 grant from the king of France.[17] As the counterpart of Hubert's land across Bayou Road, this was the choice high land to the left, with cypress swamps behind and extending to the plantation of Bienville. Joachim de Gauvrit had died by this time, and the Superior Council records of 1753 listed an account of his past and present holdings within his succession. These were filed by his widow, Marianne de Lesterie.[18]

Although Gauvrit, like Hubert, left New Orleans for Natchez, one of his daughters, Marie Elizabeth de Gauvrit Bauré de Monléon, reappeared on Bayou Road with a land grant that included some of her father's original land concession. On May 10, 1758, she was assigned by the French government "all the vacant lands situated in the rear of New Orleans and lying upon and along and at the top of Bayou St. John between the limits of the Desruisseaux lands and the rear of the lands of the Jesuits . . . or by forty *arpents* deep if they be found."[19] Thus, two generations of Gauvrits were active in the life and land near Bayou Road.

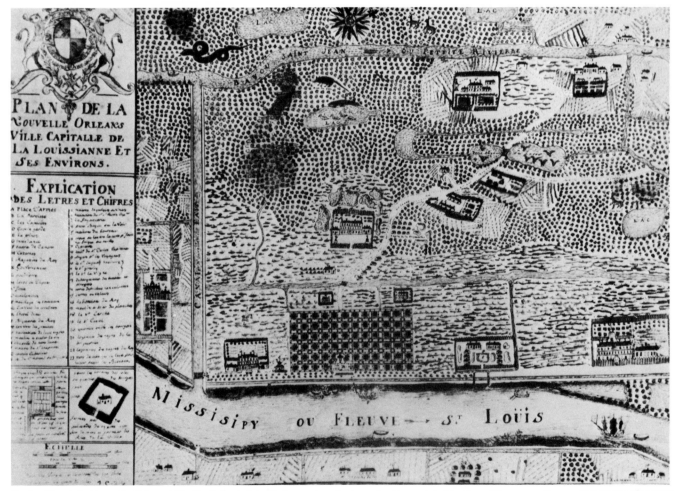

Fig. 2. Plan de la Nouvelle Orleans Ville Capitalle de la Loüissianne et ses Environs, by Dumont du Montigny. Vincennes, Guerre, Etat-Major (Courtesy of Ayer Collection, Newberry Library, Chicago)

Preserved in the French Superior Council records of 1738 is an account of another of the earliest houses along Bayou Road. It belonged to a colonist whose name appeared often in the annals of the city, Etiènne de Benac, Mousquetaire, and one of the directors of le Comte d'Artagnan's concession at Natchez in the early 1720s. On March 26, 1738, Michel Brosset sold to "M. Etiènne de Benac, Captain in the Louisiana troops and Chevalier of the Order of St. Louis, twelve lots of ground situated outside of the city on the way to Bayou St. Jean."[20] These grounds were described as being "enclosed by poles with a house *sur solle* thirty feet in width, the 'covered' walls of brick between posts surrounded by a gallery." Included in the property was a "*pigeonnier* twenty by nine feet," with a "room above covered with shingles on timber blocks, of posts and bricks, cost, 2,000 *livres*." This contract was signed, "Comte de Comtois, L. Renaudais, Jacoton, Louis Cheval."[21]

The major source to illustrate the physiography of Bayou Road during the third decade of the eighteenth century was Dumont de Montigny's "Plan de la Nouvelle Orléans, Ville Capitale de la Louisianne et ses Environs, avec Explication des Lettres et Chiffres" (fig. 2).[22] Dumont was living in the colonies from the earliest years until 1739, and the plan is thought to show the Road to the Bayou about 1730. On the left of the Road is the "Chapel of Our Lady" on a site which in the 1780s was developed as a Charity Hospital by Almonester y Rojas. It was not far from the Mortuary Chapel built a century later in 1826 on N. Rampart Street.

Dumont prophetically gave the city an extra street corresponding to the present Esplanade, which was not established until 1818 and did not continue past N. Rampart until 1835. On and to the right of this street, where the future Fort St. Jean would be, was "the house of Sieur Chaperon, lettered Y." A Chapron [sic] family was noted in the city census from the early French days. On the left side of Bayou Road, the establishment of "Comtois & Cabarriot" is defined as a small house with a flagpole in front and a row of trees to the rear. This may have been the house and tavern of Pierre Comtois who, also according to the census, lived in a house on the left of the Bayou Road until after 1753. Dumont's caption to the Bayou Road reads "chemin de la nouvelle Orléans au gran Bayou." This should clarify an occasional notarial or Superior Council reference to the Road to the Grand Bayou, which is clearly illustrated here as Bayou Road, or the Road to the Bayou called St. Jean, and used interchangeably with the "Gran Bayou." The actual Grand Bayou Saint Jean was also called by Dumont Pettite Rivièrre [sic].

Interpreting Dumont further, there were, just beyond the *fossé* (ditch) line along the right side of Bayou Road, five "houses for workmen" of the Company of the Indies. Behind these were twelve houses, "Lodging for the Negroes of the Brickyard," instituted by the company in 1719 under the direction of Charles de Morand. By 1730 Morand had increased the Negro workers from fourteen to forty. Beside their lodgings, "holes where they take out clay" to make the bricks and tiles were clearly marked. Directly across on the left side of Bayou Road was a palisaded complex, the impressive "*briqueterie* and house of Sieur de Morand" labeled "&" on the plan cipher. Outside these walls were more clay pits. Beyond the Morand house, between what today would be N. Claiborne and N. Broad, stood a small building labeled "5 Hangman's House." Crossing again over to the right side of Bayou Road were two more enclosed and

palisaded plantations. The one closest to town was designated as the "Habitation de Sieur St. Martin, Capitaine."

Raymond de St. Martin de Jauriguebery was, by the year 1735, the widower of Marie Bruslé, who had been first married to François Dugué, another property owner of Bayou St. Jean near the Bayou Road.[23] According to Superior Council records, Captain St. Martin sold his plantation in 1747 to one "Duhomel."[24] Several records in the notarial archives make references to the ancient lands of "St. Martin and Morand." As early as 1728, St. Martin and Morand were working together; Morand, one of the oldest and most influential of the earlier settlers, was acting as St. Martin's counsel or attorney in proceedings before the Superior Council on July 14.[25] Morand acquired title to this St. Martin de Jauriguebery *habitation* by a grant from the king of France in 1756. On the Dumont plan, the St. Martin *habitation* had a *maison principale*, a *magasin* or storehouse that was the French equivalent of a barn, a *pigeonnier* or dovecote with a parterred garden to the rear, the whole surrounded by palisades. Outside of these were cultivated fields, where tobacco, rice, and corn were grown.

To the rear of the St. Martin *habitation* stood another palisaded complex that housed, according to the cipher number 3, a *faïencerie* or tile-making building. At this spot there were five unidentified buildings and a garden enclosed within the palisade and cultivated fields extending to the swamp toward the lands of Gilbert de St. Maxent, later to be the Marigny property. The buildings stood on property that had been granted to Marc-Antoine Hubert in 1718 and could have belonged at this time to J. B. Brasilier *dit* Tourangeau or his lessee, Pierre Delisle Duparc.

This *faïencerie* bordered the only crossroads between the city and Bayou Sauvage, later known as Bayou Gentilly. There, Bayou Road intersected the Petit Bayou au Lavoir, over which was built the Bridge of the Washerwomen, so often referred to in French and Spanish surveys. This Petit Bayou was located near the present N. Dorgenois Street and Bayou Road or Place Bretonne. All land between the Bridge of the Washerwomen and the banks of Bayou St. John was settled before the founding of New Orleans and oriented toward these waterways.

A 1765 plan of the Road to the Bayou by English Lieutenant Philip Pittman also depicted the area (fig. 3). This plan showed the enceinte (enclosure) of the town, erected in 1760 by engineer Bernard de Verges under the sponsorship of Governor Etiènne Perrier. According to the plan, a portion of N. Rampart Street was laid out, but no name was yet indicated. Bayou Road extended from the city limits and was a continuation of the street called "Hospital," so named for the French hospital near the levee of the Mississippi River. Rue d'Hôpital ran from Rue Levée to the enceinte of the city.

Pittman placed Bayou Gate near Berry Bastion; that redoubt intruded into the parterred gardens of a house set back from Bayou Road labeled "Monsieur Latil." This was the former Charles de Morand house as it appeared some nine years after Morand's death. Alexandre Latil had been a tutor for the Morand minors, and in 1757 he married Widow Morand, Marie Renée de la Chaise. By the time Pittman drew his plan of the area, Latil was the master of this plantation. A note explains that "the whole enceinte of the town was made of stockade with a banquette and a very trifling ditch without."

During the late Spanish colonial period, the city's rear forts, particularly those between the Carondelet Canal and Bayou

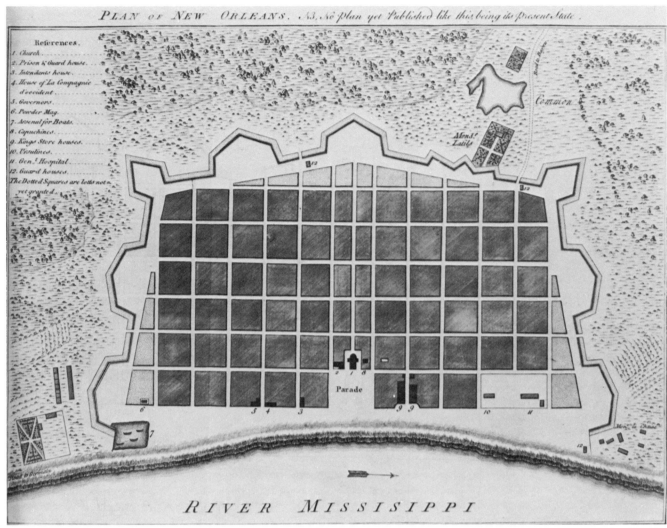

Fig. 3. Plan of New Orleans, Lieutenant Philip Pitttman, c. 1765, from *The Present State of the European Settlements on the Mississippi*, London, 1770. Original to be found at William L. Clements Library, University of Michigan, Ann Arbor (Courtesy of Historic New Orleans Collection)

Road, can be visualized through the comments of travelers to the city. French, British, and American visitors like C. C. Robin, Berquin Duvallon, Victor Callot, and Amos Stoddard wrote about the area after 1792, when Baron de Carondelet rebuilt Forts St. Jean, St. Ferdinand, and Burgundy and dug his canal. The travelers spoke of the Cuerpo de Guardia (guardhouse), which stood to the right of the Bayou Gate. Forts Burgundy and St. Jean were at the two corner angles of the town along a line that became N. Rampart Street; a third fort, St. Ferdinand, centered between these two forts, was situated in the space that would today intrude into Congo-Beauregard Square in front of the Municipal Auditorium.

Each of the forts was mounted with guns and had barracks for one hundred men. All five [including those on the two river edges of the city] were regularly constructed, furnished with banquettes and *glacis* [a mound of earth] but those at the back [Forts Burgundy, St. Ferdinand, and St. Jean] had no covered way, only stakes and palisades. Around these forts was a ditch eighteen to forty feet broad, and seven to eight feet deep. This ditch, connecting with the drainage ditches, held four feet of water even in the

dry seasons. The three-foot causeway, formed of the earth from the ditch, was planted with pickets from six to twelve feet high placed close together. A banquette was behind these palisades.[26]

A further reflection from a nineteenth-century travel account provides a glance backward:

It was the Bayou Gate opening on the Bayou Road which led from the back of the town to the cantons of Gentilly, La Metairie, Grand Bayou, and the canal which was the link with Bayou Saint Jean and Lake Pontchartrain. This back street of the town arose in a basin [Carondelet Canal] directly behind the Charity Hospital [San Carlos] and within fifty yards of it. This basin was large enough for several small vessels. Within a hundred yards of the Bayou Gate were avenues of orange trees and gardens. The banks of Bayou St. Jean were lined with handsome residences of the most varied architecture. Some of the houses were of wood and had galleries, others were of brick with Italian balconies, and others were colonnaded. There were also near the gate, tile and brickyards and a "large *hospice* (hospital) for lepers."[27]

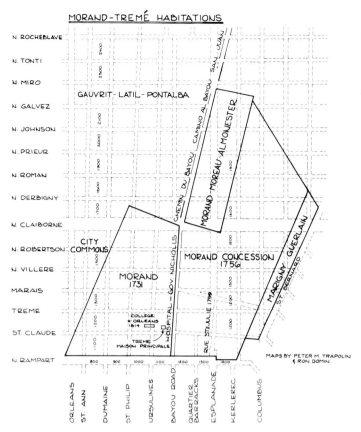

CHAPTER II

Morand

Charles Antoine de Morand was the earliest settler in New Orleans to remain on the Road to the Bayou. He came to Louisiana from near Rouen, France, as an employee of the Company of the Indies before 1720, landing first at Biloxi. As a surveyor's assistant to Adrien de Pauger and Le Blond de la Tour, he was responsible for many developments within New Orleans. Being industrious and qualified in several occupations and professions, Morand established a brickyard under the aegis of the company. It was shown on the left side of Bayou Road just beyond the city limits on Dumont de Montigny's 1730 plan, along with a *faïencerie* and several clay pits.

According to the 1727 census, Morand resided with his wife, Anne Hayes, their children, and seven slaves in a house on Chartres Street.[1] When the Company of the Indies failed in 1731, Morand saw an opportunity to purchase the brickyard and surrounding land and soon moved his family to the Bayou Road plantation. Within the next twenty-five years he more than tripled his holdings along Bayou Road and the Mississippi River, increased his political prestige, and became one of New Orleans' prominent eighteenth-century citizens.

When he died in 1756, he left his second wife, Marie Renée de la Chaise; their daughter, Felicité; and three sons, Charles, Vincent, and Louis. Among his real estate holdings were lands on both sides of the Road to the Bayou. These properties mea-

sured for the Morand estate sale and subsequent transactions ten *arpents* back of the city along the line of the city limits from Fort St. Ferdinand (Orleans Street) to Bayou Gate, and three *arpents* beyond to Marigny's canal (St. Bernard Avenue). Surveyors divided the three concessions and purchases into two tracts, distinguishing between the left and right side of Bayou Road. On the left of Bayou Road, the land extended seven *arpents* back toward Bayou St. Jean, whereas on the right side it was twenty-two *arpents* fronting the Road back toward the *Petit Bayou au Lavoir*.[2]

The lives of Morand and his family, the story of his accomplishments for the Company of the Indies, and the account of his plantations and brickyards lend a personal flavor to New Orleans' French colonial history. As a surveyor, warehouse keeper for the king, brickyard director, planter, and lawyer, Morand should be considered a major French settler. Five Morand documents and the papers relating to his purchase of the brickyard have provided historians with a vivid picture of a colonial settlement beset with bureaucracy and tales of dishonest leadership. These documents included letters to the commissioners and directors of the Company of the Indies and the lords of the Superior Council. Information concerning his public and private life between the years 1719 and 1731 was translated by architectural historian Samuel Wilson, Jr., from Morand letters addressed to the commissioners and housed in the National Archives of France. On June 1, 1724, Morand wrote:

> It is around four years that I have had the honor to be attached to the service of the Company under the orders of the engineers of the Colony with very, very moderate salary incapable of subsisting a family with which I am charged. Messrs. Legac and de L'Orme, who were Directors when I arrived in the country, counseled me to purchase a plantation and offered me some advances in negroes and merchandise as was then done for those who wished to attach themselves to the cultivation of the land, foreseeing that an employment like mine could not suffice for an honest maintenance. However, the promises which the late M. de la Tour, Brigadier of the Engineers, made me, to make known one day to the Company, if I fulfilled my employment, and . . . that it would have regard for my birth which is above that of an ordinary rodman, were the causes that I did not accept the offers of Messrs. Legac and de L'Orme, and today, by the death of said Sieur de la Tour, I see myself frustrated by all hope of being able to get along with a wife, children, and servant on seven hundred *livres* of salary.[3]

A year later, Morand continued to respectfully bemoan his financial state in a letter written to the directors of the company in 1725:

> I have taken the liberty, by the letter which I had the honour of writing to you under date of the 22nd May 1725, of having you advised of the sad situation in which I have been for the six years that I have been in your service in this Colony. . . . It has only been because of the frequent promises of assurance of protection of the late M. de la Tour to inform you of my exactitude in my duties and of my capacity for executing the advancement of the works, and to procure for myself a much more gracious employment than that which I now occupy, with an increase befitting my birth. But perceiving today that the death of said

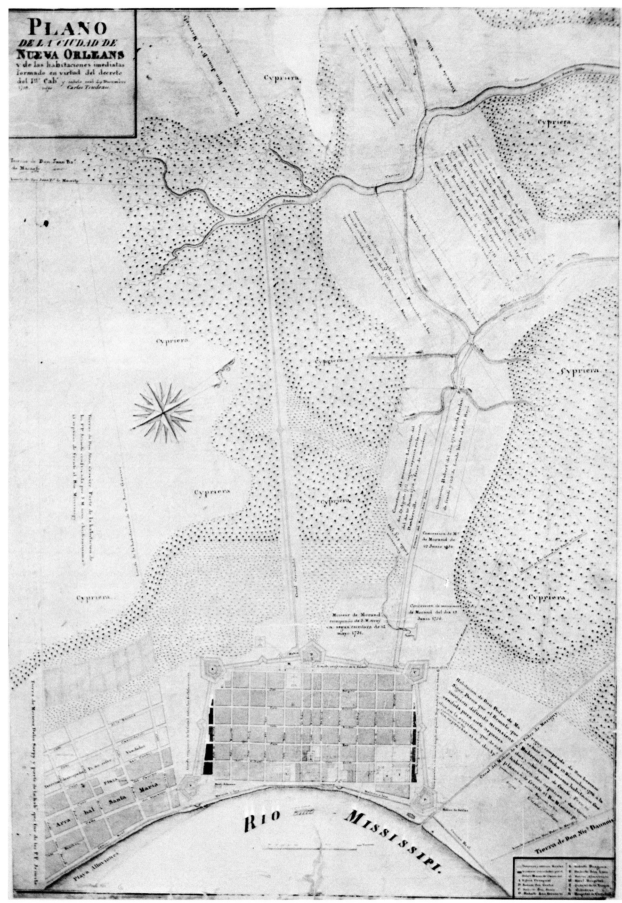

Fig. 1. Plan of the City of New Orleans and Adjacent Plantations, Carlos Trudeau, 1798 (Courtesy Louisiana State Museum, Cabildo)

Sr. de la Tour has closed up in his tomb all the expectations that he had made me hope for, oblige me, Gentlemen, to give you an ample clarification of the functions of my employment. I was detached with the late M. de Boispinel, then engineer in chief, to go from old Biloxi to Fort Louis [Mobile] with some workmen by order of the late Sr. de la Tour . . . to continue two brick yards maintained by the Company which have produced up to number of 500,000 bricks which have not been able to be transported from this place in view of the considerable expense of transportation; after which I was recalled by M. de Pauger for the advancement of the works of this city [New Orleans] and to be general warehousekeeper of all the materials suitable for use of the fortification and the navy, as well as to be charged with all the utensils concerning the artillery which does not leave off being a great occupation, with the inspection of the works, without forgetting a brickyard which the council has had undertaken on the report which I made of it, and on the necessity of having some negroes who would be able to make bricks by not being subject to the pleasure of the inhabitants, by whom the Company has always been badly served through the bad quality of their products. And so it comes back to the Company in exorbitant prices, so it forces me continually to give my attention to this enterprise. I must allude to the supplying of their enterprises, as well as to the day labourers which are considerable. This obliges me, Gentlemen, to represent to you that my salary does not answer to the different occupations which I continually have, and that my employment is one of the most fatiguing and roughest which there is in the Colony, being obliged to wander around as to the good of the services requires, during the great heats which are excessive, and without being able to count on a single moment to be able to look after my own affairs. This has occasioned the sum of 4055 *livres*, 8 *sols*, 8 *deniers* that I am in debt to the Company as you see-by a duplicate of my account which I am taking the liberty of sending you, by which I beseech you to pay attention to the moderate amounts of merchandise that I have refused to take in order not to indebt myself more with the Company. And if I am indebted for this sum, it is only because of the too slight salary and two rations of provisions which they pay me, as you will have the bounty to notice, as well as my lodging which they have never wished to give me from the first day of my arrival until today. There has never been an example of an inspector of the works not having his lodging free in view of the frequent voyages on the river which he is obliged to make for the good of the service. This had plunged me into the miserable condition in which I am, having been obliged to lodge myself in a poor hut at 50 *livres* per month while my salary only gave me 48 *livres* and two rations of provisions which have been retrenched from me on the arrival of the Councillors. This had previously been granted me by the late Messrs. de la Tour and de l'Orme in order to supplement the meager salary which I had. This is throwing me into a chagrin impossible to express to you, not knowing where to turn my head in order to find the means of acquitting myself. But I flatter myself, Gentlemen, that the probity and equity with which you are filled will relieve me.[4]

On December 15, 1726, Morand loquaciously wrote the commissioners in Paris about the death of engineer Adrien de Pauger, explaining that he, Morand, was left in charge of the works for the company until Monsieur Ignace François Broutin arrived from Natchez. He enumerated the accomplishments of Pauger in which he, Morand, was an important participant, including the building of the parish church on the site of the present St. Louis Cathedral, a horse mill, a powder magazine, the enlargement of La Direction, and the construction of lodgings for the clerks of the company. He also discussed the brickyard, which he eventually purchased:

The brickyard begins to furnish brick infinitely better than that of the private individuals, which is employed to build the chimneys of the buildings of the Company. This brickyard in a short time could supply the needs of the private individuals, and inhabitants who are asking for some . . . provided the Company wishes to increase it to ten Negroes, now having but five who are not sufficient for this enterprise, and this would by this means soon indemnify the expense which there would be for everything without being prejudicial to the works of the fortifications.[5]

Morand also told of a house built for the Company of the Indies on land of the brickyard in a letter dated December 14, 1728. The house was "of forty feet, built by Coupard the carpenter," and may have been the house in which Morand and his wife lived after the purchase of the brickyard in 1731.[6] This acquisition of the brickyard was recorded by the Superior Council, New Orleans, May 12, 1731:

Conforming to the said orders and the deliberations of the Council, [there was given] this day in perpetuity to the said Sr. de Morand the ownership of the *terrain* on which the buildings of the said brickyard are situated, bordered by four pillars of masonry, consisting of ten *arpents* on Bayou Road and seven towards the *terrain* of the Jesuits.[7]

The document indicated that partial payment for the yard was to be in bricks. A *tuilerie* or tile-works was also mentioned. The property was sold to Morand by the Company of the Indies, represented by "Perier [sic], MacMahon, and Baron [sic]." Charles de Morand and his wife, Anne Hayes, also were documented on September 15, 1736, as owing the Company of the Indies 15,314 *livres* for Negroes and merchandise.[8] Anne Hayes Morand died sometime between 1736 and 1745. There are no known records of the Morand children from this first marriage or of the death certificate of Anne Hayes Morand. A marriage contract dated 1745 between Renée de la Chaise and Morand provides a genealogical portrait:

Sr. Charles de Morand, Ecuyer, [Esquire] son of Sr. Antoine de Morand, Ecuyer, Seigneur de Bois Riad Dauquemeny and of Dame Jeanne de Heron, both deceased, a native of Dauquemeny, Bishopric of Rouen, previously widower of Dame Jeanne, [Anne Hayes], on the one part and Marie Renée de la Chaise.[9]

Preserved in the Louisiana State Museum is documentation of another plantation, acquired during the period of Morand's first marriage. The act of sale read: "Charlotte Bossua, first the widow of François Duval, then the wife of René d'Hauterive, to Charles Morant [sic] and Anne de Morant [sic]" and was dated 1729.[10] Despite his earlier complaints about his financial state, Morand continued to increase his holdings, and in 1752 he acquired a four-*arpent* plantation upriver, purchased from Andrés Jung; he added to this an adjacent tract of four-*arpents* front, bought from Joseph Delfau de Pontalba in 1754. Pontalba had acquired the land that same year from Pierre Harpain de Gautrais and his wife, Thérèse Neveux, who had received it as a gift from Chauvin de la Frenière. The plantation was described as 1½ leagues above the city fronting on the Chapitoulas Road.[11] The Morand heirs sold this eight-*arpent* tract to Antonio Barnabé in 1771.

Morand's "back of town" holdings, too, were expanded on the right side of Bayou Road when he acquired two concessions on June 19, 1756, the dimensions totaling twenty-two *arpents* on Bayou Road as seen on many eighteenth-century surveys (figs. 1, 2, 3).[12] One concession served as proof of ownership to the old St. Martin tract, which Morand had cultivated since 1747. These new lands, described years later in an estate inventory, were contiguous and bound by Bayou Road and the present St. Bernard Avenue and above, bayouward, by the Pierre Delisle Duparc plantation. The cityward boundary was the present N. Rampart Street.

Just four months after receiving his last two concessions, Charles de Morand died on October 25, 1756, leaving his widow and four minor children. Alexandre Latil, Morand's neighbor, was appointed tutor to the children and executor of the estate. Felicité de Morand's husband, Joseph d'Hauterive de Valière, became *curator ad hoc* to Charles de Morand, Jr., while Jacques de la Chaise, brother of the Widow Morand and manager of the king's stores, was undertutor to his niece and nephews.[13] Latil married the Widow Morand, Renée de la Chaise, on April 16, 1757; however, she lived only three years longer, dying on February 17, 1760. After her death, Alexandre Latil continued to live in the Morand house and manage the estates for his stepchildren.

Two years later in 1762, Latil married a second time—Jeanne Grondel with whom he had one daughter. His will, written in that same year, gave a house situated in the Vieux Carré to his wife. He bequeathed to any child he had by her the plantation he had bought from Madame d'Auberville in 1757, "on which there is a crockery factory."[14] This plantation represented eight *arpents* fronting on the left side of Bayou Road between present N. Derbigny and N. Galvez. He subsequently sold this land to Widow J. B. Voisin, and it is discussed in the Griffon and Pontalba divisions. To his stepsons—Charles, Vincent, and Louis de Morand—he gave personal items. The will listed Latil as a senior officer in the infantry.

In 1765 under Latil's management, the Morand estate leased the Chapitoulas Plantation on the Mississippi River to the partnership of Sieurs Charles de Chateaubeaudeau, Andrés Jung, Nicholas Forstall, and J. B. Garic. Chateaubeaudeau was "the overseer in charge of gardening, the brick factory, the dairy, and the general welfare and behavior of the slaves."[15] The partnership, formed to lease the Chapitoulas Plantation, contracted to pay Latil, as tutor of the Morand minors, every six months the sum of 6,250 *livres* for half the price of the lease. It is documented that both indigo and cotton were grown on these Morand lands, since "cotton was sent to France for the account of the Morand minors, and a charge for indigo" was accepted.[16]

D'Hauterive de Valière and his wife, Felicité de Morand, received as part of her dowry a three-year lease of a Morand townhouse and lots in the Vieux Carré, plus a 2½-year lease of four slaves. By 1765 a dispute had arisen between Sieur de Valière and Alexandre Latil over Latil's tutorship of the Morand children. Valière, on May 7 of that year, submitted to the Spanish judiciary "answers and observations of Tutor's account: Sieur Latil, having enjoyed the minors' plantation for 14½ months, offers to pay rent at the rate of the present lease 16,912 *piastres*, 13 *sols*, 1 *denier*."[17] At that time, Valière would not accept Latil's settlement in colonial currency but wanted real coin.

Latil had bought six lots on St. Philip Street for the minors, and Valière questioned the wisdom of this action, since the minors derived no revenue and the property needed repairs that they could not afford. In another instance, Latil submitted a bill for 3,250 *livres* for repairs to a plantation building, which Valière also refused to pay until Latil called a family meeting and showed the necessity of such repairs. Latil submitted a bill for 1,022 *livres* for stakes to repair plantation fences. Valière denied the need, testifying that "the plantation had no fences,"

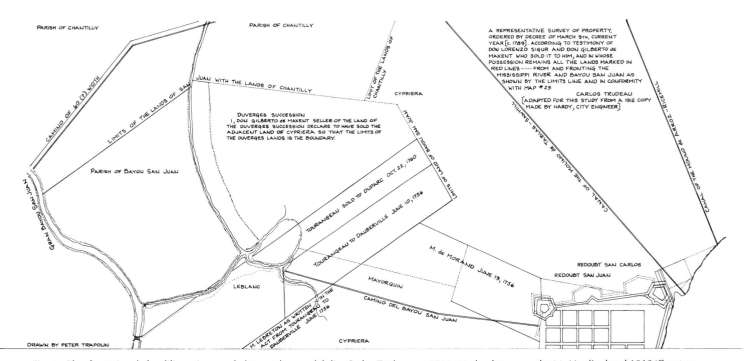

Fig. 2. Plan figurativo de las diligencias mandadas por decreto del dia, Carlos Trudeau, c. 1789. Made after a copy by M. Hardie dated 1912 (Courtesy New Orleans City Engineers Office)

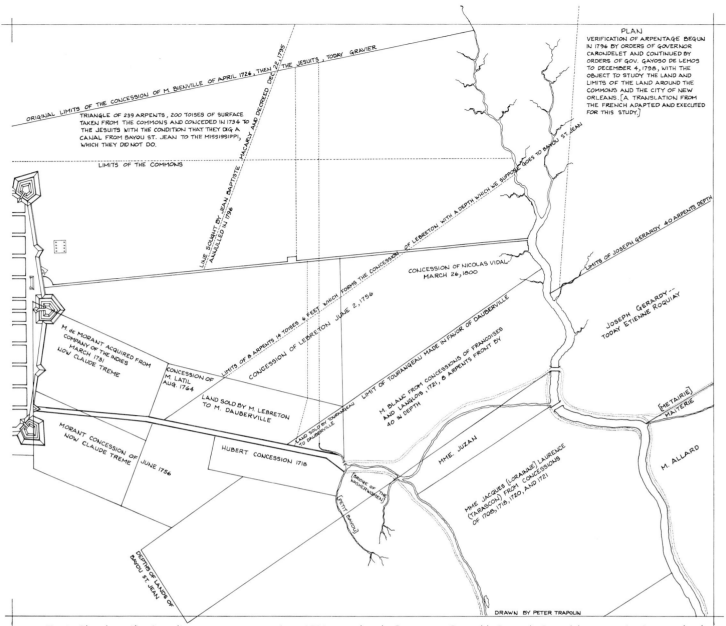

Fig. 3. Plan de verifications d'arpentages commencés en 1796 par ordres du Gouverneur General le Baron de Carondelet, et continués par ordre du Gouverneur Daniel Gayoso de Lemos, December 4, 1798 (Courtesy New Orleans City Engineers Office)

and "second, all repairs are to be made by the Lessee according to the terms of the lease."[18] He also rejected the reimbursement to Latil of 240 *livres* for the convocation of a family meeting. It is safe to conclude that these men, both litigious by nature, were destined to disagree.

A series of family meetings of the Morand minors and tutors was held between August 30, 1771, and October 19, 1772.[19] The description in French of the principal house on the left side of Bayou Road was preserved in the papers from one of these official family meetings:

On May 2, 1765, went to the principal house of said plantation which measures approximately 100 feet in length and 24 in width, a gallery in front and back in fairly good condition, the whole house with its own ironwork, locks, and keys.[20] The planks of the galleries in the back in *madrier* [thick boards], not nailed, and the front one nailed in part.[21] A brick kitchen covered with tiles, its outside shutters being detached and rotting away, the chimney pierced

in the *cocar* [flashing]. A few places of the wall have been laid bare and bricks are missing, the lower part weakened.[22] The doors are hinged with iron and lock with a key. Its roof is in poor condition and lacks a few tiles. A window in the gabled end in the back lacks hinges and iron braces. The coach house in good condition with its doors lacking hinges and braces. Another building in the *cour* [service court],[23] resting on the ground *bricté entre poteaux* [brick half-timbering],[24] covered with shingles. The front gallery has no floor planks. A dovecote of bricks and another one of *colombage*,[25] and falling into ruins, [the walls] all exposed and in need of many repairs with about thirty pairs of pigeons; I say, the one of *colombage*, the other one missing two doors and needing repairs.

The backyard is partly enclosed by a brick wall and partly by standing stakes,[26] and *jardin closé* [enclosed garden] with standing stakes on three sides, the fourth one being enclosed by the moat of the city. [This boundary proves the location of the inventoried house to be just outside the city limits, at the location of the Morand-Tremé house, which stood on the left side of Bayou Road in the square now occupied by St. Augustine Church.]The said enclosure of stakes is in fairly good condition on two sides; but the one [side] from the house toward the hospital is in complete ruin.

Two old sheds, and two new ones, to dry and mold the bricks, covered with tiles, falling into ruin; however, Mr. Latille [sic][27] had the main part of the building repaired having left the ends as such. . . . The roads going out are in need of repair at the very end. In the backyard two large doors with their two iron braces, one of which is eaten up and the other broken at the bottom; the other door, lacking a hinge and a latch, is badly hung, the door frame falling into ruin. Another door leading to the orchard is broken. A shed in the backyard serving as a stable with its roof in poor condition. The fence of the said backyard closes and is made of stakes in good condition.

The cabin lodging the cowherd in rather good condition, its door also is [in good condition]. A camp for Negroes enclosed by standing stakes, three-fourths of which are worn out and a few are missing. The thirteen Negro cabins of boards into the ground in both and bad condition.[28] There is no fence for . . . arpents while eleven arpents are enclosed.[29] Cattle: One bull, ten working oxen, twenty-five cows, eleven calves, and ten young heifers, thirty-nine sheep, eleven of which M. Latille must give back. Tools: Thirteen pickaxes, sixteen hatchets, six grindstones, two long saws, one good the other bad, two poor two-handed saws, one mane [basket], three bits, thirteen brick molds, two brass watering cans not usable, one [round] grindstone mounted on the wall, with its crank, twenty "fossils" [hoes?][30] good and bad, three spring carts, and three dung carts without wheels, a new pair of wheels and one used, two mounted plows, twenty unusable shovels [stored] in the attic, in order to give them back after the lease [expires], except for six which can be used.

Another older house known as the St. Martin maison principale was mentioned in an inventory of October 19, 1772. This inventory in Spanish described in detail the St. Martin-Morand house:

casa principal or casa alta,[31] which was 100 feet long by 48 feet wide, with the galleries both in front and behind, and a brick wall below 6½ feet in height, constructed of ladrillado entre madera [brick bats between posts], having in it a sala principala [living room], a dining room, and five more rooms and aposentos [small rooms] . . . the kitchen made of brick, roofed with tejas [tiles], 50 feet long and 20 feet wide, almacen [storeroom] of 50 feet long and 20 feet wide with gallery in front, said almacen of ladrillo entre madera [brick between posts as opposed to the brick bats between posts used in the house] roofed in tajamanil [shingles] with its doors and windows having iron fastenings. A paloma [dovecote] of bricks, 15 feet square, roofed in tajamanil, with iron hinged door, a stable of vigas [stakes] set in the ground and roofed in estacias [stakes cut into small shingles].

Two ovens for bricks, one holding 80,000 and another 90,000, and another of 70,000, all of brick roofed in tejas, drying rooms for bricks, a patio enclosed with a wall of bricks 7 feet high with great entrance doors. A garden of about three arpents lined with estacias montadas [mounted stakes] and fifteen cabañas [cabins] for Negroes.[32]

The Morand family advisors concluded that a public auction must be held to settle the estate. It was agreed that a town crier

would call "first the house situated at the corner of Dauphine and St. Philip; second the plantation at the Chapitoulas; third, the plantation at Bayou Road." On April 7, 1772, the plantation on Bayou Road, together with improvements, livestock, and furnishings as per inventory, was auctioned and bought by Carlos de Morand, Jr., for 2,370 pesos, an incredibly low sum. He agreed to give to his minor brother, Luis Daucmeny [sic] 5 percent of his share, as attested before J. B. Garic, notary. The presale inventory listed the estate's contents as "carpenter's tools, iron, land, houses, livestock, farm implements, carts, and slaves."[33]

The great Morand tract behind the city on both sides of Bayou Road was sold by Charles de Morand, Jr., on April 25, 1775, to Paul Moreau; and the sale was recorded by notary J. B. Garic:

I, Carlos de Morand, sell to Don Pablo Moró of this city ten arpents fronting the city by a depth of seven arpents which run along Bayou Road, thereon contained, a kitchen of wood, brick ovens, four sheds, circumstances and dependencies, bound on one side by land of two arpents belonging to Don Luis Daucmeny [sic] [youngest brother of Morand] behind the city [on the left], and on the other side where Guard Houses are, on one side, and on the other the lands of Pedro de Lisle alias Duparc, [all of] which belongs to me from having bought it at el remate [the highest bid at a resale] after a public auction of lands of my father Don Carlos de Morand; free from mortgage, approved by Don Luis Docmeny, brother. [The document was signed]: De Morand, Pablo Moró, Docmenille Morand [this is one of many spellings of this name].

Paul Moreau died soon after this purchase in 1775; and his widow, Julie Prevost, began proceedings in 1780 to disperse the lands of the great Morand habitation. On September 7, 1780, before L. Mazange, she sold a portion of land on the right side of Bayou Road, measuring ten arpents along the Road by three in depth, to Andrés Almonester y Rojas, the well-known Spanish colonial royal notary and public-spirited citizen:

I, Doña Juliana Prevotier [sic], widow of Don Pablo Moreau, sell to Don Andrés Almonester ten arpents of land facing the Road which they call of the Bayou, and on the other side of the Cuerpo de Guardia [guardhouse] which is at the Gate of said Road, by three arpents depth which goes to the Sipriera [cypress swamp] bound on one side by lands of the seller [Moreau] and on the other [toward the bayou] by lands of Don Gabriel Perault [Peyroux]; which ten arpents front, or a major portion I inherited from my deceased husband, and he acquired it from Don Carlos de Morand before J. B. Garic, April 25, 1775.[34]

Almonester kept the ten by three arpents and a two-arpent parcel beyond it, which he had bought from Alexandre Latil, for less than a year.[35] He sold these twelve arpents by three arpents to Joseph Chalon, a lawyer and well-known property owner on Bayou St. John. This sale took place on May 4, 1781, before notary Mazange, and the property was described as "bound on one side by the lands of Don Gabriel Peyroux, and the free Negress, Martina [the widow of Pedro Martina], and on the other by lands of Madame Moreau." Five months later, on October 2, 1781, Chalon sold "ten arpents by three arpents bound by lands of Doña Juliana Prevotier [sic], widow of Don

Pablo Moró, and on the other side, a road reserved for royal service."[36] This sale did not mention the Peyroux or Martina boundaries. Chalon also sold one thousand cypress stakes that were on the land. He made this sale to Carlos de la Chaise, who signed the act in that manner. When de la Chaise sold this land, he was referred to in the act as, "Carlos Chesse," a Spanish adaptation of the French name, de la Chaise.[37]

The remainder of the Morand estate was retained by Madame Moreau, who died in 1794. Her son, Martin Moreau, had predeceased her, leaving a daughter Julie who became her grandmother's principal heir. Julie Moreau married a Frenchman named Claude Tremé, who came from Sauvigny in Burgundy to New Orleans in 1783.

CHAPTER III

Tremé

Claude Tremé, the man for whom most of the land between N. Rampart and N. Broad streets was named, actually owned only a portion of it and that just for a decade. He acquired much of the former Morand plantation from his wife's inheritance and purchase from her grandmother Julie Prevost in 1794. The circumstances surrounding Claude Tremé's life in New Orleans, his marriage, his acquisition of land, and the subsequent disposition of it are unusual at best.

The archives of the Cabildo have a Spanish document dated March 21, 1793, that bears the title, "Marriage License of Don Claudio Tremé." This eight-page manuscript contained neither a marriage contract, a dowry agreement, nor even the signature of Tremé's bride. Instead, the contract was a testimony to the character of Tremé and his fitness for marriage according to a number of witnesses who had known him socially and in New Orleans business circles. Coincidentally, a major witness was Luis Docmeny de Morand, whose family plantation would belong to Tremé within a year. Another witness to Tremé's good character was Jean Joseph Duforest. Their testimony was given in French and thus had to be translated into Spanish and signed by Carlos Ximenes, Spanish notary. Prominent New Orleanians Antoine Bonnabel and Alexandre Bauré (Boré) were also called upon as witnesses. Portions of the document, translated from the Spanish, are presented in the following passage:

I, Don Claudio Tremé, native of Sauvigny in France, legitimate son of Don Antonio and Doña Francesca Simon, as will appear later, come before your Honor and declare that I have sought to marry Doña Julia Moró of this vicinity, daughter of Don Martin and Doña Julia Dosat [sic]; and that since to accomplish this purpose I cannot obtain from my parents or relatives the permission required by the Royal Pragmatic Sanction concerning matrimony, because all of them are in France, making it necessary in accord with the above-mentioned Royal Decree, that this Court allow me to substitute for paternal consent the testimony of witnesses presented by me to corroborate not only what I have already stated, but also the fact that they know I am single, that the above mentioned Doña Julia, my betrothed, is a pure white person by birth, respectable and of distinguished qualities, for which reason there can be no objection, and it is sufficient to grant me the permission that I request, providing me with the corresponding certification to appear before the Ecclesiastical Tribunal in order to take the steps required. I beg your Honor to approve my petition which is just, and I swear free of malice. Claude Tremé.

Following this statement, each witness testified to Tremé's character. The testimony of each witness was almost identical, so that only that of Luis Docmeny de Morand is reiterated here:

In the City of New Orleans on March 21, 1793, I, the clerk of the court by virtue of the Commission granted me by the aforesaid decree took the oath of Don Luis Daumegerig [sic] de Morand native of this city sworn by God and the Cross according to law who promised to tell the truth on the subject as far as he knew and was asked in accord with the preceding document submitted by Don Claudio Tremé, stated: that about ten years ago he who presents himself came from France to this city, where he has made his living for which reason he knows him well by social contact and communication, and knows that his parents and relatives live in France, and he has no one here from whom to ask consent to marry; that he is a bachelor, and that Doña Julia Moró is a pure white person because her parents are of this condition and as such are all members of this family held, considered and reputed by the general public; and that he knows no obstacle to this marriage and responds, after hearing this declaration read, that it is the truth as charged by this oath, and that he is 38 years old and he signed it, as I attest. Luis Dauquemanil [sic] de Morant before me: Carlos Ximenez.[1]

Claude Tremé engaged in hatmaking with Juan Francisco Jacob soon after he arrived in New Orleans. Clues to his life are revealed within legal transactions in which he was involved throughout his lifetime. On July 2, 1785, he was brought before the governing body, the Spanish Cabildo, with Claudio Chavot.[2] On March 1, 1787, he and his business associate Jacob sold a thirty-year-old slave named Samba to Pierre Camus for 600 pesos; this slave had originally been bought from Alexandre Dupont.[3] In 1787 Tremé also sued M. Delery Desilet for 96 pesos, and in 1788 he won a judgment against Stephen Lalanne d'Apremont for 252 pesos.[4] A Spanish document of the same year listed him as a member of the New Orleans Militia.[5]

On December 21, 1787, criminal action was taken by the Cabildo charging Claude Tremé with the shooting and fatal wounding of a Negro slave who belonged to François Bernoudy. Spanish documents related the testimony of Claude Tremé; his housekeeper, Francisca, who witnessed the shooting; the victim, Alejo, who was interrogated before his death; and the doctor, Juan Senac, who examined the victim before he died.

Don Estevan Miró, governor of this province, was notified at seven in the morning of October 20, 1787, that at four in the morning the same day that Claudio Tremé had shot a gun at a Negro named Alejo, a slave of Francisco Bernoudy, and that the slave had been gravely wounded and, in order to verify the reality of this deed, the matter was investigated. The surgeon, Juan Senac, went to the house and examined the wounded man testifying that said wounded man was shot by Tremé with the latter's gun. Another group of officials with interpreter Demarest took the deposition of the Negro Alejo, inhabitant of the other side of the river fronting this city. Alejo testified that he was a creole [Negro] of this city, thirty years old, a bachelor and worker in the *molino de anevar tablas* [sawmill] on the *habitation* of Bernoudy. Asked why he was on this side of the river, Alejo said that with desire to have a wife, he had left the house of the mother of his declared at four in the morning in order to return to his habitation, and on passing the front of a *casita*[little house] belonging to Joseph Wiltz situated on Delphina Street [Dauphine] some dogs barked and at this instant a man whom he did not know opened the door asking Alejo to declare himself and to stop, but Alejo said that he continued on his route without wanting to stop. Alejo went a short distance and the man shot him and commenced to shout "thief" six times, then he quit. The slave, knowing himself to be gravely wounded, dragged himself as well as he could to the lodgings of his mother which is one block distant from the site of the shooting, where he entered and they put him to bed in the *sala principal*, or main room.

The testimony of the free Negress Francisca favored Tremé:

She said that Claudio Tremé was in the house at four in the morning. He left the house to go into the front yard where he encountered a Negro who leaped the fence. Tremé shouted to the person to stop which he did not. Tremé entered the house taking his gun, left the house and began to shout "stop," not wanting to kill the man. He let go a volley and felled the Negro in the street. The judge asked her why the Negro entered the yard. She said she presumed he was going to rob but he did not have time because the dog alerted herself and Tremé. Asked if she knew the result of the shot, she said she heard the Negro say "Death." Then asked if she knew that this was Monsieur Bernoudy's Negro, she responded that she did not know him.

Juan Doroteo del Postigo y Balderamos, attorney general and official of Guadelajara, ordered during the trial that Victoria Garsin, free mulatto, daughter of Francisca, appear.

She was not in the house at dawn of the 29th, but, according to what she heard, Claudio Tremé was leaving the yard from the house which her mother occupied as housekeeper to Tremé; that a Negro jumped through the stakes and Claudio Tremé chased and shot him. Asked if the mother had any knowledge of the wounded man, the daughter said that the mother did not know him. Tremé testified that he was a native of Burgundy, a hatter, twenty-eight years old. Asked what his motives were in shooting the gun, he said that he had rented a room in Delphina Street where he had his clothes and ate although he worked in a shop, in the interior of the city, in which he slept. A [free] Negress [Francisca], whom he had to care for said room, his clothes, and effects had advised him that the night of the 27th two Negroes had come into the yard for the purpose of robbing, and had cut the cord which locked the door, and when they heard the dog barking they ran away. The next morning the Negress told Tremé this, and he said that he would come to the house [that night]. Then, between 2:30 and dawn he heard the dogs barking in the yard and . . . Tremé ran into the yard where he encountered a Negro and asked the man, who was carrying a large sack, to stop. Not being able to follow the Negro because of the man's raised stick, he shot to wound, not to kill the man. The sack which Tremé thought would contain stolen goods contained a mosquito net, meat, and

a white rag which all fell into the street. The Negress in the house heard the entire incident.

Tremé's testimony was validated by "Pedro Lambert, Pedro Memourette, St. Cartier, Joseph Dugué, and Carlos Pascal," who heard Tremé shout "Stop" and "Thief," and they heard or saw the wounded Negro shot. Mathias Alpuente, public prosecutor in the case of *F. Bernoudy v. Claudio Tremé* presented the death certificate from the priest, Antonio de Sedella, who buried Alejo in sanctified church ground.

Governor Miró wrote to Balderamos of the Tremé case:

The decrees and merits of this case have been brought to my attention . . . for the fault against the said accused, it results that he be condemned for the unforeseen accident that took place according to the declaration of all the witnesses . . . that he, Tremé, be sentenced to punishment of five years imprisonment in the garrison of this plaza and that he not attempt to escape, under pain of completing another five years of time. In addition to this sentence, he must pay the cost of the trial by the seizure of all his goods. For this, my sentence, I sign Estevan Miró and Juan del Ponca. Given and pronounced sentence in the city of New Orleans, March 6, 1788. Don Francisco Soss, Don Manuel Guerro, Don Fernando Rodrigues and Pierre Pedesclaux.

Another document signed by Governor Miró ordered an accounting of Tremé's property: "Went to the house of Claudio Tremé and took inventory: seventy-six hats in a show case, a writing desk of walnut with papers inside, a bed with mosquito net and mattresses, a wastebasket, twelve gold buttons and eleven of silver, twelve pieces gold braid."[6]

Tremé had been incarcerated before some of the testimony was taken, since he was brought from the jail to testify. However, on September 9, 1791, Tremé was the defendant in a lawsuit brought by Nicholas Cayeux. Tremé had signed a note in favor of Alejandro Baudin, who passed the note on to Nicholas Cayeux who wanted to collect it.[7] Pedro Lassalle, the lawyer for Cayeux, tried to collect 579 *pesos* from Tremé. Tremé appeared in court with Philippe Guinault, his lawyer, to testify that the case was invalid because Lassalle did not have the right to represent Cayeux, who lived eight leagues below the city. This lawsuit took place during the time that Tremé was serving his jail term. Reportedly, Tremé finished serving his five-year jail term for the shooting incident; however, the 1791 census of New Orleans listed him as a hatter and a militiaman, living on Royal Street.[8] His partner at that time was still François Jacob. This may be an error in the census brought about by copying information from previous years. By 1793 Tremé was out of jail. And on March 14, 1793, he asked permission of then-Governor Carondelet to resume his business of "hatter of this Province"; this was granted on March 16, 1793.[9] Just five days later, Tremé was petitioning for permission to marry Julie Moreau. They were married in that year, probably just after the death of Julie's guardian, her grandmother Julie Prevost Moreau.

Julie's grandmother, as the widow of Paul Moreau, had owned the Morand plantation since 1775. After her death, an estate sale took place on August 6, 1794, at which time Claude and Julie Tremé purchased the Morand-Moreau plantation on both sides of the Road to the Bayou. They moved into the plantation house on the left side of Bayou Road, the possible home of Charles and Renée de Morand and their children and, for a

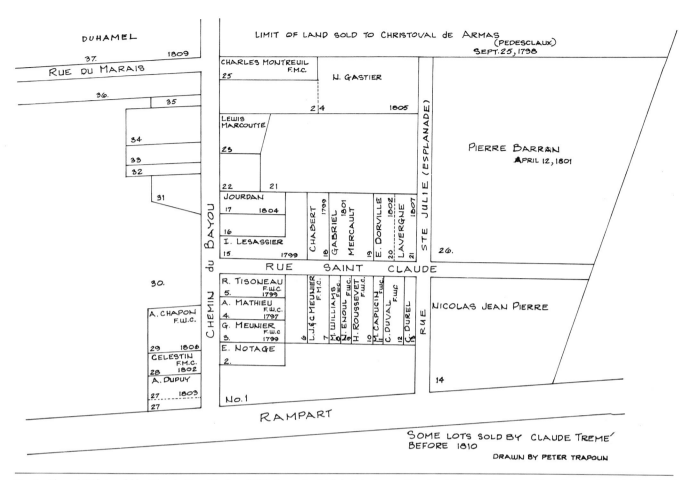

Fig. 1. Plan of 37 lots sold by Claude Tremé before 1810. See acts of Michel de Armas, October 12, 1810. (Courtesy New Orleans Notarial Archives)

time, that of Alexandre Latil. However, Tremé had little intention of cultivating the old French concession or of running the various brickyards and tile factories on the property. He first tried to make a private subdivision near the house. By early 1798 he had laid out Rue St. Claude perpendicular to Bayou Road and the present Esplanade. He also established Rue Marais, from present St. Philip to Bayou Road. Another street called Ste Julie (later widened into Esplanade) ran parallel to Bayou Road and extended from the limits of the city to the Cristoval de Armas property, later Rue Marais. St. Claude was named after Tremé's patron saint, just as Ste Julie was named to honor his wife.

Tremé began selling lots along his new streets and Bayou Road in 1798. Enumeration of thirty-seven persons who bought lots in the Faubourg Tremé between 1798 and 1810 reveals a pattern of purchases by free people of color, French and Spanish colonial settlers, and recent immigrants, like Claude Tremé himself.[10] Attached to the act of sale of the Tremé plantation to the Corporation of the City in 1810 is a numbered sketch that included thirty-seven lots presold by Tremé on the right side of Bayou Road (fig. 1). In 1799 Tremé sold three 60-by-180-foot lots, facing the right side of the Road near the limits of the city, to three *femmes de couleur libres*: Gotton Meunier, Agnes Mathieu, and Rose Tisouneau. All of the lots facing St. Claude in this square also were sold to free persons of color, again mostly

women: Marie Jeanne Willamine, Nanette Enoul, Henriette Rousséve, Marianne Capucin, and Chalinette Duval. Among the earliest purchasers in the square immediately across from the Tremé plantation house were François Lesassier, Théodore and Bazille Chabert (free persons of color), Louis Marcoutte, and Louis Desa. In 1799 they bought lots that today comprise the 1200 downriver block of Bayou Road. Creole cottages were built by 1807 on these sixty-foot lots, and the large galleried Tremé plantation house was suddenly surrounded by urban cottages.

One of the largest sales accounted for in this presale list was to Pierre Dulcide Barran in 1801; this land bordered that of the prominent attorney Cristoval de Armas, which had been purchased from Tremé in 1798.[11] The lot measured 463 feet on Rue Ste Julie, which stopped at that time at the De Armas property facing the right side of Bayou Road, one *arpent* by six *arpents* or to Faubourg Nouvelle Marigny. The next square across St. Claude, bound by Ste Julie and St. Claude streets, the limits of the city, and Faubourg Nouvelle Marigny, was sold in its entirety to Nicholas Jean Pierre in 1807. These two squares constituted the two largest sales accomplished by Sieur and Dame Tremé prior to the sale to the city. On the left side of Bayou Road where the Tremé house stood, some of the lots had 100-foot frontages. Alexandre Duhamel de Bellecourt's property purchased in 1807, however, had but 30 feet on the Road and formed a triangle with a depth along the new Marais Street for three *arpents*. Between the property of Duhamel (Marais) and Charles Griffon (N. Claiborne), nine individual purchasers were listed, five of whom were free persons of color.

These first purchases were private ones. Public auction notices for sale of lots and *habitations* from the Tremé lands were not posted until March 18, 1806, and June 9, 1809. After sporadic sales during a twelve-year period beginning in 1798, Claude Tremé sold the remainder of the Morand-Moreau plantation to the city of New Orleans in 1810 for $40,000.[12] Faubourg Tremé became the city's first subdivision. Earlier subdivisions—Faubourg Marigny, dating from 1804, and Nouvelle Marigny, begun in 1809—were the private and successful projects of Bernard de Marigny. The 1788 subdivision of Faubourg Ste Marie had been accomplished by Beltran Gravier and his wife, Marie Josephe Deslondes, after whom the suburb was named.

The Tremé family reserved the use of the house and gardens for six months, according to the 1810 act of sale:

> Seeing the necessity for Sieur and Dame Vendors to continue their residence in the principal house of the same *habitation* which they occupy, Mayor James Mather, in the name of the Corporation, declares to leave Sieur and Dame Vendors for six months the rights to the house with the court, kitchen, and gardens, *tout fruitier que potage* [the harvest of the kitchen garden].[13]

The Tremés moved to the plantation about two miles below the city, where they lived with their four sons and three daughters and where Claude Tremé died on March 17, 1828. This river plantation, which is designated on the Zimpel survey of 1834, was listed in the Tremé estate inventory (filed March 5, 1829) "as situated in this parish, two miles distant from the city of the left bank of the Mississippi River, measuring 3½ *arpents* front by 80 *arpents* depth, bound on one side by M. Martin Duralde and on the other by Charles Caffin, together with a brick kiln and other buildings and improvements."[14] Additionally, Tremé had property in Pointe Coupée Parish; he claimed 236 square *arpents* there on the west side of the Mississippi River.[15] The Tremé sons were Adolph, Benoit, Edouard, and Hortaird. One daughter, Delphine, married Philippe Lanusse; another, Nanette, was the wife of A. Lesseps; and a third daughter, Eugènie, was Madame Jean Pierre Cotteret. The inventory of Tremé's estate enumerates thirty-four slaves, classified by color and training.[16]

This Frenchman who partitioned and sold a great French colonial plantation behind the city was a transient on the land that he acquired through his wife. An active litigant, father of seven children, and real estate investor, he is remembered best for the land he sold the city for its expansion. It is the city's largest faubourg. His tomb is located in St. Louis Cemetery II, square one, not far from his former home.

One of the first official acts of the city, after the purchase of the Tremé plantation in 1810, was a survey of the master house, outbuildings, and immediate grounds (which measured 158 feet on the left side of Bayou Road and 647 feet along St. Claude. The survey, dated August 11, 1811, by Jacques Tanesse, was inscribed by Mayor James Mather.[17] This property was set aside for an educational institution for the French-speaking population, to be called Collège d'Orléans. The house and grounds were transferred to the regents on May 20, 1812.

The college chancellor was Governor Claiborne; and the regents included James Mather, Charles Trudeau, Noël Destrehan, Paul Lanusse, Pierre Derbigny, banker Joseph Saul, Dr. Joseph Montegut, Evan Jones, Louis Moreau Lislet, Elizius Fromentin, and F. Duplessis. It was agreed that if the regents did not use the thirty-seven lots for the college, they must pay the city $25,000. The city also reserved the right to send four boarders free to the new institution and ten day students.[18] Classes were held in the Tremé plantation house, and the grounds included the gardens and outbuildings. Improvements were determined by the board when architects Gurlie and Guillot contracted with its members to build a new college building. The elegant brick structure was a two-story galleried one with gabled ends, but the regents frugally retained the plantation house in the expansion program (fig. 2).

The first president of the college was Jules D'Avezac, a native of Santo Domingo. He practiced law in the city and was the brother-in-law of Edward Livingston. Both Livingston and D'Avezac had served as military aides to General Andrew Jackson at the Battle of New Orleans. Another president, Joseph Lakanal, was also an important historical figure. A prominent participant in the French Revolution, he had served as a secretary to the National Convention in Paris in 1792. He wrote the rules for the French Institute and established L'Ecole Normal, L'Ecole Poly-Technique, and the State Botanical Gardens at Versailles. With the overthrow of Napoleon and the restoration of the monarchy in 1814, he emigrated to Kentucky and later moved to New Orleans. Lakanal, having voted for the execution of Louis XVI as well as having been a priest who abandoned the priesthood to marry Marie Barbé François, was hardly acceptable to most New Orleanians when the facts of his past were revealed. He resigned after three years, at which time the college closed; and Lakanal joined the French colony in Alabama on the Tombigbee River. Returning to France in 1836, he was pardoned and given amnesty by Louis Philippe.

The Gurlie and Guillot building for the college survived intact just nine years after the failure of the institution, being partially demolished in 1827 when Ursulines Street was projected.[19] When the college closed in a storm of controversy and financial crisis in 1823, Gurlie and Guillot had not been paid, and they were awarded the buildings and grounds by the sheriff in lieu of payment. The suit, which was decided in favor of the plaintiffs, was filed on January 5, 1826, by D. Seghers, representing the architects, and Isaac T. Preston, the college. Gur-

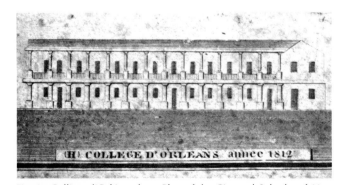

Fig. 2. Collège d'Orléans from Plan of the City and Suburbs of New Orleans, from an actual survey made in 1815, published in 1816 by Jacques Tanesse, city surveyor (Courtesy Historic New Orleans Collection)

Fig. 3. Tremé House, c. 1925 (Courtesy Tulane University Library, Richard Koch Collection)

lie and Guillot immediately sold the property to the city for $4,850. The latter subdivided the land into lots and prolonged the streets of Ursulines and Tremé. By 1828 developers Félix Pinson, Evariste Blanc, and Bazile Raphael Crocker (Crokin), free man of color, had developed the property.

The Tremé plantation house, which had been used by the college, was purchased soon after 1826 by Frenchwoman Mlle Jeanne Marie Aliquot, who opened a school for free colored children there. In 1836 the Ursuline nuns bought the house and immediate grounds from Mlle Aliquot for $5,000, the act of sale stipulating that the school would be continued.[20] The Sisters of Mount Carmel purchased the house and property from the Ursulines in 1840. Participating in the act of sale was Felicité Aliquot (Sister Françoise de Sales), a sister of the founder of the colored school. The Carmelites continued the school for free colored children and also opened a French school for white children.

Norman's *New Orleans and Its Environs* portrays the Carmelite Convent as it was in 1845 when the old Morand-Tremé house was its main building:

> The Carmelite Convent is a frame building [actually brick-between-posts construction, covered with weatherboards], which stands upon ground adjoining the church of St. Augustin and is occupied by nuns of this order. They have an excellent school under their care, divided into two apartments, one of which is appropriated to white and the other to free colored children; many of the latter

class have wealthy parents and pay a high price for their education.[21]

According to a 1926 edition of the *Daily-States*, the Morand-Tremé plantation house, in which the Sisters of Mount Carmel had lived and taught, was demolished in that year and replaced by a playground along St. Claude behind the Church of St. Augustin.[22] What would now be the city's most important early landmark, along with the Ursuline Convent, was replaced with an asphalt playground. A tangible link with eighteenth-century French and Spanish New Orleans as well as with Claude Joseph Tremé and his wife, Julie, was lost (fig. 3).

CHAPTER IV

Plantation to Faubourg

The year that the Collège d'Orléans was established, Jacques Tanesse, city surveyor, laid out the new Faubourg Tremé. The survey was inscribed: "Plan of the town and incorporated faubourgs of New Orleans comprising the Commons and property acquired by the Corporation from M. Claude Tremé, the said Commons divided into *terrains* and squares, *islets conjoinment a l'arrêtides. Conseil de Ville,* June 20, 1812, Jacques Tanesse, Surveyor to the Town."[1] By utilizing four nineteenth-century maps and surveys, one can trace the lands between N. Rampart and N. Broad that Claude Tremé sold, through their development from smaller *habitations* and suburban country seats to city blocks with urban homes. The story, "Plantation to Faubourg," is interpreted through the works of Boqueta de Woiserie, 1803 (fig. 1), Jacques Tanesse, 1816 (fig. 2), Joseph Pilié, 1822 (fig. 3), and Charles Zimpel, 1834 (fig. 4).[2]

The Tanesse survey of 1816 illustrated the pre-1810 houses along Bayou Road, as well as any built between 1812 and 1816. When this survey was made, lots were being carved from the lands of the Collège d'Orléans, along Ste Julie, and from part of the site of old Forts St. Ferdinand and St. Jean. The Morand-Moreau-Tremé house on this survey was set back on Bayou Road near St. Claude with rows of trees and outbuildings behind it. Rue Ursulines terminated at the new Gurlie-Guillot Collège d'Orléans building. The college property in 1816 consisted of four future city squares and would, by the late 1820s, be dissected with the continuation of Ursulines and Tremé. The 1200 and 1300 blocks on the left side of Bayou Road, therefore, remained the college buildings and gardens with the exception of six lots that had been sold by Sieur and Dame Tremé prior to the 1810 sale to the city.

Notary Michel de Armas in 1810 meticulously recorded each lot, its measurement, the names of the purchasers, and the date of the transaction, often including pertinent facts to aid in identification. In orderly fashion, each lot presold from Rampart to Claiborne, along both the right and left side of Bayou Road and within the boundaries of the faubourg, was documented. At the corner of Rue Rampart, referred to at the time as the limits of the city, and le chemin du Bayou St. Jean, a 30-by-145-foot lot was given by the Tremés to Louis Alex-

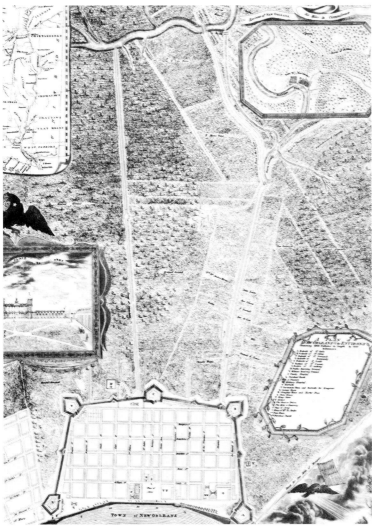

Fig. 1. Plan of New Orleans Riverfront and Fort St. Charles, 1803, by Boqueta de Woiserie (Courtesy Historic New Orleans Collection)

Fig. 4. Map of New Orleans and Vicinity, 1834, by Charles L. Zimpel (Courtesy Historic New Orleans Collection)

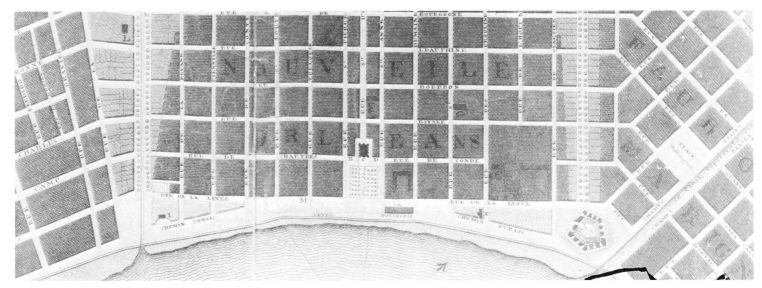

Fig. 2. Plan de la Nouvelle Orleans, 1816, Jacques Tanesse (Courtesy Historic New Orleans Collection)

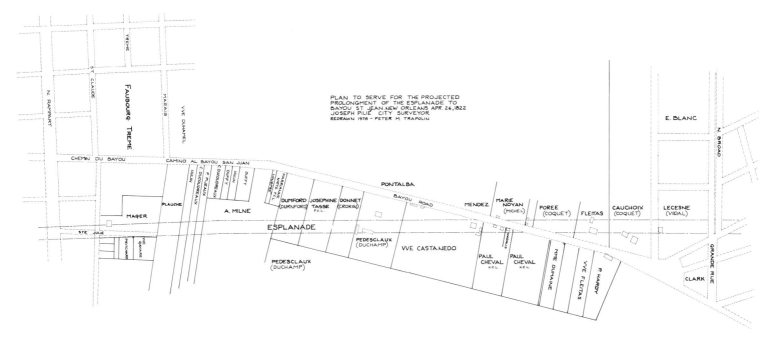

Fig. 3. Plan au prolongement projeté de la rue de l'Esplanade jusqu'au Bayou St. Jean, April 26, 1822, Joseph Pilié (Copy by Peter Trapolin of original in City Engineers Office, City Hall, New Orleans)

andre Dupuy under private signature on October 10, 1803, with the consideration that he improve the property. The Tremés reported that, since M. Dupuy had abandoned the land and left the city, the agreement with him was now void and thus they should reaquire this small lot. The adjoining 60 feet fronting the Road the Tremés had sold to M. Dupuy in an act five days earlier than their donation. Sieur Godefroy had acquired this lot from M. Dupuy before 1810, and there was no challenge to his title.

The next 60-foot lot facing Bayou Road Tremé sold to Celestin Jun, a free man of color. Adelaide Chaperon, also a free person of color, acquired the following 120 feet, allowing approximately 240 feet from her property line and the Tremé plantation house. Almost immediately adjacent to the large house on the bayouward side Rosette Toutan, free woman of color, purchased 110 feet on February 18, 1802. Sieur Peyroux and Marceline Cornu had the largest lots to the corner of Marais Street, which ended along this square and did not cross Bayou Road. Their lands and three smaller properties constitute the 1300 block, left side, of Bayou Road at this time. Tanesse used an artist's method of "hatching" to indicate separate ownership of this land, for only the Tremé mansion and college building occupied this large square.

Tremé had sold property across Marais to Alexandre Duhamel de Bellecourt in 1809, and this maison de maître, with cultivated fields behind it, appeared with the land between Marais and the line on which N. Villere Street was later cut through. Tanesse's 1816 survey indicated three urban-style creole cottages built on this same square. Pierre Laurent Montinard built one of the earliest creole cottages at the banquette on this property, and Simon Meilleur later constructed his home, set back on the lot, at 1418 Bayou Road (Governor Nicholls).

Jean Louis Dolliole, free man of color and noted builder, was established in the 1500 block of Bayou Road, on the left side, from the year 1807 (fig. 4A).[3] His maison de maître, now demolished, was still standing in 1883. The present 1600 block,

left side of Bayou Road between N. Robertson and N. Claiborne, contained the house of Pierre Ducoudreaux, free man of color, who had bought the property from Tremé in 1808. It may be the urban cottage indicated on the Tanesse survey. The wealthy Joseph Chalon family, who owned vast acreage near Bayou St. Jean, purchased the Ducoudreaux maison de maître in 1820 and after thirty years replaced it with the present 1624 Bayou Road. On the same Tanesse survey was shown, just above the Morand-Tremé boundary line across Claiborne, the habitation of Charles Griffon with its maison principale.

Crossing to the right side of Bayou Road and tracing the habitations down the Road back to N. Rampart Street, one begins at the 1600 block of Bayou Road, which was the Alexander Milne property. Well illustrated on the Boqueta de Woiserie map of 1803, it was also indicated on the 1816 Tanesse survey and further defined on the 1834 Zimpel map. Milne acquired the land in two parcels from Claude Tremé. The first sale in 1798 was "of land 70 by 200 feet on the right side of Bayou Road, bound by land of Marianne Bodaille, free woman of color, and on the other side by more land of Claude Tremé."[4]

Milne bought another area toward the Bernard Marigny line (St. Bernard Avenue) in 1800, on March 20, before Pierre Pedesclaux. A Pintado survey showed this as 17⅔ superficial arpents, roughly from N. Villere to N. Claiborne, bound cityward by land of José de Lisa and by property of Don Juan Lugar toward the bayou.[5] Milne kept both properties until his death in 1838, building his own home (now demolished) facing Bayou Road within the land of his first purchase.

Milne's succession sales, beginning in 1843, offered all of his property for development; the money derived from the sales was to be used for charitable purposes. Among the finest and the earliest urban homes built on the Milne tract was that located at 1253-55 N. Villere. This house was designed by the architectural firm of Gurlie and Guillot in 1839 for Nancy or Jane Milne, former slaves. Milne had freed the two women in his will with directions that four houses were to be constructed

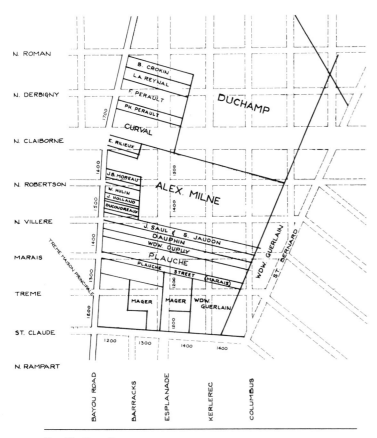

Fig. 4A. Trapolin

N. ROMAN
N. DERBIGNY
N. CLAIBORNE
N. ROBERTSON
N. VILLERE
MARAIS
TREME
ST. CLAUDE
N. RAMPART

B. CROKIN
LA REYNAL
F. PERAULT
PH. PERAULT
CURVAL
DUCHAMP
E. RILIEUX
J.B. MOREAU
W. HULIN
J. HOLLAND
DUCOUDREAUX
ALEX. MILNE
J. SAUL & S. JAUDON
DAUPHIN
WDW. DUPUY
PLAUCHE
PLAUCHE STREET (MARAIS)
WDW. GUERLAIN
ST. BERNARD
MAGER MAGER WDW. GUERLAIN
TREME MAISON PRINCIPALE

BAYOU ROAD
BARRACKS
ESPLANADE
KERLEREC
COLUMBUS

and that these would provide, through rental, for their support. Subsequently, Jane Milne married Gustave Auguste Dauphin, the free man of color who owned a small *habitation* nearby.[6]

Françoise and Charles Ducoudreaux, free persons of color, purchased sixty feet on the right side of Bayou Road by seven *arpents* in depth from Claude Tremé, establishing a *maison de maître* and other edifices. These were extant on the land when a part was sold by Charles Ducoudreaux to Philippe Pijeaux, free man of color, on July 16, 1816, for $3,250.[7] The Pilié 1822 survey showing the projected route of Esplanade marks the Pijeaux property (fig. 3). In 1826 when the small *habitation* was sold by the Pijeaux heirs to James Garside, the auction notice of December 28 described "*une maison de maître* with four rooms, two with fireplaces, a gallery of eight feet in front, a kitchen and stable sixty-six feet long."[8] The property was valued at just $1,515.

Years later in 1831, after speculators James Hanse and Edmond de Soniat had owned the house and lands, Soniat sold for $3,500 to a partnership of S. Jaudon, cashier of the U.S. Branch Bank, and James Saul, cashier of the Bank of New Orleans.[9] This 1831 sale described the property "on the right side of Bayou Road when passing to the Bayou about four *arpents* beyond the old Collège, sixty feet front on Bayou Road by seven *arpents* depth with buildings and improvements bound by the property of Joseph Urquhart and Françoise Ducoudreau [*sic*], free persons of color."[10] Jaudon and Saul are shown as owners in the Zimpel map of 1834. In 1835 Jaudon sold his half of the property to Saul, and the land was subdivided soon after 1855, when Saul sold to Victor Seré.[11] Gustave Auguste

Dauphin also purchased part of Ducoudreaux's holdings, establishing by 1828 a small *habitation* on the right side of Bayou Road as illustrated on the Zimpel map. His *maison de maître* survived the extension of Esplanade but was demolished soon after 1843 by the intrusion of N. Villere Street, as seen on plan book 90, folio 36, by L. Bringier.

The Tanesse 1816 survey is as informative concerning house placement and development as the 1730 Dumont de Montigny plan from the previous century. A small *habitation* on the right side of the 1300 block of Bayou Road, which belonged to François Auguste Armand Hulin, is marked on the Tanesse survey. Tremé had sold the land in 1802 to François Rocheblave of Gentilly.[12] The tract of land measured sixty feet fronting on Bayou Road by seven *arpents* in depth to the Marigny or St. Bernard Avenue line. Rocheblave sold to Hulin in 1804. Hulin built a *maison principale* and cultivated the tract until his widow sold the property for $4,000 to Azemia Doriocourt, Mme James Dupuy, in 1828. Mme Dupuy ultimately subdivided the tract of land, retaining some of the lots until 1858.[13]

Cristoval de Armas had bought a tract of land on the right side of Bayou Road from Tremé in 1798, and by 1816 the J. J. Isnard family had a *maison principale* and outbuildings there. Widow Isnard married J. B. Plauché, and the tract of land became known as the Plauché *habitation*, now corresponding to a portion of the 1300 block of the right side of Bayou Road with Marais Street (once known as Plauché) a boundary.

Immediately riverward of the De Armas-Plauché property was that belonging to Pierre Dulcide Barran, after his purchase from Claude Tremé on January 12, 1801. This land encompasses today the two 1200 blocks of Esplanade Avenue. Tremé Street does not cut through this large square even today. Barran was the syndic procurator of the Spanish Cabildo in New Orleans. He was a native of Ville Neuve d'Agen, France, and was born in 1766. He sold this large property to Jean Mager. In 1801 the property was bordered by Ste Julie and St. Claude streets and reached downriver to the Faubourg Nouvelle Marigny (see fig. 4B).

Across St. Claude at the corner of Ste Julie, Nicholas Jean Pierre had purchased the next largest square from Tremé in 1807. On this square in 1816 facing St. Claude is shown Etoile Polaire, the first New Orleans Masonic Lodge. Next to it at the corner of Rue St. Julie stood the *maison de maître* of Monsieur Joseph Pavie, which was standing in 1814. By 1816 Pavie was subdividing his land into nine lots. The *maison de maître* is illustrated in the acts of Marc Lafitte, January 10, 1814, and is described as a house of "brick, roofed in tile with kitchen, cabin for Negroes, *remise* [stable], well, garden, latrines."[14] The house was one of six bays set low to the ground with hip-roof and without a front gallery. Two of the nine lots to be subdivided were cultivated in "*jardins potagers*" (kitchen gardens).

The Tanesse survey also illustrated St. Bernard Avenue, formerly a canal constructed by Philippe de Marigny just two *arpents* inside his property line from the Morand *habitation*. Joseph Pilié, surveyor, was employed to lay out Faubourg Nouvelle Marigny on November 10, 1809; and Bernard Marigny sold the narrow, long strip parallel to St. Bernard to Prosper Foy on September 20, 1814. Marigny had heretofore retained this land in order to service both sides of his canal. Foy also bought land with a *maison principale* in Faubourg Tremé in 1817 from Emile Sainet. This plantation house was just inside the Tremé boundary line between Faubourgs Tremé and Nou-

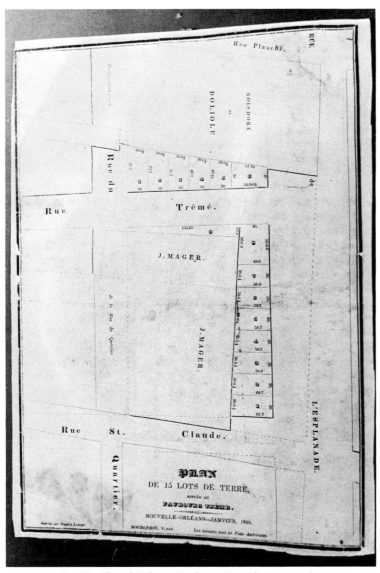

Fig. 4B. Plan of 15 lots in Faubourg Tremé by Bourgerol, 1832

velle Marigny.[15] Foy advertised his new plantation for sale in the *Louisiana Courier* on October 29, 1817:

A beautiful property, settled as a Tile and Brick Kiln, situated in the suburbs Tremé and Marigny, near the city, having about 500 feet in front of St. Claude Street, and 1,020 feet in depth along St. Bernard Street, the whole divided in lots of the aforesaid suburbs. There are on said land a number of buildings, to wit: A beautiful dwelling house covered with tiles, with a gallery all around, supported by brick piles—a fine Flower garden, all the walks of which are paved with brick—A large kitchen garden, kitchen, Negro cabins, stable, coach house, shed, etc., etc. A double oven covered with tiles, strongly built, with shelves to dry the clay. A very large octagonal mill covered with tiles, having good machinery to work the clay, and a gallery all around to shelter the materials; two large drying kilns full of shelves, and all the utensils and machinery necessary for making all kinds of square and hollow tiles and bricks. There will be sold together or separately, as will best suit the purchaser, seventeen slaves, all accus-

tomed to the work of that plantation. The above property yields a considerable income, and its neighborhood to the city secures to it a prompt and easy sale, and the owner sells it only because his business obliges him to go to Europe. For the terms, which will be very accommodating, apply in town to M. Antoine Abat, or on the premises to Prosper Foy.

As advertised, the plantation sold to Marguerite Melanie Plauché, Mme Jean Vital Marius Michel, for $35,000 on March 30, 1820, before H. Lavergne and was acquired just one year later by Manuel Andry at public auction. On February 8, 1823, before M. de Armas, Manuel Andry sold the *habitation établié en briqueterie* to Louis Honoré Guerlain. The land was described as "an irregular hexagon bound on the southwest by 460 feet belonging to James Martin, bound on the southeast by 500 feet along St. Claude, on the northeast by 1,019 feet along St. Bernard Avenue, on the northwest by properties pertaining to Milne, Philippe Doquesmenil [sic], Hulin, Dame Isnard [later Mme Plauché]."[16] The sale included "*maison de maître, cuisine, remise, briqueterie, sécherie, fourneau, moulin et tous les établissements édifices et batisses généralement*," plus five slaves, valued at $11,000. In lieu of cash, Guerlain's riverfront plantation two miles above the city, valued at $20,000, was exchanged. Guerlain had bought this river property from John McDonogh.

Guerlain subdivided the former Marigny-Foy property, retaining thirty-three lots in Faubourgs Tremé and Nouvelle Marigny. These were valued at $2,750 when his widow, Miriam Fowler, bought them at his estate auction in March, 1826. The widow subsequently married George William Boyd who, after incurring many debts, deserted her. In 1838 she was forced to sell her house and twenty-four lots in both faubourgs, all of which Jean Mager, her neighbor, bought for $30,000. Mager, a French immigrant, had advanced $10,000 to Mme Boyd in 1836. When he died, he bequeathed all of his property to his sister, Widow Agathe Collard of Metz, France. In 1845 and 1848, Mme Collard added the Guerlain lots to other land she had inherited from Mager and held an auction of ninety-three lots. The Foy-Guerlain *maison de maître* was replaced by new creole cottages, and the next decade was a boom period of expansion.

Since most of the lots in the new suburb of Tremé as far as N. Claiborne were purchased, the necessity to extend into new neighborhoods continued bayouward from N. Claiborne. On the right side of Bayou Road, beyond the land of Alexander Milne, was the ten-*arpent* lower part of the ancient Hubert eighteen-by-three-*arpent* concession. A title review forward from Hubert's 1722 departure from Louisiana revealed this land to have been owned by Charles de Morand and his heirs from his second 1756 concession through 1775. Paul Moreau bought this, along with the entire Morand plantation; and his widow sold this ten by three *arpents* of high land (equivalent today to the area from N. Claiborne to N. Galvez) to Almonester y Rojas in 1780. Widow Moreau's sale reads:

I, Doña Juliana Prevotier [Prevot], widow of Don Pablo Moró, sell to Don Andrés Almonester y Rojas, ten *arpents* of land, facing Bayou Road, by three *arpents* depth, which is to the cypress swamp, bound on one side by lands of the seller and on the other by lands of Gabriel Perault [Peyroux] Boticiara [sic], in the units of which, in the olden days the king reserved one *arpent*. . . . These ten *arpents* came to me from my deceased husband, and Carlos Morand before him, from whom it was bought April 25, 1775, before J. B. Garic for 700 *pesos*.

Almonester sold this same land the next year to Joseph Chalon and his wife, Marie Elizabeth Desruisseaux; the description was the same as the previous sale.[17] Chalon did not subdivide but sold the land intact to Carlos Chesse (de la Chaise), who sold the same land to Joseph Cultia in 1785. It was Cultia who divided the property into four small *habitations*.[18] He sold four *arpents* fronting the Road to the Bayou in 1786 to Antonio Ramis, who again subdivided them into three tracts by 1803.[19]

According to the De Woiserie map of the year of the Louisiana Purchase, Ramis' four *arpents* were divided among his stepson José de Lisa, François Perrault, and Joseph Suarez. By 1822 the same property from N. Claiborne to N. Roman was owned by Thomas Durnford, Josephine Tassé, and Donnet, all free persons of color. Durnford was a prominent real estate speculator and godson of John McDonogh, who had sent him to Baltimore for his education. By 1834 Curval and Company owned the de Lisa-Durnford tract. Within that land, which became N. Claiborne Avenue, was the Curval house, designed in the French colonial style with front gallery as well as a rear *cabinet* gallery.

François Perrault had sold to his brother, Philippe, one-half of his Bayou Road frontage; and the remainder was sold at his succession sale in 1834. A plan of eighteen lots, March 26, 1835, in plan book 14, folio 32, shows that Esplanade Avenue had not been extended to the Perrault *habitation*; but its projection had precipitated a subdivision into lots on each side of the proposed new Esplanade. The *maison de maître* fronting Bayou Road was to survive the Esplanade extension but probably was moved or demolished to make way for the projected N. Derbigny Street. The house, French colonial in style with an *L*-shaped gallery, had a *cabinet* at each end. Philippe Perrault had a galleried, hip-roofed creole cottage with two large outbuildings; it was not offered for sale.

The remaining one *arpent* and third parcel of the Ramis holdings were sold to Joseph Suarez on March 5, 1793, in an act before P. Pedesclaux. Suarez sold it January 11, 1796, to Joseph Cabaret, free man of color; and Cabaret's land is noted on the 1803 De Woiserie map at the present N. Roman Street.[20] Cabaret held this property until 1819, at which time he sold to the Cousin-Rouquette family. They passed the land on to Terence Carrière on July 1, 1828, who sold immediately to August Reynal and his wife, Suzanne Hazeur, free persons of color. Antoinette Hazeur, Suzanne's daughter, married Basile Raphael Crokin (Crocker), who acquired through his wife the Reynal land in 1835.[21] The Zimpel map records Crokin's as the last small *habitation* of the lower Hubert land.

Most of the houses indicated on the four nineteenth-century maps and surveys—De Woiserie, Tanesse, Pilié, and Zimpel—have disappeared or have been incorporated into existing houses. Nonetheless, Faubourg Tremé, consisting of the original three Morand tracts, developed so rapidly that the larger farms with *maisons de maître* were soon subdivided. Urban-style creole cottages with overhangs, built at the banquette, often were placed every thirty feet. These houses, dating primarily between 1830 and 1850 with few exceptional early examples, comprise the major part of the housing inventory found today between N. Rampart and N. Claiborne, Dumaine and St. Bernard (fig. 5). The third Tremé section of land, a trapezoidal section, will be covered in the chapter, "Lugar-Pedesclaux-Duchamp."

Some of the finest houses remaining today include buildings on N. Rampart, Bayou Road, and Barracks and toward St. Bernard on Columbus and Kerlerec. The riverward boundary of Faubourg Tremé (N. Rampart) has several outstanding house-types. Altered from its original appearance is 1035 N. Rampart, illustrated in plan book 40, folio 11. It is one of the earliest urban-style creole cottages and was built for Pierre Roup, free man of color, between 1816 and 1823 (fig. 6). Roup was active during this period in building homes on the new Esplanade and was an officer in the Masonic Lodge, Perseverance No. 4. A later owner of this cottage was free Negress Fanchonette Robert, who left the house in her will to free man of color Armand Clague, half-brother of the well-known landscape painter Richard Clague.

The present townhouse at 1201–09 N. Rampart Street, built by investor Julien Le Blanc of Cienfuegos, Cuba, stands on the site of an earlier creole cottage that belonged to French artist Edgar Degas from the time of his birth until 1862 (fig. 7). When Degas was born in Naples, Italy, the senior Degas, a banker, requested his wife's cousin Michel Musson to purchase a building in New Orleans in honor of the birth. Musson, a prominent cotton factor, purchased the creole cottage in the name of Edgar Degas. Degas, as an adult, signed the act of sale through his Paris notary when he sold the house; the signature is preserved in the New Orleans Notarial Archives.

One of the first urban cottages built at the banquette on Bayou Road near the city stood on the *maison de maître* ground,

Fig. 5. 1100 Block Barracks Street

Fig. 6. Plan book 40, folio 11; signed and dated, "J. A. Pueyo and F. Cosnier, April 3, 1845"; Rampart between Ursulines and St. Philip backed by St. Claude; 1035 N. Rampart

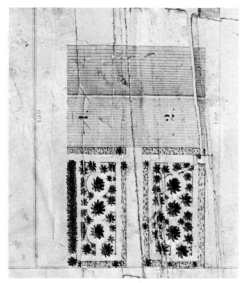

Fig. 8. Plan book 53, folio 18; signed and dated "L. H. Pilié, January 12, 1849"; Bayou Road between St. Claude and Tremé backed by Quartier (Barracks)

of Pierre Lambert (fig. 8, plan book 53, folio 18); it remains as the store-house at 1201–03 Bayou Road (Governor Nicholls) (fig. 9). François and Terence Cousin built the two creole cottages at 1225 and 1231 Marais in the 1830s. In 1838 efforts to cut Quartier (Barracks) Street through these two houses failed, and they stand today separating Barracks Street into two parts (fig. 10, 1231 Marais). One of the most important residential landmarks in Faubourg Tremé is the Meilleur Villa dating from 1829, set deep in a lot at 1418 Bayou Road (fig. 11, A – E). From 1840 St. Augustine's Church has served as the hub of this creole neighborhood (fig. 12, A; see history in "Inventory").

Although the double-dormered creole cottages constructed of brick between posts covered with weatherboard and placed at the banquette were the norm in Faubourg Tremé, a simpler

Fig. 9. 1201–03 Bayou Road (Governor Nicholls)

Fig. 7. 1201–15 N. Rampart Street

Fig. 10. 1231 Marais, Cousin Cottage

architectural version developed between Esplanade and St. Bernard avenues. The Parisian absentee owner Mme Collard did not auction the property until the late 1840s; and as late as 1838, Kerlerec did not extend past St. Claude. The preponderance of house-types remained creole cottages, but here they were usually more modest, few having dormers and still fewer of masonry construction. Early-Classic-style galleried shotguns abound dating from the 1850s and 1860s, such as the two at 1340 and 1342 Kerlerec and the fine example shown in plan book 48A, folio 67, by H. Strehler, dated 1871 (fig. 13). Most of these shotguns feature recessed side galleries, like the one at 1351 Columbus (fig. 14,A). Interspersed throughout the area are a number of fine center-hall cottages both with and without front galleries, like the one seen at 1233 Kerlerec, the Bernard Villa (fig. 15). Seraphim Maspereau, a tinsmith, lived in the area and is responsible for some of the fine rental housing, such as 1317–19 Columbus, dating from soon after 1856 (fig. 16).

Fig. 11B. Service Building, Meilleur Villa

Fig. 11. 1418 Bayou Road (Governor Nicholls), Meilleur Villa

Fig. 11A. Rear Elevation, Meilleur Villa

Fig. 11C. Mantel, Meilleur Villa

Fig. 11D. Mantel, Meilleur Villa

Fig. 12A. St. Claude between Esplanade and Bayou Road (Governor Nicholls)

Fig. 12. St. Claude at Bayou Road (Governor Nicholls), St. Augustine Church

Fronting St. Claude Str.

Fig. 13. Plan book 48A, folio 67; unsigned, dated, "March 18, 1859"; St. Claude between Columbus and Kerlerec backed by Plauche

Fig. 14. 1351 Columbus.

Fig. 14A. Plan book 78, folio 48; signed and dated, "H. Strehler, January 26, 1871"; Columbus between Marais and Villere backed by Laharpe (1351 Columbus)

Fig. 15. 1233 Kerlerec, Bernard Villa

Fig. 16. 1317–19 Columbus, Maspereau Cottage

CHAPTER V

Lugar–Pedesclaux–Duchamp

Continuing bayouward on the right side of Bayou Road beyond the land of free persons of color Reynal and Crokin (Crocker), Zimpel's map shows a plantation belonging to Bernard Duchamp. This land, originally the *habitation* of St. Martin de Jauriguebery until he sold in 1747 to M. Duhomel, reverted to the French Crown and became a grant in 1756 to Charles de Morand. The Morand heirs sold this section, as well as the other two tracts acquired by their father through purchase and concession, to Paul Moreau, April 25, 1775.

The Bayou Road frontage of this *habitation* had been part of the ten-by-three-*arpent* Hubert land that Widow Paul Moreau partitioned and sold from the Morand plantation to Andrés Almonester in 1780. Juan Rodriguez by 1790 had acquired two by three *arpents* via Joseph Cultia. Rodriguez bequeathed the property to his daughter, whose husband was Antonio Ramis. Spanish colonial subject Juan Antonio Lugar bought the two *arpents* of Bayou Road frontage on June 19, 1797, from Ramis; and notary Carlos Ximenes recorded: "I, Antonio Ramis, sell to Juan Lugar a piece of land of two *arpents* fronting with three *arpents* depth, which I have from Maria Ignacia Rodriguez [his deceased wife] bound by lands of the seller."

Three years later Lugar purchased from Claude Tremé another portion of land behind his new Bayou Road frontage, widening and extending his property to the lands of Marigny.[1] The acquisition was made in three acts: February 27, 28, and March 1, 1800. Spanish surveyor Pintado recorded on March 1, 1802:

In the presence of Juan Lugar . . . there was measured and with assistance of Tremé, vendor, 8¼ *arpents* front, less 6 *arpents*, two fathoms in depth reduced, forming a total of 48 superficial *arpents* . . . which tract is situated to the northeast of the Bayou St. Jean. The tract is in the figure of an irregular trapezoid, the sides of which are bound by Antonio Ramis and Suzanne Caüe, Widow Peyroux, the boundary line northeast between the land measured in favor of Alexander Milne, running north to Pierre de Marigny. Said tract is part of a grant to M. de Morand, June 19, 1756, with one *arpent* given by Pierre de Lisle [Duparc] in favor of Tremé in order to terminate the altercation between them with regard to mistakes in their acts of sales.[2]

Lugar's service sheet, preserved in the Archivas de las Indias in Sevilla, Spain, reveals that this Bayou Road investor was born in Alicante, Spain, in 1756 and served in the New Orleans battalion of the Royal Navy for fourteen years after action in the campaigns at Oran in 1775. He served with the Spanish Royal Navy at the Battle of Pensacola before settling in New Orleans, where he had the franchise from the city to supply wagons and labor for the collection of garbage.[3] Lugar did not hold his plantation long after the Louisiana Transfer, even though he is noted as the owner on the De Woiserie map of 1803. He sold the two *arpents* of Bayou Road frontage to Pierre Pedesclaux, as well as his eight by six *arpents* to the Marigny line. Pedesclaux almost lost his new plantation because of a suit with a debtor that resulted in a sheriff's sale of the land. Pedesclaux was able to repurchase; and the *Louisiana Courier* of June 23, 1809, advertised the auction to be held as a result of the suit, *Pintat v. P. Pedesclaux*:

In the Superior Court will be sold at the Exchange Coffee House, Saturday, July 8, 1809, at auction, an *habitation*, situated on the Road to Bayou St. Jean, on the right side, containing two acres front and six in depth, and at that distance it has eight acres front and continues in depth six acres more, bound on one side by land of Joseph Casta-

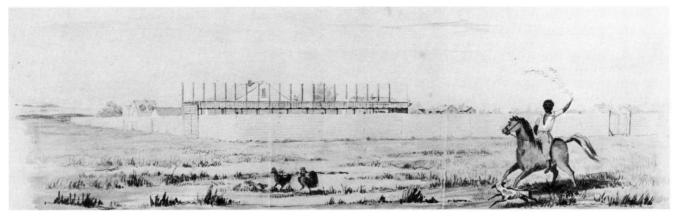

Fig. 1. Plan book 6, folio 23; signed and dated, "Eugene Surgi, November 16, 1843"; Derbigny between Kerlerec and Columbus

nedo and on the other by lands of Joseph Cabaret [free man of color] seized in execution in the above suit and it being the third and last auction. The above described property will be finally adjudicated to the highest bidder for the price which shall be offered at one year's credit with mortgage and security. B. Cenas, Sheriff.[4]

Despite the French appearance of his name, Pedesclaux was a native of San Sebastian in the Spanish Basque province of Guipuzcoa. As a Spanish colonial notary, his official records until the Louisiana Transfer were in Spanish. His knowledge of French, however, was evident in his thousands of pages of notarial acts in that language after 1803. After coming to New Orleans, he married a French Creole, Clarisse LeDuc; and their sons, Philippe and Hughes, also became notaries. Both Hughes and the Pedesclaux daughter, Basilice, are listed as property owners along the Bayou Road.[5]

After Pierre Pedesclaux's death, his widow purchased the *habitation* at her husband's succession sale, March 5, 1827.[6] Through their daughter, Basilice, the Pedesclauxs continued to operate this as a working plantation on the right side of Bayou Road for almost forty years. Basilice was first married to Sieur Thomeguez, a native of Geneva, Switzerland. They had a daughter, Louise, before Thomeguez's death, after which Basilice married Bernard Duchamp on November 11, 1820. Bernard and his brother Eugène were from Bordeaux, France, and came to St. Martinville, Louisiana, where two Duchamp homes

remain today.[7] Basilice and Bernard Duchamp had three daughters and a son. Bernard's untimely death at forty-two years of age was followed by the tragic deaths of both their son, Henry, and her daughter, Louise. Although Caroline married Pierre I. Durel, daughters Adèle and Clarisse never married. An outstanding mourning portrait of the widow and her five children is housed in the Louisiana State Museum.

The plantation, identified as the Duchamp plantation, was subdivided in 1839 after a plan made by surveyor J. A. Bourgerol. The property was offered first on June 7, 1839, when there was "a sale of lots in the tract belonging to the [Duchamp] estate situated in the rear of the city near Bayou Road."[8] Due to the depreciated value of the real estate, some of the lots less favorably situated could not be sold, so that Mme Duchamp's property was reauctioned on May 12, 1841, at the Bourse de la Cité.[9] On May 24 of that year, a family meeting of the Duchamp heirs was held before notary Lucien Herman, at which time the family advisors convened and "unanimously approve the intended leasing of the remaining lots unsold . . . with this reservation . . . that the buildings or improvements to be put on the lot or lots so leased shall be none other than those intended for dwelling houses and dependencies . . . and the expiration date of the ten years or twenty years shall be estimated according to the additional value which they . . . may give to the lot upon which they may be built."[10]

The leasing project apparently was not successful because

Fig. 2. 1500 block Derbigny

Fig. 2A. Plan book 90, folio 43; signed and dated, "G. Strehler, July 16, 1870"; Derbigny corner Laharpe backed by Claiborne, Columbus

in 1848 Norbert Vignie auctioned the remaining property, "sold by Norbert Vignie, *Encanteur, Mardi 2, Mai, 1848, a la Bourse de la Cité, rue St. Louis,* the properties of the community of Marie Théodore Basilice Pedesclaux and Bernard Duchamp, deceased."[11]

The Duchamp townhouses on Toulouse Street—bound by Chartres, Royal, and St. Peter—were inherited by the Widow Duchamp. A group of lots facing Esplanade backed by Quartier (Barracks), N. Derbigny, and N. Roman was sold to John McDonogh for $2,375. Hughes Pedesclaux, Mme Duchamp's brother, bought *"une îlet de terre borné par les rues Esplanade, Roman, Prieur, Quartier, et Chemin de Bayou* together with the house and all the dependencies for $11,400."[12] The house was not mentioned in the act of sale when the property was described as eighteen lots. The Duchamp daughters—Clarisse, Adèle, and Caroline, Mme Durel—bought some of the lots on Columbus and Kerlerec streets and some facing Esplanade, each measuring thirty-two by ninety-nine feet.

An archival drawing dated November 16, 1843, by E. Surgi in plan book 6, folio 23, shows the swampy Duchamp tract during the early years of subdivision (fig. 1). The lots sold for between $30 and $50, with each having a minimum thirty-foot frontage along Kerlerec, Columbus, or Laharpe. They were developed in the 1840s with modest, frame, dormerless creole cottages costing about $500 to $1,000, as seen in plan book 90, folio 43, two of which are found in the 1500 block of N. Derbigny (figs. 2, A). Many such cottages remain, as do separate kitchen and outbuildings of substantial size. These charming structures often lie hidden from the street.

Louis Bringier, the surveyor, and Michel Doradou Bringier, the banker, emerge as major investors in the Duchamp tract. As partners they bought and sold one another's property in efforts to avoid foreclosures, and often Louis Bringier bought lots with his partner William Israel. Prominent speculators also included free persons of color, such as Pierre Colvis, Joseph Dumas, and the Soulié family. They built entire blocks of Classic-style shotguns, with and without galleries, in the 1850s and 1860s.

An important early *maison de maître* in the Duchamp area is 1505–07 N. Prieur, built between 1841 and 1847 for Joseph Bruneau, a feedstore owner (fig. 3). Such single family dwellings were mixed among the rental houses. At 1717 Kerlerec the Martinez-Muro creole cottage epitomizes the excellence of this house-type (fig. 4).

Fig. 3. 1505–07 N. Prieur

Fig. 4. 1717 Kerlerec

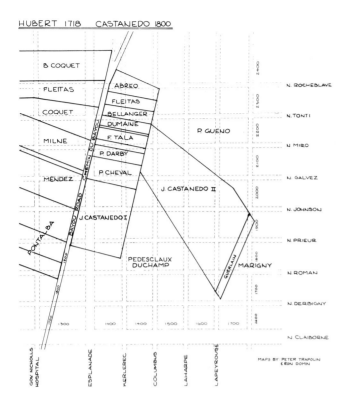

B COQUET

FLEITAS

COQUET

MILNE

MENDEZ

ABREO

FLEITAS

BELLANGER

DUMAINE

F. TALA

P. DARBY

P. CHEVAL

J. CASTANEDO II

J. CASTANEDO I

PEDESCLAUX
DUCHAMP

P. GUENO

MARIGNY

N. ROCHEBLAVE

N. TONTI

N. MIRO

N. GALVEZ

N. JOHNSON

N. PRIEUR

N. ROMAN

N. DERBIGNY

N. CLAIBORNE

GOV. NICHOLLS
HOSPITAL

ESPLANADE

KERLEREC

COLUMBUS

LAHARPE

LAPEYROUSE

MAPS BY PETER TRAPOLIN
& RON DOMIN

CHAPTER VI

Ramis – Castanedo

Bayouward from the Duchamp tract, the next large *habitation* on the right side of Bayou Road belonged to the Spanish colonial Castanedo family by 1800 and was divided into two parts that barely missed joining. The frontage on the Road was part of the Hubert concession, which became the Morand-Moreau land. Joseph Cultia, a subsequent purchaser, divided and sold to Antonio Ramis, before F. Rodriguez, December 3, 1786:

> I, Joseph Cultia, sell to Antonio Ramis my own *habitation* situated on the Bayou Road, composed of four-*arpents* front by three-*arpents* depth, with all buildings which are built on it. Bound on one side with lands belonging to Don Gabriel Peyroux and on the other with some more land belonging to the vendor, all of which belongs to me from a purchase from Don Carlos Delachaise before Rafael Pérdomo, March 16, 1785.

Antonio Ramis, a native of Huecha, Majorca, came to Louisiana early in the Spanish colonial regime. In 1775 he married Maria Ignacia Rodriguez, the daughter of Juan Rodriguez and the widow of Cristobal de Lisa. Ramis became the stepfather to Maria Josefa, José Joaquin, and Manuel de Lisa. Their daughter, Maria Rosa, born in 1776 survived, but Maria Rodriguez died soon after the birth. On January 24, 1788, Ramis proved the purity of his blood before the Cabildo, stating that his parents were Sebastian Ramis and Anne Pascals.[1]

No record of remarriage by Ramis has been found, but many documents remain to give evidence of him as a major land speculator in Faubourg Tremé. He collected much of the original Hubert eighteen *arpents* of high land on the right side of Bayou Road. This was accomplished in four separate transactions. His distribution of the first four *arpents* has been recounted in the chapter, "Plantation to Faubourg," with final sales going mainly to free persons of color. His division of two *arpents* was sold to Spaniard Juan Lugar and then another four *arpents* to his son-in-law, José Castanedo. He acquired four of the upper Hubert *arpentage* in property, which will be identified in the next chapter, "Peyroux-Cheval," as the holdings of Paul Cheval, free man of color.

Maria Rosa Ramis, upon reaching her maturity in 1797, married José Castanedo. Castanedo, a native of Santander, Spain, was born in 1769 and emigrated to Spanish colonial Louisiana under the sponsorship of Bernardo de Gálvez. Three days after Ramis sold the Bayou Road plantation to his son-in-law, in March of 1800, Castanedo sold his Rue Ste Anne house in the city to Ramis in partial payment of the debt:

> I, José Castanedo *miliciana carabinero* sell to Antonio Ramis, my father-in-law, *majordomo* of the works of *la Santa Iglesia Cathedral*, a house of mine on Saint Anne constructed principally of *carpinteria con una fábrica de ladrillas* [brick between posts] which I built in the patio, on a lot 43 by 150 feet, with the buildings built toward the rear of the lot. I bought the house at the sale of the goods of the deceased Pedro Gautien . . . before Don Francisco Broutin, February 20 of the immediate year, bound by land of Juan Federique and of a free Negress Margarita Trudeau. I sell this house and land for 2,000 *pesos* which go toward the debt I owe the purchaser, Antonio Ramis, of 8,571 *pesos* for the sale he made me of his *habitation* on the right side of Bayou Road on March 1, 1800. Of the 8,571 *pesos* that remain to me by the purchase of my plantation on the right side of Bayou Road and for which quantity of 2,000 *pesos* as value of the referred to house, so that I deduct that much of the selling price of my plantation.[2]

The rest of the Castanedo *habitation*, which had no Bayou Road frontage, had belonged in the early French colonial period to J. B. Brasilier *dit* Tourangeau, and by 1730 Pierre Delisle Duparc was leasing it. The ownership of the land passed from Brasilier Tourangeau to Vincent Le Senéchal d'Auberville on June 10, 1756.[3] Duparc, the lessee, then bought it from the d'Auberville estate in 1757. Delisle Duparc sold the property to Jean Enoul, his son-in-law, in 1775.[4] Enoul sold to Gabriel Peyroux about 1781, according to Mme Peyroux who stated, "my husband bought from Enoul about fifteen years ago," in a notarized act of 1796. She sold to José Castanedo on October 22, 1800, before Pierre Pedesclaux:

> I, Suzanna Caüe, widow Peyroux . . . sell to Don José Castanedo a cypress swamp four *arpents* front with a depth of fourteen *arpents* three feet to the limits of land of Don Lugar [the Duchamp tract] of twelve *arpents*, ten *toises*, and one foot, and the limits common with the rest of my land of fifteen *arpents*, twenty-two *toises*, five feet . . . situated in the *barrio* of Bayou San Juan bound on the southeast with lands of mulatto Pablo Dulcido Barran, on the south with lands of Don Juan Lugar, on the east with land of Don Bernard Marigny, and on the north with my lands belonging to me from the succession of my deceased husband.

José Castanedo died in 1819, and the inventory of his estate described his two properties:

On May 14, 1819, Philippe Pedesclaux, then notary of the city, proceeded to take inventory of the goods relating to the succession of José Castanedo and of the community which existed between him and Dame Marie Rose Ramis, his wife and mother of the children. It consists of land situated on the Road to Bayou St. Jean measuring 3 *arpents* and 140 feet facing the Road by 3 *arpents* depth together with the buildings there constructed, bound on one side by the land of Madame Widow Pedesclaux, now that of Monsieur Bernard Duchamp, and on the other by land of Paul Cheval, free man of color, plus other land connected to or beside the preceding . . . situated between the property belonging to Pierre Guenon (Gueno), Widow Pedesclaux, now Bernard Duchamp, Bernard Marigny, today Maunsell White, Paul Hardy, free man of color, and Widow Guadali [Guadioli], communicating to the Bayou Road by a road situated between the property of Paul Cheval and Castanedo, all valued at 8,000 *piastres*. Eleven slaves and diverse animals and furniture, bringing the total up to 17,181 *piastres*.[5]

Widow Castanedo subdivided her Bayou Road frontage at an 1832 auction after her purchase of the entire *habitation* from the coheirs, her children. This partition referred to Faubourg Castanedo in all early sales of the lots. A typical villa in the Castanedo tract today is 1435 N. Johnson, built in the late 1860s for Paul Augrain (fig. 1). The faubourg had an abundance of three-bay shotguns built in multiples by investors in the 1860s. Some rows have galleries and others overhangs. The monumental landmark is the Convent of the Little Sisters of the Poor. It occupies the square bound by N. Galvez, N. Johnson, Columbus, and Laharpe (figs. 2, A,B,C).

Fig. 1. 1435 N. Johnson

Fig. 2. Square bounded by N. Johnson, N. Galvez, Columbus and Laharpe; Little Sisters of the Poor Convent

Fig. 2A. Little Sisters of the Poor, Gate

Fig. 2B. Little Sisters of the Poor, Guardhouse

Fig. 2C. Little Sisters of the Poor, Main Building

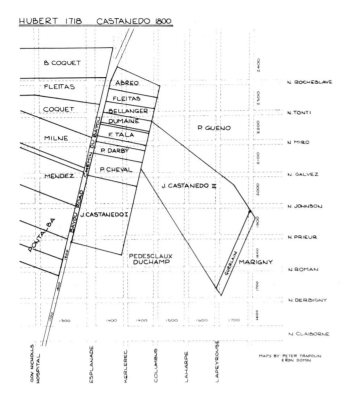

CHAPTER VII

Peyroux–Cheval

The remaining eight *arpents* of the Hubert concession ran from the Castanedo boundary following Bayou Road along the Gueno plantation to present N. Dorgenois Street. In the late eighteenth century free Negroes appear as owners in these upper eight *arpents* of the Hubert tract, and they include Jean Baptiste Mayorquin,[1] San Luis Lanuitte, Pedro and Suzanna Martina, Pedro Dulcido Barran, Gabriel Bick (alias Bic, Dic or Pic), Charles Montreuil, Paul Cheval, and Pierre Darby. Alexandre Latil, Gabriel Peyroux and his wife Suzanna Caüe, and Antonio Ramis are, however, important French and Spanish colonial owners who controlled the eighteenth-century disposition of these eight *arpents*.

M. d'Auberville had acquired six *arpents* of this land from present N. Galvez Street bayouward to approximately N. Rocheblave by 1756, shortly before his death. At his estate sale in 1757 Alexandre Latil purchased them.[2] Latil sold the first two *arpents* to Almonester y Rojas in 1780. On May 4, 1781, before L. Mazange, when Almonester sold twelve by three *arpents* on the right side of Bayou Road to Joseph Chalon, the act read: "In addition to the ten by three *arpents* which I bought from Widow Morau [sic] . . . also, I sell to said Chalon two *arpents* of land more or less which they call *Sipriera* located on the Road to Bayou San Juan behind the referred to ten *arpents*; I bought said [two *arpents*] from Don Alejandro Latil before this notary; land bound on one side by lands of Don

Gabriel Peyroux [future Castanedo] and on the other by free Negress Martina." Subsequent owner Joseph Cultia sold these two *arpents* by 1788, and Antonio Ramis acquired them.

In 1774 Latil sold the remaining bayouward four *arpents* to San Luis Lanuitte on December 23, before J. B. Garic. "Also, I [Latil] sell four *arpents* of land or cypress swamps on the Road to the Bayou behind the lands of Charles de Morand with the depth it can have, bound on one side by lands of the seller [Latil's Bayou Road, left side property], and on the other by Dupart [sic], lands also belonging to me by purchase from the d'Auberville estate [1757]." Lanuitte divided these four *arpents* between free Negro Pedro Martina by 1781 and Gabriel Bic or Bick, *mulatto libre*, by 1800.

By 1800 Paul Cheval owned the two Pedro Martina *arpents*, as well as the two Antonio Ramis had purchased from Joseph Cultia (which had come via Latil and Almonester).[3] The Cheval lands conform to the properties of Cheval, Darby, Zardais, and Tala on the Zimpel map. Also shown was the narrow right of way that Ramis retained as important access from Bayou Road to the Castanedo *habitation* belonging to his son-in-law.

Paul Cheval was married to Isabelle Dupart (alias Fanchon), also a free person of color. Their two children, Adelaide (Mme Ferrand), and Paul, Jr., inherited their father's *habitation* measuring almost two *arpents* on Bayou Road in 1830, selling it together with a house and other constructions to François Girod who in turn sold for $16,000 to Elie Norbert Henry in 1833.[4] The Henry heirs did not subdivide the property until 1855, when a survey in plan book 9, folio 2 indicated this land divided into twenty-eight lots. The projection of N. Galvez Street and Esplanade Avenue had already carved away much of Cheval's land and had resulted in the demolition of his *maison principale*, which had dated from soon after his purchase from Antonio Ramis (fig. 1).

Pierre Darby, free man of color, Sieur Zardais, and Widow Félix Tala had bought subdivisions of the lands of Cheval, Sr. Zimpel clearly indicated these small country seats. Darby's one-story frame house stood on Bayou Road in the center of the projected N. Miro Street.[5] His estate sold the land at a public auction held February 21, 1860; the proceeds went to his widow, Marie Françoise Darby. Little is known of Martin Zardais; his will was indexed but not found in the Book of Wills. Fèlix Tala received title to his property from his sister Marie Rose, Mme Pierre Peyroux. She died October 17, 1830, leaving the small *habitation* to Tala, who died four years later. His widow, Louise Euphrosine Rouzier, a native of New Orleans, inherited it.

The bayouward portion of the last two *arpents* of the d'Auberville-Latil six *arpents* pertained to "Gabriel Bick, *mulatto*" in 1800.[6] Bick's land corresponded to that of Widow Dumaine as seen on the Zimpel map. Marianne Pertuit had inherited her small country seat from her husband Jean Dumaine, who died in 1832 at age fifty-two. According to the city directory, they had lived at old number 372 Bayou Road since 1822.

The final segment of the Hubert tract toward the bayou had been incorporated into the vast plantation of Brasilier *dit* Tourangeau by the 1730s. His *habitation* fronted both sides of Bayou Road for an eight-*arpent* width and extended from the banks of Bayou St. John forty *arpents* in depth, to the land of Gilbert de St. Maxent (later St. Bernard Avenue).[7] The part of Brasilier Tourangeau's land that corresponded to the upper Hubert trace fronted Bayou Road on the right side between present N. Tonti and N. Dorgenois streets, to the depth of three *arpents* or present Columbus Street.

Brasilier Tourangeau sold the Hubert portion, along with a depth to St. Bernard Avenue, to Vincent d'Auberville on June 19, 1756, just a year before the latter's death.[8] Delisle Duparc, who was leasing this property, purchased it from d'Auberville's 1757 estate sale. Duparc's son-in-law, Juan Enoul, acquired this same four *arpents* fronting on Bayou Road, right side, as well as the depth of the land to St. Bernard Avenue in 1775, as detailed in the following chapter. He resold in 1781 to Gabriel Peyroux de la Roche Molive.[9]

That same year Monsieur Peyroux contracted with Mauricio Milon, builder, to remove his house from this upper four *arpents* of Bayou Road to his corner lot within the city.

I, Maurice Milon bind myself to take apart the house of M. Perot [Peyroux] situated on Bayou Road and to reassemble it in town at the corner of his *islet* just as it is shown on the attached plan, with a cabin serving as kitchen together with two privies. M. Perot [Peyroux] will furnish the necessary bricks for the chimneys and ironwork for one chimney, also the nails which he has gathered from the house. There will be wood for the chimney in the kitchen. The house will be *bousillier entre Colonbage* [sic] [mud and moss between posts] and covered by wooden boards. Outside the house will be lifted on blocks [measuring 2½ feet]. I certify having been paid in cash for all the work mentioned, January 31, 1781. M. Milon.[10]

On July 22, 1782, Peyroux filed a suit against Milon for the return of his money, claiming that "the construction of a house formerly situated on Bayou Road" was unacceptable. On February 13, 1783, a declaration was made in court that "Mauricio Milon agreed and contracted to take down a house for M. Peyroux on his plantation on the Road to the Bayou and re-erect same in city." The court declared that this rebuilding was worthless, and Milon had to reimburse Peyroux.

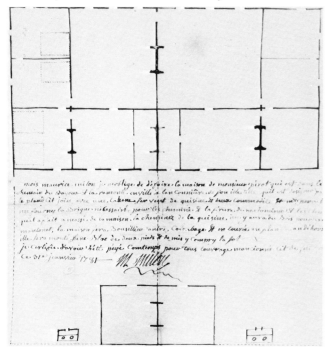

Fig. 1. Retrospective plan of New Orleans, 1838 copy Pilié. (Courtesy Louisiana Historical Center, Archives)

Attached to the 1782 litigation records is the floor plan of this house and kitchen. The original Bayou Road house may have had two large main rooms behind which were four smaller rooms, each having a fireplace. The plan indicates alteration of the floor plan for the city dwelling; small *cabinets* were to be carved from the main rooms. The plan shows the beds in place in the small *cabinets*.

Gabriel Peyroux was a prominent citizen during both the French and Spanish colonial regimes. He was among the first French citizens to swear allegiance to the Spanish government in 1769 in order to continue his transactions to supply grain to the ruling government. Notary J. B. Garic records a May 17, 1775, contract between Peyroux and the Ursuline nuns in which Peyroux arranged for his mother-in-law, Anna Caü, wife of Francisco Caü, native of Calais, France, to live at the convent. As resident of the right side of Bayou Road, Peyroux owned the Petit Bayou, known also as the Pequeño Bayou de la Cruz. One of the two Bridges of the Washerwomen was within the property of Peyroux, whose popularity was not improved in 1781 when he removed one bridge, forcing the Negro washerwomen to use the one remaining bridge belonging to him. His express purpose was to make each laundress pay a half *real*. The city council under Governor Miró on May 25, 1781, commented that Peyroux's "depraved intentions" were reprehensible. Further testimony indicated that the ditches along the road were filling up and blocked because of overuse, and the "Most Illustrious Council" ordered Peyroux "to clear and keep clean the ditches and replace the other bridge."

Widow Peyroux, who appears in many titles and land transfers throughout Faubourg Tremé, reconstituted the boundaries of the high land of the upper Hubert tract when she sold a three-by-three-*arpent* portion to "Pedro Dulcido Barran, free mulatto, on July 1, 1800."[11] She retained the remainder of her land until a future sale. Barran's new land corresponded to the nineteenth-century *habitations* of Bellanger, Fleitas, and Abreo and portions of the Bayou Road *habitations* of Pierre Gueno, as seen on the Zimpel map of 1834.

Two historic houses have stood on the land attributed by Zimpel to M. Bellanger: the Zeringue House and the Benachi-Torre House, now 2257 Bayou Road. Simon Favre had bought a total of 1½ by 3 *arpents* from Pedro Barran, including the entire 2200 block of Bayou Road in 1803. On December 30, 1805, notary Narcisse Broutin sold the same property to Joseph Zeringue. He commissioned Barthélémy Lafon to design a house the following year (figs. 2, A, B).[12] Zeringue kept his beautiful house only until 1814 when his son sold it back to Broutin. By 1832 the Antoine de Villier Guesnon family had sold the house and grounds to M. Guillaume Bellanger, a former Collège d'Orléans professor, who opened his school there. The *Louisiana Courier*, May 1, 1834, advertised:

Boarding School, under F. Bellanger, on the Bayou Road. The building is a new and spacious brick house, the second story whereof contains dormitories, which are cool in summer, and comfortable in winter. The several classes are taught in spacious halls erected in the center of a quiet and retired lot of a depth of 540 feet, and which is appropriate to the recreations of the pupils; also, a basin dug out in the interior of the establishment so as to facilitate the wholesome and frequent use of Baths to the students [see Zimpel]. Such are the advantages which the establishment offers in regard to health.

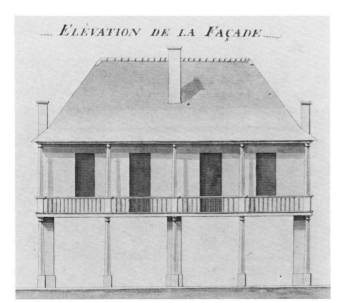

Fig. 2. Joseph Zeringue House Elevation, by Barthélémy Lafon, 1805. (Courtesy Historic New Orleans Collection).

PLAN
au Rez-de-Chaussée.
_N.° 1._

Cheminé

Gallerie.

Fig. 2A. Zeringue House Plan, Ground Floor.

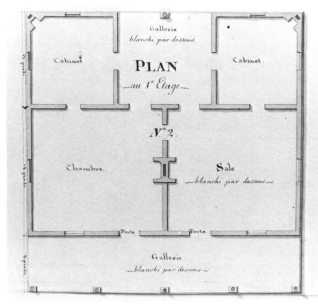

Gallerie
blanchi par dessous.

Cabinet.

PLAN
au 1.er Étage.

Cabinet.

_N.° 2._

Chambre.

Sale
blanchi par dessous

Porte   Porte

Gallerie.
blanchi par dessous.

Fig. 2B. Zeringue House Plan, Main Floor

On December 28, 1838, before T. Seghers, the syndic of creditors of Bellanger auctioned the house "where the college of said B. Bellanger was formerly situated, bound on the other side formerly by Fleitas, now Beaulieu." Etiènne Carnaby bought the *maison principale* and other dependencies," which he sold the same year to Leonard Packwood Bureau for $13,000.

Nicholas Benachi bought a lot 135 by 540 feet containing the Zeringue-Bellanger House on June 28, 1852. It was then bound by the land of M. Dumaine toward the city and property of the Beaulieu family bayouward. Benachi, a partner in the counting house of Ralli and Company at 64 St. Charles Street, bought the land and house from J. E. Holland for his wife, Catherine Grund, and their four children for $11,134. Just one year after the purchase, Mme Benachi and two of her children died at their summer house in Biloxi in the tragic 1853 yellow fever epidemic. Benachi requested that Antoine Bidault be appointed as cotutor of his two surviving motherless daughters.

Benachi then married Anna Marie Bidault, daughter of his friend, on November 13, 1856. He demolished or had moved his former home (the Zeringue House) and built for her the present house at 2257 Bayou Road in 1858–1859 (fig. 3). *The Daily Crescent* of Monday, September 12, 1859, mentions that recent improvements "for the year ending August 31, 1859, include the $18,000 dwelling of M. Benachi near the intersection of Esplanade and Bayou Road, a beautiful and expensive cottage." It has had but one owner subsequent to Benachi. Peter Torre, a native of Italy, bought the house in 1886, living there with his family until his death in 1917, after which his family retained the house, residing continuously through the 1970s.

Torre was the owner of a line of steamships plying the waters between New Orleans and the ports of South and Central America. He had a contract to carry English mail to Belize and to other English tropical possessions. His vessels sailed under the name Royal English Mail Line; Torre ultimately sold his interests to the United Fruit Company. Upon the death in 1978 of Miss Venetia Torre, Peter Torre's daughter, this outstanding nineteenth-century house was bequeathed to the Louisiana Landmarks Society. Miss Torre's will noted that her brother Louis J. Torre had donated his one-half interest to her on the condition that it would eventually be given to the Landmarks Society. The document further provided that her surviving brother, Dr. Mottram P. Torre, may live in the house during his lifetime. Architect-historian Samuel Wilson described the house: "It features a wide gallery on both the first and second floors with four sets of double, square columns across the front. The Gothic cast-iron fence was cast from the design of a Philadelphia firm with probable New Orleans connections. A fountain, placed between the front gate and the entrance to the house is a pleasant amenity to the grounds which are shaded by many large trees. This impressive building is one of the more beautiful mansions of New Orleans."

Standing beside the Benachi-Torre House is the historic Fleitas House at 2275 Bayou Road, which makes this block of Bayou Road one of the most spacious and handsome residential squares in the city (fig. 4). The containing grounds for the Fleitas House share the early history of its neighbor. In 1832 the Antoine de Villier Guesnon family had subdivided their tract; and Manuel Fleitas purchased a vacant lot, once part of the grounds of the Zeringue House. The vacant lot is shown on the Zimpel map as belonging to Fleitas.

Fig. 3. 2257 Bayou Road, Benachi-Torre House

The Fleitas House probably was moved to this site by the family in 1836, from its former location on the left side of Bayou Road. As early as the Pilié survey of 1822, the Fleitas *maison principale* was shown as standing in the route of the projected Esplanade, thus creating the necessity of demolition or relocation. At the time of its relocation it was enlarged and remodeled. Three-quarters of a century later, Mr. and Mrs. Joseph Chauffe purchased the house when they were married in 1901. It is from this period that Victorian-style additions were built, forming a wing on the left and a bay on the right.

The Fleitas-Chauffe House and grounds now terminate at the corner of N. Rocheblave. Adjacent to Fleitas' land was a small *habitation*, the 1822 owner of which was Paul Hardy, free man of color, according to the Pilié survey. Vincent Abreo owned the same land and *maison principale*, in 1834 according to Zimpel, until Abreo's death on October 14, 1844. The buildings on the Abreo *habitation* were destroyed by the extension of N. Rocheblave Street.

Fig. 4. 2275 Bayou Road, Fleitas-Chauffe House

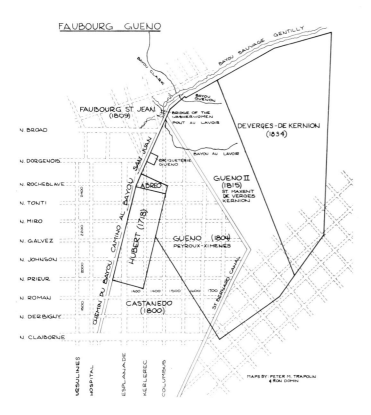

FAUBOURG GUENO

MAPS BY PETER M. TRAPOLIN
& RON DOMIN

CHAPTER VIII

Duparc–Gueno

In 1727 Pierre Joseph Delisle *dit* Duparc was living in New Orleans on St. Ann Street.[1] The Superior Council recorded his purchase of a house on Dumaine Street in 1729.[2] A planter-merchant, he held a contract with the Company of the Indies, and then the French colonial government, to supply much of the grain and goods for the colony. The Superior Council records reveal that he was an infantry captain and a Commissaire des Nations Indiennes, acting as an interpreter. By 1744 he had "a cow farm in the city on the Road going to Bayou St. Jean near the Washerwomen's Bridge."[3] Notary Garic documents Duparc's one-time ownership of Petit Desert, the early French concession later developed as Seven Oaks Plantation in Westwego, now demolished.

Duparc was among the first Frenchmen to swear allegiance to the king of Spain in a document dated August 26, 1769. Other Bayou St. John and Bayou Road residents who felt it in their best interests to cosign the oath of allegiance were Duparc's son-in-law Bartholomeo McNamara and his neighbor Gabriel Peyroux de la Roche Molive. They swore "to disclose anything that we know to be detrimental to his [the Spanish sovereign's] supreme authority."[4]

Duparc's will, dated September 17, 1775, disclosed that his six children, through their marriages, controlled a large part of the land along Bayou St. John and Bayou Road.[5] Nicolas mar-

ried Julia Larche (Larchevêque), whose father owned great tracts across the river from New Orleans. Francisca married Antoine Philippe Mandeville de Marigny, whose plantation was adjacent to her father's. Catalina married Bartholomeo Magnemassa (McNamara), who with Governor Alejandro O'Reilly's nephew, Maurice Conway, played a prominent role in the Spanish administration. Duparc's third daughter, Mariana, married Jean Arnoult (Enoul), son of Santiago Enoul Livaudais, who through his Dugué-Livaudais connections had large holdings on the Bayous Sauvage (Gentilly) and St. Jean. The youngest son, Francisco Delisle, was a minor in 1775.

Delisle Duparc's "cow farm on the Road to the Bayou" was first leased and then bought from Jean Baptiste Brasilier *dit* Tourangeau in 1760. Duparc's entire plantation, as indicated in the 1789 Trudeau-St. Maxent retrospective survey, was on the right side of Bayou Road angling from N. Broad to St. Bernard Avenue, to a point halfway between N. Galvez and N. Johnson, and from Bayou Road at N. Rocheblave angling downward again toward St. Bernard Avenue to N. Derbigny. The acquisition of this large tract was made by Duparc in two purchases: one directly from Brasilier Tourangeau and the other from the d'Auberville estate in 1757.[6] The latter had emanated from the original ownership of Brasilier Tourangeau.

The four *arpents* of Duparc's land closest to Bayou Sauvage passed to his son-in-law Juan Enoul in 1775; the latter sold them to Gabriel Peyroux de la Roche Molive around 1781.[7] Widow Peyroux inherited this important stretch of land, which bordered both Bayou Road and Gentilly Road. She sold 1½ *arpents* by 3 *arpents* of the Bayou Road frontage to free mulatto Pedro Dulcido Barran in July of 1800 for 1500 *pesos*. This land and the large Peyroux *habitation* became the Pierre Gueno plantation as seen on the Zimpel map.

Widow Peyroux sold the large tract first to Manuel Ximenes on May 22, 1801, before P. Pedesclaux. The land was described as:

> two pieces of land, one next to the other located in the *Barrio* of Bayou San Juan composed of seventy-five superficial *arpents* . . . bound on the west with the edges of the Road to Bayous San Juan and Chantilly [*sic*] to the north, with land of the Señoras Duberges [De Verges], to the south with land already sold to M. Barran and Don José Castanedo, and to the east with lands of Bernard de Marigny as surveyed by Royal surveyor Don Carlos Trudeau on the seventh of this month. . . . The land belonging to me by inheritance from my late husband . . . I sell for 2,694 *pesos*, 3½ *reales* to be paid in three years.[8]

Ximenes is shown as owner of this land on the De Woiserie map of 1803. However, the same land retroceded to Mme Peyroux on November 15, 1802, from Ximenes; and Mme Peyroux sold the same land directly to Pierre Gueno, the sale recorded May 4, 1802, in act number 44 of Pierre Pedesclaux.

Gueno, a native of Barrège, departement de Tam, France, also added Bayou Road frontage by a purchase of 1½ by 3 *arpents* from free mulatto Pedro Dulcido Barran, which Barran had bought from Widow Peyroux on July 1, 1800; this sale by Barran to Gueno before Pierre Pedesclaux was dated June 15, 1803.[9] In the same year, Gueno continued to collect acreage by acquisition of Bayou Road frontage from free man of color Carlos Montreuil: "I, Carlos Montreuil, sell to Pierre Gueno land which I bought from Claude Tremé in 1800 bound by lands of P. Cheval, free man of color, and Widow Peyroux."[10]

Another of the Gueno *habitations* bordered Bayou Gentilly and shared an easterly boundary with a canal dug by the Marigny family to service their sawmills closer to the city. Antonio Gilbert St. Maxent was one of the first owners of all these "back lands" in the second half of the eighteenth century. He sold the tract measuring sixteen *arpents*, fourteen *toises*, three *lines* in depth to Pierre De Verges on January 5, 1780.[11] De Verges's three daughters inherited the land; and on July 18, 1806, René Huchet De Kernion and his wife, Modeste De Verges, bought out Prudence and Constance De Verges after a partition of their father's estate.[12] Pierre Gueno expanded his plantation with the purchase from Mme Huchet de Kernion's holdings on September 25, 1815, thus consolidating acreage for the largest single *habitation* along the Road to the Bayou at that date.[13]

Gueno established a major brickyard and a *maison principale* that was situated at a point along Bayou Road where N. Dorgenois Street eventually came through, near the Petit Bayou, which became known as Bayou Guesnon (Gueno). Gueno died not long after assembling the equivalent of forty-eight city blocks. His will is dated October 12, 1821, 8 A.M., according to which he was born in 1759, the son of Raymond Jean Gueno and Françoise Carrier. He recognized his natural child Mathieu Gueno of France, and he freed the slave who was his mulatto mistress. Executors were Jean Ximenes and Simon Cucullu. His wife, Felicité Françoise Loubie, is listed in the 1822 city directory as a widow living at the *briqueterie*. Her children included Pierre, James, Marie, Catherine (Mme Manuel Ramos), and Madeleine (later Mme Buss).

Gueno's succession went through the probate court on January 19, 1825. It was not, however, until 1835 that Faubourg Gueno was laid out by the surveyor Louis Bringier and the lots sold by Mme Gueno. The acts of sale were passed before O. de Armas, June 20, 1835. There were more than fifty pur-

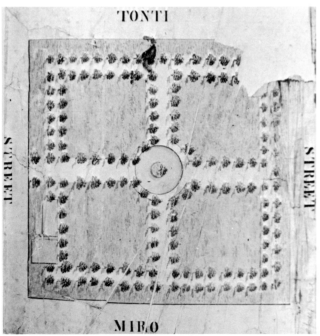

Fig. 1. Plan book 39, folio 4; signed and dated, "Bringier, April 15, 1836"; square bound by Tonti, Miro, Laharpe, Lapeyrouse

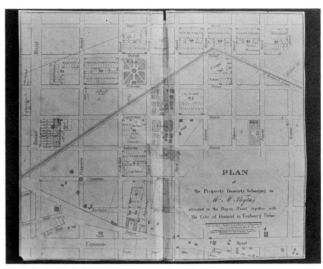

Fig. 2. Plan of the Property formerly belonging to Mr. M. Fleytas, drawn by Hirt, architect and engineer; lithograph by J. Manouvrier & Co., Corner Magazine and Poydras; see acts of Edward Barnett August 30, 1842 (Courtesy New Orleans Notarial Archives)

chasers, and they bought entire squares and groups of squares creating small farms, as well as single lots. One square, bound by N. Tonti, N. Miro, Onzaga, and Lapeyrouse, had been set aside for a public promenade and is illustrated in an archival drawing, plan book 39, folio 4 (fig. 1). Some suburban estates soon developed. An impressive one belonged to Pierre Soulé, who built a *maison de maître* amid expansive gardens in the square bound by N. Rocheblave, Onzaga, D'Abadie, and N. Tonti, now the site of McDonogh No. 9 Public School. Monsieur Viosca's residence (fig. 2) was on the square bound by Lapeyrouse, Laharpe, N. Tonti, and N. Miro.[14]

The part of Faubourg Gueno between Bayou Road, N. Dorgenois, Gentilly Road, and Onzaga was considered a prime portion of the suburb because of its relatively high elevation. An 1836 newspaper advertisement offered:

> at Hewlett's Exchange, the fine property belonging to Mr. Rouselin [*sic*] situated in Faubourg Trémé [*sic*] formerly Guesnons [*sic*], *viz* Eight fine squares of ground divided into 175 lots, a part of which front on the Bayou and Gentilly roads—those lots are the most high of the property formerly belonging to Guesnon—they have never been inundated, not even at the time of Macartys crevace [*sic*], they being on a bluff. The fine situation of these lots and the improvements which are being daily made in this faubourg, hold out great inducements to purchasers and to persons disposed to build summer residences.[15]

Charles Rousselin had bought this property soon after the October 13, 1835, estate sale of Widow Gueno. As a result of Rousselin's ownership, a street three blocks long, parallel to N. Broad near N. Dorgenois, between Laharpe and d'Abadie, was named for him. The history of one of the squares sold by Rousselin illustrates the early development of large squares for summer or suburban homes and their late-nineteenth-century urban development.

Hélène Barnett, Mme Solomon Audler, purchased property from Rousselin in the square bound by Onzaga, Lapeyrouse, N. Broad, and Paul Morphy (White) streets in the 1836 sale. She augmented this purchase in 1846, ultimately acquiring the entire square. Solomon Audler lived in the French Quarter at the time of the first land purchase in Faubourg Gueno, but by 1846 he and his family are listed in the city directory as living "on the Broadway near Columbus." The 1851 directory further refines the location: "Solomon Audler, collector of licences on Coffee-Houses, Broad between Lapeyrouse and Onzaga". Thus by 1846, and certainly in 1851, the Audlers were living in their new creole cottage, the only dwelling in the square. In 1868 Mme Audler sold her house to Mary Jane Cross, wife of cotton broker George M. Gardin. The Gardin family retained the house and entire square until 1905 when the Carrollton Land and Development Company subdivided it into twenty-four lots. At that time the Audler-Gardin house was turned on the square to face a newly formed lot at the present 2616–22 Onzaga.

In 1970 Dr. and Mrs. Thomas Whitecloud recognized that hidden behind the present twentieth-century façade lay the nineteenth-century Audler creole cottage, to which the Gardin family had added double dormers after 1868 (fig. 3). Beneath the present slate roof are the rived cypress shingles from the time of Audler's ownership. The interior four rooms and the *cabinet* gallery of the creole cottage are floored in 6- to 6½-inch pine boards. Large, pilastered mantels are painted black *faux marbre*. Doors and one entire floor are of *faux bois*. The Gardin family papers were discovered under the floorboards of the attic, which they had enlarged. The present façade dates from the early 1900s, the time of the relocation of the house.

Fig. 3. 2616 Onzaga, Dr. Thomas Whitecloud Cottage

Fig. 4. 2607 Laharpe

Its restoration by analogy would include placement of four evenly spaced French doors and a gallery with box columns and a wooden railing.

The adjacent square, bound by N. Broad, Laharpe, Lapeyrouse, and Paul Morphy (White), also contains a house that dates from soon after an 1868 subdivision (fig. 4). The Orleans Railroad Company bought two squares, including this one, for a total of $12,000, from Gustave François Weisse of Paris, France, in 1868. Weisse had owned these squares in 1862, after purchase from Eugène Rochereau, also an absentee Parisian investor. The two squares were first subdivided by the railroad company in 1868, at which time a Magny lithograph illustrated them divided into fifty-two lots for an auction sale in the St. Louis Hotel rotunda.[16] The only house existing at that time, used as the depot for the New Orleans Railroad, was set back on the square bound by Gentilly, White, Laharpe, and Lapeyrouse.

Evidently these lots did not sell, and the Orleans Railroad Company ordered a new survey the next year; an auction was scheduled at the St. Charles Hotel. At this time the orientation of four lots at the corner of N. Broad and Laharpe was changed to front Laharpe Street. The lots on which 2607 Laharpe stand were lots 9 and 10 on this 1869 subdivision and were purchased by Samuel Solomon Schoenfield. This present house is the first residence to be built on the square and dates from soon after the subdivision. It would appear from the low foundation that the house was moved within its containing lot to its present site, making it occupy only two of the original four lots. It is now a center-hall villa with hip-roof and double chimneys and has been remodeled from its original appearance. Development of the square continued slowly, but by 1883 seven houses were recorded on the Robinson atlas. The rail line from the Gentilly depot ran past 2607 Laharpe, turning upriver at the corner of N. Broad.

The Solomon Villa across N. Broad at 1572 is another important historic landmark; it remains deserted today in a garden measuring half a square of land (fig. 5). On the Lapeyrouse side of the spacious lot stands one of the largest pecan trees in the city; the parterred gardens with overgrown boxwood, huge sweet olive trees, and specimens of the plants popular in nineteenth-century New Orleans are valuable testaments to a past era. The house with its wide center hall dates from the 1870s; but it incorporates an earlier creole cottage, the floors of which are seen in the present house, giving a clue to the size of the original cottage.

Such farms and farmhouses were to be seen in Faubourg Gueno from the time of the estate sale into the twentieth century; plan book 38, folio 54 illustrates two farmhouses on Gentilly Road with galleries, stables, picket fences, shrubbery, and trees as they appeared in 1867 (fig. 6). Many of these farms were owned and run by Germans. At 2418–20 Laharpe is an important, galleried creole cottage built by one of the early Germans in the faubourg (fig. 7). The Lotzes were from Darmstadt, and there were at least four carpenters in the family. Leonard Lotz built this house and continued to live there until his death in 1907; his descendants occupied and maintained the house until 1978, representing a single-family occupancy for over 130 years. Details including millwork and a circular stairway in a rear *cabinet* reflect the careful workmanship of the craftsman who built the house.

Another former landmark, but one that retains only its early-

Fig. 5. 1572 N. Broad, Solomon Villa

Fig. 6. Plan book 38, folio 54; signed and dated, "Charles A. de Armas, December 10, 1867"; farm on Gentilly Road near Fairgrounds

Fig. 7. 2418–20 Laharpe, Lotz Cottage

Fig. 8. 2632 Lapeyrouse

nineteenth-century roof contours, is Lebreton Market. An earlier Indian market had previously been located there, prior to the time of Bienville. A galleried house at 2632 Lapeyrouse is a superior example of the enlarged creole cottage, a house-type peculiar to Faubourg Gueno (fig. 8). Four-bay width, gabled sides, and double dormers are the traditional vocabulary, here enlarged to a full two-story building with service wing extending from the rear. Built in the late Classical style, the house dates from 1872. In 1872 Augustin Viavant, Sr., who had acquired three vacant lots here, sold them to Henry Viavant for $1,500. Viavant built this house immediately, taking out a loan with the New Orleans Credit Finance Association, which allowed him a finished house for $6,728. The house remained in the Viavant family until January 12, 1886, when Viavant sold it to Ernestine Jacquet, widow of Dominique Develle, for the low price of $3,500 (P. A. Conand). As a whole the Faubourg Gueno of the late nineteenth century reflects architecture exemplifying Italianate and Victorian versions of the villa-type cottage, galleried townhouses, and twentieth-century bungalows intermixed with the gamut of shotgun variations.

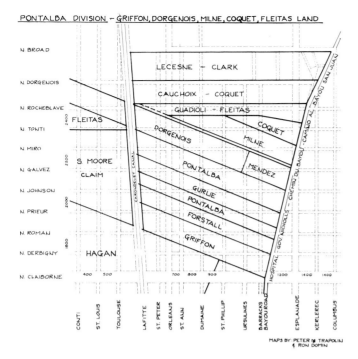

N. BROAD

LECESNE – CLARK

N. DORGENOIS

CAUCHOIX – COQUET

N. ROCHEBLAVE

GUADIOLI – FLEITAS

FLEITAS
N. TONTI
2400

DORGENOIS

COQUET

MILNE

N. MIRO

S. MOORE
N. GALVEZ
2200
CLAIM

PONTALBA

MENDEZ

N. JOHNSON

GURLIE

N. PRIEUR
2000
PONTALBA

FORSTALL

N. ROMAN
1800

GRIFFON

N. DERBIGNY

HAGAN

N. CLAIBORNE

400   500   700   800   900   1200   1400   1400

CARONDELET CANAL

CHEMIN DU BAYOU – CAMINO AL BAYOU SAN JUAN

HOSPITAL – GOV. NICHOLLS

CONTI
ST. LOUIS
TOULOUSE
LAFITTE
ST. PETER
ORLEANS
ST. ANN
DUMAINE
ST. PHILLIP
URSULINES
BARRACKS
BAYOU ROAD
ESPLANADE
KERLEREC
COLUMBUS

MAPS BY: PETER M TRAPOLIN
& RON DOMIN

CHAPTER IX

Lebreton –Griffon

Tracing of the early ownership of all the land between N. Rampart and N. Broad on the right side of Bayou Road to St. Bernard Avenue, all three Charles de Morand tracts, the ancient Hubert concessions, and Tourangeau-Duparc lands has been completed. The land beyond the Morand plantation on the left side of Bayou Road extending from N. Claiborne to N. Dorgenois was abandoned by Boissière who had purchased it from Joachim de Gauvrit in 1729.[1] Under Governor Vaudreuil in the 1750s, it became one of the numerous land grants of Louis Césaire Lebreton, a Frenchman who was "King's Councillor to the Mint in Paris, Lord of Bassan, Charmeaux, resident of Paris, on the Street of Fasters, in the suburb of Montmârtre in the house of Monsieur Coudrée."[2] Lebreton's appearance in Louisiana is further indication that men of high standing came to the colony, both for administrative purposes and to find well-placed concessions.

In 1748 Lebreton was Councillor Assessor in Louisiana and was married to Jeanne Marguerite Chauvin de la Frenière. She was a member of an illustrious early family, whose major concessions faced the Mississippi River at present-day Kenner and ran back to Lake Pontchartrain. On August 9, 1752, Lebreton received as a land grant eight *arpents* of the former Gauvrit land on the left side of Bayou Road, extending from the boundaries of Morand to the boundaries of Brasilier *dit* Tourangeau.[3] With the acquisition of Gauvrit's land, Lebreton's property almost met the Lafrenière holdings, since it spread diagonally back toward Lake Pontchartrain from Bayou Road.

Lebreton sold most of this original Gauvrit tract to Dame

Françoise Petit de Coulange, widow of Sieur Vincent Senéchal d'Auberville, on May 30, 1757, before notary Chantalou.[4] He retained two *arpents*, which he deeded to "Monsieur Louis Docmeny de Morand, his godson—a minor, assisted by his tutor Monsieur Alexandre de Latil—to settle forever the difficulties of the Morand boundary."[5] On November 13, 1776, Latil and young Morand sold these two *arpents*, along with six more bayouward belonging to Latil by purchase from Widow d'Auberville, to Dame Marie Corbin, Widow Voisin:

> I, Alexandre Latil and Luis Docmeni de Morant [*sic*] of this city sell to Anne Marie Corbin, Widow Voisin, a *habitation* composed of eight-*arpents* front, with depth it can have, situated on the Road to Bayou St. Jean bound on one side by land of Pablo Moró and on the other by that of free Negro Lanuitte, which belong to us from having, I, said Latil, bought six *arpents* at the *remate* [auction] of the estate of M. d'Auberville, June 30, 1757, and I, said Luis Morand, two *arpents* which are mine by donation given by Don Luis Césaire Lebreton, for the price of 1,200 *Pesos*.[6]

Mme Voisin gave the two *arpents* that had belonged to Louis de Morand fronting Bayou Road (left side between present N. Claiborne to N. Derbigny) to her daughter, Jeanne Voisin, on December 11, 1781, before notary Leonard Mazange. It was part of the dowry in her marriage to Charles Griffon Derneville. In Jeanne's will dated November 12, 1787, before Fernando Rodrigues, she declared "that she was pregnant and recognized for her sole and only heir the child that she was carrying, and in the case that it did not come into the world, her husband, the said Sieur Charles Griffon." Jeanne died without children that same year. Her husband, Griffon, retained this small *habitation*, living there with his second wife, Suzanna Peyroux, daughter of Gabriel Peyroux and Suzanna Caüe.

The Griffon *habitation* remained intact until 1832, with the exception of the sale of two 60-by-200-foot lots facing Bayou Road, which Griffon sold to two free Negroes in 1800 and 1801. Griffon proved his ownership of the *habitation* in the 1800 sale to Jean Baptiste Derneville, the boundary of which

Fig. 1. 1826–28 St. Philip

was contiguous with the remaining Griffon *arpents*. Trudeau made a survey that confirms this sale to Derneville, in which Griffon's *habitation* was described as "two *arpents* facing Bayou Road by donation of his previous mother-in-law, Anna Darby, Widow Voisin, December 11, 1785."[7]

The other lot toward town was sold on April 12, 1801, to Cupidon Carrés, *homme de couleur libre*, in another act before notary Pierre Pedesclaux. Griffon lived on the *habitation* until his death in 1810.[8] His heirs sold a portion of it to the city for the opening of the Girod Canal under Mayor Roffignac in 1827 and subdivided the remainder in 1832.

Within the Griffon tract, one cottage that suggests the early suburban or semirural appearance of the neighborhood soon after subdivision stands at 1826–28 St. Philip (fig. 1). It was probably built for Louis Dubrueil, free man of color, when he purchased three lots at the Griffon sale in 1832. Immediately noticeable on a present-day tour of the Griffon tract are the substantial numbers of single, three-bay, Greek Revival creole cottages having one dormer at front and rear elevations and a built-in overhang. The earliest examples of this house-type date from the 1830s, but the majority throughout the Faubourgs Marigny and Tremé date from 1845 and 1850. A rare house-type by all considerations, it is outstandingly characteristic of the Lebreton-Griffon *habitation*. The excellent example at 1803 Ursulines Street was built in the late 1850s for free man of color José Azemar (fig. 2).

Fig. 2. 1803 Ursulines

Pontalba – Forstall and Gurlie

Adjacent to the narrow *habitation* established for the newlyweds Charles and Jeanne Voisin was the remaining land of Widow Voisin, which she had bought from Alexandre Latil on September 13, 1776, measuring six *arpents* on Bayou Road from N. Derbigny back to N. Johnson Streets.[1] It was within this land in 1718 that Joachim de Gauvrit, captain of the troops in the new city, built a house on Bayou Road. Gauvrit had sold on October 5, 1728, ten by forty *arpents* from the present N. Claiborne to Milne Road to M. Boissière who abandoned the land, after which Louis Césaire Lebreton received it as part of a French grant (fig. 1). Lebreton sold the above six *arpents* on May 30, 1737, to Widow d'Auberville.[2] Alexandre Latil bought these six, with the entire depth of forty *arpents*, from the Widow d'Auberville.[3]

Latil is known to have had a *faïencerie* on the property; and he soon established a slaughterhouse there, since he obtained a franchise from the city for the provision of meat for the public market. Years later, on October 31, 1771, Latil signed a contract for the leasing of the slaughterhouse.

> Know ye that I, Alexandre Latil, inhabitant of this city, rent to Don Antonio Le Blanc, inhabitant of the same city, the slaughterhouse for this city which had been adjudicated to me on the 13th of September past, and at the same time a corral and pasture for the animals with *un mattadoso* [slaughterhouse] within, and a hut, situated at a *habitation* that I have outside of the city on the Camino del Bayou San Juan for four years, from February 1, 1772, to the same day 1776. With the condition that all the renderings will be turned over to Don Bartolomeo Magnemasa [McNamara] and Don Mauricio Conway [owner of a tannery across Bayou St. John]. Also all the skins of the animals for two years to go to them for one *peso* each and those after that for two years to be sold for four *reales* without any exception. I cede all the rest which can be seen of said slaughterhouse with said provisions for 1,060 *pesos* which will be paid each year to the *majordomo* of properties of this city and another 1,000 *pesos* to be paid to me, but I am to be paid every three months and the first payment on the first of April, 1772, to continue each three months to the end of the time. Also if anything happens to Don Antonio LeBlanc, no one can succeed him in this agreement.[4]

Latil kept the slaughterhouse and tile factory until 1776, when Anna Corbin (Darby) Voisin bought them.[5] Widow Voisin's daughter, Mme Griffon, had died by 1781; and the widow sold the former Latil tract to Andrés Almonester y Rojas.

This area along Bayou Road between N. Derbigny and N. Johnson became known as the Pontalba division when Almonester's daughter, Micaela de Pontalba, inherited it. Almonester owned it at the time of his death and left it to his wife, Louise de la Ronde, who subsequently married J. B. Castillon. In 1811 when Almonester's daughter, Micaela, married Joseph Xavier Celestin Delfau de Pontalba, her mother, Mme

Fig. 1. Plan book 31, folio 32; signed and dated "L. Lafon, 1812, copied by John Pilié"; plan of property of M. de Pontalba on the Bayou Road

Castillon, gave as part of Micaela's dowry "a plantation on the Bayou Road with the front and depth as shown, bound above by the land of the heirs of Sieur Griffon and to the rear with land which belongs to Almonester, he having built a leper's hospital."[6] The very next year Celestin de Pontalba and Micaela, who resided in France, arranged a public auction to be held on January 9, 1812, to sell this property, which they had divided into eleven strips between N. Derbigny and N. Johnson (fig. 1).[7]

The auction notice was advertised three times prior to the sale by Dutillet and Peyrelade:

> The plantation of M. Pontalba, formerly Almonester, belonged to Madame Castillion [*sic*], situated on the left side of the Bayou Road in leaving the city will be sold by the above-named auctioneers in lots of half an *arpent* fronting the Road, with depths at the Canal Carondelet. The house is in the centre of a lot of 142 feet, the whole conformable to the plan now posted up at the Commercial Coffee-House. This land is the highest in that quarter and too well known to require further particulars. The sale will take place on the premises on the tenth of February next [1812].[8]

This 1812 auction sold the divided property from N. Derbigny to N. Roman streets and from Bayou Road to the Carondelet Canal to Edmund Forstall, Louis Gilles, Louis Aimé Pigneguy, Tremé Lahuttière, and François Jean Pierre. Forstall began reconsolidating these lots, adding one closest to the city, which he purchased from Denis Gaston in 1820. Gaston had built a house soon after his 1817 acquisition from Gilles. The house was described in an act before Philippe Pedesclaux, May 27, 1820, as "a house of four rooms and two *cabinets* with a *galerie* front and rear, brick between posts and roofed in slate. A wood kitchen with many rooms, two large warehouses of wood in one of which is a furnace and *chandière* [candlemaking equipment] mounted over the furnace; a vast edifice with *moulin a poudre* [flour mill]."

In 1826 Forstall mortgaged one of these 90-foot lots on Bayou Road, with its extreme depth of 15 *arpents*, in favor of his wife, Clara Durel.[9] On December 23, 1828, he bought 250 feet more on Bayou Road, land contiguous with his own, from Jean Louis Gras. Forstall and his wife occupied this *habitation* until 1843, at which time he and his brother, Placide, were in serious financial trouble. On August 10, 1843, they sold the entire property to Manuel Lizardi, who resided in England. The sale to Lizardi included, in addition to the Bayou Road property, a plantation below the city next to the plantation of Widow Tremé.[10] Forstall also sold Lizardi six lots in Faubourg Marigny bound by Greatmen, Craps, Poets, and Franklin, as well as a plantation known as "*Grande Terre* in Barataria, *Parish of Jefferson*, established in a *sucrerie* [sugar refinery] together with all the animals, *machines à vapeur*, and slaves."

Lizardi, who had arrived in New Orleans via Cuba, had large real estate holdings all over the city, including homes on Esplanade and at 1600 Prytania. After this sale, Edmond and Placide Forstall became attorneys for the absentee landlord Lizardi who resubdivided the Pontalba-Forstall tract and sold the lots on June 25, 1847, averaging about $400 for a lot 30 by 120 feet.

Adjacent to the Forstall division, measuring approximately one city block on Bayou Road and extending in depth to the Carondelet Canal, was that part of the Pontalba lands associated with Louis Gurlie. A house within this area may have been built by Almonester and purchased by Etiènne Débon at the Pontalba auction. Débon sold this Bayou Road frontage between N. Roman and N. Prieur to Louis Gurlie, and the city engineer's office preserves the survey of L. Bringier, dated July 26, 1836, for a subdivision of the Gurlie property. This land had a pond or swamp that could well have been the clay pit for Latil's *faïencerie*. An October 27, 1834, mortgage described events leading to the partitioning of the Pontalba-Gurlie division:

Were present M. Louis Gurlie and Dame Nancy Claire Farragut, his wife, by him duly authorized, living in this city; who have declared that the said Sieur Louis Gurlie, having undersigned and acquired 200 shares of stock of 100 *piastres* each, forming together the sum of 20,000 *piastres* in the capital funds of the Banque des Citoyens de la Louisiane. . . . And to guarantee their said shares in the capital funds of the said Banque . . . they accept and mortgage jointly and separately by these present in favor of the Banque de Citoyens de la Louisiane, the following property: A lot of ground situated on the Road of Bayou St. Jean, to the left side of the said Road when leaving the city, and formerly forming two distinct lots, measuring the said lot in English measure 232 feet facing the said Road, with a depth running as far as Canal Carondelet; the said lot being bound on each side by properties of Monsieur de Pontalba *fils*; Together with the house of bricks and all other buildings, circumstances and dependencies with no exception of reserve; and to charge of all usages and servitudes attached to this same lot of ground, such as they are built, and indicated on a plan drawn by the Sieur Barthélémy Lafon, January 8, 1812, deposited in the study of the late Philippe Pedesclaux notary of this city. It is expressly excepted by the present mortgage a portion of the said lot of ground, which portion is part where passes the Canal Girod, and is the measure of 9,873 feet superficially, which is shown more clearly on a plan drawn by the Sieur Joseph Pilié, surveyor of the city, and annexed to an act carrying the transaction in the report of Felix de Armas, notary of the city, July 14, 1825; The said portion thus excepted having been ceded and abandoned to title of transaction to the Corporation of this city of New Orleans, by act of October 8, 1825 in the report of the said notary Felix de Armas, by Sieurs Gurlie and Guillot who were then owners of the above described lot.[11]

The remaining Pontalba division land was dedicated for the establishment of a lepers' hospital. A letter from Andrés Almonester y Rojas was read to the Cabildo at its meeting of April 22, 1785. He wrote that he had constructed a "hospital for lepers, composed of four separate sections large enough to house many white families . . . and other separate quarters for Negroes." He also constructed a canal for the bathing of sick people; this canal served as a boundary to the hospital. The City Council recorded:

The St. Lazarus Hospital, established outside the City on a bend of the Bayou Road, has funds of 2,500 *pesos* which are placed at rent or interest under mortgage guarantee, 1,500 *pesos* at a rate of 5% per annum, and the remaining 1,000 *pesos* at 5% which the person interested voluntarily agreed to donate for charity. In said Hospital are three sick Negroes and they are given ten cents every day for their meals. There is a guard maintained at the Hospital in order to prevent the patients from going beyond the allowed

limits and the Corporal in command of the guard received from the Overseer or City Treasurer the money alloted for the sustenance of the patients, the same Corporal attending to the purchase of the required foodstuffs. As to the other expenditures, they cannot be figured beforehand.[12]

The act of donation of this property to the city by Almonester is dated April 20, 1785. The hospital was so successful that leprosy was almost eradicated from the city. Governor Estevan Miró on August 10, 1790, in a letter regarding Almonester's many charitable works and his expectations of royal honor, wrote that "since the death of the five lepers who were caught, no others have been seen in the province."[13]

The hospital ceased to function soon after 1803; the buildings were destroyed by fire, and the city decided to lease the land in 1808. On April 7 of that year the *Moniteur de la Louisiane* advertised: "Thursday the 21st, current, at noon there will be proceeded with, in the office of the Mayoralty, the adjudication to the highest offerer and last bidder, a lease for rent for the space of one year, of the dependant land of the old Lepers Hospital, situated on the Road to Bayou St. Jean. James Mather, Mayor."[14] Leasing by the city continued until 1833 when, as a result of a plague that killed over one thousand citizens in September alone, a new cemetery was urgently needed. The City Council, at a special meeting on September 25, 1833, authorized "the opening for burials of Almonester's land on 'Leprous Road.'" Micaela Pontalba filed suit in the Third District Court to recover possession of the property, since it was no longer used for the charitable purpose for which it had been donated by her father. The court ruled in her favor; but when the city took the case to the Supreme Court of Louisiana, the judgment was reversed.

On the 20th of April, 1785, Don Andrés Almonester y Rojas the father of the plaintiff, made to the *Ayuntamiento* of the city of New Orleans, a donation. The donation was accepted unconditionally, and the *Ayuntamiento* proceeded to take possession of the property, and to apply it to the use contemplated by the donor. Up to 1805, lepers were admitted in the hospital. After that period it was abandoned and became the refuge of Indians, who, after some years, set fire to it and burned it down. The ground then ceased to be used for any purpose, till 1833 when the City Council passed an ordinance converting it into a cemetery. This change of destination gave rise to the present controversy. Apparently, due to the swift action of Mme Pontalba, few, if any, burials took place. The Supreme Court reported that "the parties . . . entered into a written agreement by which the property was to be sold, and its proceeds deposited in a bank, subject to the final decision of the court."[15]

A compromise partition of the land provided Mme Pontalba with half of the proceeds from the sale of the land. The hospital strip from N. Prieur to N. Johnson at Bayou Road was finally subdivided in 1836, according to an advertisement in the *Louisiana Courier*, on December 23, 1836, which auctioneers Mossy and Garidel posted at the St. Louis Exchange:

One thousand twelve lots of Ground being a part of the estate of Madame de Pontalba, comprising the high grounds of the well known *Terre de Lepreux* and extending from the Bayou Road as far as Common Street in the 2nd municipality. The plan and the division of the lots as made by M. d'Hémécourt will be found at the store of the auctioneers. This fine property is too well known to require a particular description and . . . Acts of sale before Felix Grima, notary public at the expense of the purchaser.

A happier use for the Carondelet Canal section of the *terre de lepreux* was Le Jardin du Rocher de Ste Hélène. Built and landscaped along the Carondelet Canal at N. Miro Street, it became a major attraction and pleasure garden. An 1844 drawing in plan book 35, folio 16 shows this elegant park replete with two plantation-style galleried structures, billiard pavillions, a large kitchen, parterred gardens with fountains and statuary, and a long bower (fig. 2).

A cohesive building style prevailed in the former Pontalba division beginning with the 1830s sale of lots. Reminiscent of the plantation origins of the area are the galleried creole cottages at 927 N. Galvez and 2014 Ursulines (figs. 3 and 4); the latter is illustrated in plan book 44, folio 36 with a drawing by C. A. de Armas dated 1855 (fig. 5). The four-bay, two-story creole house at 1027 N. Roman blended well as part of the interpretive creole architecture (fig. 6). To be found, too, is the four-bay gable-sided creole house, which is an enlargement of the cottage type, exemplified by 1228 N. Johnson (fig. 7). Houses of 2½ stories with large front and rear dormers like this often have attached dependencies. Frame, double-dormered, Greek Revival creole cottages are particularly evident, as seen in plan book 46, folio 46 (fig. 8). In contrast, the Pontalba division has one of the finest detached Italianate townhouses to be found in Faubourg Tremé, the Bouchard-Costanza house at 2014 St. Philip dating from 1867 (fig. 9). Providing a unifying and important addition to the area is St. Anna's Church, now renamed St. Peter Claver at 1923 St. Philip Street, dating from 1852 (fig. 10).

Fig. 3. 927 N. Galvez

Fig. 4. 2014–16 Ursulines

Fig. 2. Plan book 35, folio 16; signed and dated, "Bourgerol, September 5, 1844"; Du Jardin du Rocher de Ste Hélène, Carondelet Canal at Miro (demolished)

Fig. 5. Plan book 44, folio 36; signed and dated, "C. A. de Armas, February 20, 1855"; Ursulines between Johnson and Prieur, backed by St. Philip

Fig. 7. 1228–30 N. Johnson

Fig. 6. 1027–29 N. Roman

Fig. 8. Plan book 46, folio 46; unsigned and undated; Roman between Bayou Road and Hospital backed by Prieur

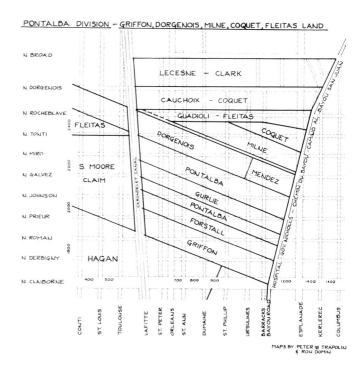

MAPS BY PETER M TRAPOLIN
& RON DOMIN

Fig. 9. 2014 St. Philip, Costanza House

Fig. 10. 1923 St. Philip, showing steeple of St. Peter Claver (formerly St. Anna) with silhouette of St. Joseph's Academy (now Bell Junior High) in background

CHAPTER XI

Dorgenois – Mendez

Beyond the Pontalba division lay a 1¼-*arpent habitation* associated at the time of its subdivision in 1844 with the heirs of Louis Gatien Lebreton-Dorgenois and Antonio Mendez. The land was part of the ancient Lebreton concession of 1758 and, like the adjacent land toward the city, came down through Almonester who, however, separated this tract from his leper colony. He sold the *arpents* "with their entire depth to the land of the Jesuits (Common Street)" to Joseph Cultia in 1781.[1] In 1786 Cultia sold them to Antonio Ramis, from whom François Lebreton-Dorgenois purchased them in two separate transactions—November 16, 1805, and January 20, 1806, before Pierre Pedesclaux. An act by Pedesclaux on September 24, 1807, describes the front portion of the property facing Bayou Road: "Appeared Monsieur Antonio Ramis of this city who has told us that on July 16, 1805, he sold before this notary to Monsieur François Lebreton-Dorgenois of this city 1¼ *arpents* facing Bayou Road on the left leaving the city by 4 *arpents* in depth for 1600 *piastres*." This section ultimately became the Mendez *habitation*.

After acquiring the land, Dorgenois immediately began to disperse it. His daughter, Anne Marie, had married Joseph Dusau de la Croix; and on November 6, 1807, before notary François Broutin, her father gave the couple the house and land facing Bayou Road that he had purchased from Ramis. Subsequently, the estate of M. de la Croix sold this house and land on Bayou Road to Martin Palao, who sold it to Antonio Mendez on August 1, 1825.[2] The Mendez family resided there for a short while; but in 1831 Elizabeth Mendez, with agent Thomas Dumas, subdivided the property into lots and began to sell them (fig. 1). Most of the lots were purchased, along with the house, by Charles Maurion, a prominent judge, and M. Guignan. Maurion's purchase was for speculation, since he sold his portion almost immediately in March of 1832.

The rest of the Lebreton-Dorgenois tract from St. Philip Street to Common Street was inherited and bought by Louis Gatien Lebreton-Dorgenois from his father's estate. He, in turn, left it to his daughter, Marie Louise Josephine Estelle, wife of Joseph Volant Labarre, and to his son, Louis Joseph Lebreton-Dorgenois. On November 9, 1843, the latter sold his undivided half of the property to S. W. Oakey, thus causing a partition that took place on November 2, 1844, before notary P. P. Labarre. Jean Communy, city surveyor, made a plan of the property dividing it into lots; and a sale was held "by virtue of an order of sale to effect a partition . . . will be offered at public sale at the City Exchange, St. Louis Street between Chârtres and Royal, Wednesday, October 23, 1844, at twelve o'clock . . . twenty-three squares and parts of squares and lots of ground situated in the First Municipality . . . extending from Ursulines Street to Canal Street."[3]

The lots sold in groups to speculators; prices ranged from $13 to $83 a lot. Those fronting the Carondelet Canal were considered most valuable. Mme Labarre retained about ninety lots extending from Dumaine to Canal. Prominent purchasers were Pierre and Paul De Verges, who bought eight lots at $138 each on Carondelet Walk, and John Kemp, who bought one lot at N. Broad and Iberville for $69. Pierre Passebon, who owned and built four houses on Esplanade Avenue and a number of properties in Tremé, bought twenty-one lots fronting Canal at N. Dorgenois and some at S. Broad and Common. Jacques Demourelle bought thirteen lots on St. Peter and on St. Ann between N. Rocheblave, N. Miro, and N. Tonti. John McDonogh bought forty-two lots for $4,107 at Ursulines in the square bound by St. Philip, N. Galvez, and N. Miro.

Archival drawings dating from the late 1840s indicate that modest creole cottages, as well as large masonry complexes, were built soon after the subdivision. Most of the homes were rental houses of frame construction. Plan book 38, folio 13 and plan book 52, folio 43 give an indication of the appearance of these cottages (figs. 2, 3).

Fig. 1. Plan book 44, folio 69; signed and dated, "A. Castaing; February 12, 1862"; Bayou Road between Johnson and Galvez backed by Barracks; Mendez Plantation House (demolished)

Fig. 2. Plan book 38, folio 13; signed and dated, "A. Castaing and J. A. Celles, July 26, 1865"; Dumaine corner Tonti, backed by Miro and St. Philip (demolished)

Fig. 3. Plan book 52, folio 43; unsigned, undated; St. Ann corner Miro backed by Dumaine and Tonti

CHAPTER XII

Milne Gardens, Coquet, and Fleitas

Beyond the Dorgenois and Mendez *habitations*, the next plantation shown on the Zimpel map was Milne Gardens, so named in the 1844 estate sale of Alexander Milne because of that gentleman's extensive vegetable and fruit tree farm.[1] It reached from the present N. Galvez, across Milne Road, and passed N. Miro along the left side of Bayou Road. Its history extended back to Alexandre Latil. In 1774 Latil sold four *arpents* to free Negro San Luis Lanuitte.[2] Prior to receiving his freedom from Jean de Pradel, who held large plantations across the Mississippi River from New Orleans, Lanuitte had acted as his master's agent, traveling to France in that capacity. Lanuitte owned land in the French Quarter in 1777, when he sold a lot on Rue Dauphine to Rosa and Juana Malet, free Negresses. He also owned four *arpents* across Bayou Road, which he had acquired from Latil in the same 1774 purchase.

In 1777 Lanuitte also sold his four *arpents* on the left side of Bayou Road in two acts, April and December. Two *arpents* went to free Negress Martina, and two *arpents* were purchased in December by Jean Baptiste and Marguerite, married free persons of color.[3]

By the early nineteenth century these four *arpents* on the left side of Bayou Road were owned by two other free persons of color—one by Marie Michel, alias Noyan, the other by Catin Marc. The one sharing a common boundary with the Dorgenois and Mendez *habitations* belonged to Marie Michel, who built a *maison principale* as early as 1806. By 1822 Mme Michel had sold a small strip adjacent to her bayou-side boundary to free woman of color Marthe Lebreton, as seen on Pilié's survey. There Mme Lebreton had a house and outbuilding that are shown to be in the center of the projected Esplanade. In 1829 James Powell, agent for Alexander Milne, bought the entire two-*arpent* Bayou Road frontage from the Michel estate; and Mme Lebreton had by then left Bayou Road, her land reverting back to Marie Michel. Milne, who was curator of Mme Michel's estate, bought the land through the offices of Powell for $1,000. The act of December 1, 1829, before L. T. Caire described the property "about a mile from the city, 300 feet on Bayou Road, bound by property of Antonio Mendez, and on the other side by property of Catin Marc, free woman of color, with buildings and improvements."

It is to be hoped that Milne represented the best interests of the testator, Marie Michel, for he was at this time the largest landowner in the city, living in the 1600 block of Bayou Road (Governor Nicolls). His holdings along Lake Pontchartrain stretched from the present Pontchartrain Boulevard, along the line now marked by Robert E. Lee Boulevard, all the way to Chef Menteur. This land was swampy most of the year but was an excellent source of lumber, furs, and seafoods and an important basis for the fortune accumulated by Milne during his residence in New Orleans. When he died in 1839, he was buried in the center square of St. Louis Cemetery II; above his grave is a magnificent granite obelisk on which his entire will

is engraved. A shrewd Scotsman, land speculator, and planter, he left his entire fortune to the city. Milne owned the Michel property at the time of his death. When his estate was settled in 1844, it was described as follows:

> The property known as Milne's Garden situated in the First Municipality and extending from the Bayou Road to Orleans Street, divided into squares and lots according to a plan of L. Bringier, surveyor general, dated November 4, 1843, the lots numbered from 1 to 75, having their dimensions expressed in English measure on said plan, will be sold with reference thereto.[4]

Plan book 36, folio 9 shows Milne Road between his former lands and those of the Dorgenois *habitation*. Barracks Street was cut through the tract at this time. Antoine Doriocourt purchased most of the Bayou Road frontage of Milne Gardens on June 3, 1844, before C. Pollock. He paid $250 for a fifty-foot frontage on Esplanade and $350 for just twenty-six feet on Bayou Road. Paying more for less land on Bayou Road lends proof to the early-nineteenth-century reality that Bayou Road continued to hold prominence and desirability over the new Esplanade Avenue. The Doriocourts kept the lots until 1859, when André Doriocourt sold three of them to G. Jumonville for $1200, keeping the rest. A Jumonville center-hall cottage is thought to have been moved from Bayou Road to the present 2229 Barracks Street. The line between Milne Gardens and the next *habitation* is drawn through the middle of N. Tonti Street so that one of the prominent remaining houses in Milne Gardens stands on the even side at 1124 N. Tonti (fig. 1). Built by architect-owner Hubert Gerard in 1860, it is a double-galleried, side-hall dwelling.

The next portion of the former Latil-Lanuitte *habitation* belonged to Thomas Porée in 1822 and to free Negress Catin Marc by 1829. Later, entrepreneur Bernard Coquet bought this small pie-shaped tract, measuring two *arpents* fronting on Bayou

Fig. 1. Plan book 101, folio 14; signed and dated, "John F. Braun, archt., March 3, 1883"; Tonti between Ursulines and Hospital (Governor Nicholls) backed by Miro; 1124 N. Tonti

50

Road between N. Tonti and N. Rocheblave, but extending in depth just two blocks where it abutted the Domingo Fleitas *habitation*, as indicated on the Zimpel map. Within this study it is referred to as Coquet I. Coquet, a modest real estate investor in comparison with Milne, bought an additional two *arpents* on Bayou Road immediately above the Fleitas property. To differentiate between the two parcels, the bayouward Coquet division is identified as Coquet II. Bernard Coquet is particularly remembered for his establishment of the famous Tivoli Gardens fronting Bayou St. John and for the omnibus that he established in Coquet II. When he died, Bazile Brosset Beauregard purchased the small Coquet I, "two *arpents* front on Bayou Road bound above by Fleitas and below by lands formerly belonging to Marie Michel." The act was passed on June 28, 1836, before notary Carlisle Pollock. Beauregard began selling lots immediately, and a new neighborhood emerged.

The major landmark of Coquet I is the historic Lafon Home of the Holy Family at 1125 N. Tonti (fig. 2). Thomy Lafon, a wealthy free man of color, bought two large lots from Beauregard in 1836; the lots remained empty between 1836 and 1850. By 1866 the value of the property had jumped from

Fig. 2. 1125 N. Tonti, Lafon Home

$500 to $14,000, proof that the present 1125 was standing.[5] Lafon donated this property to L'Association pour l'Assistance des Orphelins de couleur de la Louisiane. This association had been chartered in 1865, and in 1877 the home was handed over to the Society of the Holy Family by M. le docteur and Mme L. C. Roudanez, who represented the association and were witnesses to the Lafon donation of the building and grounds.[6]

The Société de la Sainte Famille was founded in Faubourg Tremé in 1845 by Marie Aliquot, a Frenchwoman and well-known educator. It was established as an order "exclusively for colored women" devoted to the keep and support of old and infirm free women of color unable to care for themselves. This important order of nuns was assisted financially through contributions from a prominent Frenchwoman, Agathe Mager Collard, to whom her brother, Jean Mager, had bequeathed vast holdings in Faubourgs Tremé and Marigny. The nuns ran the home on N. Tonti for over a century; in 1974, advised that repairs to the structure were not to the best interest of the order, the nuns abandoned the asylum and moved to 6901 Chef Menteur Highway. That decision broke a link in black history

Fig. 3. 2510 Dumaine

in New Orleans. Not only was this order of nuns a black one, but it was assisted by the city's wealthiest black entrepreneur, Lafon, and held property that had belonged to a series of black owners since the eighteenth century. Innovative and informed planning on the part of the advisors could have provided the Sisters with a feasible method of retaining their original building. An act of sale was passed on March 9, 1976, between Mother Rose de Lima Hazeur, president of the Society, and the Odyssey Institute, a nonprofit corporation from New Jersey. One of the ironies of the entire situation lies in the name Hazeur, one of the earliest and most prominent free black families of Faubourg Tremé.

Both of Coquet's former plantations exhibit fine examples of the Classic-style shotgun ranging in date from 1850 to 1875. The late-Classic-style, side-hall shotgun at 2510 Dumaine is reflective of the sophistication of the early shotgun, dating from the mid-nineteenth century (fig. 3). The General Laundry at 2550 St. Peter, built in 1929, is an unusual landmark. This unique structure in the Mayan Revival style stands alone as one of the most atypical buildings, not only in its Coquet division but the entire city (fig. 4).

Fig. 4. 2550 St. Peter, General Laundry

Between the two Coquet *habitations* lay a narrow strip of land, the boundaries of which follow the present street alignment. On May 20, 1801, Carlos Guadioli, a Spanish colonial tavernkeeper, received a grant from the king of Spain for this *habitation*, fronting fifty-three *toises* on the left side of Bayou Road between the present N. Miro and N. Tonti streets. The land extended westward for fifteen *arpents* to the Carondelet Canal, where it widened to two *arpents* front, continuing seventeen *arpents* more in depth to the boundary of Faubourg Ste Marie. Guadioli increased his Bayou Road frontage by purchasing a small trapezoid of land, two *arpents* by three *arpents* in depth, from Madame Bertrand. She had acquired it by purchase from Mme Gabriel Peyroux.

Guadioli held his plantation for less than two years. The abrupt end of Spanish rule brought about his decision to leave the city. On June 5, 1805, in an act before Narcisse Broutin, he sold his *habitation* to another Spanish colonial citizen, Domingo Fleitas. Unlike Guadioli, Fleitas' roots were firmly established in Louisiana. His wife was a French Creole, and he owned property in the 900 block of Rue Bourbon. Fleitas died in 1826, leaving the plantation to his wife, Marie Josephe Guesnard, and children, Jean Manuel, Barthélémy Paulin, and Virginie, Mme Louis Aimé Pigneguy. After the death of Widow Fleitas, Jean Manuel sold the Bayou Road frontage, in depth to the Carondelet Canal, to Jean Dufour, a speculator, before notary G. LeGardeur on August 4, 1836. Dufour sold the *habitation* to the First Municipality for 30,000 *piastres* just two months after his purchase.[7] The city incorporated this specific land into Faubourg Tremé and by 1846 was selling lots in it.

Esplanade Avenue had been projected as early as 1820 to extend across the Fleitas *habitation* just where the *maison principale* stood. This master house might have been built soon after the 1805 purchase from Guadioli, or it is possible that it was built for Guadioli soon after his 1801 land grant. Indications are that Jean Manuel Fleitas moved this house in 1836 from the left side of Bayou Road to a bare lot just across it. The extant house at 2275 Bayou Road may well be the Fleitas *maison principale*, moved and renovated about the time of the sale of the *habitation* to Jean Dufour. It was described in its original location in the inventory of the estate of Mme Fleitas, who died there June 27, 1834, as a six-room house with a rear gallery having one *cabinet*. It was raised on brick piers and built of *colombage* construction. There was a kitchen, stable, dependencies, a *cave*, office, courtyard, gardens, and fruit trees, with a number of farmyard animals also inventoried.[8]

The portion of the plantation between the Carondelet Canal and Common Street (Faubourg Ste Marie boundary) went to Joseph Kenton on May 19, 1835, after Mme Fleitas' death. Kenton paid $50,000 for the land, described in an act before T. Seghers:

> Situated on the southwesterly side of Carondelet Canal, at the first half-moon . . . measuring two-*arpents* front on said Canal and extending in rear as far as Common Street by a depth of seventeen *arpents*, ten *toises*, two feet on one line, and seventeen *arpents*, five *toises* on the other . . . together with the privilege of navigating on said Canal for the transportation of the produce of the land.

Kenton found that there were other claimants to the land that he had bought. These included Samuel Moore, who had purchased from the Canal and Banking Company, and Baroness de Pontalba, who claimed the land as part of her inheritance from Andrés Almonester. Her claim indicated that the land was part of a French concession to d'Auberville in 1756; therefore, in 1801 it was not the king of Spain's land to concede to Guadioli. After years of litigation, a partition between the claimants resulted in an 1850 subdivision.

The Fleitas plantation house is a major landmark of the entire Faubourg Tremé, standing today at 2275 Bayou Road on the lot that Manuel Fleitas purchased in 1832 from the estate of Antoine de Villier Guesnon (fig. 5). Analysis of the structure reveals the basic Fleitas house, with both 1836 reconstruction and early-twentieth-century additions dating from the Joseph Chauffe purchase. The French doors, shutters, hardware, flooring, front room proportions, hip-roof, dormers, and wide rear gallery, now enclosed, reflect the early date of the house. Greek Revival mantels, molding, and other decorative details, as well as the kitchen extending from the main house, date from 1836 when Jean Manuel Fleitas moved and rebuilt. Also in 1836 a rear gallery was appended to the earlier one, which was enclosed. Three-quarters of a century later, Mr. Chauffe added a wing to the left, providing two bedrooms, and enlarged a *cabinet* with a bay, creating a master bedroom on the right.

The Clément Duhamel house at 2434 Barracks, built after the Civil War on the Fleitas division, illustrates the continuing

Fig. 5. 2275 Bayou Road, Fleitas-Chauffe House in 1974

preference for the creole floor plan, here built on the banquette (fig. 6).

A tract that the Zimpel map identifies as another Coquet *habitation* originated from Suzanna Caüe, Widow Peyroux, and Joseph Suarez.[9] In 1796 Widow Peyroux sold Suarez a small part of this land fronting Bayou Road; he then augmented his holdings with an 1801 Spanish land grant between the present N. Rocheblave to N. Broad streets at the Carondelet Canal, narrowing to a triangle with its point near N. Broad at Bayou Road. In 1806 he sold that portion of the above described land, which is identified for this study as Coquet II, to Philippe Gabourdet for $2,500 with buildings and improvements.

A year later Gabourdet sold to François Joseph Lebreton Dorgenois, whose *maison de maître* could well have been one built by Suarez in 1801.[10] Dorgenois died at this Bayou Road home on September 24, 1813. He had been the first United States marshal after the Louisiana Purchase and was a descen-

Fig. 6. 2434–36 Barracks, Duhamel Cottage

dant of Louis Césaire Lebreton, who coincidentally had held a land grant including this property in 1756. The *Louisiana Courier* of March 25, 1816, advertised: "Bayou Road, two *arpents* front and extending to the Canal Carondelet [bound by the Fleitas line, just behind N. Rocheblave to N. Dorgenois], with a mansion and servants' houses heretofore occupied by Lebreton Dorgenois, deceased, formerly Marshal of the United States for the District of Louisiana."[11]

Three years later in 1819, the estate was settled and the plantation sold to Thomas Edouard Joachim Cauchoix, an attorney, who held it until his death in 1825, when his heirs sold it to Jean Manuel Fleitas. At the time the *habitation* included "*une maison de maître briquetée entre poteaux et couverte en bardeaux, ayant sept chambres et galeries avec columns en briques devant et derrière.*" The price quoted in the title transfer was $3,750.[12] The translation of this important description reveals that this house, perhaps the one constructed by Suarez, was a brick-between-post house, roofed with shingles. It had seven rooms, which is an unusual number, and brick-columned galleries both in front and rear. (Most of the rural creole cottages, even those that were constructed of brick between posts, had galleries with turned wooden columns.)

In 1828 Jacques Bernard Coquet bought the *habitation* from Fleitas in the names of his six unmarried children. They paid $7,763 for the same property, which included "*tous les édifices, batisses, charrettes, tombereaux, instrumens aratoires, caves, et un cheval nommé Jack* . . . all of the buildings, outbuildings, wagons, wheelbarrows, agricultural tools, raised cellar, and a horse named Jack."[13] In 1836 the death of Mme Coquet resulted in a partition of the property between Coquet and his children.[14] The father bought out one son, François, and retained the Bayou Road frontage with the *maison principale* and outbuildings. His choice land measured 383 feet on Bayou Road with 371 feet on Esplanade (a new boundary at this time), the rear property line, 209 feet on N. Dorgenois, and 118 feet on the Fleitas line. Each child received an equal share of the remaining six squares, which fronted Esplanade and stopped at the Carondelet Canal. One daughter, Eulalie, had died by 1836, but her succession was granted an equal fifth. Another daughter, Marie Rose, soon after the partition, married her neighbor Jean Manuel Fleitas, son of the Spanish land grantee Domingo Fleitas. Thus, land that had belonged to separate owners was joined by marriage, a traditional social condition that throughout history has united even kingdoms.

CHAPTER XIII

Blanc – Vidal – Clark

Ownership of the land between Bayou Road, the Carondelet Canal, N. Dorgenois, and N. Broad streets stems from *habitations* that fronted both Bayou Road and the banks of Bayou St. John. When the Corporation of the City of New Orleans purchased all the undeveloped land between N. Dorgenois and Bayou St. John in 1822, they incorporated the area into Faubourg Tremé. A short review of the history of Bayou St. John is recounted to establish its relationship to this strip between N. Dorgenois and N. Broad streets.

One of the earliest maps of the area, dated c. 1723, allocates the prime section between Bayou St. John and the Joachim de Gauvrit *habitation* boundary at the present N. Galvez Street to "Française" and "Langlois."[1] It is designated in the retrospective Gayoso de Lemos plan of 1796 as "Concessions of Française and Langlois of 1721, each eight *arpents* fronting the Bayou by forty *arpents* in depth." The Trudeau retrospective of 1798 attributes these same lands to "Stephen Langlois and Daniel Provanché, concessions dated October 20, 1720, and April 21, 1721. Lands at present occupied by Louis Blanc." Daniel Provanché's association with Bayou Road and Bayou St. John was shortlived; he does not appear in title transfers. Provanché probably abandoned his land to "Française,"[2] who must be Françoise Duval, an attorney-general in Louisiana. By 1729 Duval had died, and the entire tract was acquired by Langlois.[3]

Most of his large swatch of land between N. Dorgenois and Bayou St. John was swamp, except the part bordering the bayou and the Bayou Road ridges. In 1756 this marshland was regranted to Louis Césaire Lebreton, along with the Joachim de Gauvrit tract that had also reverted to the French Crown.[4] Within a few years Louis Brasilier *dit* Tourangeau had purchased that part of the Lebreton land between present N. Galvez and Bayou St. John. His son, Jean Baptiste, through marriage into the family of the original concessionaire, Stephen Langlois, acquired the remainder of the tract between Bayou St. John and N. Dorgenois.

Brasilier Tourangeau had come to Louisiana as valet for Captain Lauzes and was listed as gardener to the priests of the parish church in the city.[5] He married Jeanne Charlotte Treman of Pascagoula. Jean Baptiste Brasilier, their son, married Pélagie Loraine Tarasçon, on August 17, 1748. Her stepfather was Stephen Langlois, the original owner of the huge tract, from N. Dorgenois to Bayou St. John.[6] Brasilier Tourangeau's daughter, Madeleine, married François Henri Duplanty and, shortly after his death in 1770, Enrique Desprez of Opelousas.[7] Pélagie Loraine and her second husband, Andrés Jung, a ship chandler and shipbuilder whom she had married by 1779, lived across Bayou St. John on a plantation where the king's warehouse stood, although she still owned one-half of her family tract across Bayou St. John, between that body of water and all the swampland up to present N. Dorgenois Street.

The other half of the land fronting Bayou Road, bound by present N. Dorgenois and Bayou St. John, was owned by her sister-in-law Madeleine Brasilier. The latter wrote her will December 13, 1773, leaving to her second brother, Louis Braziler [*sic*], "a *habitation* composed of eight *arpents* front by a depth of twenty-two, situated on the Bayou St. John, fronting on the Bayou, bound on one side by the Camino Real [Bayou Road] and by lands of my brother Luis Brazilier . . . with the condition that one warehouse of eighty feet and one rice mill may be used by my husband Henrique Desprez although he cannot sell it."[8]

Madeleine, however, altered her will and sold this land the next year to Joseph Chalon and his wife, Elizabeth Desruisseaux, on October 15, 1774.[9] M. and Mme Chalon in 1780 also acquired the adjacent eight *arpents* by twenty-two *arpents* (approximately between the future Dumaine, Carondelet Canal, N. Dorgenois, and the bayou) by purchase from Madeleine's sister-in-law, Pélagie Loraine, and her second husband, Andrés Jung. The Chalons added this resulting sixteen-by-twenty-two-*arpent* tract to their numerous holdings on both sides of Bayou Road and Bayou St. John but sold it within a year to the notary and eminent Spanish colonial citizen, Andrés Almonester y Rojas. Almonester paid 6000 *pesos* for "sixteen by twenty-two *arpents* . . . situated in the Parish which they call the Bridge of the Bayou St. John, one-half league distant from New Orleans . . . with various buildings built of wood and brick, three Negroes, twenty-four head of cattle, one horse, three wagons and all the pigs and other animals."[10]

This land was just one of Almonester's many holdings; and two years later, in 1783, he offered the products of the plantation for the support of San Carlos Hospital, specifying that an abundance of lime and lumber were to be had on the place. Within ten years, however, Almonester sold the plantation in two acts to Louis Antoine Blanc, one-half in 1793 and the other in 1798.[11]

It is from the time of the Blanc ownership that the blocks between N. Dorgenois and N. Broad began to take their present configuration. Louis Blanc and his wife, Louise Gauvin, lived in a *maison principale* fronting Bayou St. John (924 Moss Street), where he cultivated the high portion of his land and grazed his cattle. Blanc managed a tannery belonging to Mauricio Conway, which used hides provided by Alexandre Latil's slaughterhouse located just cityward of the Blanc *habitation*.

Soon after Louis Blanc appeared as a property owner on Bayou Road, Nicolas Maria Vidal, an important Spanish official, began making investments in the same area. In 1800 he bought part of Blanc's new plantation, six *arpents* fronting the Camino Real (Bayou Road).[12] Vidal then added four more purchases of adjacent land, which he bought from Joseph Suarez, Pedro Juzan, Suzanna Caüe, Widow Gabriel Peyroux, and free Negress Fanchon Montreuil. The newly acquired land measured four *arpents* fronting the right side of the Camino Real, adjacent to his holdings via Blanc, and extended to the Bridge of the Washerwomen and Petit Bayou. It bordered the present Grand Route St. John, then the edge of Juzan's plantation.[13] His holdings also included Bayou Fanchon, formerly part of the *habitation* of Fanchon Montreuil. These waterways were a crucial objective in Vidal's purchase, giving him water transportation, irrigation, and drainage facilities.

The largest portion of Vidal's property was from Joseph Suarez, who had received an 1801 Spanish land grant that covered the area between the present N. Rocheblave to N. Broad Street at the Carondelet Canal, narrowing to a triangle with its point near N. Broad Street and Bayou Road. Suarez, according to his 1806 will, lived on Bayou Road. He was a native of the Canary Islands and was married twice, first to Françoise Seja and then to Catherine Cavalier, by whom he had four children—aged twelve years to six months when he died. At the time of his death in 1806, he owned a lot outside and below the city acquired from Brognier Dudonet and a *habitation* three *arpents* facing each side of Bayou Terre aux Boeufs. Immediately after completing his will, he sold the remaining Bayou Road land grant to Philippe Gabourdet for $2,500 *piastres*. That part of Suarez's land grant that Vidal did not buy was acquired by Widow Peyroux and became the Coquet division, previously discussed (fig. 1).

Finally, to consolidate a sufficient area to comprise a major plantation, Vidal requested and received a Spanish land grant from Carlos III, king of Spain, of vacant lands behind his new plantation. The land grant was authorized April 16, 1800, under the intendant general, Ramon de Lopez y Angulo.[14] Vidal, who was identified within the transactions as lieutenant governor, attorney general, and acting governor of the province of Louisiana and West Florida, immediately built a *maison principale* with supporting farm buildings. The house and outbuildings faced Bayou Road, left side, just bayouward of N. Broad; the area between N. Dorgenois and N. Broad was cultivated land without structures.[15]

Within a year, Daniel Clark came to Bayou Road and began to collect land from both Vidal and Blanc. Spain's loss of her colonial province and the subsequent Louisiana Purchase may well have caused Vidal's unexpected removal from Bayou Road. Clark, born in County Sligo, Ireland, in 1766, came to Louisiana under the auspices of an uncle, whose business he inherited in 1800. Daniel Clark purchased Vidal's entire *habitation* in 1804,[16] and in 1806 Louis Antoine Blanc gave Clark a receipt for final payment of six additional *arpents* fronting Bayou Road.[17] In two years the Irish-American had acquired the original French concessions of "Française and Langlois" and the additional acreage previously acquired by Vidal. Blanc retained for himself the house and grounds fronting Bayou St. John.[18]

Clark planned a suburb, which Barthélémy Lafon surveyed in June of 1809.[19] Lots sold immediately; and on June 15, just six days after the new Faubourg St. Jean was laid out, Clark sold the first two squares between then Rue D'Orgenois and Grande Rue (Broad Street) beginning at Bayou Road, to Henry Lecesne.[20] Lecesne built a country seat near Bayou Road, which he offered for sale April 29, 1811, soon after the completion of his main house. The *Louisiana Courier* advertised: "In the suburb St. Jean, a very elegant new house, built with bricks between posts and covered with shingles, divided into five commodious rooms with back and front gallery, kitchen, yard, well, etc., the whole in the best order . . . built upon a lot of about 180 feet fronting Orchard Street [Seventh Street], by about 360 feet on Dorgenoy [*sic*] Street, including in whole nine regular lots . . . has a very fine and well-cultivated garden with a double row of sweet orange trees . . . is everywhere newly fenced with standing stakes."

Lecesne did not sell the country estate, however, until 1825 when it was purchased by Dame John Watkins. Her son sold the squares to Joseph Barthet in 1837.[21] A lithograph by X. Magny dated April 4, 1853, of the Lecesne property to be auctioned through the office of N. Vignie, illustrated the blocks between N. Dorgenois to N. Broad at that time (fig. 1A).[22] The lithograph identified several of the neighboring dwellings: Mme François' large, hip-roof residence facing the new Esplanade with stables and outbuildings along N. Broad; M. Brugier's home in the large triangular area between the Halle Bretonne

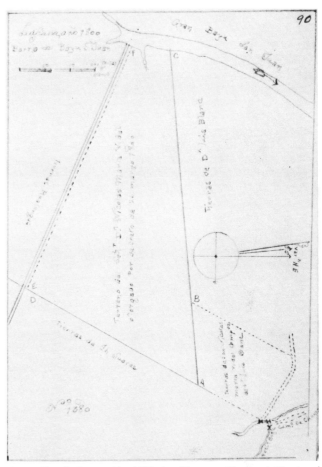

Fig. 1. Pintado Papers, No. 1380. Land between Dorgenois Street and Bayou St. John (Courtesy Louisiana Historic Center)

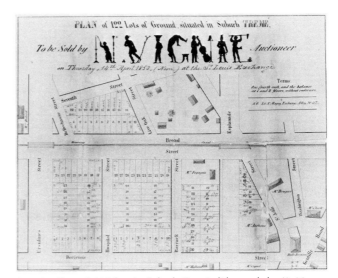

Fig. 1A. Plan of 122 lots in Suburb Tremé, lithograph by X. Magny, 1853

and N. Broad, across from M. Jartoux; Daniel Clark's former residence at the juncture of St. John (Bell), Washington (Desoto), and Gentilly Road at the Halle Bretonne.

Clark had died at the house in 1813, leaving his good friends Richard Relf and Beverly Chew as executors of his much-contested estate. An ad in the *Louisiana Courier*, March 2, 1814, advertised: "To rent, the beautiful house before occupied by Daniel Clark situated on the Bayou Road." The house ultimately fell into ruin and was demolished. Relf and Chew had sold the remainder of the undeveloped land between N. Dorgenois and N. Broad to Evariste Blanc, son of Louis Blanc, in 1813.[23] Between 1811 and 1816, he also purchased other lands bayouward that his father had owned before selling them to Clark. Then on September 26, 1834, Blanc sold to the Corporation of the City of New Orleans his "land or plantation, irregularly shaped having about twelve *arpents* frontage on Bayou St. John and bound by said Bayou, Carondelet Canal, Bayou Road, and Dorgenois . . . for $50,000."[24] Faubourg St. John, as indicated on the Zimpel survey, fronted Grand Route St. John and extended in an irregular pattern from Bayou St. John to N. Dorgenois. After 1834 the City Corporation incorporated the rest of the Clark-Blanc lands into an extension of Faubourg Tremé, the city's suburb; and houses were built by the mid–nineteenth century.

A major residence in the N. Dorgenois to N. Broad section of this land is 2654 Dumaine, the Esnard villa dating from 1853 (fig. 2). There are also a number of imposing, single-family frame houses that stand on the boundary line of the Evariste Blanc land; 929 N. Dorgenois, dating from the 1860s, is among them. It is a two-story, side-hall, double-galleried house. A later example of the two-level, single-family architectural expression is 1201 N. Dorgenois.

Fig. 2. 2654 Dumaine

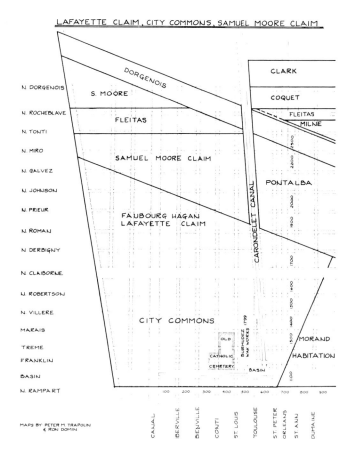

MAPS BY PETER M. TRAPOLIN & RON DOMIN

CHAPTER XIV

City Commons

The plantations and divisions thus far discussed were related to the Road to the Bayou, whereas the adjacent vacant land toward Canal Street did not share a bond with that important eighteenth-century artery. The City Commons were considered useless, cypress swampland. They were not sought for purchase or concession but were used for public grazing and as a source of free firewood and fill during the dry season. For the remainder of the year citizens avoided the steaming, inundated spaces. Between the City Commons and the city limits were the Military Commons, a two-*arpent*, twelve-*toise* strip of land established uniformly around the entire city in 1718 by the French engineers and reserved by the Crown for the city's eventual fortification. From 1718 the City Commons were situated between the boundary (Common-Tulane) of Military Governor Bienville's riverfront plantation and the Charles de Morand *habitation*. They extended from the Military Commons (N. Rampart Street) toward Bayou St. John and its branches.[1]

This area remained vacant between 1718 and 1743 except for The Chapel of Our Lady, shown as *X* on the 1730 Dumont de Montigny plan of the city and its environs (fig. 1). Then in 1743, a new Charity Hospital was planned on a 300-foot-wide section located partially on the rear Military Commons at Tou-

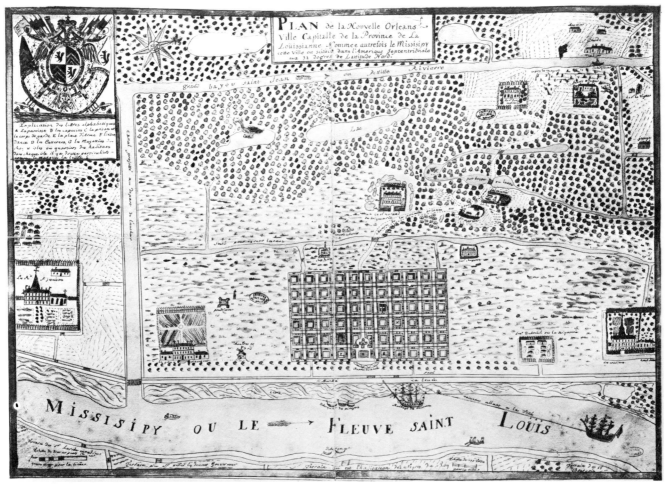

Fig. 1. Plan de la Nouvelle Orleans, Ville Capitalle de la Province de la Loüissianne by Dumont de Montigny, c. 1732, Archives Nationales, Paris (Courtesy Library of Congress, Washington, D.C.)

louse Street, back 600 feet into the City Commons. Called L'Hôpital de St. Jean, it was built under the supervision of Père Charles de Rambervilliers, Capuchin Superior, and blessed on March 9, 1752. There were other minor intrusions into these lands, but many years later a witness was to declare: "The inhabitants of the City were in the constant habit of using all the land to the rear of the City according to their own use and doing other acts as suited their convenience or necessities."[2]

The French colonial authorities in 1760 constructed fortifications around the city, the palisade of which cut across the hospital property. In 1764 the hospital directors petitioned the acting governor, d'Abadie, to grant them another site to replace the one encroached by fortifications. The hospital apparently remained in the same building, and some additional land within the fortifications was given to it as compensation. Lt. Philip Pittman's manuscript map c. 1765 (fig. 3, Chapter 1) illustrated the rear of the city as it appeared after Bernard De Verges's 1760 stockades were established: beginning at the south or Canal Street side of the city ramparts was St. Louis Bastion; extending from Bienville Street was "Fort Bourgoyne"; then, along the ramparts came the large Choiseul's Bastion, beside which was St. Jean's Hospital; the center bastion on the site of the later Fort St. Ferdinand was Orleans Bastion; the next bastion was reduced considerably in size to

avoid infringement upon the Morand house and gardens, and it was called the Bayou Redoubt; just to the right of the Bayou Gate, leading to the Chemin du Bayou, was the Corps de Garde and Berry's Bastion, which occupied the site of future Fort St. Jean; squares laid out just inside the fortification, backed by what later became Rampart Street, were "squares destined for artillery."

Along the Bayou Road on the left side, Pittman showed the Morand house and gardens, then inhabited by Alexandre Latil and his second wife, Marie Grondel, and the Morand minors. Toward the bayou from the Morand lands, Latil's slaughterhouse and plantation was indicated. On the right side of Bayou Road, the second Morand house and brickyards on the old Raymond St. Martin de Jauriguebery lands was designated. A note on Pittman's map stated, "The streets now called Rampart, Customhouse, and Barracks were then laid out as marked on this plan but had no names at the time," and "the whole enceinte of the town was made of stockades with a banquette within, a very trifling ditch without."[3]

A 1766 "Inventory of Government Property" by the French Intendant Foucault further described the rear of the city: "The *corps de garde* of the Bourgoyne gate . . . is of the same construction as the one previous of the gate of the Chapitoulas," a building in wood frame to lodge the guard of the powder

57

magazine. "The *corps de garde* of the gate of the Bayou . . . similar to the preceeding one," a building in wood frame.

Moreover there are on the two wings of the small sides of the city, as well as on its rear to the Southwest, Northwest, and Northeast, several parcels of land and islands forming trapezoids of different sizes as is seen by the plan of the city, which locations are produced by a trace of the stockade or fortification, and are still neither figured conforming to the said plan nor employed to any usage, although their destination is determined. On a few of the bastions of this enclosure are platforms to place two cannons in battery for the defense of the avenue of the city as well as for the school artillery, and on the outside of the enclosure, there is a mound of earth for the said usage.[4]

Extensive repairs were made to St. Jean's Hospital in 1769, yet ten years later in 1779 a severe hurricane almost destroyed it. Two more hurricanes completed its ruin in 1780. A kitchen and storehouse, however, had remained standing; in these a provisional hospital of six beds was established. Late in 1782 Andrés Almonester y Rojas made an offer to Governor Miró and the parish priest to rebuild the hospital at his own expense. Upon receiving approval, he then salvaged all possible materials on the site. The land remained under the jurisdiction of Governor Miró because it was part of the City Commons and trespassed somewhat onto the city fortifications. Unfortunately, Almonester's new hospital, situated at the end of Toulouse Street at present N. Rampart, would obstruct the extension of Toulouse, a situation noted by the Cabildo authorities of the period. Since the governor did not want to demolish the extant storehouse and kitchen, a new main building on the site was begun in 1783 and completed in 1786 at a cost of over 100,000 *pesos*. The new building was brick and was dedicated to San Carlos in honor of Carlos III, king of Spain.

The hospital contained a church fifty-two feet long, a sacristy of twenty feet, a chapel of twenty-four feet, four wards for beds, the first of eighty feet, the second of sixty, the third of forty, and the other of twenty, and the pharmacy. A vestibule at the opposite side from the church served as an entrance. The chapel was placed under the invocation of the Virgin of Consolation and the wards were dedicated to St. Joseph, St. Matthew, St. Bernard, and St. James. These descriptions were set forth in Almonester's petition to the King dated May 1, 1784.[5]

To support the hospital, which was a charitable institution, Almonester offered to donate the proceeds from a number of plantations and properties, including those from a fifty-*arpent* dairy farm known as La Metairie, located on the Bayou Tchoupitoulas beyond Bayou St. John and extending back to Lake Pontchartrain. Milk from the dairy was sold in the city and also supplied to the hospital. When Almonester sold the plantation to Mauricio Conway in 1787, the land acquisition was described:

Sixteen to twenty-one *arpents* of land situated in the parish, name La Metairie, Matheo Dereaux [*sic*] on one side and Madame Desruisseaux on the other. Lake Pontchartrain in the rear, the major part bought from the Capuchin fathers, August 2, 1784."[6]

He also offered, for the support of the hospital, produce from an additional sixteen-by-twenty-two-*arpent* plantation fronting Bayou St. John, which he had bought from Joseph Chalon in 1781.[7] The farm was to supply the hospital with vegetables, chickens, and milk, as well as an income from the sale of quantities of lime and timber. However, Almonester sold the plantation to Louis Blanc in two transactions of 1793 and 1798.

When Almonester died in 1798, his daughter Micaela inherited the patronship, exercised for her by her mother. This patronship continued until September 22, 1809, when the entire hospital was destroyed by a fire. According to Samuel Wilson, Jr.:

No plans or sketches of the Hospital of San Carlos have been found, and few descriptions of it have survived. Its location and form appear on Pilié's map of August 18, 1808, which shows that one of the wings, probably containing a chapel, was located almost on the axis of Toulouse Street, terminating the vista from the river and the Government House. A map of the city in 1793, contained in the journals of Mathias James O'Conway, also indicated the hospital, but erroneously shows it outside the fortifications. It does, however, clearly indicate an H-shaped plan with a pedimented central bay with small circular attic windows above an entrance doorway. The architect of the building is unknown, but it may have been Gilberto Guillemard, who was in Louisiana at that time, having participated in Galvez's campaigns against Manchac and Baton Rouge in 1779.[8]

Fig. 2. St. Louis Cemetery showing Iberville Housing Project and City Skyline

In the rear of San Carlos Hospital a new cemetery was established in 1788, with the present N. Rampart, Conti, St. Louis, and Tremé streets as its boundaries. This cemetery is now known as St. Louis Cemetery I and is the only colonial cemetery in the city. The earliest remaining marked tomb in St. Louis I is that of Antoine Bonnabel, dated 1800.

Another cemetery was planned by the City Council in 1820, and the city dedicated four squares as St. Louis II, bound by Canal, N. Robertson, N. Claiborne, and St. Louis streets (fig. 2). Iberville, Bienville, and Conti streets were later cut through the cemetery, which previously was one continuous property from Canal to St. Louis Street. These cemeteries remain today as major national landmarks; they contain the earliest and the most sophisticated architecture within the City Commons today. The world-famous, arched, wall vaults, which partially enclose two sides of St. Louis I, are occasionally used for burial; whereas, the interior vault sections separating the Catholic area from the segregated Protestant space are abandoned and being demolished by total neglect.

In St. Louis II, nine city blocks of four-tiered, vaulted tombs are condemned by the city as unfit and exist in a limbo between preservationists' attempts to save them and the Archdiocese of New Orleans' plans to demolish them. Many important inhabitants of Faubourg Tremé and the City Commons are recalled only by their tombs in St. Louis Cemeteries I and II. General Jean Baptiste Plauché, the De Armas family, Jean Mager, Claude Tremé, and Alexander Milne are buried in St. Louis Cemetery II. Milne's will, which established charitable institutions throughout the city, is engraved on his granite oblisk (fig. 3).

Near the cemeteries stands the Mortuary Chapel of St. Anthony of Padua, now called Our Lady of Guadalupe Church, planned in 1819 when the City Council offered to sell the Archdiocese ten lots on N. Rampart at the corner of Conti for a chapel. The purchase, accomplished in 1825, was announced to the populace by an architect's competition advertisement in the *Louisiana Courier*, which invited "architects and builders to 'come forth and present their plans, devices and estimates of the cost of said edifice.' " According to Leonard Huber in his 1976 publication for the church's 150th anniversary:

> Some of the best known architects and builders of the day competed: Gurlie and Guillot, François Correjolles, William Brand, who later constructed the Hermann-Grima House [820 St. Louis Street], and James Moony and M. Lissuate.
>
> The wardens awarded the contract at a price of fourteen thousand dollars to the French architect-builders, Gurlie and Guillot, who had done work for the wardens before, having completed the second floor of the Presbytère in 1813. The firm had built for the Ursuline nuns their new convent in lower New Orleans. The wardens, also impressed with the pains taken by architects Brand and Moony, awarded them each fifty dollars for their trouble. . . .
>
> The resulting structure had a triple-arched façade, reminiscent of the first story of the Cabildo, and a belfry surmounted by a low dome and cross. Three substantial doors set in fan-lighted frames marked its entrance, and the small nave was lighted by twelve windows with rounded tops. [The façade of the church today is essentially the same except for the steeple and a clock that was added to the belfry (figs. 4,A)⁹.]

By 1853, however, although the chapel continued its usefulness, the establishment of numerous churches throughout the city obviated the need for a single mortuary church. After the Civil War a soldier-priest of the Confederacy, Father Isidore-François Turgis, renewed interest in the church by celebrating a daily mass for his old companions-at-arms. In January of 1875 the most Reverend Archbishop Napoléon Joseph Perché converted the former mortuary chapel into a parish church for the growing Italian population of the city.

On September 25, 1944, fire damaged the altar, sacristy, and sanctuary; temporary repairs were made until a 1952 renovation and new construction were completed. Adjacent to the church, Diboll-Kessels and Associates, Architects, also had constructed in 1949 a new twelve-room rectory and community hall at a cost of $150,000. It replaced a three-story, nineteenth-century storehouse bought by the church and used as St. Vincent Hotel, a place for transient men. In 1969 the church and rectory were again remodeled, repainted, and air conditioned. Artist Charles Reinicke painted six ceiling murals depicting the history of the church. The pastor, Peter V. Rogers,

Fig. 3. Tomb of Alexander Milne

Fig. 4. Mortuary Chapel (Italian Church) (Courtesy New Orleans Public Library)

Fig. 4A. 411 N. Rampart, Mortuary Chapel (Our Lady of Guadalupe–St. Jude)

Fig. 4B. Iberville Housing Project

O.M.I., organized the Policeman and Fireman's Holy Name Society and turned the community hall into a neighborhood center for the residents of the old City Commons and those living in the Iberville Housing Project (fig. 4B).

CARONDELET CANAL

The Spanish Governor Baron Luis Hector de Carondelet began planning the construction of a canal in 1792 to serve as a waterway and drain for the swamps between the city and Bayou St. John. He asked permission of the Spanish king to utilize black convicts in its construction and requested the citizens' donation of their slave labor. Through the efforts of sixty Negroes, the canal opened in 1794; its cost in actual cash was $30. A basin, located almost at the central gate of the rear of the city near what is now the corner of St. Peter and N. Rampart streets, formed the canal's terminus. As first built, the depth was scarcely six feet; an eight-foot embankment on either side provided facilities for rope twining, flatboats, and promenading. The canal's drainage value to the city was immediately demonstrated. Ambition to reach Mobile and Pensacola through the bayous and lakes from the gates of the city resulted in plans to enlarge this original canal immediately. With 150 convicts the canal was widened to fifteen feet.[10]

The legislature of the territory of Orleans chartered the Orleans Navigation Company in 1805 to improve the canal following the line laid out by Carondelet, connecting Bayou St. John with the city. This company, eager to widen the canal, found to its distress that it crossed not *"tierras realenguas"* (abandoned lands), but the properties of Daniel Clark, U.S. Marshal F. J. Lebreton Dorgenois, Louise de la Ronde Castillon (Widow Almonester), and the heirs of Charles Griffon. After many years of litigation, a "right of way purchase" took place in 1828 and thereby rectified Carondelet's error in taking colonists' private land for the Crown. The canal was widened to thirty feet with a sixty-four-foot-wide embankment on each side.[11]

The canal grew into an important artery of commerce through which flat-bottomed sailing scows brought lumber, tar, pitch, turpentine, brick, charcoal, fish, oysters, and cordwood from the Tchefuncte and Tangipahoa rivers, Bayous Lacombe and Bonfouca, Pearl River, and the Gulf Coast, taking back merchandise and miscellaneous freight. One of the main routes of travel from New Orleans to the east and north was by small boat through the canal to Bayou St. John to Lake Pontchartrain and, via steamer, to Mobile. Thus, a drainage convenience became the navigable Carondelet Canal, later to be known as the Old Basin Canal.

In 1852 the Orleans Navigation Company, directed by Joseph Faurie, Francis Duplessis, Julien Poydras, William Kenner, William Wyckoff of Opelousas, Louis Blanc, and George Pollock, went bankrupt. The charter was forfeited, and the property of the company was sold to the New Orleans Canal and Navigation Company, which then took over the project with members of the old company continuing to serve. In the same year, the Carondelet Canal was sold at auction, with its navigation rights and other property, to James Currie of New York. In 1858 the legislature chartered a new board of commissioners and bought back the property. A statute provided that after fifty years the state should take over the canal and property by paying an award to be fixed by three commissioners.[12]

When railroads became major means of transportation, the Southern Railroad was established alongside the old canal, with a terminal built in 1904 at Basin and Canal streets. In 1927 the canal was deemed unnavigable and ordered by the state to be filled in; the canal bed became Lafitte Street. This ended the farsighted efforts of Governor Carondelet. The irony

of the inscription that appeared in Spanish, French, and English over the windows of San Carlos Hospital is evident:

> The Baron de Carondelet, Governor General
> Having planned executed and perfected
> Almost without expense this Canal,
> The Council in the name of the inhabitants
> As a testimony of the public gratitude,
> Has decreed that it shall forever
> Bear the name of the
> Canal of Carondelet.[13]

BERMUDEZ GRANT

During the waning years of the Spanish colonial period a small tract of land around the Carondelet Canal basin was ceded to Francisco Xavier Bermudez (fig. 5). At a meeting of the Cabildo, July 14, 1797, Bermudez presented a request for "three *arpents* square of the community lands of this city at the edge of the left side of the Carondelet Canal, to build an apiary and laboratory to bleach wax, having previously built a waxworks on a lot within the city limits, where the dust from vehicles causes him great loss."[14] His request was beyond the jurisdiction or authority of the Cabildo, and a matter to be taken up with the Crown; but Bermudez requested a letter

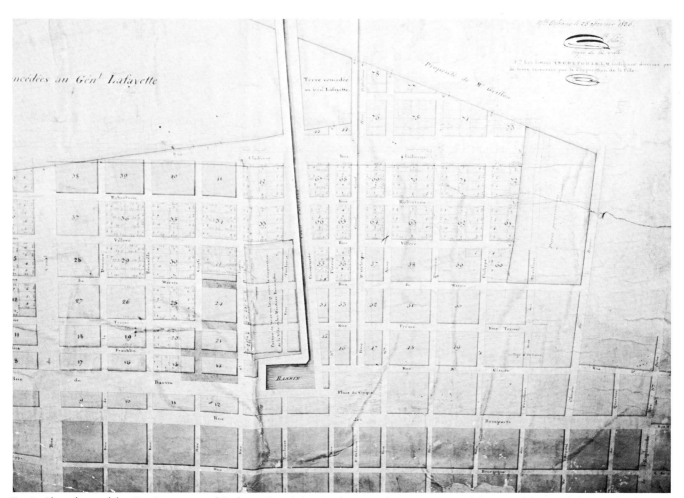

Fig. 5. Plan of part of the City Commons and Faubourg Tremé showing the Bermudez Concession and the Carondelet Canal, by Joseph Pilié, 1826 (Courtesy City Engineers Office)

from the Cabildo recommending the grant, "certifying how useful this project will be to this Province with this new line of business, by increasing the culture of bees, which development will be profitable to the Royal Finance, due to the collection of export duties." Bermudez's grant was approved after an investigation by the attorney general, with the condition that "between the land he intends to obtain and the levee of the Carondelet Canal, a strip of land be left vacant, wide enough for a main road."[15]

The State Land Office validated this Bermudez grant in 1812: "Francis Bermudez claims a tract of land situated in the county of Orleans on the South side of the Canal de Carondelet, containing 2 *arpents* front by 4½ in depth, bounded on the remaining sides by vacant land. A royal order from the Court of Spain being exhibited to the Board, dated at Aranjuez, 3rd day of May 1799, in favor of the claimant for the land in question, the Board do hereby confirm the claim aforesaid."[16] When the City Commons were laid out and subdivided by the city in 1812 along with Faubourg Tremé, the new streets circumvented the area of the Bermudez grant.

Francisco Bermudez was a Spanish colonial who came to New Orleans via Havana, having appeared in the city by February 16, 1775, when he was noted as a defendant in a suit brought by Jean Lafitte. His heirs, who had moved to Havana after the Louisiana Purchase, were restrained from selling the land by the City Council in 1823. The City Council minutes of July 19, 1823, noted that the Spanish Crown had specified: "If the lands were used for anything but a wax-bleaching factory, the property would revert to the Commons of the City." Lawsuits followed, and according to the City Council records of May 14, 1825, "the Mayor went to the Bermudez grant by the Spanish government and found neither beehives nor wax factory, conditions under which the grant was made."[17]

The Corporation of the City claimed the land was to be reinstated as the City Commons. Finally, the City Council renounced rights to the Bermudez land on condition that "plans and surveys of the area be drawn up and the land auctioned for the benefit of the creditors and heirs of F. X. Bermudez, with one-half of the proceeds going to the Corporation of the City, the creditors and heirs to abandon the necessary land for roads to the city."[18] The land was surveyed and subdivided according to a plan by Joseph Pilié, dated April 14, 1829. The auction took place, and the Bermudez heirs and creditors received half of the proceeds, $13,422.57. José Antonio Bermudez of New Orleans and Charles Darcantel represented the heirs: Julian Francisco Leoncis, Rafaela Théodorea, and José Antonio Bermudez, residents of Cuba. George Morgan, sheriff of Orleans Parish, acted as syndic for the creditors.[19]

The area was developed industrially because of its location at the Canal basin. The Robinson Atlas of 1883 shows that most of the Bermudez squares became part of a complex housing the L'Hote Lumber Company, Mill, and Sash, Door, and Blind Factory. The L'Hote family was from Alsace-Lorraine and lived nearby.

When the Carondelet Canal and its basin were new in the early 1800s, the land drained by it was premium property. When it became known in 1804 that President Thomas Jefferson anticipated claiming all of the City Commons beyond the fortifications as a special land grant to the Marquis de Lafayette for his participation in the American Revolution, numerous claimants appeared for the uncultivated tract. These included the City Corporation, which declared that the city owned 1,800 feet beyond the fortifications by virtue of an old law decreed by Governor Carondelet. The council produced Spanish records dated 1797 that indicated, according to the corporation, that the land had been granted to give the city a revenue for public works. This claim was settled by congressional action of March 3, 1807, when ownership of the City Commons adjacent to New Orleans and within 600 yards of the old fortifications was recognized as valid, provided the city relinquish within six months all pretensions to more extended claims. A letter from Governor Claiborne to President Thomas Jefferson, dated December 22, 1804, clarified the status of the Commons:

> The Commons of the city as explained by the Mayor, and as he said, were defined many years ago, included Forts St. Charles and St. Louis, all the minor fortifications erected by the Baron de Carondelet, several handsome adjoining lots, and extend about one-quarter of a mile on the Canal [Carondelet] towards the Bayou St. John: . . . the balance of the land on each side, quite to the Bayou is vacant; I do not know its width; the length is near a mile . . . a survey of at least 600 acres may be obtained. The claim of the City, if a good one, will not only enable the Corporation to increase their funds, but to add greatly to the beauty of New Orleans, and to the comfort of the inhabitants by preserving several open squares, and the laying out and improving several public walks.
>
> When I advised the laying of a part of General Lafayette's grant on the unappropriated land adjoining this City . . . the interference of this claim, may prevent the obtaining of as valuable a tract, as I at first contemplated. . . . But I nevertheless think that the land on each side of the Canal, to which there is no claimant but the United States, will greatly enhance its value; and that the General's interest would be served by locating the same in his name. [He was proven incorrect by the Supreme Court of the United States and five federal statutes.] I would propose that an area of 250 feet on each side of the Canal, should be preserved, in order to admit of its enlargement and of a road to be ornamented with a double row of trees. It is probable that New Orleans will in a few years extend quite to the Bayou, and therefore I think that the lands on the Canal, will soon meet with lucrative sales. . . . Mr. Isaac Briggs, who is now nearly restored to health, has promised in a few days to visit with me, the Canal of Carondelet, and to give me his opinion as to the quality, quantity, and relative value of the vacant land.[20]

Although the 1807 congressional action determined the boundaries of the Commons, ownership of the vacant lands beyond Claiborne Avenue was still unsettled. At this point the federal government claimed ownership, via the Spanish Crown, of swamplands from Carondelet Canal to Faubourg Ste Marie, and Claiborne Avenue to present N. Dorgenois. Forty-eight years of litigation transpired before the ownership was permanently established.

Nevertheless, the area between Rampart and Claiborne, between Faubourgs Ste Marie and Tremé, and the City Commons were free for urban development by the city after 1807. Jacques Tanesse laid out the subdivision in 1812, and lots began to sell. In 1822 the Girod Canal (Orleans Street) was dug parallel to the Carondelet Canal for drainage, and the City Commons was distinguished by having two commercial waterways. These two projects predisposed much of the land to commercial and industrial development. There were warehouses, lumberyards, coal yards, and shell depots; but efforts were also made to reserve prestige lots for residences along both waterways. La Compagnie des Architects de Huitième District, a creole contracting company, owned and sold many lots in the vicinity of these canals during the 1830s and constructed hundreds of creole cottages. St. Louis Cemeteries I and II, Perseverance Hall, Our Lady of Guadeloupe Mortuary Chapel, Parish Prison, and the Tremé Market were major landmarks during this period of development. The appearance of the area was also greatly enhanced by the Public Square (Circus Place-Congo-Beauregard Square). The wide, tree-lined levees along the Carondelet Canal were popular promenades. The waterways, indeed, gave the City Commons an unusual character in the nineteenth century. Old prints and photographs indicate that sailing vessels, or their masts, were visible from every viewpoint. The Carondelet Canal and its basin, Girod or Orleans Canal, and the drainage canal along N. Claiborne combined to make the City Commons a picturesque neighborhood, albeit seasonally odiferous from stagnant water.

PARISH PRISON

In 1831 there was a need for a new parish prison, and the City Council and Mayor Denis Prieur authorized a purchase from Oliver Blineau of land, 240 by 131 feet, in the small square bound by Orleans, St. Ann, Tremé, and Marais. The prison site replaced a soap factory on the square at the time. The purchase of the ground took place just as residences were being built in the vicinity, and within a few years the Tremé Market was established in the next square. Perseverance Hall had been built recently nearby. The prison site was also just a square away from Circus Place on N. Rampart and three blocks from the Carondelet Basin.

The new prison was planned by Joseph Pilié, city surveyor, whose drawings, dated April 8, 1833, are preserved at the archives of the New Orleans Public Library. Contractor Samuel S. Slack began work on the prison the same month and built the foundation and first level. His contract was annulled, and the work was continued by François Correjolles and Jean Chaigneau. Pilié then resigned as architect and A. Voilquin made new plans for the third level, which was yet to be built. Voilquin's plans were adapted by the City Council on April 27, 1836; then A. J. Bourgerol was replaced by engineer Colonel C. Crozet, who completed the project for a total cost of almost $200,000. Colonel Crozet's specifications for the completion of the prison, preserved in the archives of Félix de Armas, dated October 17, 1836, are signed by Gobet and Larochette, contractors, who completed the work. The contract calls for

the eight façades of the two buildings to have in their complete height mortar to imitate granite. The lower part of the façades, up to six feet, the pediments, pilasters, capitals, and the cornices will be rough cast, or pushed to the gauge, of quality of hydraulic mortar mentioned above. . . . The interior of the vestibule, halls, officers' rooms . . . cells, kitchens, waterclosets, stairways, chimneys, dungeon galleries, piers and galleries, façade walls, and enclosures opening to the courtyard, and in a word all the surfaces, to have two coats of grey mortar and one coat of white. All ceilings to have the same plaster treatment except for the gallery ceiling of the cells of the two lower floors which will have *voliges de cypres* [cypress

lath], although the galleries of the cells of the [third] will be lathed and plastered three coats.[21]

Aesthetically, the prison was a major architectural landmark for the city, and its demolition in 1895 a serious loss. It had represented the combined effort of two architects, as well as an important nineteenth-century social statement. The interior featured large courtyards with arcaded walkways and tiers of galleries. There were separate accommodations and yards for women, white men, black men, and debtors; those accused of nonviolent crimes had a separate area apart from other convicts. The "Orleans" was a large room on the third floor, used for prisoners who paid for their accommodations.

Pilié's plan of 1832 for the prison recalled the original Hewlett's Exchange, with a balustrade that obscured the roofline. The final building, however, had a hip-roof and arcades at the first level and continued the French and Spanish building traditions. The plan shows the influence of the French military handbooks of the eighteenth century, which had been used by the chief engineers of the city. The handsome prison complex is illustrated in an etching by Edmunds preserved in the Historic New Orleans Collection (figs. 6, A, B). The neutral ground on Orleans was planted in sycamore trees; the two towers of the prison were complemented by the tower of the Tremé Market, which could be seen straddling Basin Street as it met N. Claiborne Avenue. Eleven years after its demolition in 1895, its empty site was filled with the City Pumping Station building. Its architecture introduced a twentieth-century, Spanish Revival type in public buildings.

TREMÉ MARKET

Tremé Market was begun in 1839, spreading across the present Basin Street and extending two blocks between Marais to N. Robertson Street. Streetcar tracks ran along Basin, passing through the middle of the market. Richard Clague's painting of the 1860s shows the market a block away from the Old Basin (Carondelet) Canal (figs. 7,A). The Girod Canal, directly behind the market, ran along what is now Orleans Street; it intersected canals on N. Claiborne and N. Broad. A building contract dated November 28, 1839, by Bourgerol, city surveyor, was recorded in the acts of J. Cuvillier. A drawing of the market's Basin Street façade was attached to the acts of the same notary, May 20, 1839, along with the contract by Gobet and Larochette, builders for the First Municipality. The market was to be erected for $27,000 along the center of Orleans Street (present Basin Street) according to Bourgerol's plans.

Eleven years later, James Lilly agreed to paint "the meat, vegetable, and Tremé Markets" for $1,650.[22] John McVittie agreed to repair the "meat, vegetables, and Tremé Markets for $1,500." These 1850 contracts specified that the columns were to be painted black and "the outside of the awnings shall be painted with blue stripes." Materials were supplied by the contractors. The work was to be finished in forty days, or Lilly was to pay a daily $25 fine. The *Picayune* of April 27, 1858, reported that "the Council voted use of the Canal neutral ground in extending Tremé Market a square beyond its existing boundaries."

CONGO-BEAUREGARD SQUARE

The square in front of the Municipal Auditorium had been open space since the demolition of Fort St. Ferdinand in 1804.

Fig. 6. Parish Prison and Tremé Market on Basin Street, Jewell's Crescent City, 1879 (Courtesy New Orleans Public Library)

Fig. 6A. Parish Prison (Courtesy New Orleans Public Library)

Fig. 6B. View of City Commons from Canal and Tremé streets in 1849 crevasse; Parish Prison shown (Courtesy Historic New Orleans Collection)

Fig. 7. Tremé Market (Courtesy New Orleans Public LIbrary)

Fig. 7A. Tremé Market from Carondelet Canal, watercolor by Richard Clague (Courtesy Felix Kuntz Collection, New Orleans)

The land was immediately incorporated into the City Commons, except for that small portion which was claimed by Claude Tremé. He successfully sued for a part of the fort's *glacis* in 1815, claiming the *glacis* exceeded the alloted Military Commons that surrounded the city.[23] Maps and surveys through 1845 referred to the square as Circus Place, but it was popular from 1806 as a site for slaves to congregate on Sundays and was known also as Congo Square. A law dating from 1806 stipulated that "slaves must be free to enjoy Sundays, or they were to be paid fifty cents a day if they worked." On October 15, 1817, a city ordinance was passed that forbade all assemblies of slaves except for worship, funerals, games, and dances. It stated that "the assemblies of slaves for the purpose of dancing or other merriment, shall take place only on Sundays, and solely in such open or public places as shall be appointed by the Mayor, and no such assembly shall continue later than sunset." Two years later, on a Sunday in 1819, J. Benjamin Henry Latrobe happened upon a gathering of 500 to 600 Negroes in Circus Place:

They were formed into circular groups, in the midst of four of each group there were two women dancers. They each held a coarse handkerchief extended by the corners in their hands, and danced in a miserably dull and slow figure, hardly moving their feet or bodies. The music consisted of two drums and a stringed instrument which no doubt was imported from Africa. On top of the finger board was the rude figure of a man in sitting posture and two pegs behind him, to which strings were fastened. The body was a calabash. It was played upon by a very little old man, apparently eighty or ninety years old. . . . A man sung an uncouth song to the dancing, which I suppose was in some African language, for it was not French, and the women screamed a detestable burthen on a single note.[24]

By the 1820s activities among the Negroes in Circus Place had gotten out of hand, and Paxton's *New Orleans Register and Directory* recorded in 1822: "The Circus public square is planted with trees, and enclosed, and is very noted on account of its being the place where the Congo and other Negroes dance, carouse, and debauch on the Sabbath, to the great injury of the morals of the rising generation . . . but if it is not considered good policy to abolish the practice entirely, surely they could be ordered to assemble at some place more distant from the houses."[25] This plea was understandable because there were large townhouses and *maisons de maître* nearby, like that of Benoit Milbrouck, and the Collège d'Orléans. Louis Moreau Gottschalk lived in a townhouse in the next block. Although the music may have disturbed his family, it inspired the young composer. In later years, while living in France, he wrote "Bamboula" and other music based on the rhythms he had heard at his own N. Rampart Street home, so near Circus Place.

By the late 1830s N. Rampart Street, the Commons, and Faubourg Tremé had developed so heavily that, although no law forbade activity on Circus Place, it became restrained. In April of 1845 an unusual petition was made before the First Municipal Council requesting that the ancient privilege of dancing in Circus Place be restored to the Negroes. The council agreed that "from May 1 to August 21 each year, slaves, with written consent from their owners, could gather in Congo Square on Sundays from 4 to 6 P.M. The dancing must not be offensive to public decency and eight policemen must be present."[26] The name Circus Place was hereby officially noted as Congo Square by the council.

Then, on January 25, 1851, the First Municipality renamed the Place d'Armes (in front of the Cabildo, Cathedral, and Presbytere), Jackson Square, and the redesignated Congo Square as the new Place d'Armes, where the militia would drill on Sundays. In 1879 the *Daily Picayune* reported the activities at the "Old Square" as "serene, nurses strolling babies, the tinkling bells on the car mules, the drowsy drumming of the cicadas on the tall sycamore trees."[27] On March 24, 1893, the square was renamed Beauregard Square after a resolution by the City Council to honor General P. G. T. Beauregard, New Orleans Civil War hero and recently deceased resident. Beauregard Square was landscaped, oaks planted and whitewashed, and benches set in place (fig. 8).

Behind this square the Municipal Auditorium was built in 1929 by the Caldwell Brothers and Bond Brothers, builders, after the Italian Renaissance-style designs of Favrot and Livaudais. The first theatrical star to appear was Al Jolson, who per-

Fig. 8. Beauregard Square (Courtesy Historic New Orleans Collection)

formed to an audience of 4,500 on January 30, 1930. The structure seats 6,000 for balls and concerts and can be divided to house a small (2,000) performance in one side and a large one (4,000) in the other simultaneously, making it quite a versatile hall. The city of New Orleans dedicated the auditorium to World War I "Heroes who gave their all in Her defense and for Her Honor," as recorded on a bronze plaque.

Intermittently, from the time of the completion of the Municipal Auditorium, various city administrations have tried to embark upon a cultural center project on the squares surrounding the auditorium and Beauregard Square. For the most part, these projects were ill-conceived and badly designed. One, dating from the 1920s, included a large, two-story structure that was to be built across N. Rampart Street, extending two blocks into the French Quarter. It was not, however, until 1955 that any money was set aside by the city for the acquisition of land for the expansion of a cultural center, of which the Municipal Auditorium and Beauregard Square were the base. Under Mayor DeLesseps Morrison, the 1955 capital budget recommended that $1,000,000 be approved for the acquisition of four squares around the auditorium. The request was cut in half, but in 1958 arrangements were made for $200,000 to be allocated that year and $400,000 each year in 1959 and 1960. Then, in 1961, with urban renewal funds from the fed-

eral government, the city reacquired the area of the City Commons extending from the Basin-Orleans connection, St. Philip and N. Rampart to N. Villere. An unfunded project for the construction of five major buildings designed for culture-oriented use was unfolded, and clearance of the land began.

LOUIS ARMSTRONG PARK

Unobserved by members of the City Planning Commission was the fact that the area, which had appeared to them a slum, was in reality a living history of the city, reflecting one and three-quarter centuries. Hundreds of the brick-between-post creole cottages and center-hall, side-gable houses had been designed, built, owned, and lived in by the prosperous free black community of the first half of the nineteenth century. These were the early *entrepreneurs* of the suburbs opened by the city in 1812, who had built investment housing in great quantity—lasting testimonials to their socioeconomic affluence in Faubourg Tremé and the City Commons. Archival drawings, auction notices, building contracts, and old photographs indicate that more brick structures and historic buildings of quantity were demolished by this urban renewal project than remain on any similar number of squares in the area beyond N. Rampart. One of the important creole buildings demolished was the birthplace of the black poet Rodolphe Desdunes and numerous historic homes of black nineteenth- and twentieth-century musicians. House-types and styles, like those considered worthy of National Register status in the Vieux Carré, were razed, along with 150 years of history (figs. 9,A-E).

By 1965 the city funded relocation for inhabitants of the former City Commons, many of whom were descendants of early settlers. Several years later Elizabeth McDermott at the University of New Orleans ruefully commented within a sociological treatise:

The relocation policies are interesting when considered from three viewpoints: that of the government, the tenant and the landlord. The City Government first notified the

Fig. 9A. 900 block Tremé (demolished)

Fig. 9. 1141–43 Dumaine (demolished)

Fig. 9D. 1227–25 Dumaine

Fig. 9B. 1301–03 Dumaine (demolished)

Fig. 9E. 936 St. Claude

Fig. 9C. 1233–35 Dumaine (demolished)

tenants by leaflets or notices . . . [informing] them of the City's intention to utilize the site for a Cultural Center Project. They were also told that information booklets, explaining both residential and business processes, would be available in the near future. Soon after, a relocation office was established in the area. Its function was to help the displaced find suitable housing according to their income, family size, site preference, and place of work. Eventually as the National Urban Renewal Program became more stabilized and the City Planners more experienced, the Relocation Office was to work with Real Estate Boards to find housing that met strict standards.

The office was to help find mortgage financing to purchase new homes, to obtain relocation payments to cover moving and temporary rental, to handle eviction policies, and to reestablish businesses in other lucrative areas. The relocation staff included seven persons, and there were comprehensive plans for a smooth and satisfactory transition. In reality, relocation became "dislocation."

When the information booklets were finally mailed, at least 70% of the citizens did not receive them. Those who did could not understand the complex procedures . . . and moved out without receiving relocation funds or assistance. Many moved in with families or friends in the Tremé area, increasing an already existing high density problem.

The property owners also felt victimized. The landlords, almost all absentee, were notified of the City's plan after the tenants . . . that the area was to be redeveloped and their property expropriated. Although demolition was not imminent, the tenants, confused and distrusting, moved out almost immediately. At least a year elapsed before the City got two appraisals on each property and began to negotiate with the owners on the price. Then the City had to wait a considerable time until necessary purchase funds [were received] from the Federal Government. It was even a year or more later until the houses were torn down. In the meantime, the landlords received no rent, were expected to meet mortgage payments, and had to contend with transients and indigents who moved in and out of the property at will. Owners agreed the purchase price was fair, but they suffered from inconvenience and the necessity of hiring lawyers.

The first actual construction within the cleared complex began in 1971 after eight years of negotiations. A Center for the Performing Arts, designed by Mathes and Bergman and Associates, Inc., with architect Harry Baker Smith as consultant, was completed in 1973 for eight million dollars. The remainder of the cleared site lay unused, but grandiose schemes were being discussed.

When the famous New Orleans Jazz musician Louis Armstrong died, city officials decided that the cleared area adjacent to the Performing Arts Center could be developed as a memorial for the New Orleans–born black musician. As the Performing Arts Center foundations were being laid in 1971, a San Francisco architectural firm, Laurence Halprin and Associates, was given a three-month contract to design a park fronting on N. Rampart, immediately adjacent to Beauregard Square to extend to St. Philip and N. Villere and the Orleans-Basin connection. The plan was to include a lush green space, interspersed with berms (mounds) with large shallow pools, above which one could stroll by connecting walkways while admiring splashing fountains. A botanical garden, a community gymnasium and archives, a casino, a restaurant, even a Mt. Armstrong were considered. The plan was based on the refined principles of the Victorian pleasure parks, which offered a combination of indoor and outdoor experiences. The spectrum of culture, recreation, and leisure activities were to be subtly entwined to induce visitors and natives to frequent the ten-block space throughout the day and evening.

This plan was controversial and unfunded. The black community, awakened to their personal loss, objected to this effete plan. Further consternation surfaced when it became apparent that the San Francisco plans included an attempt to recapture, with twentieth-century plasticity, nineteenth-century reality, which had been swept away with urban-renewal-funded demolitions.

After further delay, in 1974 the City Council authorized the spending of $8,200,000 for the development and improvement of the entire thirty-one acres owned by the city. Included were the Municipal Auditorium, the Theatre for the Performing Arts, Congo-Beauregard Square, and the proposed Louis Armstrong Park area. The entire site was enclosed by a concrete and steel fence. Parking areas were specified, as were a 2¾-acre lagoon and fountain system, extensive regional planting, paths, lighting, seating, and other public amenities. Congo-Beauregard Square was allocated $1,200,000 from the Department of Commerce and the Economic Development Agency. Architectural portions were to include creation of a jazz museum complex and outdoor performing areas. Robin Riley was named project architect, with Cashio-Cochran as landscape architects.

The plan for the park that emerged according to Riley's design included preservation of the four buildings that remained within the compound after the urban renewal clearance: Perseverance Hall dating from 1826, at former 901 St. Claude, and its separate, two-story kitchen dating from 1830; the Rabassa-De Pouilly House, formerly 1125 St. Ann; and a gable-sided, brick fire station, successfully designed for the city in the 1940s to blend with the creole architecture of the vicinity. Another frame building, the Reimann House, was moved from city-owned property at 618 S. Gayoso to Louis Armstrong Park as part of the newly oriented jazz complex.

The history of these buildings is an initiation into the relevancies of social activities in this area. The story of the Fraternal-Masonic organization and its lodge and the activities of musical performances, both white and black, are related. The other nineteenth- and early-twentieth-century buildings now incorporated into the complex are symbolic of the former history and appearance of Faubourg Tremé and City Commons.

La Loge Persévérance, numéro Quatre was organized in 1806 at Jérémy, St. Domingue, under a charter issued by the Grand Lodge of Pennsylvania. In 1808 the Lodge established itself in New Orleans, with membership chiefly comprised of refugees from St. Domingue and Cuba. First they met in the Etoile Polaire, then facing St. Claude on a site behind the present location on N. Rampart, between Esplanade and Kerlerec. A new charter was obtained in 1810, and a site for another lodge was selected and purchased from the city of New Orleans in 1819.

The members contracted with architect-builder Bernard Thibaud for "erecting and constructing . . . a building to serve for the holding of said Lodge, the dimensions of which were decided and agree upon and this for a sum of $5,272." The build-

Fig. 10. Perseverance #4 in 1974

Fig. 11. Perseverance #4 in 1979

ing was completed and accepted by the Lodge on April 1, 1820 (figs. 10,A). The building contract has not been found, but much information about it is contained in a subsequent agreement between the Lodge and Thibaud regarding payment for the work, in an act passed before notary Marc Lafitte, October 15, 1821. However, the extant building is substantially the one erected by Thibaud in 1819, with 1850 alterations.

This building was saved from demolition largely through the efforts of local architect Samuel Wilson, Jr. It is now undergoing interior restoration according to consultative advice of Monroe Labouisse after exterior restoration in 1974–1975 according to specifications by Mathes and Bergman with Samuel Wilson, Jr., consulting architect. It will be used as a cultural and social hall, thus continuing its nineteenth-century functions.

On March 11, 1830, eleven years after the main hall was built, the Lodge, represented by Adolphe N. Pichot and Jean Labadie, entered into another building contract with François Correjolles and Jean Chaigneau, *entrepreneurs de batisses*, for the construction on the Lodge's grounds of

une maison a étage [two-story house] . . . foundations 18 inches deep in the ground, first floor raised 18 inches from the banquette, ceilings 10 feet high first story, 10 feet 8 inches high second story, each floor divided in two rooms, each apartment with a chimney, and three of them paneled. The apartment or room in the front to serve as a kitchen will be floored in lake brick, the other floors in boards 6 inches or 7 inches wide, tongue and grooved, ceilings of mortar, three layers, first floor to have three doors and two windows, second floor to have two doors and four windows, balcony to run the whole length of the house facing

on the yard to 4 feet wide with columns and balustrade with stairway. The front of the building under the balcony will be paved in lake bricks for a total width of 8 feet. Walls to be 9 inches thick except the side of the neighboring property which has 1-foot thickness to the height of the second story. Walls on the road and yard to be plastered two coats, one black mortar, the other white. Slate roof with gutters. All wood painted with two coats exterior, doors and windows green, all others pearl grey. Also, a well, mounted in bricks, 10 feet deep, 3 feet high above the banquette. Entrepreneurs promise it will be ready for occupancy by the 30th of June next for $1,800; $600 beginning of building, $600 on delivery, and $600 with interest six months later.[28]

The interior of the resulting building was altered in the nineteenth and twentieth centuries and the roof rebuilt. It has not been restored, but was renovated by the city for adaptive use as an office, after plans of architect Robin Riley and Mathes and Bergman and Associates, Inc. (fig. 11).

Architects Freret and Wolf in 1940 designed the yellow brick fire station, which, with its proportions and parapet gabled sides is compatible with the nineteenth-century character of the adjacent Faubourg Tremé. The fire station is undergoing renovation; the façade will be reconstructed by analogy, with four French doors and batten shutters like a creole cottage.

Perseverance Hall and its kitchen have been placed on the National Register of Historic Places and are excellent memorials to architects Bernard Thibaud, designer also of the 1816 Theâtre d'Orléans, and to François Correjolles. The latter was born in Baltimore, after his parents had fled the uprisings and massacres in San Domingue. The importance of the Perseverance Hall complex stretches beyond its architectural value and its historic importance as the oldest Masonic Lodge in the Mississippi Valley. Like many benevolent and church-related institutions in the city, the building was rented for social and cultural events. The main hall, with its wooden balcony and outstanding stairway, was appropriate for concerts, dances, musicales, recitals, poetry readings, and theater. From the documented 1870s performances by educated Creoles of color and those performances by early-twentieth-century black bands, evidence is preserved of the building's importance through entertainment use.

Other music halls associated with the early years of New Orleans jazz have been destroyed. Economy Hall (San Jacinto Hall) at 1422 Ursulines, where Louis Armstrong played, was demolished after a 1964 hurricane. St. Ann Hall at 1315 Barracks and Co-operation (Hope's) Hall at 922 Tremé Street were also razed, as of course have been most of the bawdy houses, bars, and restaurants of Storyville.

Part of the jazz complex within the Cultural Center, is the Rabassa-De Pouilly House, a historic residence used for many years as the St. Ann Street annex for McDonogh No. 41 School (fig. 12). It is a major example of a high, raised creole cottage, of brick-between-posts construction. Indeed, except for an 1805 drawing of the Zeringue House on Bayou Road (fig. 2, Peyroux-Cheval), the Rabassa House is the only existing record within New Orleans of the creole cottage wherein the *rez de chausée*, or main level, is raised eight feet on brick piers. Jean Louis Rabassa built it soon after he purchased the site from

Lewis Fuller on May 17, 1825. Fuller had purchased the property in two parts, one on November 18, 1816, and the other on October 21, 1819, both from the Corporation of the City of New Orleans when Augustin Macarty was mayor. The plan of four rooms, two across the front and two deep, with two *cabinets* or small rooms at the ends of a recessed rear gallery (now enclosed) is that of every typical creole cottage. Across the front a gallery supports a heavy wooden parapet, part of a later Greek Revival cornice. The house has gable ends, with a straight sloped roof in front and a double sloped (canted) roof in the rear to extend out over the rear gallery and *cabinets*. The gable ends are covered with small wood shingles that appear to be original and, if so, are a unique surviving example. Most of the doors and windows and the interior trim were replaced in the 1850s with late Greek Revival details. The timber frame with its members dove-tailed, mortised and tennoned, and numbered with Roman numerals is another unusual feature of the house. When Rabassa sold the property in 1833 to Jean Baptiste Seraphin Cucullu, it is stated in the act of sale that the land belonged to him by his purchase from Fuller and "the buildings as having had them built."[29] Edith Elliot Long's research on the famous early-nineteenth-century architect, J. N. B. de Pouilly, revealed that he resided in this house at the time of his death in 1875.[30]

Louis Armstrong Park reflects the effort of the community to recognize in a suitable manner the musicians of New Orleans who developed jazz as a national art form. "To be jazz, as identified by scholars, the music must be (a) improvised, (b)

Fig. 12. Rahassa-De Pouilly House

played in 2/4 or 4/4 time, and (c) retain a definable melodic line."[31] But jazz, to a New Orleanian, is far more than that. It is a way of life and a way of death, an inextricable part of history and of daily life in Faubourg Tremé and the City Commons. It is the outgrowth of musical development from the time of the establishment of the Commons. Slave chants had blended with the improvised rhythms of the New Orleans black in Circus-Congo-Beauregard Square from its beginning. Music was an essential part of the classical education of numerous well-to-do free men of color, many of whom studied in Paris and returned to New Orleans where they performed in the lodges, churches, and fraternal halls of the Commons before and after the Civil War. Dixieland and jazz grew out of this musical tradition. It is and was neighborhood music for dancing, parades, weddings, picnics, wakes, and burials. It developed in the churches and lodge halls, and by 1889 it was the music played by the brass bands of fraternal organizations. The neighborhood saloons, corner bars, cabarets, dance halls, and honky tonks made possible the growth of the jazz tradition; and the brothels of Storyville, where jazz musicians appeared between 1897 and 1917, helped to spread the popularity of the music.[32] The dixieland and jazz music, like the buildings where it was played and the houses where the musicians were born and lived, are a visible link between the early-nineteenth-century free Negro community and their twentieth-century descendants.

STORYVILLE

Throughout the 1850s the area between N. Rampart and N. Claiborne, Common and St. Ann continued to grow, with numerous boardinghouses run by Irish and German immigrants and free women of color. By the Civil War, it was teeming with newcomers; by the end of Reconstruction occupation, many of the boardinghouses had become bordellos. Before these brothels moved to the north side of Canal Street, Basin Street on its south side between Gasquet (Cleveland) and Common held the most famous houses of the day. One of the first of the "elegant" pleasure palaces belonged to Kate Townsend, a four-

story frame house on Customhouse (Iberville) and N. Villere, from 1863. She was quickly followed by the beautiful Negro madame called "Minnie HaHa" at 45 S. Basin by 1868. Then there was Fannie Sweet, who used voodoo to lure and hold customers in the late 1860s at S. Basin and Gasquet (Cleveland). In the late 1870s Hattie Hamilton also located across Canal Street at 21 S. Basin.

On September 22, 1870, the city's German daily, *Taglische Deutsche Zeitung*, reported that the citizens of the area were seeking an injunction to stop Hattie Hamilton's operation. But the pre-Storyville era was launched, and local politicians joined the rush to buy the bars, restaurants, and houses, some of which commanded a high rent. Tom Anderson, political boss of the Fourth Ward, owned 209 N. Basin Street, and from that saloon guided the destiny of Storyville through the intricacies of political chicanery. Neighbor Josie Arlington at 225 N. Basin ran his sporting house, which "rivaled Lulu White's in splendor and gaudiness. The Arlington was a narrow Edwardian house, four stories high with a cupola. Inside was a succession of parlors . . . Japanese, Turkish and Viennese . . . a hall of mirrors and . . . elaborately furnished boudoirs".[33] In 1892 Anderson also opened a restaurant at old number 12 N. Rampart frequented by police and politicians (fig. 13,A).

Efforts of local residents to abate the trend were futile. George L'Hote and members of the Methodist Episcopal Church on Bienville Street lost a battle against the district's expansion in 1897. "Out of all this clamor, came one thin voice of reason, that of Alderman Sidney Story. He proposed a law that there be a 'certain district, outside of which it will be unlawful for prostitution to be carried on'. . . . For the first time in the history of the Western Hemisphere, there was established by law a district wherein prostitution could be practiced as a profession, with the full support of the law."[34] For his artful solution to the problem of rampant, city-wide prostitution, Story was memorialized in the thirty-eight-block red-light district. Storyville,

Fig. 13. Storyville on Basin Street (Courtesy Historic New Orleans Collection)

Fig. 13A. A 1925 view of Canal Street showing the Jung Hotel built for the Peter Jung, Sr., family by architects Weiss, Dreyfous and Seiferth, J. B. Burks Construction; Storyville from Lasalle Street to N. Robertson; Tulane Medical School, attributed to architect Thomas Sully (1890s), between N. Villere and N. Robertson; St. Louis Cemetery II bound by Iberville, N. Claiborne, N. Robertson, St. Louis (Courtesy Historic New Orleans Collection)

a city within a city, held an infamous position throughout the nation.

N. Rampart and N. Basin streets were the sites of the best-known and most successful establishments, and some of the 1830s townhouses and creole cottages in the 200 block of N. Basin were replaced by large, gaudy, late-Victorian and Edwardian mansions. By running the classiest sporting house, Lulu White, an "octaroon from the West Indies," soon won the title of Queen of Storyville. She was located before 1908 at Mahogany Hall, which she had built for $40,000 at 235 N. Basin, recalled in "Mahogany Hall Stomp" by musician Spencer Williams. In its day Mahogany Hall was the gaudiest, most expensive sporting palace, built primarily of marble and mahogany. Four stories high, it contained five parlors on the first floor and fifteen bedrooms, each with a bath.[35] She later moved to a small saloon next door on the corner of Basin and Bienville, a brick two-level building dating from 1909, the first story of which remains as the equipment building of Krauss Department Store.[36]

Emma Johnson, a Cajun, started at old number 20 Gasquet in 1892, but moved to 331 and 333 N. Basin, Greek Revival townhouses, which are now demolished. She was considered one of the most evil madames, engaging in acts of great perversity. Willie V. Piazza, an octaroon, was at 317 N. Basin, a brick, mid-nineteenth-century house, after moving her location from 172 Customhouse. "It was at Willie's that the great piano men played—Jelly Roll Morton (Joseph Le Menthe), and the equally great but lesser known, Tony Jackson."[37]

Many of the "cribs" were but sparse, partitioned spaces or rooms in the old Greek Revival, Classic-style townhouses, creole cottages, and shotguns. Each crib rented nightly for $3 to the women of the street (fig. 14).[38] Despite the rule of Tom Anderson from his Fair Play Saloon, corner N. Basin and Iberville, the boundaries of Storyville began to spill over into the rest of the City Commons and into Faubourg Tremé. At the corners of St. Claude and Marais at Dumaine, cribs were rented by white girls; on N. Villere and N. Robertson at Dumaine they were rented by Negro women, and frequented by Negro men and white teenaged boys.[39]

Payments for these rooms were made each week to managers, who usually ran bar-restaurants at each corner storehouse, like Joe Victor's Saloon at 1534 St. Louis (fig. 15). These establishments also featured dixieland music and jazz. Two other lonely buildings, remnants of Storyville, remain: Frank Early's Saloon at 1909–13 Franklin Street (Tremé) at the corner of Bienville, a late Victorian frame store-house, used today as a grocery store (fig. 16); and the building next door on Bienville, behind Early's, a frame, mid-nineteenth-century house of two stories with a second-level gallery that was partitioned into ten cribs.

Many of these houses were owned by descendants of the original German, Irish, Creole, or American families of the City Commons who had moved out or had begun to rent their property before Storyville was established. A double-dormered creole cottage with a two-story service wing could be partitioned into perhaps fourteen cribs, each cottage bringing in $42 per

Fig. 14. Storyville Cribs: a two-bay creole cottage and a two-bay shotgun (Courtesy Leonard Huber)

Fig. 15. 1534 St. Louis, Friebault House

Fig. 16. 1909–13 Franklin (Tremé), Frank Early's Saloon

night, or $294 per week. Comparable property elsewhere might produce rent of only $15 a month. The price for virtue has always been high, and many of the elite in New Orleans found it expedient to resist. Storyville real estate has been the base for more than one New Orleans fortune.[40]

While sin raged, jazz reigned in Storyville. Played in the fancy houses and in nearly every corner store-house in the district and throughout Faubourg Tremé, jazz became a New Orleans export to St. Louis, Chicago, and New York. At old number 101 Franklin [Tremé] Street was the 101 Ranch, and trumpeter Muth Carey recalled it in "Hear Me Talkin' to Ya," and the "Franklin Street Blues." The well-known piece, "St. James Infirmary," was inspired by the St. James Methodist Church building in Storyville. Gasquet, now Cleveland Street, is recalled in "Gasquet Street Blues" and the record "Every Man a King" by Tony Fougerat and His Kings of Poverty.[41]

By 1917 when the United States Department of the Navy caused the district to be closed down by law, Storyville and its political power had already begun to wane. Prostitution had been reduced as early as 1915 by one-half, with just 700 cribs remaining; those outside the district, like the ones on N. Robertson and N. Villere, were almost empty.[42]

Once Storyville closed down in 1917, the city began to obliterate its excesses. In 1938 the neighborhood, considered a slum, caused the founding of the Housing Authority of New Orleans. That authority, within a year of its organization, purchased and demolished much of Storyville. At the time, in 1939, it was felt that the proposed Iberville Project would stimulate the depression-racked economy by providing jobs and low-rent units; it would deter further blight by furnishing a wedge against construction of substandard housing by private investors. A requirement between 1938 and 1950 was that projects could be built only where slum housing had existed.

In 1939 architects Hubert A. Benson, George H. Christy, and William Spink began the construction of seventy-five brick buildings with 858 apartments: 362 having one bedroom, 363 having two bedrooms, and 134 having three bedrooms. The total cost was $847,986.76. The resultant Iberville Project was sensitively conceived, and designed to blend in scale and material with the old neighborhood. The proportions of each unit recall rowhouses of the nineteenth century, displaying the traditional gabled ends, galleries, chimneys, ventilators, and ironwork. The complexes, H.A.N.O.'s first, are by far the most aesthetically pleasing of all subsequent efforts. It is ironic that the city repurchased their own City Commons on which to build public housing.

LOST NEW ORLEANS

Watercolor drawings in the New Orleans notarial archives of auctioned City Commons buildings afford pictorially a view of this "Lost New Orleans." The land belonged to private owners after resting a hundred years within the public domain. Its early-nineteenth-century development was rapid; its late-nineteenth-century deterioration, associated with the musical art form, jazz, continued the pace. Archival drawings show sophisticated urban housing with major public institutions and religious buildings. These were not in conflict with the industrial character of the neighborhood emanating from the Carondelet Canal (figs. 17,A).

Houses in the style of the 1820s through the 1850s are seen: plan book 34, folio 46, 1835, by A. J. Bourgerol, illustrated an urban creole cottage with extensive gardens comprising a half-square at St. Ann, corner of N. Robertson, backed by N. Claiborne and Dumaine (fig. 18). Plan book 43, folio 19 depicts a charming center-hall house with three front dormers, facing Basin at the site of Krauss's running through to Franklin (Tremé). Built probably in the 1820s as a major single-family dwelling, by the end of the nineteenth century it was used by prostitutes (figs. 19 A,B). The house was an atypical type, but early Greek Revival and Creole in decorative style. A large two-story service building with long wings was illustrated in the 1850 drawing by Louis Pilié.

By the 1840s, modest rental shotguns of the two-bay, hip-roof variety, as well as gable-sided, two-bay creole cottages, were erected along the banquettes. These joined double, detached creole cottages, which were identical and in even rows. Genre scenes by Louis Surgi depicting daily activities are recorded in the 1844 drawing of common-wall creole cottages, both for single or double occupancy as seen in plan book 16, folio 1 (figs. 20,A). The full two-level creole house is seen at the height of its development in an 1850 drawing of a Greek Revival double house having four bays on each level and an outside stairway. A more modest version of this house-type

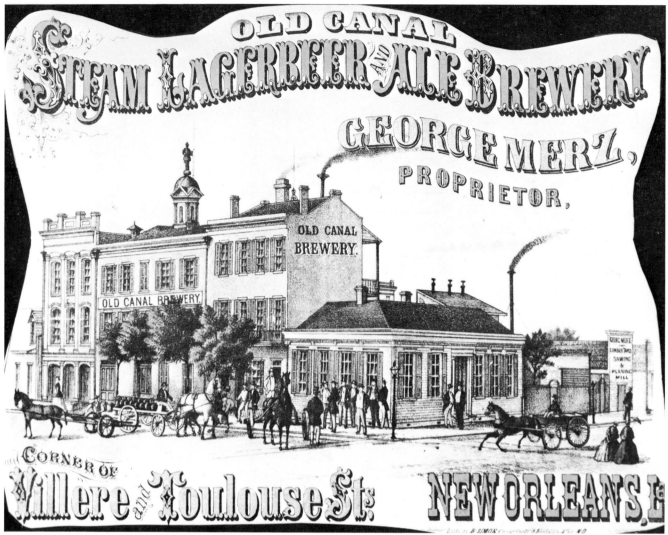

Fig. 17. View of Villere and Toulouse showing five buildings facing Villere with businesses belonging to George Merz, 1871, B. Simon Lithography

Fig. 17A. View of Merz property showing Toulouse Street buildings, the Carondelet Canal with schooners, and bridge near Tremé Market by I. E. Boeher, lithographer, 1867, Graham's City Directory

stood on St. Peter Street in 1847, according to J. N. B. de Pouilly, plan book 44, folio 2.

A street scene at the corner of Conti and N. Villere, as it appeared in 1860, is charmingly depicted by artist-architect A. Persac in a drawing, plan book 74, folio 16, which showed a corner store with a house behind and a row of cottages dating from the 1830s (fig. 21). The French style of building, now associated with the Vieux Carré, flourished in the City Commons; there were *porte cochère* houses, *entresol* houses, and hall-less townhouses having a series of arched openings as illustrated in plan book 46, folio 23 (A. Castaing, April 12, 1859) and plan book 5, folio 11 (Strehler, June, 1873). Others, handsomely illustrated for these nineteenth-century auction advertisements, were designed in the Greek Revival style, though making free use of both American and French details and floor plans, as in plan book 59, folio 1 (A. de Armas, 1870) (figs. 22,A).

Among the few remaining fine buildings within the City Commons is 1429 St. Peter Street, near N. Basin (fig 23). The city of New Orleans has recently renovated and adapted this 1850s common-wall townhouse and outbuildings for use as a firehouse. An excellent, brick, corner store-house at 1534 St. Louis Street remains near the Iberville Project and across from a row of brick railroad warehouses that replaced the former levees of the Carondelet Canal. On N. Rampart Street in the

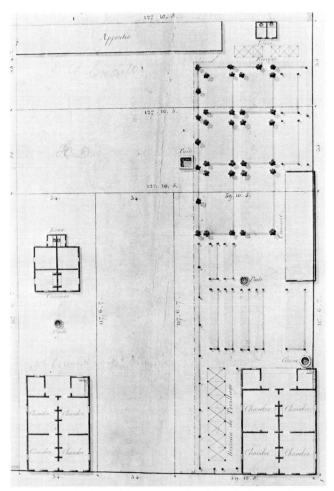

Fig. 18. Plan book 34, folio 46; signed and dated, "Bourgerol, August 6, 1835"; St. Ann corner Robertson backed by Claiborne and Dumaine

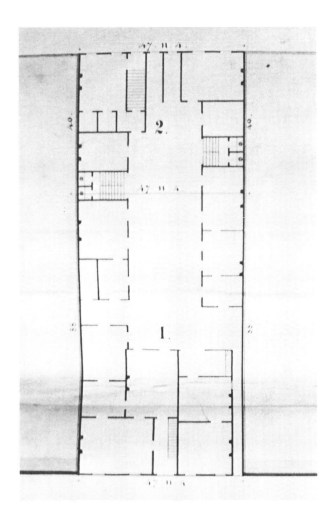

Fig. 19B. Plan book 43, folio 19; floor plan (demolished)

Fig. 19A. Plan book 43, folio 19; service building (demolished)

Fig. 19. Plan book 43, folio 19; signed and dated, "Louis H. Pilié, April 9, 1850"; Basin between Customhouse (Iberville) backed by Franklin (Tremé)

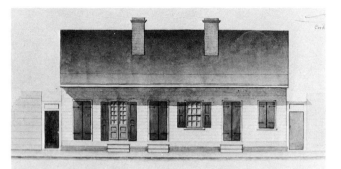

Fig. 20. Plan book 16, folio 1; signed and dated, "Cosnier, February 12, 1845"; Villere between Bienville and Customhouse (Iberville) (demolished)

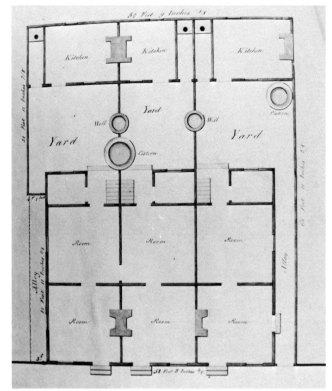

Fig. 20A. Plan book 16, folio 1; plan

Fig. 22. Plan book 59, folio 1; signed and dated, "Arthur de Armas, February 11, 1870"; Rampart corner Conti backed by Bienville and Basin

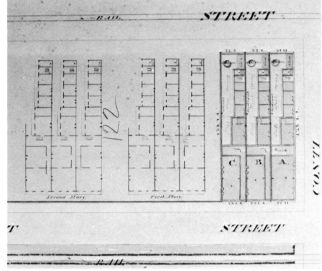

Fig. 22A. Plan book 59, folio 1; plan

Fig. 21. Plan book 74, folio 16; signed and dated, "E. Surgi and A. Persac, January 16, 1860"; Conti corner Villere backed by St. Louis and Marais (demolished)

Fig. 24. Burnham Station (Courtesy Historic New Orleans Collection)

200 block stand the remnants of a row of three-story 1850s townhouses. Such rowhouses are rare in this area, and these are of historic importance.

BASIN STREET

The name Basin Street, recalled in Spencer Williams' "Basin Street Blues," emanated from a section of land that was used as a turn basin for the Carondelet Canal. The basin was filled and the land transformed into portions of a railroad artery that terminated at Canal Street in a station designed in 1904 by E. K. Burnham and Company of Chicago. This internationally known firm also designed the New Orleans Hibernia Bank Building on Carondelet Street in the central business district.

The Burnham Railroad Station was an imposing structure, measuring 82 by 200 feet (fig. 24). It was a major twentieth-century landmark, being an important architectural expression and link with the transportation saga of New Orleans; it was demolished when the Union Passenger Terminal opened under the aegis of Mayor DeLesseps Morrison in 1954. Removed to pay court to the then-popular concept of "open spaces," it made land available for gardens and memorials. Between Canal Street and the Municipal Auditorium three monuments dedicated to Latin American heroes were erected along Basin Street,

Fig. 23. 1429 St. Peter.

and the neutral ground was designated as the "Garden of the Americas."

At Canal and Basin, the cast granite statue of Simon Bolivar, a twelve-foot-high sculpture by Abel Vallmitjana, was a gift to the city from the people of Venezuela and was erected in 1957. It stands in a small plaza ornamented by a pool and fountain designed by Mario Bemerqui and Casieles Asociados, S.A. Ramps and platforms are combined with shallow, tiled, meandering waterways. Varied textures include quarry tile, lava stone, glazed tile, iron supports, and bronze replicas of the coats-of-arms of countries freed by El Liberador. The combination of materials reflect mid-twentieth-century Venezuelan architecture.

Next along the broad, double-laned street is a bronze statue of Mexico's greatest hero, Benito Juarez, who in the 1840s lived in New Orleans' Faubourg Marigny. Placed in position on Basin at the corner of Conti in April, 1965, by a Mexican delegation led by former president, Miguel Alemán, its marble base is inscribed, "People of Mexico to the People of the United States of America—In homage to the Restorer of the Republic and President of Mexico from 1858–1872."

The third Latin American monument guards the neutral ground in front of St. Louis I Cemetery, at the corner of St. Louis Street. A bronze statue of General Francisco Morazón, hero of Central America who was executed by Costa Rican rebels in 1842, was dedicated October 21, 1966. Two countries, Honduras and El Salvador, participated in the gift.[43]

The Krauss Company Department Store at 1201 Canal, corner of Basin, opened in 1903, predating the Southern Railroad Terminal by one year. The first firm was founded by Leon Fellman and the Krauss Brothers, but the Heymann family has held the ownership continually since 1920. The Italianate-style building features pairs of arched windows. In addition, the building has rusticated elevations on three sides and a handsome cornice with heavy modillions and refined dentils. The original three-level structure built in 1903 has had a series of four additions. Warehouses and parking lots belonging to the Heymann family replace the 200 block of Basin Street, which once was emblazoned with the great Storyville mansions of Tom Anderson, Josie Arlington, and Lulu White.

The Saenger Theatre is located at 1111 Canal Street, between Basin and N. Rampart, on a narrow block allowing access from four streets (fig. 25). The theater was built between 1925 and 1927 after designs of the New Orleans architectural firm of Emile Weil and Associates for $2,500,000. Eugene J. Gibert, Sr., a partner in the firm, was director of the project. Designed in the atmospheric manner, the most fanciful of all movie palace genres, it followed a concept created by John Eberson, a European-trained architect. According to John W. Stewart:

> The Saenger was decorated with a deep azure blue Mediterranean sky enhanced by moving clouds, twinkling stars, a moon, and a sunrise-sunset effect. The auditorium was set in a Florentine garden with controlled lighting. There were four magnificent crystal chandeliers from a French chateau and extensive marble statuary.

> The arcades are sheathed in Travertine marble with terrazzo and tile floors. The lobbies have columns of black marble and stairways of white marble. Cast plaster ceilings and walls have polychromatic detailing. Generous smoking rooms separate the rest rooms from the corridors,

Fig. 25. Saenger Theatre

and the theatre is replete with ancillary gathering places.

The exterior is built of poured in place, reinforced concrete, on a foundation of pilings, one of the first such concrete structures in New Orleans. Due to a cautious and conservative attitude toward the new technology, it was constructed considerably stronger than similarly fabricated, contemporary buildings.

The original air conditioning was an ice system replaced by a 225-ton air distribution system in the 1940s. The two Utica-Imperial Super Smokeless steam boilers fired by Truli-Radiant Upshot natural gas burners were built in 1926.

The Saenger was the dream theater of the four men who ran the Saenger Amusement Company: Julian H. Saenger, E. V. Richards, A. D. Saenger, and L. M. Ash. Julian Saenger entered the theater business while operating the Saenger Drugstore in Shreveport, Louisiana. The New Orleans Saenger was the ultimate achievement of the company before it was sold to Paramount-Publix Corporation in 1929 for over ten million dollars.

Prior to the building of the theater, this square was filled with three-level townhouses; six faced Canal Street, at least four overlooked the side of the Burnham train depot on Basin Street, and four fronted N. Rampart. Most of these had galleries or

Fig. 26. Moody Mansion

balconies and when constructed were elegant homes, several having side gardens.

MOODY MANSION

One can visualize the grandeur of residential living on Canal Street in the last half of the nineteenth century through the recollection of Lillian Lyman Campbell, whose grandfather, Samuel Nadin Moody, resided at 1411 Canal from 1858. The three-level, three-bay masonry house described by Mrs. Campbell in 1939 was built for Moody in 1858 by Crozier and Wing, builders, after designs of Howard and Diettel, architects (fig. 26). Its contracted price was $15,500.

Our Grandfather Moody . . . a shirt manufacturer on the corner of Canal and Royal . . . lived at 253 Canal Street near Marais. The mansion, shorn of all its former iron grilled galleries, its white marble vestibule, its garden, its carriage entrance and its grandeur, still stands, a skeleton of the past. I recall the huge saloon parlor, on the first floor. There was a smaller reception room, and a general sitting room on the second floor, and these two, served for informal gatherings of family and friends. But I gazed with childish awe, when the parlor doors were opened. This room was large enough to contain two carved white marble mantelpieces, and above them, large mirrors, in much curlicued, wide, gilt frames, reached to the top of the 18-foot ceilings, which was much ornamented with a plaster cornice, and figures, and a floral plaster circle surrounding the chandeliers. These crystal chandeliers were my greatest admiration, for they were very large, and had three tiers of gas globes. The lights were reflected in the mantel mirrors, and in the long pier looking glasses at each end of the room; and these pier mirrors had the same much ornamented gilt frames, which extended across both windows on each side of the glasses, and formed the decorative band from which hung the heavy yellow damask draperies, cords and tassels, and the lace curtains brought from Belgium. There were five windows altogether, for there was one on the side, between the two mantels. Near this side window was a large gold-colored grand piano, with picture medallions, a copy of one that belonged to Louis XVI of France. Beyond the mantels were two tables of inlaid tortoise shell and brass, made by Charles André Boule, and the cabinet that matched the tables, stood between the two doorways into the entrance hall.

There were two large sofas upholstered in yellow damask, many arm chairs also covered with yellow damask, and numerous small gilt framed chairs (which I was always afraid to touch) with tufted seats in pale pink, pale blue, pale yellow, and pale green damask. Two upholstered "shell" chairs, so called because of their shape, were my special admiration, for they had silk cord, between the divisions of the back.

I recall the Dresden China clock, with its cupids, that stood on one mantel. And the pair of red Bohemian glass vases, enameled in white, that stood on the marble console, at the base of the front pier mirror. Of the paintings on the wall I specially recall three, which caught my childish fancy: "The Bay at Venice," Landseer's "Two

Dogs Pointing a Partridge," and "The Old Shoemaker." An all-over deep plush carpet, with pale pink roses, covered the floor. This saloon parlor was the scene of many lavish entertainments, and the carpet was then covered with a heavy linen crash.

Every Christmas for years there was held a Christmas Fancy Dress Ball, with a tree to the ceiling, and a present on it for every guest. Mrs. McCook, the seamstress, used to interest me, for she came for months in advance to dress dolls for this tree. I can remember my pride in one costume I wore to one of these Christmas parties, when I represented "just a little snow drop", in white cashmere, trimmed with maribou feathers. My cousin, Belle Labuzan, was "just a little star" in another white dress with a band on her curly light hair, and a silver star, that bobbed about on a wire right in front. We sat side by side, and did not leave our seats until we were called to get our gifts off the tree.

During the years from 1858 to 1860, Grandpa Moody gave two or three additional balls on Twelfth Night. Those years the Christmas ball was for the children, and the other ball was for the grown-ups. This second ball was not only a costume ball but the guests were also masked. He remembered the tradition that Mary Queen of Scots had a ball to celebrate Twelfth Night, and he wanted to revive the custom in old New Orleans. He had a bean in a cake, and the queen was the young lady who drew it. Grandpa Moody was an Englishman by birth, and a great contributor to the Confederate cause, for which he had keen sympathy. This may have been because he was Treasurer of the British Funds, which were contributed to the Confederate cause.

It may have been due to the fact that his sister, Sarah Moody, had married General Charles A. Labuzan, who commanded the 2d Division, Louisiana Volunteers, C.S.A. General Labuzan was an intimate friend of General Beauregard, and had charge of the drilling of raw recruits for the Confederate Army at Camp Beauregard, located where Audubon Park now is. He was also a veteran of the Texas-Mexico War.

When General Butler took possession of New Orleans in April 1862, he tried to confiscate our grandfather's property, under the plea that my grandfather was aiding the Confederacy. He could prove nothing; and because our grandfather had been very careful to retain his British citizenship, Butler could do nothing with a Queen's subject.

Here are some of the names I recall as guests at my grandfather's house:

The Valcour and Lacestière Labarre families. Dr. Hitchcock, who was Dentist to the Court of Belgium, and his wife, Marie Durant, the singer. The Bailey family, also Dr. Walter Bailey. The Butlers. The Pierce family. Dr. Bruns. The Denegres. Dr. Chauncey Stone. The Dolbears. The Ainsworths. The Walmsleys (he was President of one of the Banks). The Semmes. Dr. Holcombe. The Morgans. The Van Wickles (Jacob Van Wickle lived on Esplanade Street, and was the Father of Amanda, who married for her second husband, John G. Devereux, President of the Hibernia Bank,—Stephen Van Wickle, who lived on a plantation at Point Coupée, and was the father of Adeline, who in turn was the Mother of Stephen Coulon,—and both these Brothers were members of the Louisiana State Legislature at one time.—Remsen Van Wickle, who had a cotton pickery on Claiborne St. near Canal—and his brother Jacob who was in the Cotton Compress business with his Uncle Wood.)

The John Budd Slawson family (who lived on Canal Street. He was President of the first Omnibus line, and later the first Street Car Line, in New Orleans. He was a member of the Louisiana Secession Convention, and had to flee to Europe when General Butler took possession of the City. Grandpa Moody shipped him gold in boxes of shirts. When Mr. Slawson returned to this country he settled in New York City, and owned the first cross-town Car line there. He invented the, "Drop your nickel in the Box" fare box). There were the Boulignys. The family of Captain William Campbell, corner Claiborne and Bienville. (He was Captain of the famous Robert E. Lee steamboat, that acme of Mississippi River's elegant travel in its day.) The Townsend family. (Mrs. Mary Ashley Townsend, sister of William R. Lyman, was a Southern poetess of much fame in her day. Her Husband, Gideon Townsend, of the Banking firm of Townsend and Lyman, used to enjoy reading his wife's poems, and did it so well he was in much demand as a guest.) The Increase Stoddard Wood family. He owned the first Cotton Compress in the City at the corner of Canal and Claiborne. His residence was the large brick house opposite, but on the next River corner from Claiborne. His family went to Europe when Butler was ruling in New Orleans, and after Lee's surrender they returned to New York City, but later settled in Baltimore, Maryland. Judge Bonner was one of the young beaux who was a frequent caller. Judah P. Benjamin, the noted lawyer, was a friend of my grandfather. Phineas T. Barnum, was also a warm friend and visited at Grandpa Moody's home. The Grand Duke Alexis, brother of the Tsar, was also entertained at the Moody home when he visited New Orleans. "Mark Twain" was another honored guest. Charles Dudley Warner, editor of Harper's magazine, also was entertained there. Emma Abbott was another guest I remember. She was a noted singer in her day. Dr. Theodore Clapp, minister of the Unitarian Church, was another friend. My father, William Remsen Lyman, was the first President of the New Orleans Stock Exchange. Later he became President of the Crescent Insurance Company, on Camp St. corner Exchange Alley. My Grandfather Moody died January 1st, 1872, [and the Moody family mansion sold in 1884 for $16,500.][44]

Lafayette –Hagan and Moore

Ownership of the lands beyond N. Claiborne Avenue between Common and St. Philip streets was not established until five decades after the Louisiana Purchase in 1803. The United States government claimed the lands from N. Claiborne to N. Dorgenois, Faubourg Ste Marie to the Carondelet Canal, as part of the Louisiana Purchase, supposing that they were *tierras realenguas,* or abandoned lands that had belonged to the Spanish Crown. Under this assumption, the United States Congress awarded this land to General Lafayette. Generals of the Revolutionary War were entitled to up to 11,500 acres each, according to a congressional bill of 1800. Thomas Jefferson, knowing that Lafayette was in need of funds after his financial reversals during the French Revolution, planned to obtain a grant for Lafayette. Armand Duplantier, as the appointed agent

for him, was instructed to locate lands which might benefit him in the newly acquired Louisiana Territory.[1]

Property selected by Duplantier was 1,000 acres near New Orleans for which he filed a warrant. The application specified "lands belonging to the United States lying around the city of New Orleans, including the fortifications in the parts thereof not received by this government and on the Canal Carondelet as far as the Macarty Plantation."[2] Myriads of problems beset Lafayette as a result of Duplantier's choice of land; and when lawsuits were settled, Lafayette's heirs and partners owned just over 114 acres. The area is shown on Zimpel's map as Hagan's subdivision, ultimately forty-one city blocks, a triangular-shaped space between S. Claiborne and S. Galvez at Tulane, narrowing to a point near St. Philip and N. Claiborne.

To raise money to continue the litigation over his land claims in Louisiana, Lafayette sold one-half of his United States grants to Sir John Cogshill, an English baronet who lived in Ireland. Soon afterward, the baronet died, and his nephew Sir Josiah Cogshill inherited the shares. He sold them to the Irish-American entrepreneur John Hagan, a speculator in New Orleans real estate and an owner of the first St. Charles Hotel. The heirs of Lafayette continued their partnership with Hagan, but by 1840 Hagan persuaded Lafayette's two daughters to sell him

Front Elevation on Customhouse Street.

Fig. 1. Plan book 21A, folio 36; signed and dated, "C. A. Hedin, February 1851"; Customhouse (Iberville) between Roman and Prieur, backed by Canal

their share of the Louisiana tract for 100,000 francs. Despite Hagan's entreaties, Lafayette's son, George Washington Louis Gilbert Dumottier Lafayette, persevered in his refusal to sell, thereby, ultimately retaining some thirteen acres. After selling a few lots privately, Hagan held a public auction on May 11, 1840, at the St. Louis Exchange. By the end of 1841 nearly all lots were sold, and a minute portion of the proceeds was paid to young Lafayette.

Archival drawings dating from the early 1850s suggest the atmosphere of Faubourg Hagan as it appeared then. Modest, frame dogtrot creole cottages often with common-wall or common-roof were the norm as shown by C. A. Hedin in plan book 21A, folio 36 (fig. 1). Set back on their lots were double-level, Lower Garden District-style, side-hall houses, which accommodated the needs and tastes of the German immigrants who settled in the neighborhood, as seen in plan book 45, folio 30, 1852 C. A. De Armas (fig.2).

Château D'Arcy at 1800 Canal Street, an ice cream parlor and billiards hall dating from about 1879, remains today one of the outstanding buildings in Faubourg Hagan (fig. 2). This building was restored in 1978 by the Orleans Parish Medical Society for its office. Along Bienville and Iberville streets stand pretentious, two-level, single and double detached townhouses, as well as multiple-family dwellings in the Greek Revival, Classic, and Italianate styles. These houses are replete with double-level galleries of lacy cast-iron, box cornices, and handsome kitchen wings.

Hidden in the 1700 block of St. Ann Street and cut off from the rest of the street by the expressway and N. Claiborne Avenue stands one dead-end block of creole cottages dating from the 1830 decade, which, if restored, would re-create an entire block as it appeared about mid-century. The major structure here is a brick creole cottage with dentiled cornice. The appearance of one of these cottages in plan book 94, folio 46 (fig. 3) was recorded in a drawing made for auction, and the 1800 block of St. Ann remains an excellent exhibition of other extant creole cottages.

The major extant monument of Faubourg Hagan is the French Hospital (fig. 5). La Société Française de Bienfaisance et d'Assistance Mutuelle de la Nouvelle Orléans, organized in 1839 and incorporated in 1843, was "a society for fraternal, benevolent, and charitable purposes."[3] Its first hospital had been established in 1844 on Bayou Road near N. Robertson in a center-hall, gable-sided, double-galleried residence, old number 27. The French Society had purchased the land for $300, and a French visitor to New Orleans contributed 300,000 bricks to build the early infirmary known as Asile de la Société Française.

The property on which the extant French Hospital (Peter Claver Hall) stands was subdivided in 1832 by the Griffon heirs. A plan illustrated in plan book 55, folio 1 was made showing the Griffon *maison principale* on Bayou Road, but at the time—1832—there were no buildings on this square. Oliver Blineau acquired the entire square bound by Orleans, N. Ro-

Fig. 2. 1800 Canal, Château d'Arcy

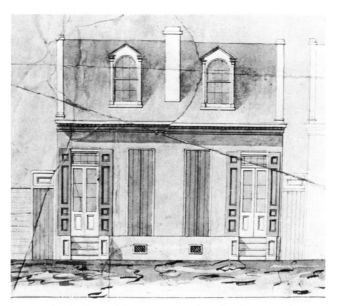

Fig. 3. Plan book 94, folio 46; unsigned, undated; St. Ann between Claiborne backed by Dumaine

Fig. 4. 1800 block St. Ann

man, N. Derbigny, and St. Ann in two separate purchases: one from the Griffon heirs and one from the Corporation of the City on the same date, May 14, 1832.[4] Blineau, president of the society, held the entire property until 1859, when he donated a lot running through its center to La Société Française. This lot had frontage of 124 feet on both St. Ann and Orleans streets. Blineau's donation was "to give witness to the price that he attaches to its success and future prosperity."

Preserved in the acts of O. Drouet, June 15, 1860, is a building contract between "Joseph Jouet, *entrepreneur* and Oliver Blineau, president of the French Society, for construction of a new asylum, a brick building of multiple stories, roofed with slates, to cost $29,500."[5] Nine pages of specifications are attached to the act. Two years later Blineau donated two additional lots, one on each side of the already established site, to the Société. Each one fronted 25 feet on Orleans Street and 25 feet on St. Ann, bound by the asylum on one side and by more

Fig. 5. Peter Claver Building (formerly French Hospital)

property of Oliver Blineau on the other. Each lot was valued at $2,000 and contained dependencies. The society's property then fronted 174 feet of Orleans and St. Ann. In 1881 it acquired the rest of the block from four separate owners.

According to the Robinson Atlas of 1883, the building was a modified *T* shape that faced St. Ann Street, but in 1914 a two-story annex was built facing Orleans Street, making the building resemble an *H*. The original 1861 building was a three-story, hip-roof structure, a late example of the Greek Revival style. Two-story pilasters articulate the façade into three segments; rustication and arched openings at the ground level and small dormers above the entablature recall the French tradition in New Orleans architecture. The roof is encircled by a parapet interrupted by a low pediment above the original St. Ann Street entrance. The two-story addition on Orleans Street is sensitive in scale and detailing. It repeats the rustication of the ground floor and its arched openings with keystones. The cornice and parapet share a similar restrained design.

The French Benevolent and Mutual Aid Society of New Orleans, referred to commonly as the French Hospital, operated a hospital here until 1949. In 1951 in a meeting conducted in French, the society sold the hospital and land, which measured 297 feet on Orleans and St. Ann by 151 feet on N. Roman, by 149 feet on N. Derbigny for $82,600.[6]

The purchasers were the Knights of Peter Claver, who used the buildings as their national headquarters. A Roman Catholic fraternal organization for blacks, it is "a society for fraternal, benevolent, and charitable purposes," having 116 councils and 10,000 members in sixteen states. The organization in 1974 constructed a new headquarters in an adjacent building, abandoning and threatening the future of the historic French Hospital. The existence of an important black institution within Faubourg Tremé is a natural connection with the history of the black community. With proper restoration this building could provide an elegant place for receptions, as well as offices for neighborhood organizations.

New Orleans hospitals were among the finest and most historic buildings. This one remains for the present with all its historic associations, while other important hospitals have been demolished. The First and Second Charity Hospitals, dating from the French and Spanish colonial days, which once stood on N. Rampart Street, have been razed, as have the Latrobe Charity Hospital on Canal Street (later used as the First Louisiana State House), the First Charity Hospital on Common Street,

Dr. Stone's Infirmary at the corner of N. Robertson and Canal within the City Commons, Hotel Dieu on Tulane Avenue, Mercy Hospital in the Saulet plantation mansion on Annunciation, and Sara Mayo on Jackson Avenue.

Parallel to the claims of the United States government and General Lafayette for the area beyond Faubourg Hagan were the cross claims of New Orleans' French and Spanish Creoles, as well as those of new Americans like Samuel Moore. Their petitions were related to the supposition that all French and Spanish colonial Bayou Road frontage purchases and grants extended to the boundary of the Jesuits-Pradel-Gravier *habitation*, Faubourg Ste Marie. These were lands between Lafitte Street (Canal Carondelet) and Common (Faubourg Ste Marie), N. Johnson to N. Dorgenois, as seen on the Zimpel map.

Charles Griffon's heirs claimed that their Bayou Road frontage extended in depth to the borders of the Pradel-Gravier lands. They asserted that Louis de Morand had been given the entire depth by his godfather Lebreton and that Madame Voisin, through whom their father, Charles Griffon, had acquired the property, bought the entire depth from young Morand and his tutor-stepfather, Alexandre Latil. According to them, the Carondelet Canal was cut through their property; but it never served as a boundary, for Griffon had owned the land beyond prior to the establishment of the canal.

In a similar fashion, the Baroness de Pontalba claimed ownership of all the land between the Griffon boundary up to the Dorgenois claim by virtue of her father's purchase of the Bayou Road frontage, with the entire depth to the Jesuit-Pradel-Gravier boundary. This too emanated from Mme Voisin, who had purchased the land from Latil in 1776. In two acts in 1805 and 1806 Ramis sold François Dorgenois 2 *arpents* fronting on Bayou Road by 4½ *arpents* in depth.[7] Then on September 24, 1807, Pedesclaux notarized an act stating that those two *arpents* extended to "all the depth they can have," a standard verbiage from French colonial days to mean either 40 or 60 *arpents*, or up to another surveyed boundary.

The Fleitas lands between the present Common and Lafitte streets, N. Tonti and N. Rocheblave, were claimed by three parties: Joseph Kenton, the Marquis de Lafayette, and Baroness de Pontalba. Their lawsuits continued up to 1854. On May 19, 1835, the heirs of Widow Fleitas had sold to Joseph Kenton for $5,000 "land situated on the southwesterly side of Carondelet Canal at the first half moon measure, 2 *arpents* fronting on the said Canal extending in rear as far as Common Street by a depth of 17 *arpents*, 10 *toises* on one line and 17 *arpents*, 5 *toises* on the other, together with the privilege of navigating on the said Canal for the transportation of the produce of the land." The evidence that Kenton presented to uphold his right to the land was the unbroken chain of title from Carlos Guadioli through Fleitas.[8]

Lafayette was defeated in his claim and the Baroness de Pontalba attested that the Spanish land grant to Carlos Guadioli in 1801 was invalid since it crossed land that her father had rightfully owned since July 2, 1772.[9] A suit brought by the baroness against the 1850s owner, Joseph Kenton, resulted in a partition in 1854 of the contested land, with the proceeds divided.

Various lawsuits and claims to additional land beyond Faubourg Hagan, including two triangles of land separated by the Fleitas claim, were further complicated by the injection of claims by Samuel Moore. He produced documents of his own-

ership of land between the Carondelet Canal and the Gravier plantation line. He had bought the land from the New Orleans Canal and Banking Company; this sale was executed by Laurent Millaudon, John Slidell, and Joachim Kohn shortly after their purchase in 1831 from the heirs of Barthélémy Macarty.[10]

Jean Baptiste Macarty, the father of Barthélémy Macarty, purportedly received a land grant from Governor Carondelet on December 22, 1795.[11] The validity of this grant was questioned from the earliest days, and the Land Office of the new territory supplied evidence that the grant was unproved.[12]

Whether or not the land grant was valid, it traversed property claimed by the Baroness de Pontalba, which had been surveyed by Olivier de Vezin in 1765 as part of the D'Auberville estate purchased by Latil, then by Widow Voisin, and eventually by Almonester; it was inherited by his daughter, Micaela de Pontalba. Almonester had filed suit against Macarty in 1795 when Macarty requested a land grant. Almonester then had proved his ownership of the tract, according to evidence presented half a century later at the trial May 10, 1853, in suits of the *Heirs of Lafayette v. Madame de Pontalba, et al.*[13]

The persevering Macarty heirs, however, finally succeeded in having their claim to this same land confirmed by an act of Congress on February 28, 1823. The fact that neither Almonester nor the Baroness cultivated the land under litigation gave credence to the supposition that the land may have been vacant, or *tierras realenguas*:

> It is a historical fact that during the colonial existence of Louisiana grants of land were frequently relinquished by the grantees for the purpose of avoiding the charges which they imposed, and that the lands were reunited to the national domain. When the title has remained in the land office during a long space of time, without the heirs of the grantee having set up any claim to the land they cover, the presumption is strong that they were abandoned; particularly when the same land was subsequently granted to other persons.[14]

The notary P. Cuvellier recorded a partition of the properties claimed by the two parties, Pontalba and Moore and their partners and heirs, on November 5, 1853. By this time Mr. Moore had died and his widow, Marie Françoise Malvina Lovell, was heir to one-half of his property and Moore's partner, Bailly Blanchard, was heir to the other half. Moore's son had also

Fig. 6. 315 N. Miro

died, and his estate was represented by attorney Théodore Nicolet in a case in which Blanchard and Mrs. Moore were the defendants.

Although the area was subdivided at the time of the partition ordered by the court, development of this section, N. Johnson to N. Broad, Lafitte to Canal was slow. The Robinson Atlas of 1883 reveals many empty squares; however, houses such as the common-roof creole cottages at 315–25 N. Miro remain as early examples of residential architecture in the area (fig. 6). These houses are separated by dogtrots and have both Classic- and Italianate-style decoration. The major landmark, the House of the Good Shepherd, has been demolished. The handsome complex covered the square bound by N. Broad, N. Dorgenois, Bienville and Conti.

CHAPTER XVI

Role of Free People of Color in Tremé

From the time of Faubourg Tremé's earliest settlement to its urbanization, free persons of color played a predominant role within the entire geographic area. Because of their integrated participation in the social, economic, architectural, agricultural, military, and religious development, they created an area unique in the history of the United States. Eighty percent of the lots between Dumaine and St. Bernard, N. Rampart and N. Broad were owned by persons of mixed heritage one or more times since the Spanish colonial period.

Their activities are traceable because they were distinguished as a group from white and slave ancestry by designations that followed their names: *homme de couleur libre, femme de couleur libre, gens de couleur libres* and *negre libre*. Abbreviations of the above terms appear on legal and church documents: h.c.l., f.c.l., g.c.l., and later in the American era, f.p.c., indicating a free person of color. There are hundreds of examples of eighteenth- and early-nineteenth-century ownership of large and small land areas in Faubourg Tremé by free persons of color. As the suburb expanded, so did the real estate and building activities of these people. The story, only partially told in this chapter, was interwoven throughout the preceding chapters and expanded in the succeeding "Architectural Inventory."

The time sequence of their appearance and that of their descendants spans two and three-quarter centuries, and it is constant. As early as 1726, Luis Congo, a free Negro, was the official keeper of the Chemin au Bayou St. Jean, and lived on the Road with his wife.[1] San Luis Lanuitte, a former black slave of Jean de Pradel, had obtained his freedom by 1774; he then purchased eight *arpents* along Bayou Road, four on the right side and four on the left, from Alexandre Latil via the Dauberville estate.[2] This land was near the Bridge of the Washerwomen and was subsequently sold to a series of free persons of color. Pedro Martina and his wife purchased two *arpents* of Lanuitte's property in 1777 and added more adjacent land be-

fore Pedro's death. His widow sold some of the land to a member of the Montreuil family, free men of color and owners of Faubourg Tremé land since the last quarter of the eighteenth century.

The free Negro couple known only by the names Juan Bautista and Margarita are thought to be the first generation of freed persons of the Montreuil family and are known through the wills and land purchases of two of his children. The parents, too, were land investors who acquired property from Lanuitte: "On December 16, 1777, he (Lanuitte) sold to Juan Bautista and Margarita, *negros libres casados*, two *arpents* of land on the left side of Bayou Road with all the depth it can have, bound on one side by land of Widow Voisin, and on the other by the free negress Martina."[3] Other purchases in the same vicinity provided the Montreuils with a *habitation* of at least six *arpents* frontage on Bayou Road. Of his children more is known about the daughter Françoise than the son François.

Françoise Montreuil (recorded in her will in the Spanish manner, Francisca Montreuille), also referred to as Fanchon Carrière, owned land on Bayou Road, some of which she acquired through purchase from her father's estate, the remainder from shrewd buys that provided her with three separate plantations. Her residence between Bayou Road and Grande Route St. Jean was indicated on a number of late-eighteenth-century maps and surveys.[4] A small bayou that ran from the juncture of Bayou Road and Bayou Sauvage toward Bayou St. Jean was known as Bayou Fanchon.[5] Her neighbors were the French colonial Juzan family, Nicolás Vidal, the Spanish colonial attorney general, and Louis Blanc (French colonial planter and tanner). The overseer for her lands was Matthew Austin (Mateo Hostén), a white man, for whom she provided in her will. As a slave owner, Fanchon did not through her final testament emancipate the slaves claimed by her as property. She recorded her will in Spanish before notary Narcisse Broutin in 1801:

I, Francisca Montreuille, alias Fanchon, *negra libre*, inhabitant of Bayou San Juan, native of this city, natural daughter of the deceased Juan Bautista and of Susana, also dead, [I] having been sick for a long period . . . First, I command my soul to God [thirty-three lines testifying to her faith follow]. . . . I wish to be buried as humbly as possible. . . . Second, I want three masses celebrated for my soul, and I leave two *reales* for each one. I declare that I am *soltera* [unmarried] and have for my natural children Naneta Cadiz, *mulata libre*, now dead, who was married to Pedro Bahy [Sergeant First Class of Free Mulatto Militia Company of New Orleans], *pardo libre*, having left three children, two boys and one girl; Pedro of about nineteen years, Andrés of nine years, Leonora of four and one-half years; Carlos, *mulato libre*, of forty years; Maria Genoveva, *mulata* married to Gabriel Geronimo, *pardo libre*, and Agatha, *mulata soltera* of twenty years which I declare as my heirs.
I declare that I am in debt to Luis Gallot, *pardo libre*, for 400 pesos. . . .
I declare that my goods consist of a house in the city, three *tierras* [lands] situated at Bayou San Juan, and some slaves, some animals, etc.
It is my wish that Mateo Hostén (Matthew Austin) remain living in my house at the Bayou San Juan all his life without my heirs being able to ask for any rent.
I name as my heirs of all my goods and actions, etc., my four cited children, Naneta Cadiz, Carlos, Maria Genov-

eva, and Agatha so that they may have and inherit equally. I name as my testamentary executor Santiago Le Ouf, *pardo libre*. I name as curator *ad bona* and *ad lites* for my minor daughter Agatha, Francisco Broutan, free Negro, relieving him of proving his honesty."[6]

She did not sign the will, but placed her mark. The witnesses who did sign were white settlers Juan Bautista Poeyfarre, Antonio Fromentin, and Claudio Francisco Girod.

In 1798 Fanchon Montreuil had sold a plantation on Bayou Road to white Spanish colonial José Suarez in an act before notary Carlos Ximenes on December 4: "Fanchon Montreuille sells to José Suarez four *arpents* of land fronting on the Road to the Bayou bound on the side of the Little Bayou by land of Widow Peyroux, which land I bought at the estate sale of Pedro Martina, three years ago before Pierre Pedesclaux." Four years later, in 1802, before Pierre Pedesclaux, "Fanchon Montreuille, free *negra*, sells to Don Antonio Magnemassa [McNamara] of this city a piece of land situated on the Road to the Bayou leaving from this city right side . . . land bound by my own, having bought it at the succession of Pedro [Martina] before Carlos Ximenes four years ago [1798]."[7]

François Montreuil, Fanchon's brother, wrote a will in 1814 in French acknowledging himself to be the son of Jean Baptiste, mulatto, and Suzanne.[8] He recognized his wife Marianne Montreuil and four children: Jean, Louis, Charlotte, and Bazile. He first owned a lot on Burgundy between Ursulines and Hospital (Governor Nicholls), which he had acquired from Mme de Villier. By the 1820s, he was a major developer in Faubourg Nouvelle Marigny, also owning lots in Tremé and plantations outside the city. In the St. Louis Cathedral funeral records of 1840, Joseph Louis Dédé, a blacksmith, was declared to be the natural son of François Montreuil (alias Louis Dédé) and Antoinette Gravier, both deceased. Joseph Dédé resided with his wife Marie Charles on Rue Robertson, between Ursulines and Bayou Road.

The utilization of aliases and the constant phonetic spelling of surnames by the French and Spanish record keepers create genealogical chaos and encourage historians to speculate on the relationships of families. The example of Fanchon Montreuil's 1801 will names her forty-year-old son Carlos as one of her heirs. Carlos Montreuil was listed at this time in the records of the mulatto militia as corporal second class[9] and was the Charles Montreuil listed as the owner of property on Marais Street purchased directly from Claude Tremé.[10] In 1803 he sold one *arpent* by three *arpents* on the right side of Bayou Road to Pierre Gueno; the land had once been held by Fanchon Montreuil.[11] In his will, dated 1825, Charles Montreuil declared that he and his wife, Constance Maignieu, and their seven children lived on Gentilly Road. Their home was noted as being two miles from the city when the document was written.[12] At least one of their children was a girl, Agatha, whom it is thought later married Jean François Dubreuille of San Marcos, who identified himself in 1805 as a *pardo libre*.

An Etiènne Bique alias Montreuil, declared himself to be the natural son of Charles Montreuil and Maria Chalos when he was married on July 20, 1825, to Pélagie Leblanc of New Orleans. She was the natural daughter of Jacques Leblanc and Jeanne Derneville, both free persons of color. An Ovid Maurice Charles Montreuil, mulatto, was identified in church records as being alias Bique, when in 1840 his natural son of seven years of age by Marie Hypolite Lavois died of influenza.

A man named Bique or Bic was listed as owner of two *arpents* on the right side of Bayou Road, and one title referred to someone owning this property as mulatto Gabriel Bique alias Montreuil. This was land that Fanchon Montreuil had once included in her estate.[13]

Charles Montreuil's younger sister Agatha, the daughter of Françoise (alias Fanchon), was, like Charles, the third generation of her family to live on Bayou Road. Through her purchase of a lot from Claude Tremé in 1809, it was possible to follow her to the construction of a house on the land opened after Quartier (Barracks) was extended (1310–12 Barracks). She left the property to her natural son Joseph Guillaume. Guillaume married Marie Castellain, and after his death she married Jacques Meffre-Rouzan, a *mulato libre* of distinguished origins. She retained the Montreuil-Guillaume house until 1852, selling then to free man of color Joseph Blouin. Thus, the activities of four generations of Montreuils is recorded in the land transactions within Faubourg Tremé.

By the end of the Spanish colonial period, many French- and Spanish-speaking free persons of color owned *habitations*. Jean Baptiste Mayorquin (or Mallorquin) was one such person; he was a black freeman whose plantation was near the Bridge of the Washerwomen on Bayou Road. According to his will of December 2, 1814, he was the natural son of François and Rose Dubreuil, *gens de couleur libres*.[14] On October 20, 1812, Mayorquin witnessed the marriage of his Negro slave Francisco Beaulea to Julia, the Negro slave of Catherine Monplessis, a *negra libre*.[15] Mayorquin himself never married; but in an accounting of his property in 1814, he acknowledged six daughters by three different women. Two of these were free women of color, but Marie Thérèse Broutin, mother of Charlotte and Marie Joseph, was the slave of Mr. Broutin. Mayorquin owned part of the ancient Antoine Hubert concession on Bayou Road, as well as an *habitation* in La Métairie, four *arpents* fronting the Bayou by fourteen *arpents* depth. Also listed in his inventory was a brick house on St. Philip, a lot 23 feet by 150 feet, a wooden house on a lot 16 feet by 120 feet, and fourteen slaves.[16]

A year after his 1814 testament, a son, Juan Baptiste, was born to Mayorquin and Genevieve Meyon. Funeral records of the St. Louis Cathedral show that in 1840 a Juan Baptiste Mallorquin, the natural son of Mayorquin, died at age twenty-five at his mother's house at number 83 Love (Rampart Street in Faubourg Tremé).[17] The 1838 directory lists a Mme Maignan, free woman of color, as living at this address.

Paul Cheval was one of the early inhabitants of Faubourg Tremé, mentioned on the Pilié and Zimpel maps of 1822 and 1834, respectively. He owned four *arpents* on the right side of Bayou Road, and throughout his life he cultivated his land and leased or sold other small portions of it. In addition to legitimate children, Paul Cheval is named as the father of Joseph Cheval by Maria Louisa and of Adelaide Paul Cheval by Barbara Francisca. Both mothers were *mulatas libres*. In October of 1818, Paul Cheval, Jr., registered as the legitimate son of Paul Cheval and Isabella Dupart, when he married Melania Olivier, natural daughter of Rosa Guillard.[18] Cheval, Jr., was listed in the city directory as a grocer living at 1318 Ursulines from 1826 until 1850. His mother, Isabella, owned the house from 1826 until 1858, after which it was left to him in her will. Isabella Dupart *dit* Fanchon is credited also with owning 1322 Ursulines and 1012 Marais in 1826.

The continuity of land ownership in Tremé by the Chevals is indicated by several of its members. Christoval Léandre Cheval, *mulato libre*, was the natural son of Prudence Cheval, *negra libre*. He married Aimeé Viavant, quadroon, the natural daughter of Susan Viavant, *mulata libre*, in October of 1816.[19] They owned 1514 Dumaine from 1831 to 1853 and retained 1518–20 Dumaine for forty-four years, from 1831 to 1875. Their son, Auguste Cheval, was part owner of 1514 Dumaine in 1840–1841. In the 1849 city directory, A. D. Cheval was listed as a slater who lived on Claiborne between Ursulines and St. Philip.

Another property owner was José Cabaret, listed as a quadroon but the natural son of Margarita Lalande, *negra libre*, and an unknown father. He owned a small property on the right side of Bayou Road near Claiborne from 1796 through 1819. He was registered at the parish church of St. Louis as a free mulatto, a native of Mobile who had been baptized in New Orleans. In March, 1801, he married Maria Juana de Iustis (Eustis), *mulata libre*, native of New Orleans, and the natural daughter of Angela Forest (sometimes listed as Faust), *negra libre*.[20] When she died, he married a free *griffe* from Ste Domingue, Maria Magdelina Herbeau, in March of 1817. He was literate and served as a witness to many marriages performed at the parish church, sometimes signing as José Cabaré, without indicating his color. Besides dealing in real property, he was listed in the city directory as a carpenter. During the Battle of New Orleans, he is registered as a quartermaster in Pierre Lacoste's First Battalion of Free Men of Color.

Pierre Dulcide Barran is known as a free person of color only through one title transfer for property on the right side of Bayou Road near the Bridge of the Washerwomen in 1800, when in a sale of land by Widow Peyroux, Barran is referred to as a *mulato libre*.[21] A man of the same name, assumed to be white, was born in Villeneuve d'Ange, France, in 1776, and was a lawyer and colonial official within the Spanish government in New Orleans, as well as a real estate investor owning the entire 1200 block of Esplanade through to St. Bernard Avenue. No absolute relationship between the men has been established. According to surveyor Pintado in 1800, when he was commissioned to calculate boundaries under dispute by a Pierre Barran and Claude Tremé, the latter was declared the rightful owner of one *arpent* by three *arpents* of the Bayou Road frontage.[22] As soon as the title was secured in 1800, Tremé sold the land to free mulatto Charles Montreuil, who in 1825 declared himself to be a resident of Gentilly Road.

Firmin Perrault, listed as a free quadroon and the natural son of Francisca Perrault, *mulata libre*, and an unknown father, married Hortense Toutant, a free quadroon and natural daughter of Rosita Toutant in 1807.[23] He was, like Cabaret, a member of the battalion of free men of color under Pierre Lacoste in the Battle of New Orleans. The Perrault families, one white and one colored, both owned small *habitations* on Bayou Road near Claiborne in the early nineteenth century. Joseph Firmin Perrault, free man of color, owned 1526–28 Ursulines (1832–1836). Appollinaire Firmin Perrault, free man of color, owned 1504 Dumaine in 1836 and was listed as a tailor at 440 St. Claude in 1861. Emma Fleitas, wife of Appollinaire Perrault, owned 1220 Columbus from 1856 to 1858.

Among the distinctive *gens de couleur libres* in the Faubourg Tremé area are two generations of the Crocker family. They were eminent as both plantation owners and real estate devel-

opers. The name appears in a variety of spellings, such as Crokin, Croker, Croquier and Crokère, although it probably stems from Raphael Croquier, a Guatemalan native, appearing in the Spanish Grenadiers in New Orleans from 1793. At that time Raphael was twenty-two years old and unmarried. By 1807 he was promoted to captain and was a member of the Company of Royal Guards.[24]

Basile Raphael Crocker, free man of color, owned a small plantation on the right side of Bayou Road in 1835; the same plantation belonged earlier to free man of color José Cabaret. Crocker acquired a portion of the plantation through his wife, Antoinette Hazeur; the property on the Zimpel map is identified as that of B. Crokin. Antoinette Hazeur, daughter of Suzanne Hazeur, was a member of one of the oldest free families of color in Faubourg Tremé. She was the natural daughter of Auguste Reynal, free man of color, who as early as July 1, 1828 had bought the plantation she later inherited.[25] Records of children from the marriage of Antoinette and Basile have not been uncovered; however, Basile had a natural son, Pierre, by Celeste Maldonado. Pierre's marriage record of 1829 revealed that on February 17 he married Rosa Gignac.

Basile Crocker was also a major developer of the Collège d'Orléans properties after the school closed in 1826. With architect Felix Pinson and investor Louis Blanc, he bought and built houses in the 1200 and 1300 blocks of Ursulines. His son Pierre's properties were nearby at 1022–24 N. Rocheblave and 1110 Tremé in 1826–1827. In the 1844 directory, Basile was listed as a fencing master on Bayou Road, near Claiborne. According to the 1861 city directory, he lived at old number 349 Villere in the third district.

Rodolphe Desdunes, the prominent colored author, has this to say about Basile Crocker:

> Basile Crokère was a remarkable member of the Creole population. He was born in New Orleans and it was there that he developed his talents, particularly as a fencing master. He was likewise a skilled mathematician and a craftsman of some reputation. Mr. Crokère, like a number of his compatriots, applied himself both to work and to study. In time, thanks to his intelligence and courage, he was able to overcome the difficulties of his environment. As a carpenter he became one of the most skilled builders of staircases in New Orleans. Only one other man was his equal in his trade, his friend Noël J. Bacchus. It was, however, because of his success as a swordsman and as a mathematician that he won the honor he holds today in the history of distinguished men of Louisiana.[26]

A composite of contemporary memoirs depicts Basile Crocker's appearance and lifestyle: "His *Salle d'Armes* [fencing school] was always crowded with students. The Creole gentry did not scruple to cross swords with him in private assaults. . . . Crokère was one of the handsomest men of New Orleans. With dignity he walked down the street in his green broadcloth suit with spotless linen and the widest of black stocks around his neck. He was famous for his collection of cameos. He wore cameo rings, breast pin, and even a cameo bracelet."[27] Crocker was seventy-nine at his death in 1879 and was survived by his wife, according to his obituary in *L'Abeille de la Nouvelle Orleans* on January 30.

There is abundant evidence of the early real estate activities of these freed people of color. Land acquisition, like freedom, was received for efforts and affections; nevertheless, disagreements and misunderstandings caused many activities to reach the stage of suits and arbitrations in the colonial courts. According to Spanish Cabildo records of August, 1781, a free Negro named Bartolomé agreed to clear six *arpents* of land in exchange for the ownership of four *arpents*. Bartolomé presented the Cabildo four certificates dated July 25, 1781, signed by four French colonials attesting to the fact that they witnessed in 1778 one M. Arlu, on behalf of Alberto Bonne, make a donation of four *arpents* front to Bartolomé. "Bartolomé cleared the six *arpents*, established himself on the four he had received, built a cabin and other small buildings, placing fences and working the land as well."[28]

Bartolomé attested that when he was on a military expedition to Pensacola and Mobile with other free Negroes who had been ordered to assemble, M. Bonne sold the land for eighty *pesos* and evicted Bartolomé's mother and the rest of his family. Upon his return, Bartolomé was able to repurchase the property for eighty *pesos* from Juan Baptiste Barsson, who had bought it from Bonne. Bartolomé then sued Bonne before the Cabildo for the eighty *pesos* and the price of the crops that Bartolomé had planted. The case was dismissed upon Bonne's evidence that he had never transferred the title by notarized act of sale to Bartolomé. The record ended in 1782, Bartolomé having reacquired his four *arpents* but not just compensation from Bonne.

PROVENANCE

The French *Code Noir* of 1724 specifically forbade interracial marriage, and the unions of those of disparate blood could neither be legalized nor sanctified. The children of these persons were *gens de couleur*; if they were free, the word *libre* was appended to the appellation. *Gens de couleur* could be the issue, born in Louisiana or elsewhere, of slaves and white persons, free persons of color and white persons, or two persons of color, free or slave. A free person of color might be entirely black or of mixed blood; however slaves, whether black or mixed, were described in specific terms, such as *esclave mulâtre* or *esclave griffe*. As the colony grew and more slaves were brought to Louisiana, repeated incidents of emancipation were recorded.

The origins of freedom of Louisiana's *gens de couleur* varied. Military assistance to the colony during the first Indian conflicts provided one of the earliest examples, although the 1732 census of New Orleans revealed only six free persons of mixed heritage. Throughout the colony, slaves were freed as a result of colonial wars of the French (1699–1769), and Spanish (1769–1803). Manumission for any reason became legally difficult after Louisiana became a state and totally illegal from 1852 until the fall of New Orleans in 1862. The colonial and American governments supplied funds to reimburse slaveowners for men freed, killed, or lost because of military service.

Slaves might be freed by their masters; this was effected by official governmental acts and later by notarized ones. The usual stated reasons for emancipation were standard verbiage, such as: "freed for the love and affection I hold for said person" or "because of the good service rendered by said person." As early as 1737 François Trudeau, a member of the Superior Council, asked for authorization to free a Negress named Jeanneton to reward her fidelity and zeal in his service. The petition was granted and signed by Governor Bienville. *Gens de cou-*

leur Louis Connard and his wife Catherine petitioned M. de Bienville for their freedom, which they claimed had been granted them and their four children through the will of M. de Coustillhas, their former master. A collated copy of the Coustillhas will confirming the manumission of these slaves was filed with the Superior Council on March 6, 1739, and adherence thereto signed by Governor Bienville and the Intendant Simon.

A mulatto slave of Pierre Gueno was identified as his mistress and freed by him in his 1821 will. Superior Council and Spanish Judicial records contain hundreds of emancipation acts granted for housekeepers as well as mistresses. When slaves were emancipated by former masters, they traditionally took the surname of the liberator; this neither denoted nor denied blood relationships. Most slaves, like Jane and Nancy Milne who were freed in 1838, were not necessarily related to their masters, although a freed slave might be the child, mistress, or sibling of the former owner. Free Negro Louis Alexis freed Sophie Peyroux on February 28, 1833, according to Notary Seghers. She was forty-three in 1841 when she registered at the sheriff's office and listed herself as an immigrant from Africa, an Hibo who was once owned by the Peyroux family.

Sometimes the surname indicated the plantation or townsite where the slave first worked after arriving from Africa. The name Mayorquin (Mallorquin) appears Spanish in derivation but probably stems from Miragouin or Miragouene, a French-Canadian name given to a settlement (and named for an early settler in 1706) near Mobile and Fowl River.[29] Thus, the Faubourg Tremé resident, free Negro Juan Bautista Mayorquin, probably belonged to the originator of that settlement or to persons coming from there.

It is not known where François and Françoise Montreuil acquired their last name, since their parents were not credited with surnames in known acts of sale and numerous notarized boundary references. Charles Montreuil, Françoise's son, had natural children who were known as Bique, though this was not the name of the mother. Other persons named Montreuil called themselves Dédé. A son of Charles named Bazile is listed on the Sheriff's Register of 1856 as Basile Dédé. The Montreuils, Dédés, and Biques through marriages and aliases remain related but separated by surname selections.

At least one Dédé, who may or may not be related to this family, achieved prominence in the field of music and was considered a master of tonal art. He was born in New Orleans on November 20, 1827. Impressed by his rare musical gifts, the free people of color, his fellow citizens, raised funds with which to enable him to complete his musical education in Europe. In 1857 he entered the Conservatoire. A master of the violin, a composer of many works for orchestra (probably the best known among which is "Le Palmier Overture"), and a conductor of the orchestra of L'Alcazar in Bordeaux, he became an intimate friend of Gounod. After forty-six years in Europe he visited New Orleans, where he was accorded the honors that his achievement merited. He quickly returned to France, however, for he found conditions in his native city intolerable. He died at Bordeaux.[30]

Slaves often purchased their own freedom, borrowing money from other slaves and free persons of color or earning by extra work, such as that performed on Sundays. Marie Françoise Bernoudy, a former slave, wrote her will on March 16, 1830. She had lived with Marie Austine White, a free woman of color, who had lent her the money to buy her freedom. Mme Bernoudy was "born in Africa of the Ibo nation."[31]

The freedom of others was bought by friends and relatives. Jonathan Darby, a plantation owner in the 1720s, was director of the Cantillon concession when he appeared before the Superior Council on November 28, 1727, to authorize the marriage of John Mingo, free Negro of the English nation from the Carolinas, to Thérèse, a slave Negress of the Cantillon concession. Mingo was to pay as much as possible each year to redeem 1500 francs, the price of Thérèse. "Darby meanwhile is to allow rice, corn, beans, and sweet potatoes to feed Thérèse, and to provide clothing. When the price is paid, Thérèse shall have her liberty. Meanwhile, children born prior to payment shall also be free." By 1729 Thérèse was not yet emancipated, but she nonetheless had left the plantation with Mingo. On October 21, 1729, M. D. Chavannes agreed "to hire free negro Mingo and his wife Thérèse, bought by Mingo of Monsieur Darby, for three years. Mingo to work as overseer of slaves in the cultivation of tobacco, cotton, and other crops; Thérèse to engage in woman's work. Hire for Mingo to be 300 francs a year in current funds besides eight percent of plantation produce except increase of Negroes and cattle. Hire for Thérèse to be 200 francs a year payable to Darby until Mingo's contract with him be discharged."[32]

On June 28, 1737, free Negro Diocou, who had been emancipated for his assistance and work in the Natchez War, claimed a credit of 450 francs due to him from the St. Julien estate. Since he had partially paid for his wife, he requested that the above credit be further applied to her purchase, so that she could be completely redeemed. The action was approved by the king's attorney D'Auseville.[33]

A contract on July 12, 1737, before the notary royal and before Inspector Jean Baptiste Raquet, the director of Charity Hospital then called St. John, and François Tiocou, a Senegalese free Negro, was agreed upon with terms. He obligated himself to serve the sick and the poor in the hospital for six consecutive years without wages, on the condition that he be fed and clothed and that freedom would be granted to his wife, Marie Aram. The fulfillment of this contract occurred in 1744, when Governor Vaudreuil signed the judgment granting freedom to Marie Aram. Both François and Marie elected to remain in the employ of the hospital and receive wages for their efforts.[34]

Jean Baptiste Marly, free Negro, agreed to serve M. Jean Joseph Delfau de Pontalba, infantry officer at Pointe Coupée, as a cook for three years from December 1, 1745, to December 1, 1748. The terms in this contract were for Marly's maintenance and medical care and freedom at the end of the third year for Marly's wife, the Negress Venus.[35]

Ana, a slave of the Capuchin Fathers, asked in 1783 to be released from servitude and slavery because of her advanced age of fifty-one years. She offered to pay for her freedom at whatever price experts might place upon her. She had evidently saved the funds herself, although slaves were not legally allowed to accumulate capital.[36] The notification was given to Reverend Father Antonio de Sedella, the beloved Père Antoine. An appraisal estimated her value at 220 pesos. Ana placed the money before the court and asked that the Reverend Fathers draw up the act of emancipation; it was necessary also for her to pay all the court costs incurred by her emancipation.[37]

On September 23, 1784, free Negro Valentin attempted to buy the freedom of his brother Sylvestre, who belonged to the estate of Andrés Jung. The slave was appraised at $300; but that amount, according to testimony, was rendered for the special interest of the inventory and did not represent the true value of the slave, who was said to be valued at between $800 and $1,000 at public sale. The court ordered a new appraisal and asked that Dr. Joseph Montegut certify the state of health of the slave. Dr. Montegut, royal physician, established that Sylvestre, a Negro carpenter, indeed was partially lame but that his infirmity did not totally cripple him. One appraiser valued Sylvestre at $1,000 and another at $500, and the court ordered a third appraisal. The third appraiser offered to the court the valuation of $800, and this was the amount that Valentin paid for his brother's freedom.[38]

Marguerite, a free mulatress, did not provide for the freedom of her mother and brother until her death. On March 1, 1770, before notary Garic, "Marguerite, a free mulatress, declares that . . . her estate consists of a house on Royal Street which she wishes sold after her death, the proceeds are to be devoted to the purchase of the freedom of Genevieve, her mother, slave of Monsieur Andry, and Louis, her brother, a slave of Monsieur Maxent."[39]

Martha Dauphin, femme de couleur libre, emancipated her slaves August 26, 1801: "I, Martha Dauphin, free griffe, have for my slaves Gideon, griffó of two and one-half years and Caroline, griffa of five years, children of the Negress, my slave Genevieve, and for the much love and affection I have for the cited children I give them liberty from captivity and servitude."[40]

The city of New Orleans purchased the freedom of a mulatto, Celestin, according to City Council records, on March 19, 1806. At that date the council asked the authorization "to claim from the Territory a sum of two thousand dollars which the Council advanced on City funds as payment for the freedom of the mulatto Celestin, who discovered the conspiracy plotted by one Grandjean by name in order to incite the slaves, set fire to the city, and to cut the white people."[41]

Considering the many methods of earning or receiving freedom, it would be thought that a man or woman having achieved the desired state would never again be returned to enslavement. During the French colonial period a free person of color could be reduced to slavery by action of the Superior Council, as provided by the Code Noir, Article 34. This action was taken for theft, nonpayment of debt, or immoral conduct.[42]

In August of 1743 Jean Baptiste fought to maintain his freedom after being accused of stealing from his employer some shirts and handkerchiefs, which he claimed to have purchased from a slave, Marie Pantalon. She and another slave testified against him, and he was convicted. Even though he had spent twenty years as a slave of M. Coustillhas and had been freed, he was reduced again to slavery and sold at public auction, with restitution for debts being paid from his sale. Any profit was to benefit the Charity Hospital.[43] Jeannette, another former slave of M. Coustillhas, also lost her freedom in 1747 on a conviction of theft. She, too, was resold to compensate for the theft; any profits were destined for Charity Hospital.[44]

This means of setting an example to discourage crime by free persons of color was prohibited under Spanish law in the Third Partida of their Siete Partidas, or black code equivalent. Efforts were made to revive the reversal to slavery custom after 1803; however, in 1824 the Supreme Court of Louisiana held that a white person could not legally reduce a free Negro to slavery following the legal formalities of manumission.

An example of the method by which slaves of a deceased plantation owner were freed by will related to the Brasilier-Blanc plantation, which ran from Dorgenois to Bayou St. Jean and from the Jesuits' land to Bayou Road. Pélagie Lorraine, first the widow of Jean Baptiste Brasilier, then the wife of Andrés Jung, died at the Bayou St. John home of her brother, Santaigo Lorraine Tarasçon, in 1781, soon after writing a will dated September 3. Her will stated: "The estate consists of twenty-four slaves and a plantation on Bayou St. Jean. I free my slaves, Alexis, Luis, Opal, Catalina, Maria Luisa, and the latter's child Francisca. My testamentary executor must give to each freed slave a cow and a calf."[45]

The entire family was distressed by the will and agreed to have it considered null and void, a decision in which the Tribunal of the Cabildo concurred, if the family paid the costs of the proceedings. The slaves contested this agreement and asked for their freedom in accordance with their mistress' will. Carlota first took action, stating that since the time she reported to M. Jung that his wife was unconscious, M. Tarasçon, the deceased's brother in whose power she remained, had punished her frequently. She asked the court to remove her from Tarasçon's power and deliver her to Andrés Jung, which the Tribunal did.

The other slaves testified that they were to be set free as soon as Mme Jung's death took place. According to them, testamentary executor and guardian of the estate, Carlos Tarasçon, was charged in the will to grant them their liberty. Nonetheless, Tarasçon had continued to hold them and to make them work. When they asked him about their freedom, he told them to work until after the harvest. They petitioned the court to order the will of their mistress carried out. Judge Dufossat ruled in their favor ordering Tarasçon to draw up the acts of emancipation within one day precisely before giving each one of the slaves a certified copy for his protection.

The designation of free persons according to the color of their skin was part of the legal procedure during French, Spanish, and American periods and continued until the 1860s. These descriptions were enforced by the church records and the legal transactions that transpired throughout the colonial period in acts of manumission and the many lawsuits.

During the French colonial period, all church records—whether pertaining to whites, slaves, or free persons—were included within the same books. Entries of marriages, baptisms, and interment were specific, and they provided as much detail as could be gleaned by the recorder's observation and information furnished by the participants. One of the earliest church marriages of free persons of color in New Orleans was between Jean Baptiste Raphael, an immigrant from Martinique, and Marie Gaspar, whose origins were unknown. Jean Baptiste's father was Jean Raphael and his mother Marguerite de St. Christophe, both of whom continued to reside in Martinique. Marie stated that her father was a drummer in the company of M. Le Blanc. The Capuchin Father François Raphael officiated at the marriage, which took place in the wooden church of St. Louis at the Place d'Armes on August 14, 1725.[46]

The decision by Spanish officials in New Orleans to continue to invoke the French Code Noir officially extended the policy against miscegenation and marriages between races. This was not forbidden, however, in the Spanish Siete Partidas,

the black code for the Spanish colonial empire. The result was that Spanish officials in New Orleans did not refuse to hear matters related to mixed marriages. One of the early Spanish judicial records after Governor O'Reilly's arrival is a marriage contract, recorded in French on November 16, 1769. Jean Paillet, a native of Martigue, bishopric of Arles en Provence, France, son of Antoine Paillet and Marianne Paillet, contracted to marry Catherine (Catiche) Villeray, natural daughter of Charlotte, a free mulatress, and the late Sieur Roy Villeray, a white man. The contract was signed by both principals, indicating their literacy.[47]

The church registers of marriages, baptisms, and burials used the color distinctions, although there were many contradictions. Jean Baptiste Mayorquin (Mallorquin) was always correctly identified as a negro libre, or black. However, José Cabaret was a quadroon according to an 1801 Spanish designation by the parish church recorder; but in 1817 when he remarried, another curate, this time in French, documented him as a mulâtre. A person of color was assigned a color, usually mulato, quarteron or griffo, or the equivalent derivations in French. After 1820 the church began to designate a person only as free person of color, with no reference to tonal shade; that is, personne de couleur libre (p.c.l.), homme de couleur libre (h.c.l.), or femme de couleur libre (f.c.l.), after the individual names. After the end of the Civil War, many church records continued to designate a colored person as either homme de couleur or femme de couleur. The sheriff's register of free persons designated them from 1841 to 1862 by color, and among Faubourg Tremé residents there were "brique, marabon, griffe, octarona, quarteroon, mulatto and negre."[48] When the records were kept in English, they were often as descriptive in tonal shade, such as a "yellowman." Whereas a griffe may be the issue of a Negro and a mulatto, a marabon that of a mulatto and a griffe, a quadroon of a white and a mulatto, the realities were not always so exact. A person who appeared to be quite light-skinned could be referred to as a griffe, though he might be one-eighth Negro or an octaroon. Identification was most often an on-sight decision rather than a qualified evaluation, and this in a society further complicated by legitimate and natural children who used many names and aliases. It is obvious that the mathematical amount of black blood was of little consideration, whereas the appearance as to color was a valid means of identification.

Françoise Montreuil, alias Fanchon Carrière, seemed very specific, however, when she identified herself and her children by color in her will. She was a negra; Naneta Cadiz, a daughter, was a mulata married to a pardo. Her son Carlos was a mulato, and her daughters Maria Genoveva and Agatha, mulatas. Her executor was a pardo, and curator for her minor daughter was Francisco Broutan, negro.

Between 1803 and 1810 the population of the gens de couleur libres in New Orleans grew to 3,332 out of a total population of 12,225, and most of the increase constituted émigrés from Ste Domingue.[49] The Louisiana Courier of May 2, 1808, noted: "Thanks given to Mr. McIntosh [a white man] for efforts in rescuing many people and getting them [free people of color] out of Santo Domingo during Christophe's Revolution." A dinner was given in McIntosh's honor. The free gens de couleur prospered in New Orleans as their ranks grew. Immigration from Ste Domingue, Haiti, and Cuba had brought a huge influx of talented French- and Spanish-speaking families. Their arrival coincided with the subdivision of Faubourg Marigny in 1805, Nouvelle Marigny in 1809, and Faubourg Tremé in 1812.

The social, cultural, legal, and economic position of *gens de couleur libres* in the eighteenth and early nineteenth centuries was superior in New Orleans to perhaps anywhere in the United States. Political changes, however, throughout the country were filtering into the city, and restrictive laws were forcing separateness. Prior to the mid-nineteenth century, certain statistics provided a plausible explanation for factual cultural cohesiveness.

The 1805 census listed the population of the city as 8,475 persons, of whom 3,551 were white, 1,566 free persons of color, and 3,105 slaves; Indians and others numbered 253. The census did not include residents of Bayou Road. Rampart Street, *derrière de la ville*, was included as having 21 whites, 26 free persons of color, and 21 slaves.

Fifteen years elapsed before another census was taken, with the results of the August, 1820, census appearing in the 1822 city directory. The 1820 census did not designate free persons of color in individual entries but collated results, attesting that the city of New Orleans had 29,000 persons, including 8,590 white males, 5,318 white females, 2,432 free colored males, 3,805 colored females, 2,709 male slaves, and 4,646 female slaves. By this date Faubourgs Tremé, Marigny, and Ste Marie had been incorporated into the city so that Bayou Road citizens to N. Galvez were included. Outside of the city proper there were 3,576 white males, 2,251 white females, 403 free men of color, 521 free women of color, 4,622 male slaves, and 2,969 female slaves.

In categories of both censuses, males far outnumbered females except in the urban area, where there were more women of color and slave women than men. The excess of free colored women and the shortage of white females from the time of the city's founding encouraged, if not caused, the formation of *plaçage* relationships. The interracial relationships of the French and Spanish soldiers inevitably led to an increased population of *gens de couleur*. The acceptance of these social conditions was further strengthened by the location of individual residents. Title transfers for hundreds of years reveal white and free persons of color maintaining *habitations*, and later whole neighborhoods, together. The existence of more slave women than slave men in urban areas may well have precipitated relationships of white men and free men of color with these slave women. There are also long lists of baptisms indicating both legitimate marriages and concubinage among *gens de couleur*.

Law pertaining to inheritance applied to natural children of both free Negro and white paternity. A natural child was one acknowledged by the father, with neither father nor mother married at the time of the birth. If paternity was acknowledged before a notary and two witnesses, a natural child became a legal heir. Nicholas Vidal, the famous Spanish colonial official whose family founded the city of Vidalia, included in his will that his four natural colored children share "an equal portion of his estate."[50] After Vidal's death his succession papers were placed in the Pensacola Cabildo, New Orleans having become American territory. A *mulata* daughter of Vidal demanded reopening of the succession, claiming she had not received her allotted inheritance. By that time, 1822, Pensacola, too, had become American territory, and military governor Andrew Jackson made the papers available to Vidal's acknowledged

daughter after incarcerating the former Spanish governor who had refused them.

The quasi acceptance of the *plaçage* arrangement between white men and free women of color continued after Louisiana became part of the United States. In the last quarter of the Spanish colonial period and early American one, some of the most noted Faubourg Tremé liaisons were stable family communities with white male émigrés. In these cases more often than not, the *plaçage* was the man's only home. A monogamous state with his *placée* produced natural children who were his heirs, and automatically free. The *placée*, however, could legally inherit only movable property, making intervivos donations of real estate a custom.

Pierre Passebon, Jr., and his father, both white Frenchmen, migrated to New Orleans from France in the 1820s. The senior Passebon married Emilie Guidry, a white woman from New Orleans, who was the widow of James Armitage.[51] They lived in the French Quarter where she died in 1839 at age thirty-six. They did not have children. Pierre Passebon, Jr., was a builder in New Orleans and forty years old at the time of the 1850 census, when he lived on Bayou Road with Athalie Drouillard, a thirty-year-old mulatress, and their two-year-old daughter, Caroline Passebon.[52] The home belonged to Mme Drouillard, whose holdings were valued at $10,000. Mme Drouillard also owned 1221–23 and 1225–27 Rue Tremé from 1841 to 1857. Residing with them was Marie Noël Cordier, a seventy-five-year-old free mulatress from the West Indies, perhaps the housekeeper or mother of Mme Drouillard. In 1839 Mme Cordier purchased 1110 Tremé for $3,000 from Auguste Guerin, selling it a year later for an $850 profit.

Louis Dolliole, another white Frenchman, immigrated to the city near the end of the Spanish colonial period and became a prominent builder. He too formed a permanent *plaçage*. His will, dated November 18, 1815, declared that he lived on Chemin du Bayou St. Jean, that he was indisposed but of sound mind, that he was a native of La Sene en Provence (France) and the legitimate son of the deceased Louis Dolliole and Dame Catherine Bertonne. He was Catholic and never married, but he had four natural children: Jean Louis, Madeleine, Joseph, and Pierre. He recognized them and left them everything that he possessed except the four hundred *piastres* that he willed to his brother Jean, and the silver, furniture, and utensils that he left to his *placée* Geneviève, nicknamed Mamie. He gave a special bequest of his property in France to a granddaughter and to his niece, daughter of his sister Thérèse Graselles.[53]

The same Louis Dolliole lived on Bayou Road but owned property in the French Quarter. The City Council gave him permission on April 16, 1822, "to turn and place his house on Burgundy Street between St. Philip and Ursulines with the gable facing south in order that the said house be on the rear of the same lot on which it is constructed at the present time, but said Louis Dolliole shall have the house covered with tiles; and that he has constructed on the frontage of said lot another house made of brick, covered with tiles, in conformity with his proposal."[54] He died ten years later in 1832, leaving a colored family that has distinguished itself in New Orleans in the building trade. Most of the male Dolliole progeny married other mulatto freed persons.

His brother, Jean François Dolliole, like him a builder and immigrant to the city, wrote a will in 1816 at his residence, corner Dumaine and Promenade Publique (probably Claiborne). According to his will, he lived with a free woman of color, Catherine, who bore him four children: Louis Laurent, eleven years old; Etiènne Adam, aged seven; Joseph Panthelion, who was six; and Edmond, an infant of nine months. He appointed his brother Louis as his executor and left Catherine and each child $100.

Jean Louis Dolliole and Joseph Dolliole, quadroon brothers, sons of Louis and Geneviève Dolliole, were leaders in the development of Faubourg Tremé. They were important builders and speculators. Jean Louis was born in 1779 and by 1815 lived in a *maison de maître* on Bayou Road (the present 1500 block of Governor Nicholls). He married Hortense Dussau, free woman of color, in February of 1818. She was the natural daughter of Monsieur and Catherine Dussau, and at the time of the marriage they already had three children: Mathilde, born in 1809; Luis Drausin, born in 1812; and Euphrina Hortense, born in 1816.[55] His wife, Hortense, had died by 1820.

Jean Louis accepted the legal responsibilities for many free people of color and was listed in the *Moniteur de la Louisiane*, July 10, 1820: "Notice—Those who have claims against the estate of the late Marie Françoise Robert, free woman of color, are requested to make them known to the subscriber. L. Dolliole." An 1822 census credits Jean Louis as being both a cabinetmaker and a planter. He was listed in the census of 1850 as a seventy-one-year-old male mulatto and builder with an estate or cash of $10,000. He lived with his second wife, Marie Dolliole, aged sixty, mulatto from the French West Indies. His son, Louis Drausin Dolliole, was a third-generation carpenter-builder and was thirty-five in 1850. The latter's brother or cousin, Drausin, was listed in the 1840 census, aged twenty-nine, a male mulatto carpenter living in Faubourg Tremé with a wife and three children under ten years of age. By 1861 Gardener's New Orleans directory listed no less than eight Doliols (Dollioles), including three who were carpenters, one a brickmason, a shoemaker, and a free woman of color, Marie Doliol, a grocer in the Vieux Carré.

Joseph Dolliole, the second son of the white progenitor Louis, was married in March of 1822 to Magdelina Hobé (probably Jove), a free woman of color of New Orleans, the natural daughter of Nicolas Hobé and Margarita Jason. [56] In 1827 Joseph purchased much of the Collège d'Orléans property facing St. Philip with his brother Jean Louis and was engaged in the building trade. Joseph was married to Josepha Rodriguez when he died in 1868. Pierre Dolliole, another brother, was also a carpenter and owner of 1127 St. Philip Street between 1816 and 1821. In the 1850 census he was listed as being a fifty-nine-year-old "joiner" with an estate of $12,000. Another Dolliole, Rosette, was listed as buying and selling many of the St. Philip Street properties between 1827 and 1834.

Achille Barthélémy Courcelle was a white builder of Faubourg Tremé and was married to Felicité C. Dupin; they owned 1523 Ursulines from 1832 to 1837. After his wife's death, he established a *plaçage* with Louise Vitry, free woman of color. By 1850 they lived with their four small mulatto children on N. Derbigny between St. Philip and Ursulines. At the time of the 1850 census, Achille was forty-five years old, a native of Louisiana worth $4,000; Mlle Vitry, a mulatress, was thirty-two. The natural children were Achille, thirteen; Rosalina, ten; Laura, six; and Emilie, four. The Courcelles were active in

Tremé real estate through both their male and female lines. Charles E. Courcelle, free man of color, lived at old number 245 Claiborne in 1849, indicating that Achille was not the only progenitor of the racially mixed Courcelle family line.

Achille Courcelle's colored counterpart and contemporary, also a prominent builder, was Myrtil Courcelle. He was a real estate broker and builder, living on St. Philip between Marais and N. Villere in the 1840s; but he owned and built other houses, such as 1622 Dumaine (1850–1854) and 1523–25 St. Philip. He died in 1872 and left a substantial estate.

White men of many nationalities continued through the first half of the nineteenth century to form stable alliances with mulatto women. A typical alliance was that of Jean François Chatry in 1850, a "landlord and white native of France" living with his *placée*, forty-two-year-old Josephine Rey, a Louisianian and mulatress. [57] She probably was the daughter of free man of color Barthélémy Rey, a Faubourg Tremé builder. Their children, named Chatry, included Josephine, fifteen; Idalie, fourteen; Ophelia, four; Clémence, three; Charles, ten; Alfred, twenty-two; Ernest, eighteen; and August, sixteen. The last three young men were all identified as clerks. Jean François was a captain under Colonel Michel Fortier's Battalion of Free Men of Color. In 1818 he was "promoted to major and given command of the colored militia." This was a peacetime volunteer group whose members were difficult to rouse to monthly musters. It was not until the Mexican War that the militia was mobilized again in a meaningful way.

José Florez was a white broker, born in 1804, in Spain who lived with his *placée* Apolline Florez. [58] She was a thirty-two-year-old mulatress from Louisiana, and their son at the time of the 1850 census was listed as six years old and a male mulatto. Juan Peyrura, a forty-year-old Portuguese fisherman, had as a *placée*, Antoinette, from Louisiana; they had two children during the time of the same census: John, seven, and Auliana, five, both male mulattos. [59]

Estevan Cordeviola, native of Genoa, Italy, lived with Maria del Rosario, a Negress of Guinea. Two of their four children were baptized in 1821 and 1823, respectively. By 1840 both elder Cordeviolas were deceased, and their youngest daughter, Mme Louis Fernandez, had died at the home of her brother, Etiènne Cordeviola, who lived on Claiborne between Rues Ste Anne and Dumaine. Etiènne Cordeviola was born Antonio Estevan Cordeviola on March 25, 1806. He became a notable builder and real estate speculator as well as a tailor in nineteenth-century New Orleans and was known as Etiènne Cordeviolle. His partner was distinguished, wealthy François Lacroix. [60] In 1841 Louise Commagère, the Cordeviola's granddaughter, was baptized. The paternal grandparents were Louis Commagère and a descendant of the Mayorquin family, Bernardine Raphael.

Among the most notable Louisiana colonials with *plaçages* were Hughes Pedesclaux, Narcisse Broutin, François Meilleur, and Louis Doquemeny de Morand, all of whom had *placées*. In some cases these alliances were begun after the death of a wife or wives, and in many cases the men had legitimate and illegitimate heirs. In numerous examples within their wills it appears that they bequeathed equal amounts to both sets of offspring.

Hughes Pedesclaux, brother of Basilice Pedesclaux Duchamp (see Chapter 5) and son of the noted Spanish colonial notary, was a lawyer and notary in 1850, aged forty-eight, living on Bayou Road with Mme Cabaret, a twenty-five-year-old mulatress, whose relative José Cabaret had a Bayou Road plantation. There were three Cabaret children, and four Pedesclaux minor mulattos, according to the 1850 manuscript census. Also in the *ménage* was a seventy-five-year-old female mulatress named Cabaret.

A similar *plaçage* took place between another prominent lawyer-notary, Narcisse Broutin, and Mathilde Gaillau. Broutin owned the Bayou Road Zeringue-Bellanger *habitation* in 1802.

> He was a descendant of one of the earliest settlers of the city, the king's engineer-in-chief during the French colonial period, who had designed the Ursuline Convent. In his will, deposited in the records of Carlile Pollock, July 12, 1819, Narcisse Broutin declared that he had never been married and had no legitimate descendants. "I hereby acknowledge," he added, "Rosalie and Augustine and Frumence to be my children, born of Mathilde Gaillau, free woman of color, who now resides together with our said children with me in my present dwelling." Broutin bequeathed to the children one-half of all of his property, which was the maximum allowed by law even though he had formally recognized them and had no legitimate heirs.[61]

François Meilleur, a white man, had a *plaçage* and acknowledged colored children. His mulatto *placée*, Elize Baumier, was from the West Indies, and in 1850 they had free children ranging in age from one to nineteen. At this time Meilleur was fifty and Elize, thirty-nine. One of their sons, Pierre Alphonse, died in 1841 at their home on Rue Tremé. Several children of this alliance survived. The 1850 census enumerates them as Francillette, 19; Rosa, 17; François, 10; Louisa, 5; and Laperle, 1.[62] François was in business with a free man of color named Bruslé, who may have been the free mulatto Captain Charles Bruslé, who distinguished himself as a member of the Spanish *pardo* group. François' white relative, Michel Meilleur, was a state senator; and Simon Meilleur built a beautiful villa at 1459 Bayou Road.

Louis Doquemeny de Morand was the son of the French colonist Charles de Morand, eighteenth-century developer of the great plantation from which a large portion of Faubourg Tremé is derived. He married Suzanne Perault, a white New Orleans Creole, by whom he had a son, Louis Joseph Doquemeny de Morand, born about 1791. Soon afterward Mme Morand died. Morand then took a *placée*, free Negress Marie Françoise Decoudreaux, member of a family of free persons of color who owned land in Faubourg Tremé. Her father, Charles Decoudreaux, held a small *habitation* on the right side of Bayou Road by 1812. The Decoudreauxs also had a *maison de maître* in the 1600 block of Bayou Road across from philanthropist Alexander Milne and next to wealthy French creole Joseph Chalon and his wife of French Canadian descent, Elizabeth Desruisseaux.

In addition to his legitimate heir and three natural colored daughters, Morand had another illegitimate child, a white son; "Louis Azenor Dauqueminy, twenty-two years old, who was living with him but was at the moment of the writing of the will (March 30, 1821) traveling together with his legitimate son to Campeche." The mother of this young man was a white woman, but Morand avowed that "delicacy does not permit him to name her."[63]

White men did not have exclusive rights on a *plaçage* ar-

rangement; however, when engaged in by free men of color with either free or slave women, the terminology applied was more biblical—concubinage. The natural children of such unions were accepted socially, religiously, and legally as legitimate as were the issue of *plaçages*.

Free people of color shared another unifying factor with their white brethren, that of religion. Whether native Louisianians or émigrés, free persons of color were Roman Catholic. During the early history of the area, both *gens de couleur libres* and their white neighbors propagated the faith. Those who owned slaves arranged for and were witnesses to marriages, baptisms, and funerals within the parish church of St. Louis. Of course, in doing this, they were following the laws of the *Code Noir* and the early decrees of Bienville. Carlos Decoudreaux and Euphrosina Ysnard (Isnard), *gens de couleur libres* of Bayou Road, were two witnesses at the wedding in August of 1803 in the parish church of the Negro slaves of M. Vidal, white plantation owner along Bayou Road. The church kept careful records of such marriages, baptisms, and funerals.[64]

In the Spanish period *gens de couleur libres* and their slaves were recorded in separate books from white persons. On each occasion the parents of the subject, their color and condition of servitude, as well as that of the principals, were recorded. The exactness of these entries, as in the French period, was subject to the intelligence and disposition of the recording curate.

Among married couples with substantial land holdings in Faubourg Tremé were Gustave Auguste Dauphin, a Louisiana native mulatto, and his wife, Jeanne Milne, the freed slave of Alexander Milne. In 1850 she was listed in the census as a thirty-five-year-old mulatress, a native of Louisiana. Their estate at the time was valued at $5,500, his profession that of carpenter and landowner of a small Bayou Road *habitation*. Her sister Nancy lived with them at 1253–55 N. Villere Street from 1841 to 1858, but Jeanne continued to live there as owner until 1875.

Other Dauphins in Faubourg Tremé were Françoise, *mulata libre*, native of Paris, and natural daughter of Francisco Isnard, and Marianne, *negra libre*. J. B. Dauphin, *mulato libre* of New Orleans and natural son of Martin Dauphin, married in 1805 Francisca Larase, *mulata libre* of New Orleans, legitimate daughter of Juan and Maria Juana Larase. Witnesses were Francisco Marco, Francisco Dauphin, Bazile Demazilière, and Pierre Colvis.[65]

The Boisdoré family were prominent for over a hundred years in the development of Faubourg Tremé. Between 1800 and 1841 François Boisdoré, free man of color, owned land on Esplanade between Tremé and Marais.[66] In 1828 he contracted to build a *maison de maître* on Bayou Road at Rue Tremé for Marcely Cornu. In that same year on May 24 Boisdoré married Josephine Sophia Livaudais, attesting in the marriage record that he was the natural son of Dubruisson Boisdoré and Adelaide Boisdoré. Plan book 85, folio 14 in the New Orleans notarial archives shows F. Boisdoré buying three lots on Villere corner Bayou Road in 1841. He sold 1260 Esplanade in 1844.

This François Boisdoré and his neighbor Louis Dolliole thwarted the city's attempt to widen Esplanade through their plantations until a fair and proper price could be agreed upon. The negotiations lasted from 1832 to 1837. A plan ordered for the sale of fifteen lots by another neighbor, Frenchman Jean Mager, was drawn by surveyor Bourgerol in January of 1839.

The Boisdoré and Dolliole land was clearly shown. Boisdoré had the remainder of his land surveyed and auctioned in 1844.

The family continued to be prominent in land development, business, culture, and politics. "François Boisdoré, Jr., was a bookkeeper for Pierre Cazenave, a leading undertaker and embalmer. Boisdoré was a talented orator, engaged in frequent debates for the Republican cause . . . and became a school teacher after the Civil War. He died in the late 1890s."[67]

Louis Boisdoré, free man of color, is probably the cousin of the above François, because at his marriage to Louise Fernandez on December 27, 1827, he stated that he was the natural son of free person of color Louis Boisdoré and Charlotte Morand.[68] A Louis Boisdoré, white native of New Orleans born in 1762, was a member of the Company of Distinguished Carabineer Militia of New Orleans and the New Orleans Militia Company in 1802. His 1802 service sheet stated that he was in robust health and not married.[69] A Marguerite Boisdoré, free woman of color, was the cousin of Henriette Delille, who was the founder of the Sisters of the Holy Family. Marguerite owned 1609–11 St. Philip for at least a year between 1836 and 1837, indicating that she and her family were selling property in this neighborhood at the same time François, Sr., was selling so much land.

When Julia Boisdoré, *mulata libre*, married Felipe Hazeur, also a *mulato libre*, they joined together at least three influential free colored families. The marriage was consecrated in the Church of St. Louis in December of 1801, and the record listed her father as "Francisco d'Orville, captain of the company of *Pardos* of this *Plaza*"; her mother was Isabelle Boisdoré, daughter of either Louis or François. Felipe, the natural son of Rose Hazeur, was probably educated in France as were many of Rose's natural children; his father, probably white, was unnamed.

Louis Barthélémy Rey, free person of color, was an immigrant from Santiago, Cuba. He was the natural son of Joseph Rey and Elizabeth Mirlen. In July of 1829 he married Rose Agnes Lacrisle.[70] Rey joined with others to complain that Mme Bernard Couvent's legacy was being diverted from indigent orphans and that her will was not being honored. As a result of his interest he became the first member of the board of the Institute for Indigent Colored Orphans.[71] Rey owned 1424 Derbigny in 1847 and was the builder of 1924 Bayou Road; a building contract for a house on this site remains. Josephine Rey, a daughter, was the *placée* of white immigrant Jean François Chatry and bore him eight mulatto children. His sons, Octave (born in 1837), Henry, and Hippolyte, became well-known for their efforts to help the Union cause. Octave was a member of the New Orleans Metropolitan Police Force of the Fourth Precinct from 1868 to 1877. He died in 1908 and was survived by four sons and one daughter.[72] The Rey family were influential Faubourg Tremé citizens, pewholders at St. Augustine Church from the beginning, where they financed a stained-glass window.

Bazile Demazilière was a distinguished free person of color who had a *maison de maître* in the 1600 block of Bayou Road, which ran three blocks through to Dumaine. His marriage contract to Antoinette Dubreuil in 1821 specified that a house was to be built on the land at her expense. The priest of St. Louis Church recorded this marriage in June of 1824, at which time the groom identified his mother as Marie Bienvenu and stated that his father was unknown.

When the Battalion of Free Men of Color was officially mustered into the United States Army on December 16, 1814, one of its companies was led by Captain Bazile Demazilière in command of fifty-one soldiers. A relative, Baltazare Demazilière had preceded him into the *pardo* militia as a first lieutenant under the Spanish regime.[73] After the Battle of New Orleans, the Demazilières bought on Bayou Road and became the neighbors and relatives of the Decoudreauxs.

On December 1, 1798, Charles Decoudreaux, a *quarteron libre*, son of Fanchonette Decoudreaux, *mulata libre*, and an unknown white father, married Margarita Castanedo, *quarterona libre* of Havana, Cuba, the daughter of Maria Juana de Iustis and an unknown father. Her mother, Maria de Iustis, was listed as marrying free man of color José Cabaret in 1801 and was declared at that time to be a native of New Orleans and the natural daughter of Angela Forest (Faust), *negra libre*. At the Decoudreaux wedding, the witnesses were white: Manuel Serrano, Doña Josepha de Lisa, and M. Doquemeny Morant, all Bayou Road property owners.[74]

The Decoudreauxs owned 1608 Bayou Road (Governor Nicholls) from 1831 to 1851. Pouponne Decoudreaux owned 1119–21 Robertson in 1806, selling it in 1821 to Bazile Demazilière. Josephine Decoudreaux, daughter of Charles and Margarita, became the wife of Paul Trevigne. Their son Paul was born in 1825 and became a linguist, teacher, and editor in chief of *L'Union*. Later he was the editor of another newspaper, the daily *La Tribune*, which ceased publication in 1869. From 1892 to 1896, *Le Crusader* enjoyed Trevigne as a collaborator.[75] His cultural contributions reached beyond the boundaries of Faubourg Tremé and New Orleans; his works for the cause of people of color were acknowledged at the Philadelphia Centennial Exposition in 1866. By living until 1909 this man, whose forebears had enjoyed at least one hundred years as free persons, observed slavery, freedom with restrictions, political upheaval through Reconstruction, and the local animosities raised against his people in their quest for social justice.

MILITARY

The contributions of the *gens de couleur libres* and *negres libres* to Louisiana's military activities extended back to the Natchez Massacre of 1729. On May 13, 1730, before the French Superior Council, a proposal to liberate Negroes for military merit was made by Attorney General Fleuriau. He urged that a military company organized among select Negroes be on instant call against the occasion of Indian uprising. Freedom had already been given to certain Negro volunteers in the wake of the Natchez affair. Under command units instituted by Jean Baptiste Le Moyne, Sieur de Bienville in 1736, there were "140 Negroes, both slaves and free. . . . Of these, the free Negroes comprised a small unit or cadre for a company. . . . The slaves were promised their freedom for risking their lives . . . yet only the bravery of Simon, a free Negro, and Captain of the Negro Company, enabled [his company] to escape censorship [because of the initial panic under fire]."[76]

By 1739 at least fifty free Negroes were part of Bienville's permanent command, although the majority of Negro troops were requisitioned slaves from New Orleans. Bienville used the *corvée*, or method of forced labor, to raise soldiers for his campaign. Under this system the Crown reimbursed the owner for the loss by escape or death of the slave soldier. In the event of freedom an appraised value was established to provide compensation to the slaveholder by the Crown.

During the French colonial years there evolved a tradition of *gens de couleur libres* in the militia, but it was the Spanish who firmly established the New Orleans militia units of free men of color. Spanish policy throughout its vast colonies provided for the organization of separate militia units based on color. Governor Alejandro O'Reilly, leaving from La Coruña, Spain, with troops for New Orleans, stopped in Havana to augment his forces in 1769. Among his recruits were 160 men, 80 each from the mulatto (or *pardo*) and Negro (or *moreno*) militia of Havana, who came with him to New Orleans.[77] Most of these men remained with O'Reilly when he departed New Orleans and returned to Cuba in 1770, but most French-speaking free colored soldiers, some of them free natives of the colony or free emigrés, others freed slaves, remained. These persons were therefore available to be organized under the leadership of new Governor Bernardo de Gálvez.

The longstanding Spanish enmity with England caused Louisiana's involvement in the American Revolution, and Governor Gálvez formed Louisiana *moreno* and *pardo* militia companies. The *moreno* militia company was composed of dark-skinned Negroes, and the *pardo* militia unit comprised mulattos and light-skinned persons—including eighty free colored men, with a white superior officer and colored officers. Among the individuals within these two companies who were cited for bravery and who received freedom and monetary reward were several residents of Faubourg Tremé: Captain Bautista Hagon and Captain Francisco Dorville, both of the *pardos*; Captain Noël Carrière, Captain Nicholas Bacchus, and San Luis Lanuitte, all of the *morenos*.[78]

Subsequent governors continued to utilize the two militia units of the free men of color, and these defended the three forts in the rear of the city in 1797 after Governor Francisco Luis Hector, Baron Carondelet, reinforced the city forts and those around the parish. This military precaution was provoked by fear of another British attack. Carondelet assigned mulatto Captain Francisco Dorville with fifty mulattos to defend the Redoubt San Juan (N. Rampart and Bayou Road) in January of 1797; thirty Negroes commanded by First Lieutenant Pedro Thomas, a free Negro, held Fort San Juan (N. Rampart at Esplanade). Forty free mulattos commanded by Captain Charles Simon, a free mulatto (probably the son of the man who won fame during his service to Bienville), were assigned to defend Fort Bourgogne (N. Rampart, Canal, and Iberville) at the city limits, between the City Commons and the Gravier-Pradel *habitation*. Thirty-five free mulattos guarded Fort San Luis (Canal Street at the river).[79]

Captain Noël Carrière was in charge of Fort San Fernando, the center fort to the rear of the city, which jutted into a part of the Charles de Morand plantation and Congo (Beauregard) Square. Carrière had been a slave of the Carrière family after he or his parents were brought to Louisiana from French West Africa during the French colonial period. He was free by 1777 when he married Marianne Thomas, probably daughter of his confederate, Lieutenant Pedro Thomas. He was a second lieutenant under Governor Gálvez and became the captain and commander of fifty men from the company of free Negroes when assigned to Fort San Fernando. Carrière died in 1835, and his son, also named Noël, became a significant property owner in Faubourg Tremé. His father, a black man and a cooper by profession, was prominent in the Spanish *moreno* unit, whereas the son was a member of the *pardo* unit. The younger Carrière was a first Lieutenant under mulatto Captain Basile Demazilière of the Chosen Free Men of Color Division in the Battle of New Orleans.

San Luis Lanuitte had been the Negro slave of Chevalier Jean de Pradel, acting as purchasing agent for his master at their plantation, Monplaisir, across the Mississippi River from New Orleans. Pradel died in 1764, and the slave continued as a personal aide to Mme de Pradel and in that capacity traveled to France as her representative in 1767.[80] He probably was freed by Mme Pradel in her will in 1768. Known to be free in 1774 when he purchased plantations on Bayou Road, he was a sub-lieutenant in the Negro Militia Company of New Orleans in 1779 and fought under Gálvez in Baton Rouge where he was cited for valorous conduct. He was in the first line in the 1780 siege of Mobile and was wounded January 7, 1781, in the Battle of the Village against the English near Mobile.[81]

Between wars, veterans and slaves were called upon to aid the city in times of crisis. Levees broke; fires were a constant threat and reality; slave uprisings and runaways occurred with regularity. Into these areas free persons of color, particularly those formally involved with the military, assisted white leaders and officers. The Cabildo issued an order in 1790, recorded in the Black Book, that "all free Negroes and mulattos in the city and such slaves as their masters wish to hire out" were to report to repair the levee for one month's duty at three *pesos* a day per person. Free *pardo* Pedro Bahy, member of the militia and son-in-law of Françoise Montreuil of Bayou Road, sent his slave to work as his substitute, which was permitted. The slave died during his work on the levee and Bahy presented a claim to the Cabildo for the price of the slave, Felipe. The Cabildo rejected the claim since the death, according to the Royal Physician, was a natural one. Furthermore, according to Cabildo records, "it was Bahy himself who had been called to work; therefore if his substitute had been accepted, it was to accommodate Bahy." In March of 1783 an expedition was sent out against several fugitive Negroes, under the command of Guido Dufossat. Within his pirogue were four free mulattos, Pedro Bailly (Bahy), Pedro *dit* Conway, Claver, and Dédé Montreuil. The fugitive slaves, called *cimarones*, were apprehended; and the sentence issued by Governor Miró ranged from lashing, branding, and shackling to condemnation on the gallows.[82]

Spain returned Louisiana to France in 1803, and the Spanish military officers and troops departed for Havana, Cuba, or the remaining Spanish colonial centers at Pensacola or Mobile. French-speaking *gens de couleur libres*, both native Louisianians and emigrés from Ste Domingue, remained in the French-speaking Louisiana. When Pierre Clément de Laussat arrived in November of 1803 as prefect of Napoleon to reclaim the colony for France, he ordered an inventory of military forces within the city. Intact was a battalion of *gens de couleur libres* under Captain Charlot Brulé. The Fuseliers were headed by Captain Joseph Simon and José Cabaret; Louis Dussier and Louis Gallout were officers. Captain of the Grenadiers was Vincent Populus. The Negro militia was commanded by Captain Augustin Fazande; the Negro Fuseliers by Louis Thomas and Lieutenants Vincent Cupidon and Alexander and Nisle, Jr. Within twenty days, however, these same troops found themselves citizens of the United States under orders of Governor W. C. C. Claiborne.[83]

Among the men known to be residents of Faubourg Tremé who declared their allegiance to the United States in an address to Governor Claiborne soon after the Louisiana Transfer were: Baptiste Hardy (1012 Marais and 1322 Ursulines), Bazile Demazilière (1119–21 N. Robertson from 1821 to 1835), Louis Liotau, Charles Porée (the Porée family once owned the Coquet division).

Claiborne personally seemed to trust the colored militia, but political intrigues during his entire political career plagued him in his decisions regarding the arming of blacks and mulattos. Finally on

September 7, 1812, an act to organize a corps of militia for the service of the State of Louisiana, as well as for its defense, as for its police, a certain portion of chosen men from among the free men of color. . . . This corps was limited to four companies . . . of sixty-four men, including officers. Its personnel was restricted to free men of color "chosen from among the Creoles" who not only paid a state tax but who for two years previous had been the owners or sons of owners of landed property worth at least $300. . . . Governor Claiborne soon thereafter appointed Isadore Honoré (of Faubourg Tremé) second lieutenant in the battalion, one of the earliest examples where a state of the union commissioned a colored officer and the first time in the United States that a Negro volunteer militia with its own Negro line officers was authorized by state legislative enactment.[84]

The War of 1812 and the threat of English attack at some point on the Gulf Coast finally brought about activation of the Battalion of Free Men of Color. General Andrew Jackson issued a proclamation from his headquarters at Mobile on September 21, 1814, to the free colored Louisianians, acknowledging the fluctuating treatment of the colored militia by the American administration and promising better treatment:

Through a mistaken policy you have heretofore been deprived of a participation in the glorious struggle for national rights in which our country is engaged. This no longer exists. . . . Your country, although calling for your exertions, does not wish you to engage in her cause without amply remunerating you for the services rendered. Your intelligent minds are not to be led away by false representations. Your love of honor would cause you to despise the man who should attempt to deceive you. In the sincerity of a soldier and the language of truth I address you.

To every noble-hearted, generous freeman–men of color, volunteering to serve during the present contest with Great Britain, and no longer, there will be paid the same bounty in money and lands now received by the white soldiers of the United States viz: one hundred and twenty-four dollars in money, and one hundred and sixty acres of land. The non-commissioned officers and privates will also be entitled to the same monthly pay and daily rations, and clothes, furnished to any American soldier.

On enrolling yourselves in companies, the Major-General commanding will select officers for your government from your white fellow-citizens. Your non-commissioned officers will be appointed from among yourselves.

. . . To assure you of the sincerity of my intentions and my anxiety to engage your invaluable services to our country, I have communicated my wishes to the Governor of Louisiana, who is fully informed as to the manner of enroll-

ment, and will give you every necessary information of the subject of this address.[85]

The result of this decree was the reactivation, in effect, of the Spanish colonial militia with changes conforming to Jackson's specifications. A battalion of free men of color consisting of four companies under the command of white Major Pierre Lacoste marched under Captain Vincent Populus of Faubourg Tremé, the ranking colored officer. They were assigned to proceed to Chef Menteur on December 17 with Maximilien Brulé, Faubourg Tremé property owner, as *porte drapeau*.[86]

On December 12, 1814, a company of colored militiamen under free man of color Captain Ferdinand Lioteau of Tremé was officially enrolled in the United States Army. On that date the First Battalion of Free Men of Color had a strength of 353 including an 11-piece band and staff officer. Populus remained the ranking colored officer with a grade of second or aide major, a rank rarely awarded by the U.S. Army to a colored officer at such an early date.[87]

One company, that of Captain Louis Simon, was then commanded by Lieutenant Maurice Populus with seventy-one men. Captain Charles Porée led sixty-three men, Captain Bazile Demazilière led fifty-one, and Captain Ferdinand Lioteau forty-five men. Privates in the battalion included Jean Dolliole, Voltaire Auguste, Louis Dauncy and Pierre Bailly, father and son, all of whom appear on property titles of the creole faubourgs. José Cabaret was quartermaster; Louis Hazeur, Sr., was in the band; Firmin Perrault, Baptiste and François Macarty, Charles and Pierre Dupart were sergeants. Among the troops were Antoine and François Boisdoré.

Another group of free men of color forty-five years and older responded for service as the home guard. Among these seventy-nine free men of color, many had served in the Spanish colonial wars, and some were from the Bayou St. John area. Assigned to duty at Fort St. John at the mouth of Bayou St. John and Lake Pontchartrain, under Corporal Jean Pierre Labau, were d'Orville and Rochon, names familiar to the area. Another contingency of *gens de couleur* was stationed at the Bridge of the Bayou between new Faubourgs Pontchartrain and St. John.

A second battalion of free men of color was raised, this one comprised of émigrés, from Ste Domingue recruited by Joseph Savary, a colored émigré who was a distinguished officer in the French army. There were 210 men serving under Major Louis Daquin, a white émigré from Ste Domingue. Savary served under him as the first free man of color appointed to the rank of second major in the United States Army.[88] Those of his soldiers who are recognized as familiar to the Faubourg Tremé area, and property owners there, were Camille Brulé (a third lieutenant), François Cazenave, Jean Charles, Julien Gobette, Louis Ferrand, François Hardy, Louis Monsignac, and Angel Robert. This second battalion of four companies was mustered into the United States Army December 19, 1814.

Additionally, there were two separate companies of free men of color with troops composed of some Tremé residents. Captain Alexandre Lemelle led sergeants Charles Darby and Narcisse Rochon and privates Pierre Darby, Louis Frilot, and Jean Macarty, among others. Captain Charles Forneret's company had as second lieutenant Augustin Blouin, and Charles and Hyacinthe Blouin were privates.[89]

Public memories of valor and good works are short-lived,

however, and many of these colored veterans had to negotiate for their pensions and even the right to be included in the festivities honoring General Lafayette in 1825. They were successful, and the April 19, 1825, *Le Courier de la Louisiane* announced a public appeal for: "the Commandant of the Corps of free colonial men who eminently contributed to the defense of this country, should come with the officers . . . to put themselves at the feet of one of the Heroes of the American Independence as a tribute to their respect and admiration."

Soon after the secession of Louisiana from the United States in 1861, *gens de couleur libres* of New Orleans, many of whom were slaveholders themselves, met to discuss participation in the Confederate war effort. The *New Orleans True Delta* of April 23, 1861, noted that "these men [of color] whose ancestors distinguished themselves at the Battle of New Orleans are determined to give new evidence of their bravery." On May 12, 1861, Governor Thomas O. Moore issued a proclamation providing for a free colored regiment of 440 free men of color designated as the First Native Guards, Louisiana Militia, Confederate States of America.[90]

The free colored population of Louisiana in 1860 was 18,547, with 11,000 living in New Orleans. By 1862 there were 3,000 members of colored military organizations from throughout the state; among the officers were citizens and propertyowners of Faubourg Tremé. Noël J. Bacchus, a forty-year-old mulatto carpenter and second-generation soldier, was a captain. His relatives Juan Bautista and Nicholas had both served the French and the Spanish in defense of New Orleans. He was listed in the muster rolls as having property valued at $800 in the Seventh Ward. Louis Rey, son of Barthélémy Rey of Tremé, was a captain; and a younger son, Armand, a drummer.

At the time of the fall of New Orleans, the Confederate regiment of color was stationed in the city and refused to leave. They hid their arms in Economy Hall, Claiborne Hall, and the Couvent School in Faubourgs Tremé and Marigny.[91] Ultimately a committee including Henry L. and Octave Rey, Edgar Davis, and Eugène Rapp reported to General Butler and formed the first black regiment in the Union Army. In the fall of 1862 three companies were formed of Louisiana free persons of color to fight for the Union; they armed and uniformed themselves. The First and Third Louisiana Negro Regiments, raised in New Orleans by General Nathanial Banks, fought for the Union in the Battle of Port Hudson. François Ernest Dumas, wealthy Faubourg Tremé man of color, joined the Second Regiment and attached a company of his own slaves to it.

RESTRICTIVE LAWS

The events of the Civil War, Reconstruction, and the bitter continuation of its effects found the *gens de couleur* affected by laws more confining and ruinous than the restrictive laws that had governed them during both colonial periods. From their earliest days the freed people and the slaves were under the French *Code Noir*. The French had instituted a *Code Noir* for its Caribbean colonies in 1685, but Bienville promulgated the *Code Noir* of 1724 as the official document to guide the lives of slaves and *gens de couleur libres* in Louisiana. In 1769 Spanish Governor O'Reilly caused a *Code Noir ou Loi Municipal Servant de Règlement* to be published in French and distributed among the population. This document, essentially

a continuation of the French Code, was revived by Governor Gálvez in 1778.

The Spanish colonial administration from Seville had circulated black codes called *Las Siete Partidas* for their vast territories as early as 1540 and 1641; but another revised code of 1789, which applied to Louisiana under Governor Esteban Miró, recognized the growing mixed population and sought to control its progressiveness.[92] Local decrees and ordinances during the Miró administration reflect this growing sensitivity of the white population toward the *gens de couleur libres*. In 1786 Governor Miró ordered that the free women of color tie up their hair and dress themselves modestly without jewelry. This became known in oral history as the Tignon Law; it was the application of the Spanish *Copilación* regulation regarding Indian women to New Orleans free women of color. Miró hoped by the Tignon Law to discourage *plaçage* relationships. He further re-enforced the laws forbidding intermarriage, which continued to take place in Mobile despite the *Code Noir*.[93]

According to the Spanish Cabildo records of January 19, 1781, "because of the great multitude of troops and crews from ships, due to the state of war between Spain and England, the great number of free Negroes and slaves in the city," the attorney general recommended that masking and public dancing by the Negroes be prohibited during the carnival season. In 1801 the Spanish governor refused *gens de couleur libres* the right to dance in Bernard Coquet's pleasure garden (Tivoli, on the shore of Bayou St. Jean). On the other hand, by 1810 during the American domination, the newspapers announced that pleasure gardens were for subscribers on the first and third Sundays and for free women of color on the second and fourth Sundays.

The great influx of French-speaking émigrés from Ste Domingue had begun in 1790. In 1803 when the blacks defeated the French in Haiti, thousands of black and white refugees came to New Orleans. In 1809 the French-speaking Creoles of Ste Domingue who had gone to Cuba were evicted by Spanish officials angered by French occupation of Spain. Between May and July of 1809, 6,000 refugees departed Cuba—2,000 of them, many *gens de couleur libres*, coming to New Orleans. Immigration continued despite an 1804 order by Governor Claiborne barring entry to all persons of color from the Antilles. On May 16, 1806, the *Moniteur* reported a legislative act "to prevent the introduction of free people of color from Ste Domingue and other French islands to the Territory of Orleans."

The enforcement of these laws was weak and ineffectual. Claude Tremé, himself from France, had new immigrants who spoke his native language, to whom he made private real estate sales of lots from his plantation adjacent to the rear limits of the city. This new population certainly influenced the decision by the city to buy the Tremé plantation and create a city-owned faubourg.

Although these émigrés between 1790 and 1810 included many well-educated free persons of color who became leaders in education and business, their very large numbers also brought unrest among segments of the white community and resulted in more restrictive laws. The mass immigration coincided with the arrival of even larger numbers of Anglo-Americans who were unaccustomed to *gens de couleur libres*. The native free persons of color and the recent French émigrés achieved a standard of acceptance within New Orleans society; nevertheless, they had been and continued to be subjected to periodic legislation, decrees, ordinances, and resolutions that caused personal indignation as well as financial inconvenience. A legislative act dated March 7, 1816, read: "An individual coming into this state from a foreign country, or from any one state of the United States, and desirous of requiring residence therein, shall give notice in writing to the judge of the parish where he proposes to reside of his intention to require residence."

The editor of the *Louisiana Courier* of 1820 wrote in a letter to the director of the Orleans Theatre:

Sir, From all sides a report is spread, that after having hesitated a long time to cede to the free people of color the second boxes of your theatre and the amphitheatres belonging thereto, you have at last come to a determination favorable to them, and which is nothing but the result of mature and sound reflection. All those, sir, who feel interested for your prosperity, and for that of your establishment, had long ago, thought that it was an error on your part, to suppose that the white population were sufficiently large, to occupy all the year, the great number of places which had been destined to them. . . . At all time, in New Orleans, those Boxes have been assigned to the colored population, and it was a kind of injustice to deprive them of a right which time and usage had secured to them. . . . You deprived yourself, during the long year, of more than fifteen thousand dollars, which those boxes must produce, had they been occupied . . . that social laws are by no means offended by [your decision] and finally, that among the public you will find very few censors, but a great number of people who should regret that he, who has been so enterprising as to give so fine establishment to one of the most flourishing towns of the union, should not be encouraged. [signed] Justice.

The legislature of 1830, however, following public outrage after a March, 1829, slave uprising forty miles from New Orleans, inaugurated a series of restrictive laws that became broader each year and severely hindered the *gens de couleur libres* in their economic and educational opportunities, as well as their social and business relationships with white persons. The documented restrictions, attacks in the press on many Faubourg Tremé inhabitants, and police harrassments are reflected in their lives.

One 1830 law prevented free people of color from entering Louisiana and forced those who had entered after 1825 to leave within sixty days. Those who had entered between 1812 and 1825 were required to register themselves in their towns. However, those who had immigrated before 1812 were specifically exempt. The same law contained a clause restricting communication by blacks or whites that "caused unrest among slaves or free people, or caused the latter to forget their place."[94]

Others forced to register were indentured persons. Whether *gens de couleur libres*, white, or slaves, they were recorded by notarized acts of indenture and through the sheriff's and mayor's registers. In 1811 a mulatto slave Michel, belonging to Faubourg Tremé resident Mme François Montamet, was indentured by her to Louis Leroy for one year to learn the trade of carpenter. Leroy was to pay Mme Montamet $8 a month. That same year Louis Isnard, born in Jeremie, Ste Domingue, bound himself to A. Lacarrière Latour, architect, to learn the trade of bricklayer. The document stated that Isnard and his mother were white. In 1811 Jean Louis Moreau, a fourteen-year-old orphan boy of color born in Baradue, Ste Domingue, had with the advice of his aunt Louise Lominil, free quadroon, bound himself to Ferdinand Lioteau, free man of color. He was to learn a trade as a cabinetmaker, to dwell with Lioteau for five years, and to receive good and sufficient meat, drink, and lodging. Six months of night school were to teach him to read, write, and do arithmetic. He was to be furnished clothing, opportunity for washing, and care in case of sickness.

A young, aspiring surveyor, Joseph Pilié, who became very important to the history of Faubourg Tremé, was a white native of Ste Domingue. He indentured himself to Barthélémy Lafon, surveyor, in 1805:

The private engagement of Mr. Joseph Pillier [*sic*], towards B. Lafon, engineer: I undersigned, Joseph Pilier [*sic*], of the island of San Domingo, presently residing in New Orleans, obligate and engage myself to work during the space of two consecutive years which follow in a year from this day, for Mr. Barthelemi [*sic*] Lafon, engineer geographer in the same city, in his geographer's office or any place suitable to him. I obligate myself to work at all sorts of drawing which shall be brought to me and particularly at that of geography, copying, reducing, and tracing as necessary, the plans, charts, and drawings which he shall present to me, and moreover to aid him in his geographical or geodesic operations if he finds it suitable, without my being able to refuse; to oversee the meteorological observations in the course of the day, and to occupy myself with other works of this nature if he requires it. Which things here above named I obligate myself to do in consideration of sixteen dollars per month which Mr. Lafon obligates himself to give me at the end of each month. The aforesaid Mr. Lafon being also obligated to feed me during the whole time that I am in his office, and to lodge me. N. Orleans the 17 February 1805, Jh. Pilié.[95]

According to Greiner's digest, the Legislative Act 1533 of 1841 re-enforced the obligation to register: "It shall be the duty of all free Negroes, griffes, and mulattos of the first degree, who came into this state after the adoption of constitution thereof, and prior to the first day of January, 1825, within sixty days after the promulgation of this act, to enroll themselves in the office of the parish judge of the parish where they may be resident, or in the office of the mayor of the city of New Orleans; setting forth their age, sex, color, trade or calling, place of nativity, and the time of their arrival in the state; for which enrollment the parish judge or mayor shall be entitled to demand and receive the sum of fifty cents."

The free persons of color who registered after this legislation often did not include the prominent Faubourg Tremé families. Such unregistered colored persons were among the wealthiest families in the city: the Macartys, Meffre-Rouzans, Souliés, Dumases, Colvises, and others. These were people who had business offices and homes in France as well as New Orleans; they or their families had arrived in Louisiana before 1812. These same families sometimes were not even noted as *gens de couleur* in the city directories; nor were they consistently designated thus in notarized acts. They traveled back and forth to France. Some left the United States permanently; but many of their descendants remained, creating an educated, hardworking upper class of free persons of color.

The legal sheriff's register provided not only a rough census of the number of free persons who came into Faubourg Tremé, but an invaluable historical resource. Color was listed as black, mulatto, quarteroons, yellowmen, griffes, and *briques*. Of those registered, as many black men were listed as lighter-skinned persons. One of the tallest persons was 5 feet 11 inches, but the average male was between 5 feet 3 inches and 5 feet 7 inches. Among the professions enumerated for 1840–1857 were planters, foundrymen, barkeepers, coopers, saddlers, boardinghouse keepers, and cotton press hands. Most common professions were those of seamstress, carpenter, bricklayer, plasterer, washwoman, steamboat caulker, slater, steward, cooper, *charretier*, drayman, and cigar maker.

In 1841 Hughes Pedesclaux, a white man of Faubourg Tremé who had his own acknowledged colored children, freed Jean Louis Pedesclaux, a *negre* who registered at the sheriff's office in that same year. Jean Lambert, a French-educated free man of color of Faubourg Tremé and member of a wealthy family, freed Marie Louisa Dalila, a Negress from Port-au-Prince, Haiti, in 1828. She was sixty in 1841 when she registered at the sheriff's office. In one instance in 1841 both the liberator and the emancipated slave registered together. Marie Thérèse Villanueva, alias Zelmire, a Negress from the Congo, was freed in 1826 by Charles Leseur, a free man of color. Villanueva herself in turn freed Carlos Fernandez, mulatto, born in New Orleans, who was thirty-eight years old in 1841. Antoine Benjamin, free person of color, registered in 1841; he had freed Mathieu, alias Jean Joseph, a *griffe* of English Turn, aged fifty-two. In 1835 Benjamin had also freed Joseph Honoré, a painter born in New Orleans in 1793 and perhaps the relative of the Isadore Honoré of military fame.

EDUCATION

The tentacles of restrictive laws reached beyond the political, social, and economic realm into the religious life of the *gens de couleur*. Because of their acceptance, indeed forced enrollment, into the Roman Catholic Church, most *gens de couleur libres* and slaves were baptized, married, and interred within that religion. Unlike some of the areas of discipline and control, the *gens de couleur libres* accepted the Church as a symbol of distinction. It was within the Church that some humane and educational advances were possible. In 1836 the establishment within the faubourg of an order of nuns, all of whom were *gens de couleur libres*, brought about definite participation by the Catholic Church in education in this area. As Faubourg Tremé residents whose families were benefactors to the order, the nuns took their vows at St. Augustine's Church on St. Claude Street. Their first school, ironically, was in the original Tremé plantation house; and their major asylum, the Lafon home on N. Tonti, established in 1865, was run by their successors, the Sisters of the Holy Family, on the site until 1970.

The founder of the order was Henriette Delille, born in 1813, natural daughter of Jean Baptiste Delisle-Sarpy and Pouponne Dias, a "*quarterone libre*." She lived with a sister, Cecilia, six years older, and her brother Jean, on Burgundy between St. Peter and Toulouse; one grandmother, Henriette Labeau, after whom she was named, lived with them. Cecile Marthe Basile Dubreuil, the other grandmother, was born a slave in 1742 in New Orleans. By 1760 Mme Dubreuil was free and owned a house on Orleans between Royal and Bourbon. Among Henriette Delille's relatives were cousins Pierre and

Basile Crocker and Marguerite Minion Boisdoré. Her uncles Narcisse Labeau and Raphael Roig, free men of color, were planters and neighbors of school philanthropist John McDonogh.[96]

Laws against the education of slaves were stringent, and those for free persons of color were under constant scrutiny. One of the earliest advertisements for a school for colored children appeared in the *Louisiana Courier* on January 13, 1813, and was evidently in open violation of the law: "I intend to establish a school for the education of colored children. Such an institution is entirely lacking in this portion of the country, and the enlightened persons who heretofore were desirous of having their children educated—I refer to the prudent colored people—were obliged to send them to the North. On them I depend for support. Eighteen or twenty pupils having been already promised, the school will be opened on Monday."

Henriette Delille attended a school opening in 1823 for free people of color on Rue Barracks in the French Quarter, run by Sister Ste Marthe Fortier of the Dames Hospitalier, the only member of the French order in New Orleans at the time. Influenced by Sister Ste Marthe, Henriette worked among poor persons of color and slaves in New Orleans, aiding, assisting, and teaching them. She worked with Juliette Gaudin, natural daughter of Theresa Ste La Cardonie and Pierre Gaudin. Juliette had immigrated from Cuba with her parents, and her father had opened a school for *gens de couleur* in New Orleans.

Meanwhile, Mlle Marie Jean Aliquot, a young white Frenchwoman born in 1783, immigrated to New Orleans where she devoted herself to the aid of poor Negroes, both slave and free. Her sister Félicité was a Carmelite nun in New Orleans; another sister, Adèle, arrived in New Orleans in 1831 but died in 1832.

Mlle Aliquot, Juliette Gaudin, Henriette Delille, Josephine Charles, and six others (names unknown), in November of 1836 formed the "Sisters of the Presentation." Mlle Aliquot purchased the Tremé plantation house at Bayou Road and St. Claude after the 1826 closing of the Collège d'Orléans. The sisters taught free colored children until 1840 when, because of lack of funds and racial harrassment, Mlle Aliquot was forced to sell. The Ursuline nuns were the purchasers with the condition in the act of sale that they continue the school for colored children.

An act of the legislature of 1830 stated "whoever shall write, print, publish, or distribute anything having a tendency to produce discontent among the free population or insubordination among slaves or make use of language in any public discourse . . . in private discourse or conversations, or shall make use of language in any public discourse . . . or shall make use of signs or actions . . . should be punished by imprisonment at hard labor for life or suffer death." Mlle Aliquot, as the white member of the group, could be prosecuted by this law; and the Archdiocese arranged intermittently for her to leave Faubourg Tremé to help slaves in the county parishes.

On November 21, 1842, the Soeurs de la Ste Famille (Sisters of the Holy Family) were incorporated, but Henriette Delille and Juliette Gaudin were not ordained as nuns; they acted in that capacity with the sanction of Father Janssen and other religious leaders of the city. In 1847 the state legislature passed an act in which members had to exceed six to incorporate a literary, scientific, or religious association. This meant that the society with only three members would be disbanded. With the help of Cecile Edouarde Lacroix, wife of François Lacroix (a well-known colored *entrepreneur*, broker, and tailor), a group was formed of free men and women of color called the Association of the Holy Family. Officers included Etiènne Cordevielle, builder in Tremé, Armand Richard Clague, Joseph LaVigne, François Boutin (Broutin), and Chazel Thomas. François Lacroix raised money and helped finance and build for them their first *hospice* on St. Bernard Avenue. Joining them was Agathe Mager Collard, a white Frenchwoman, who with her brother Jean Mager was a prominent landowner in Faubourg Tremé and one-time president of the society.

In 1850 the society, with $1,600 from Mlle Aliquot, bought a small residence on Bayou Road between N. Rampart and St. Claude, a block from the new St. Augustine's Church. This replaced their former home at the Tremé house, where a school continued then under the auspices of the Sisters of Mount Carmel, who had succeeded the Ursulines. That same year Magdeleine Chaigneau, of a Faubourg Tremé family, joined the group.

Henriette Delille, Juliette Gaudin, and Josephine Charles were finally permitted to take their formal vows October 15, 1852. The ceremony took place at St. Augustine's Church, recently designed by French architect Jacques de Pouilly to serve the growing population of Faubourg Tremé, largely the French-speaking *gens de couleur libres*. This order of amazing women organized and administered five major institutions for the education and protection of young and old people of color. They enlarged the *hospice* on St. Bernard Avenue in 1860 and expanded with the Asylum of the Children of the Holy Family on Dauphine in the French Quarter. In the meantime, the small school in the house on Bayou Road continued and was incorporated as a School for Children of the Holy Family in 1875.

Thomy Lafon aided these courageous women when he provided an asylum for old and infirm persons of color. In the late 1860s he built a large brick edifice at 1221 N. Tonti for these Sisters of the Holy Family. He also gave land and some funds for another building, the Providence Asylum for Colored Orphans, in the same block in 1867. Louis Charles Roudanez, member of another prominent Tremé family, gave the money to lay the foundation. The institution became known as the Louisiana Asylum when the Sisters of the Holy Family merged their orphanage with the one run by the Louisiana Association for the Benefit of Colored Orphans. This association had been founded in 1865 also by wealthy *gens de couleur*. The first domicile for their orphans was the home of Pierre Soulé, which Union General Stephen A. Hurlbut requisitioned in 1865 as a school for freed slaves.

Henriette Delille died at the Bayou Road residence of the Sisters of the Holy Family in 1862. Her efforts and those of Mlle Aliquot had longlasting results. The school on Bayou Road at the Tremé house continued in operation under the leadership of the Carmelites. The second school, in the 1100 block of Bayou Road and now demolished, educated many Faubourg Tremé children. The order remains in existence today, residing in the Gentilly area.

Another woman, a free black, Mme Gabriel Bernard Couvent, founded a school in nearby Faubourg Marigny for free persons of color. This, the Couvent School, had as its directors, benefactors, and students many Faubourg Tremé *gens de couleur*. Mme Couvent's husband, Gabriel Bernard Couvent, free person of color and a carpenter, died May 22, 1829, at the age of seventy-one, leaving his wife a considerable estate. Mme Couvent was born Justine Fervin, a black African woman, an illiterate former slave who died at eighty on June 28, 1837, and was buried in Faubourg Tremé's St. Louis Cemetery II. She left property in land and several houses to provide funds and domicile for poor, black, Catholic orphans of the Third District (Faubourg Marigny). Her will was written in 1832 and executed in 1848. During Reconstruction, persons of color began to attend public school, and the Couvent institution was almost deserted; but it did reopen after 1884. The colored directors and benefactors who provided leadership were L. A. Desdunes, R. L. Desdunes, clerk and author; Eugène Luscy and Noël Bacchus, builders; and François Lacroix, *entrepreneur*.[97]

The most successful institution for higher education among Negroes in New Orleans was Straight University. Chartered by the Louisiana state legislature in 1869 it was founded by the American Missionary Association. The school was named for Seymour Straight, the white New Orleans produce merchant who donated the original land for the school. Edward and Charles Heath, well-to-do Englishmen and property owners in the American commercial district, were also active in the promotion of the institution. The Freedman's Bureau donated $20,000, and the school temporarily opened in a church in 1869.[98]

After an 1877 fire destroyed the school building at Esplanade and N. Derbigny, it was housed at Canal and N. Tonti streets. In 1881 Mrs. Valene G. Stone of Malden, Massachusetts, donated $25,000 enabling the institution to purchase half a square off Canal Street and erect Stone Hall, a dormitory and teachers' home. In 1883 William C. Whillen and Mr. Straight donated money for the construction of Whitten Hall, a boys' dormitory. The school buildings were used as Vermont headquarters at the New Orleans Exhibition of 1885. It developed a library housing over 5,000 volumes and a much-needed industrial department with the Slater fund. The university also developed schools of medicine and law, as well as classical and normal departments.

Aristide Mary and other New Orleans leaders from the *gens de couleur* community had objected strenuously to the formation of a separate school for Negroes, proclaiming the move devisive during a crucial time when black Republicans held the political leadership in Louisiana. Thus, support for the school by many of their people was withheld. Straight University played a major role in the evolvement of the postwar Negro community in the city, but primarily it contributed to the education of the emancipated, Protestant slaves from Louisiana's country parishes and their descendants. Few French-speaking, Catholic *gens de couleur* attended or supported it.[99]

Nonetheless, this school and the other, the New Orleans University begun in 1869 by the Freedmen's Aid Society, through the benevolence of the Methodist Episcopal Church, were the important post-Civil War institutions. The school was called the New Orleans University and was above Canal Street in an area now called the Lower Garden District. Sixteen schools listed exclusively for Negroes were reported in the New Orleans area in that same year, 1869, as well as fifteen private schools designated at the same time for "free colored people."[100] (In 1935 Straight College and the New Orleans University merged to form Dillard University on Gentilly Road.)

BUSINESS

Attitudinal changes immediately prior to the Civil War deprived many Louisiana free persons of color of former opportunities and caused a migration by some to Haiti through the port of New Orleans. The press and the politicians had continually presented challenges and obstacles to their progress, and this was duly noted in an account on January 15, 1860, in the *Daily Picayune.*

The bark Laurel . . . will leave today for Port au Prince, Hayti, having on board, as passengers, ninety-one free persons of color, who are emigrating from this state to try their chances in Hayti—these people are all from the Opelousas parishes and all cultivators. . . .

Of the various expeditions which have left New Orleans for Hayti, this is certainly the most important, from the peculiar class of emigrants and the fact of their taking away with them a considerable amount of capital. . . .

We have rarely had occasion to complain of the free colored people, who, born on the soil of Louisiana, have grown up in our midst. As distinct as their position from whites, no hard feeling exists between the two races. They cannot, and do not, attempt to come out of the sphere of inferiority in which they were born, but within that sphere they enjoy their rights, and privileges in full security. They contribute their quota of usefulness, and in return receive the protection of our laws. No dangerous influence upon our slaves need be feared from them. With people of color from other parts who might come to us, unknown, tainted, perhaps, with fanatical notions, the case is different, and our state Legislature has had to enact laws, stringent, perhaps, in their effects, but dictated by prudence, as necessary to the maintenance of order and the happiness of our blacks, as well as to the security of property of their masters. Hundreds, therefore, who have lived for some time among us, and who may be well-thinking and useful individuals, find themselves proscribed by the provisions of the law, and it is well that they should seek, in Hayti, the quiet life they cannot, by law, enjoy in the slave states, and which they will not seek in the free states, convinced, by experience, that *there* they will not find it. If following their example, and seduced by the inducements held out by the Haytians . . . our native free blacks follow the tide of immigration, we have more to rejoice than to complain, for although we give them due credit for their usefulness and the respect for our institutions and love of country, of which they have given many proofs, we can but give them the God-speed when they make a determination which may better their position, socially, whilst it relieves us from the painful task of maintaining the proper equilibrium between them and the whites, their superiors, on the one side, and the slaves, their inferiors, on the other.

At this same time, 1860, the property holdings of the free persons of color in New Orleans were estimated between $13,000,000 and $15,000,000.[101] It was not uncommon for estates to range in property values from $40,000 to $100,000. The basis of economic power and the social positions of most of these free colored people was in the land; it was through, not only the building trades that they mastered, but the accumulation of large and small land acquisitions. Most men were both builders and land brokers, like Myrtil Courcelle, who lived in Faubourg Tremé throughout his lifetime, built, traded, and died there in 1872.

Etiènne Cordeviolle was the first colored generation of a leading family of Faubourg Tremé. A builder, he lived on Claiborne between St. Ann and Dumaine in 1840. His father was an immigrant from Genoa; and his mother, Marie Rosalie, a Negress, native of Guinea. In 1850 his father, the white Italian, was a builder living with his mixed family in Faubourg Tremé. The two generations, white father and colored son, were responsible for many houses built throughout New Orleans between 1830 and 1860.

Pierre Théodule Olivier was a prominent colored builder; among his remaining houses is the Chalon House in the 1600 block of Bayou Road and 1717 Kerlerec, which was planned and constructed for his sister Adèle and her husband, Charles Martinez. Olivier's building contracts for both of these outstanding creole cottages exist. On July 28, 1842, Martinez entered into this contract with his brother-in-law and François Muro, free man of color and *entrepreneur* for the *maison principale* and kitchen at 1717 Kerlerec with the cost set at $1,100.

Martinez and his wife, Adelaide Adèle Olivier, were propertied individuals as evidenced by their marriage contract of November 7, 1836, before C. Pollock. The future husband brought to the marriage nine lots in the Vieux Carré and Faubourg New Marigny, property in Mandeville and Attakapas, a grocery store, and four slaves. Adèle Olivier's dowry consisted of one-third interest in a lot in the Vieux Carré, and one-eighth interest in land in Attakapas, which she had inherited from her father Pierre Olivier, free man of color, in 1805.

After building the *maison principale*, Mme Martinez, a resident of Plaquemines Parish, sold nearby lots to the builder Muro's widow, who built houses for speculation. One of these remains set back in the lot at 1725 Kerlerec, now undistinguished because of a front wraparound. Notary L. Herman, on December 19, 1848, recorded "half a lot closest to Derbigny street sold independently of buildings now on it, which belong to Mme Muro for having had them built for her account and at her expense" (1725 Kerlerec). The following year, "on May 26, 1849, Dame Louise Olivier [Mme Martinez], free woman of color, sells to Dame Emelie Augustine Thezan, widow François Murow [*sic*], free woman of color, a lot on Kerlerec to Columbus between Derbigny and Roman, acquired November 9, 1843." The Thezan family, mentioned in many books, was particularly well represented by Sidney Thezan, a wealthy moneylender, commissioner, and estate planner. He lived on Esplanade, and with his son Joseph he invested in many properties; he died in 1875.

Julien Colvis and Joseph Dumas, free people of color, were partners, speculating and developing Faubourg Tremé from 1830 until 1869. They were also tailors with a business at 124 Chartres (1849). As wealthy citizens they owned property not only in Louisiana but in France and visited there often. Title research reveals their dual ownership of 1933 Ursulines, 1820 and 1824 Dumaine (1836–1869), 1209–11 St. Philip (1830–1869), 1933–35 Ursulines (1837–1846), and 1609–11 St. Philip (1837–1846).

Julien Colvis, a native of Santiago, Cuba, the natural son of Joseph Colvis and Charlotte Colvis, married Marguerite Bernoudy of St. Charles Parish on September 14, 1829. Colvis' son Joseph married Marguerite Dumas, and in 1869 the couple lived in Paris; his daughters both married white Frenchmen. Marguerite Hermina Colvis married Jacques Goupil of Paris, and Jeanne alias Amelia Colvis married Auguste Coutanceau of Bordeaux. A third daughter, Marie Mathilde, also lived in Bordeaux; her husband was Pierre Elie Sicard, and in 1869 they owned 1209 St. Philip, purchasing it from the Colvis-Dumas partnership.

The Joseph Dumas family lived on St. Philip near St. Claude in 1844. Francis Ernest Dumas, a son, served in the Second Regiment of volunteers of the Union Army, utilizing his own slaves to help the cause. He was reported to be one of the wealthiest free persons of color in Louisiana. This influential former slaveowner chose to remain in New Orleans as a leader for the rights of the Negro, whereas most of his family moved to France. He ran as the Republican candidate for lieutenant governor in 1868 and lost.

In an 1850 manuscript census, Bernard Soulié was listed as a forty-year-old male mulatto merchant from Louisiana. He had at least two children, then, Victor and Emile Léon, the latter a student. At the time of the census his estate was valued at $50,000. His neighbor was an important white Irish immigrant and significant builder, John McVittie. Bernard and his brother Albin were active Tremé realtors. Among their many properties were 1226–28 Tremé and twin townhouses in the second block of N. Rampart, where they had their real estate brokerage firm. Emile Léon, Bernard's son, moved to France, where, as absentee landlord, he continued to rent houses and buy Tremé land. Bernard and Albin's partner and relative was Lucien Soulié, who shared ownership of 1529 Ursulines with Bernard from 1838 to 1845.

The Gignac name appears repeatedly in title transfers of property on Bayou Road. François Gignac, free person of color, was a native of New Orleans. He married Celestina Vela, free woman of color and daughter of Maria Calen, in May of 1825. Gignac was the natural son of Joseph Gignac and Maria Montreuil and the brother-in-law of Pierre Crocker. He owned 1110 Tremé from 1836 to 1838, and in 1841 he was domiciled at 236 Ursulines, listing his profession as carpenter. In 1849 Mme M. Gignac ran a school for colored children next door at 233 Ursulines.

A brother, Jean Baptiste Gignac, was born in 1799, also in New Orleans. François and Jean Baptiste could well be the grandchildren of Françoise or François Montreuil, which would make them fourth generation Tremé residents by 1800. When Jean Baptiste died on January 19, 1840, he was living on St. Philip between Marais and Villere with his wife, Adelaide Campanel. He was a tailor who, with his brother François, also bought and sold property.

Pierre Roup, free man of color, was an émigré from Ste Domingue. He owned property both on Esplanade Avenue and N. Rampart Street. He is listed in the marriage book of St. Louis Cathedral as a free man of color, son of Pierre Roup and Hélène Lesseige of Ste Domingue. His bride was Catherine Lafitte, daughter of Pierre Lafitte and Marie Louise Velard of New Orleans. As organizer of Perseverance Hall in 1820, he served with white émigrés, friends from Ste Domingue. As an officer of the organization, he signed the contract for the building of the complex at Perseverance Hall and was listed as an assessor for the Third District. Mme Roup predeceased her husband, dying in 1840 at their home on St. Claude between Rue Quartier (Barracks) and Esplanade.

The white progenitor of the white and colored Meffre-Rouzan families of New Orleans was Jacques Meffre-Rouzan, native of Chateau Roux in Dauphine, France. He was the legitimate son of Sieur Meffre and Catherine Rouzan. He married Rose Angelin and had two children who, in 1814 when their father wrote his will, were eight-year-old Jacques Philippe and Antoine Julien, aged two. They lived at the corner of St. Louis and Levée in a one-story brick house with a mortgage of $6,000 owed to the heirs of M. Favre. Meffre-Rouzan also owned a lot on Rue Levée behind the customhouse on which there was a small wooden house. By 1850 another or the same white man named Meffre-Rouzan of the same place in France was living in Faubourg Tremé with his wife Constance Meilleur.

Jacques Meffre-Rouzan, a free person of color, recorded his parents as Michel Rouzan and Maria Piquery, a free woman of color. In an October 17, 1825, ceremony he married Catherine André Cavalier, the daughter of Andrés Cavalier and Pélagie Gaudin. By 1850 they were living in Faubourg Tremé, and the census listed him as a fifty-five-year-old mulatto carpenter.

The Cavalière family, possible relatives of Mme Rouzan, were established in the area by 1830. Jean Théophile owned 1514 and 1518–20 Dumaine in 1831. Bernard Jules Cavalière owned 1454–58 St. Claude from 1835 to 1858. Antoinette Cavalière and her husband, Ursin Manuel Heins, lived on Rue Robertson between Ste Anne and Dumaine when he died.

Nelson Fouché was a Jamaican immigrant to New Orleans, the natural son of Thomas Fouché and Maria Niclarn. At St. Louis Church in New Orleans in 1823 he married Maria Francisca Lefebre, a native of Cuba, the natural daughter of M. Lefebre and Maria Dusseau. Although he was an enterprising builder in Tremé, his home was in Faubourg Marigny, where he had land holdings. As a literary man, he contributed to Paul Trevigne's L'Union, a weekly newspaper geared to informing black residents of political events. Desdunes described him as "a brilliant but exceedingly modest man, whose genius was respected by all races. He has left us a small volume entitled Nouveau Recueil [A New Harvest]. The book reveals the ambitions and hopes he had for progress in our society. Fouché busied himself mostly with painting, surveying, and the arts."[102]

Mme Fouché, née Dusseau, was a member of an early colored Tremé family. On January 2, 1818, St. Fort Dusseau, free person of color and native of New Orleans, married Eulalie Rillieux, widow of Thenencio Voisin, the natural daughter of Pierre Rillieux and Rosalie Dusseau. St. Fort's parents, according to the St. Louis Church marriage register, were "Louis Dusseau and Maria," unmarried. The Rillieux family through Norbert received international fame. In the applied sciences, according to Rodolph Desdunes,

> Norbert Rillieux, a colored Creole, was unequaled in Louisiana. A machinist and engineer of first rank, especially skilled in large-scale scientific work, he invented and patented in 1846 a vacuum cup that revolutionized sugar-refining methods in that day. Among his recorded achievements is a practicable plan for a sewerage system in New Orleans, which local authorities refused to accept, for the reason that at the time sentiment against free people of color had become sufficiently acute to prohibit the bestowing of such an honor upon a member of this persecuted group. After a time he must have moved to France, for he is mentioned as head of the Ecole Centrale of Paris. . . . M. Norbert Rillieux était le plus célèbre de nos Creoles.[103]

The following men included here for their business acumen would have been exceptional during any period of New Orleans history, but they are particularly notable because they steadfastly surmounted all obstacles that reduced many free men of color and survived the chaos of the Civil War and Reconstruction.

The father-son brokerage team of free persons of color Francis and John Raquet Clay was among the prosperous group. They made most of their loans to whites with building interests, including Christian Roselius, Cristoval Toledano, and architect James Freret. John Clay demanded 8 percent annual interest with loans for no less than $500. The Clays prior to the war had been most successful, however, as estate executors of wealthy Negroes. When free colored financier and builder Myrtil Courcelle died in 1872, Clay received 2½ percent commission as the executor of a greatly diminished estate worth $36,482.[104]

The Macarty families, both *gens de couleur* and white, were leaders in the evolution of Faubourg Tremé. Barthélémy Macarty was the white son of Jean Baptiste Macarty and Mlle Fazende. He received a large land grant in the area at the end of the Spanish colonial period. His 1832 will revealed that he was unmarried and childless; he left his estate to his friend Armand Pitot.

The colored branch of the Macarty family was one of the most prominent in the financial affairs of Faubourg Tremé. Drausin Barthélémy Macarty, mulatto, married Anna Louise Courcelle, free woman of color and member of Myrtil Courcelle's family. Among the properties Macarty owned were 1612 St. Philip (1846–1879), 1523–25 St. Philip (1840–1843), 2204 St. Philip (1855), and 1018–20 N. Robertson (1847–1855). He utilized his skill to increase his legacy from $35,000 in 1860 to $77,300 in 1870.

Eugène V. Macarty, free man of color, was born in New Orleans in 1821. In 1840 he was sent to France to study music under the sponsorship of Pierre Soulé, French ambassador from New Orleans. He attended the French Conservatory in Paris; and upon returning to his native city, he performed at the Theâtre Orléans.[105] Other black Macarty descendants remained in France, like Isadore Barthélémy Albin Macarty, who became a resident of Bordeaux, where he lived in 1881 when he sold 1223 St. Philip Street in New Orleans. In the 1850 census one of the Macarty mulattos was listed as a forty-four-year-old landlord worth $25,000.

Substantial information has been published regarding Thomy Lafon, wealthy black philanthropist, both during his lifetime and for many years afterward. He was important to Faubourg Tremé as resident, realtor, broker, and contributor to two major charitable institutions in the area—the Lafon Home for the Aged and the Providence Asylum for Colored Orphans.

Lafon was born on December 28, 1810, in New Orleans. His mother was the free woman of color Modeste Foucher. A notarial reference of October, 1776, collected by Dr. Ronald R. Morazan, sets forth the emancipation agreement of Modeste's mother Julia and her children. "René Brion and his wife Dame Piguery emancipated their slave named Julia, age twenty-two, and her three children, Benedicta, Achilles, and Modesta, for all the love and affection which they had for them and the loyal service they had given." This indicates that Thomy Lafon was a third generation New Orleanian; his grandmother Julia, born in 1754, was a slave in New Orleans before 1776.

Julia, the emancipated slave, took the name of her former master Brion. She owned property in the French Quarter by

1794; Governor General Carondelet's report of the 1794 conflagration included a list of the property owners of the 212 buildings that burned, indicating that Julia Brion, *mulata libre*, owned two 2-storied houses which burned. She died in 1809, leaving children by different fathers. The father of one was a Negro; the father of Modeste Foucher was either white or a mulatto free man of color. Modeste may have been the *placée* of a Frenchman, "a native of Castelnaudary, in Languedoc," according to Louise M. Laralde's succession deposition, taken in Cincinnati in 1937. Mme Foucher had at least four children: Thomy Lafon, Edouard Laralde, Alphée Bodin (Baudin), and Josephine Lacoste (married surnames).[106]

Three of Modeste Foucher's children were residents of Faubourg Tremé. Thomy Lafon resided most of his adult life at the corner of N. Robertson and Ursulines with his widowed sister Mme Alphée L. Baudin. It is assumed that Josephine Lacoste resided in Tremé, but an actual address has not been forthcoming.

The 1850 manuscript census listed Lafon as thirty-eight years old, a mulatto, and a broker with an estate of $10,000. He resided with his sixty-five-year-old mother Modeste, a free mulatress; Alphée Baudin; and her husband, Lavinski Baudin, a forty-year-old free man of color who was employed in Lafon's shoe store.

Lafon's will, published in the *New Orleans Picayune* December 27, 1893, listed his large bequests to different charitable institutions:

> Probated this afternoon in Judge Monroe's division (C) of Civil District Court . . . the handwriting of deceased, in French, [it] is a voluminous document. The bequests include: $10,000 to the Charity Hospital ambulance fund, $5,000 and one square of ground bounded by Common, Gravier, Clark, and Genois streets to the Lafon Home, $20,000 to the Little Sisters of the Poor, $3,000 to the Shakespeare Almshouse fund, $15,000 to the Catholic Colored Indigent Hospital. Various bequests of valuable real estate are made to several charitable institutions, notably the Louisiana Asylum, corner of Tonti and Hospital [Barracks] streets, properties on Burgundy, Dauphine, Dumaine, and St. Ann streets, also to the Holy Family religious order $10,000; the Straight University is left $3,000 in cash; to his sister, Alfée Lafon, he leaves property on Ursulines and Robertson streets, and $5,000 in cash; to his niece, Mme Cronille, $10,000; to each of his godchildren, namely, Valentine Crocker, Emma Guerineau, Alvarez Macrois, Henry Burel, and Joseph Greer Le Blanc, $1,000 each; to a number of cousins $1,000 each; to Hon. Carleton Hunt $500 as a mark of esteem. There are two codicils dated April 14 and Dec. 18, 1893. In the latter testator increases the bequest to the Little Sisters of the Poor to $20,000. The executors named are P. A. Bacas and Robert Clay, and are made exempt from bonds.

Another account in the *States* newspaper on the same day reported that:

> Lafon was in many respects a peculiar man. Although he possessed several fine residences, he preferred to reside in a humble abode, with no other companion save his aged sister to whom he was devoted. He was always a thrifty man, and this readily accounts for his immense acquirements. However, he was ever open-handed and generous when parties deserving of charity made calls upon his purse. As a business man he was shrewd and sagacious and was generally successful in his speculations.

Lafon was a devoted art student and was especially fond of music. Though extreme age weakened him considerably, he was always erect and dignified looking, courteous and affable to all, and charitable to many. He readily won friends and kept them. He was never married. His death was caused by a combination of maladies. In his last hours he was attended by Rev. Father Mignot of the Cathedral. His funeral will take place at 3 o'clock this evening from his late residence, corner of Ursulines and Robertson streets.

The wealthiest *gens de couleur* in New Orleans were brokers, all associated with Faubourg Tremé. By 1873 Alexandre Aristide Mary, Drausin B. Macarty, and Thomy Lafon owned $238,800 in property throughout the city, much of it leased to white citizens. Alexandre Aristide Mary, *homme de couleur*, described by Rodolph Desdunes in *Nos Hommes et Nos Histoire* as "wealthy, educated, and refined," inherited his money from his white father along with valuable real estate, much of it on Canal Street, as discussed in Volume II of *New Orleans Architecture: The American Sector*. He inherited so many commercial buildings from his father that he preferred to lease them rather than engage in the active real estate buying and selling.[107]

Mary was instrumental in the organizing in 1890 of the Comité des Citoyens. Comprised largely of Faubourg Tremé *gens de couleur*, it had eighteen members, with Arthur Esteves as president and C. C. Antoine as vice-president. Among the members were Rodolphe L. Desdunes; Numa E. Mansion, son of Lucien Mansion; and L. A. Martinet, founder of the *Daily Crusader*, which the organization used as official organ. The committee worked with two objectives in mind: to wage legal battle against discrimination and to create a public sentiment unfavorable to these injustices. On February 5, 1892, the Comité des Citoyens reported $2,767.25 collected toward a fund to test the constitutionality of the Jim Crow law. According to an advertisement in the *Crusader*, the Comité asked for donations to help it in its patriotic enterprise, which was to inaugurate judicial procedures to fight racism. Members listed were: C. Antoine, Firmin Christoph, Laurent August, Eugène Luscy, R. L. Desdunes, Alcée Labat, R. B. Baquet, M. J. Piron, L. J. Joubert, and others.[108]

Among their major endeavors was instigation of the far-reaching lawsuit *Plessy v. Ferguson*, led by Faubourg Tremé citizens Homère Plessy and Rodolphe Desdunes, with the financial backing of Mary. They lost the lawsuit which resulted in the establishment of the separate but equal doctrine as being permissible in public areas. Homère Plessy, a courageous man, was buried in his beloved Faubourg Tremé in the city's oldest cemetery, St. Louis I. His family continues to honor and use the tomb today. Thus it was the French-speaking Tremé citizens who championed changes for Negroes on the national level.

The accomplishments of Alexander P. Tureaud served as a finale in the civil rights field to the nineteenth-century *gens de couleur* of Faubourg Tremé. As a young man he left New Orleans for Washington, where he graduated from Howard University in 1925. A life-long resident of the creole suburbs, he lived at 1975 N. Rocheblave in 1927 when he was clerk for U.S. Comptroller of the Customs. He died at 3121 Pauger on January 22, 1972. Active in the civil rights movement from his law offices in the City Commons at 1821 Orleans, he repre-

sented numerous descendants of free woman of color Modeste Foucher in their claims to the $400,000 inheritance of Louise M. Laralde in 1938. Miss Laralde of Cincinnati was a granddaughter of Mme Foucher, free woman of color, and niece of Thomy Lafon.[109]

The post–Civil War infiltration into New Orleans of freed Negro slaves from the country brought major social and economic consequences to the *gens de couleur*. The new arrivals, Protestants and English-speaking, and the native *gens de couleur* were forced into an unstructured social condition with magnetic pulls of the past and pressures of the future. The French language, the higher degree of whiteness of the *gens de couleur*, their situation as property owners and taxpayers, as well as the financial and educational opportunities afforded them, resulted in a people entirely foreign to the country freeman. Role models for the *gens de couleur* were based on white relatives and neighbors. Freed slaves from postwar Louisiana and Mississippi had no time for roles; their needs were endemic. Immediate assistance was required, and the solutions came weakly through the government, through the church, and to a degree through mutual aid and benevolent associations.

In political and legal reality, the property-owning and once slaveowning Catholic *gens de couleur* after Reconstruction found themselves considered equivalent to the freed slaves in New Orleans. Louisiana legislative code number 111 of 1890 designated a person of any African ancestry as a Negro. This finalized a total change among the inhabitants of Faubourg Tremé. The war that resulted in freedom for slaves brought oppression to the former *gens de couleur libres*. They lost their white clients in all fields of business. Small businesses in the corner store-houses were barely able to operate, their customers being the poverty-stricken Negroes and Creoles of color who had lost their means of support. Real estate brokers lost their property.[110] Housing patterns were altered. Many *gens de couleur* lost their homes and began to rent, often from white Creoles who had moved out of French Quarter homes to the more modest frame cottages of Faubourg Tremé. Well-to-do white Creoles who had lived among the *gens de couleur* before the war moved away if they could, renting their run-down creole cottages and townhouses to freed slaves.

The mutual aid societies and benevolent associations that had long been established among the *gens de couleur libres* assumed a major role in efforts to solve these postwar social problems. The freedmen also formed parallel groups and associations. The societies provided insurance in the event of poverty, sickness, and death, since white insurance companies would not accept free persons of color as clients. The benevolent associations, therefore, were groups formed to blanket all social needs, including aid to asylums, schools, homes for the aged, and even burial expenses. These societies and associations also provided space, funds, and audience for brass bands and musicales, thus fostering the continuing development of musical tradition among *gens de couleur* and the former slaves.

La Société des Artesans, an organization of free colored mechanics, had been organized in 1834. Formed by colored war veterans ostensibly as a literary organization, it was also a group to study and address political conditions germane to their people. According to author Desdunes, the Société d'Economie was begun about the same time for more upper–class, professional, free persons of color who desired even more exclusiveness within their social set.[111] Les Jeunes Amis was organized in 1867, composed of French-speaking *gens de couleur*. The admission fee was $1 to $2 with 50¢ to $1 monthly dues. According to the constitution, no *placée* or mistress could be registered as a family member. In 1880 a domicile for Les Jeunes Amis was built at 1321 N. Robertson.

La Concorde was organized in 1878 by sixty-five *gens de couleur*. Between 1878 and 1884 the society paid $1,838 for burial expenses for fifty-five members, $2,453 in doctor and druggist fees, and $1,085 for pensions for aged and infirm members. They met at 159 Camp Street. Concorde Lodge #3 was domiciled in Perseverance Hall on St. Claude, which they rented for meetings on Tuesdays. The Perfect Union Hall, also known as the French Union Hall, was at N. Rampart and Dumaine. The Francs Amis met at 1420 N. Robertson.

Monied real estate brokers, factors, and merchants who were trained in the musical arts adjusted first as laborers and clerks, then combined these practical trades with professional musicology. Once the *gens de couleur*, schooled in classical music, had held formal musicales and concerts and were esteemed by the community as advocates of the most refined European musical traditions. Financial and social devastation ended their musical pursuits on this level. They clung to the past as Creoles of color, endeavoring to maintain their traditions. Some taught the classical music that they had learned in Europe before the Civil War. When the opportunity afforded, they accepted money to play at social engagements for white society. Ultimately, it was through music that the Creoles of color regained prestige in the compromising and changing ambience of late-nineteenth-century New Orleans. Paul Dominguez, a Creole violinist, who may have spoken Parisian French but broken English, explained:

You see, we Downtown people, we try to be intelligent. Everybody learn a trade, like my daddy was a cigarmaker and so was I. . . . We try to bar jail. . . . Uptown, cross Canal [Street] yonder, they used to jail. . . . There's a vast difference here in this town. Uptown folk all ruffians, cut up in the fact and live on the river. All they know is—get out on the levee and truck cotton—be long-shoremen, screwmen. And me, I ain't never been on the river a *day in my life*. . . . See, us Downtown people, we didn't think so much of this Uptown jazz until we couldn't make a living otherwise . . . they made a fiddler out of a violinist—*can* be a fiddler. If I wanted to make a living, I had to be rowdy like the other group. I had to jazz it or rag it or any other damn thing. . . . Bolden cause all that. He cause all these younger Creoles, men like Bechet and Keppard to have a different style altogether from the old heads like Tio and Perez. I don't know how they do it, but goddam, they'll do it. Can't tell you what's there on paper, but just play the hell out of it."[112]

A roster of the names and addresses of musicians who played in New Orleans dixieland, brass, and jazz bands between 1880 and 1915 indicates that well over half lived in the creole suburbs, primarily Faubourg Tremé.[113] Many of these Creoles of color were responsible for the recognition of jazz as a native New Orleans art form and as an international style of music and were descendants of well-known previously discussed property holders and *gens de couleur libres* of Faubourg Tremé.

Adams, Thomas, laborer, 2229 North Prieur
Alexander, Adolph, shoemaker, 1801 St. Philip
Baquet, George, laborer, 2126 Annette
Baquet, Theogene V., cigarmaker, 1820 Conti
Barbarin, Isidore, musician, 1750 St. Claude
Beaulieu, Paul W., carrier, Post Office, 1026 Burgundy
Bechet, Leonard, dentist, 1716 Marais
Boisseau, Joseph, musician, 413 North Roman
Brown, James, musician, 724 North Derbigny
Chaligny, Paul, tailor, 919 St. Claude
Collins, Walter, laborer, 322 North Galvez
Cottrell, Louis, musician, 1121 North Robertson
Cousteau, Sylvester, cigarmaker, 1446 North Derbigny
Decker, Sylvester, laborer, 238 South Basin
DeLille, Louis, musician, 1631 North Robertson
Dominguez, Paul, laborer, 1700 Elysian Fields
Dominique, Aniate (Natty), cigarmaker, 1723 Urquhart
Filhe, George, musician, 1704 Laharpe
Glenny, Albert, laborer, 1817 Marais
Jackson, Frank, laborer, 1529 Gasquet
Jeanjacques, Alcibiades, cigarmaker, 1413 North Villere
Keppard, Frederick, musician, 1813 St. Ann
Keppard, Louis, musician, 1813 St. Ann
Laine, Alfred, musician, 632 Port
Lyons, Robert, musician, 421 South Liberty
Martin, Louis, cigarmaker, 808 St. Claude
McCullum, George, sexton, 3514 South Liberty
Moret, George, cigarmaker, 1818 St. Anthony
Nicholas, Joseph, laborer, 2266 North Villere
Parker, William, laborer, 1905 Marais
Perez, Emanuel, musician, 1714 Urquhart
Phillips, Octave, laborer, 2237 Orleans
Picou, Alphonse, tinner, 1720 St. Philip
Piron, Albert L., artist, 1525 Columbus
Piron, Armand, musician, 1818 Columbus
Ray, Louis, laborer, 212 Port
Remy, Dominick (T-Boy), laborer, 1923 Bienville
Rena, Henry (Kid Rena), musician, 2032 Conti
Tillman, Cornelius, screwman, 2912 St. Philip
Tio, Lorenzo, painter, 1621 St. Bernard
Tio, Louis, cigarmaker, 1704 Laharpe
Vinet, Joseph, cigarmaker, 108 Annette
Williams, Norward (Gigi), porter, 1830 St. Philip

The Tio family appear as free persons of color in Faubourg Tremé by 1822. Luis and Lorenzo Tio, Sr., Creoles of color, were born in Mexico in 1863 and 1865 respectively. Their father, whose progenitors had come to New Orleans from Spain, may have emigrated to Mexico as a result of the Civil War. Both were graduates of the Mexico Conservatory of Music. They returned to New Orleans as music teachers, playing in the Excelsior Brass Band in the 1880s. Lorenzo lived at 1723 Kerlerec, with Marguerite his mother, the widow of Marcos Tio. He was listed as a cigarmaker at 301 N. Roman in the 1880s and 1890s. Lorenzo Tio, Jr., was born in New Orleans in 1884, growing up in Faubourg Tremé. By 1910 he was with the Onward Brass Band although he was also a concert musician under his father and Théogène V. Bacquet.[114]

The Bacquet family had three musicians playing in New Orleans brass bands. Théodule, or Théogène V. Bacquet, was born in New Orleans about 1858. He was a music teacher and the leader of the Excelsior Brass Band from about 1882 to 1904. His sons, George and Achille, made jazz history. Achille was born in 1885 at 312 Tonti and became a clarinet player.

His elder brother George was born in New Orleans in 1883. The three musicians lived together at 2002 Iberville by 1906. George lived at 1953 N. Miro by 1911.[115]

The Bechet brothers, Sidney and Leonard, were well-known Faubourg Tremé Creoles of color. Leonard, a dentist, was born in 1877 and played the trombone in his own Silver Bells Band. He lived at 1716 Marais Street. His brother Sidney was born in New Orleans in 1897 and played clarinet with his brother's band. He emigrated to France in the 1950s.[116]

Alphonse T. Picou was a celebrated clarinetist from the faubourg. He and his brothers Etiènne and Joseph rented creole cottages in the area most of their lives. Alphonse, born in 1880, supported himself as a tinner and lived variously at 1421 Orleans (1897), 912 N. Prieur (1899), 1660 N. Johnson (1906), 1630 N. Galvez (1907), and 1664 N. Johnson (1910). His musical career began in 1892 in a band led by Creole of color Bouboul Valentin.[117] Etiènne Picou was a barber by trade and Joseph a cigarmaker, typical professions for the Creoles of color in the 1890s.

The Domingues family produced two musicians raised in the creole suburbs. Paul, Sr., was born about 1865. He was a classical musician who played string bass with jazzmen. His son Paul, Jr., a barber by trade, was also a concert musician playing the violin and guitar; but he played with various jazz bands in the Storyville cabarets. He played with Louis Armstrong in 1923 at Andersons on Basin.[118]

Armand J. Piron was a barber and at least a second–generation musician, born in New Orleans in 1888. By 1908 he lived at 1523 Columbus with Milford Piron, a cigarmaker. His father was a successful music teacher and led the Piron-Gaspard Orchestra. Armand, his son, crippled by an accident when he was seven years old, studied violin and played with the Peerless Orchestra about 1912.[119]

Piron, like so many of the musicians who played creole music, moved frequently within the creole faubourgs. He was listed as a professional musician at 1818 Columbus in 1914, at 1734 Annette in New Marigny in 1923, back in Tremé at 1916 N. Prieur in 1925, and at 2117 Lapeyrouse in 1942 shortly before his death. Louis Nelson de Lille (Delisle), born January 28, 1885, in New Orleans, grew up in the Creole of color community and was related to Baptiste DeLille, a trombonist born in New Orleans about 1868.[120] They were descendants of early settlers in the area and at least share a name, if not a kinship, with the foundress of the Sisters of the Holy Family, Henriette Delille. Louis Delisle, known as Big Eye Louis Nelson, studied with the Tios.

Alcide Pavageau's name has also had a long association with Faubourg Tremé. In 1836 his family owned 1621 Dumaine, and in 1850 his relative Nelson Pavageau was listed as a forty-three-year-old mulatto tailor from the West Indies. Known as "Slow Drag" Alcide, he played the guitar and bass though he is best remembered as Grand Marshall of the Second Line.[121]

Louis Dumaine, born about 1898, shared the surname and neighborhood of the early-nineteenth-century planters of Bayou Road. A trumpet and cornet player, he taught music and played in the Tupelo Brass Band. He lived at 1924 and 2014 N. Rampart. Milford Dolliole, a descendant of the Dolliole family, was born in 1903. In the early 1920s he played the drum with the Young Tuxedo Orchestra. Daniel Desdunes, Rodolph's son who grew up at 928 Marais, became a musician and taught

music at Boys Town in Omaha, Nebraska. Clarence Desdunes, born in 1896, was also a concert-trained bandleader and with Armand Peron formed the Joyland Revelers.

There were over sixty well-known musicians from among the Creoles of color who lived and played in the creole suburbs between 1880 and World War I. Like most mentioned above, they were primarily tradesmen, such as barbers, cigarmakers, bricklayers, or coopers. Among familiar names is Octave Gaspard, born in 1870, both a cooper and concert pianist. He lived in a double house with his brother, Vic Gaspard, also a cooper, born in 1875 at 2022–28 Bourbon. Another brother, Ed Gaspard, played the bass drums for the Onward Brass Band before the Spanish–American War. Associated with the Gaspards during World War I was Raymond Glapion. Born in 1895, he was a member of a long established Tremé family and an educated musician.

George Guesnon, known as Creole George (1907–1968), was a musician and musicologist who preserved Gombo–French dialect songs. Sylvestre Coustat, born before the Civil War and dying in 1910, was a founding member of the Onward Brass Band and played in the dance band of his brother Manuel Coustat and Daniel Desdunes in 1890. He was a cigarmaker, living at 1446 N. Derbigny. Manuel Perez, a fine classical musician and teacher (1873–1946), organized the Imperial Orchestra in 1900 and lived at 1714 Urquhart. Joseph de la Croix Pierce (1904–1973) was known for his songs in Creole French. Henry (Kid) Rena (1898–1949) learned to play at the Waif's Home with Louis Armstrong.

Storyville, located in the Commons adjacent to Faubourg Tremé, presented an opportunity for struggling musicians to supplement their incomes. For many Creoles of color, according to musician Danny Barker, playing in Storyville meant a loss of status within their own community. "Ferdinand Le Menthe's [Jelly Roll Morton] grandmother kicked him out of the house when he was fifteen for playing in Storyville."[122]

Surrounding Storyville was an almost unbroken line of cabarets, dance halls, and honky tonks comprising the Tango Belt. Those having names and locations preserved in Faubourg Tremé are Abadie's (1906–1917), Marais and Bienville; Alley Cabaret (1920s), N. Claiborne and St. Bernard; Anderson's Annex (1901–1925), Basin and Iberville; Artesan Hall, 1460 N. Derbigny; and Big 25 (1902 to the late 1950s), Franklin (Crozat) and Iberville. A building at N. Villere and St. Ann was known variously as the Brown Derby, Gypsy Tea Room, and Japanese Gardens. Casino Cabaret at 1400 Iberville, Hope's Hall at 922 N. Liberty, Frank Early's (1909–1913) at Franklin and Bienville, Globe Hall at St. Claude and St. Peter, the Frolic (Top Hat) at St. Ann and N. Dorgenois, and the Frenchmen's (1900–1915) at N. Villere and Bienville were a few of many. There was a boxing arena at Conti and Burgundy called the Coliseum in the 1920s. Dixieland bands on wagons advertised prizefights and entertained in the arena; others evolved from the corner groceries and bars of the neighborhood.

Although marching bands of Creoles of color were active in Faubourg Tremé by the 1860s, it was in Storyville and the Tango Belt of the Commons and Tremé that both black, uptown, Protestant Negroes and downtown, formally educated, Catholic Creoles of color played. Here is where jazz developed its distinct identity. Louis Armstrong, a black man, was born and lived on the periphery of the neighborhood. He was born on Jane Alley between Gravier and Perdido and grew up at the Waif's Home at Canal Boulevard and City Park Avenue.[123] He met and played with Creoles of color both in the Waif's Home and in Storyville; fame found him on a Mississippi riverboat, and he blew his way into the heart of the world. Although he is buried away from his city, he is honored in New Orleans' Faubourg Tremé with an entire park.

It is not coincidental that Local 496 of the American Federation of Musicians was organized in Faubourg Tremé and was once housed on N. Claiborne at Columbus, where the jazzmen of New Orleans lived and played in the early twentieth century. The building is a fine, frame, two-story, Classic-style townhouse with a cast-iron gallery at the second level. It has been altered for commercial use at the first level but could easily be restored as a landmark to jazz.

Music was not the only art form by which Creoles of color preserved their traditions. Prior to the Civil War, the greatest literary achievement of these people was the 1845 publication of *Les Cenelles*, compiled by Armand Lanusse. The 210-page book contained poems by seventeen Louisiana Creoles of color.[124]

The nineteenth-century newspapers established by *gens de couleur* of Faubourg Tremé also provided a forum for the literary set and served as major organs of education and the promotion of political policy. The *Tribune* was published daily after October 4, 1864, the first Negro daily newspaper in the nation. It was until 1869 an official organ of the Louisiana Republican party. It was edited by Paul Trevigne, who lived in Faubourg Tremé; and Dr. Louis Charles Roudanez was a major contributor.[125] In 1850 Trevigne was a twenty-nine-year-old schoolmaster, a mulatto, who with his wife, Josephine Decoudreaux, owned 1608 Governor Nicholls.[126] In 1862 he started another newspaper, *L'Union*, a monthly published in French and English in an effort to communicate with both the French-speaking Creoles of color and the English-speaking freedmen of Louisiana.

The *Crusader*, another daily local newspaper founded by Creoles of color, was used for publicity by the Comité des Citoyens.[127] Rodolph Desdunes contributed to it from 1889 to 1898. Desdunes was among the first Creoles of color to publish memoirs about his fellow poets and other prominent free persons of color. His book *Nos Hommes et Notre Histoire* was published in Canada in 1911. Desdunes was born in New Orleans on November 15, 1849; his father Jeremiah was from Haiti, and his mother Henrieta was Cuban. He had two brothers: Pierre Aristide, a cigarmaker and poet, and Daniel, a prominent politician, social leader, and philanthropist.[128]

Rodolphe married Mathilde Chaval (probably a descendant of Tremé early settlers Pierre or Leándre Cheval). Their children were Wendell, Daniel, Coritza, Agnes, Lucille, and Jeanne.

They lived at 928 Marais. In 1879 Rodolphe was appointed a messenger at the U.S. Customs Service. In 1885 he lost his job, a political appointment, but he returned from 1891 to 1894. He retired, blind, in 1910 and is buried in the Desdunes family tomb in St. Louis Cemetery.[129]

Another well-known author Charles B. Roussève, a native of the Tremé area, wrote *The Negro in New Orleans* published in 1969. He was descended from J. B. Roussève, born January 2, 1820, the legitimate son of J. B. Roussève and Alexandrine Barbé. J. B. Roussève, Jr., died in 1841 at his mother's home on the corner of N. Rampart and Esplanade. Another Roussève, Ferdinand L., was born in 1904 and was educated in the New Orleans Catholic school system. He finished his education at Massachusetts Institute of Technology and became the first Negro architect registered in Louisiana.

The newspapers were largely backed by Aristide Mary and other leaders of the colored Creole community. Although few Creoles of color were active in the Republican party, one of the most outstanding was Tremé resident Antoine Dubuclet, state treasurer from 1868 to 1879. Dubuclet, an *homme de couleur libre* from Iberville Parish, was a sugar planter at his Dubuclet-Durand plantation, ninety-seven miles from New Orleans adjacent to Nottaway. He owned ninety-five slaves in 1850; and his property was valued at $206,400 in 1860, making him the largest slaveowner and richest planter from among the *gens de couleur* in the state. Between 1871 and 1873 he was also receiver of the State Land Office. His New Orleans residence was at old number 25 Robertson until he moved to 75 N. Rampart in 1874, now the 300 block; by 1876 he lived at 268 Canal.

Most of the *gens de couleur* who have been discussed were born and lived their entire lives in the Tremé area. Most also have found a final resting place in one of the three St. Louis cemeteries. Florville and Octave Foy, free men of color, were Marigny residents, but they were buyers and builders of Tremé property. They were also active workers in the monument business. Florville's name appears on many of the marble tablets of St. Louis Cemeteries I and II. His family tomb stands proudly on the main aisle of St. Louis II, square 2.

Another well-known sculptor of cemetery monuments of both St. Louis I and II was Eugène Warbourg, free man of color, born in New Orleans about 1825. His importance, however, reached far beyond Faubourg Tremé and New Orleans; he was recognized in France, Belgium, England, and Rome. He studied in New Orleans under a French artist, called Gabriel, and contracted for sculptures for the St. Louis Cathedral and the Hotel Grunewald-Hermann. He left New Orleans permanently in 1852, dying at thirty-six in Rome about 1861.[130]

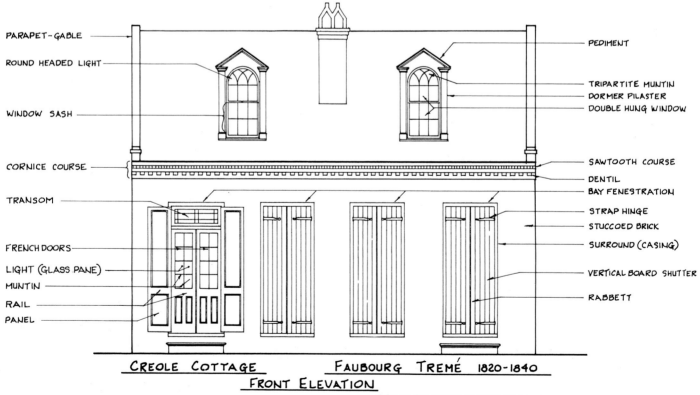

PARAPET-GABLE

ROUND HEADED LIGHT

WINDOW SASH

CORNICE COURSE

TRANSOM

FRENCH DOORS

LIGHT (GLASS PANE)

MUNTIN

RAIL

PANEL

PEDIMENT

TRIPARTITE MUNTIN
DORMER PILASTER
DOUBLE HUNG WINDOW

SAWTOOTH COURSE
DENTIL
BAY FENESTRATION
STRAP HINGE
STUCCOED BRICK
SURROUND (CASING)
VERTICAL BOARD SHUTTER
RABBETT

CREOLE COTTAGE   FAUBOURG TREMÉ 1820-1840
FRONT ELEVATION

DRAWN BY PETER M. TRAPOLIN

RESTORATION BY ANALOGY

Tremé House -Types and Styles

The description of the development of Faubourg Tremé, the tracing of the history of individual plantations, and the recording of the house-types and styles that distinguished each one make it readily apparant that there are thousands of historic structures of distinctive character. Even though there are no buildings of the monumental importance of the U.S. Customs House on Canal Street or the Old U.S. Mint on Esplanade Avenue, the 181 squares are worthy of national historic district distinction.

The entire area is predominantly residential, its dwellings small in scale, and builder designed and constructed. A few well-known nineteenth-century architects were active here, but essentially the neighborhoods were developed by black and white entrepreneurs and building companies. The architecture, which can be substantially differentiated according to type and style, is that of the average man. It is vernacular architecture, evolved from the French and the Spanish and adapted to the current mode of the time and locale. Because of the overall importance of this large residential space with its proximity to the Vieux Carré and the central business district, it should be seriously considered for protection against façade desecration, demolition, and tasteless intrusions.

Restoration by analogy is a term used herein to explain a common nineteenth-century building practice that is suggested as a proven method for recapturing the historical integrity of that bygone era. As in logic, analogy infers that certain admitted resemblances imply probable further similarities. Scores of creole cottages, townhouses, and shotguns were built as specific types. It is essential, therefore, that owners, contractors, and planners comprehend this system of parallellism and employ analogous examples in recycling the buildings for twentieth-century use. Faubourg Tremé's potential renaissance could be further enhanced by understanding the authors' definitions of restoration, renovation, and rehabilitation, as well as the methodology of achieving them.

Restoration is the process whereby a structure is returned to its original appearance. It can be an intentional and deliberate re-creation. Recognition of the original appearance and identification of the components is a requisite. Preservation of all original materials is an integral part of restoration, as is their reinstallation or replacement with reasonable facsimiles. The knowledge needed to reproduce may be acquired in several ways, but in the case of buildings in most areas of New Orleans, it can be accomplished by turning to analogous examples provided from available sources. These are to be found in nineteenth-century watercolor drawings, building contracts, auction notices, old photographs, and comparable extant houses. Analogy in the nineteenth century provided easy answers to otherwise difficult decisions; likewise it aids the twentieth-century owners' endeavor to recapture the fabric and spirit of another time.

The New Orleans Notarial Archives preserves over five thousand drawings of elevations and floor plans of specific New Orleans houses and commercial buildings sold at public auction. These watercolor drawings were commissioned by the sheriff as display advertisements and placed in auction exchanges. Architects, surveyors, and artists were hired to provide these renderings; and many notaries who passed the ensuing act of sale attached the drawing to that act.

These drawings were gathered and bound into 117 volumes, known today as plan books, by the Works Progress Administration in the late 1930s. The large drawings were placed indiscriminately, neither chronologically nor according to artist, notary, or geographical location. In 1953 Rudolph H. Waldo, an outstanding former custodian of notarial records, indexed these plan books according to district and municipal squares. Although the drawings were crudely glued and bound, they remain for researchers, scholars, and individuals as one of the greatest visual links to New Orleans' nineteenth-century architecture (figs. 1, A, B).

The Friends of the Cabildo have photographed in black and white all elevation drawings within the plan books and produced a card file with descriptions of the unphotographed plans. The Historic New Orleans Collection has photographed every folio (page) with elevations and plans within the 117 plan books in color and in black and white. A complete series of index cards describing in detail every attached auction notice, signature, and house description, replete with notes relative to color and architectural details, accompanies these photographs. These color slides of the drawings are accessible to researchers and easily reproduced by the Historic New Orleans Collection.

The tools for unraveling house information are well documented in *Researching the History of Your House* by Wayne M. Everard, available through the Louisiana Division of the New Orleans Public Library. The booklet stresses the importance of the title search, and lists every place and method for research. The reward of investigating a title could produce an attached building contract between the owner of the property and the architect or builder, a rare and valuable find. Sometimes the building contract is a general one, which nevertheless may contain some measurements. A contract that includes specifications along with elevations and attached floor plan can facilitate a more exact restoration.

The "Architectural Inventory" within this volume includes translations and extracts from contracts for houses of most types and styles; all can be helpful to restoration. Contracts give instructions as to *faux bois* (false wood) and *faux marbre* (false marble) treatment, painting methods and colors, treatment of lintels and sills, types of sashes and kinds of glass panes. Gallery railings, whether of iron or turned wood, are described. Measurements and materials for entrances, fanlights, plaster work, and millwork often are specified. When contracts do not give exact sizes of moldings or similar details of dormers,

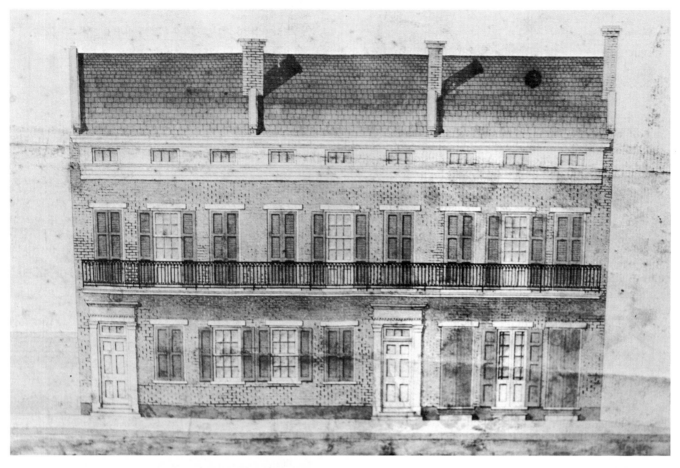

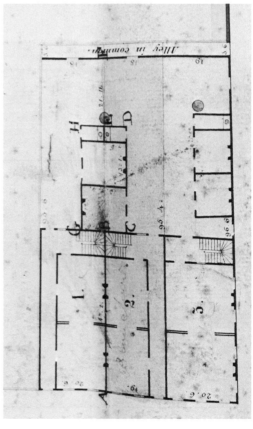

1, A,B. Plan book 84, folio 2, Bayou Road (Governor Nicholls), corner Tremé, backed by Barracks, Plauché (Marais). Still standing at 1301–05–07 Governor Nicholls.

entrances, etc., the practiced eye of the careful and knowledgeable designer can be responsive to the overall character of a building.

Although a building contract for the specific house to be restored may not be forthcoming, there are analogous ones for comparable houses. Because these contracts are often in French or Spanish, translators are essential. General information may be culled from reading a collection of contracts, available in translation within the Friends of the Cabildo's *New Orleans Architecture*, Volumes I-VI. If title research does not reveal a building contract, sometimes an inventory of an owner's estate indicates the floor plan and furnishings of each room.

Auction notices that appeared in the local newspapers also can facilitate restoration. When a house was to be sold at public auction or sheriff's sale, the sale was advertised three times over a two-week period in local newspapers both in French and English. After the ensuing auction, when the act of sale was passed, the notary often attached the newspaper notice to the act; some were also glued directly to the watercolor drawing made for the sale. These auction notices can be quite illuminating, and through them the floor plan and façade might be restored. For example, the Ganel townhouse at 1501 Dumaine appears today as a flat, boxlike structure without cornice, gallery, balcony, or correct three-bay fenestration. The *New Orleans Republican*, December 3, 1868, advertised the three-bay townhouse for sale, having on the ground floor, "hall, double parlors with sliding door, dining room and pantry under the staircase, three rooms above, two *cabinets* and balcony on the street, and two-story frame building in the yard of six rooms, paved yard, cistern, water works, privy, etc." In this case an archival drawing of the house also exists in plan book 1, folio 25. These are aids for both an interior and exterior restoration.

An 1879 newspaper description of the Bernard Villa at 1233 Kerlerec reveals information useful for garden replanting as well as room arrangement: "A large, frame, well-built, slate-roofed house with hall in centre, two parlors, dining room, two bedrooms, two rooms in attic, with four *cabinets*. A two-story frame, slate-roof building, having on first floor a kitchen, pantry, and stairway, two rooms, *cabinet*, and stair landing on the second floor, gas throughout, cistern, privy, brick yard, shed, etc.; fine orange and other fruit trees, ornamental trees, shrubs, water works."

The Charvet House at 1622 Dumaine appears today as a mutilated store-house with weatherboard front and large show window. Its 1901 estate sale by Bernard A. Kernan noted "a splendid frame, slate-roofed residence, with plastered front etc. . . . a rear building adjoining main house with two rooms, gallery on each floor, etc." The front and rear elevations and floor plan can be restored via this auction notice.

Old photographs of many New Orleans buildings are preserved in the vertical files of the various libraries. Diligent research or advertising for old photographs often uncovers them in private collections. General street-scene photographs also serve to illuminate former building appearances. No matter how incomplete or mutilated a photograph might be, it serves as a building record frozen in time.

Two 1970 photographs of 1400–08 Bayou Road (Governor Nicholls) reveal an already altered, common-wall creole cottage (figs. 2, A,B). The photographs indicate that the present mansard roof of the building was not original; indeed, it is out of character and is a roof-type never employed in the area until after 1870. The photographs indicate weatherboarded gabled ends, having a slight cant. Three dormers are proper for this size gabled roof and were placed at both the front and rear elevations. Brick chimneys also should be reinstalled. The Governor Nicholls Street façade was of plastered brick with two rows of cornice decoration, one sawtooth and one of

dentils. The Marais Street side of the cottage had been replaced with concrete bricks by the time of the 1970 photograph, but its restoration could be accomplished by copying the opposite original side or by using another extant corner creole store-house as a guide. Its front should be of plastered brick with six casement openings with shutters. The 1970 photograph shows batten shutters with strap hinges, which have been repaired or copied correctly, and French doors with four pairs of lights above solid panels. Wrought-iron grill transoms, if original, indicate commercial use.

Nineteenth-century designer-builders often availed themselves of published catalogs and pattern books similar to the local Robert's catalogs first published in 1857. These builders' guides were particularly popular during the period following the Civil War; but as early as the 1830s, façade millwork could be ordered from local sash,

2, 2A, 2B. A 1969 photograph, illustrates the building at 1400–08 Bayou Road (Governor Nicholls) prior to further 1970s alteration. 2B indicates the appearance of rear elevation before removal of the roof and dormers.

111

door, and blind factories. Thus, one street might have twenty houses with Greek Key entrances ordered within the same decade from catalogs. A door of a particular type and style might grace every entrance of a block, though the houses were built for separate owners.

Since building by analogy was the norm in the nineteenth century, careful observation of houses similar to the one to be restored is beneficial. Once the building-type and style are understood, a module can be fashioned from the combination of appropriate facets. As early as 1811 a building contract was signed between John Wolfe, carpenter, and Joseph Quegles to build a "brick-between-posts mansion house similar to that of P. T. L. Godefroy" who resided in 1810 at the corner of Bayou Road and the Ramparts (1100 block side of Governor Nicholls, house now demolished). This is one of the earliest analogous examples of buildings found in Faubourg Tremé. An 1855 building contract that exemplifies the continuing nineteenth-century custom applies to the townhouse at 1212 Barracks (now mutilated), where builder Nicholas Duru agreed to build

> a house and kitchen of two stories just like the one occupied by M. Jourdain on St. Bernard Avenue with the exception of the front gallery. . . . The balcony will be 4 feet wide, with a cornice according to the plan. The house to measure 42 feet by 21½ feet. Inside to be the same as the Jourdain house except louvered shutters on the first floor. The outside may be painted in white or color of taste of proprietor, but shutters and exteriors to be a beautiful green. House to be raised 2 feet off ground. Cast-iron balcony with pilasters supported by iron bars and crowned with capitals and a beautiful cornice. Between the pilasters there will be cast-iron or wood.

If a valid house-type has been altered and restoration seems desirable, particularly for the front elevation, it can be planned and executed after a study of the proportions, including those of all openings. These are extremely important to reconstitute. Measured drawings, based on scale proportions of the archival drawings, will provide clues to exact architectural details, such as roof height, cornice treatment, bay spacing, and the size and placement of shutters and steps. These details may also be secured by following the list of house-types included herein with analytic comment. Because of the restorer's purist intent, close documentation of the building's construction should be made. This includes, wherever possible, identifying and dating evolutionary alterations and additions to the structure. It is through this method that a decision to return to the original building date may be mediated to retain some changes. Restoration, therefore, differs from both renovation and rehabilitation, although elements of each are included.

Renovation is the task of house renewal. It is synonymous with remodeling; and when sensitively done it should incorporate restoration of the façade and retention of extant original features, millwork, mantels, and decorative detail. Renovation for an adaptive use can be consistent or inconsistent with the original property use. With extreme renovations, a building's interior and exterior spaces often are reorganized as part of the remodeling. Exterior work may produce an alteration of façade doors and windows; this is regrettable, as is the introduction of materials and forms incompatible with historic integrity. Additional space secured by closing in galleries and balconies is abhorrent; correct solutions again may be found in observation of wing treatment found on similar houses among the archival drawings. All original façade openings must be maintained or reconstructed. They may be permanently closed by hinged shutters, but the proportions of the façade are defaced if they are filled in, shortened, or altered.

Today any renovation of a preindustrial residential structure almost invariably introduces features, such as plumbing or central heating, that depart from the original conditions. The tendency is to make these as unobtrusive as possible. For each particular case there may be several possible solutions, depending on the program of adaptive use. As a general rule, particularly where there have been crude, makeshift changes, it is preferable to return at least to the exterior appearance of the building. There are instances where decorative modifications of the original appearance—for example, Victorian jigsaw ornament on a Greek Revival building—represent interesting interim phases that become built-in evidences of historic changes.

In restoration, renovation, and rehabilitation, exterior paint color selection is important. Archival drawings again are extremely useful. Trim, foundation splash (course), and shutter colors are depicted, as are roof colors and finishes for railings.

Rehabilitation suggests the act of putting a structure into good condition, thereby meeting city building codes. Electrical and plumbing requirements are determined after inspection. Roof, gutters, walls, steps, and foundations are checked for safety conditions, as are windows and interior surfaces. Little or no major reconstruction is involved; however, painting often is.

Rehabilitation usually involves short-term goals of making a dwelling livable. It may include faulty renovation practices, such as the replacement of front steps with large concrete landings framed by ornate, incongruous, iron railings. Aluminum windows and siding often are substituted, unfortunately, for original wood sash and six-inch cypress weatherboard siding. Tasteful compromise for economy is possible; it is practical because destruction of exterior features important to the building's truths reduces the future monetary value of the building.

Tremé House-Types

Faubourg Tremé exhibits over a dozen mutations of six major house-types; the full gamut of nineteenth-century decorative styles is represented. Each type in its original plan had probity of proportion; and through scale, texture, and overall massing it produced neighborhoods with identifiable characteristics. The creole cottage with its multitudinous variations is the most abundant type. Other house-types include the one- and two-level side-hall house, the center-hall villa, and the shotgun.

Creole cottages may be divided into at least ten modifications of type within Faubourg Tremé, many exemplifying the development period of a former plantation or a city subdivision. Whether galleried, set at the banquette or back on the lot, whether with side-gabled roof, hip-roof, or a combination of the two, the floor plan, the garden, and kitchen placement retain a similar and interpretive pattern. The standard form is the four-bay creole cottage, with openings evenly spaced across the façade, and four rooms within, of equal or similar size, two across the front and two across the back. Two chimneys providing four interior fireplaces frequently are placed between double dormers, one in front and one in the rear roof slopes. To the rear there is usually a gallery up to ten feet wide with *cabinets* (small rooms). A house width of twenty-eight feet balancing a forty-foot depth, which includes a rear gallery between *cabinets* leading to a rear courtyard, is a prototype.

A kitchen may have been set across the rear of the lot parallel to the main house or placed midway, producing a courtyard between the house and kitchen. Plan book 77, folio 9 illustrates a house set back on the narrow lot with front gardens (fig. 3). Beyond the house was a courtyard with a cistern and kitchen building, followed by its *potager* (kitchen garden); both house and kitchen have side gables. A detached kitchen was often placed along a side property line; and after mid-century, these separate buildings often were attached to the rear of the main house. (Many cottages and kitchens have been altered with wraparound front and side additions; others were demolished when their lots were resubdivided.)

The most common type of creole cottage is detached, built at the banquette, with gables at the sides, double dormers, and a front overhang or *abat-vent*. Dating primarily from the 1840s like the one illustrated in plan book 99, folio 3, these abound throughout the entire area but are most characteristic of the vicinity between N. Rampart and N. Claiborne, Dumaine and Esplanade, the first Morand-Moreau-Tremé plantation (fig. 4). Outstanding surviving examples are 1317, 1431–33, 1529 Ursulines and 1505 St. Philip. Such cottages may be constructed of frame, brick, brick between posts as in plan book 86, folio 46, or a combination of these (fig. 5). The façade may be marked by four long casement doors or two long single doors with two short windows. The doors may be centered or placed at the corners. An arrangement of alternating doors and windows was also commonly employed.

Although the decade of the 1840s saw the heaviest development of Faubourg Tremé's creole housing, fine examples remain from the 1830s and earlier. Plan book 40, folio 11 illustrates 1037 N. Rampart, an 1820s house, as it appeared when auctioned in 1845 (fig. 6). In plan book 84, folio 46, a drawing dating from 1838 depicts another cottage that dates from the 1820s or early 1830s (fig. 7). The outstanding feature of the latter is the *faux marbre* treatment of the entire façade. (The cost factor of duplicating this nineteenth-century affectation may be prohibitive.)

The earlier the date of the house, usually, the smaller the dormer proportions. In most cases, roundheaded dormer lights denote an 1830s building date whereas small, segmental-arched dormers spring from either the 1820s or the previous century.

Another variant cottage still standing is 1719–21 St. Ann near N. Claiborne. Plan book 94, folio 46 shows this 1839 cottage with batten shutters that have panels on the inside (figs. 8,A). The steps are enclosed in paneled boxes. The plastered façade is painted grey, matching the slate roof. The Terence Cousin House at 1231 Marais Street, dating from the 1830s, is an outstanding single-family creole cottage, showing American influence with a single Greek Key entrance and three double-hung windows, an unusual arrangement.

Comparison of a gabled roof, as seen in plan book 4, folio 8, to that of an extant house at 1114 Barracks illustrates the proportions possible in a creole cottage (figs. 9,10). A beak roofline seen at Conti, corner N. Prieur, differs in profile from the slightly canted roof at

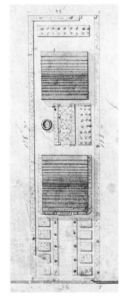

3. Planbook 77, folio 9.

4. Plan book 99, folio 3, St. Philip, corner Marais, backed by Tremé, Dumaine, demolished; signed and dated "September 30, 1880, Louis H. Pilié, deputy city surveyor." This 1880 drawing depicts a standard 1840s Faubourg Tremé cottage. Hundreds of these dormered houses line the streets. This one, constructed of brick between posts, has a scored plaster façade finish; the corner boards indicate that the gable sides are covered with weatherboards. Each side has a covered balcony on the gabled ends. Two casement openings have no transoms, and the cypress is grained to resemble oak. The plastered, pedimented dormers have square-headed lights in the sash windows; these, with the enlarged dormer size, are also sings of the 1840s decade. The overhang is supported by wrought-iron bearers, traditional to brick and brick-between-posts construction.

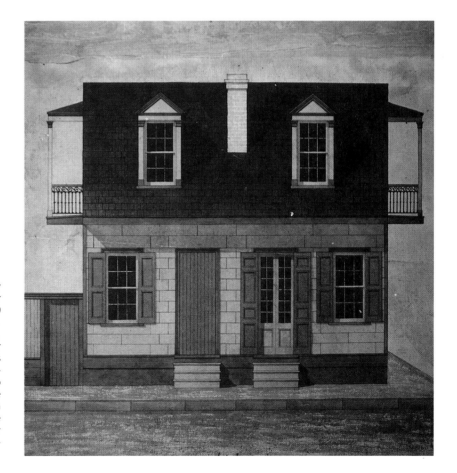

5. Plan book 86, folio 46, Rampart between Hospital (Bayou Road, Governor Nicholls) and Barracks, backed by St. Claude, demolished; drawing signed and dated "January 26, 1866. A. Persac." Adrien Persac depicted the brick-between-post construction of this simple cottage. The boarded gable sides contrast with the plastered front elevation. Vertical board shutters have plain battens rather than panels. Yellow ochre paint with Paris green shutters and off-white woodwork is a common color combination for such houses.

2035 Governor Nicholls (figs. 11,A). Gable-sided cottages may have incorporated front and rear overhangs, semi-incorporated ones, or an appended *abat-vent*. The roofline may be straight, have a double pitch toward the roof ridge or toward the overhang, or may terminate with a graceful cant.

The creole cottages between Esplanade and St. Bernard avenues from N. Rampart to N. Galvez streets, covering the former Milne, Guerlain, Duchamp, and Castanedo holdings, were generally of a more modest character than those upriver between Esplanade Avenue and Toulouse Street in Faubourg Tremé. Built as rental units in the 1840s and 1850s, many of them are of flatboat-board construction, covered with weatherboards. Others are brick-between-posts or brickbats-between-posts constructions, but they appear as frame buildings because of weatherboard siding. Entire blocks of these were built by single speculators, investors, or builders; and hundreds remain today.

Draftsman Eugène Surgi made especially picturesque, and sometimes picaresque, drawings of street scenes with rows of these frame creole cottages. Plan book 21, folio 27 shows two rows in a square

in the Commons as they appeared in 1844 (figs. 12, A). Many blocks on the right side of Esplanade and in Faubourg Hagan are lined with such houses like those of the 1500 block of N. Villere (fig. 13). If restored to the correct fenestration, with shutters and simple wood or precast concrete steps, the blocks of such houses would present a charming nineteenth-century neighborhood. Many such houses have lost chimneys, and most do not have original slate roofs or wooden picket fences. Brick sidewalks often remain, as do some granite curbings. Although the façades of these rows are quite simple, repetitive, and anonymous (like those seen in plan book 88, folio 7), the original service buildings and detached kitchens, courtyards and rear galleries introduce variation in proportion, scale, and decoration (fig. 14).

The detached kitchen is an essential part of the creole cottage complex. Often it has as many square feet as the main house. Most often it is situated facing a parterred garden and *cabinet* gallery of the main house, an area of aesthetic importance. Sometimes entire rows of two-story, gable-sided, or pitched-roof kitchens were built with common walls, like the remnant at 1505 St. Ann (fig. 15). Arched openings with stairwells, second-level galleries with turned

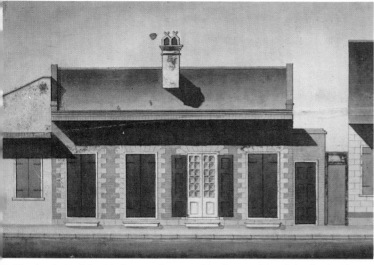

6. Plan book 40, folio 11, Rampart between Ursulines and St. Philip, backed by St. Claude, still standing; signed and dated "April 3, 1845, Pueyo and Cosnier." Exposed brick contrasting with masonry texture forming the opening surrounds distinguish this unusual creole cottage dating from the 1820s. The low elevation of the house, one step from the banquette, and ten small glass panes or lights in each side of the French doors are visible clues to the early date of the house, a date verified by conclusive title research. The cottage has brick gabled ends and central chimneys at the front and rear elevations.

7. Plan book 84, folio 46, St. Philip between N. Robertson, N. Claiborne, backed by Dumaine, demolished; drawing signed and dated "December 14, 1839, J. A. Pueyo." The small proportions, four French doors, small dormer with segmental-arched lights beneath the usual pediments, and the *abat-vent* or overhang treatment suggest that this creole cottage might date from the 1820s. The *faux granite* color scheme presented in this archival drawing makes it a valuable documentary.

8. Plan book 94, folio 46, St. Ann near N. Claiborne, backed by Dumaine, still standing, unsigned and undated. Title research verified the 1839 building date of this extant brick cottage at 1719–21 St. Ann. Outstanding architectural details include the boxed step enclosures, rectangular foundation ventilators, paneled pattern on the batten shutters seen on those that are opened, proportion of the arched lights on the dormers, and the parapet gable ends. Relatively large glass panes, three on each French door panel, are more typical of the 1840s when larger panes of French glass were available.

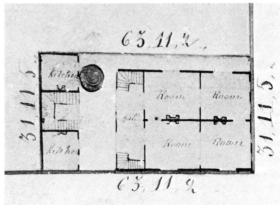

9. Plan book 4, folio 8, St. Philip, corner of St. Claude, backed by Tremé and Dumaine, demolished; drawing signed and dated "March 9, 1869, J. Strehler." The side elevation indicates a wide, tall creole cottage with a built-in overhang and canted roofline at the front with a narrower overhang and slight cant at the rear elevation. As with most Faubourg Tremé creole housing, the front elevation of flushboard or plastered finish contrasts with weatherboard sides. Although the house is located at a corner, the side elevation has double-hung windows with protective iron grills as well as vertical board shutters with panels; often a side elevation at a corner has casement openings. The detached kitchen of two stories is of wood with the usual second-level built-in gallery supported by box columns. Two chimneys and a skylight may be seen at the roof. The plan indicates double occupancy.

10. 1114 Barracks. Front cant to gable may be seen.

columns or pillars, batten shutters, original roofs, and painted plaster may be found in kitchens hidden in Faubourg Tremé, like the one at 1100 N. Rampart (fig. 16). Sometimes the original *maison de maître* has been demolished or burned, as noted on the lot at 925 N. Robertson with its 1839 kitchen shielded from view behind a newer house (fig. 17). The kitchen was often built of brick with a slate roof, a fire preventive measure (as seen in plan book 5, folio 11), although the house that it served may have been of frame construction with a wooden roof (fig. 18). Many existing brick kitchens show evidence of terra-cotta, yellow ochre, or salmon-colored paint, with Paris green or deep aqua-colored trim and shutters.

Galleried Creole Cottages

Rarest of all creole cottage types in Faubourg Tremé today is that designed with a front gallery. Rural by nature, examples usually represent the earliest cottages along the Road to the Bayou. They once constituted most of those identified in the period building contracts as the *maisons de maître*. The construction of front-galleried houses, also known as *maisons principales*, began in the early eighteenth century and continued as a popular idiom into the 1870s. The Martinez-O'Brien House at 1717 Kerlerec Street, dating from 1842, is a two-room plus *cabinet* gallery variation (figs. 19, A). There are fewer than twenty documented galleried creole cottages in Faubourg Tremé.

Notable examples remain at 2418 Laharpe, 927 N. Galvez, and 1505–07 N. Prieur, which dates from 1841 (fig. 20). The Marrioneaux *maison de maître* at 2218 Dumaine also shows the continuing popularity of the galleried creole cottage in the mid–nineteenth century. This house has three handsome dormers and a *cabinet* gallery with original railings. Also galleried in the late Classic style is 2307–09 Iberville, built after 1867, which contrasts well with 2409–11 D'Abadie, a modest frame example with 1890s period jigsaw work decorating the gallery.

The traditional usage of the creole cottage was as a single or double residence. However, the four corners of many squares in Faubourg Tremé held store-houses, the ground levels reserved for commercial use. Creole cottages made handsome store-houses, with the first level devoted to taverns, bakeries, booteries, or sweetshops.

11. Conti corner Prieur. Weatherboard on all elevations, low side gables, front beak-roof, and simplicity of style of this dormerless cottage is a model that is repeated block after block in Faubourg Hagan and to the right side of Esplanade. Most, like this, have a small, one-story detached kitchen with gable sides.

11A. 2035 Governor Nicholls. The drop-siding may postdate the original construction of this creole cottage, but it is an appropriate finish. Wear reveals the bricks of the chain wall at the foundation. Beneath the louvered shutters, not original but suitable, are four casement openings.

12, 12A. Plan book 21, folio 27, Orleans and St. Peter in square bound by Orleans, Tremé, Marais, and St. Peter; drawings signed and dated "May 23, 1844, Eugène Surgi."

13. 1501–05–09–13 N. Villere. The scale, beak-roof lines, opening arrangements, and chimney placement make this row an attractive part of the nineteenth-century neighborhood. Reinstallation of original-style doors, batten shutters, and missing chimney as well as repainting, would rejuvenate the group, creating a street scene similar to that seen in the 1844 Surgi drawings (figs. 12, 12a).

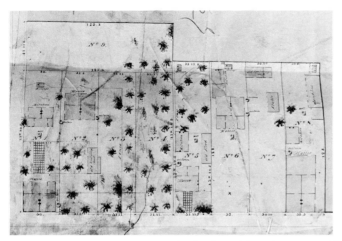

14. Plan book 88, folio 7, between N. Villere and Kerlerec, backed by N. Robertson, demolished; drawing signed and dated "February 16, 1856, Arthur C. de Armas, deputy surveyor general." Variations of textures seen on shutters, picket fences, weatherboard, slate, and brick combine with repetition of shapes in the beak-roofs, gable sides, and opening rectangles to create an abstract composition encompassing entire blocks.

15. 1505 St. Ann. This kitchen was once part of a common-wall row that extended across lots containing a group of 1830s creole cottages. The second-level gallery has almost disappeared. However, central stairwell arches, blue-green batten shutters with strap hinges, terra-cotta-colored plaster over soft bricks, and some beaded boards remain to indicate the quality of this kitchen.

16. 1100 N. Rampart. A view from Ursulines Street of an outstanding kitchen that served an early cottage on N. Rampart. Brickwork on the chimney, at the parapet ends, and the splayed-brick lintels of the openings are indications of the fine quality of the building. Wood colonettes and square balusters defined the second-level gallery at one time.

17. 925 N. Robertson. This photograph shows the second level of an 1820s or 1830s kitchen on a lot that has lost the original cottage. Colonettes or box columns and railings have been replaced with two-by-four boards. Some shutters and transoms have been removed. Notwithstanding these and other alterations, the parapet ends, fenestration arrangement, and building proportion bespeak a handsome edifice.

18. Plan book 5, folio 11, St. Ann between N. Claiborne, N. Robertson, backed by Dumaine, demolished; drawing signed and dated "June 1873, Strehler." Slender colonettes, a delicate arched opening at the second level, and a small pilastered dormer date this sophisticated kitchen from the 1820s or 1830s.

The attic or dormer level was, and still is, used as a residence, usually for the proprietors. Over thirty creole cottage store-houses like those at 1529–33 Ursulines and 1532 St. Philip Street merit restoration by analogy. The archival drawing in plan book 74, folio 16, offers an excellent example of such a structure in 1860 when E. Surgi and.A. Persac depicted a bakery on Conti at the corner of N. Villere Street (fig. 21).

Common-Wall Creole Cottages

Common-wall creole cottages are quite unusual, and the existing examples are handsome. Most creole cottages are detached buildings with narrow, guttered walkways on one or both sides that lead to the rear courtyard. Plan book 2, folio 2 illustrates a pair of common-wall creole cottages with brick-gabled parapet ends (fig. 22). A common-wall row dating from the 1840s is seen at 1300–06 St. Claude, corner of Barracks (fig. 23). Most were designed utilizing Classic-style traditions with sophisticated millwork, as seen in plan book 85, folio 23 (figs. 24, A).

Common-roof creole cottages with a central dogtrot passageway are found in great numbers in Faubourg Hagan and once were plentiful in the City Commons. They are rare in other sections of the city. Plan book 51, folio 20 illustrates one like those that once lined Iberville, Bienville, Conti, and Orleans and the cross streets between N. Claiborne and N. Broad (figs. 25, A). Most date from the mid–nineteenth century, with the earliest constructed in 1841 soon after Faubourg Hagan was laid out. Nearly all are designed in the Classic or Greek Revival style. Hundreds are detailed with Greek Key surrounds, small box steps, two full-length openings, and two double-hung short windows on a frame, side-gabled house. These are divided in the center by a dogtrot or ground-level passageway. The

19. 1717 Kerlerec. This galleried 1842 creole cottage is one of the few in Faubourg Tremé that has been renovated. Designed and built by Pierre Théodule Olivier, free colored builder, for his sister and her husband, Charles Martinez, the cottage represents the two-room and rear *cabinet* gallery floor plan variation of the type. It is decorated in the Classic style,

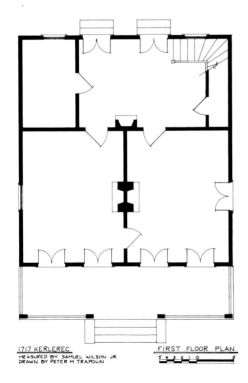

1717 KERLEREC
MEASURED BY SAMUEL WILSON JR.
DRAWN BY PETER M TRAPOLIN

FIRST FLOOR PLAN
5 4 3 2 1 0   5

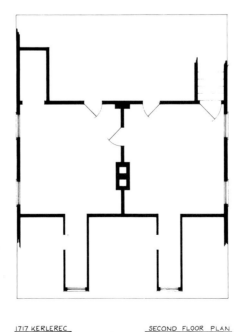

1717 KERLEREC
MEASURED BY SAMUEL WILSON JR.
DRAWN BY PETER M TRAPOLIN

SECOND FLOOR PLAN
5 4 3 2 1 0   5

20. 1505–07 N. Prieur. Galleried creole cottage.

21. Plan book 74, folio 16, Conti, corner Villere, backed by St. Louis and Marais, demolished; drawing signed and dated "January 16, 1860, E. Surgi, and A. Persac." This street scene typifies numerous Faubourg Tremé corners. A hip-roof, one-level corner store-house is seen in front of a two-level frame kitchen with gallery. Beside the store-house may be seen the brick parapet of a gabled, dormered creole cottage.

entrance doors have double, oval, glazed panels above rectangular or oval, lower wood panels; above the doors are matching glazed transoms. The majority of existing cottages in the area do not have dormers. Sometimes the dogtrot appears in common-roof multiples, as illustrated in the 1866 drawing of the row at N. Prieur and Canal, plan book 41, folio 19 (fig. 26). An outstanding row of three remains at 315–319–323 N. Miro, as illustrated in the chapter on Faubourg Hagan.

Two-Bay Creole Cottages

Two-bay versions of the creole cottage were built having two rooms, one behind the other, with a gallery or *cabinet* to the rear.

The traditional detached kitchen is found beyond a courtyard that contributes the space necessary to adapt such houses to modern use. These cottages, because of their unusual proportions, are rare and have special charm. Most have high, gabled sides with a single front and rear dormer. Nearly all are decorated in the Greek Revival style and date from the 1840s and 1850s. Excellent examples may be seen at 1308 St. Claude (figs. 27,28), 1518 N. Robertson, 1227 and 1819 St. Philip, and in the 1400 block of Columbus Street. Plan book 5, folio 1 shows another two-bay creole cottage that in 1858 stood on St. Peter Street (fig. 29). Plan book 90, folio 14 illustrates an example demolished for Louis Armstrong Park; it shows one gabled end, with the opposite side sloping in a steep hip-roof (fig. 30).

22. Plan book 2, folio 2, N. Derbigny between Customhouse (Iberville), Bienville backed by N. Claiborne, demolished; drawing signed and dated "September 25, 1854, De Armas." This handsome, common-wall, brick creole cottage features stepped gable ends, each having a pair of chimneys. Still standing at 1300 St. Claude is a similar masonry pair of common-wall creole cottages (fig. 23). Loss of original doors and shutters and alteration of fenestration are temporary mutations that might be restored.

23. 1300–04–06 St. Claude. This common-wall creole cottage at the corner of Barracks dates from 1847. Restraint in decoration is characteristic of the Classic period, and here the only evident motifs are cap-molded lintels and standard pilastered, pedimented dormers.

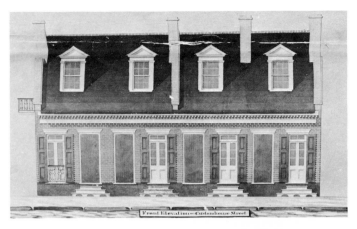

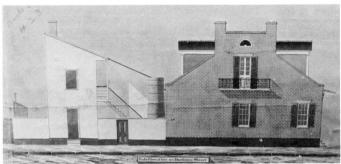

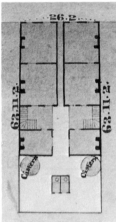

24,A. Plan book 85, folio 23, Customhouse (Iberville) corner N. Derbigny, backed by N. Claiborne, Bienville, demolished; signed and dated "June 12, 1854, Hedin and Schlarbaum." Numerous archival drawings show now-demolished common-wall creole cottages in the Commons and Faubourg Hagan. The building type was more prevalent there than elsewhere in Faubourg Tremé. This complex is a handsome reflection of the type, decorated in the Classic style of the late 1840s. The steps are unusual, each riser diminishing in size; and they appear to be of marble. Vertical board shutters, paneled on the inside, are not hung with strap hinges. The casement openings have three glass panes on each side above a solid panel. Each pair has a simple transom divided by one muntin. The narrow opening surrounds of wood are recessed and surmounted by molded cornices. Three projecting courses of brick-below-brick lintels form a distinguished cornice. The foundation bricks are exposed, the front elevation is finished with red paint and penciling to suggest hard northern brick, and the chimneys are of yet another brick. Well-proportioned, standard, pilastered, pedimented dormers with double-hung windows pierce the roof at both front and rear elevations. Double chimneys on gabled ends and between are important design elements. The detached two-story kitchens are frame with beak-roof and built-in gallery.

25,A. Plan book 51, folio 20, N. Villere between Common, Gasquet (Cleveland), backed by Marais, demolished; drawing signed and dated "February 9, 1856, C. A. Hedin." The dogtrot, double creole cottage was built extensively in the decades of the 1840s, 1850s, and 1860s in the City Commons and Faubourg Hagan. The distinguishing feature is a narrow opening having a door or lattice screen that opens directly onto the banquette. Within is a narrow flagged and guttered walkway leading to a rear courtyard or service area of the complex. The majority are of frame construction, weatherboarded on four elevations, having a combination of doors and short, double-hung windows. The doors may be casement, but most are single doors with either a Greek Key surround or a similar one without the dog ear. Most such houses found in the area have no dormers.

26. Plan book 41, folio 19, N. Prieur, corner Canal backed by Customhouse (Iberville), N. Johnson, demolished; drawing signed and dated "August 15, 1866, Paul Charles Boudousquie." Common-roof, dogtrot rows similar to this group may be found throughout Faubourg Hagan. They began to be built in the 1840s, but the idiom continued as a popular rental housing investment through the 1860s. Five small units face N. Prieur with a garden area on Canal that abutted a two-story, Classic-style, single-family dwelling.

27, 28. 1308 St. Claude, Cottage and Kitchen. The two-bay creole cottage retains its original features, including a masonry, pitch-roof, two-story kitchen across the rear of the lot. The façade is entirely outlined in a course of projecting plaster. A Classic-style cornice may be seen beneath the overhang, which is appended in the old style. The pilastered, pedimented dormer has arched lights complete with arched, louvered shutters that contrast with batten shutters on the side elevation. The cottage is set low to the ground, two steps off the banquette, and the brick chimneys rise high from one sharply angled parapet gable. The kitchen completes a sculptural presentation of the complex. Replacement of the roof parapet, repair of the overhang, and replacement of box columns and railing would restore the exterior to its 1830s appearance.

29. Plan book 5, folio 1, St. Peter between N. Derbigny and N. Claiborne, backed by Carondelet Walk (Lafitte Avenue), demolished; signed and dated "A. Castaing, December 2, 1858." The two-bay variation of the creole cottage type most often has gabled sides and a single dormer at front and rear elevations. Greek-Revival or Classic-style decoration is the norm.

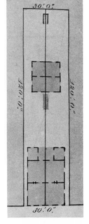

30. Plan book 90, folio 14, St. Philip between Tremé, Marais, backed by Dumaine, demolished; drawing signed and dated "December 28, 1877, A. Toledano." The two-bay creole cottage may have a hip-roof, gabled sides, or like this one, a parapet gabled side at the property line with a hip-roof opposite. The floor plan indicates three rooms, one behind the other, an unusual central chimney, and a two-room service wing extending from the rear of the house. Like most such cottages, it has Classic-style decoration, here a dentiled cornice. Note the absence of millwork around the slightly recessed opening surrounds.

Three-Bay Creole Cottages

The three-bay creole cottage appeared as a result of Anglo-American influence on the local architecture. A full-length entrance beside two short windows, or three evenly-spaced casement openings, heralded the arrival of the entrance hall or semi-hall in creole architecture. 1313 Ursulines is the earliest documented example in Faubourg Tremé, dating from the 1830s. Most three-bay cottages are located in the Pontalba and Griffon divisions, between N. Claiborne and N. Galvez, on the left side of Bayou Road. Most have large, single dormers front and rear, Greek Key entrances, and two double-hung windows. Some, like 1143 Marais, have one brick side and one weatherboard side (fig. 31). Others, like 1249 Kerlerec, have recessed side galleries behind the entrance door rather than a hall or anteroom. The Labranche cottage at 1217 Kerlerec has an 1868 building contract, which could prove useful for other restorations of three-bay creole cottages. An exceptionally large, three-bay cottage in the Greek Revival style, with a large box overhang and a deeply recessed entrance, is seen at 1450 N. Johnson. It dates from the 1870s. An Italianate entrance on a masonry façade with two 3-quarter-length windows characterizes 1016 N. Roman. There are fewer than thirty 3-bay creole cottages in Faubourg Tremé. Three-bay creole cottages with high hip-roofs are usually in the Greek Revival

31. 1143 Marais. Greek Revival in style, this three-bay creole cottage has a brick front, one brick parapet gabled side, and another weatherboarded side. Combinations like this are found throughout Faubourg Tremé. Modern louvered shutters and a lowered door are minor disfiguring alterations to a typical cottage. Photograph by Ben C. Toledano.

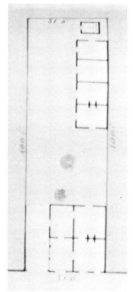

32. Plan book 65, folio 8, N. Claiborne between Esplanade, Kerlerec, demolished; drawing signed and dated "January 20, 1859, Tourné and de L'Isle." The three-bay, hip-roof creole cottage type begins to resemble the Classic-style shotgun, resulting in an overlap of building types in Faubourg Tremé. This mid-nineteenth-century example with Greek Key entrance is only two rooms deep. The four-room service building and kitchen is detached, running along the side property line of the 100-foot-deep lot.

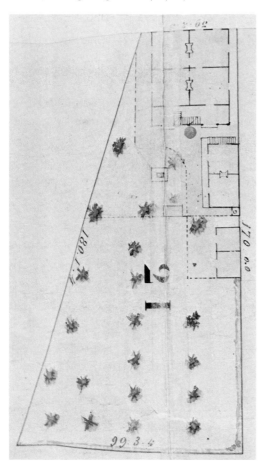

style, built in the 1840s and 1850s; plan book 65, folio 8 exemplifies this type (fig. 32).

Creole House

Yet another example of the creole building type represented in Faubourg Tremé is the full two-story creole house. In the late 1840s these appeared as a two-story version of the four-bay, gable-sided dwelling. An urban phenomenon, these houses were built at the ban-

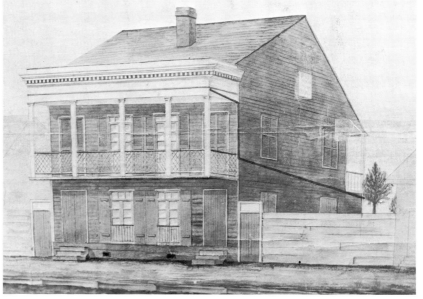

33, A. Plan book 85, folio 15, Dumaine between N. Johnson and N. Galvez, backed by St. Philip, demolished; drawing signed and dated "March 31, 1869, J. A. Celles." This full two-story creole house is characteristic in both type and Classic style: four rooms at each level, gable sides, stairway piercing the second-level gallery at the rear, chimneys centrally located, beak-roof incorporating gallery overhang at the rear, and front box cornice above box-columned gallery. This example illustrates four casement openings at each level of the front elevation; there are batten shutters below with louvered ones above.

quette, of frame, brick, or brick-between-posts construction with four openings, usually full length, at each of the two levels. At the second level, a balcony, or more often a gallery, decorates the simple façade. Used as both single and double houses, there are one or two sets of front steps. Plan book 85, folio 15 illustrates a typical example built with a Classic-style box cornice above box columns in the 1850s (figs. 33,A). The drawing shows the central chimneys piercing the roof at the front and rear, as is traditional with one-level creole cottages. The rear elevations are designed with a full gallery at both levels, sometimes with *cabinets*, and with the stairway to the second level. The interior floor plan is identical to that of the standard, four-bay creole cottage, but having two full stories rather than a dormered attic. Although most have been demolished, there is an example remaining at 1218 Ursulines, which dates from the 1840s.

These creole houses also appeared set back on the lot, with double-level galleries and the stairway placed on the front gallery (fig. 34). Some surviving examples of this type have been observed with

just two rooms at each level in the colonial tradition. All have detached kitchen buildings along the sides or back of the lot. An extant example, just one room deep with wide front galleries, may be seen at 927 N. Prieur Street. There is an 1850s example at 1219–21 St. Claude; at 1325–27 Governor Nicholls stands one with double galleries, built after the Civil War.

Adaptations and modifications of the creole cottage continued well into the second half of the nineteenth century. Enlarged, four-bay, gable-sided creole cottages, with or without front galleries, were built along N. Claiborne Avenue toward N. Broad. At 1228–30 and 1240 N. Johnson stand two examples of this type, one with and one without a gallery. The gabled sides extend a full two-and-one-half stories, although the façades each retain two dormers, but very large ones. The interior floor plan at the first level continues the eighteenth- and early-nineteenth-century creole cottage floor plan, but with the four main rooms of a larger scale. The late-Classic example at 2632 Lapeyrouse in Faubourg Gueno dates from the 1860s; it provides a luxurious dwelling near the former bed of Bayou Sauvage (Gentilly) beyond N. Broad (fig. 35).

35. 2632 Lapeyrouse. Galleried 2½-story creole cottage is an outgrowth of the traditional smaller type.

34. Plan book 38, folio 14, N. Derbigny between Esplanade and Kerlerec, backed by N. Claiborne, demolished; drawing signed and dated "November 15, 1865, A. Persac." This double-galleried variation of the two-story; gable-sided creole house was a handsome mid-nineteenth-century Classic-style addition to the Duchamp tract. It represents a building type that has all but disappeared from the streets of the city. An example much like this remains on Grand Route St. John bayouward from N. Broad. The two levels of galleries at front and rear elevations with gables on the sides articulate the house-type. They were set back in the lot, creating a spacious, rural atmosphere. Pretentious as the house seems with rows of Classic-style columns, it contained just two large rooms; outbuildings are detached, situated to one side of the lot.

Villas and Center-Hall Cottages

Galleried, villa-style or center-hall houses represent several major landmarks of Faubourg Tremé. Among the finest is 1418 Bayou Road (Governor Nicholls), the Meilleur-Lansford Villa. Except for the addition of oversized dormers, this outstanding home, built in 1828, retains its original appearance within and without (figs. 36, A). Like most creole versions of the villa, it is not raised as high as its later, American counterparts uptown and in the Garden District. A Classic-style villa at 1511 Ursulines dating from about 1849 is a major anchor to the neighborhood (fig. 37). It is set back on a large lot with traditional planting. Except for the removal of the chimneys and inappropriate metal louvered blinds in the dormers, it retains its original appearance. Although the sides are covered with weatherboards, the façade is lathed and plastered, and, as with interior rooms, has baseboards, a customary architectural treatment. Examples seen at 1486 N. Miro, 1433 N. Galvez, 1435 N. Johnson, 1221 N. Conti, 1233 and 1917 Kerlerec, and 1523 and 1574 N. Dorgenois illustrate the increasing popularity of the center-hall cottage after 1850 (fig. 38). By this time American influence had penetrated the creole suburbs.

The Solomon Villa at 1572 N. Broad is an outstanding late-nineteenth-century example, once set amidst vast orchards and gardens in Faubourg Gueno. Examples remain at 1433 N. Galvez and 1116–18 N. Dorgenois Street. They were once fine country seats, presently so mutilated that only comparison with archival drawings or other center-hall cottages makes it possible to discern the original fine appearance. Over twenty-five documented examples of the villa-type in the area exhibit an interesting combination of Louisiana colonial, creole, and American building traditions.

36, A. 1418 Bayou Road (Governor Nicholls). Meilleur-Lansford Villa, interior doors.

37. 1511 Ursulines. The more traditional, center-hall, villa-type cottage has a gallery across the façade, here in the late Classic style. Traditional to the villa is a wide central entrance flanked by two openings on each side; this one is in the Greek Revival style. The villa, as exemplified in Faubourg Tremé, was seldom raised high on brick piers; the elevation here is relatively low.

38. 1233 Kerlerec. The center-hall, five-bay, 1½-story cottage is found in Faubourg Tremé set at the banquette without front gallery and set low on a chain wall. This Classic-style example has a recessed door with sidelights and transom beyond a pilastered entrance having an entablature with dentiled cornice.

Townhouses

Some fifty detached townhouses, rowhouses, and double-level galleried, side-hall houses remain scattered through Faubourg Tremé. These single-family dwellings were built from the 1830s until World War I and number among the most expensive structures in the area, contributing a height module as well as economic stability in the area. Archival drawings and building contracts indicate that many rowhouses were removed from N. Rampart Street and the area that eventually became Louis Armstrong Park. Archival drawings like plan book 4, folio 2 illustrate them. These records are a retrospective of the former Commons between Canal and N. Rampart, N. Claiborne and Dumaine (fig. 39). N. Rampart Street once had entire blocks of these handsome rowhouses like the ones illustrated in plan book 59, folio 1, dated 1847, which might serve as a model for the restoration of two remaining examples in the 200 block of N. Rampart (figs. 40, A). Important rowhouses at 1301–03–07 Bayou Road (Governor Nicholls) are illustrated in 1850 in plan book 84, folio 2 by Louis H. Pilié (fig. 41).

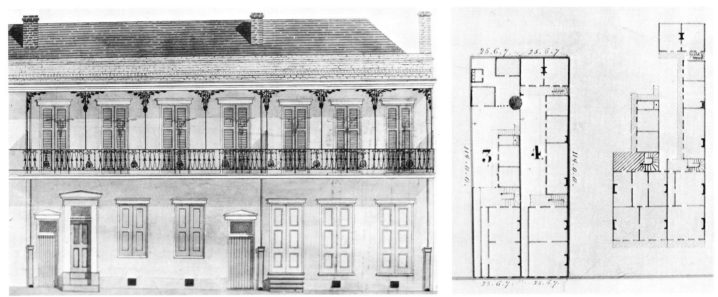

39, A. Plan book 4, folio 2, Customhouse (Iberville) near Marais, backed by Canal, demolished; drawing signed and dated "December 2, 1877, E. E. Seghers." These common-wall rowhouses in the Greek Revival style exhibit some variation of fenestration in each unit. Low openings lead to service alleys, flagged and guttered.

40. 229, 231 N. Rampart and plan book 59, folio 1, N. Rampart, corner Conti, backed by Bienville and Basin, demolished; drawing signed and dated "February 11, 1870, Arthur de Armas." Common-wall rowhouses abounded on Rampart Street in the Commons and Faubourg Tremé. Those illustrated in the archival drawing were constructed in 1847 by builder Joshua Peebles and could serve as a guide for the restoration for the extant Soulié rowhouses at 229 and 231 N. Rampart, also Greek Revival in decorative style.

The detached townhouse with balcony or gallery across the façade developed particular proportions in Faubourg Tremé; plan book 1, folio 10 and the extant L'Hote house at 2013 Dumaine are examples of the relatively low, wide, and boxlike configuration as compared to examples elsewhere in the city (figs. 42, A). An outstanding frame detached townhouse in Faubourg Tremé is the Constanza residence in the Italianate style at 2014 St. Philip Street. The exterior condition of these houses provides few clues to the fine architectural details of the interiors, which contain original light fixtures, mantels, moldings, and luxurious medallions (fig. 43).

The double-galleried, side-hall house that flourishes on Esplanade Avenue is noticeably absent elsewhere in Faubourg Tremé and the Commons. Those documented are of frame construction and remain on N. Claiborne Avenue and Canal Street. They were once fine examples but are now mutilated by insensitive alterations. The identical 1870s galleried, side-hall houses, replete with ornate brackets and turned balusters, formerly at 908 and 910 N. Rampart Street, were demolished in 1970 (fig. 44).

42. 2013 Dumaine. This townhouse exhibits a Greek Key surround behind which is a recessed entrance with sidelights and panels. Large dentils at the cornice line are almost obscured by the second-level cast-iron balcony. The iron work is the major decorative element to the otherwise extremely restrained Greek Revival façade. The paucity of decoration is itself a reflection of the Greek Revival and Classic style according to Faubourg Tremé usage.

41. Plan book 1, folio 10, Customhouse (Iberville) between Franklin (Saratoga), Tremé, backed by Canal, demolished; drawing signed and dated "May 1, 1866, C.C. Vetinel." This detached townhouse is decorated in the Classic style. The variant of the townhouse type is built at the banquette and has a second-level iron balcony and a dormer to be seen above the cornice. Such townhouses are characteristic of the type as seen in Faubourg Tremé.

43. 2014 St. Philip. The Bouchard-Costanza townhouse dates from soon after 1857 and represents the Italianate style of decoration. The deeply rusticated wooden façade, the heavy box cornice with brackets and dentils, and the handsomely detailed entrance with its heavy box cornice with pilasters having decorative consoles are all Italianate motifs.

Two-Story Center-Hall Houses

The full-scale, two-story, center-hall house is virtually nonexistent in most of Faubourg Tremé. Such houses are large, built for single-family use. Highly visible along the Esplanade, they remain prestigious architect-designed homes. One outstanding, though atypical Classic-style, center-hall, double-galleried house is immediately off Esplanade, the Benachi-Torre House at 2257 Bayou Road (see back cover). The Wogan House at 1425 N. Prieur, now mutilated, was an example, representative of the type in the Classic style.

Shotgun Houses

Shotgun houses are associated with American, late-nineteenth-century architectural development; however, two-bay and three-bay shotguns, just two or three rooms deep with a relatively high hip-roof and Greek Revival decoration, were built in Faubourg Tremé beginning in the late 1840s. A galleried example is seen in plan book 48A, folio 67, dated 1859 (fig. 45). At 1120 N. Miro is a mid-nineteenth-century, two-bay shotgun with a front gallery and side overhang, the latter a characteristic of early shotguns.

The entire 1700 block of Laharpe Street in the Guerlain tract is a series of two-bay shotguns in the Classic style, having as documentation an 1853 archival illustration, plan book 47, folio 26. There are a number of Classic-style shotguns in the 1400 block of N. Prieur, dating between 1857 and 1862, built by investor Jules LeBlanc of Cienfuegos, Cuba, and New Orleans. At 1223 Ursulines is a frame, Classic-style shotgun with pilasters flanking the entrance and a side

44. 906, 908 N. Rampart. Demolished for Louis Armstrong Park were two identical, frame townhouses of large scale decorated in the Victorian style with jigsaw-work galleries at the second level. Fancy, fluted, full-length window frames had bull's-eyes and were crowned with cornices having shell-motif central elements. Supporting the heavy galleries were unusual pierced-work brackets and pilasters with sunburst design extending from the porch floor to the second-level gallery and projecting out to the edge of the gallery, a highly unusual arrangement. The placement and combination of shapes and motifs made a rhythmical and highly creative combination; of special interest was the gallery frieze-band where two variants of spindles alternated. A combination of motifs from a variety of decorative styles—classic dentils and bull's-eyes, Italianate doors and molded cornices, high Victorian pierced work—resulted in a forthright and forceful composition full of vitality. These two late-nineteenth-century examples of the townhouse illustrate the continued usefulness and popularity of this English import type to the creole suburbs. Photograph by Ben C. Toledano.

45. Plan book 48A, folio 67, St. Claude between Columbus and Kerlerec, backed by Plauché (Marais), demolished; drawing unsigned and dated "March 18, 1859." The transition to the three-bay, one-story cottage having a floor plan similar to the first level of a side-hall townhouse suggests American influence in Faubourg Tremé building by mid-century. Emphasis on the handsome entrance, the louvered shutters, and a deep box cornice with parapet in the Classic style all herald the influx of Anglo-American influence.

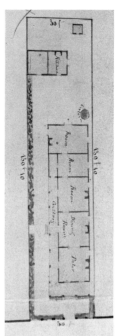

46. Plan book 44, folio 83, Hospital (Bayou Road, Governor Nicholls) between N. Galvez and N. Johnson backed by Ursulines, demolished; drawing signed and dated "May 4, 1857, F. N. Tourné." By mid-nineteenth century the equivalent of the familiar shotgun had begun to appear in Faubourg Tremé, especially beyond N. Claiborne. This one has a gallery across the front and along one side of its five rooms. The chimneys on this early shotgun are placed along the side of the hip-roof. Late Victorian shotgun chimneys are usually along the roof ridge. In the creole tradition the two-room kitchen is detached from the cottage.

gallery dating from the 1850s. In plan book 44, folio 83, a drawing dated 1857 depicts a Greek Revival shotgun with front and side galleries (fig. 46). The second room, a dining room, had an outside entrance making it accessible to the detached rear kitchen. Similar to many Classic-style shotguns and creole cottages, it had a plastered front and weatherboarded sides.

Investors Albin Soulié, Michel and Louis Bringier, Pierre Colvis, and Joseph Dumas built many such galleried shotguns in the Duchamp and Castanedo divisions in the 1850s and 1860s. Those areas are characterized by alternating groups of frame creole cottages and frame shotguns in the Classic style, both with and without galleries. The 1200 block of N. Galvez has three outstanding Greek Revival and Classic-style shotguns, and the block illustrates the variety of façade trim. At 1526–28 St. Philip stands a very rare example of a Classic-style, double shotgun with frame construction and a plastered façade, dating from the late 1860s or early 1870s. There were also several double shotguns built of brick in the Greek Revival style in the Commons.

The late Victorian, frame shotgun in two-, three-, four-, or six-bay interpretations is a genre apart from the mid-nineteenth-century Classic or Greek Revival-style examples. After Reconstruction the New Orleans economy slowly began its revival; and with the influx of Sicilian immigrants and the expansion of the creole and black population in the "back of town" area, many late Victorian shotguns were built as rental units, both on vacant lots and as replacements for early creole cottages and garden-embellished *maisons de maître*. The former Bayou Road Lambert *maison de maître* was replaced by two Victorian double shotguns at 1211 and 1213–15 Governor Nicholls. Although vast numbers of creole cottages and houses were built by black owners and builders, as were Classic-style and Greek Revival shotguns, the late Victorian shotgun was the popular building

idiom for white entrepreneurs. The black community, having lost its economic base, joined the newcomers as tenants. According to the traditional living patterns of New Orleans, these inhabitants were of all races and nationalities.

Shotguns are associated most obviously with uptown New Orleans, but outstanding examples may also be found throughout Faubourgs Gueno and Tremé and the City Commons. After creole cottages, they are the base of the housing inventory, and the most plentiful type is the double, four-bay shotgun with bracketed overhang, having a low hip-roof (fig. 47). It is a plain building type wherein the selection and mode of assembling and arranging standard mass-produced elements create the characteristic style of decoration. They depend on façade decoration, proportion, and roof profile for exterior articulation. The chimneys, ridge tiles, overhang, bay placement, gallery colonettes or supporting brackets and accompanying frieze-band and railing, the steps, and foundation are all important components of a frequently repeated composition. As single buildings or detached multiples in rows edging the street, they serve as sculptural entities.

Jigsaw work provides the decoration in this late-century rental housing, and the exuberant effect is directly in contrast to that of the Classic- and Greek Revival-style decoration found on early houses of the same building-type (fig. 48). Late Victorian shotguns might have galleries, but the less expensive type had an overhang supported by scrollwork brackets above a porch. In the 1880s a low hip-roof extending and incorporating the overhang was common; front gables with aprons to form an overhang appeared in the 1890s and early 1900s. Vergeboard and apron edges provided a surface for icicle, fleur-de-lis, or scalloped jigsaw-work motifs. A gallery across the front denoted a greater expenditure and provided increased surface for jigsaw work. Ursulines Street, especially, exhibits blocks of shot-

47. 2100 block Conti. This block in Faubourg Hagan illustrates the most evident type of the late Victorian shotgun to be seen in the area covered by this volume. Four-bay double shotguns with bracketed overhangs provide a repetitive theme fitting in scale with the four-bay, gable-sided creole cottages that also abound.

48. Window surround on late Victorian shotgun. This detail illustrates a tripartite window cornice crowned with pierced-work cresting. Sunbursts, scallops, icicles, paired brackets, bosses, quoins, drop-siding, and fluted window frames are decorative devices flamboyantly combined and evident in this photographic detail.

guns decorated with extravagantly original and imaginative jigsaw work (fig. 48A).

Component gallery sections included turned colonettes, a spindle or pierced-work frieze-band, and spandrels of applied work or pierced work with bosses. Balusters were turned or of the more unusual sawed work. In the 1890s decoration of the stylish front gables became a challenge; surfaces were shingled or filled in with wooden sunbursts. Within the gable a stained-glass window or panel with applied-work decoration contributed additional texture to the already busy surface. Drop siding covered the front, usually with boards eight inches wide, and there were wood quoins for corners. Decorative cornices above each façade opening were essential elements, and sometimes the opening had fluted surrounds with fancy cornerblocks; the carved wooden cornices were topped with pierced-work crestings (fig. 49). Etched glass within the door was above an applied-

work panel in the 1870s; blue and yellow flash squares edging plain glass panels furnished alternative door choices in the 1880s.

In these Victorian examples, light and shadow played a role in the entire composition (fig. 50). The profusion of wooden ornaments, raised or flattened, heavy and delicate, whimsically repeat elements of grand architectural statements and complete the integrity of their vernacular type. The major interest in jigsaw work was not the design of each piece, those being available by the thousands at sash, door, and blind factories, but in the creative combinations of the decorative forms. Brackets supported overhangs but were used also as spandrels between colonettes or with pillars to form a purely decorative ornamentation. Spindels, associated with the band between colonettes, were interspersed among pierced or applied-work panels to simulate an entablature. Such indiscriminate combinations and usage of jigsaw work results in an eclectic mixture. Designs obviously Classic in inspiration are incorporated with pierced work recalling Moorish designs. Motifs like the bull's-eye and shell, once used as simple Classic-style ornamentation, are used in multiples or highly decorative rows.

49. 2017 St. Philip. Texture and surface variations as well as variety of form and shape, are multiplied by light and shadow in this outstanding example of jigsaw composition.

50. 2455 Laharpe. A simple boxlike house-type is transformed by its decorative style—the creative combination of jigsaw elements into a street sculpture of high sophistication.

51. 2455 Laharpe. Individual jigsaw pieces were the mass-produced product of a newly industrialized society; but highly individualized selection, combination, and application resulted in a spontaneous art form in Faubourg Tremé.

There was a progression in popularity of jigsaw pieces from larger, nonangular, and simple forms in the late 1870s to extremely light and lacy decorative work in the 1890s (fig. 51). The proliferation of jigsaw forms seemed as endless as their combinations. This ornamental woodwork was sold by catalog number, and the different forms have been given names applying to their method of manufacture. Categories include pierced work, applied work, sawed work, turned work, and scrollwork. Panels, brackets, scrolls, cornices, and other decorative surfaces might be composed of any of these; occasionally, a fanciful name suggestive of shape may be offered, for instance "steamboat," "fan," and "snail" brackets.

The predominant four-bay, double, frame shotgun had certain characteristics reminiscent of creole housing: the four-bay arrangement with no emphasis upon the entrance, the door and windows sharing a full length, the lack of an interior hallway. The side-by-side double, built as a detached dwelling, was also a creole tradition; however, the shotgun, usually larger, followed the narrow lot configuration. Rooms of equal size, usually twelve by fourteen feet, progressed one behind the other; four rooms on each side was standard. Without interior halls or side galleries, the floor plan forced the occupant to go through each room to get to the rear of the house where the kitchen and plumbing were located. The first room was the living room; the second, the dining room followed by two or more bedrooms, behind which was the kitchen.

Individual rooms on each side were served by interior separating

wall fireplaces with brick chimneys along the central roof ridge. Roofs were slate with decorative, red tile roof ridges. Often fancy brickwork chimneys and terra-cotta chimney pots embellished the shotgun roof. Segmental-arched front openings predominated in the creole suburbs, whereas square-headed openings were more popular in uptown shotguns. The segmental arch first appeared in New Orleans during the early French colonial period through 1820, but it had a city-wide revival during the Italianate period of the 1860s and 1870s. Such surrounds with their accompanying louvered shutters or screens were available at local sash factories from the 1880s through the turn of the century. The segmental-arched windows might be, like the transomed entrances, full length; the sashes were double-hung with large panes. A common façade arrangement was two, full-length doors, one at each outer wall, with segmental-arched transoms and two short segmental-arched windows between. The houses were set at the banquette or slightly recessed on the lot, raised on brick piers between one and three feet off the ground or raised on a chain wall, perforated on the front by square or oval cast-iron ventilators.

The shotgun may have been built as or converted to a camelback, with a two-story rear section (fig. 52). These two-story portions, usually of four rooms, may have gable sides and side galleries, but most have low hip-roofs. Extant camelback shotguns dating from the late 1860s are found in the creole suburbs, but the first archival drawing of the camelback yet found dates from the early 1870s. The camel-

52. 2224–34 Bienville. Camelbacks appear on shotguns of the two-bay through six-bay types. The two-story portion may have side galleries, and it may have gable-ends or a hip-roof. A street view in many cases will not reveal the camelback or two-story part of the dwelling.

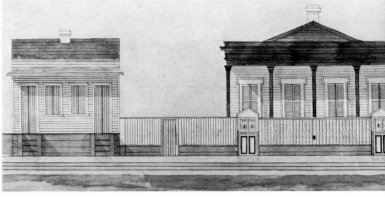

54. Plan book 5, folio 23, N. Dorgenois between Hospital (Bayou Road, Governor Nicholls), and Barracks, backed by N. Rocheblave, demolished; drawing signed and dated "March 21, 1874, Oct. J. Morel." The familiar four-bay, double shotgun began to appear in Faubourg Tremé in the late 1860s. This galleried example is decorated in the late Classic style.

back as a separate building type was an outgrowth of the creole tradition wherein a separate two-story kitchen across a courtyard from a one-story dwelling was connected to the house by filling in the courtyard to provide living space. Ultimately, houses were built according to this traditional development, and the building type was established. It made possible the separation of the living and cooking quarters from the sleeping area. The height increase away from the street, on narrow lots, resulted in a consideration to architectural massing. The one-level along the banquette continued a human scale.

The full six-bay, late Victorian shotgun is rare throughout the city, and most examples are found in the creole suburbs (fig. 53). In effect, it is two 3-bay, side-hall houses with common wall and roof, serving as a double house. It most often seems to date from the 1890s and has a wide front gable with either porch or gallery. Often entrances on the outer edges of the façade lead to open or recessed side galleries.

Archival drawings of shotguns with jigsaw work are rare. Plan book 5, folio 23, dating from 1876, illustrates a Classic-style shotgun

having a paint scheme associated with late Victorian shotguns (fig. 54). It was customary to paint the woodwork dark brown or light buff, rather than white, which is so often used today. Window sashes were oxblood red or dark green with contrasting surrounds. Recessed portions of the drop siding were often painted a darker shade of the house color to emphasize shadow, resulting in an increased decorative effect of all combined surfaces. An auction drawing in a private collection depicts the twentieth-century "ell" shotgun painted grey with green shutters. Pink shingles appear in the front pediment (fig. 55).

Bayed cottages of the late nineteenth and early twentieth centuries also appear in relatively large numbers in Faubourg Tremé (fig. 56). Toward N. Rampart Street, they too usually replaced creole cottages or their garden areas; but near N. Broad, they were built on empty lots. These frame cottages were single-family dwellings set back on their containing lots. They are characterized most obviously by protruding bay windows, galleries, multiple rooflines, projecting segments, recessed entrances, and side ells.

53. 1211–15 Bayou Road (Governor Nicholls). Decorative ridge tiles with roosters and matching brick chimneys create a sculpture effect on shotgun rooflines. The six-bay shotgun variation here has a shingled front gable with apron covering a gallery.

55. Drawing of unidentified house. Private collection. Authentic color schemes for late Victorian and Edwardian houses are difficult to find.

56. 1221 Marais. Although the late Victorian bayed cottage is a house-type that appears throughout the United States, it lags far behind the shotgun and camelback in numbers in New Orleans. Among local neighborhoods, Faubourgs Tremé and St. John exhibit more examples of the type and style.

Atypical House -Types

Of the thousand and more buildings inventoried for this book, only thirty-five are characterized as atypical; they are neither creole cottage, villa, two-level galleried side-hall house, rowhouse or detached townhouse, shotgun, or bayed cottage. These are a departure from the above categories and are so unusual that they must be considered different and apart. The addition of a fifth opening to a creole cottage provided floor versatility (fig. 57). The Greek Revival-style creole cot-

57. 1130 Ursulines. The 1820s Levasseur creole cottage of brick between posts was remodeled in the Greek Revival style and given a fifth opening, used as an entrance. There are numerous such examples in Faubourg Tremé. One or two may have been built in this manner.

58. 1318 Ursulines. The 1836 Biamonti creole cottage has been transformed into a Second Empire-style residence.

59. 1317–19 Columbus. The Maspereau House is an 1850s, Classic-style, double dwelling having unusual galleries with stairs and *cabinets* on each side. They are reached by façade entrances with Classic-style surrounds.

tage at 1130 Ursulines was increased in size by a fifth opening. Wrapped around the Greek Revival-style cottage at 1318 Ursulines stands a Second Empire-style dwelling; a creole cottage, built in 1836 according to its building contract, has a wraparound front (fig. 58). Its strange proportions result in a moderately successful composition. Other atypical buildings include 1319 Columbus and 1231 and 1436 N. Villere, all six-bay creole cottages, each half designed with side galleries (fig. 59).

There are a few examples of early-twentieth-century residences that present combinations of established types and styles. The raised basement, galleried, center-hall villa forms an architectural continuum with floor plan variations and eclectic stylistic considerations. The bungalow, a twentieth-century building type and style, incorporates influences; it is rare throughout the city. Some appear characterized by brick piers with Egyptian-style half-columns of wood to support a gallery. The roofline extends beyond the walls to form deep eaves, giving a rustic treatment with wood bearers. The shotgun also continued through the 1920s, utilizing Neoclassic-style decorative motifs with Ionic columns, diamond-pavéed windows, garland friezes, and narrow weatherboards.

Any of the six major house-types and their variants within Faubourg Tremé may be restored, renovated, or rehabilitated. Analogy is the key; the success is dependent upon identification, analysis, and a careful program of procedures. The emphasis in this volume has been on the historical development of the area and the visible elements of the architectural ensemble. The neighborhood differences are blended together by house-types of similar scale, materials, and placement. This was accomplished by local builders sensitive to the economy of lot sizes and regard for a street pattern.

Historians most often concentrate on well-known national and local architects. The innovative designs of a Latrobe, Towne, Davis, Richardson, Gropius, Wright, or Kahn filter down and create trends of national and international architectural determinations. Their works are recorded in hundreds of books and exhibitions. This in no way reduces the value of expressions by local builders; it simply means that few vernacular builders and their works have been elevated to the scrutiny of scholarship. Since their work represents the vast majority of houses and commercial space throughout New Orleans and its creole faubourgs, it behooves us to present them and study their simple but delightful buildings.

ARCHITECTURAL INVENTORY

The inventory presents a photograph, description, and history of some 500 edifices in Faubourg Tremé and the former City Commons between N. Rampart, N. Broad, Canal, and St. Bernard. At least 100 more structures with history and analysis are not photographed but are included and may be located by boldface headings of many entries and by additional boldface references flagging these addresses as they appear in the inventory text.

The inventory begins with Bayou Road, the ancient portage from Bayou St. John to the rear gate of the city. For this study Bayou Road retains its ancient name, rather than the twentieth-century appellation Governor Nicholls, assigned to it between N. Rampart and N. Claiborne. At N. Claiborne, a new street called Governor Nicholls was carved through the nineteenth-century plantations between 1830 and 1850. The city, in an effort to aid the citizens in street alignment, renamed Hospital Street (which began at the Mississippi River and stopped at N. Rampart) Governor Nicholls and changed Bayou Road to a continuation of old Hospital. Thus today only the Bayou Road that continues from N. Claiborne to follow its circuitous route to N. Broad has retained its original name.

The history of Bayou Road in historic documents refers to the street between N. Rampart and N. Claiborne as the Road to the Bayou. Therefore, for this study, where so many quotations from original wills and acts of sale are included, the authors reinstituted the use of the name Bayou Road for that sixteen-block stretch between N. Rampart and N. Claiborne. Whenever this is done, the old name is given and the present name, Governor Nicholls, is given in parentheses. When Bayou Road appears without being followed by parentheses, it indicates the section today known as Bayou Road.

This inventory of Faubourg Tremé streets is presented in alphabetical order with the exception of Bayou Road (Governor Nicholls) as the first street. All other streets may be found according to the alphabet, and their block numbers discerned by the presentation of the even block side before the odd.

The exclusion of any structures from either the "Early History," "Restoration by Analogy," or the "Inventory" by no means suggests the authors' condemnation or disinterest. There are many worthy examples of each house-type and style to be found in this vast and densely built neighborhood. Structures analagous in type and style to those included in this volume are potential objects for restoration and renovation by analogy.

BAYOU ROAD (GOVERNOR NICHOLLS)

1130–32

Morand Habitation. This double creole cottage provides an example of an early Faubourg Tremé housetype. Probably built of brick between posts covered with weatherboards, the house has retained its two original chimneys. The foundations have been raised in recent years; the roof and overhang have been reworked several times in the 150-year existence of the cottage.

1138–40

Morand Habitation. The land on which this house was built belonged originally to the front section of the Morand-Tremé house and gardens. St. Claude was cut through from Bayou Road to Ste Julie (Esplanade) about 1799 by Claude Tremé, and soon creole cottages lined both Bayou Road and the new street. This substantial double house probably replaced one of the cottages, but it was standing in 1883 when Robinson published his atlas of the city. The ornamentation on its two-level gallery was ordered from a builder's catalog of millwork. The center separators, called "plank dividers" by builders of the period, provide a maximum sense of privacy to the occupants of this multifamily dwelling. Photograph: Gypsy Van Antwerp.

1131–33

Ross Cottage. This property, located across from the now demolished Morand-Tremé plantation house, was among the many lots sold by Claude Tremé at the end of the eighteenth century to free persons of color. Philippe Ross, f.m.c., purchased a lot, 30 feet fronting on Bayou Road by one *arpent* in depth, from speculator Françoise Lemaydel, Widow Couterie, on August 22, 1806 (P. Pedesclaux). She had owned the property just one year, purchasing it from free Negress Agnes Mathieu, the owner since 1795. Ross built a stuccoed creole cottage, perhaps brick between posts, during his twenty-year ownership. It was not shown on the Tanesse map of 1816, for it was probably built about 1837, when it and a slave were sold to Adèle Alvar, f.w.c., for $5,300. A retrocession two years later returned the property for the same price to Ross. The creole cottage has its original dormers with pilasters and arched lights and retains its French doors and transom with original muntins. Batten shutters with panels on the inside have large, early-nineteenth-century strap hinges. The Ross family continued to own 1131–33 until 1890, when Widow Ross's sister, Widow P. I. Favré, died. The cottage sold at the Auctioneer's Exchange to P. A. Perrault for $1,335 (February 26, 1890, J. F. Meunier) and was advertised in the *New Orleans Bee* on April 6 and 7 and May 4 and 11, 1889, as "the double cottage with attic, numbers 181 and 181½ Bayou Road." Around the turn of the century, it was owned with other rental property by J. M. Lafferanderie. Recently it was included in the real estate holdings of Dr. Anita Crozat Kohlsdorf.

1137–39

Laizer Property. This lot was one of the earliest Claude Tremé sold from the original Morand plantation and was bought by Agnes Mathieu, a free Negress, on May 17, 1795. Jean Laizer purchased it from Henry Metzinger on September 4, 1817, for $900; Laizer improved the property with a creole cottage and sold it to Paul Laurent Retif for $1,554 ten years later (December 27, 1827, L. T. Caire). After a seventeen-year ownership, Retif sold it to Mme J. B. Guigon in 1844. Mme Guigon gave the house to her daughters of a previous marriage, Eliza and Honorine Mercier, whose families held it until 1875. The creole cottage behind a disfigured brick façade was altered in the twentieth century for commercial purposes; it has been gutted and is now used as a garage. A twentieth-century dwelling adjoins it in the rear. Although the extreme mutilation of the exterior makes dating this structure difficult, portions of an original façade and the low foundation point to a construction date sometime between 1817 and 1827 during the Laizer ownership. Even in its present condition, this façade is compatible with the street scene because it includes proportions and materials utilized in nineteenth-century building.

1141–43, 1145–47

Camus Property. The lots on which **1141–43** and **1145–47** stand were sold by Claude Tremé to Rose Tisoneau, f.w.c., as early as May 12, 1799. On the corner, 1145–47, is thought to be the principal house mentioned in the 1829 inventory of François Aimé Camus. Recorded by J. Arnaud, the inventory mentioned "one lot 34 feet by 130 feet on Bayou Road, a major house with a courtyard, service buildings and construction, value $1,200." This house and an empty lot (now 1141–43) were inherited by Marie Fratel, wife of Benjamin Mercier, from her uncle, François Camus. She was remarried in 1830 to J. B. Guigon, and they built the creole cottage at 1141–43, as well as six other houses, on land inherited from her uncle. In 1864 Guigon sold the seven houses to his wife's daughters, Honorine Mercier Cifreo and Eliza Mercier Bougère. The act of sale, February 8, 1864, took place before J. Cuvillier. 1145–47 now appears as a two-story, four-bay creole cottage, used as a store; it was probably altered and raised when St. Claude was widened during the Mercier ownership. The two Mercier sisters partitioned their property in 1875: Mme Bougère retained 1145–47 until widowed in 1886, at which time she sold the house back to her stepfather, J. B. Guigon. He sold it to Marie St. Martin, widow of John Garrau, for $2,225 (September 24, 1889, M. Voorhies). 1141–43, also one of the earliest creole cottages in Tremé, was designed with brick-gabled parapets and arched lights in the pedimented dormers. The house remains in its original condition, with four arched openings across the rear and remnants of a parterred garden. The mantels with Greek Key surrounds and a kitchen within the main house are later additions. The present owner is Mrs. Charles Bracquet, née Natalie Lasbriques, who was born in the house and is a descendant of Marie Fratel.

53/18 (site of 1211–1215)

1201–03, 1205–07

Pierre Lambert Properties (1201–1227). In 1810 Pierre Pedesclaux recorded a land sale by Claude Tremé to the Corporation of New Orleans. The act included a list of property previously sold by Tremé to individuals, which included the square bound by St. Claude, Ste Julie (Esplanade), Chemin du Bayou (Governor Nicholls) and stretching to the limits of the Cristoval de Armas holdings. The first three lots from the corner of St. Claude and Chemin du Bayou measured 60 feet fronting on the Chemin. According to the Pedesclaux survey, the first was sold by Tremé to F. Lesassier in 1799, the second to Louis Desa in the same year, and the third to Jourdan in 1804. Adjacent to the three above properties, a lot measuring 80 by 80 feet was sold to Louis Marsoutte in 1799. By 1819 Pierre Lambert owned all these Bayou Road properties; one he purchased from the Solomon Prevost estate (May 12, 1813, Pierre Pedesclaux), a second from Benoit Milbrouck (April 17, 1819, John Lynd), and a third from Marcelite Hazeur, f.w.c., who had vast holdings in Faubourg Tremé and resided in both New Orleans and Paris. The Jacques Tanesse survey of 1816 clearly indicates the existence of three urban cottages in the present 1200 block. One was a corner creole cottage on the site of **1201–03**. It appears to have been demolished by Lambert and replaced with the present structure in the 1830s. At Lambert's death, it was sold to Louis Martin, whose family retained it until 1890. In that year, it was sold as "lot and building" for $2,800 by auctioneer Albert Pane. It had been advertised in the *Daily-Picayune* in July and August of 1890, being finally purchased by other Martin heirs. Five years later, two of these, Mrs. A. J. Schoenfield and Mrs. C. L. Martin, sold it again at auction for $2,450. In 1849 the Lambert estate also sold the adjacent creole cottage at **1205–07** Chemin du Bayou, which Lambert also had built in the 1830s. Joseph Lieutaud purchased it on a lot, measuring 32 feet on Chemin du Bayou, for $1,275. His family kept **1205–07** until 1883, when it was sold to John Costé, f.m.c., for $2,300. A description of the house at that sale stated: "The improvements comprise a one story and attic frame [only the front elevation is plastered] dwelling divided into two tenements having two rooms and one gallery to each tenement, brick yard, waterworks to each tenement, privies, etc. The property bears numbers 191 and 193 Bayou Road. Being the same property acquired by purchase from the heirs of Pierre Lambert as per act passed before the notary Adolphe Mazureau dated February 28, 1849." These are two of the more architecturally significant houses in Tremé and merit removal of dormer awnings and replacement of lowered doors and reinstallation of batten shutters. The corner cottage (1201–03) has architectural sophistication implied in its scale, its brick-gabled parapets, and its scored, plastered, and well-proportioned dormers. French doors with five pairs of lights in the upper panels are still visible in the remaining openings.

BAYOU ROAD (GOVERNOR NICHOLLS)

Pierre Lambert, Jr., inherited his father's *maison de maître* in 1849, when L. H. Pilié illustrated it for the succession sale (plan book 53, folio 18). The drawing shows the house set back from the roadway and surrounded by gardens; it was on a lot 60 feet from the corner. The structure is shown on the Robinson Atlas of 1883 but was demolished shortly thereafter to make room for the late-Victorian shotgun houses now numbered **1211** and **1213–15**. Segmental arches over the doors, full-length windows, drop-siding, and gables covered with shingles indicate that the houses were built in the last decade of the nineteenth century.

André Doriocourt purchased the next two lots from the Pierre Lambert estate in February of 1849 for $810 each. At this time, there were no buildings standing on the lots, which ran from Bayou Road (Governor Nicholls) through to Barracks, since the land was Pierre Lambert's rear garden. According to a building contract brought before notary Antoine Doriocourt in July, 1853, the house at **1219–21** Bayou Road was built for the Doriocourt children by *entrepreneurs* J. G. Plicene and George Abry for $2,600. The contract specified that the house was to "measure 28 feet by 58 feet with six rooms, four to be 14 feet by 17 feet, two to be 14 feet by 17 feet with a gallery divided into two by *une cloison en planches* (planked dividing wall). . . . There will be a kitchen 35 feet long and a gallery to have two stories of wood with two stairs . . . brick courtyard and banquette." It was to be built in 2½ months. Throughout the nineteenth century, the masonry-front cottage with weatherboard sides bore the municipal numbers 199 and 201 and was owned by various members of the Doriocourt family. The four-bay, shotgun house next door at **1223–25** Bayou Road was indicated in outline on the Robinson Atlas of 1883. The Doriocourt family had also purchased this lot from the Lamberts in the early nineteenth century. The site of **1227** Bayou Road, which once extended from Bayou Road to Ste Julie, was sold by Claude Tremé to Narcisse Gastier on June 10, 1805, and was later acquired by Lambert. The present house is the second dwelling built on the lot. The pleasant, late-Victorian, three-bay townhouse with a side hall has a second level with bay, front gable, and balcony. It is outlined on the Robinson Atlas of 1883. Photograph: Ben C. Toledano.

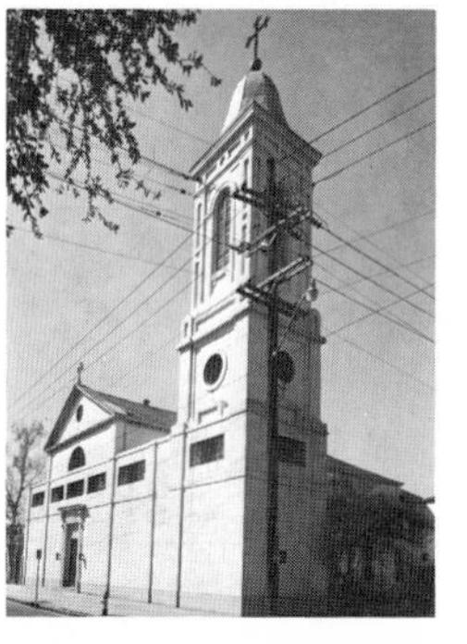

St. Augustine's Church and Rectory. St. Augustine's Church, designed by architect J. N. B. de Pouilly, was built in 1841–42 by Ernest Godchaux and Pierre Vidal at a cost of $25,000, according to a building contract entered by P. Cuvellier on December 22, 1841. The new parish was bound roughly by N. Rampart, N. Claiborne, St. Peter, and Elysian Fields. Although French and Spanish creoles, as well as free Negro patrons, took up a collection to finance the church, Bishop Antoine Blanc personally paid most of the building costs. The list of donors for the building fund included the Creole families of Landeaux, Rousseau, Garidel, Capdevielle, Landry, and Poursine, as well as the free colored families of Dolliole, Reynal, and Reggio. At the time of its construction, half of St. Augustine's congregation consisted of Creoles of French and Spanish ancestry and recent French immigrants; the other half was composed of free people of color, with a few pews reserved for slaves. The church was designed in the Greek Revival style by its French architect, yet it reflects a knowledge of Italian Renaissance buildings and has an international flavor not expressed in the architecture of other New Orleans churches. Attention is given to the clerestory level with the circular windows along the side and extensive use of wrought iron on the front rectangular clerestory. These contrast with the simplicity of the façade. Pilasters articulate the central pedimented block and the corner bell tower. The 1841 building contract, preserved in the archdiocesan archives, specifies: "The foundation to be in country brick bordered in good mortise 3½ bricks deep. . . . All the walls will be of lake bricks, painted in oil [plastering is the result of a 1926 renovation] . . . all carpentry to be of good cypress. The roof will be slate. The casement windows and the interior doors to be built of cypress, first quality, and the wood paneling painted to resemble mahogany or other wood chosen by the Bishop. . . . The windows to work with hinges. . . . Pews will be of well-dried cypress bleached and assembled . . . each [pew] to have a lectern, a kneeling stand, a bar, also an iron grate, all painted to resemble mahogany or other wood, also the balustrade of the sanctuary. The confessionals, the altar, and the pulpit will also be of first choice cypress and will be assembled and painted conforming to plans approved by Monseigneur. The main door will be cypress two inches thick, assembled, equipped with hardware, painted after the plans, and with casing, counter casing, brackets, and cornices. The base of the casing, counter casing . . . and foundation between the bases of the principal door and the said threshold will be granite or white marble as will be the steps of the doors on the façade. The entrance will be in asphalt with a star in stone or other ornament instead. The capitals and cornices of the interior will be cypress painted in oil, except the cornice of the ceiling of the nave which will be in plaster. All the plastering of the walls and ceiling will be of the manner of the country. The ceiling of the nave will be arched and ornamented with brushes in *grisaille* [tint drawing] or in *plâtre* [plaster]. . . . All the painting and the glazing of color and other will be made with first quality materials. The tableaux of sacred history will be painted in fresco after the subjects chosen by Monseigneur. . . . In general all will be executed after the plans approved by Monseigneur for $23,500. [Signed]: Wednesday October 13, 1841; Jacques de Pouilly, Pierre Vidal, Bishop Antoine Blanc." The original murals, may have been repainted by Mrs. George de Jahan (Marie Bernard), since the *Daily-States* (January 3, 1926) reported, "Jahan murals were left intact" during the 1926 renovation. They were described then as "four murals after Murillo," but they have since been destroyed or concealed. The church was renovated in 1925–1926 according to plans of Weil and Bendernagel, Architects, with R. P. Farnsworth as contractor, at a cost of $60,00. According to the *Daily-States*, (January 23, 1926, p. 8, cols. 5–8), the exposed bricks of the church were then plastered and present stained-glass windows installed. These were donated by members of the French-speaking congregation. The bells of St. Augustine's Church were bought by Father Joseph Subileau at the New Orleans Exposition of 1883. The present interior of the church has been spoiled by subsequent renovations since 1950, but old photographs preserved in the rectory, along with the building contract, would serve as a guide for restoration. Murals remain today in the apse along with a handsome marble-balustered communion rail decorated with iron, bronze, and brass. However, paintings on the walls of the nave and clerestory have been covered over with paneling and those above with a modernizing ceiling. Photographs in the rectory indicate that the ceiling had panels painted with fleur-de-lis and rondels, including a Murillo-style Madonna, Isaiah, and Jeremiah. The clerestory walls were plastered and decorated with swags and garlands. Marbled wood columns divide the nave and narthex. The latter has been spoiled by a wall beneath the choir loft, and an unsuitable, modern dividing wall obscures the church entrance.

1210, Rectory

The rectory probably dates from the pastorship of Father J. B. Jobert, pastor of St. Augustine's Church from 1856 until 1874. Italianate fenestration and the dentiled entablature suggest a Neoclassic structure of the 1870s. Bands and courses of plastered brickwork and a hip-roof, however, continue creole traditions. Beyond the rectory is a two-story, plastered brick-and-frame building used for many generations as the parish school. The front and rear elevations have four dormers each, and the rear elevation retains its handsome double galleries, although the box columns have been removed.

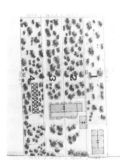

94/30

1322–24

Jonau Properties, 1310–1324. Once part of the eighteenth-century Morand-Moreau-Tremé holdings, this property was included in that sold by Claude Tremé to Henri Peyroux. Between 1805 and 1807, Peyroux sold 200 feet facing Bayou Road by 70 feet in depth to Louis Alexandre Lefaucheu. Research reveals that Dame Louise Calendreau, Widow Jean Marie Henry, bought a large portion of the tract in 1809 and built on it a *maison de maître* complex, probably in the 1820s. At her death in 1832, her estate was willed equally to her grandson Jean Louis Jonau and four other persons, among them Joseph Costé and Caliste Caubert, both f.m.c. On November 5, 1833, Jonau bought out his fellow heirs and became sole owner of the property. By 1849 Paul Lieutaud was owner of a portion of the land. On June 15 of that year, he sold it to William Perine Ellison for $2,525 before J. Holland. The present 1310 Governor Nicholls was constructed for Ellison in what had been the side yard of Mme Henry's *maison de maître*. It is a two-level, three-bay, double-galleried, side-hall, frame house. The Classic-style residence was sold by Ellison to Caroline Schwartz, Widow Adam Busch, in 1856 for $8,000. H. J. Montagnet purchased it from her in 1884 for $3,500, the low price indicating that the property had been reduced to its present size of 34 feet facing Bayou Road. Although altered, the house could easily be restored to its mid-nineteenth-century appearance. The double, camelback house at **1312–14** was built of frame construction with shingled front gable and an apron-covered gallery supported by Doric columns with piers. The use of drop-siding and quoins dates this house to the last decade of the nineteenth century; however, the garland swag decoration on the gallery apron is characteristic of the first decade of the twentieth century. The present concrete porch and steps have replaced earlier wooden ones. The adjacent dwelling at **1316–18** appears as a late-nineteenth-century shotgun; however, a close look reveals a large, weatherboarded creole cottage set back on a lot that has been filled in to the street with a front appendage or wraparound shotgun. At **1322–24**, a four-bay, masonry-fronted creole cottage with hip-roof and overhang is the earliest remaining building from the Henry-Jonau complex. Plan

book 94, folio 30 contains a drawing that depicts a plan of the house and is dated March 7, 1849. Louis Jonau sold 1322–24 to Louis Frigière on March 30, 1849, for $3,000 (L. T. Caire). Frigière held the building for nine years until he sold it to Victor Conand for $4,300 on May 12, 1858 (A. Ducatel). The Conand family owned the house until 1908. Alterations presently obscure the original appearance of the cottage. It has a plastered brick façade and cornice with dentil molding; the sides, which are now covered with weatherboards, may be of *colombage* construction. Dr. Richard Levy has recently acquired the house, and it has been restored under the direction of Mel Graziano.

1304–06

Peyroux Property. This frame, four-bay shotgun probably was built in the 1880s, even though many of its stylistic characteristics reflect the following decade. Houses of this type were raised after the advent of the automobile and are difficult to date. It is safe to comment that the dormer and Corinthian columns were never part of the original design of Victorian shotguns or altered creole cottages. The land on which the house now stands belonged to Henri Peyroux in the early 1800s and then in 1806 to L. A. Lefaucheu. This was part of the eighteenth-century Morand-Moreau-Tremé plantation house and gardens, but it was not included in that land sold for the Collège d'Orléans.

1326–28

Vincent-Mallard House. This two-level, four-bay house with galleries across the front was built of frame construction in the late 1850s. The original doors with oval glazing, rusticated wooden façade, and cornice with paired brackets and dentils are characteristic features of a Classic-style house. The property was acquired by the Joseph Vincent family in the 1840s from the noted investor J. B. Sauvinet at a sheriff's sale (COB 36/123). Vincent probably built the present house, which he sold to Prudent Mallard, the cabinetmaker and furniture dealer, in 1868 for $4,000. Mallard kept the property less than one year before selling it to Jean Numa Avegno on April 6, 1868, for $3,500 (A. Ducatel). The Avegno family kept the house until Charles P. Avegno sold it in 1944 for $5,250. The owner in 1974 was F. Cantelli.

1301–07

84/2

Monrose Row (1301–07), 1311–13. Three, masonry, 2½-story, Greek Revival rowhouses at **1301** through **1307** were begun in 1839 for Charles Monrose and were completed in 1840 by Louis Janin. Monrose began extensive purchases within the square by buying in 1836 from Bazile Beauregard, in 1837 from architect Jacques de Pouilly, and in 1838 from the city. This land included 152-foot Tremé Street frontage by a depth of 145 feet along Bayou Road. Barracks had not yet been cut through this square, and in 1838 (December 5, F. de Armas) Monrose sold five of his lots to the city for the prolongment of Quartier (Barracks). Monrose, who had a bakery and residence at old number 262 Bourbon until 1838, moved to the corner building, the first of his planned row, opening his business at 1301–03 by 1840. The same year, Monrose's creditors held a public auction (September 2, 1840, L. T. Caire), and he lost his new property to attorney Louis Janin for $8,000. Janin immediately completed the row of three houses. An 1850 archival drawing (plan book 84, folio 2) depicts them as they appeared when Janin sold each to separate owners at public auction. 1307 Bayou Road brought $3,500 from Mme Jean Lalaurie; the others, $3,200 each. Mme Lalaurie sold 1307 in 1853 to Mme Placide Forstall. Both women owned large amounts of real estate and used the house as a rental unit. The Forstalls owned 1307 until the end of the century. The purchase agreement from Janin on October 10, 1850 (R. J. Ker), described the house as "built of brick, three stories high and the use of an alley leading to its rear from Tremé Street having 3 feet 6 inches width." The middle house, number 1303, was bought by Mme Eliza Field, who lived there until she sold to Widow Franz Steubenrauch in 1867. Baker Jean Lafferanderie, also an owner of 1221–23 Tremé, bought the house in 1890 as rental property. Number 1301, the corner dwelling, was rented by Monrose from Janin for ten years, after which it sold in 1850 to Eugène Mioton, an importer and dealer in earthenware, china, and glass. Mioton lived at the address but later moved to Esplanade Avenue. From 1854 until 1857, the French Market butcher Dominique Monlezun lived in 1301, which then changed hands four times before being acquired by Mme Jacinto Aleix, the proprietress of a Vieux Carré coffeehouse and a resident of Union Street. An 1890 auction notice (J. E. Meunier) described the property: "A two-story and attic building with a verandah on both streets, having a large store on the ground floor with store fixtures, two fine rooms on the second floor, and two rooms well finished in the attics, closed gallery to each story and pantry, a two-story brick building adjoining the house having a large kitchen." The adjacent house toward Marais at **1311–13** Bayou Road, a late-Victorian double house with two stories, replaced an earlier *maison de maître* that was included in the Monrose-Janin acquisition and survived into the mid-1880s. This present frame residence, built sometime after 1883, is characterized by a front gable covered with shingles, a roof overhang supported by brackets, and a balcony at the second level. The original wood railing was replaced with a wrought-iron one.

1315

Dumontil Property. Here a two-bay townhouse of frame construction was built with a roof overhang and a cantilevered balcony at the second level. The roofline is hipped, and the front façade is surmounted by a shingle-covered gable. Brackets support the roof on the second level. The addition of gable and brackets in the late nineteenth century may obscure the appearance of an 1850s Classic-style house; the Gothic-style iron railing may be an indication of the earlier date. The land on which this house is built was part of the ancient holdings of Demahy Dumontil, who bought the land from Claude Tremé in 1807.

1400–08

21/9

1400–08, 1410–12. This is a triple, common-wall creole cottage built at **1400–08** on the garden portion of the Demahy Dumontil *maison de maître*, which was still standing in 1831. By 1816, according to the Tanesse map, Marais Street had been cut through a portion of the garden. These corner urban buildings were built between 1831 and 1836 for Louis A. Neil, who bought the lots from Arnold Myers in 1831. The cottages have retained their original splayed brick lintels, batten shutters, and strap hinges; the original roofline has been mutilated by the recent addition of a modern mansard roof. It is possible that the E. Surgi drawing of June 4, 1838 (plan book 21, folio 9), shows this corner, common-wall cottage to the left. The drawing shows an adjacent, hip-roof, side-dormered creole cottage, indicated as number 1, and described

as "composed of two rooms with fireplace, sleeping room, and *grand galerie* across from Plauché and Widow Dupuy's property." This cottage occupied the site of **1410–12** Bayou Road, a double shotgun built at an angle to the street; however, the original cottage seen on the plan may remain behind the newer house.

1418

Meilleur-Goldthwaite House. Simon Meilleur and his Philadelphia-born wife, Catherine Flack, had this house built in 1828–1829, after buying the lot on October 10, 1828 (O. de Armas), from Jean Jacques Isnard. When Isnard had assumed ownership in 1824 for $700 at the auction of the Pierre Laurent Montinard estate (February, C. de Armas), the property was described as "a lot of ground on the Bayou Road . . . on which stands a house consisting of two rooms and a shed and

several other buildings." These structures were still standing when Meilleur made his purchase in 1828, measuring 60 feet on Bayou Road (Governor Nicholls) by a depth of 540 feet. After Meilleur built this home in 1828, he lived in it for several years before selling on November 22, 1836, to Auguste Belloquet. The latter sold it April 29, 1839 (A. Ducatel), to Delphine Bégonier Marmillon, widow of Louis Dufilho, of Jefferson Parish. At the time of this sale, a plan of the property was exhibited, drawn by J. N. de Pouilly, copied from a plan by city surveyor Louis Surgi, dated February 15, 1839. Because of this plan, de Pouilly has been erroneously thought to be the architect. However, the house could have been designed by William Brand, who was in New Orleans in the 1820s and designed the Hermann-Grima House at 823 St. Louis, or by Joseph Correjolles, who designed the Beauregard House. Mr. William Franklin Goldthwaite, after whom the house is popularly named, was a later owner and prominent bookseller. For many years Mr. and Mrs. Alonso Lansford, noted art historians and painting conservators, owned the house and resided there. All architectural and decorative details of this outstanding house remain intact. The oversized dormer was added later. Photograph: Marcus Fraser.

Dauphin Property (1415). As late as 1834, this property was part of a small *habitation* facing Bayou Road owned by Gustave Auguste Dauphin, f.m.c. The extension of Esplanade Avenue caused the subdivision of Dauphin's property. Dauphin had married Jane Milne, a former slave of Alexander Milne. Milne freed Jane and left instructions in his will for a house to be built for her on his property. That house, at 1253–55 N. Villere, was where they lived. The extant, post-1883, two-story, frame house at 1415 Bayou Road has been considerably altered; but it retains its original stairs. The façade is now marked by six square brick pillars supporting a second-level balcony that has been filled in. The Pelican Brewery was located in the middle of this square of land facing N. Villere, according to the Robinson Atlas of 1883.

1510–12, 1516

Murphy Houses (1510–12, 1516), 1518, 1522. On this site in 1830 stood Lewis Levy's *maison de maître*, which he sold to William E. Murphy in 1839. After fifty years of ownership, Murphy gave the *maison de maître* and grounds to his daughter Citye Ann Murphy of Paris, France. During his long ownership of this land, Murphy subdivided and built the two houses at **1510–12** and **1516** Bayou Road (Governor Nicholls). An attorney, Murphy married Citye Rose Alvarez in a ceremony in Mobile in 1843. Their daughters, Citye Ann and Zoë Marie both married Frenchmen, lived in Paris, and inherited their parents' real estate

holdings, which included 1510–12 and 1516 Bayou Road, 1132 N. Robertson, and 1123–25 Marais. The façade of 1516, a three-bay, hip-roof, brick shotgun, has retained its brick dentils, original *abat-vent*, and supporting iron bearers. The three openings are surmounted by wooden lintels, typical of houses in the early nineteenth century. The side-wall placement of three chimneys at 1510–12 Bayou Road, the full-length openings, the recessed side galleries, and the position of the house on the lot provide clues that this house was part of the early Murphy *maison de maître* complex. However, the present front gable, brackets, and brick facing give the house the appearance of an ill-proportioned shotgun. Restoration would include reroofing and removal of added architectural details. The houses at **1518** and **1522** Bayou Road (Governor Nicholls) were built after 1883 as replacements for a row of common-wall creole cottages that were owned first, in 1834, by J. L. Dolliole and later, in 1838, by Félix de Armas. 1518 was built as a two-bay, frame shotgun with a front gable and apron. 1522 was built as a four-bay, double shotgun, with the same architectural features as the house at 1518, including the shingles on the gable, fleur-de-lis vergeboard, and border on the apron.

1507–09

Dupont House. The two-story, double house with front gable was built after 1907 when Louis A. Dupont purchased the lot from Mrs. Alcide Valeton. An earlier house at the corner of Bayou Road and Villere, old number 245 Bayou Road, was owned by the artist John Pemberton in 1850, when he sold it to Adolphe Avenel. It was described as late as 1892 as a "double tenement, frame, slated cottage with double story back building known as 245 and 247 Bayou Road." Adjacent toward N. Robertson was a creole cottage, "a brick cottage known as 249 Bayou Road." Behind the corner on N. Villere Street was a "two-story, frame dwelling known as 271 Villere." The entire subdivision of three houses belonged to Adolphe A. Avenel

from 1850 to 1892. Rooftops of old numbers 245, 247, 249, and 271 were shown on a sketch by D'Hémécourt dated January 6, 1892 (J. Duvigneaud).

1519

Hulin Property 1513, 1519. Part of the 1500 block of Bayou Road on the odd side was once the site of the *maison de maître* of Widow J. Hulin, as seen in plan book 38, folio 31, a drawing dated 1866. She owned the property as early as 1820, and a building is seen on the site of **1519** Bayou Road on the Tanesse map of 1816. Some remnants of the Hulin *maison de maître* may be incorporated in this present house, which has a graceful hip-roof and brick sides covered

with weatherboards. **1513** Bayou Road, a three-bay shotgun, was built with an entrance leading to a recessed side gallery. Hexagonal bays at each end of the side gallery are unusual, but the façade characteristics of drop-siding, bracketed overhang, and full-length openings with molded cornices are common to late-Victorian houses.

1606

Demazillière Property. An early *maison de maître* in the 1600 block of Bayou Road was that of Bazile Demazillière, f.m.c. His property was located at the corner of N. Robertson in the same block as that of Joseph Chalon and the free persons of color, Foucher and Hazeur. Demazillière's house was built in 1821 as part of a marriage contract between him and his fiancée, Antoinette Françoise Dubreuil, f.w.c. Before the marriage, Demazillière sold to Mlle Dubreuil a lot on Bayou Road "30 feet by 3 *arpents* bound by Dame Veuve Blaise Cenas and Jean Foucher," for $100. The vendor specified that he "promises to build in four months *une maison en colombage, couverte en bardeaux* 26½ feet by 24 feet divided into four rooms with double chimneys in the front two rooms, a gallery front and rear, and *une cave* below, a kitchen in the court to measure 20 feet by 12 feet with a chimney,

also two latrines. The vendor reserves the right to rent the finished house" (see 1119–21 N. Robertson). This *maison de maître*, demolished in the late nineteenth century, was replaced by the present two-level, double, frame house having four bays, wooden brackets supporting the overhang, and applied jigsaw millwork.

BAYOU ROAD (GOVERNOR NICHOLLS)

1608, 1614

Louis Chalon House (1608), 1614. Louis Théodule Chalon, one of Joseph Chalon's sons (see 1624 Bayou Road), built the Classic-style, double-galleried house at **1608** between 1851 and 1860. It features a double gallery with fluted Corinthian columns and a cast-iron railing. On the side is a covered balcony with cast-iron railing and supporting cast-iron brackets. The recessed entrance is framed by pilasters and cornice and enclosed by louvered shutters; molded cornices surmount the full-length windows. Neither the steps nor the façade siding is original. Louis Chalon bought the lot with earlier buildings from Louis Decoudreaux, f.m.c., on June 4, 1851, before A. Doriocourt for $2,000. The Decoudreaux family had held the property from their acquisition from Claude Tremé in the early 1800s until this 1851 sale. It had been developed with property lines running parallel and perpendicular to Bayou Road, and the placement of this house continues the tradition. In 1860 when Chalon sold the lot with this house to Jean Baptiste Preau, the price jumped to $8,000. The site of **1614** Bayou Road was the *maison de maitre* of a free man of color, Prosper Hazeur. The lot measured 33 feet front on Bayou Road and 420 feet deep, reaching back to Ursulines, where it formed the corner of N. Claiborne. The house was constructed of brick between posts with a shingle roof and contained the usual four rooms, with a *galerie et cabinet*. There is no mention of a front gallery in the March 23, 1850, inventory of Hazeur's estate, and his house may be the one set back on the lot indicated in the Tanesse survey of 1816. According to the inventory of 1850, there was *une mauvaise cuisine en bois*, and *un vieux hangard*, appraised at $8,000—a considerable sum. Hazeur's wife, Felicité Robert had died December 11, 1844, leaving three children. They were Léocadie Hazeur (who married Nelson Pavageau), Lise who married Norbert Picou, and Prosper, Jr. The inventory enumerates a "slave named Juliette born in New Orleans, of 18 years, who was a cook and washerwoman, a milk cow, and small creole cottage." The back gallery contained "an old mahogany bureau, a *garde-manger* [pantry], and a cypress armoire." In the yard were 2,000 lake bricks, old irons, and *la batterie de cuisine* (a set of kitchen utensils). In the bedroom were "a mahogany armoire, a smaller armoire, mahogany tester bed, another small bed, a cherry easy chair, three old tables, and a pair of *cylindres de cheminée* [hurricane lamps]." The present house at 1614, with its beveled-glass double doors, was built with a side hall and Classic-style double gallery with a dentiled cornice, probably in the 1860s. However, late-nineteenth-century alterations on the first- and second-floor galleries have altered the original façade proportion, shortening the columns and adding entablature arches.

1624

36/5

Chalon-Coiron House. An early owner of this last lot on the left side of the Morand tract was Françoise Dubreuil, née Fanchonette Decoudreaux, f.w.c., who had acquired it from Claude Tremé on July 26, 1808 (Pierre Pedesclaux). She also held through marriage the land presently occupied by 1608 and 1614 Bayou Road. Charles Lamerance acquired the first lot in Mme Dubreuil's succession on February 11, 1811. A recapitulation of this ownership was recorded by T. Seghers on June 9, 1836, as evidence in a lawsuit between Charles Decoudreaux, f.m.c., and Charles Lamerance. By that date, 1624 had long been the property of Joseph Chalon and his wife, Elizabeth Desruisseaux, who had purchased it from James Hopkins on June 12, 1820 (John Lynd). Monsieur Chalon, a prominent lawyer, had married the daughter of Joseph Desruisseaux and Francisca Girardy, and had vast holdings along Bayou Road and Bayou St. John. The Chalons probably built their house, illustrated in plan book 36, folio 5, soon after 1820. Their neighbor across the street was Alexander Milne, who built the large home often described erroneously as a Scottish castle reproduction. The economically and socially prominent Chalon family and Milne joined distinguished and prosperous free persons of color in ownership of both sides of this block. In 1836 Chalon subdivided his property but donated lots adjacent to his house to his children: Joseph Octave, Louis Théodule, and Hermogène. He had already given his daughter Celèstine, Widow François Lamolère Dorville, a lot to which he added thirty more feet (June 9, 1836, T. Seghers). Other property was sold to Nelson Fouché, f.m.c., and Jean Firmin Pepin. Widow Chalon sold the house at 1624 Bayou Road and the immediate grounds to her son Joseph Octave in 1850 for $2,600. Soon after buying the house and grounds, Joseph Octave entered into a contract with Pierre Théodule Olivier, f.m.c., to build a new house at 1624. This contract suggests that the early Chalon house was moved back and altered by the son to serve as a kitchen for a new creole cottage. Excerpts from the French contract recorded before Cyprien Ladreyère on January 12, 1850, are as follows: "Joseph Chalon and Pierre Théodule Olivier contract for the construction of a house, building, and dependencies on a lot of ground on Bayou Road between Robertson, Claiborne, and Ursulines, the lot 60 feet facing the road by 100 feet on Claiborne and 116 feet on the Robertson Street side. The builder to furnish materials to build a house 30 feet by 46 feet deep and 12 feet tall, divided into four rooms, a gallery and *cabinet*. Each room will be 14 feet 3 inches by 16 feet deep. The gallery will be 10 feet by 20 feet, the *cabinet* 8½ feet by 10 feet. The floor will be 30 inches above the banquette level. The attic will be floored with two small halls between two attic bedrooms. There will be four windows, two on the façade and two on the side of the house opening on the court. . . . There will be two windows on each of the side gables. The two rooms of the main floor facing the street will each have two doors. . . . There will be on one side a sliding door to get to the rear rooms, and on the other side a paneled door. . . . The gallery will be closed; there will be two doors and one window onto the court and one door for the *cabinet* and a staircase to the attic. The builder will take for a model the house of Monsieur Joachim Courcelle on Claiborne between St. Philippe and Dumaine. The house will be made of wood on a brick foundation, covered in slates, the façade brick between posts, the rest brick to three feet only. The façade will be plastered, the gables and sides covered with boards. The house which is now found standing on the land will be moved and relocated on the back of the lot. The gallery and brickwork will be lathed and plastered and the roof covered with shingles of good quality. The façade and rear elevation will have a double covering in lathes or in planks, the façade whitewashed and the back of raw wood. The enclosure of the land on the side of the house will be made in planks of white pine and grooved and will be placed upright. There will be a door to the court from each side of the house, having a movable panel with grill. There will be a latrine of 4 feet by 7 feet divided in two *cabinets*, a well of brick with wood cover, a cistern of 1,200 gallons. Cost, $2,680." This new house was obviously retardate in style, and indeed, except for the gallery, was similar to Chalon's parental home. It was 1850, yet he used brick-between-posts construction and decorative details reminiscent of the 1820s, as seen in the elevation of the house in the possession of Coiron descendants. Elizabeth Desruisseaux Chalon died in 1854, and her son Joseph was the executor of the estate. In that capacity, he sold two lots to the rear of 1624 Governor Nicholls to a free man of color, Louis Mathé. Then on October 3, 1856, before P. E. Laresche, the Chalon home was sold to Jeanne H. Millaudon, wife of Casimir Cardanne. Subsequent owner Albin Rochéreau sold the property, then known as 270 Bayou Road, at auction for $3,600 to François S. Coiron on May 9, 1877, before James Fahey. Coiron donated the house to his wife, Aimée Strata, in 1899; their daughter, Aimée Coiron, wife of Leon M. Roubion, retained it until her death in 1964. The house has been enlarged, probably by the Coiron family, to five façade openings with an enclosed and recessed side gallery. The hall has a segmental entrance, leading to a *cabinet* with stairwell. The façade siding and brackets were added in the 1890s. Retained are the original French doors, front and rear batten shutters with hardware, and the original enclosed back gallery with a small fireplace. The other rooms also have typical wooden pilastered mantels. Across the rear of the lot is a two-story service house with brick fireplaces. This may be a portion of the 1820 Chalon *maison de maître*. It is coincidental that within this house lived descendants of Claude Tremé's daughter, Eugènie, who had married François Ste Marie Coiron. Their heir, François Stanislaus Coiron, was born on Lesseps Plantation (Réunion Plantation) in St. Bernard Parish and, after the Civil War, bought 1624 Governor Nicholls, residing there until his death.

BAYOU ROAD*

*Bayou Road between the 1700 and 2600 blocks retains its original name.

1836

Sutterlin House. A mid-nineteenth-century house with double-galleried façade and side hall stands on a larger parcel that once belonged to Edmond Forstall. By 1834 this lot was owned by C. Janin, according to the Zimpel map. It was the only property subdivided from the Forstall *habitation* before 1847. An auction held on April 25, 1854, revealed that much of this square was to be partitioned because Samuel Moore "failed to comply with the terms of the adjudication made to him of said property on the 11th day of February last." Eugène Guyot acquired the site of 1836 Bayou Road for $2,000, selling to George Sutterlin at the same price one year later. The present house was built in 1855 for George Sutterlin who, upon his death in 1856, left the house to his widow and five children. They kept it until 1879, when Widow Sutterlin, Elizabeth Kuhn, sold to Widow Joseph Armbruster for just $600. She apparently completely remodeled or rebuilt and sold 1836 Bayou Road to Henry Bentz for $5,100 on June 4, 1892, as recorded by notary Zengel.

1924

Gautier Villa. The site of 1924 Bayou Road was part of the land Claude Tremé sold before 1810. Jean Baptiste Larieux, f.m.c., who was married to Josephine Dolliole, obtained the property from builder Barthélémy Rey, f.m.c., on May 11, 1847 (A. Doriocourt). He sold the lot at auction for $800 to Aimé Gautier on February 15, 1848. By 1853 Gautier acquired three lots facing Bayou Road and had the extant house built. He retained ownership for twenty-five years, selling the property on March 29, 1878, to Jules Joseph D'Aquin (E. Boundy). The frame villa-type house was built with five bays. The entrance leading to a wide center hall is ornamented with Greek Key medallions, and a dentil cornice. The gallery supports, railing, garlands, and dormer were added sometime in the early twentieth century, but remnants of the original parapet can be seen. One gabled-end has a cast-iron balcony and a dentiled overhang.

1903–09

Crocker Property. This four-bay Victorian house is flanked by two wings. The façade has segmental arches, a spindle course of pierced panels, turned spindles, and brackets. The 1900 block on both sides is characterized by 1890s shotguns similar to this, with a variety of decoration. The odd side of the street was part of the Morand concession of 1756, which was sold by Widow Paul Moreau to Andrés Almonester in 1780. A series of subsequent owners followed, including the family of Pierre Crocker, a prominent, free black investor and draftsman for many archival drawings.

2116

Pontalba Division. The double-galleried, two-story, frame house was built in retardate Classic-style in the 1880s. The features of the façade include a cornice articulated with dentils and paired brackets, turned baluster railing, Classic door and window surrounds, box columns, and a central dormer on a steeply pitched roof. The side elevations are gabled.

2122

Barron Villa. A galleried, frame villa with five bays was built by Archibald Barron, after he purchased this lot in 1847. In May of that year, Barron, who had invested in much land beyond N. Rampart, bought "two pieces of contiguous land situated on the Road to Bayou St. John" from D. Seghers and Joseph Abat. The lots were originally part of the Pontalba division, and at the time of the sale, Barracks Street had not been cut through. Barron built this handsome house between 1847 and 1869, when he sold it to William Francis. It was described as "a one-story house at 368 Bayou Road" (May 15, 1869, A. Doriocourt). Joseph Eugène Léon Joubert de Villemarest sold the house to Mme Marie Adèle Communy, widow of Dr. Yves René Le Monnier at an auction on September 22, 1883, when the property was advertised as "a handsome cottage with hall in the centre, and having modern improvements."

2257 Kitchen

Benachi-Torre House. The outstanding, center-hall, Classic-style house built in 1859 for Nicholas Benachi and his second wife, Anna Marie Bidault, cost $18,000. This was the site of an earlier Bayou Road residence designed for Joseph Zeringue in 1806 by Barthélémy Lafon. The earlier building housed the Bellanger boarding school from 1832 to 1838. Benachi purchased it with grounds measuring 135 feet front by three *arpents* depth in 1852 for $11,134 (June 28, T. Guyol). He lived in the early *maison de maître* with his first wife and children for a short time, but Mme Benachi and two of the children died of yellow fever in 1853 at their summer home in Biloxi. When Benachi remarried, he demolished the early house, building this one for his new wife. The Benachi family kept its residence until 1886, when Peter Torre purchased it. The house and grounds remained in the Torre family, although the three-*arpent* depth of the lot has been cut by the extension of Laharpe Street. The house and detached, two-story service building are enclosed on the spacious grounds by a high cast-iron fence having a Gothic-style gate. The ensemble is one of the city's major landmarks. Although the floor plan reflects the traditional, American, center-hall plan, the single windows on either side of the entrance and second level door are unusual for New Orleans. Paired box columns supporting the double galleries are another variation from the norm. Adding sophistication to the façade are the pilasters at the corner of the flushboard front. The $18,000 building price in 1859 is high and is reflected in the excellent quality of interior millwork and plaster decoration. The complex was donated to the Louisiana Landmarks Society in 1978 by heirs of Peter Torre.

2275

Fleitas-Chauffe House. This *maison principale* may well be a Spanish colonial residence built for Domingo Fleitas about 1802 and moved to this site and remodeled in 1836. The Fleitas family owned property in the French Quarter on Burgundy, but they lived most of the time on the left side of Bayou Road at their narrow *habitation*, measuring only 53 *toises* front but extending in depth to Common Street. When Domingo Fleitas died in 1826, his estate was sold (July 21, 1826); but the family repurchased the portion of the plantation that contained the *maison principale*. There Madame Fleitas died on June 27, 1834. Her will, dated March 21, 1832, before T. Seghers, left her property to her four surviving children: Jean Manuel, Barthélémy, Paulin, and Virginie, married to Louis Aimé Pigneguy. An inventory of the

estate described the following rooms of the house on the left side of Bayou Road (July 21, 1834): "Southeast room, Northwest room, *cabinet* behind southeast room, *salon* on courtyard, bedroom of Madame Fleitas, dining room." The house was described as *en briques au rez de chaussée*, that is, raised on a brick basement, and *haut en colombage*, the upper part half-timbered. It is not mentioned whether it was *bousillage* or brick-between-posts construction. Recorded were the "kitchen, stable, dependencies, the whole cultivated in gardens and fruit trees." There were also "office, cave, cour, and animals," appraised at $14,000. The inventory describes the present site of 2275 Bayou Road, right side, as undeveloped, with a garden, as it also appears on the Zimpel survey of 1834. The lot on the right side measured 135 feet front on Bayou Road by three *arpents* or 576 feet deep and had been purchased by Domingo Fleitas in 1812 from his son-in-law, Louis Aimé Pigneguy (May 30, N. Broutin). By 1835, Jean Manuel Fleitas had bought out his relatives and was the sole owner of the *maison principale* and lands on both sides of Bayou Road. Just two years later, in 1837, he sold the property on the right side, with this extant house, to Frederick Furst (January 6, A. Ducatel). The act of sale mentions that "the buyer is not to begin enjoyment of the *maison de maître* on the lot until the 6th of March next—until then Jean Manuel Fleytas [*sic*] reserves the right to inhabit the said house and its dependencies." Since the Fleitas plantation on the left side of Bayou Road (where the *maison principale* had stood) was sold by Fleitas to speculator Jean Dufour in 1836, it is thought that Jean Manuel Fleitas moved the old house, which stood in the projected route of Esplanade, across to the right of Bayou Road just after the August 4 sale of the land to Dufour. Then he renovated it, adding the present Greek Revival-style moldings and mantels and appended kitchen wing. The floor plan, room proportions, front and rear gallery supports, fenestration, hip-roof line, dormers, hardware, and shutters indicate eighteenth-century origins. After Fleitas sold to Furst, the house was purchased in 1843 by B. Poydras de Lallande for $4,300. Mrs. Joseph Leach sold to Henry S. Chauffe on May 20, 1901, and Mr. Chauffe brought his bride to the historic house. They made twentieth-century additions. On the left is a wing in the form of a shotgun, which provides two bedrooms. On the right, the Chauffes added a bay to the rear *cabinet*, creating a large master bedroom. The present dining room and kitchen area are appended to the rear and date from the 1836 relocation. The Chauffe son and daughters lived in the house, keeping it in fine condition until 1977, when it was sold. Photograph: Janet Urian.

2545

Sainte Rose de Lima Church. Ste Rose de Lima Parish was established in 1857, two years after Fanny Labatut, widow of Evariste Blanc, donated a lot on Maurepas Street, near Mystery across N. Broad. Her gift to Monseigneur Antoine Blanc was made, according to the act of sale (June 21, 1855, O. de Armas), "for the greater good of the Catholics residing between the city and Bayou St. John." In the same act, Madame Blanc pledged to furnish "300,000 bricks of good quality destined for the erection of a church or chapel on said lot, also a presbytery or residence of the priest serving the said church." The lot and bricks were appraised at $4,000, and the Archbishop pledged to start construction within three years. First, the small house already on the lot at Maurepas and Mystery was converted into a chapel in mid-April of 1857. This early location was abandoned for a more favorable lot along Bayou Road in Faubourg Gueno, which was donated July 2, 1857, by Madeleine Gueno Buss (Mme James Joseph), a daughter of Pierre Gueno. A small frame church was completed on the new lot adjacent to the present church in November, 1857, and named Ste Rose de Lima. The new parish was bound by N. Dorgenois to St. Bernard to the Old Basin Canal. In 1870 a new church was planned for the parish, and a contract drawn between Father Mittelbronn and Alexandre Castaing, architect (March 5, O. de Armas). This third church cost $13,000 and was enlarged in 1891. It burned October 24, 1913, along with the earlier frame chapel, which had been moved and converted into a school. When the present church was built in 1914, the building association was chaired by John A. Wogan, and Paul Andry was selected as architect. He designed the new brick church in the Tudor or English Gothic style; the cost was $70,582. The present brick school, facing Columbus Street, dates from 1925 and was also designed by Andry, with George J. Glover, the builder. A loan of $78,657 covered the cost of the school.

Bayou Road continued on its winding route, but Governor Nicholls beginning at N. Claiborne Avenue was established in the 1840s and was called Hospital all the way to N. Broad. In 1909 the street, including what the authors have identified as Bayou Road, was named Governor Nicholls and ran from the Mississippi River to N. Broad. Bayou Road, the original Road, continued by its own name from N. Claiborne to N. Broad.

1714

Griffon Division. Hidden behind this mutilated façade is an outstanding example of a two-bay, dormered, gable-sided, creole cottage with semi-incorporated overhang. The house is on land that Charles Griffon sold to J. B. Derneville, f.m.c., in the early 1800s. Such creole cottages abound in Faubourg Tremé, especially in the Griffon and Forstall tracts, the area between N. Claiborne and N. Prieur. This one, stucco to the gable, is of handsome proportions, retains its arched-light dormer, and probably dates from the early 1840s.

1722

Griffon Division. This *petite maison* is an outstanding remaining example of a house-type peculiar to the creole suburbs. An entrance, now mutilated by lowering, leads to a recessed side gallery covered by a hip-roof with a sloping cant; the other side property line elevation is gabled. Façade rustication and short windows suggest that the house was built in the 1830s, after the heirs of Charles Griffon subdivided the family *habitation*. An 1893 sale on November 16, by Zoë Dusau de la Croix (widow first of Charles Fortier, then William Chapman) to Pierre Racheu at auction for $880 described the property: "284 Hospital, the improvements consist of a cottage having four rooms, side gallery, two-story rear building with two rooms, cistern, privy, etc." The two-story kitchen has been demolished and replaced by an appendage to the house.

1826

2/7

Forstall Division. The history of this property can be traced back to Alexandre Latil in the eighteenth century. Latil sold it to Don Andrés Almonester y Rojas, whose widow gave it to their daughter Micaela for her dowry. In 1812 she and her husband, Joseph de Pontalba, sold it to Edmond Forstall. Manuel Julien de Lizardi, a subsequent owner, subdivided it in 1847. The 1840s-style creole cottage was built soon after. It is illustrated in plan book 2, folio 7 as it appeared in 1878. The gallery overhang has been removed and a front appendage added, probably in this century. The density of the population of the Forstall division increased and the rural atmosphere diminished. The stump of a sycamore, which once shaded the deep front garden of the yard, remains beside the herringbone-patterned brick sidewalk. The original wooden picket fence has been replaced by an inappropriate chain-link one.

1828

Noël House. Disguised behind a twentieth-century renovation that encloses half of the gallery, there stands a fine, late-1840s, two-story, four-bay, gable-sided house in the creole tradition. The original house, with front and rear galleries supported by box columns, was just one room deep. The rear gallery and kitchen building have been removed. Yorick Noël bought two lots in 1848 for $400 from Marie Manuel Elliot, who had acquired them after the 1847 subdivision of the Forstall *habitation*. Noel sold one lot, with the present house, to G. G. Gaibisso for $2,000 on November 25, 1859, as recorded by A. Doriocourt.

1915

Pontalba Division. Here stands a good example of the three-bay, single-dormer creole cottage. Probably built in the 1840s, it occupies a portion of the Pontalba division retained by the Baroness from 1812 until the 1830s sale. The high, pitched, canted roofline gives it visual charm. Beyond the entranceway there is a recessed side gallery.

1929–31

Gurlie Division. The weatherboarded creole cottage was built on land that was part of the Gurlie division, subdivided in the 1830s. Adolphe Duhart, f.m.c., lost an undeveloped lot to his creditors on August 26, 1840, as recorded by notary T. Seghers. Subsequently, Quirin Muller sold it to Mme Jean-Jacques Trosclair for $500 in 1860. Three years later, she sold the land with a new creole cottage on it to her son-in-law, George Bernard Ittmann, for $3,000. The excellent pilastered dormers are now disfigured with louvered "fill-ins." The cement steps and the present railing are not appropriate to the style of the house.

2033–35

Jumonville Cottage (2033–35) 2037–39. The dormered creole cottage pictured was built for Gustave Jumonville soon after 1857. He bought two lots from Joseph Girod for $500 on December 22, 1857, before A. Doriocourt. He sold the house and grounds January 20, 1866, before the same notary, to Victor Henry Hattier for $4,500. The property had been part of the second Pontalba division, that strip which Mme Pontalba did not sell in 1812 but kept until January 12, 1837 (F. Grima), when she sold four lots to J. M. Lee. His creditor Louis Bringier acquired them that same year. The Baroness sued Bringier over the property, and she reacquired it in a sheriff's sale August 27, 1839. She held the lots until 1848, selling them June 14 to Eugène Delazzèrie (T. Guyol) for $600. The corner, double shotgun at **2037–39** Governor Nicholls, with front hip-roof, probably dates from a few years after its mid-nineteenth-century, side-gabled creole neighbor. They are compatible in style, proportion, and banquette position. The banquette is the original brick.

2219–21, 2223

Cohen Cottages. These two creole cottages were built in 1853 by John McVittie for Michael Cohen, who had owned the lots for a decade. As soon as the houses were completed, Cohen sold one of them to McVittie for $400. After a thirty-year ownership, the builder sold **2219–21** to Martin Broderick in 1883. The house never brought more than $640 on any of the eight occasions it changed hands between its construction date and 1927. The weatherboarded, beak-roof, urban-style cottage originally had open galleries on each side, as seen in an 1876 survey by Allain d'Hémécourt attached to the act recorded by A. Dreyfous on March 29, 1877. The survey showed the alignment of Milne Road, which still exists today for only one block from Esplanade to Governor Nicholls, formerly Hospital Street. The lots were part of the holdings of Antonio Mendez, a Spanish colonial citizen, who had bought the Bayou Road frontage of the Dorgenois *habitation* in the early 1800s. The three-bay, beak-roof creole cottage at **2223** Governor Nicholls is the smaller of the two built as a single but now having double entrances.

2316

Milne Gardens. According to title research, this camelback shotgun dates from 1906. The gabled front with shingles and recessed side gallery suggests a return to Neoclassic tastes and blends well with the attached gable-sided camelback. The two-level structure recalls the standard, two-story, gable-sided, detached creole kitchen, once built across the rear of lots in most New Orleans eighteenth- and early-nineteenth-century housing. Moses Raymond and his relative Ernestine Orelia financed the building of the house between 1906 and 1907, and Raymond sold it to Edwin William Rosenmeier in 1917 (March 3, O. Schreiber) for $1,500. The property was part of the Milne Gardens, which Alexander Milne acquired from the estate of Marie Noyan Michel, f.w.c., September 29, 1829, in probate court. Milne's estate subdivided the tract according to specifications in his will; the purpose was to raise money for the establishment and support of his charities.

2523

Monsseaux House. Paul Hypolite Monsseaux bought this property in 1869 and built the present three-bay, side-hall, galleried house. It was sold in the succession sale of his wife, Marie Adelaide Guesnon, on August 2, 1890 (A. Doriocourt). The house shows evidence of a remodeling between 1900 and 1910, as indicated by the gabled front with shingles and stained glass, the sparseness of decorative details, and the Neoclassic columns. The detached service wing, with batten shutters, has the original slate roof and five pillars. The main house is of brick-between-posts construction, with machine-cut posts. A large magnolia tree in the ample side yard and a palm tree enrich the spacious setting.

147

1114–16

Soulié Property. The history of a single house often reveals the history of the entire square; so it is with 1114–16 Barracks. Laurent Alpuente owned this land after purchasing 64 feet facing N. Rampart from the City Corporation in 1819. He built two creole cottages at the N. Rampart Street banquette, and Joseph Pilié depicted them in 1828. This plan was attached to the acts of Félix de Armas on August 12. Another plan of one of these cottages by D'Hémécourt was drawn forty-nine years later for free men of color Bernard and Albin Soulié, of Paris and New Orleans. They sold a quarter of this square including the N. Rampart Street house in that transaction of April 11, 1867, notarized by E. Eude. At that time, the only structure at the banquette on the site of the present 1114–16 Barracks was a chicken house, part of the Alpuente-Soulié Rampart Street complex. Blaise Pradel bought the entire parcel for $12,000 from the Souliés in the 1867 sale. Four years later, he moved to Bourg, France, and resold the same property for $10,500 to Jules Le Blanc, who resubdivided and developed the land. Mlles Marie Oscarine and Simone Louise Vignaud were the recorded owners of the house at 1114–16 Barracks in 1879, when they sold to Mme Louis C. Lange for $2,100 (May 19, O. Morel). Even though the brick-between-post construction, masonry front, and beaded-wood side covering suggest a building date as early as the 1820s, this house was not on its present site in 1867. Although such construction has been documented as late as the 1870s, it is also possible that this is an early house moved here in the 1870s by Jules Le Blanc from one of his vast real estate holdings. The rough plaster, pierced-work cornices, and overhang brackets probably date from the Lange ownership after 1879. The three-room, two-story, brick kitchen in the rear predates the house at this location. Shown on the 1867 D'Hémécourt plan, it was the kitchen of the N. Rampart Street creole cottage, now the site of 1225 N. Rampart.

1122

Mioton House. The three-bay, semi-detached, Greek Revival, masonry-fronted creole cottage has an entrance door opening onto a side gallery. A round-headed dormer light, a roof flare at the overhang, and a single side chimney next to a brick parapet are distinguishing features. A one-story, frame service wing forms an ell in the side yard; a two-story, brick kitchen extends across the rear. This house is situated on part of a large tract of land that Claude Tremé sold to free man of color Charles Meunier in 1803 (P. Pedesclaux, act 60). Fortuné Armand, f.m.c., paid $200 for this portion of Meunier's property in 1824, and the lot was vacant when Armand's widow, Félicité Denuy, exchanged it for $700 worth of construction work by builders Duru and St. Martin, to build a house on St. Antoine between Marais and St. Ann, backed by Esplanade. The house at 1122 Barracks was built in 1846–1847 by Jacques Michel St. Martin and Nicholas Duru as a speculative venture. They sold it to Eugène F. Mioton for $3,000 in 1847. Mme Mioton retained this cottage until 1865, selling it to Edmund Breaux for $1,912 (November 17, R. Ker). The house has had a long series of owners since; its highest selling price through 1920 was $1,750.

1124–26

Roy Cottage (1124–26) 1123. Claude Tremé sold a parcel of ground including this property at **1124–26** to Charles Meunier, f.m.c., in 1801 (April 21, P. Pedesclaux). In 1834 Bernardo Santos purchased part of the present lot at an auction of Meunier's estate for $1,500. Two years later, builder Frederick Roy bought the Santos lot and an adjacent one from Marie Louise Bernard for $430, providing a wide site for this house, (April 3, 1836, H. Pedesclaux). Roy built the present structure soon after 1836, selling in 1839 to Pierre Dupeux for $7,000. Dupeux sold the property within the year to Mme Aimée D'Arensbourg, f.w.c., for the same price. In 1853 Armand Richard Clague, f.m.c. and half-brother of well-known artist Richard Clague, purchased this house at auction, keeping it as rental property until 1856 (February 5, O. de Armas). The house then changed hands almost every two years until after the Civil War. It is a fine, semi-detached, double-dormered creole cottage with masonry front and four French doors, gabled ends of brick, and small arched dormers with simple pilasters—all indicative of the 1830s building date. An outstanding, two-story, masonry service building rests across the court to the side of the house. This is now a separate property, but it was once part of 1124–26. Across the street at **1123** is a two-story, two-bay, frame house which could predate the present façade embellishments. The first-level gallery and second-level balcony and overhang reflect the style of the 1880s. The French doors and simple surrounds, however, suggest a mid-century Classic-style dwelling.

1204

1212

Larribeau House (1212), 1204. These frame, three-bay townhouses in the Greek Revival style date from 1855 and 1857. Recessed entrances have doors with sidelights and transoms, and second-level galleries are supported by box columns. **1212** has lost its gallery railing, and **1204** has one of cast-iron. The two properties were the rear garden of the large Bayou Road holdings of Pierre Lambert, whose estate was settled in 1849. Lambert had bought property from early Tremé purchasers Solomon Prevost (1813), Benoit Milbrouck (1819), and Marcelite Hazeur (1849). A building contract dated May 7, 1855, before A. Chiapella, indicates that Lambert's daughter Mme Louis Larribeau, acquired one of her father's lots and had Nicholas Duru build the house and kitchen at 1212 Barracks in 1855 for just $2,500. The contract specifies "a house and kitchen of two stories just like the one occupied by M. Jourdain on St. Bernard Avenue with the exception of the gallery in front. . . . The balcony will be 4 feet wide. It will be made with a cornice according to the plan. The house to measure 42 feet by 21½ feet, the kitchen 24 feet by 12 feet. Inside to be the same as the plan except *parisian* [louvered] shutters on the first floor . . . four grates at 10 dollars each for the four fire-places of the house. Paint in two coats of good paint of oil and in white. The outside may be in white or color of taste of proprietor. Shutters and exterior doors to be a beautiful green. The house to be raised 2 feet off the banquette. The windows of the kitchen will be glass as well as the doors of the rooms of the second floor. The hall door will be paneled. A wall 8 feet high, 78 feet long, in lake brick to be built. Cast-iron balcony with pilasters supported by iron bars and crowned with capitals and a beautiful cornice; between the pilasters there will be cast iron or wood. Cost: $2,500." The lot at 1204 Barracks was formed by Hugh Dowling, who purchased land from Hugh Frigère in 1847 and later from the Lambert heirs. Dowling built two or more houses, including 1204, on his lots about 1857. It is obvious that Dowling copied Mme Larribeau's nearby house at 1212. He kept this and other adjacent houses until 1881, when Jean Marie Lafferranderie acquired them. Lafferranderie had huge holdings in the area in the 1880s, and his widow, Olympia Quivard, left 1204 Barracks to her daughter, Mme W. G. Crozat, in 1920. Numerous subsequent owners paid less than $1,500 for the house until a sale in 1946 grossed $3,000. Title research indicates that Lafferranderie acquired property to the rear of this lot from the succession of Thomy Lafon in 1894.

1218

Doriocourt House. This and adjoining lots extending to Bayou Road became part of the Doriocourt estate in 1865 (November 1, A. Doriocourt) and remained in the family until 1882 when André Doriocourt sold this house to Brandao and Gintz for $1,800. The frame, single shotgun with Greek Key entrance had been built for André and Joseph Doriocourt soon after 1867 and represents a Greek Revival style prevalent in Tremé. Victorian window cornices, bracketed overhang, and fleur-de-lis vergeboard were added later; originally there were three full-length façade openings. This property shares an early history with its immediate neighbors across the street.

1224

Bacas House. The entrance of this modest frame cottage leads to a recessed side gallery. This house is not illustrated on insurance maps of 1883 or 1890, but it was probably constructed soon after. Mrs. Bernard Saulay lost the vacant lot for $30 in back taxes to P. A. Bacas in 1895. Two years later he sold to Louis Lafferanderie for $600. Lafferanderie, a large landholder in Tremé, probably bought this house after construction. There are many records of his owning property used for rentals; there are no sources indicating that he built within the area. There is, however, much evidence that he and his family retained ownership for long periods; his widow held this property until 1933.

1200 Block

Le Blanc Row. This row of frame, single, Greek Revival creole cottages located at **1213**, **1217**, **1219**, and **1221** Barracks is one of the more outstanding in the Tremé area. Each cottage was once identical, with one Classic-style pilastered dormer to the front and another in the rear, a recessed side gallery, Greek Revival-style dentils on the cornice, and Greek Key door frame. Although the façade of 1213 has been altered, some surrounds retain medallions. Victorian brackets and lintels were added to all the houses. The municipality sold property in this square in 1830, when Paulin Le Blanc bought the front part of the lots to a depth of 30 feet. He built the houses after he had acquired the back 28 feet of each lot in 1847 and Barracks Street was cut through. His widow sold them to Eugène Surgi, architect-surveyor, in 1870 (March 15, E. Commagère). Surgi probably added the Victorian brackets. Jean M. Lafferanderie, a well-known developer, purchased the houses in 1892; his heirs sold them to separate owners in 1909. The early history of the property goes back to Demahy Dumontil, who bought most of this square from Claude Tremé and sold it to Pierre Lavergne in 1807. Jean Mager purchased it in 1814, after which the city acquired the property as part of a parcel through which Esplanade was to extend. Plan book 85, folio 14 indicates that in 1841 Rue de Quartier (Barracks) had not been completed in this square, although Tremé Street was established. Plan book 36, folio 15 depicts a creole cottage and service building adjacent to these lots at the corner of Barracks and St. Claude in 1849 (December 1, L. Surgi). Now the corner site at 1201 is vacant.

1305–07

Tiblier Cottage. In 1849 Aribert Desjardins sold Claude Tiblier land, which he had purchased at a sheriff's sale the same year. C. A. de Armas drew a plan of the property showing six lots, measuring 67 feet on Barracks by 200 feet on Tremé by 28 feet on Esplanade by 240 feet on Marais (July 17, 1849, A. Mazureau). The site of **1305–07** Barracks was one of these lots. Tiblier may have used builder A. Hypolite Sampson to construct this masonry creole double on the site at the same time he contracted with him for the building of 1240 Esplanade. The cottage is a perfect example of an 1850s creole style, with brick fire-extension walls bordering the side-gabled roof. Two, well-proportioned, pilastered dormers with arched lights are separated by a tall chimney. The rustication of the façade may be original, but the four full-length openings now have Victorian door surrounds with bull's-eye and scallop design on the frame lintels. A fleur-de-lis vergeboard decorates the built-in overhang, which is supported by Victorian brackets similar to those of its 1890-style, frame, camelback neighbor at **1301**. Tiblier sold 1305–07 for $3,500 with two lots to Anthony Perault (January 15, 1866, A. Boudousquie). The Perault family retained ownership until 1879, then sold to Mme J. D. H. Herman. Jean Baptiste Laporte's widow, Sophie Dorn, acquired the house from Mme Herman's legatee, J. Pierre Picheux, for only $1,000 in 1895 and probably is responsible for the Victorian decorative additions.

1310–12

Guillaume-Blouin House. An early *maison de maître* occupying this and adjacent land was part of the 1809 inheritance of Agathe Montreuil, f.w.c., from Narcisse Harker (August 10, N. Broutin). The property, which faced Bayou Road, had previously been sold by Claude Tremé in 1803. Joseph Guillaume, the natural son of Agathe Montreuil, inherited the early *maison de maître* and large lot. In 1847 Widow Guillaume, Marie Castelain, sold the back half of the Bayou Road property for the prolongment of Barracks (July 12, J. Cuvillier). The present, urban-style creole cottage was probably built soon after the street was cut through for the widow, then wife of Jacques Meffre-Rouzan, f.m.c. She sold the new house to Joseph Blouin, f.m.c., March 15, 1852 (P. E. Laresche). This double, frame creole cottage with gabled ends was built higher above the ground than its neighbor at 1305 and was a more modest version of the creole style. Chimneys pierce the roof, but it is unlikely that the dwelling ever had dormers. The attic rooms were ventilated then, as today, by gable windows covered by batten shutters. The side elevations retain the batten shutters with strap hinges, but the façade was updated in the 1890s with segmental-arched Victorian doors, windows, drop-siding, quoins, and overhang brackets.

Barracks Street and Bayou Road. Barracks Street was opened from N. Rampart to Marais in the 1840s. It stopped there as a result of litigation between the city and owners of the Boisdoré, Dolliole, and Plauché *habitations*. Mme Plauché refused to sell, and the city realized that signatures of not fewer than nine other property owners would be necessary to acquire land for the continuation of Barracks through to N. Claiborne. They abandoned the project, and today Barracks ends at Marais and begins again five blocks away at N. Prieur. This photograph shows the island created by the turning of Bayou Road toward Esplanade and the commencement of Barracks directly to the left.

2012–14

Jean Saux House. This two-story, masonry, Greek Revival-style building was built with four bays at each level, in the creole manner. Presently there is a work area and auto-repair space below, apartments above. Stylistic features are the gabled sides, wrought-iron balcony, and four French doors at the second level, along with a simple string course cornice and scored façade. The house was built soon after 1848, when Jean Saux bought the lot from Baroness de Pontalba (June 14, T. Guyol). When Saux sold the property to Dominique Meunier on August 28, 1861, before A. Doriocourt for $2,500, the act specified that the buildings "belong to Sauce [*sic*] for having had them built since the said acquisition" in 1848. André D. Doriocourt bought the building from Meunier on August 27, 1867 (A. Doriocourt); and the act described "the buildings thereon, consisting of a two-story brick house, having in the garret two openings, one on each side, slate roof, back buildings . . . the brick walls on both sides of the buildings being built on the lot sold exclusively." Mme A. D. Doriocourt and André Doriocourt, Jr., sold the property (January 23, 1869, Antoine Doriocourt) to François and Jean Meda for $2,525. It is coincidental that the Meda heirs included Mme Justine Lauga, wife of Louis Tremé, who inherited the house or bought it from other heirs for $4,000 on November 3, 1944 (COB 534/178). Thus the Tremé name reappears in twentieth-century ownership.

2110

Mendez Division. The three-bay frame shotgun with hip-roof and segmental-arched openings has a handsome entrance with cornice and dentil work. The original door has a new glass panel above, and recent façade renovations have resulted in a slight alteration of the proportions of the three bays. Pierced-work overhang brackets postdate the Italianate surrounds of a house, probably dating from the 1870s. Two side alleyways provide easy access to the rear.

2226

Boyens House. The irregular square of the "Milne Gardens," bound by Barracks (Quartier), Milne Road, N. Miro, and Rue de L'Hôpital (Governor Nicholls), was bought by J. G. Coulter, June 3, 1844, from the Milne estate with lots facing N. Miro. Speculators, including Pierre Passebon, were among the owners until 1854, when Jean Valsain Jourdain sold the large undeveloped parcel to C. I. Montrond and Edward George Gottschalk for $1,350. A survey by J. A. D'Hémécourt showed the 1854 extension of Barracks Street (December 5, A. Chiapella). In 1858 this lot was resurveyed and laid out 56 feet 2 inches facing Barracks by 101 feet. It was purchased from Emma Pollock by Arin Boyens for $300 (October 8, 1858, A. Doriocourt). The present house was standing in 1878 when Henry Boyens died; and his heir, Theodore Boyens, bought it from other relatives at the appraised price of $1,200. Built in the 1860s as a four-bay, dormered, creole cottage with front overhang incorporated into the canted roof, it is set back somewhat from the street. A twentieth-century modernization had completely obscured the original façade, which should be restored. Milne Road remained open in 1858, but a 1922 survey for the title to 2226 indicated that the road had been closed and sold for residential property sites.

2234–38

Milne Gardens Estate. Having the same early history as 2226 Barracks, this lot was sold by the Milne estate to J. G. Coulter in 1844. Reoriented in 1849 from N. Miro to face Barracks, the lot was developed after Barracks was extended in 1854. A feature of the large, four-bay, frame, corner cottage is the two-story, frame service wing extending from the rear. It now serves as a separate dwelling, and features gabled ends and a balcony at the second level with new supports and railing. The ensemble with its handsome, wide gables and decorative restraint reflects its 1850s building date. Brackets and verge have been added.

2229–31

Jumonville House. This wraparound attached to a frame, double-dormered creole cottage stands on the "Milne Gardens" tract. Alexander Milne's estate sold some Bayou Road frontage on this square bound then by Milne Road, N. Miro, Ursulines, and the merging of Bayou Road and Esplanade to Antoine Doriocourt on June 3, 1844 (C. Pollock). Milne had acquired the entire tract between N. Miro and Milne Road, left side of Bayou Road back to the Carondelet Canal, by purchase from free woman of color Marie Noyan Michel's estate (which Milne represented) on December 1, 1829. The vendor, according to notary L. T. Caire, was James Powell, representing the Michel estate. Gustave Jumonville, by a series of purchases from André Doriocourt and others in 1859, acquired the entire irregular square created by the extension of Barracks. The square was planted then in fig, peach, and orange trees, which Doriocourt specified were his to move (June 23, 1859, A. Doriocourt). Jumonville built a creole cottage facing Bayou Road at Esplanade in the 1860s, with the garden facing Barracks. He sold it in 1880 to Eulalie Virginia Arnous. The house at 2229–31 Barracks is thought to be the Jumonville residence, moved back to face Barracks after 1883. Its configuration compares with the Barron villa at 2122 Bayou Road. The present appearance resulted from a remodeling in the bungalow style of the 1920s. Original dormers have been reworked and the side-gabled roof extended. The side elevation retains clues to the original early character of the once-elegant home.

2434

Duhamel House. The city held an auction of this and other Fleitas property on January 9, 1837. Buyers included such well-known builders, architects, and *entrepreneurs* as J. L. Dolliole, J. N. B. de Pouilly, Charles Monrose, A. Peyroux, and B. Soulié. The lot at 2434 did not sell, although its adjacent neighbor was purchased by Adolphe Soraparu for $500. Then in 1850, Jean Charles Allan D'Hémécourt bought the lot after another auction held by the city on December 17 for just $190. In 1861 Clement Duhamel combined this corner lot and adjacent ones by purchases from D'Hémécourt and others. He built the urban cottage on the banquette with gardens beside it. After his death in 1873, the property was sold at auction and acquired by Charles Lafitte (October 29, A. Ducatel). Finally, on November 15, 1879, Lafitte sold the complex to Jean Louis Tissot with buildings and improvements for $3,000. Eventually the gardens were sold and developed, but the lovely cottage remains one of the finest urban houses on the former Fleitas plantation. Although dating from after 1861, the house continues the creole type and style developed in the 1830s.

2500 Block

2500 Block. The trio of similar, frame, double, Victorian camelbacks at 2526–30, 2532–34, and 2536–38 have segmental-arched openings, steamboat brackets, and scalloped vergeboards. The original wooden porches on all three houses have been removed, as have the turned balusters and wooden railings. Poured concrete porches replace the original ones; and precast concrete steps, the former wooden box steps. Recessed from the street, the houses represent an agreeable 1890s street scene. The shallow gardens enclosed behind iron picket fences enhance the repetitive module created by the house, fence, and garden placement.

BIENVILLE

1208–12

City Commons. This two-level, side-gabled frame dwelling resembles detached service buildings that proliferated in the residential area of nineteenth-century New Orleans. Essentially, **1208–12** is a triplex that retains its original wooden balcony trim, window and door surrounds, and drop-siding. It could date from the mid–nineteenth century and is one of the few nineteenth-century buildings remaining in the City Commons.

1810

Guillemain House. This typical example of the late-Classic-style houses built as rental units in Faubourg Hagan dates from the late 1850s. Its lot without improvements had been owned by Paul Tulane in the 1840s as one of his many real estate investments. L. A. Guillemain owned the property from 1848 to 1857, sold it to William K. McIntosh for $1,300 in 1857, and reacquired it in 1859, probably as a way to finance construction, since he sold it again in 1866. The first family to own the house for a long period of time was that of Henry Pedarré, whose heirs held it from 1866 until 1890. Pedarré's widow sold it at that time for $850 to the Mutual Loan and Building Company. This company, in turn, sold the property to Victor J. Jaeger for $2,215 on December 6, 1890, as recorded before the notary Legier. Built directly on the banquette, the double house was designed with a Greek Key entrance and overhanging gallery at the second level, where box columns support the heavy cornice with its paired brackets and dentil molding. The railing of the gallery is cast-iron.

BIENVILLE

1838

Faubourg Hagan, 1836, 1838. The masonry creole cottage illustrated with its detached two-story kitchen, was built in the early 1850s. Like the rest of the block, the corner house was once part of land owned by Paul Tulane, who bought the property from the Lafayette-Hagan partnership in May of 1841. He sold this lot and several others to L. A. Guillemain in 1850. Guillemain built immediately, and he sold the lot measuring 27 feet by 109 feet, along with a cottage, to Patrick Mulledy for $1,100 on February 26, 1853, as recorded by notary A. Dreyfous. Mulledy owned the house until 1874, when his heirs sold it for $2,000 to Martin Caulfield. Caulfield held title for twenty years. Originally, the cottage was designed with the traditional four façade openings on each street elevation. The corner entrance and new windows mar the exterior and destroy the otherwise excellent cottage proportions. The detached kitchen in the rear has retained more of its original character. Next to 1838 Bienville is a frame creole cottage at **1836**, which has been raised and remodeled several times since its construction in the late 1850s.

1803–05

Leber House. Although the double creole cottage was a preferred design in Faubourg Hagan, 1803–05 Bienville represents one of several two-story, four-bay, double houses built in the area. Title research indicates that a house or houses (probably modest, frame, 1850s creole cottages) occupied this and the corner lot when Zelie Ruty, wife of Guillaume Fargue, purchased the two in 1854 from John Davis for $1,900. Davis had bought the lots from the son of General Lafayette of France. The sale to Madame Fargue was made on the condition that she pay for the draining and shelling of that portion of Bienville Street. The Fargue family held both properties for eight years, selling them to Philippe Leber on February 28, 1862, according to the act before S. Magner, notary. Mr. Leber, subsequently built this house at 1803–05 Bienville, and sold it in 1884 to Peter Grieff. Leber and Grieff represented the influx of German immigrants who moved into Faubourg Hagan around 1850. In 1896 when Rosa Fisher bought the house from Louis Kottwitz for $3,725, it was numbered 313 and 315 Bienville (February 8, F. J. Dreyfous).

1912

Weber House. The three-bay townhouse was built in 1859 on land that Louis Barthélémy Macarty bought from the Hagan-Lafayette interests in 1840. Henry Weber purchased the vacant lot at an auction on May 27, 1859, from the heirs of Achille St. Dezier for $910, according to an act before notary A. E. Bienvenu. Architect Charles Lewis Hillger designed the house for Weber, who then hired Henry Saenger to build it. The building contract, recorded in English by notary R. J. Ker on August 16, 1859, reads in part: "the front cornice and the galleries to be made as per elevation drawings with pilasters having molded brackets, caps, and cases. The cornice to have large brackets, dentils, and moldings all as indicated. The rear galleries to measure 8 feet by 3 feet with solid posts with strong nails and square balusters between same. The side galleries to have fascias and cap. All baseboards, water tables, corner boards, and fascias to be put up in best workmanship manner. All of above work to be of sound and seasoned heart of cypress of suitable thickness. The joists for support of kitchen gallery to be planed. The sides of main building and the back building and rear gables to be inclosed [sic] with dressed clear and seasoned pine weatherboards not to expose more than 5½ inches to the weather.... Sliding doors 10 feet high, 7 feet 8 inches wide by 1⅞ inches thick, in two leaves each, framed with molded panels and to be properly set on brassways, with suitable sliding door lock having silver-plated knobs and furniture. The openings to be trimmed with 10 inches wide double-faced and diminished architraves with 1½-inch band and 2¼ inches molded, the whole to be set on plinth blocks. The partitions to be true and well brased [sic].... Iron bars of ⅝ inch by 2¾ inches wrought iron to be properly fastened for support of side gallery, as said bars to be about 32 inches from centers. Cast-iron ornamental pattern balcony railing to be furnished ... a folding gate of the same pattern of castings to be constructed and hung into the railing and over the front steps. Said gates to be properly fastened with suitable bolts, springs, latches. A molded wood rail to be screwed to the top rail of said iron railing.... Neat pilaster pattern wood mantels to be made and set in the fireplaces of parlours, bedrooms, dining room. Plain mantels for the fireplaces of rear building. Parlors to have $12 grates and bedrooms $9.... The bathroom to be furnished with a plunge and shower baths, the bathtub lined with lead weighing four lbs. to the superficial foot, furnished with all necessary supply and waste pipes, stop, corks. The water is to be laid on from the hydrant in the yard. The bath to be neatly encased with woodwork.... A dresser to be set up in the kitchen to be lined with zinc.... Fence in the yard to have a large gate made in two folds of two neat ... wide pickets and 3 inches by 4 inches railings and baseboard all dressed for painting.... The interior was to be lathed and plastered three coats, and the parlors to be finished with marble dust. The parlors to have a neat stucco cornice 12 inches on the ceiling and 9 inches on the walls. And each parlor to have an ornamental centre flower of choice pattern about 4½ feet in diameter. . . . The parlor chimney mantels to be marbled and varnished, also the chimney pieces. . . . The front door to be grained oak and varnished. . . . All sashes to be painted mahogany color. All blinds to be painted Paris green. The doors of the dining room and the wood dado to be grained oak and varnished. . . . The wood caps of railing to be painted mahogany colors. The mahogany work of stains to be varnished and polished in best manner. The iron gate to be varnished black, japanned. The brickwork of front foundations to be painted red and pencilled. Cost of building to be $3,400." The Weber family retained their fine Classic-style house until 1887, when they sold it to the American Homestead Company for $3,500.

1916

1936–38

Bettinger House (1916), 1926–28, 1936–38. Like its neighbor at 1912, the frame townhouse at **1916** Bienville was built in the late 1850s. The façade features include an entrance with segmental arch of keystone design, full-length segmental-arched second-level windows, a cast-iron balcony railing, and a roof overhang supported by brackets. These features may be later additions, for they represent the Italianate style of the late 1870s. John Hagan sold this lot to James Flint in 1849. A subsequent owner, William Joseph Huet, sold the vacant lot to François August Bettinger for $480, and during the 1850s Bettinger probably built the house. In 1859 he sold it to his daughter Anna, Widow Simon Grisham, for $4,200 (February 17, A. Ducatel). In 1878 Widow Grisham married Louis Gauchez of France, and she sold the property to Christopher Erne for just $600. In 1887 it was valued at $2,250 in Erne's succession. His family owned the house until 1895, during which time they probably remodeled it in the Italianate manner. **1912** retains more

of its original mid-nineteenth-century appearance and appears far more handsome because of the Classic-style cornice hiding the roof, in front of which is a fine cast-iron gallery with cresting. In contrast to the two-story townhouses is a small creole cottage at **1926–28** Bienville. It is designed with four bays and gabled sides and has a detached one-story, gable-sided kitchen building to the rear. Serving as an anchor to the block is the six-bay, two-story, double house of frame construction at the corner of Bienville and N. Prieur, number **1936–38**. A second-level, cast-iron balcony supported by wooden brackets extends around three sides of the building. The low, hip-roof with projecting eaves and underlying brackets, as well as the segmental arches framing the doorways contribute to the thoroughly Italianate design. There are neither box cornices, columns, nor dentil moldings to suggest the transition between the Greek Revival and the heavier Italianate style. Stylistic analysis places the construction of this house in the early 1870s.

1903–07

1909–11

Hildebrandt House (1903–07) 1909–11. Formerly one of the finest multiple-family dwellings in Faubourg Hagan, the once-handsome, Greek Revival-style house at **1903–05–07** was built between 1850 and 1857 for John H. Hildebrandt. Purchasing the lot from other German immigrants, Theodore Schoenheit and Carl Steinback, on July 1, 1850, Hildebrandt sold the building seven years later to Henry Bruning for $5,700 (January 28, 1857, R. J. Ker). Built at the banquette, the frame house has a tongue-and-groove front with fine Greek Key entrance surrounds and pedimented cornices. A second-level gallery has a cast-iron railing, box columns, and an entablature with paired brackets and modillions. The double creole cottage at **1909–11** Bienville with central, open passageway or dogtrot has walls flush with its neighbors. Although of smaller scale, it is a variation of the Classic style. Windows and doors have slightly projecting cornices and the two entrances have neat Greek Key surrounds. The side-gabled roof has a built-in overhang; it was once covered with slate. The simplicity of design and ornament suggests a date between 1841 and 1850. Crowded between adjacent houses, it retains much of its original appearance.

2018–20

Weber Cottage. In 1858 Leon Queyrouze sold an undeveloped lot at 2018–20 Bienville to Jean Sauvage, who in turn sold it to Henry Weber (December 27, O. Drouet). Between 1859 and 1862, Weber made three additional purchases, which gave him a total frontage of 81 feet on Bienville. By 1862 he had built this masonry, Greek Revival-style shotgun cottage and an identical adjacent one, now demolished. Number 2018–20 remained in the Weber family until 1916. The house is an outstanding example of the double, Greek Revival-style, brick shotgun. Masonry construction is not often used in this building type. The front gable and the

millwork brackets supporting the roof overhang were added in the late nineteenth century and the porch railing in the twentieth. Like other documented examples of this type, the rear elevation has a brick-gabled parapet. A service wing is attached and extends the depth of the property.

2114

2128–30

Griffon Division, 2114, 2128–30. A good example of a frame, three-bay, shotgun house with millwork in the Italianate style stands at **2114.** The segmental arch over the recessed entrance door, the roundheaded windows, and the heavy box cornice are typical features of this style, which was popular from 1870. At **2128–30** stands a fine, two-story townhouse with gabled sides, wooden façade rusticated to resemble stone, and simple Greek Revival doorways with Greek Key surrounds. The detailing on this building is transitional, balancing the slender proportions of the Greek Revival style with the heavier, more ornate Italianate style. The house was built after 1853. The land on which it stands was partitioned in 1853, having been many years in litigation between the heirs of Samuel Moore and Charles Griffon.

2226–34

Frobus Cottage. This entire square was part of a large tract claimed by the heirs of Lafayette, Samuel Moore and his partner Théodore Nicolet, the Griffon heirs, and the Baroness de Pontalba. A partition recorded by notary P. C. Cuvellier on October 25 and November 5, 1853, decided in favor of Théodore Nicolet's estate, which accepted ownership of this square. On December 22, 1858, the attorney for the Nicolet estate, Louis Janin, transferred ownership to Hippolyte Griffon who subdivided the square into twenty-two lots. John H. Frobus acquired two of the lots by 1861 and contracted with builder Elijah Cox to construction "a one-story frame house with kitchen, privy, cistern, and fences on two lots on Bienville between Galvez and Miro." The house was intended "to be similar in every respect to the houses of Mr. Baker, assistant street commissioner, on the same street . . . to have three rooms 16 feet by 17 feet, one pair of sliding doors, one fireplace with a grate in the front room. This house to be one foot higher than the houses of Mr. Baker. Kitchen and privy to be covered with slate. Both lots to be enclosed with rough fence similar to Mr. Baker's, but one-half of front to have neat paling fence. Cost to be $1,000." This contract was recorded by notary E. Barnett on March 30, 1861. Frobus sold this lot, possibly with the above-described house to Louis Dessomes of Matamoros, Mexico, for just $1,813. This was a loss, since his original investment for the lot and house was $2,200. The cottage, now used as a store-house, was built with a hip-roof and rear gable. Large modillions and paired rafter ends mark an unusual roof overhang.

2415–17

2431–39

2229, 2415–17, 2431–39. The three-bay, frame shotgun with Classic-style detailing at **2229** was built after the 1853 partition of the Samuel Moore estate. The house has a hip-roof that incorporates the porch, and the entrance is flanked by pilasters typical of the late 1850s. Two blocks away at **2431–39** is an example of a rare, common-wall creole cottage, a type seldom built in the city's suburbs. It is situated on land belonging originally to the Fleitas succession. The heirs sold this property to Joseph Kenton in 1834. His ownership, like that of the neighboring Samuel Moore land, was disputed by the Baroness de Pontalba, who claimed the land as an inheritance from her father, Andrés Almonester y Rojas. Kenton, not the Baroness, however, won the ensuing lawsuit by 1850, and the houses were a part of the new development. The six-bay double house with hip-roof at **2415–17** is a restrained example of the Classic-style double shotgun type. Behind each entrance are recessed side galleries. The house appears to date from the 1860s.

2600

Baker Cottage. This corner creole cottage built of brick between 1862 and 1865 is retardate in style. In 1858 John Budd Slawson purchased the entire square where the house is now situated from Romanzo W. Montgomery for $6,000. Montgomery had purchased "339 lots in the Macarty plantation" from the New Orleans Canal and Banking Company for $18,711 on May 2, 1850 (O. H. Perry). The property had been part of the J. B. Macarty Spanish Concession, described in the title as "26 *arpents* on the Mississippi River by all the uncertain depth it can have." The depth was contested by the heirs of L. C. Dorgenois. John Budd Slawson, already the owner of an omnibus line and other property in the 2300 block of Esplanade, subdivided his square in 1862, selling this lot to Joseph Motzen Baker for $900. Baker built the present house, which remained in the family until 1895. The house was sold at auction to Rudolph J. Goebel for $1,430 to settle the succession of Mary Hopkins, Widow Patrick Kaveny, January 31, 1895 (J. J. Woulfe).

134

Immanuel Lutheran Church. The Chapitoulas plantation of Jean Baptiste Macarty stretched along the Mississippi River for twenty-six *arpents* to an uncertain depth, which according to title research appears to have included this section of N. Broad Street. The Macarty heirs valued the plantation, buildings, animals, and 110 slaves in excess of $100,000 in 1826. Bernard Marigny and Samuel Kohn in 1831 bought a half-interest in it. Twenty years later John Slidell and Laurent Millaudon bought interest in the property. At that time the land closest to the river was subdivided into the township of Carrollton. In 1866 Laurent Millaudon's wife sold this corner lot with other properties to Edward Keenan via a three-month owner, Benjamin Wadsworth (January 16, S. Magner). Keenan appears to have subdivided the land and created this 34-foot front lot by 1885. The cornerstone of the Immanuel Lutheran Church is inscribed: "Erected 1918. C. E. and E. E. Reimann contractors. Building Committee Ernest Edward Reimann,Chairman,Oswald Stierle,John Wirth, John Mathes,Emile Wendling, R. H. Schindler, J. Schilling, pastor." It is a Gothic Revival, frame building with a multi-gabled roof and a bell tower, as well as two pointed-arch windows of stained glass and tripartite tracery pattern. The entrance door is framed by a pointed arch.

Pumping Station

St. Louis Street Pumping Station #2. Within the N. Broad Street neutral ground between St. Louis and Conti streets is a typical pumping station built in 1899 for the New Orleans Drainage Commission. The commission was composed of R. M. Walmsley (president), W. Flower, A. Britten, J. C. Morris, L. Cucullu, Otto Thoman, P. Capdeville and M. Abascal. It is one of three pumping stations in the area covered in this book; and like its counterparts, it exhibits fine brickwork and architectural detailing. Splayed bricks form lintel patterns at the wide machinery entrance, and the elongated windows have keystones and are covered by iron shutters. Pilasters surround the building, and above them are terra-cotta, caplike decorations. The bricks are burnt-sienna color and the window trim is green.

636

Macarty Property. The Spanish Mission-style, commercial building was built of brick with an overlay of stucco in 1923. In 1908 Victor Lambou bought five lots, each 30 feet by 100 feet, from Maurice Pivert for $4,800 (January 28, B. Ory). Lambou probably built this structure as an investment, and he immediately sold it to Anthony J. Sciambra and Paul Masino, Jr. The property had formerly been part of the eighteenth-century holdings of J. B. Macarty. The design of the building utilizes the baroque devices of plasticity, scrolling curves, and a row of arches divided by Corinthian columns. The red tile roof is typical of the building style.

800

930

800 and 900 Blocks. Within the Daniel Clark land that paralleled N. Dorgenois and N. Broad streets from Orleans to Bayou Road are nine blocks that were laid out as Faubourg St. John in 1809. Several late buildings of importance remain. A two-story, corner store-house at the downriver corner of St. Ann at **800** N. Broad reflects a traditional usage of a corner location. Beneath a gabled front roof are an apron and other appendages covering the second-level balcony. The balcony covers the banquette along N. Broad and is supported by turned wooden colonettes. The store-house dates from after 1883. At **930** is a fine, center-hall, raised basement, villa-type house probably built in the late 1870s. It appears on the Robinson Atlas in 1883. The deep, front gable has sunburst applied-work decoration, which generally suggests a building date later in the century, although the roofline could postdate the rest of the building and could be the result of a reroofing. The villa has pairs of full-length openings flanking the central entrance. Raised on brick piers, the "basement" remains open. At one time, herringbone-patterned brick sidewalks and small front gardens behind wrought-iron fences provided a neat appearance to this spacious home and its neighbor at **924**. The latter is a double frame shotgun also pre-

dating 1883, which is presently being "bricked-over" and raised high off the ground. Whereas raising a house can sometimes be architecturally harmonious, "bricking-over" is wrong without resetting all window and door frames. Another double frame shotgun with bracketed overhang at **922** postdates 1883 but completes a pleasant small grouping of nineteenth-century frame houses.

1572

1500 Blocks, Solomon House (1572). A later development on this back edge of the Gueno *habitation* includes **1530**, a one-story, bayed cottage with Ionic columns. It represents the early-twentieth-century, City Beautiful style, expressed by a deep front gallery and large brackets that serve as dentils. The pleasant façade has screened transoms, a decorative element above each bay window. The turn-of-the-century house is well-kept today as a physician's office. Its neighbor at **1520** is a galleried, frame shotgun with a front bay. It predates 1530 by twenty years and is recorded on the Robinson Atlas of 1883. The second 1500 block of N. Broad is the only one along N. Broad between Canal and St. Bernard that is unmixed with commercial establishments. The rural or open character of the street persisted until the late nineteenth century, and the canal that ran its length remained uncovered until the 1940s. Presently, four varieties of late-Victorian shotguns with lacy jigsaw millwork reflect the mode of the period. Standing in a row from the corner, they include **1542–44, 1546, 1554,** and **1556**. The appearance of the entire row has been adversely affected by concreting the small front garden spaces, which probably had been enclosed by simple iron-post fencing. At **1562** and **1578–80**, the early-twentieth-century, City Beautiful style blends well in scale. 1562 incorporates an open side-gallery, a retardate treatment from the nineteenth century. **1558** is a twentieth-century bungalow, which also blends because of scale and proportions. The center-hall cottage at **1572** and its gardens once filled this entire square until the property was subdivided after 1877. The Joseph Solomon family built the center-hall, side-gabled, single-dormered cottage at 1572 sometime during their thirty-five-year ownership of the property (1842–1877). The house is one of the most important historic buildings still remaining in old Faubourg Gueno. Alterations and renovations through the decades by subsequent owners have made exact dating of this house difficult. The façade is characterized by a box cornice with a raised parapet supported by Doric columns, behind which are French doors flanked by sidelights. The gallery across the front has lost its railing, and the porch steps have been altered. When Solomon's widow sold the house to Matheus Poelman for $5,321.50, the property included the house with seventeen lots. The act of sale was recorded by notary A. Hero, Jr., on August 7, 1877.

1700–02

1600–02, 1682, 1700–02. This part of the former Pierre Gueno plantation ran from Gentilly Road between Columbus and D'Abadie back along an uneven line to N. Prieur. Only a portion of the riverside of the 1400 block of N. Broad is included in the Gueno tract. It was once separated from the 1500 block by the St. Bernard Canal, which began at St. Claude Street and drained lakeward, crossing the Broad Canal to join the natural bayous, Sauvage and Clark. The 1600 block and most of the 1700 were also within the Gueno boundaries. The Kernion, Howe, and St. Martin families owned the next plantation in an easterly direction along Bayou Sauvage bordering Chemin au Chantilly (Gentilly Road). The house at **1600–02** N. Broad was designed in the traditional late-nineteenth-century manner, utilizing ready-made millwork ordered from a catalogue, a gabled roof with scrolled brackets supporting the roof overhang, and pierced panels for the cornice cresting over the windows and doors. The relatively recent addition of the railing detracts from the charm of this cottage. At the other end of the second 1600 block stands **1682** N. Broad. The house was designed as a corner, three-bay, frame house with an attached doorway. The segmental-arched doorway, shutters, and screens lend dignity to the façade. The corner building at **1700–02** now has Art Nouveau motifs in relief plasterwork and probably was built in the 1840s as a masonry, gable-sided, creole cottage with a detached service building to the rear. Even with the complete fenestration alteration, the configuration of this creole cottage is evident. This and **1572**, the Solomon House, are probably the two earliest remaining structures on N. Broad within the reviewed stretch, which was once included in Faubourg Gueno.

CANAL

1800

Château D'Arcy. The design of this house with its virtuoso combination of millwork patterns and styles is most imaginative. The millwork, particularly the oriental-influenced railing pattern, the lattice frieze, scrolled brackets, and pendills (an American colonial term for boss) appear to be specially ordered rather than catalog stock. The irregular roofline of gables, dormers, chimneys, and turrets, along with the façade projections and recessions of bays and porches, are characteristic of the Queen Anne style. The millwork details of the cornices and the dormers are reflective of the Second Empire style. The front galleries, framed by shoulder arches with pendills and ornamental brackets, further amalgamate exuberant architectural periods. The plantings of oak and magnolia trees complement the architecture and are probably the remnants of a nineteenth-century garden. This portion of Canal Street was included in the land granted to French General Lafayette for his "assistance to the United States in the American Revolutionary War." John Hagan bought out the interests of the Lafayette heirs and sold four lots in this square in 1840 to James L. McLean. He improved the lots and sold them in 1854 to Mary Henrietta Pintado for $4,125. The auction description of these four lots in 1859 told of the prevailing rural condition, "the above lots are in a high state of cultivation, with flowers, vegetables, fruit trees, shrubbery, etc." Abraham De Meza purchased the property then for $7,000 and sold it soon after for an $871 profit to Ann Eliza Horton, widow of Jabez Barney and later the widow of George Freeman. Mme Freeman sold the same property six years later in 1866 for $10,000 to another twice-widowed lady, Jane D'Arcy. It was during the D'Arcy ownership that 1800 Canal was built. In 1886, when it and two other of the original lots were auctioned, it was described: "The improvements consist of a frame, slated building known as the 'D'Arcy Château' built for an ice cream saloon and garden with high ceilings, extensive gallery, covering sidewalk on Canal Street, summer-houses in rear, etc. All in fair order, with gas throughout and elegantly adapted for public garden or public resort, livery stable, or other purposes, or can be easily and cheaply converted into residences with apartments, price $4,600." By 1934 notary J. A. Casey was recording an act of sale from Orleans E. Allen to C. Walter Mattingly for only this house, price $13,750. The Orleans family had concluded a forty-eight-year proprietorship.

2011

Tiblier-Girod House. This double-galleried townhouse was built of frame construction about the year 1857, judging from stylistic details and title research. The house now represents the transitional styles of Greek and Italian Renaissance Revival periods. In Greek Revival designs, the box cornice usually had dentil moldings rather than brackets, and the raised rounded parapet would have been square; the present forms are Renaissance Revival. The contrast of round Corinthian columns on the second level with Ionic capped box columns on the first is also associated with the more florid Italianate style. Window hoods with dentil moldings and Greek Key door and window surrounds are typical Greek Revival motifs, which blend harmoniously with other revival styles. Claude Tiblier, who purchased this lot in 1857 from John Hagan and the heirs of Lafayette, was an ambitious Frenchman who involved himself in New Orleans real estate along Esplanade and in Faubourg Ste Marie (*The American Sector*). With a partner, Joseph Girod, he constructed this house, selling it in 1861 to Catherine Ustick, wife of Erasmus Darwin Beach, for $2,500 (April 5, T. Guyol). The octagonal bay on the right side of the second level and the first-level wing addition on the left side indicate that the Italianate features of this house were probably added.

2331

2300, 2400 Blocks. The 2300 block of Canal retains three frame, two-story, nineteenth-century residences at **2311**, **2331** and **2335**. These once-comfortable, single-family dwellings suggest the appearance of many blocks of Canal Street as they were at the turn of the century. Primarily a residential avenue, it was convenient to the Canal mule-drawn streetcar, which ran its length out to the cemeteries and back to the foot of Canal Street where ferries crossed the Mississippi to Algiers. The atmosphere was verdant with large gardens and trees; commercial establishments were rare until one approached the Claiborne intersection, and even there many residences survived until the 1930s. The 2400 block of Canal has contemporary office buildings on each side of the street. The Pan American Life Insurance building at **2400** was built in 1952 by Skidmore, Owings, and Merrill, with Claude Hooten as associate architect and George J. Glover, builder. Across the street at **2475** stands a building constructed by Curtis and Davis, architects, in 1958, featuring a

N. CLAIBORNE

2335

façade screen of Moorish-style, terra-cotta tiles over glass and concrete blocks. An interview with architect Arthur Q. Davis revealed his firm's philosophy governing the design of the Caribe Building: "It was our intention to build a simple, straightforward, rectilinear structure which would be attractive and at the same time inexpensive. It is a very efficient building with a central elevator core . . . readily subdivided for rental purposes and has proved to be very efficient. The concept of an exterior sun control screen around all four sides of the building was conceived well before the need for concern with energy conservation. Also, the decorative screen permits us to have an exterior wall of a much simpler construction, recessed approximately three feet behind the sun screen. We actually used industrial windows and an economical concrete-block wall which is not visible from the street."

2547

Dorgenois Division, 2507, 2547. This house pictured was built on one of the many parcels of land owned by Andrés Almonester y Rojas, Louisiana's earliest Spanish notary and philanthropist. The land was purchased from Almonester by Juan Rodríguez, who passed it to his son-in-law Antonio Ramis, who then sold to François Joseph D'Orgenoy. The D'Orgenoy family held it from September 24, 1807 (Pierre Pedesclaux), until a grandson sold half of his interest to Samuel W. Oakey. Oakey sold the half-interest to Mme Joseph N. Volant Labarre, née Marie Louise D'Orgenoy. The D'Orgenoy family did not fully leave the scene until 1865, when J. M. Baker bought the Canal Street lot for $1,833. The lot measures 30 feet on Canal by 79 feet on N. Dorgenois. In 1866 Baker sold to Joseph and Bonaventura Puig of Florida. These men built this masonry, four-bay, two-level house with step-gabled ends. In 1875 when the Puigs sold the house to Hugo Redwitz, it was described as "a double tenement [meaning rental unit], two-story brick dwelling, containing six rooms on each side, also a small cottage, containing three rooms, cistern, etc." The depth of the lot at the time was 137 feet along N. Dorgenois. François Meunier of Paris purchased the lot and house from the Redwitz succession in 1883; one can only speculate that Meunier may have been an absentee landlord during his decade of ownership. The outlines of a fine, nineteenth-century home still remain in this building, now utilized as a restaurant in an area of mixed residential and commercial use. At **2507** Canal, a three-bay, two-story, side-hall townhouse retains the original etched-glass entrance transom. It was built with a balcony and deep overhang at the second level, which displays the original cast-iron gallery. Stained-glass windows may be seen along the side elevation. Presently, the first-level façade is filled in with a brick protrusion.

N. CLAIBORNE

500 Block

City Commons. Railroad warehouses were built along the banks of the Carondelet Canal, and in 1905 the waterway was filled in and renamed Lafitte Street. These warehouses were built in the 1880s; their architectural attributes include fine brickwork, regularly spaced pilasters, string courses, cornices, and iron bearer overhangs. The building is now the headquarters for the New Orleans Shippers Association. The flagstones, granite, and slate blocks in front date from the enlargement of the old Carondelet Canal by the New Orleans Canal and Banking Company in the 1830s. During the eighteenth and nineteenth centuries, this area served the city as a water transportation route, but the railroad replaced shipping for commerce as the nineteenth century progressed.

732

800

732, 800. An early-twentieth-century, plastered brick building at 732 is a fanciful version of the Neoclassic Revival style. Attention is given to the corner position with extra height and parapets at both street elevations near the corner. Adamesque sculptural relief motifs abound and are given correct attention by duotone painting. The name F. P. Prout is worked in sculpture and incorporated in the façade decoration. At **800** the brick building on the St. Ann Street corner dates from 1924 and was built as a branch of the Hibernia National Bank. It is an excellent example of the brick commercial-institutional buildings of the period. Terracotta decorations and fancy brickwork distinguish this building, which is articulated by rhythmically spaced brick pilasters with tile caps at both street elevations. The St. Ann Street elevation has triple windows, arched with console keystones; four plaques of relief sculpture are inset above grille windows. A tile roof, variegated brown brick, tile string courses and capitals, ironwork in grilled windows, relief scuptures, cartouches, and bronze entrance details animate the building, giving a textural and sculptural effect. Since the 1960s the building has housed the Pizzo Leather Company.

1240, 1234

1241–1243

1245

1200 Blocks. One of two remaining residential buildings in the 1200 block of N. Claiborne, the large, late-nineteenth-century, bayed, turreted cottage at **1240** is in outstanding condition. The large round posts at the gate and carriage entrance are stamped by Hinderer's Iron Works and are embellished with Egyptian and Greek motifs and caryatid heads. Beyond the fence is a cemented area with parterres planted in boxwood, a central circular fountain, and a pair of lamp posts. The recessed entrance has original louvered storm doors, beyond which is a carved door with stained-glass transom. The interior of this post–1883 dwelling reflects the continuing preference for the standard 1850s-style double parlors with screen divider, medallions, and Classic motifs in millwork and moldings. There are cove ceilings, gas-electric lighting fixtures, mantels of marble and wood, and large medallions of cast iron throughout the first level. The interior walls and part of the façade have received a rough stucco treatment in the twentieth century. Antonia Jackson has owned and resided in the house for twenty-three years. **1234** N. Claiborne is a two-level, Edwardian, frame, single-family dwelling converted for use as the Straight Business School. Across the wide street a four-bay, two-story, frame double at **1241–43** was built facing tree-lined N. Claiborne Avenue by 1883. The wooden gallery at the second level has graceful shoulder-arches between the supporting colonettes. Doors and windows on both levels are tall and narrow. Next door at **1245**, a lone, double-dormered creole cottage remains, hidden under a brick modernization and a huge outdoor billboard. Once one of a pair of creole cottages, it is a sad vestige on a prominent New Orleans avenue, which once boasted a promenade replete with large oak trees and colorful mule-drawn carline.

1424, 1428

1424, 1428, 1438. 1424 N. Claiborne Avenue, a frame, post-1883, vernacular, Edwardian cottage features a projecting front bay, recessed doorway, and two projecting front gables covered with shingles. A third shingle-covered gable is centered over the side gallery. The front gallery roof is supported by turned columns and a spindle course of pierced panels and smaller turned spindles. Scallop-patterned vergeboards emphasize the gables of the roofline. The irregular façade and roofline of the building reflect the popular taste of the early 1900s. Set back from the banquette, **1428** is a large, two-story dwelling with galleries. It reflects a return to the Neoclassic style with Palladian features of modest revival expression. **1438** N. Claiborne (not shown) is also a comfortable single dwelling with verandas and wide porches suggestive of a rural late-century period.

1417

Denis-Cenas House. This brick townhouse once had a first-floor gallery and a second-level overhang supported by brackets. These features are characteristic of 1870s buildings, although the details of masonry façade with full-length openings and flat stone lintels are associated with earlier ones. In 1842 the lot was sold in the auction of the Duchamp plantation. Arthur Denis built a house on this corner property, which faced Esplanade, and in 1867 sold it to Widow H. B. Cenas for $7,000 (September 12, A. Mazureau). The Cenas family opened a school, for which architect Samuel Jamison built a back building charging $4,650 in 1874. The property at that time was described as "the remaining part of a certain portion of ground which measured 90 feet front on Esplanade by 130 feet depth and front on Claiborne." The building pictured could have served as the Cenas School building. The school is remembered as an exclusive private establishment, which appeared in the directories from 1875 until 1910. The Cenas heirs owned the building until June 12, 1913.

1423

Duchamp Division. On March 19, 1842, Madame Bernard Duchamp sold lots numbered 1 and 2 to Philip Young, f.m.c. Young sold them, "together with an unfinished building and construction material," for $900 in 1844 to another free Negro, Rose A. Bruslé. Mlle Bruslé sold the improved property twelve years later to Margaret Thompson, f.w.c., for twice her purchase price; and Mlle Thompson sold to Arthur E. Denis for the handsome sum of $2,250 (October 19, 1858, P. C. Cuvillier). Denis also bought a third and adjoining lot from Eugène Petitpain, which contained buildings and improvements. The three properties were purchased by Philip Thomas Philips from Denis in 1864. Elise Bienvenu, wife of Pierre Frederick Thomas, probably built this house between 1866 and 1871 after demolishing the other building. She sold it in 1871 to the American Missionary Association. The handsome, double-galleried

house has a bowed center front, a feature of several houses built along N. Claiborne Avenue in the 1860s. The house was designed with late-Classic detailing including: four fluted columns, pilaster-flanked entrance with dentil cornice, weatherboards forming a rusticated façade, and cornice with parapet accented by paired brackets and dentil molding. Although the ell to the rear of the house is not original, it was designed so that its cornice complements that of the main house. The banquette is laid with flagstones.

1427–29

1427–29, 1433, 1439. The two-story, three-bay townhouse at **1427–29** was built of frame construction in the late-Classic style. The façade is articulated by double doors beyond a recessed entrance and a gallery at the second level. The pierced-work cornices, entrance surround, and the doors are not original to the house. Like 1423 N. Claiborne, this lot was sold by P. T. Philips in 1866, and the house was built soon afterward. The house is similar to ones at 2003 and 2013 Dumaine, both of which were built in the 1860s. At **1433** N. Claiborne, an early-twentieth-century, Neoclassic Revival, single-family home contrasts in scale and detail with its immediate but earlier neighbor at **1439**. The latter, a tiny bayed cottage built between 1890 and 1910, is more typical of the frame houses built at the turn of the century throughout New Orleans. The large, flamboyant house at **1433** elegantly reflects the architectural preferences of Albert Toledano and Emile Weil, who are credited with mansions on the major city avenues. The remaining houses on both sides of N. Claiborne in this 1400 block are residential relics of a street now desecrated by an elevated expressway and filled with commercial establishments unharmonious with the character of an important city artery.

1442–44

1442–44, 1448, 1449. In the second 1400 block of Claiborne, a creole cottage and double shotgun recall the street's appearance at the end of the nineteenth century. The four-bay, frame creole cottage at **1442–44** has a pitched and canted roof supported by brackets and gabled sides. Simple, straight-molded window hoods and batten shutters with strap hinges complete the façade features. Except for the brackets, which were added, the house appears to date from the 1850s. It retains its front and rear chimneys and some original shutters. **1448** is a four-bay shotgun with front-gabled roof; it replaced a creole cottage that stood there in 1883. The pair of houses, creole cottage and shotgun, illustrate here the compatibility of the two house-types. Conformity of scale and fenestration and contrast of roofline and decorative details result in a pleasing presentation, further enhanced by the herringbone-patterned sidewalk. A funeral home at **1449** encompasses two N. Claiborne Avenue houses behind a new monolithic brick façade. The corner structure probably represented an 1870 Queen Anne style with a slate-covered turret. The second home retains none of its original front, but the rear octagonal bay indicates a large, two-level, galleried home.

1480

Duchamp Division. At **1480**, the one-time three-bay, two-story, side-hall townhouse with Greek Revival-style surrounds and recessed door is built in the style of the 1850s. This once-gracious house in the second 1400 block retains its box cornice with dentils and cast-iron balcony. A fine, two-story, side-galleried service wing is attached and set away from Columbus Street, affording space for a rear garden at the side. Greek Revival in style, the frame, three-bay, side-gabled creole cottage at **1506** has an extremely steep roof. The left side has a graceful, cast-iron balcony at the attic level. A two-story, attached service wing affords tremendous square footage to this narrow house. The wide, recessed entrance and exterior finish of the façade are alterations.

1522

Circle Market. On April 30, 1859, surveyor D'Hémécourt drew a plan of a "valuable tract of land in the 3rd District," in which a market house across from the present Claiborne Circle market at St. Bernard Avenue was indicated (plan book 74, folio 7). The present market is in the Spanish Revival style popular in the early twentieth century. The hexagonal cupola roofed in bright red tiles and the startling white stuccoed brick walls make it an attractive sight from the ground-level circle, as well as from the elevated expressway above. A covered archway includes the banquette area on both N. Claiborne and St. Bernard elevations. Although the structure itself appears twentieth century in style, the site itself, the covered walkway, and the character of the market reflect a colorful nineteenth-century neighborhood style.

1126

1100 Block. The even side of Columbus between St. Claude and N. Rampart is a pleasant combination of four frame double shotguns with bracketed overhangs contrasting with single-dormered creole cottages. The altered façade openings at **1130** should be restored by analogy to the appearance of **1126**. Across the street at **1139** Columbus is a post-1883, four-bay, frame, double shotgun with deep gabled roof and bracketed overhang. Full-length, segmental-arched openings have highly decorative architraves with sawtooth-edged cornices.

1220

1220, 1231–33, 1235–37, 1243–45, 1249–51. The two squares bound by Columbus, Kerlerec, and St. Claude as well as Columbus, Marais, St. Claude, and Laharpe emanated from the Pierre Marigny plantation strip, which Widow C. Guerlain owned and sold to Jean Mager on June 22, 1838. A group of investors, including Seraphim Maspereau, acquired lots on the even side of Columbus in the 1848 sale of the estate of Agathe Mager, Widow Collard. In 1856 Maspereau sold the still-vacant lot at 1220 Columbus to Emma Fleitas, f.w.c., wife of Appolinaire Perrault, f.m.c. Mme Perrault sold the vacant lot with improvements to Achille Tardie in 1858 for $550. Tardie built the present house on the 30-foot lot, selling it to Alfred P. Archinard for $3,050 in 1859. Post-reconstruction prices were low; on December 17, 1877, Archinard sold to Antoine Du Gardin St. Alexandre for $1,000 before notary A. E. Bienvenu. 1220 Columbus, even in its dilapidated condition, exhibits fine characteristics of its type and style. It is a three-bay, single-dormered, Greek Revival-style creole cottage with gabled sides and built-in overhang. A well-proportioned Greek Key entrance leads to an entrance hall that was once a recessed, open, side gallery but is now enclosed. Remnants of a side balcony from the attic level retain a cast-iron railing. The herringbone-patterned brick sidewalk remains intact along with granite curbing. Across the street at **1231–33** and **1235–37** Columbus are a pair of four-bay, double shotguns with bracketed overhangs built after 1883. A different Victorian house-type at **1243–45** was built about the same time. It is a five-bay, frame, double-dormered, late-Victorian, rural cottage with a deep front gallery. The house has an elaborate cornice decorated with scallops and brackets, whereas a band of spindles and turned columns support the gallery; side gables and side entrance complete the design. **1249–51** Columbus is a two-level, four-bay, double-galleried, frame creole house. In 1883 this house was numbered 49. A house-type indigenous to the Tremé–Bayou St. John area, this one, although somewhat mutilated, is similar to many in the Faubourg St. John area. It probably dates from the mid-nineteenth century but has received later alterations.

78/48

1321

1300 Block. The 1300 block of Columbus, odd side, is rich in mid-nineteenth-century creole house-types. Three- and four-bay, early-Classic-style, frame shotguns intermingle with a variety of creole cottages. Archival drawings of demolished cottages further reflect the rich creole heritage that developed on the block in the continuing decades. The square had its beginnings as the property of Widow Guerlain and Alexander Milne. The Guerlain portion of the land was sold off in lots or groups of lots beginning in 1848. Milne's share was subdivided as early as 1838. An architectural anchor on the block is the engaging, Classic-style, double, six-bay creole cottage at **1317–19**. It features entrances at each end leading to side galleries beneath gabled ends with exterior stairways, backed by *cabinets*. It was built soon after 1856 for tinsmith and lampmaker Seraphim Maspereau on portions of three lots acquired separately by Maspereau: one in 1846 from H. Pedesclaux (May 14, A. Doriocourt); a second in 1848 from Widow Collard; and the third in 1856 from Collard's estate (September 16, P. Lacoste). Maspereau's will indicated that he never lived in this creole cottage, nor in the one he owned next door at **1321**. Maspereau's three-bay and six-bay creole cottages were numbered 58 and 61 Columbus Street at the time of his death. He resided at 92 Esplanade in 1850, 359 St. Claude in 1870, and 356 Marais in 1875, with his business address at Condé (Conti) and Mandeville from 1846 onward. At his estate sale in 1878, the house at 1317–19 Columbus sold to P. J. B. Marchand for $1,800. Marchand sold it to Lise Eldridge Langville (Mrs. Joseph Cantrelle) for $2,300 in 1883 (August 14, G. Legardeur). The owner of this outstanding house in 1968 was Miss Bonnie Ann Jolly. Maspereau's adjacent house at 1321 Columbus, a three-bay, frame creole cottage with gabled sides, has a Greek Key entrance that leads to a short hall and recessed side gallery; the brackets were added later to this 1860s house. Seraphim Maspereau's ownership of both of these cottages, as well as of 1501–03 Marais, spanned the 1870s. Maspereau owned nine other lots in this square and others in an adjacent one, including his dwelling in 1875 at 1476 Marais, which he probably built about 1860. **1325–27**, a

modest, late-nineteenth-century, frame, double, camelback shotgun, replaced an early Maspereau rental unit. Underneath a twentieth-century wraparound at **1331** Columbus is a creole cottage of frame construction, perhaps another of Maspereau's rental units. Plan book 7, folio 6, depicts a similar house, which might be used as a guide in restoring 1331. Following this series of creole cottages are fine examples of early-Classic-style shotguns like the one at **1339** Columbus, a three-bay, frame camelback with Classic-style entrance, side gallery, and bracketed overhang. This house has been spoiled by the 1920s addition of an ill-proportioned porch and gable, which could, however, easily be removed to restore the house to its former mid-nineteenth-century appearance. Of similar age is the single, frame, three-bay shotgun with hip-roof at **1351**. The Greek Key entrance (obscured by awnings) leads to a recessed side gallery behind which is a bayed *cabinet* that appears as a twentieth-century addition but is shown on the archival drawing, plan book 78, folio 48, by H. Strehler, dating from 1871. This house is an example of a Greek Revival shotgun and has a separate kitchen wing extending from the rear. The brackets postdate the construction of this fine house. An excellent drawing gives the appearance of the house shortly after its 1840s construction on the Alexander Milne tract. The banquette retains the herringbone-patterned brickwork shown in the archival drawing, although the high plank fence has been replaced with a later iron one. **1355–57** Columbus is a four-bay, frame shotgun with hip-roof and bracketed overhang. Four, full-length, segmental-arched openings indicate a late-1870s building date.

1415–17

1400 Block. The 1840s-style creole cottage at **1415–17** Columbus has had its doors and windows greatly altered. The double dormers, central brick chimney, and semi-incorporated overhang, as viewed from the gabled ends, are clues to a fine architectural type. **1423–25, 1427–29,** and **1431–33** are once-identical, double shotguns with hip-roofs and bracketed overhangs. These simple, small shotguns, only three rooms deep, enhance the street scene. While segmental-arched openings and brackets suggest an 1880s date, the small size and hip-roofs indicate the 1870s.

1500

1500–1800 Blocks. A creole cottage has been adapted to a corner store-house at **1500** Columbus. At one time, this cottage probably had a deep, front garden behind a wooden dowel fence. This area was filled in over fifty years ago, judging by the roof and overhang configuration. The brick banquette along the front and side retains the spirit of a semi-rural setting. The **1600, 1700,** and **1800** blocks of Columbus have many two- and four-bay Victorian shotguns with ill-conceived façade alterations. The entire street from N. Rampart to N. Claiborne needs resurfacing, gutters, and curbing. The square bound by Kerlerec, N. Prieur, Columbus, and N. Roman was owned by M. Ay Fernandez, with his house located at Columbus and N. Prieur in the 1850s.

2226

Tala Property, 2220–26. At **2226** is a well-kept cottage with entrance recessed behind a shallow, side gallery. The gallery is supported by turned columns with a simple band of spindles and pierced panels. Cap-molded lintels accented with pierced work, original iron fence, and side yard with old-fashioned plantings contribute to the charm of this house, which was probably built in the 1890s with a shallow ell to the rear on the N. Miro Street side. The property here was part of the small Tala *habitation* bound by Castanedo Alley, as shown on the Zimpel survey of 1834. Prior to the late-Victorian development of the square, there were creole cottages built in the 1850s. Tranquille Bachelin sold to Joseph LeBlanc a property at public auction in 1865, described as "the buildings No. 268 Columbus Street and improvements consisting of two, small, frame houses built in the interior of said portion of ground having each two rooms, front and back galleries, *cabinet*, cistern, well, privy. Stable, oven, chicken house, a large fruit, flower and vegetable garden." The price for this property was $1,600 according to the act recorded by notary A. Dreyfous on June 20, 1854. **2220–22** Columbus is a double shotgun with façade decoration matching that of the house at 2226.

2221–23

2217–19, 2221–23, 2237–39. A well-kept double shotgun with hip-roof at **2221–23** illustrates the continuing popularity of simple, classic forms into the 1870s. The drop-siding, segmental-arched transom, and the large applied-work brackets with finials, supporting the overhang, are Victorian embellishments to an otherwise restrained façade. **2217–19** is also a double shotgun with restrained, Classic-style decoration but also having the bracketed overhang and segmental-arched openings associated with late-Victorian decoration.

COLUMBUS

2324–26

2309

Hubert Concession. The opposite sides of the 2300 block of Columbus emanate from different plantations. The even side, landmarked by **2324–26**, was the rear portion of the Zeringue-Bellanger-Fleitas holdings, being in effect the backyard of the Zeringue *habitation* and Bellanger College, then the Fleitas-Chauffe house. The land on which this relatively recent house at 2324–26 stands is part of the eighteenth-century Marc Antoine Hubert Concession, one of the earliest concessions granted by the French government before the founding of the city. In the early 1800s the grounds housed the Bellanger School; other owners of the strip were Joseph Zeringue and Norbert Broutin. The grounds here contained "framed stables, pigeon and fowl houses, cistern, etc." in 1856 when the lot facing Columbus was sold separately for the street to be cut through. The present house was probably built for Joseph Molaison soon after 1890 when he bought the 75 feet on Columbus on August 27, before J. Fahey for $500. The house, as it appears today, is an interesting, three-bay version of a raised, Victorian home with hip-roof and center hall. Segmental-arched openings and a deep gallery are supported by Classic-style pillars with pierced-work brackets, bosses, and a band of spindles and pierced-work panels. The porch railing is comprised of the original turned balusters, but the entrance balustrade is a new iron one; the façade has drop-siding. The odd side of the street—the square bound by Columbus, N. Tonti, N. Miro, and Laharpe—was part of the Faubourg Gueno, as purchased from the heirs of René Huchet de Kernion, husband of Dame De Verges. Antoine Gilbert St. Maxent had purchased a large portion of land in this area, selling it on January 5, 1780, to Pierre De Verges. De Verges's three daughters inherited the large *habitation* measuring six *arpents*, fourteen *toises*, three lines by twenty-one *arpents* depth. Huchet de Kernion and his wife bought out Prudence and Constance De Verges on July 18, 1806, before N. Broutin; on September 25, 1815, Pierre Gueno bought the full tract. This square, including the 2300 block of Columbus, was not developed until 1889 when Sidney Joseph Poupart purchased the site of **2309** from the Commercial Homestead. He probably then built this villa-type house, which was designed with a central-hall plan and a façade articulation of segmental-arched openings in the late-Victorian style. It is unknown whether the house stood on brick piers at one time or was raised and a cement porch and enclosed first level added.

CONTI

1834

Faubourg Hagan. The 1800 block of Conti between Roman and Derbigny, odd side, now has eight shotgun houses that predate 1883. Some of these retain their original entrance doors, shutters, and decorative details. Others were updated in the late nineteenth century. Any of them may have been built by Theo Broudner for John Monnergham, as early as 1860. On February 29 of that year the two men signed a contract, recorded by notary E. Barnett, for three houses to be built for $3,850 on this street. Across the street at **1834** Conti, the shotgun house with Greek Revival-style façade was built after 1850. It has lost the wooden columns that once supported the box cornice with dentil molding. Eliza McIntyre, wife of Robert Walker Fishbourne, sold the house to Samuel Moore on August 15, 1850, for $1,500, according to the act recorded by A. Chiapella. Mme Fishbourne had bought this lot and six others for $1,225 just one year earlier from Robert Burton, the first to purchase the land after the Hagan-Lafayette partition of 1842. She built this house and others for speculative purposes, selling them soon after they were constructed. Removal of the chain-link fence and screen doors, along with replacement of the box columns to support the gallery roof, would restore this property to its original appearance.

1836

Lafayette Property. Michael Kopfer bought the site of 1836 Conti along with another lot from Lafayette's heirs and their partner, Pierre Riviere, on October 23, 1848, for $347.32, according to notary B. Phillips. At that time the banquette had just been built; thus Kopfer had to pay the vendors for it, in addition to the cost of the property. Kopfer built this house sometime after 1848, probably in the middle 1850s. The house was sold at a sheriff's sale to Martin Joseph Farrell to settle a lawsuit with Frank Miriam on May 20, 1880 (3 DC#25956). The three-bay, camelback cottage was designed with a heavy, box cornice with brackets, roundheaded windows surmounted by straight-molded cornices, and a narrow, segmental-arched, recessed entrance with pilasters flanking each side of the doorway. The camelback section of the roof is hipped. An open gallery extends along one side at both levels of the house.

CONTI

7/33

1726–1736

1726–28, 1730–32, 1734–36. Henry Weber bought the lot at **1726–28** Conti in Faubourg Hagan from the heirs of Lafayette on April 1, 1851, as recorded by notary M. Gernon. Soon thereafter, he built this double creole cottage. On May 3, 1856, as recorded by R. J. Ker, Weber sold half of the new house to Henry Gulle for just $800. The property, measuring 12½ feet by 100 feet, included "the one-half or tenement of the frame house and dependencies thereunto attached on said half-lot of ground." In 1860 Gulle purchased the other half of the house from Franz Wayand for $850. He sold the double to Joseph Keller on May 11, 1872, for $2,100. The Keller family followed by Charles Bruning owned the house until 1919. George Nami then took over the title; his family still owned the house in 1952 (COB 587/573). The house at **1730–32** Conti was built in the 1850s also. The two creole cottages have identical fenestrations but slightly different roof heights. It is uncertain whether the house was built as a speculative investment by T. Mathews or by Jacob Bopp. On April 1, 1851, Thomas Mathews bought the land from the Lafayette heirs. When he died in 1858, Jacob Bopp purchased the property for $1,075 at the March 13 estate auction. This price suggests that either the house was already there or Bopp bought other property along with this lot. The house was surely standing by the late 1850s, since Bopp's family resided there. After Bopp died in 1886, his heirs kept it until 1891. The side view of the creole cottage shows the gabled side and attic opening with strap-hinged batten shutters, as well as a detached kitchen in the rear. The side gable is regularly proportioned with a built-in overhang forming a beak. This cottage and the adjacent one are illustrated in plan book 7, folio 33; French doors and *faux-granite* steps with three risers are depicted in this illustration. The steps are now gone, and the sidewalk has been raised so that the ventilators along the foundations are scarcely visible. The chimneys have been removed as well as gutters and drains. The detached kitchen remains intact behind the house. At **1734–36** is a corner, two-level, frame, double house. The second-level gallery crosses the façade and returns around the side with cast-iron railing. Louvered shutters at the second level protect full-length openings. The well-kept house probably dates from the mid–nineteenth century.

1918–1938

Faubourg Hagan. Studying this photograph of six houses in the 1900 block of Conti, one can readily comprehend the original character of Faubourg Hagan. Frame creole cottages, mostly double, sometimes triple or quadruple, abound; as do single and double shotguns, particularly those constructed in the 1890s. Galleried, two-level houses appear on the main thoroughfares but are less common on the side streets, particularly the grid section between N. Claiborne, N. Broad, Canal, and Basin. The most popular types, affording excellent use of narrow lots, were the creole cottage and the shotgun. **1936–38** Conti is a four-bay, frame creole cottage with the beak-roof popular in the 1860s. On these corner creole cottages, the side elevation often had batten shutters. A detached, side-gabled kitchen remains with this property. The adjacent **1932–34** is a common-roof creole cottage with center dogtrot passageway, as is **1924–26**. Side-gabled, beak-roof creole cottages are often similar, but the house size causes a variance in roof heights. **1928** Conti is a three-bay shotgun with Italianate details. An open side gallery gives access to the rear rooms. **1922** is also a shotgun, but a two-bay with detached service wing. Stylistic analysis of the two-story frame house at **1918** Conti suggests that it was built in the 1850s. Principal features are Classic detailing, such as the box cornice, and the cantilevered balcony with cast-iron railing. This railing returns along the sides of the house, which has side entrances rather than front ones. Since Faubourg Hagan was subdivided in 1841, this house was one of the earlier structures in the area. The chain of title ended with a sale by deed on November 13, 1905, when Thomas Capo sold it to Frank Black as recorded in COB 208/187.

1927–31

1927–31, 1939. The common-roof creole cottage illustrated includes a four-bay double and a two-bay single separated by a dogtrot passageway. Built in the late 1850s, this house-type is found almost exclusively in Faubourg Hagan. The corner creole cottage at **1939** Conti may have been built soon after 1853 when lawsuits involving disputes over this land were settled. The heirs of Lafayette, the heirs of Griffon, and the heirs and partners of Samuel Moore all claimed title. The dispute was settled in 1853 with a partition between the Moore and Griffon claimants.

2100–2118

2100 Block. Spanning much of the block is an excellent row of shotgun doubles. It forms a pleasing rhythm of rooflines, brackets, segmental windows, and doors with molded cornices. Shiplap board fronts and weatherboard sides are satisfying in repetitive treatment; even the concrete steps, which were once wooden box ones, create a neat pattern. These houses probably were built in the last decade of the nineteenth century; the land was vacant in the 1880s. The historic provenance of the block refers back to the Baroness de Pontalba and property inherited by her from her father, Almonester y Rojas.

2101–03

Faubourg Hagan. This mid-nineteenth-century corner creole cottage appears to be of masonry construction; it has undergone unfortunate twentieth-century alterations. Replacement of the present façade with a traditional four-bay arrangement would help restore this property to its former state. The kitchen building in the rear remains. Baroness de Pontalba sold the lot, a part of her 1812 dowry, to Frederick Keiner in 1850. Mr. Keiner probably built the dormerless cottage soon afterward, and the house remained in the Keiner family until 1905, when George H. Keiner sold it to Thomas Capo. It was then listed as municipal numbers 2101 and 2103 Conti and 413 Johnson and was sold for $3,050 (October 20, 1905, A. Guilbau). The New Orleans Terminal Company owned the structure from 1909 until 1921.

2216, 2220

Faubourg Hagan. The early shotgun at **2216** is characteristic of those found in Faubourg Hagan. Such design features as the entrance leading to a side gallery, Greek Key surrounds on the front openings, and a high hip-roof are repeated in the houses of this area, which were built during the 1850s. This one has retained its wooden box steps, louvered shutters on the front, batten side-wall shutters, and wooden side railing. **2220** Conti is also a three-bay, Greek Revival shotgun dating from the mid–nineteenth century.

2232–34

2200, 2300 Blocks. The Griffon family acquired most of this block in 1862 after the partition between the heirs of Samuel Moore and the heirs of the Baroness de Pontalba, both of whom claimed the land behind Faubourg Hagan. The smaller, double creole cottage at **2228–30** retains the lower roof height of an early creole cottage, but like its neighbors, probably dates from the 1860s. At **2232–34**, the double, corner creole cottage has a high beak-roof incorporating an overhang and a small detached kitchen now joined to the house; Victorian brackets and window hoods have been added. These houses were finished in either white or buff-tan paint with Paris green shutters at the time of their construction, and this unpainted exterior is inaccurate. At **2224–26**, speculators bought and sold the lot until Henry Huger purchased it from Charles Beddiges in 1866 for $500. He built the frame, dogtrot creole cottage soon afterward and kept it for forty years. In 1905, he sold the property for $2,500 to Thomas Capo who owned real estate in the area, according to the act recorded by notary A. Guilbaut. In the 2300 block Mme Samuel Moore, Françoise Malvina Lovell, in 1853 acquired the square that contained the lots on which the houses at **2326–28** and **2334** were built. The square was subdivided into twenty-eight lots by Mme Moore, who sold them to J. H. Rahders for $5,600 on July 28, 1857 (P. C. Cuvellier). In 1860 Jacob Gräff bought the vacant lot at 2326–28 and built this frame, four-bay, Greek Revival cottage with detached, gable-sided kitchen. Gräff owned the building until his death in 1903. His heirs held the property until 1906, when they sold it to Thomas Capo for $4,000 on February 6, as recorded by notary A. Guilbaut. 2334 Conti, a frame, corner creole cottage, continues the tradition of modest residential dwellings built as rental units in the original Pontalba division. In 1857 Adam Spies purchased two lots in the square from J. H. Rahders for $1,275 (March 28, P. C. Cuvellier) and built the house at 2334, which he retained until 1876.

2600 Block. The square bound by N. Broad, Conti, Bienville, and N. Dorgenois was once the site of the House of the Good Shepherd, a landmark for many years until its demolition around 1960 for the Schwegmann's Supermarket. Across the Conti Street side of the Schwegmann's store, in the 2600 block, stands a group of two-bay and four-bay shotguns, some of which predate publication of Robinson's Atlas of 1883.

2129, 2335. The unusual, double creole cottage at **2129** appears to be one of the oldest remaining houses in the square. A tin roof, supported by brackets, covers a double cement landing; neither is original. The cottage is austerely simple and very small, allowing for each apartment no more than one room and a small attached service space at the rear. Built of vertical flatboat boards, directly on the sill, the front and rear are covered with weatherboards. The gabled sides of the building are now plastered. No stylistic details remain to indicate a construction date, but it is known that the Gueno plantation was not subdivided until 1835. Standing among more recently built neighbors, **2335** is also one of the oldest houses remaining in this area. Twentieth-century stucco pillars and an attached porch roof alter what was originally a two-bay, frame shotgun with hip-roof. The door and full-length windows have simple wooden surrounds topped by a plain cornice. Although architecturally repetitive, it was a common house-type in the mid–nineteenth century.

2409–11

Jones Cottage. The main body of this four-room, galleried house is creole in plan. To the rear is a connected shed having two windows on each end; a simple, cast-iron picket fence crosses the front of the lot. This rural-style cottage dates from after 1855, when on March 30, before A. Bienvenue, André Gregoire sold two lots, each 30 feet facing D'Abadie to Henry Jones, f.m.c., for $140. The residence remained in the Jones family until 1926 when the succession of Miss M. A. Jones sold the house "in that part formerly known as Faubourg Gueno designated as 4 and 5 of square 36 on plan made by N. Fouché, dated March 27, 1848, deposited in the office of Amedée Ducatel as plan number 3 in book number 3 (CDC number 163681, July 28, 1926)." The delicate frieze and spandrels of pierced work and turned columns of the gallery suggest a post–Civil War building date. However, such decoration could have been added to the façade during a renovation, when the segmental-arched openings and drop-siding were perhaps applied to an 1850s façade. The mid-century date is suggested by the set-back, galleried house, built low to the ground with four full-length openings, as well as by the 1855 Henry Jones property purchase. The seventy-five-year continuous ownership by a single black family marks this house as an unusual site in Tremé.

2815

Faubourg Gueno. This area has a large number of early, two-bay shotguns both with and without front or side galleries. The side gallery on this example was built as an integral part of the house, and the hip-roof extends to cover it. The roof hip is high, with central chimneys piercing the ridge. Such houses usually date from the mid–nineteenth century.

N. DERBIGNY

315–17

315–17, 321. After the 1841 subdivision of Faubourg Hagan by John Hagan and the heirs of Lafayette, Jacques Descrimes acquired four lots facing N. Derbigny, which he sold to François Roffiac on April 14, 1848 (A. Chiapella), for $1,150. Seven years later, Roffiac's heirs inherited the property, which by then included this high, gable-roofed, double creole cottage at 315–17. The incorporation of a front gallery supported by box columns was a technique most often employed in rural creole cottages set off from the street with gardens in the front and rear. This cottage is placed directly on the banquette, but it once had land stretching back 148 feet. The Roffiac family retained the house and the three adjoining properties until 1882. The creole cottage standing next door at 321 was probably built in the 1850s and sold in the 1899 Jules Lassère succession for $1,215.

925

Griffon Division. A two-level, frame, side-hall, galleried, Greek Revival house at **933–35** is now mutilated. Stylistically, this house seems to be one of the earlier ones in the district, which was part of the Charles Griffon estate. The box columns and ironwork of the second-level gallery lend distinction to the house, which probably dates from the late 1840s. The three-bay shotgun with overhang at **925** is structurally sound and appears on the Robinson Atlas for 1883.

1208–1216

Griffon Division. The six-bay, common-wall creole cottage at **1212–16** is a gable-sided, frame dwelling for three families. Built directly on the banquette, it retains two original, paneled and louvered doors, two windows with louvers, and Victorian brackets supporting the incorporated overhang. There are now cement steps rather than the original, wooden box-type. This rental unit replaced a mid-nineteenth-century, frame, corner store-house with two-story kitchen that had been built on the site of the eighteenth-century *maison de maître* of the Bayou Road Griffon *habitation*. The *habitation* measured two-*arpents* front on Bayou Road and extended to the Gravier plantation on Common Street. The early store-house complex appeared in an 1871 auction drawing by Henry Boudousquié, preserved in the notarial archives in plan book 90, folio 29. The extant cottages are built in a retardate style since they postdate 1883, not appearing on the Robinson Atlas. Therefore, the brackets and jigsaw work are original to the structures. The four-bay, hip-roof shotgun at **1208** is more typical of the late-nineteenth-century rental units that proliferated in all New Orleans neighborhoods.

1400 Block

Castarede Cottage (1424). The early history of this land includes ownership by Charles de Morand in the eighteenth century and Bernard Duchamp in the early nineteenth century. The Duchamp estate was auctioned in 1842 (March 19, L. Hermann). The owner of the property on Esplanade and N. Derbigny, when that street was cut through shortly after 1866, was Jesse Conner, f.m.c. At the time Conner sold to Cyprien Dufour (January 10, 1866, A. Dreyfous), the act stated, "Dufour retains in his hands the sum of $160 without interest, to meet the claim of the city of New Orleans against the property now sold, for the opening of N. Derbigny Street." Four other free persons of color, including Louis Barthélémy Rey, were interim landholders of this block on N. Derbigny between the ownerships of the Duchamp and Dufour families. When Jean Jules Aldigé sold 1631 Esplanade to General P. G. T. Beauregard in 1889, a large garden filled the rear 123 feet along N. Derbigny. This was subdivided in 1892, and the three-bay, two-level, Victorian house with side hall, standing at **1426** N. Derbigny was built. In 1895 the general's heirs inherited the property, with 1631 Esplanade and 1426 N. Derbigny appraised at $9,500 and $3,000, respectively. The empty lots on which presently stand the four-bay, vernacular Edwardian cottage at **1424** and a three-bay, Victorian, side-hall cottage at **1428** (now raised), were valued at $700 each. Alfred Lionnet purchased the entire Beauregard estate for $12,400 in 1895. His widow, Rose Lelia, sold the lot at 1424 to Judge Wiley Harvey Lyons, who built the present house in 1902 for his widowed sister, Amanda Lyons Castarede. This bayed, galleried cottage with triple gables above a spindle-work frieze was a popular turn-of-the-century house-type between N. Claiborne and N. Broad. The frame creole cottage that remains at **1432–34** N. Derbigny, corner of Kerlerec, may have been constructed by one of the early free persons of color. This dwelling, placed low to the ground with built-in overhang, is in the style of creole cottages erected in the 1840s. Beside it at **1430** is a post-1883, four-bay, two-level, frame, rental house, which replaced a creole cottage and garden. The second 1400 block of N. Derbigny Street crosses Kerlerec Street and continues the typical Duchamp architectural house-types of simple, frame creole cottages and maisonettes. Designed for rental usage, the predominant creole housing is interspersed with Victorian shotgun replacements. **1440** is a four-bay, frame creole cottage with detached kitchen in the early 1840s style. At **1442–44** and **1446–48**, two, late-Victorian, shotgun doubles complement a third frame house with gabled sides at **1450–52**, which was formerly a creole cottage until a second story was added. **1474–76** is a modest, wraparound creole cottage with an 1890s-style house attached to the front. Plan book 77, folio 39 shows the creole cottage as it appeared on June 12, 1866, in a drawing by P. N. Judice. Across the street, **1471–73** is a frame creole cottage with gabled sides; its neighbor at **1475–77** is also a creole cottage. Both could be attractive if landscaped and restored to their original crisp appearance reflective of the mid–nineteenth century.

1514

1514, 1513–15. The early maisonette in the photograph was built on the Duchamp estate in the decade after its subdivision. Characteristic of such petite, two-bay cottages is the high hip-roof incorporating on overhang returning around one side. The original chimney remains, and there is a *cabinet* to the rear; but the present concrete porch, steps, and iron railing spoil an erstwhile lovely cottage.

1530

1520–22, 1530. Many of the galleried creole cottages built in the 1840s and 1850s on the Milne and Duchamp estates are hidden behind disfiguring, twentieth-century additions. Plan book 89, folio 3, by G. Strehler, illustrates the rustic appearance of this cottage at **1530** in 1866, on the occasion of a sheriff's sale. Auctioned again in 1870, the rural, front-galleried, frame cottage was drawn by G. Strehler, plan

91/6, (1530)

book 91, folio 6; and it was shown to have a front cistern with each family sharing its collected rainwater. A very simple structure, the house appeared to be painted dark green with French casement door panels of a lighter green. House trim and simple banister rails were white. At one time this cottage had a white picket fence, large deciduous fruit trees, and vegetables in the front garden. Now a stucco, hip-roof, 1930s addition fills in the open space, and the N. Claiborne Avenue elevated expressway is clearly visible through the backyard. At **1520–22**, an early, four-bay, frame, country cottage with gabled sides has a built-in front gallery, which was once wood with box columns. The 1870 appearance of the house was probably similar to that of its neighbor at 1530, seen in the auction illustration. Only the cap-molded lintels in the Classic style and the cant of the roof give indication of a building date in the 1850s. Thomas La Bertie is the first documented owner of the house, and he began paying taxes on it in 1870. In 1878 La Bertie sold the house to Numa Dudoussat, who in 1884 sold it to Augustin Follain. The recorded owners in 1974 were Mr. and Mrs. Donald Hingle, who live elsewhere.

1542, 1538

90/43

Duchamp Division. Plan book 90, folio 43 illustrates the two houses at **1536–38** and **1540–42** as they appeared on July 16, 1870, in a drawing by G. Strehler for an impending public auction. The drawing illustrates a row of three rental units in an estate, but the third cottage has been demolished. Both remaining houses are being reroofed, and it is seen by comparison with the plan that the corner cottage has lost its front dormer. The plan further shows that the small corner cottage had two rear *cabinets*, one of which housed a stairway to the dormered garret. Fireplaces were in each of the two outbuildings. The houses are built of flatboat boards set vertically, then covered with weatherboard. They have lost their batten shutters, and doors have been lowered. Simple, beak-roofed creole cottages like these dotted the Duchamp division by the late 1840s, and their number increased throughout the 1850s.

N. DORGENOIS

215

211–13, 215, 218. The 200 block of Dorgenois Street between Iberville and Bienville was not available for development until the final 1854 settlement of a series of lawsuits initiated by various claimants of the land, including Baroness de Pontalba, Samuel Moore, and Joseph Kenton. **211–13**, a small shotgun with hip-roof and gabled back end, dates from the mid-1850s. The cottage at **215** was built in the creole style soon after the development of this swampland between the old Basin (Carondelet) Canal and Common (Tulane). Its gabled sides and one-time arrangement of four, equidistant openings were typical of a rural creole cottage raised high on piers and set back from the street with front garden. The small remaining segment of vertical board fence indicates the type of fencing that once enclosed the property. The two-bay shotgun across the street at **218** N. Dorgenois has a high hip-roof extending to cover a side gallery. The façade has a deep parapet that extends to create an entrance to the side gallery from the street. Such side-oriented shotguns with high hip-roofs were built in the 1850s.

900–02

900–02, 919, 923, 925–27. Albin Soulié, f.m.c. of Paris, was a major landholder and builder in New Orleans in the 1850s. He purchased this property on both sides of the street from Robert J. Ker in 1854, ending Ker's two-year ownership of this part of the Bernard Coquet division. Soulié sold the corner at **900** to Jean Baptiste Crevon in 1859 for $1,175 with the stipulation that "the above lots are subject to a contract . . . for banquettes to be made in front of said lots on Dorgenois . . . which contract is hereby assumed by the purchaser." Recent remodeling of the attractive, double-dormered, high gable-sided creole cottage has made stylistic interpretation difficult. Either Soulié built this house between 1854 and 1859, or Francis Mouney had it constructed soon after 1866, using the building style of the 1850s. Observations prior to renovations indicated that this was a frame creole cottage with two French doors and two double-hung windows with simple surrounds. The gabled sides have cast-iron balconies extending from the attic level. Across the street at **919**, **923**, and **925–27** are three, frame, Victorian cottages that display a variety of jigsaw decoration. As a group they enhance the street scene.

929

Badue House. The two-level, three-bay, frame house at 929 was part of the Evariste Blanc plantation prior to its purchase by the city in 1834. Jules Badue probably built this house prior to 1865, when he lost its ownership to the Hope Insurance Company. It was sold by that company to E. Abell for $3,375 in 1865, before E. Barnett, and held by him for twenty years. Isidore Newman bought and sold the house in 1885. It is probable that a Widow Hearsey, who purchased it that year, changed the lower-level windows to the early-twentieth-century fanlight style. The Greek Key entrance surround suggests that the original gallery supports might well have been two-level box columns, but the present fluted Doric ones and cast-iron railings are stylistically proper. Set back from the street, the house is framed by a pair of large magnolia trees.

1116–18

Boulanger Country Seat. This central-hall villa was once surrounded by spacious lawns and gardens. Now its land has been subdivided and the house itself mutilated. The large hip-roof retains its very fine, small dormer, and the dentiled cornice, which once crowned a columned open gallery, is visible. The gallery is now weatherboarded and enclosed. The molding outline of the original stairway remains; but a braced cement and iron stairway, narrower in scale, now services the imposing central door. The space between the original brick piers has been filled in. The rear gallery with its *cabinets* has been enclosed; a remnant of a small circular stair in the *cabinet* is crudely cut off with plywood. Some base moldings and interior door surrounds are still in place. A succession of notable families have owned this property from the eighteenth-century concession until 1916, when house and land fell to a building and loan company. Louis Sénèchal Dauberville received claim to the land from Louis Césaire Lebreton, whose heirs continually reappear as owners. Then Domingo Fleitas, Bernard Coquet, and his daughter, Pauline Josephine, held it until it was in her succession to Julien Alexandre Boulanger. Sometime after his purchase on May 1, 1862, Boulanger built this raised country seat (A. Dreyfous). He and his wife, Léonie Rosine Alexandrine Candide Avenec, lived here for the next four years. It was Mme Boulanger who sold the house, buildings, and seven lots to François Rimailho and Charles Espernan, who were partners in the Société de Commerce. They retained the house until 1869, when Espernan sold to Rimailho. The family of the latter held on until 1881, when Jeanne Desirée Cazaux, Widow Rimailho, relinquished ownership to Jules J. D'Aquin. William A. Kernaghan took over a year later, having the entire property for the next three years and selling it in 1885 to Mme Marie Bousquet Adam for $3,500. Her heir, Jean Baptiste Lucien Adam sold to the Security Building and Loan Company (December 27, 1916, F. Zengel) for $3,500.

1201

Faubourg Gueno, 1201, 1209–11. North Dorgenois is unusual in Faubourg Gueno, for both sides of the street are lined with large oak trees. A two-story, front-bay, Edwardian-style frame house at **1201** is an attractive architectural enhancement to the block despite the unfortunate addition of an attached side shed. **1209–11** is a four-bay, two-story, double house. An interesting example, this early-twentieth-century house has a combination of late-Victorian millwork on the gables, verge board, and second-level balcony, which contrasts with Classical-style dentils on the first-level gallery cornice. Slender Doric columns and Classic-style entrance surrounds reflect the Neoclassic Revival then gaining in popularity. Windows have typical early-twentieth-century muntins with a crisscross design.

1223

Faubourg Gueno, 1223, 1237–39. The early-twentieth-century cottage pictured is reminiscent of the Arts and Crafts style. It has a side gallery with spindles and colonettes leading to the entrance. A pair of tall, narrow windows is balanced above by a decorative, pierced-work gable supported by brackets. An individualistic cornice molding decorates the main roof as well as the gallery overhang. At **1237–39**, a handsome, four-bay, double shotgun has a deep gallery supported by fluted Corinthian-type columns, which support a cornice with brackets and delicate dentils; doors and windows have cap-molded lintels. The roof and siding of this

house suggest a date after 1885; the cornice and columns are Neoclassic Revival in feeling. Central chimneys indicate double fireplaces servicing both sides of this house. A cast-iron fence with heavy piers having caps decorated in acanthus motif is a sophisticated accoutrement.

1450

Second 1400 Block. The entire square bound by N. Dorgenois, Columbus, Kerlerec, and N. Rocheblave belonged to Madeleine Gueno Buss, daughter of Pierre Gueno, when she died in 1867. In her will, executed before A. Dreyfous on November 28, 1867, she left the square to her nieces and nephews, the Laforest children: Felicité, Mary, Louise, Alfred James, Jules, and Edward. The three traditional, frame, double shotguns at **1458–60**, **1462–64**, and **1466–68** N. Dorgenois, were built after the Laforest heirs sold lots in the square in 1877. Rooflines, including gabled and hipped fronts, illustrate the versatility of shotgun styles employed. The frame structure at **1450** was formerly part of a rural complex set far back on the lot; it was probably the kitchen or service wing of an early house, perhaps one belonging to Mme Buss. This one-story segment, now used as a residence, could date from the 1840s.

1504–06

Faubourg Gueno, 1500, 1504–06. Brunois's Tavern at the corner of Columbus, is a typical New Orleans corner commercial building with a diagonally set front door and deep overhang. This frame, turn-of-the-century structure also has the traditional low hip-roof. Corner stores of this type have great aesthetic appeal and lend vitality as well as services to small neighborhoods. At **1504–06** is a three-bay, late-Victorian house, converted to a double. Gabled roof, bracketed overhang, drop-siding, and quoins are architectural characteristics of this structure, as are the segmental arches with decorative architraves.

1574–76

1529

1500 Blocks. The 1500 blocks of N. Dorgenois, on both sides, continue as a handsome, tree-lined street with a variety of frame house-types and styles dating from 1854 to the turn of the century. A building contract for **1516** lends importance to this two-bay shotgun with hip-roof and gallery supported by box columns. The original door is illustrated in the Robert & Company catalogs for 1881 and 1890. The house once had the side-gallery entrance so prevalent in Tremé, but it has been altered. William Morel de Guiramond contracted with Octave Foy, free colored builder, on October 6, 1854, "to supply material and build on Guiramond's lot a one-story, frame dwelling house." This contract was notarized by Edward Barnett. Guiramond paid $225 for the lot in 1851, and he paid Foy $1,515 for his services. A far more imposing house is **1574–76**, a five-bay, frame, American-style cottage with central hall. The recessed central entrance is flanked by pairs of full-length, segmental-arched windows. The front gallery is supported by colonettes with a band of spindles and pierced-work decoration. Behind the apron forming the gallery roof is a gambrel-roof in the Second Empire style, a version of which is also illustrated in the 1881 and 1890 Robert's catalogs. There are two chimneys in the outer walls and interior chimneys to the rear. The roofline, with its Dutch influence and shingles, would date the house in the early twentieth century, although the building type had been popular for over fifty years. An anchor to the block is **1529**, a raised-basement, Edwardian house with central recessed entrance flanked by projecting bays. Wide wooden steps lead to the gallery, which has a bracketed overhang. The wooden railings and turned balusters are heavy and unusual, as is the sculptured cement foundation. A large side yard is entered through a wrought-iron trellis, often used as a garden bower. **1523** is a five-bay, villa-style house situated low to the ground on piers of six bricks. The handsome, central entrance has a doorway illustrated in Robert's 1881 catalog with two arched panels, glass above and solid square panels below. Plasters with a deep cornice are late-Victorian, but reminiscent in motif to the popular Classic surrounds used for so many years by New Orleans builders. Hip-roof, bracketed overhang, full-length windows, and a shallow ell to the rear characterize the late-Victorian version of a house-type popular throughout the nineteenth century. **1545** N. Dorgenois is a two-bay shotgun with hip-roof, segmental-arched openings, and bracketed overhang. Full-length openings feature cap-molded lintels with dentils; unfortunately, the porch railing is not original, but this three-room corner cottage is in fine repair. **1569** is a two-bay shotgun with gabled roof, apron, and rear ell. The galleries are supported by colonettes turned in the Moorish manner, with balusters, a band of spindles, and pierced work. Such 1890s-style Victorian cottages with ells necessitate larger lots, affording some spacing between houses. The Moorish motif, while unusual in the city, is found often in this neighborhood.

Chinese Laundry. At N. Dorgenois between Kerlerec and Bayou Road backed by N. Rocheblave is a charming masonry structure with a pagoda tile roof. Built as a Chinese laundry, this and several other identical buildings throughout the city represent outlets for Chinese immigrant trade dating from the 1920s. Many have closed, and have been demolished or disfigured. This, like the enamel-baked Toddle Houses, represents curious anecdotal life-styles in the first half of the twentieth century.

1726

1609, 1613–15, 1726. At **1609** is a late-Victorian, bayed cottage with an ell to the rear. A recessed gallery entrance, supported by colonettes, and small front bay are characteristic of the house-type, as is stained glass in the bay window. Both the gallery and ell roof, as well as the main roof, have gables, creating an interesting outline. **1613–15** N. Dorgenois is a more traditional shotgun cottage having a gabled roof and apron overhang with steamboat brackets. Segmental-arched openings have double-hung windows, and the cap-molded lintels have pierced-work cresting. Fleur-de-lis verge and icicle-patterned bands decorate the overhang. Drop-siding and quoins complete the standard façade design. At **1726** is one of many high-hip, slate-roofed, two-bay shotguns in the Classic style that appear in Faubourg Gueno, dating between 1850 and 1875.

2552

Police Youth Activities Building. Few Faubourg Tremé buildings approach monumentality, which heightens the importance of this 1890s version of a Romanesque château. Built as a public building by the city of New Orleans, the cornerstone reads: "Erected during the administration of Paul Capdevielle, Mayor, 1902." It has fortunately been preserved and serves now as the New Orleans Police Department Youth Activities Building. Most of the buildings in this block are modest, twentieth-century structures, although a few Victorian singles remain.

DUMAINE

1500–1510

City Commons. Among a series of creole cottages and front-gabled shotguns is **1504**, a two-level, Greek Revival, detached, frame townhouse. The entrance leads to a recessed side gallery with stairwell. The second-level balcony has wooden pillar supports and had a cast-iron railing. The Greek Key entrance and Classic-style cornice recall the former appearance of the house. The façade is now covered with modern siding; there is no service wing or outbuilding. It was probably built for Delphine Philibert, wife of Henry Train, in 1862. She had purchased this lot from Bernard Ehrenshneider after he had reoriented it from a Villere Street frontage in 1859. Ehrenshneider purchased the lot with two others from Severin Doebelle. The three faced Villere and had creole cottages built on them, one of which is 825 N. Villere. At the corner, **1500–02** is a Victorian, shotgun camelback with segmental-arched openings having original screens. Front-gabled roofline with apron, drop-siding, and quoins all bespeak an 1880s building date. Lintels have carving with a leaf motif repeated in the sill moldings. The Greek Revival, double creole cottage with dormers and masonry front at **1508–10** was documented in an 1860 sale (August 3, C. V. Foulon) by the Leon Sindos heirs to Mme Jacques David St. Herman (Louise Morin). The sale "excluded two buildings, one on the street, the other at the rear of the lot, which buildings belong to Mme Severin Latorre." The cottage had been built for the Sindos family before 1848 as rental property, since Leon P. Sindos lived on Marais between St. Philip and Dumaine, having a "Variety and Fancy Store" at 227 Royal. On December 25, 1848, the Fifth District Court handled the succession of Louise Bacilice Sindos wherein the house went to Léonide Sindos, wife of Octave Bellot, and three minor Sindos children with usufruct by Pouponne Hagan, wife of Leon Sindos.

1514

Théard Cottage. This three-bay, frame creole cottage with Greek Key entrance and two other full-length openings is typical of the Greek Revival period in New Orleans. The façade has been faced with drop-siding of the Victorian period and the foundation filled incorrectly. Gabled sides have original batten shutters and hardware at the upper level. Behind the entrance is evidence of a recessed side gallery with *cabinet*, and there is an attached shed to the rear. The house was built for René Philippe Théard who bought the property from the heirs of Léandre Cheval, f.m.c., in 1853 (March 7, O. Drouet). When Théard sold the property for $2,150 to Jean Baptiste Roudanez in 1856, J. Lisbouny, notary, recorded on November 6: "Ven-

dor built the house since his acquisition." The property, part of the City Commons, had belonged to the Cheval family from September 13, 1831, when Jean Théophile Cavelier sold the lots to Cheval for $350. Cavelier had bought them from Barthélémy Arnaud and Spire Loguet, f.m.c. In the 1831 sale, notary F. de Armas noted that "the buildings thereon are not part of the sale; vendor will remove them as soon as possible." This is another important indication of the prevalent custom in the eighteenth and nineteenth centuries of moving houses.

1518–20, 1522–24

Cheval Cottage (1518–20), 1522–24. The mutilated creole cottage at 1518–20 is on part of the property once owned by Léandre Cheval, f.m.c., as is its neighbor 1514 Dumaine. Peter J. Blumers bought the house from the Cheval succession on July 27, 1875, selling it July 2, 1890, before A. Ducatel, to Malvina Cougot, Mme Pierre St. Raymond, for $3,250. Cheval probably built this house soon after his 1831 purchase of the property from Jean Théophile Cavelier. During the Cheval family's forty-four-year ownership of the house, the widow sold the side yard in 1853, and René Théard built the neighboring house at 1514. Presently only the scale of the house, as well as its original chimney and dormers, indicates its architectural value. The façade has been mutilated by a lowering of the openings, an application of modern brick veneer, and ungainly concrete steps with inappropriate iron railings. The early, double-dormered, frame creole cottage with gabled sides and arched dormer lights at **1522–24** has a Greek Revival façade of wood rusticated to resemble stone. Four French doors have molded wood lintels in the Greek Revival manner. Decorative brackets were added in the Victorian period as well as segmental, oval-arched openings in the door. An attached, gable-ended, kitchen wing extends to the rear. This cottage, like its neighbor at 1518–20, is one of the earlier extant buildings in the area known as the Commons. Soon after the 1829 auction of the Commons by the municipality, François Desgrais built this house on the 30-foot lot that he had bought for $390. He sold the new house for $2,800 on February 7, 1830, before F. de Armas, to L. Beltremieux, f.m.c., Marthe Castenedo, f.w.c., bought it with three slaves for $2,500 from Beltremieux in 1832. An 1878 auction notice for a sale by Pélagie Hebert, alias Orphe, to Jean Fourton described "a house of six rooms, kitchen of four rooms, two cisterns, double hydrants, a brick-covered courtyard, *lieux d'aisance* [covered convenience], etc. divided into two tenements renting for $20 a month" (June 8, C. T. Soniat).

1530

Passebon Store-house. The two-story, frame, corner store-house was built with four openings at each level. The molded cornice with dentils and brackets reflects the Italianate style of the 1870s. A second-level balcony has been removed, and the first level has been mutilated. Pierre Passebon, who owned many properties in Tremé, acquired this lot from the Citizens Bank of Louisiana in 1847 without a building. Less than a year later he sold the lot with buildings and improvements to Victor Bénit for $2,400 (May 4, 1848, C. Boudousquie). Exterior renovation could return 1530 to its original appearance with replacement of the three first-level windows and an iron balcony.

1/25

1501

Ganel Townhouse. One of three identical houses built by Prosper Ganel soon after his purchase of three lots from Charles Gérard in 1859 (April 30, A. Abat), 1501 is a Greek Revival, two-level townhouse with masonry front and frame sides. Features include Greek Key entrance, wooden pedimented lintels, and granite steps. The balcony has been removed; and a two-story, frame, service building extending to the rear of the house has been demolished. In 1868 the three houses were sold in a sheriff's sale to settle the Ganel estate and illustrated by J. A. D'Hémécourt in a plan of "three, two-story dwellings with two-story kitchens, cisterns, sheds, and waterworks etc. belonging to the Succession of Widow P. Ganel." One of the houses is described further in the *New Orleans Republican*, December 3, 1868, as having on the ground floor "hall, double parlors with sliding door, dining room, and pantry under the staircase, three rooms above, two *cabinets* and balcony on the street, and two-story frame building in the yard of six rooms, paved yard, cistern, waterworks, privy, etc." Mlle Ganel purchased 1501 at the succession sale for $5,250. The third house was purchased by M. E. Gottschalk, representing E. Prieur, for $6,275. It was the residence of the Ganel family and, although now demolished, is pictured in plan book 1, folio 25, dated May 14, 1877.

1509–11

Carran Cottage. This double creole cottage retains its original batten shutters, strap hinges, and French doors, as well as molded wooden lintel openings. The property, with six other lots, was sold at auction in August of 1829 by the municipality to A. Boimaré. Boimaré sold the lots one by one; and on March 6, 1832, before C. Janin, this lot was auctioned for $430 to J. Arnaud. He sold the semi-improved lot in 1836, without this building, to Norbert Rillieux, free black inventor of a revolutionary sugar-boiling process and vacuum pan. Rillieux disposed of the property to builder Myrtile Courcelle, f.m.c., one month later on August 3, 1836, for $1,000, suggesting that arrangements had been made between Rillieux and Courcelle for the construction of the house. Courcelle sold this new house and others in 1843 (February 4, C. V. Foulon) to Eulalie, Céleste, and Marie Coralie Soulié, living in Paris, for $2,500. It is documented that Courcelle built the house by a statement in the act of sale: "including the buildings which the owner built since his acquisition" (October 30, 1850, O. Drouet). This is one of numerous buildings with which Joseph Dolliole and the Macarty family, f.m.c., were involved. In 1854 the cottage was sold by Clémence Eveline Chesse, widow of Edmund Samuel Hermann (well-known merchant), to Isabelle Macarty, f.w.c., represented by her husband, Daniel Nobé, and Joseph Dolliole. Isabelle Macarty Nobé sold it in 1870 to Félicie Deslend (November 5, E. Breaux), and John Carran acquired it from her by sheriff's sale seven years later on December 15, 1877, for $1,500. Carran and his heirs kept the house until the turn of the century.

1523–25

Pereuilhet Property. This hip-roof house with wrought-iron balcony is just two rooms deep, but a two-story, rear service wing adds additional square footage. The notarial drawing in plan book 7, folio 23 indicates that in 1867 there was a stable on this site belonging to P. Pereuilhet. A newspaper ad refers to *une grande écurie pour huit chevaux ou plus*. The stables were sold to Cayetano Pazy Conto for $1,380 in 1867 (May 1, A. Ducatel). The present house replaced them and was probably built in the late 1870s as evidenced by the façade decoration. The Robinson Atlas indicates that this house was in place in 1883, although the two-level, side-gabled service building was not.

1529

Buck Property. Here is a house with both creole and early shotgun characteristics. The Greek Key entrance leads to a side gallery, roofed by an overhang covered by an extension of the hip-roof. The other side of the roof terminates in a gabled side without windows. There is an outstanding, two-story service building across the rear of the lot. As late as 1868 the only structures on this property were two sheds. At that time John Spengler sold a house with four rooms and a detached kitchen which faced N. Robertson on the first lot from the corner. This N. Robertson Street house has been demolished and replaced by an undistinguished larger one. Included in a survey for that sale was the lot measuring 31 feet and 11 inches with sheds on which 1529 Dumaine now stands. Spengler kept the Dumaine Street property three more years, selling it in 1871 to Glassco Buck for $1,400 (March 6, O. Drouet). The Buck family retained it until 1919, when the heirs sold to O. Duconge, Jr. The present house is not on the Robinson Atlas of 1883, which shows the front of the lot vacant with a building to the rear. 1529 and its kitchen were either altered and moved to this lot or were built in a retardate style in the late 1880s.

1531–33

Demourelle Cottage. Antoine Louis Boimaré purchased this lot from the city at auction in 1829, when he also bought the site of 819 N. Villere. Boimaré sold the 30-by-120 foot lot to Jacques Demourelle in 1832 (April 3, C. Janin). The Demourelle family built this early creole cottage soon after, and it remained in the family until an 1878 succession sale. On July 18, 1878, before O. Morel, this house went to Peter Joseph Blumers for $1,550. It was described at the auction as a "family residence, divided into two tenements having four rooms, two *cabinets* and gallery, kitchen, cisterns, privy." The creole cottage is one of the few in Faubourg Tremé having a hip-roof, and thus it is quite important. The overhang returns around the side; and since the façade is almost devoid of decorative elements, the roof is emphasized. The house may be of brick-between-posts construction beneath the new weatherboard covering.

1604–06

Correjolles Cottage. The double-dormered, masonry creole cottage has part-masonry, part-wooden gabled sides. The narrow, flush frames around two French doors and two double-hung windows indicate an early date, as do the small dormers with roundheaded lights. The cottage was built by owner-architect François Correjolles, who paid $975 for a 60-foot lot on Dumaine, part of the City Commons, at the auction succession of Alexandre Benoist on January 10, 1834. When Correjolles sold the lot to investor Charles Raymond, February 22, 1836, before T. Seghers, it was with *entourages*, and the price was $2,500. In a traditional architect-client payment arrangement, the property and house reverted back to Correjolles in July of 1836, and the architect retained the house until June of 1853. He sold it then before A. Boudousquie with shares of stock, buildings, and improvements for a low $1,800 to investor, Pierre Passebon. Passebon doubled his money in four months, selling buildings, improvements, and stock for $3,500 to Jeanne Henriette Millaudon, wife of Casimir Gardanne (October, 1853, A. Ducatel). When Mme Gardanne sold the house in 1866 to Charles Thierry, it was described as "a house covered with slates, number 258, having four rooms, closed gallery, and two *cabinets*, two rooms in the *mansardes* (dormers) with *cabinets*, two-story kitchen of four rooms and gallery, gravelled courtyard, two cisterns, well, latrines, etc. The whole divided into two." A drawing of this house in plan book 86, folio 44 may date from that 1866 sale. Photograph: Bee Pollock.

1622

Charvet House. The two-level, Italianate, side-hall, frame house has a late-Classic-style bracketed cornice and a wide Greek Key entrance with original medallion decorations. The façade has been mutilated but could be restored to resemble 2003 Dumaine. The house dates from soon after the Lucien Charvet purchase of the lot from the Sindos heirs at auction on July 14, 1860. When Charvet sold the property on April 19, 1861, before O. Drouet to Henry Germain for $5,800, it was "with a *maison à étage* which has been constructed since [Charvet's] acquisition." Among the earlier owners of the lot was builder Myrtile Courcelle, who acquired it at a sheriff's sale from Rosa Gomez, wife of P. E. Barbé. When Courcelle sold to Sindos in 1854, there was an earlier creole cottage worth $1,650 on the lot. In 1901 when the estate of Bernard A. Kernan sold the house to John Mailhes for a low price of $1,950, it was described as "a splendid, frame, slated residence, with plastered front; house contains on first floor, hall, double parlors, and dining room; on the second floor, hall, four rooms, and bathroom; also a rear building adjoining main house, containing two rooms; gallery on each floor; a large yard, with side alley, cistern, shed, etc. all in fair condition. Rents for $25 per month" (September 9, 1901, F. Zengel).

1628

Paternostro House. The two-story, four-bay, Victorian, frame store-house has a front gable and decorative overhang. In 1848 realtor François Lacroix, f.m.c., sold property on this square to builder Etiènne Cordeviolle, including six brick houses: one at the corner of St. Ann and N. Claiborne, one at the corner of Dumaine and N. Claiborne, and four facing N. Claiborne. Cordeviolle probably built the group of houses for Lacroix. A plot plan of 1857 shows a building on this corner. Cordeviolle kept the property until 1870, when it was sold by his estate to Felicité Mayronne Lanaberé (January 31, O. de Armas). The Lanaberé heirs retained ownership until 1883, when they sold it to Pierre Tisné for $1,500 (June 6, E. Peyroux). Tisné sold it to Antonio Paternostro in 1892 for $1,650. The Victorian building now on the lot was probably built after 1892 by Paternostro.

1613–1619

Company of the Architects Property. The double, frame, modified camelback with hip-roof at **1613–15** has full-length, segmental-arched openings on a façade which incorporates cornices with scallops, bracketed overhang, and drop-siding with quoins. Next door at **1617–19** Dumaine is a double, frame shotgun with hip-roof and bracketed overhang, featuring two original French doors with arched panels, two French doors with original screens, and segmental-arched openings. There is very little decoration other than simple brackets with applied jigsaw work. A central chimney here is placed in an unusual location. Both houses postdate 1883 and replaced 1830s creole cottages that were built by the Company of Architects of the Eighth District. **1621** Dumaine is a masonry building with parapet and flat roof having five iron support ties across the front. The interesting old brick façade also has a decorative but primitive cornice. The wide entrance and two small windows suggest that this one-story building may have been a stable or blacksmith shop. This building also postdates 1883 and replaces an 1830s creole cottage built for Nelson Pavageau, f.m.c., who bought the two lots from the Company of the Architects on January 25, 1836, before H. Pedesclaux. When Pavageau sold the lots a year later on May 25, 1837, there were buildings and improvements; and the price had jumped to $4,500.

1820, 1824

Colvis Cottages. Both of these single-dormered, two-bay, Greek Revival creole cottages were built for investor Julien Colvis, f.m.c., soon after his purchase of the property in 1846. Colvis and his partner Joseph Dumas, f.m.c., owned most of this block in 1836 when they bought seven lots from Louis Arceuil (August 20, J. Mossy). The partners divided their common holdings, and Colvis acquired these seven lots on January 26, 1846, before T. Guyol, at which time no buildings or improvements were mentioned in the $2,800 appraisal. Colvis' heirs sold these two houses for $1,220 and $1,275 to Adam Stanislas Detez of Cuba (March 22, 1869, E. Bouny). Joseph Colvis was married in New Orleans to Marguerite Dumas, but she and their three daughters were living in France at the time of Colvis' death. Marguerite Hermina Colvis was the widow of Jacques Goupil of Paris. Jeanne, alias Amélie Colvis, wife of Auguste Coutanceau, lived in Bordeaux, as did her sister Marie Mathilde Colvis, wife of Pierre Elie Sicard. It was Mme Sicard who came to New Orleans to arrange the sale.

1924

Forstall Division. This is a good example of a turn-of-the-century double house with six openings, a late type seen in the creole suburbs. Each façade entrance opens onto a recessed side gallery behind a shallow hall. Note the decorative applied work in the front gable. The turned columns have been removed and the foundation filled in with vermiculated stone. The window and door surrounds, typical of the Neoclassic style, have fluting and bull's-eye detailing.

1909

1915–1923

Forstall Division. 1909 is a three-bay, Greek Revival shotgun with hip-roof and recessed side gallery. The overhang, brackets, and weatherboarding postdate the 1860s-style house. There were once five such houses on the block including **1915 1917,** and **1923.** All of the houses have been altered, but each has some detail suggesting the original appearance of the group. 1915 has had a camelback attached, and 1911 was demolished. Although 1909 and 1915 retain their Greek Key entrance surrounds, 1909 has recent narrow weatherboard replacement. 1915 has the original side chimneys, but 1909 retains the original roofline. Restoration of any one of these houses would require a composite analysis of the group to determine the total original appearance of one of them.

2003

Gibert Townhouse. The two-story, frame, Classic-style house with an iron gallery at the second level has a wide, Greek Key entrance with original medallions (see 2013 and 1622 Dumaine). The recessed entrance has sidelights and transom. Cap-molded wooden lintels decorate the full-length front openings; granite steps remain. This house was built soon after 1866 by Pierre Gustave Gibert on property that had belonged to his wife, Charlotte Coralie Bellocq. At her succession sale in 1882, Pierre Gibert bought the house outright for his second wife, Noémi Victoire Gibert. A newspaper article describes the house at the time of the sale from the records of notary Martin Voorhies, December 7, 1882: "Elegant well-built family residence, frame building, slated, two-stories high with iron balconies and canopies on both Dumaine and Prieur Streets, containing on first story a wide hall, double parlors with sliding door, dining room with pantry, kitchen and two other rooms, *cave*, and large side gallery, stairs, and water closets; on second story, three bedrooms, two boudoirs and hall in main building with four bedrooms and *cabinets*, with galleries on both sides, stairs and water closets in kitchen building. . . . The buildings highly finished with cornices and centre pieces, marble mantels in parlors and dining room, have gas throughout. Also on lot, one story building, containing bath room, and wood and coal room, also large washroom, chicken house, carriage house, stables and feed room . . . four large cisterns and well and a pump, spacious garden, laid elegantly in squares, circles, and diamonds . . . ornamented with shade trees and flower plants, *kiosque* and hot house . . . yard paved with bricks . . . garden alley is shelled."

2013

L'Hôte Townhouse. This townhouse is almost identical to 2003 Dumaine. Title research terminates in 1873 when the succession of Charles L'Hôte (minor) left the house to one Louise Chevral, his mother, who was first the widow of Celestin L'Hôte and then wife of Paul Duchenne. The L'Hôte family, Alsace-Lorraine natives and prominent in the lumber business along the Carondelet Canal at the Basin, probably had the house built in the 1860s. Paul Duchenne, a doctor, and his family resided here at old number 376 Dumaine from 1873 until 1880. The house was finally inherited by Paul Duchenne from his wife, and he sold it June 11, 1883, to Stephen Escoffier, Jr., for $2,500 (COB 118/191). Such townhouses of relatively low, wide proportions, built at the banquette with iron gallery or balcony at the second level, were popular beyond Rampart.

2110

Gerodias Shotgun. There are many Classic-style, three-bay, frame shotguns in the area of N. Johnson, N. Prieur, and N. Galvez from Carondelet Walk (Lafitte) to St. Bernard. Building contracts indicate that houses were built on this block in the 1850s, and by 1862 there were many Classic-style shotguns. 2110 Dumaine, however, dates from 1872, as do some others in the block. Victor Gerodias, who with his wife, Louise Hasker, built several houses facing Dumaine in this square, bought a lot with a building next door at 2118 Dumaine in 1862. Mme Gerodias sold the lot with the partially built house at 2110 Dumaine to John Beity in 1872. Acts of notary Fahey, April 26, 1872, list the building materials on two houses and lots that Beity had bought for $11,500. There was an arrangement in this building project in which M. Beity sold 2110 Dumaine back to Mme Gerodias on April 26, 1872.

2118

Jacobs Cottage. A three-bay creole cottage stood on this lot in 1862 when it was the property of John M. Jacobs. A survey that year established a property line between it and Victor Gerodias's newly purchased land (2110 Dumaine). This lot in 1862 was a triangle, the angular line being an old border of the Pontalba division, as subdivided by Baroness de Pontalba in 1812. It was resubdivided into lots conforming to present street lines in 1836, at which time Jacobs owned the lot, according to a plan of December 22, by D'Hémécourt, deposited with Félix Grima. Another plan in 1849 indicates that the lot was undeveloped at that time, and title research suggests that M. Jacobs had 2118 built in the 1850s. Flaired gabled sides, Classic-style cornices, and excellent proportions support the 1850s date. The large dormer with baroque motif and double-arched windows postdate the mid-century and probably were added during the 1870s by Mme Gerodias, who bought the house in 1862. She sold it to George Canbry on May 24, 1879; and he turned it over to Laura McGuire, Mme Maximilian Keniston, for $4,000 in 1882 (COB 117/317).

2132

2129–31

Lehman House (2132), 2129–31. This portion of the Pontalba division was subdivided by Nicholas Gurlie. Although the house at **2132** is a masonry shotgun with Greek Revival decoration, a type and style documented as early as the 1850s, it dates from about 1871. On October 18, 1870, before notary A. E. Bienvenu, Manuel Guerrier sold 66 feet on Dumaine by 106 feet in depth to Louis Ernest Lehman. The lots appear undeveloped at the time, according to a sketch attached to the act. Lehman probably built this outstanding, scored masonry shotgun replete with scalloped verge, molded cornice and lintels, and wide Greek Revival door framed with modillions. The four-bay, double creole cottage at **2129–31** is in the Pontalba division and retains its Classic-style, heavy box cornice. Molded "crown" cornices adorn the simple façade. The scale of the gable-sided cottage is harmonious with its neighbors. Its location and decoration are both suggestive of an 1850s construction date.

2218–24

Marionneaux Maison de Maître. Set back in a 160-foot-deep lot that emanated from the Pontalba division as it drew close to the Dorgenois boundary line is the outstanding Marionneaux *maison de maître*. The galleried, Classic-style residence is unusual because three dormers are seen behind the entablature. A pair of dormers at the front elevation, repeated in the rear, is the norm in New Orleans for both creole cottages and center-hall, villa-style residences. The three dormer arrangement is to be found more commonly along the Gulf Coast of Mississippi. Enclosure of half of the front gallery and vandalism have spoiled the appearance of this important house. However, decay cannot obscure the fine proportions of the gabled sides, gallery, and interior spatial arrangement. Double parlors have millwork in the Greek Revival style with wooden pilastered mantels. A lovely *cabinet* gallery to the rear contains a curving stairway to the commodious attic. A narrow central hallway in the attic is lit by the central dormer and opens onto three rooms on each side. The house is associated with the A. G. Marionneaux family who owned the property from 1848 until 1882. Mme Louise Meynier acquired about one-half of the square in a sheriff's sale in 1842 after the settlement of a lawsuit between Mme de Pontalba and the municipality over ownership of this portion of the old Leper Colony. Mme Meynier sold three undeveloped parcels of the square with portions fronting Dumaine, St. Ann, and N. Miro for just $500 to Virginie Labasterie, a f.w.c., who owned and developed numerous properties in Faubourg Tremé. In 1848 Mme Labasterie traded the corner of N. Miro and Dumaine, adjacent to 2224 Dumaine, to B. Abadie (August 16, E. Barnett). On the same day before that notary she sold an *L*-shaped lot, front measuring 67 feet and 8 inches on Dumaine going back 160 feet and having 40 feet of frontage on N. Miro by 131 feet behind the Abadie lot. The sale was for $2,300 to Antoine G. Marionneaux, and the act mentions "buildings." Mme Labasterie may have sold Marionneaux this fine, newly built house, or Marionneaux may have built it soon after 1851. He purchased two more lots toward N. Galvez from Rose Plantey, f.w.c., for $1,000 that year. The large size of the dormers and the modest parapet above the dentiled cornice would suggest that Marionneaux built the house. His heirs sold the group of lots and the residence to J. R. Bistes for $2,400 in 1882 (May 12, J. Fahey). The house and its property are landmarks of the area. Archival drawings of similar structures indicate what the complex might look like restored to its mid-nineteenth-century appearance, with parterres and rows of fruit trees.

Fleitas Division, 2422–24, 2432. The three-bay, Italianate, frame shotgun with recessed front entrance at **2432** was built by Gaston Bruslé sometime during his twenty-six-year ownership, which began in 1841 when he bought eight lots from Joseph Guillot. Bruslé sold it in 1867 to Johann Zobel (October 23, J. Cohn). There is drop-siding on the façade and louvered shutters that cover segmental-arched windows. A hexagonal wing juts into the shallow side yard, shaded by a large sycamore tree. The city probably acquired this land when street extensions were being anticipated in the late 1830s from M. Charles Dufour, speculator-purchaser of property in the Coquet-Fleitas holdings. At **2422–24** a frame, double shotgun has typical jigsaw work on a drop-siding front with quoins and segmental-arched openings and pierced-work cornices.

2510

D'Aquin House. Title research indicates that this handsome, Italianate-style house was built for Jules Joseph D'Aquin in 1872. He purchased land surrounding this lot from Mme Jean Manuel Fleitas, née Marie Rose Coquet, in 1871. D'Aquin also bought land from builders Edward Herman, Louis E. Lehman, and Alcée Nicaud in 1869 and 1872. L. E. Lehman then built for D'Aquin according to a contract before T. Buisson dated March 25, 1872. The cost was $4,100. D'Aquin left the house to his wife, Marie Guex, and their seven children. The D'Aquin heirs still owned the property in 1905. The rusticated façade in the Italianate manner blends well with the pilastered entrance exhibiting a handsome cornice with dentils and modillions. The original recessed door has arched sidelights and tripartite transom with oval lights. A heavy cornice across the front continues the Classic theme of the entrance and is modestly carried to the small hexagonal bay in the rear side yard. This area is filled with a large magnolia and palm trees. Marie Rose Coquet inherited the property in 1850, along with other lots, from Bernard Coquet, her father. She lived as a widow in 1870 on N. Villere, northeast corner of Esplanade. The history of the land extends beyond the Coquet-Fleitas ownership to the eighteenth-century holdings of Suzanna Caüe, Widow Gabriel Peyroux, and nineteenth-century owners Joseph Suarez, Lebreton Dorgenois, and Thomas Joachim Cauchoix.

2518–20

Coquet Division. 2518–20, 2526–28. This block in the Bernard Coquet division had just five houses in 1883 as shown on the Robinson Atlas. A large, frame, Victorian double at **2518–20** has a front-gabled roof with an apron and typical jigsaw work that decorates the façade in 1890s style. The entrance doors lead to two, recessed side galleries with *cabinets* to the rear. The full-length windows are double hung with six panes below and four above with segmental arches; a residence divider, called a "plank divider," separates one side from the other. The house has a small front garden now cemented behind an iron fence. At **2526–28** there is a Victorian, frame shotgun with four bays that appears to retain its original entrance doors.

2652

Blanc-Clark Division. This turn-of-the-century cottage is a whimsical version of the bayed cottage-type. Recent renovation has resulted in paint combinations that emphasize the lacy, turn-of-the-century jigsaw work. Not only is there an icicle-patterned vergeboard, but there is also a scalloped sill. An original entrance door with stained glass, shingles on the front gable with its stained glass, and a sunburst design in the gallery gable are among the variety of textures and forms combined for a fanciful effect.

2654

Esnard Villa. This raised, Greek Revival, villa-style house was built soon after 1853 for Marcelin Esnard, who bought eleven lots on N. Broad extending from the corner of Dumaine (June 16, A. Ducatel). The act stipulated that "the paving facing lot 11 corner Dumaine has been paid for." Esnard bought the lots from Benoit Oscar Vignaud, who acquired them from Bernard de Santos in 1847. Santos had bought them from the city in an 1846 auction of part of the Evariste Blanc *habitation* (September 14, J. Cuvillier). This land was among the many lots claimed by Myra Clark Gaines, who sued Esnard July 18, 1878 (Fifth District Court #3663), and ultimately received $1,850 from a subsequent owner, Henry Carrière, after which she withdrew her claim. This house was described in an 1893 auction when the heirs of Jean B. Ferchaud sold it and the remaining lots between N. Broad to N. Dorgenois to Widow Madison Robert Flautt. The description read: The improvements consist of the very elegant and delightful raised dwelling known by the municipal number 500 Dumaine Street, having on the first floor a large center hall, with double parlors with sliding doors on one side, hall, three bedrooms on the other side, a large dining room, pantry, etc; in the attic two large rooms, *cabinets*, passageways, etc. All the rooms on the first floor have recently been papered with wallpaper of the most elegant designs; gas throughout the whole building. A two-story building in the rear with eight rooms, with large shed attached; three cisterns, privies etc. Both buildings are slate covered." This excellent, center-hall house has several exterior architectural features of interest, including flush wood surrounds and tongue and grooved planks covering the façade. Flushboard is used to give the effect of a plastered front; the sides of the building are weatherboarded. A wide, Greek Key, recessed entrance is flanked by two double-hung windows on each side. Two large dormers with Classic pediments complete the style of the 1850s. Both sides of the house have hexagonal bays; the N. Robertson side is decorated with dentils and modillions.

N. GALVEZ

210–12, 214–16, 220–22

Griffon Division. 214–16 N. Galvez is a dogtrot frame creole cottage flanked by four-bay, frame creole cottages at **210–12** and **220–22**, built in the 1860s. The three properties were part of the Griffon estate, which was in dispute until a settlement was effected by partition between the heirs of Griffon and Samuel Moore in 1853. Successive owners of the lots and cottages were first free persons of color and later German immigrants, reflecting the overall character of the neighborhood in the last half of the nineteenth century. **210-12** was built for Henry Weiser after his purchase of land measuring 36 feet fronting on Iberville by 106 feet on N. Galvez from Hippolyte Griffon in 1859 for $850. Weiser formed this lot facing N. Galvez Street and built the house between his 1859 purchase and 1873, the date of his wife's estate sale. The dogtrot creole cottage at **214–16** was built soon after 1862, at which time François Gouclemus purchased property 28 feet by 120 feet fronting on N. Galvez for $370. His sister inherited this lot with buildings in 1864. The house at **220** also dates from the 1860s. Mary Jane Dudley, a Negress, owned it at the time of her death in 1899, when she deeded it to her godmother, Hagar Mathieu.

927–29

915, 927–29. The four-bay, galleried cottage at **927–29** N. Galvez was built in the Pontalba division and is recessed on the lot in a rural manner. Gabled ends have double angles, and the roofline extends out to cover the gallery. The house is situated on a low chain wall; the original box columns supporting the gallery have been removed. Although in poor condition, its simplicity and rural aspect in the midst of a high density urban area have increased its importance as an intact example of a once-common house-type. In 1850 Widow M. D. Bringier, Louise Agläe Dubourg, sold five undeveloped lots to Pierre Deverges (January 24, T. J. Beck). Deverges probably built this galleried cottage as rental property, since he sold two lots with buildings and improvements to Joseph Charles St. Romes for $3,460 on January 10, 1855, as recorded before notary J. Lisbony. The three-bay, Victorian cottage at **915** has handsome cornices with pierced-work cresting above the fenestration. A gallery is supported by turned colonettes with a spindle course of pierced-work panels. The lot shares an early history with **927**, part of the Pontalba, Bringier, St. Romes ownership. The house is seen on the Robinson Atlas of 1883, belonging to the Widow St. Romes. When she sold in 1900, the act indicated that a gun club was at the rear of the lot and that there was a dance platform facing Dumaine in the square (January 11, 1900, I. Charbonnet).

1007–1017

Dorgenois Division. These three double, Victorian shotguns at **1007–09, 1011–13, 1015–17** were built after 1883 with identical segmental-arched openings and scroll-shaped brackets supporting the overhang. The attractive trio is situated on a part of the Dorgenois *habitation.*

1202

Dougart House (1202), 1230–32. The illustrated three-bay, masonry-fronted shotgun was designed in the Classic style. Façade details include an entrance flanked by pilasters and crowned by a dentiled cornice, as well as double-hung windows with stone window lintels. A series of additions and renovations, such as the ell to the rear and the side bay, has altered its original appearance. Like 1237 N. Galvez across the street, it was built as rental property for Mathias Baptiste Dougart, probably soon after his purchase of the two lots on December 28, 1865, from A. Barran (A. Doriocourt). The two houses were originally identical. After Dougart's death, his widow married Edward Lischy and retained ownership of 1202 N. Galvez until 1882. On November 20, 1882, she sold the house to Ernest Pragst for $3,000, as recorded before notary John Bendernagel. Both this property and **1230–32** had been part of the Antonio Mendez tract, a subdivision of the Dorgenois *habitation.* A late-Victorian camelback with front gable and gallery, 1230–32 has five bays, one of which leads to a recessed side gallery. The front gallery is supported by turned columns surmounted by pierced work and spindles. Segmental-arched openings have cap-molded lintels surrounded by decorative pierced work. A tin-roofed cistern to the rear of this post-1883 house is visible from the Barracks Street side.

1237

1223, 1231, 1237. The Classic-style, side-hall shotgun is more predominant in Faubourg Tremé than any other area of the city. By 1856 A. D. Doriocourt and Hughes Pedesclaux were speculating in this area, which had formerly been the Dorgenois and Mendez plantations. It had first been subdivided in 1831, but the extension of Esplanade and N. Galvez streets caused redevelopment around mid-century. Doriocourt and Pedesclaux, both of whom owned large tracts across Bayou Road, sold lots including the one at **1237** to Archibald Barran on February 28, 1856 (A. Doriocourt). On December 28, 1865, before Doriocourt, Barran sold three lots to Mathias Baptiste Dougart. When Dougart died in 1878, his estate included this house at 1237 N. Galvez Street and the identical one across the street at 1202. The fine house at 1237 has a masonry front with Greek Revival, recessed entrance framed by pilasters and dentiled cornice. Window lintels are stone, and sills are wooden. Remnants of scored plaster on the façade and the well-proportioned hip-roof are indications of the fine quality of this 1860s house, which has weatherboard sides. **1223** N. Galvez is a Greek Revival, galleried version of the side-hall shotgun in the Classic style. It is set back on a large lot at an angle to the street. Dougart may have been the builder of this house also. **1231** is an Italianate version of the three-bay, side-hall shotgun. The chimneys are along the roof ridge in the 1870s-style shotgun, whereas those of the earlier example at 1237 are on an outside wall.

1466

1468–70

Le Monnier House (1466), 1468–70. The Le Monnier House is among the most charming homes in the Castanedo holdings. The late-Victorian frame cottage with six French doors has a projecting gallery, supported by turned columns, with a deep latticework frieze similar to 1443 N. Galvez. There are recessed side galleries on both sides. The original wrought-iron fence is by Ragen-Die's Iron Works, New Orleans. The deep, wide lot features old-fashioned planting, including sweet olive, crepe myrtle, altheas, figs, and Japanese plum trees. The house dates from between 1888 and 1902. On July 10, 1888, Paul Barrière (O. Drouet) sold the lot to Marie Louise Hermann, wife of William Le Monnier, for $400. She had the house built, selling it December 1, 1902, for $3,500 (G. LeGardeur) to her relative Marie Louise Le Monnier du Quesnay, in whose family it remains today. **1468–70** N. Galvez, a large creole house with gabled sides, was once identical to 1473–75 N. Galvez, across the street. Simulated brick, a concrete porch, and a large twentieth-century dormer disguise the Classic-style appearance of the house.

1447

Castanedo Division, 1443, 1447. At **1443** N. Galvez stands a frame, bayed cottage with entrance recessed beyond a shallow gallery. Massive millwork on the band below the gallery cornice is noteworthy. Bull's-eyes and brackets alternate in a decorative pattern. Between the paired columns is a heavy latticework design similar to that at 1446. Elongated brackets form the column caps and bosses. A very deep, hexagonal bay ells out to the rear toward the Columbus Street side. The entrance has a cut-glass transom; the bay has guttae decorating the arched openings. Cast-iron gateposts are cornstalks clustered with wrapped ivy; the finials are unshucked corn clusters. Since the house is not indicated on the Robinson Atlas of 1883, it is a late-century structure. The handsome, side-hall shotgun at **1447** is dramatically situated on a wide lot planted with a variety of palms. Set above a raised, brick basement with an ell to the rear, the well-proportioned house, with hip-roof slightly flared at the eaves, creates an impressive effect. The deep gallery is supported by narrow pillars and has a railing with turned balusters, as do the wooden steps. A porch on the side and rooms to the rear have been added, according to the present owner Mr. Rivera, whose wife's family, the Howells, bought the new house in 1900. It stands on the former Castanedo *habitation.*

1455–57

Cheval Property. Part of the land that Antonio Ramis acquired through his wife, Maria Ignacia Rodriguez, the site of 1455–57 N. Galvez was sold by Ramis to Paul Cheval, f.m.c., in 1800 (December 17, C. Ximenes). Many years later, in 1871, Christian Theodore Buddecke bought this and six other lots in a parcel from Widow Josiah Broadwell (January 2, J. Cohn). There were no buildings there in 1879 at a Buddecke partition sale. Subsequently, the lot was listed as part of the succession of Joseph Lambert Bercier in 1895 (March 29, CDC #45, 440). It is suggested that the house as it appears today dates from soon after 1895. That date is indicated by the decorative box cornice with its spindle-work frieze and paneled box columns. However, these millwork decorations could represent an updating of an earlier late-Classic-style house moved to the location.

1465–67

1465–67, 1473–75. The frame, six-bay, camelback, double house with wide and deep front gable covered with original clapboard at **1465–67** N. Galvez is similar to 1458–60 N. Miro. Title research indicates that this square had been purchased by L. Bringier and William Israel from Widow Joseph Castanedo on June 14, 1833 (H. Pedesclaux). The property remained undeveloped, and on July 18, 1868 (R. J. Ker), the Bringier heirs sold nine lots to Brou Mathé. Mathé built this house, selling it in 1902 to Helen Jouet, Widow Bercier. Although Mathé owned the lot from 1868, stylistic analysis suggests an 1880s construction date; and a house appears on this lot in the Robinson Atlas of 1883. A 1902 survey in the acts of F. J. Dreyfous October 31 outlines the present house. **1473–75** is a large, gable-sided, double creole house of frame construction with full attic. Built in the Classic style, it appears to date from the late 1860s or 1870s.

N. GALVEZ

1500 Block

Little Sisters of the Poor. Nuns from the Société des Dames de la Providence arrived from St. Pern, Brittany, in December, 1868. The *Daily-Picayune* reported April 23, 1872: "The cornerstone of the new Catholic Asylum of the Little Sisters of the Poor was laid." A building contract attests that Thomas Mulligan built for the sisters a "three-story, substantial and tasteful brick building on the river side of Johnson between Columbus and Laharpe" for $45,000. Over the years a handsome and monumental complex was developed, a landmark on the old Castanedo plantation. Frederick Wing was the architect for a three-story brick building added to the complex in 1877 at a cost of $22,300, according to an additional building contract before O. de Armas on November 29 of that year. Some of the elderly descendants of the former plantation owners along Bayou Road resided in the asylum, including the Duchamp sisters. Early benefactors of the asylum were Joseph and Louisa Avet, Monsieur and Madame D'Hémécourt, and Thomy Lafon. In 1972 the Sisters moved from the Asylum in Faubourg Tremé to a new reisdence for the elderly on the West Bank. The original complex has been preserved by the Archdiocese.

1561

Faubourg Castanedo. This unusual, four-bay, frame, camelback, Victorian house has a pyramid of front pediments, creating a roofline of four gables. The entire façade from the porch to the high camelback is covered with shingles overlapped in a sawtooth-patterned design. A fancy brick chimney adds to the variety of textures and form, giving this house a sculptured effect. A dentil motif applied to the pediments is continued on the side elevation. In contrast, the gallery supported by pillars has a frieze of delicate spindle and pierced work. Decorative opening surrounds have fluted pilasters topped with brackets crowned with tripartite pierced work. The gables contain stained-glass windows. The general effect of this unusual turn-of-the-century residence is one of sophistication.

IBERVILLE

1723

1717–19, 1723. At **1717–19** Iberville is an unusual, six-bay, common-wall, double shotgun with each half having a side hall. It postdates 1883, since it is not identified on Robinson's Atlas. The porch retains appropriate wooden planking and the original multiple-unit separator. Cement steps replace wooden originals. This version of the shotgun house is not typical but is suitable for this neighborhood where common-roof, creole cottage rental units abound. The herringbone-patterned brick banquette adds charm to the late-nineteenth-century house. **1723** Iberville is an erstwhile, side-hall townhouse with deep overhang above a second-level balcony. This façade, balcony, and roof arrangement is characteristic of the late-1870s and 1880s in Faubourg Hagan, a date that also fits the fancy cornices above the first-level openings. Mutilation has spoiled the appearance of this relatively spacious house.

1911

1908, 1911. Lucien Hermann, notary, passed the act of sale resulting from the auction in 1840 of the property belonging formerly to the Marquis de Lafayette and John Hagan. A lot was sold to Robert Montieth on June 1, 1840; and by 1848 a small, frame, four-bay creole cottage without dormers was standing at **1908** Iberville. Henry Brining had bought the lot with improvements from Montieth for $207 in 1845. Brining sold three years later to Carl Hoff (September 9, P. Laresche) for $700 with the mention of building and improvements. The Hoff family kept the property for twenty-seven years, and in the succession sale of Carl and Mathilda Hoff it was bought for $1,015 by Jacob Scherer on July 12, 1875 (A. E. Bienvenu). Unusual gabled sides halfway back on the house across the street at **1911** Iberville would indicate that not only have the exterior walls been changed, but the roofline also. Once the gable extended down to the front of the house. This is mutilation on a grand scale of a once-fine, three-bay, Greek Revival-style creole cottage. The original Greek Key surrounds and the recessed entrance arrangement remain, along with window lintels that indicate original placement. A fine, brick, dentiled cornice may be seen beneath the first-level overhang, providing further clues to a house-type of the 1860s.

IBERVILLE

1933–1939

Faubourg Hagan, 1900 Block. Matthias Haas bought the site of **1921–23** Iberville from Thomas Hagan (John's son) on February 12, 1849, for $360 before notary J. R. Beard. Haas built the early, four-bay, frame shotgun. When Haas died in 1882, his daughter Caroline, Mrs. Hermann Klein, and her son Martin Louis Klein inherited the house. This early shotgun remained in the Klein family until 1966, when Widow E. M. Klein sold it on October 3, before J. S. Quinlan, to Mrs. C. K. Capdecomme. The same family held ownership from the time of its construction in 1850 for 116 years. The pair of common-roof, frame creole cottages at **1933–35** and **1937–39** Iberville were probably built in the late 1850s for Johannes Theodore Ernst, who lost them on December 12, 1874, in a court case against Joseph Jacob. At the ensuing sheriff's sale, George Shafer bought three lots with these row cottages and another for $1,825. Shafer retained the houses until 1883, when on March 10, before C. Rolle, he sold them to Frederick Robbert for just $1,600.

2001

Grace Methodist Episcopal Church. In 1851 Henry Weber and Louis Metz purchased lots in this part of Faubourg Hagan from Karl Hoff and Karl Loeper. They were acting on behalf of a Lutheran group that was incorporated December 30, 1852 (R. J. Ker), becoming St. John's German Evangelical Lutheran Congregation. Trustees, along with Weber and Metz, were Johann Diederick Kohnke and Mathias Haas. The Lutheran congregation sold this site, at the corner of Iberville and N. Prieur, including a church building, on March 31, 1917, for $13,500 to the Grace Methodist Episcopal Church (A. G. Williams). The latter was organized in the same year, uniting the Union and Pleasant Plain churches. The building pictured is the second church on the lot, replacing the earlier Lutheran church.

2025–2033

Samuel Moore Property. Two, common-roof, frame creole cottages with dogtrots feature full-length openings and, like many other houses in the neighborhood, date from the late 1850s. The land was involved in the claims of Lafayette and Samuel Moore between 1851 and 1857. When Francis Anthony Opl finally obtained clear title by purchases from the heirs of Moore and a subsequent owner, Margaret McKion, via the Lafayette representatives, he had 52 feet by 106 feet. He built the simple, multirental units and kept them until 1891, selling them to Charles Kreher for $2,500 on July 15 before J. R. Legier.

2120–2130

2107–2113

2100 Block. Properties on each side of the 2100 block of Iberville were claimed both by the heirs of Charles Griffon and by the Samuel Moore–Théodore Nicolet partnership in the 1850s. Finally, on Feruary 18, 1858, Mlle Clémence Griffon sold three lots, sites of **2107–09** and **2111–13**, to Raimond Castille, f.m.c., for $1,200 before P. C. Cuvellier. The frame, dogtrot creole cottages were built as rental units between 1861 and 1868 by Theresa Dietrich and her husband, George William Groetsch. Mme Dietrich had bought the lots from free Negress Hermance Duplessis in two purchases in 1860 and 1861 for a total of $1,325. She later married Groetsch, and there is indication from title transfers that the houses were financed by Sigmund A. Suskind and built for about $2,500 in 1868. Groetsch sold the house at 2107–09 on May 7, 1870, to Joseph Harz before J. Cohn, notary. Across the street at **2128–30**, **2124–26**, and **2120–22** are three, detached, double creole cottages with gabled ends and beak roofs. The identical cottages postdate the 1850s partition of lands involved in the dispute among the various claimants. Here the beak roofs have overhangs supported by decorative brackets that may be original, indicating an 1870s construction. The trio of rental doubles is set low to the ground on wooden sills and retains original stoop construction as well as brick banquettes.

2224–2234

Samuel Moore Claim. A trio of detached, frame, double creole cottages having Greek Key entrances and built-in overhangs, dates from after the 1850s partition of this property. These houses may be compared with the three beginning at 2120 Iberville, which date from the late 1850s. The latter are set closer to the ground and have molded cornices and added Victorian brackets.

2235

2229–31, 2235. The corner cottage at **2235** Iberville was built for John Frederick Hennings, who bought the lot, 28 feet by 108 feet, from the P. A. Durand succession on October 7, 1865. The four-bay, frame creole cottage has a beak roof incorporating an overhang, gabled ends, and a single brick chimney at the center of the roof ridge. Hennings' heirs disposed of the house on July 22, 1893, after a succession sale, before J. J. Ward. Subsequent owners of this simple rental unit have permitted its decay and disfiguration. It now has an attached shed seen along N. Miro, although the brick sidewalk remains except for the corner intersection. Part of the *tout ensemble* of a pleasant neighborhood of rental houses, it retains appropriate proportions and could be renovated by analogy to other similar creole cottages. Adjacent at **2229–31** Iberville is a simple, three-bay, masonry-fronted, side-hall shotgun featuring a high hip-roof, also incorporating the overhang, suggesting an 1860s building date. It is a simple rental unit in the American style and compares in scale and in simplicity with its creole-style neighbors.

2310–12

Joseph Artigues House. The Griffon heirs bought this square from the estate of Théodore Nicolet, who as Samuel Moore's partner was a claimant of the land through J. B. Macarty and the Canal and Banking Company (June 6, 1857, P. C. Cuvellier). Hippolyte Griffon subdivided the property in the same year, at which time Messrs. Ward, Saunders, and Hunt bought six lots for $2,415. By 1860 these men owned the entire square of twenty-eight lots, which they sold to Abraham de Meza and Anatole Cucullu for $13,000 (March 9, 1860, J. Graham). Joseph Batt purchased five lots from the partnership in January of 1867 for $300 and a month later sold them to Joseph Artigues for the same price (E. Bouny). The present creole cottage was probably built for Artigues who, with his family, owned the property from 1867 until 1910. The simple cottage has gabled ends with a dramatic front cant terminating with fleur-de-lis decoration bordering a bracketed overhang. The handsome original doors with double oval panels and lights in the transom remain; the chimneys have been removed.

2326–28, 2330–32

Samuel Moore Property. The 27-by-114 feet containing lots of the houses pictured at **2326–28** and **2330–32** Iberville share a common history with their neighbor at 2310–12. They too were built for the Artigues family, which owned them from 1867 until 1893. In that year, Widow F. Schleichardt bought 2330–32 Iberville for just $800 from the New Orleans German-American Homestead, which had purchased it from the Artigues (August 9, W. R. Ker). The two houses are Greek Revival shotguns, featuring masonry façades with dentils, high front hip-roofs with overhangs, weatherboarded sides, and gabled rear elevations. One cottage was built just two rooms deep.

2307–09

2301–03, 2307–09. This square was one allotted to Mme de Pontalba in the 1853 partition of 549 lots worth $49,550. Sharing in the settlement were Mme Samuel Moore and the estate of Théodore Nicolet. The baroness sold the entire square to a group represented by Philip Rotchford in 1859. On July 15 of that year, before notary S. Magner, the square was bought by the Most Reverend Anthony Blanc, Archbishop of New Orleans, for $11,775. In 1867, the Most Reverend Jonathan Odin, Archbishop of Louisiana, sold two lots at auction to Peter A. McIntyre for $1,225. **2307–09** though a galleried, frame creole cottage with gabled sides in the Greek Revival style of the 1840s, was apparently built soon after 1867 by McIntyre on one of the lots. He lost the house, then known as 461 and 461½ Customhouse, at a sheriff's sale in 1876 to M. J. Birmingham for $1,450. The attractive house is set back from the banquette in a brick-paved front yard. The wooden steps, slender turned columns, dentiled cornice, straight parapet, cast-iron railing, and original oval-paneled doors and oval transoms all bespeak a nineteenth-century scene. An adjacent house, probably the Italianate shotgun at **2301–03** was built by Birmingham in 1883 when he "erected a $1,700 house," and the two properties were appraised at $3,500. The Birmingham family kept the two houses until 1905 (June 15, 1905, F. D. Charbonnet).

2311–13, 2315–17

Moore-Pontalba Claim. Faubourg Hagan and the property beyond, toward N. Broad Street, abound with dormerless, weatherboarded, side-gabled creole cottages with dogtrots or street-level central passageways. These two examples in the 2300 block of Iberville Street probably date from the 1860s, with subsequent additions of brackets and new roofs. **2315–17** Iberville has a simple shed attached to the main house, which serves as a kitchen. The property was part of the holdings partitioned to Baroness de Pontalba after litigation that lasted until the 1850s. **2311–**

13 has had doorways lowered and its chimney truncated, but it is a fine dogtrot creole cottage.

2329–31, 2333–35

Pontalba Property. 2329–31 Iberville (right) is an unusual hip-roof, dogtrot shotgun; normally, dogtrot houses in the Greek Revival style have gabled sides in the creole manner like 2333–35. Both houses have traditional latticework on the upper part of the central passageway and Greek Key surrounds. They could date from soon after 1859, when Baroness de Pontalba sold the undeveloped square to Philip Rotchford (June 21, E. Barnett), who subdivided the same year.

2401

Fleitas Division. The land on which this four-bay, corner creole cottage stands was part of an 1801 concession from the king of Spain to Carlos Guadioli. The plantation fronted on the left side of Bayou Road and continued across Canal Street ending at Common Street. After the Louisiana Purchase, Guadioli sold to another Spanish colonial settler, Domingo Fleitas. In the 1830s Fleitas sold the Bayou Road frontage to the Carondelet Canal to Charles Dufour, and in 1835 Joseph Kenton acquired the land on "the southwesterly side of the Carondelet Canal at the first half-moon measuring two *arpents* front on said canal and extending in the rear as far as Common Street . . . together with the privilege of draining the said land into the canal . . . and with the further privilege of navigating on said canal for the transportation of the produce of the land" (May 19, 1835, T. Seghers). Kenton sold this lot, a portion of the above, before A. C. Ainsworth on May 14, 1850, to William Penn for $310. Penn built the high, gable-sided cottage soon thereafter, selling it with other properties for $2,000 to Martha Campbell, f.w.c., in 1862. The wide-angle gabled ends cant slightly to incorporate the undecorated overhang and can be seen effectively from the N. Tonti Street side, where brick banquettes remain. As late as 1883 the block was undeveloped except for this building at 2401 Iberville and one other house.

2427

Fleitas Division. The containing lot at 2427 Iberville is part of the Kenton holdings acquired as investment real estate from the Fleitas heirs in 1835. The house is being raised in the 1976 photograph but had brick piers in the late nineteenth century, evident in the photograph. The galleried, side-hall shotgun has three full-length openings with Greek Key surrounds surmounted by Classic-style molding. Two double-hung windows are beside an entrance with paneled door. Such Greek Revival-style decorative details have been documented in this area and Faubourg Hagan, dating to the late 1860s and 1870s. Robinson's Atlas of 1883 shows this block with just two houses, one at 2401 Iberville and another toward N. Rocheblave set back in the lot, which is probably this house. The Greek Revival-style house predates the added gallery. Certainly the 1890s-style frieze and jigsaw-work posts with bull's-eyes and pierced-work spandrels contrast with the simplicity of the front elevation with its flushboard covering.

2639

Macarty Claim. It is difficult to determine whether this house is indicated on the Robinson Atlas of 1883, but such bayed cottages have been documented in Faubourg Tremé and the Commons from 1889 (see 1221 Marais) and continued to be built until the turn of the century. Often one finds the rear "ell" formed from an old creole cottage with a wraparound front segment. Bayed cottages are characterized by front projecting galleries, recessed side galleries, and rear bays. Here the front gables are shingled with fancy vergeboards having applied decoration.

N. JOHNSON

916

Blondeau House. Norbert Rillieux, the free black inventor, owned much of this square in 1836 when he sold five lots to Adélard Blondeau (August 23, L. Ferand). Blondeau built houses on the property, and Mme Blondeau inherited this one in 1857. Although altered, the Classic-style, three-bay, frame cottage retains its hip-roof and recessed side gallery. The entire street has brick sidewalks, as well as fine granite curbing.

1240

Pontalba Division, 1228–30, 1240. The large, double-dormered, masonry-fronted creole house at **1228–30** N. Johnson has a dogtrot alley and built-in overhang. Flat stone lintels and flush fenestration surrounds reflect the Classic style of this rare house-type. There is no façade decoration except latticework covering the underside of the overhang. It is unusual for a creole cottage of such large proportions to have a central dogtrot. Although the house dates from 1865, there is no exterior indication of such a late date other than the large size. It is retardate in style like many in this area. The lot was part of the Pontalba division that comprised the leper hospital reacquired by the Baroness de Pontalba from the city after the hospital closed. She sold six lots, including this site, to Joseph Soniat-Dufossat in 1848 for $2,330. He sold the same six lots for $3,500 in 1861 to Jean Ringé (December 19, P. C. Cuvellier). The fine, large creole house was built in 1865, when Ringé financed its construction through a business arrangement with Athanase Petit. In 1867 Petit turned over two lots with this new house to Ringé's daughter, Mme Serovich, for $5,000 (June 27, A. Barnett). Next door at the corner, another large, frame creole house at **1240** has a more recent wraparound façade. It matches the plot plan in plan book 7, folio 10, by J. A. Celles. Large creole houses, sometimes 2½ stories high like these two, often appeared beyond Claiborne toward Broad after 1850. The type is an enlargement of the original, eighteenth-century creole cottage plan, and its continued use into the late-Victorian period reflects its suitability to the New Orleans population.

1237

1200 Block. This entire block in the Pontalba division is an assemblage of mid-nineteenth-century creole cottages: **1227–29**, a standard, four-bay creole cottage like **1217–19**; **1231**, a two-bay, frame, single creole cottage with single dormers; **1239–41**, a four-bay, frame creole cottage. **1235–37** N. Johnson is masonry-fronted with canted roof, incorporating the overhang. The brackets postdate the mid-nineteenth-century cottage, and the concrete porch is even newer. Brick chimneys once pierced a slate roof at front and rear elevations.

1440

Faubourg Castanedo. An interesting combination of Classic decorative details with Victorian form characterizes this potentially attractive two-story, single-family home. The unimproved property was part of the Bringier estate and was acquired by John Cronan in 1867. Cronan's heirs sold to Edward Robert Hogan in 1871. Hogan may have built the house; he sold the lot with buildings and improvements, perhaps this house, to Joseph Jacob on May 22, 1875, for $1,700. The Robinson Atlas suggests that the front bay was added after 1883. The Jacob family retained the house well into the twentieth century.

1450

Duchamp Estate. In 1849 Joseph Bruneau purchased this lot in the second 1400 block of N. Johnson from the succession of Bernard Duchamp. Bruneau retained the property until 1875, when he sold it to E. V. Ruel (June 30, E. Boundy). At that sale no buildings or improvements were mentioned. The house was built either by Bruneau in the late 1850s or 1860s or by Ruel when he bought the property in 1875. If Ruel built it, the Classic-style, three-bay creole cottage is extremely retardate in decoration. It is now set high off the ground, an unusual arrangement that dramatizes the tall single-dormer, sloping gables and Classic box cornice. The Greek Key entrance with recessed door and two, short, double-hung windows with cap-molded lintels and wood pediments above are fine Classic-style details. The deep box cornice creates an overhang and features modillions and dentils. The original entrance door in the style of the 1860s and 1870s has two, narrow, arched glass panels. The banquette is herringbone-patterned brick with wooden curbing.

1439

Augrain Villa (1435), 1439. The villa at **1435** N. Johnson was built soon after 1867 on land that Widow Castanedo sold to William Israel in 1833. M. D. Bringier, his partner, acquired the lot from Israel along with twelve others for $3,336 in 1838 (March 13, Tureaud). These properties were sold by the Bringier estate to Félix Labatut after the public auction on July 7, 1867 (W. J. Castell). Labatut immediately sold to Paul Augrain four lots here for $2,225. The Augrain family built the villa-type house, one of the major buildings in the old Castanedo tract. The Augrain heirs retained their home until August 4, 1900 (P. Labatut). The Greek Key,

central entrance has arched sidelights and transoms. Square-headed, full-length openings lead to the deep gallery with cast-iron railings supported by fluted pillars with necking and Doric-type caps. The narrow drop-siding postdates the construction of the house, as does the hexagonal wing to the rear on the Kerlerec Street side. The new roof and absence of chimneys detract from the outstanding home. Classic entrance pilasters and cornice leading to a recessed door with narrow, arched panels suggest that the side-hall shotgun at **1439** dates from the 1860s. The lot was included in the M. D. Bringier estate sale in 1866 (*Daily Picayune*, October 21, 23, 27) and sold to Félix Labatut on July 27, 1867 (W. J. Castell). As in the adjacent Duchamp area, Faubourg Castanedo had an abundance of three-bay shotguns built in multiples by investors in the 1860s; some rows have galleries and others, overhangs.

2018–20

Faubourg Gueno. This galleried, double, frame shotgun with front gable typifies the final stage of jigsaw-work decoration in New Orleans before the return to Neoclassic motifs in the World War I period. A spindle-work band, pierced-work blocks and spandrels, as well as a decorated vergeboard, create a light and airy effect. Fancy segmental architraves have pierced-work crested cornices. Stained, flashed glass in the gabled front also indicates the turn-of-the-century building date.

2009–11

Faubourg Gueno. The simple, front-gable, double, frame shotgun has an apron overhang and brackets. Segmental-arched openings have molded cornices with scalloped borders. The front gable has lost its decoration. New, precast concrete steps are suitable here and complement a neat, original, herringbone-patterned brick sidewalk. Oval, cast-iron ventilators are an added attraction to this well-kept ensemble.

KERLEREC

1100 Block. A traditional, 1850s-style creole cottage at **1113** Kerlerec has had an extension added to the front, creating a wraparound. **1117–19** and **1121** are frame creole cottages with four bays and side gables; both 1850s-style cottages have had Victorian and twentieth-century alterations. **1125** and **1133** are similar, two-story, three-bay townhouses with recessed entrances, second-level balconies, and overhangs with brackets at the roof. The hip-roof at 1133 contrasts with gabled sides at 1125, which also has a fine bay. Across the street at **1130** Kerlerec, a two-bay, two-level frame house with front and side upper galleries is a relatively unusual type seen in the Lower Garden District and in the creole suburbs from 1850.

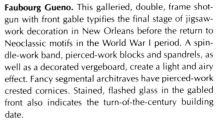

1214

Mager Property. Drop-siding, segmental-arched windows, and bull's-eye decoration on the box columns date this frame camelback in the late nineteenth century. Five bays afford a center-hall floor plan, which is unusual in a house decorated in this turn-of-the-century style. The two-level, rear building has side galleries on both levels. The front piers are a recent addition, along with the cement porch. Nineteenth-century owners Jean Mager and his sister Agathe Collard held this land until mid-century when her sons subdivided it for development.

1216

1200 Block. Louis A. Cabiro bought the lot at **1216** Kerlerec from Seraphine Maspereau, divorced wife of Ernest D'Aquin, in 1881 (July 2, C. T. Soniat). The 1885 city directory lists Charles and L. A. Cabiro, Jr., residing at a house on this lot, then number 100 Kerlerec. Auguste Cabiro, Jr., resided at 104 Kerlerec; and Auguste, Sr., a sugar broker, was listed at 186 Esplanade. The description of 1216 Kerlerec in the 1898 Cabiro succession indicates an earlier creole cottage on this lot (March 1, C. T. Soniat): "1216 Kerlerec is a handsome, one-story-with-attic cottage having side hall, gallery, four rooms, two *cabinets* in the main house, kitchen with four rooms, coal room, shed in rear, cistern and privies." The present house also has a side hall, gallery, and four rooms below; but it is a full two-story house, built or enlarged for 1898 purchaser Edward Soniat-Dufossat. The second-level, late-Victorian gallery returns around the side. The frame, villa-type camelback at **1234** has a side gallery. The house probably dates from the 1890s but has an unfortunate dormer in the style of the 1920s. The three-bay, side-hall frame shotgun with hip-roof and overhang at **1240** is an earlier house; the Greek Key entrance and cap-molded lintels date it from the 1860s, the brackets being a later addition. A third contrasting house-type in this block is **1248–50**, a four-bay, frame, Victorian creole cottage with gabled sides. All four houses are on lots from the Guerlain holdings, and the early brick banquettes remain.

Mager Property. This traditional corner store-house is on the Jean Mager portion of the Morand-Tremé property of the eighteenth century. The one-story, frame building has a hip-roof and a deep, corrugated tin overhang, which is supported by wooden posts and covers the banquette. Bayed display windows are supported by brackets, and full-length window openings have batten shutters. The dwelling portion of this complex is in the form of a camelback with double-gabled ends and a second-level balcony, below which is Bulot's Oyster House. Mager left this lot and others adjacent to his sister Agathe Collard in 1845. She, in turn, left them to her two sons, Auguste Jean Baptiste and Alfred Joseph Collard, of France in 1857. They sold the property in 1859 to Francisco Romagosa, which included four lots and "a two-story, frame house on lot 16 for a total of $5,000." In 1866 Louis Arthur Poincy sold the house, dating from the 1850s, to B. L. Millaudon for $6,500. It is now incorporated into the present store-house. The Collard sale in 1859 mentioned that it included "all buildings on said lots which form the Cockpit, which is established there, with the exception of the two-story house built on lot 16, belonging to Alfred Hurtubrise who has the right to remove them."

1217

La Branche Cottage. Like other cottages in this part of Faubourg Tremé, 1217 Kerlerec was built as an investment by an Esplanade resident. In this case, Ronald La Branche, who lived at 118 Esplanade on the Burgundy corner, was the builder. The archives yield a contract between La Branche and Eugène Surgi for the building of "a one-story, frame building with garret, kitchen, and appurtenances," for $4,100 in 1868. La Branche purchased the lot from Benjamin Millaudon, who had acquired it from Louis A. Poincy in 1866. The 1868 contract in the acts of Gottschalk, June 15, is translated as follows: "The ground floor will be 11 feet 6 inches in height and the garret will be 10 feet in height. The house will be lathed and coated on both floors. The kitchen will be lathed but not coated. The roof covered in slate, also the balcony. The kitchen covered in planking carefully done. Good carpentry with thick wood, white lathing for the house, *bruites* [natural] for the kitchen; door and window frames in wood *avec grates* with the price of $14 for the 3 facing the street. The balcony in the garret will be in wood with pilasters. Good flooring in the house and kitchen. The *barrieres* [fences] will be made in jointed boards with posts 4 feet by 6 feet 8 inches high around the lot. Gas in all the house, up and down, with three candelabra provided by the contractor for the two parlors and the dining room only. Water from the waterworks leading into the bathroom. No cornices in the house. There will be two dormer windows, one front, one rear; house to be painted with three coats, to the taste of the owner. The kitchen will be a lean-to and 10 feet high. The ditch of the privies will be in brick and covered with cement. All the work will be done well and with good materials. The house and kitchen will be supported on the ground by brick. Cost $4,100." The house is situated on the former site of Louis Honoré Guerlain's residence, as indicated in plan book 19, folio 29, dated 1838, on land that he had bought from Manuel Andry in 1823 (M. de Armas). The La Branche family held the cottage until 1871, in which year Joseph Maloney Soniat-Dufossat bought and moved into it. City directories from the early 1870s tell us that he resided here, then numbered 99 Kerlerec. In 1880 Charles F. Claiborne, a well-known resident of Esplanade, acquired the cottage. An auction notice from this transaction describes the property as "a neat and comfortable family residence having double parlors with folding doors, extra-size dining room, large hall, pantry, 2 large bedrooms, with two cabinets in main building, 3 large rooms, pantry and servants room in buildings attached to main house, wash house, brickyard, cistern, privies, etc., the whole slate covered."

1233

Bernard Villa (1233), 1237. The frame, one-story with attic, dormered, center-hall house illustrated has Greek Revival details. Its builder was F. Edward Bernard, a partner in Shumway & Bernard, sugar dealers. Bernard bought lots 20 and 21 from Alfred and Ursin Des Landes "free men of color and cigar manufacturers who operated their business from 87 Goodchildren" (St. Claude). Alfred Des Landes lived at old number 60 Kerlerec. He and his brother acquired these lots in 1848 from Widow J. J. Collard (Agathe Alexandrine Mager), who on the same day disposed of a bevy of other lots she had inherited from her brother Jean Mager, a commission merchant. Mager had bought these two lots in 1838 along with twenty-two others in Faubourg Tremé and New Marigny from Dame Miriam Boyd, a rich but unfortunate heiress who was widowed by her first husband, Louis Honoré Guerlain, and deserted by

her second, George Boyd. The large number of lots involved in the 1838 and 1848 transactions suggest that the vendors were *entrepreneurs* dealing in land rather than buildings. Bernard built the house at 1233 after acquisition of two lots, about 1864. The 1870 city directory shows Bernard residing at 105 Kerlerec, the old number for 1233. After Bernard's death, the house was sold at auction to his son Frank E. Bernard, Jr., in 1879. One of two newspaper descriptions of the cottage dates from this sale: "a large, frame, well-built, slate-roofed house, with hall in centre, two parlors, dining room, two bedrooms, two rooms in attic, with four *cabinets*. A two-story, frame, slate-roofed building, having on first floor a kitchen, pantry, and stairway, two rooms, *cabinet*, and stair landing on the second floor, gas introduced in all the house, cistern, privy, brick yard, shed, etc. . . . fine orange and other fruit trees, ornamental trees, shrubs, water works, etc." The 1881 city directory lists Frank E. Bernard, bookkeeper, at 109 Kerlerec. The last nineteenth-century owner of the house was Léonce M. Soniat, who had the property from 1893 until 1904. An auction notice in the *New Orleans Picayune*, February 18–22, 1893, describes this house at the succession of Mrs. F. E. Bernard when it sold for $4,300: "The improvements consist of a delightful, one-story attic, slate-roofed residence, with large centre hall, parlors with sliding doors, three bedrooms, large dining room, *cabinet*; in the attic two large rooms and four *cabinets*; a two-story building attached to the main building having four rooms, bathroom, also an outbuilding containing washroom, coalroom, woodroom, etc." The present, early side-hall shotgun at **1237** Kerlerec was built between 1850 and 1852 for A. Lusto, who bought this lot from Joseph Alcindor in exchange for a slave worth $650 in 1850. When Lusto sold for $1,000 on April 24, 1852, to Mlle Ephémie Laizer, the act specified that "he built the buildings after acquisition of the land." A recessed entrance leads to a side gallery backed by a *cabinet*. Fine brick sidewalks remain.

1245–47

Guerlain Tract. 1245–47, 1249. Pictured is a weatherboarded creole cottage with gabled sides and incorporated overhang, built of *bousillage* construction with rubble between posts. A. E. Bienvenu, a notary residing on Esplanade Avenue between N. Rampart and St. Claude, owned the property from 1848 until 1885. He built this rental double soon after acquiring the lot. Bienvenu's land had the same circuitous history as its neighbors: from Widow Guerlain, Jean Mager, and from Widow J. J. Collard. The Guerlain holdings included thirty-three lots in Tremé and Marigny, fronting on St. Claude and St. Bernard. Interestingly, the June 18, 1838, Pilié drawing indicates that Kerlerec was not yet cut through in this square. The three-bay, Classic-style creole cottage next door at **1249** has an entrance hall leading to a recessed side gallery, behind which is a *cabinet*. The single-dormer and gabled sides are typical. The original entrance is in the Classic style, but drop-siding, quoins, and brackets were added to the 1860s-style house.

1324, 1326

Hulin Property. At **1324** and **1326** Kerlerec, two once-identical, double-level, double-galleried, late-Classic-style frame houses have box cornices with parapets and dentils supported by wooden pillars, as well as turned balusters on the second-level railing. The cut-glass door and transom remain at 1324; the iron fence is of 1880s vintage. The houses stand on land that Claude Tremé sold in 1800 to François Rocheblave of Gentilly (March 8, 1802, P. Pedesclaux). In 1804 Rocheblave sold "60' front on Bayou Road by 7 *arpents*, to François Armand Hulin for $1,600." The Hulin's *habitation* faced Bayou Road on this narrow strip, and Widow Hulin sold it in 1828 to Azémia Doriocourt, widow first of Bernard Genois, then of James Dupuy. The act of sale before O. de Armas stated that the above-quoted dimensions were "joining on one side Christoval de Armas, today J. B. Plauché; on the other side formerly Docominique [*sic*] Morant, today Dauphin, f.m.c., in its depth the lands of Bernard Marigny." Madame Dupuy kept the *habitation*, which shows on the Zimpel map of 1834, until 1858 when she subdivided into lots. Achille Tardie bought two lots for $1,425 on December 24, 1858, before A. Ducatel. He built these houses at 1324 and 1326 Kerlerec immediately, selling to Mme Jules Armant for $8,000 in 1860 (March 30, T. Guyol).

1336

Fernández Cottage. This late-Italianate version of the three-bay, dormered creole cottage, showing American influence, was probably built soon after 1885 for Widow J. J. Fernández, who inherited the property from her husband. At that time the lot, 33 feet 4 inches on Kerlerec, extended 321 feet 4 inches to Esplanade, with a 33½-foot frontage on Esplanade. The Fernández family kept the house until 1901 (October 10, E. J. Barnett). The late building date is indicated, since the house does not appear on the Robinson Atlas of 1883. This house, then, is one of the last examples of the three-bay, gable-sided creole cottage that began to appear in the 1840s in Faubourgs Marigny and Tremé.

1338, 1340

1342

Decoudreaux Property. The site of the three houses pictured had, in 1826, *"une maison de maître* of four rooms, two having fireplaces, a *galerie,* 8 feet wide across the front, a kitchen, banquette, stable 66 feet long by 14 feet wide," which had been built by Charles Decoudreaux, f.m.c., to face Bayou Road between 1800 and 1816. Decoudreaux had bought the undeveloped land from Claude Tremé in 1800, selling the above-described complex July 16, 1816, before P. Pedesclaux, to Philippe Pijeaux, f.m.c. In 1831 Samuel Jaudon and James Saul purchased from Edmond Soniat (July 1, A. Mazureau) this small *habitation* located *"about four arpents* beyond the old college, 60 feet on Bayou Road by seven *arpents* deep, with buildings and improvements, bound by the property of Joseph Urquhart, f.m.c., on one side and Françoise Ducoudreau, f.w.c., on the other." Saul and Jaudon sold the *habitation* in 1855. In 1861 when the purchaserer George Lanaux sold a few lots including these to Francisco Pizaro Martinez (August 13, S. Magner), there were "machinery and castings belonging to Varnum Sheldon on the property which he is to remove." The present galleried, side-hall shotguns at **1340** and **1342** Kerlerec are Classic in style and were built sometime between 1861 and 1868 for Martinez or subsequent owner Félix Edgar Bernard. The two houses were once identical, featuring delicate cornices with dentils supported by four, slender, box columns forming a gallery. Unfortunately, the Classic-style columns have been replaced at 1340, where late-Victorian jigsaw cornices have also been added. The two-bay shotgun with large brackets and pendils at **1338** postdates 1883.

1418, 1422

1400 Block. The three-bay, two-level, late-Victorian frame house at **1400** Kerlerec has a bracketed overhang and a second-level gallery with turned balusters and full-length segmental arches on all openings. The house has a deep ell to the rear. It is built on land that Alexander Milne bought from Claude Tremé in 1800 and was first subdivided in 1844 at Milne's estate sale. **1418** is a three-bay, two-level, frame, side-hall house with gallery at the first level. The second level gallery has been enclosed. **1422** Kerlerec is a three-bay, two-level, side-hall house with galleries supported by pillars. Both houses are indicated on the Robinson Atlas of 1883, but both have been altered, obscuring the original decorative style. These houses were also built on land belonging to the Milne estate. Across the street at **1417–19,** is a four-bay, frame shotgun with full-length, segmental-arched openings, gabled front, and bracketed overhang.

86/17, (1725)

1717

Martínez-O'Brien Cottage (1717), 1725. At the 1841 auction of Duchamp land, Charles Martínez, f.m.c., bought six lots in this square for $753. Each measured 32 feet on Kerlerec by 175 feet; two faced Columbus, as seen in the plan of J. A. Bourgerol, April 19, 1839. Martínez and his wife, Adelaide Adèle Olivier, were quite well-to-do as seen from their November 7, 1836, marriage contract before C. Pollock. The future husband brought to the marriage nine lots in the Vieux Carré and New Marigny, property in Mandeville and Attakapas, a grocery store, and four slaves. His fiancée's dowry consisted of a one-third interest in a lot in the Vieux Carré and a one-eighth interest in land in Attakapas, which she had inherited from her father, Pierre Olivier, f.m.c., in 1805. On July 28, 1842, Martínez entered into a contract with builder Pierre Théodule Olivier, f.m.c., his brother-in-law, and *entrepreneur* François Muro, f.m.c., for a *maison principale* and kitchen to cost $1,100 (L. T. Caire). The contract stated: "The *maison principale* will be brick upon posts, 28 feet by 32 feet depth, divided into two rooms, it will have a gallery in front and one behind, the former will be open and have square columns, the latter will have a *cabinet* on one side, and on the other a cellar beneath. Each room will have a chimney with plain wood mantels. . . . The roof will be of wood shingles, the house will be lined on the exterior with bleached battens, lap-jointed and with hidden nails. It will have four openings on the front, two doors, and two windows, and a door in one of the gables, and a window in the other. All these openings will have barred doors and glazing. There will be a barred door and window in the *cabinet* and a barred door to the *cabinet* above the cellar. . . . It will be placed on brick footing 8 inches thick, 24 inches high. On the front there will be a stairway 8 feet long and another of the same dimensions in the rear. The stairway in the gable will have the dimensions of the openings. . . . All the openings will have casings 3½ feet wide inside and out, those inside will be double casings. There will be plinths 9 inches wide throughout the house.

All the floors will be thick bleached wood, grooved and nailed with hidden nails. The interior walls and ceilings to be plastered. All the visible wood to receive two coats of good paint, the panes will be of Boston glass, the iron work will be of good dimension, and locks will be placed wherever necessary. The kitchen will be made of barge planks placed upright on footings, one brick thick, 18 inches high. The kitchen will be covered with wooden staves, divided into three rooms, one with fireplace, each room to have a door and window; the floor will be of wood, and the interior and exterior will be whitewashed." After building the *maison principale* at 1717 Kerlerec in 1842, Mme Martínez sold adjacent lots to builder Muro's widow, Dame Emélie Augustine Thézan, who built investment houses on them before 1848. Plan book 86, folio 17 shows one of the houses still standing at **1725** Kerlerec as it appeared May 12, 1871. By 1864 Widow Martínez, who had moved to Plaquemines Parish, died; and her heirs sold 1717 Kerlerec, then numbered 215, to François Abadie. The auction, advertised in French and English newspapers, on April 26 and May 4, 1869, took place at the Merchant's Exchange.

1819–21

1917

2018–20

1800, 1900, 2000 Blocks. As early as 1844 there were two buildings on the square facing Kerlerec on the odd side of the 1800 block. They are shown in plan book 40, folio 5, dated June 12, 1844, by L. Surgi. The drawing shows the square established in a garden belonging to "Ay Fernández." One of the houses remains at **1815–17.** It is a dormered, double creole cottage with overhang incorporated into the roofline in the style of the 1840s. It is now covered with asbestos siding, which hides the original façade, and has late Victorian decoration. A modest, frame, double creole cottage at **1819–21** is also illustrated in the 1844 drawing. One block away at **1917** is a villa-type house raised just three feet off the ground, displaying a central entrance flanked by two segmental-arched, full-length openings on each side. A wide gable with icicle-patterned vergeboard and a gallery supported by turned columns and crowned by a band of spindles and pierced-work spandrels both suggest an 1890s construction date. The very decorative opening surrounds include fluting, bull's-eyes, brackets, and tripartite cornices. The original iron fence and old crepe myrtle trees enhance the country-style cottage, which stands on the "Castanedo division of Faubourg Tremé" (February 1, 1842, C. V. Foulon). The M. D. Bringier estate sold the Kerlerec front of the square in 1842 to Philippe Videchi (March 22, P. Lacoste). The immediate purchaser, Giovanni Polessi, sold this subdivided lot to Elizabeth Bland the same year, probably after building a modest creole cottage. The early cottage sold to a number of owners, including Joseph Bruneau, a heavy investor between Bayou Road and St. Bernard. In 1894 an heir of John Carron, who had bought this property from Bruneau in 1875, sold it to the American Homestead Company for $1,450. This was a means of financing construction of a few house on the lot. Within a year, on September 11, 1895 (M. T. Ducros), the American Homestead Company sold the present house with another lot to Paul Percy Viosca for $6,000. Jean Bernard was once an owner of the site of 1917. He also acquired the site of **2019–21** in the following block, probably at the 1841 auction of the subdivided Duchamp estate. The extant house was built soon afterward. Then, in 1876, the house was seized from Widow Bernard for nonpayment of taxes and auctioned at the tax collectors' sale. Widow Bernard, Arsène Broutin, was able to redeem the house for payment of $191.57 in back taxes, but she sold to the Little Sisters of the Poor in the following year for $600 (September 1, 1877, A. Pitot). The Sisters, in that same year, exchanged properties with Mme John Wells, who then disposed of the cottage for just $1,370 to A. E. Bienvenu (July 30, 1878, M. T. Ducros). A four-bay, late Victorian shotgun at **2009–11** Kerlerec has segmental-arched windows and two segmentally-arched French doors, bracketed overhang, undecorated gable, drop-siding, and quoins. The herringbone-patterned brick sidewalk enhances the nineteenth-century atmosphere. Across the street at **2018–20** a late Victorian, galleried, frame double shotgun is located in the former Castanedo division.

LAHARPE

1611

1300, 1400, 1600 Blocks. Squeezed within the boundaries of the former Guerlain division are the 1300 and 1400 blocks of Laharpe Street. Two, four-bay, frame shotguns with front-gabled roofs and bracketed, apron overhangs at **1368** and **1372–74** are embellished with fancy architraves around full-length openings. These houses were built before 1883 since they appear on the Robinson Atlas. At **1404,** four full-length openings with handsome Greek Key surrounds enhance a frame creole cottage, which is just one room deep with a one-story shed across the rear. A simple, Greek Revival box cornice once supported by wooden box columns is now replaced by ironwork. The original entrance door and transoms are spoiled by porch and awnings. The cottage probably dates from the late 1840s. The Bernard Duchamp estate shared a property line with Mme Guerlain and her plantation; they meet at the 1600 block. The four-bay creole cottage at **1611** is typical of those built about mid-century within the eighteen city blocks of the Duchamp plantation. It has a central chimney and gabled sides. The present unusual brackets with spindles and other late-Victorian elements are the result of a remodeling. Across the street at **1614** is a two-bay, frame shotgun, that was built in the 1880s, which replaced an earlier cottage. It has steamboat brackets, a hip-roof, scalloped vergeboard, drop-siding, and quoins.

47/26,

1722, 1724, 1726

Duchamp Division. Here stands a row of rare, early-Classic-style shotgun houses. **1718** replaced an earlier creole cottage as seen in plan book 47, folio 26. **1722** is also illustrated in the 1853 archival drawing; today it has a new door. **1724** and **1726** match the drawing and retain their French doors. The houses had plastered and rusticated façades and weatherboard sides in their original state. The hip-roofs are steeper than those on late-century shotguns.

1729–31

Duchamp Division. Plan book 45, folio 14, of May 20, 1847, indicates a row of simple, two-room, galleried, creole cottages facing Laharpe. The square was sold by the heirs of Bernard Duchamp, and the little houses seen in the archival drawings of 1847 must date from 1844. On both sides of the block today stand mid- to late-Victorian shotguns, most of which have altered entrances, porches, and steps. However, the present creole cottage at **1729–31** Laharpe is quite old, probably dating from the late 1840s. Indicative of this early date are the small dormers and cant to the gabled ends of the roof where the overhang is incorporated. The present façade, segmental openings, siding, and brackets represent a Victorian remodeling. The house must have been standing on the lot when Melanie Hastier and Céleste Porche sold it on November 21, 1860, to J. A. Langhauser, as recorded before notary N. Hahn. An 1846 building contract, which could apply to this house, was recorded by L. Hermann. It stipulated that Jesse Connor, f.m.c., hired Louis Viavant, a free colored builder, to construct a creole cottage on Laharpe between Roman and Derbigny for $700. He then paid André Gregoire, builder, to finish the job for $265 in September.

1833–35

1800 Block. A two-level, frame, store-house at **1801** has full-length openings at the second level and a hip-roof with three chimneys. The late-Victorian door is not original, and a balcony has been removed. Devoid of decorative detail to afford clues to its construction date, a twenty-year spread of 1860 to 1884 is placed on this store-house built by Widow Louis Abadie. Her husband bought two lots from Jean Agut via the Duchamp succession for $450 in 1860. Widow Abadie, Clothilde Mahalin, sold the house to Victor Hubert in December, 1884, as recorded by notary P. A. Conand. Between 1890 and 1901, the house was used as a grocery store and barroom by John Vigeaux and listed as such in his succession when his heirs sold it on May 30, 1901. **1805–07** Laharpe is a double-dormered, frame creole cottage with gabled ends. The brackets on the overhang were added. Flush opening surrounds and arched dormer lights with pediment and pilasters suggest an 1840s date. This is also the case with the house at **1833–35**, built as a four-bay creole cottage with gabled ends and service wing extending to the rear. This small, dormerless, frame cottage is doubtless one of the original row of cottages built on the Duchamp estate in the 1840s and could be either frame covering a bargeboard construction or one of brick-between-posts. Note the wide boards covering the façade. The double shotgun at **1837–39** represents an inter-mixture of later shotguns with creole cottages on this block. Across the street at **1814–16** stands an earlier, mid-nineteenth-century example of the double shotgun with Classic-style pillars supporting a gallery. The hip-roof and post-and-lintel openings with flush simple surrounds reflect the 1850s, an early date for a shotgun. The floor plan, height, and roofline also suggest this period. However, the doorway is a late-Victorian addition. A building contract, dated May 19, 1854, indicates that a $5,650 *maison a étage* was built on one side of this block for the Société des Dames de la Providence. John McVittie was the builder for the projected orphan asylum, which was "to be a model frame building with slate roof." No clue remains to the building's location.

1915–1925

Castanedo-Duchamp Land. Rows of double shotguns dating from the turn of the century are characterized by triple front gables above galleries. Such shotguns were often built on land that had been used for truck farms and small gardens from the 1840s.

2004

Castanedo Division, 1916–18, 2004. This creole cottage, as pictured, perfectly exemplifies a gracefully canted, side-gabled roof. Tucked between a twentieth-century "pillbox" and a shingled, late-nineteenth-century shotgun, it hugs the banquette and has the excellent proportions of an 1850s-style cottage. The ragged edge of asbestos siding and aluminum window and door casements do not destroy the overall authenticity of a fine house-type, but it would be greatly improved without these additions. The late-Victorian shotgun at **1916–18**, owned by Mr. and Mrs. Andrew Maderl in 1976, is typical of the street and marks the beginning of the land that belonged to the Castanedo plantation.

2001–07

Faubourg Castanedo. A common-wall, creole cottage, built as a three-family dwelling, retains its three dormers; but one door has been removed and a second shortened. The single, Classic-style entrance with pilasters, the three, well-spaced dormers, and the built-in overhang suggest an 1850s date. Common-wall, multiple-family creole cottages are rarely seen in Faubourg Tremé. On July 31, 1855, in the Fourth District Court number 8660, there was a suit and an ensuing sheriff's sale—*Gustave Sébastièn v. Hubert Gérard, builder*, in which a large number of lots were sold to F. Goldthwaite. Gérard may have built this and other creole cottages in the square for Sébastièn around 1854. The substantial house has been involved in three sheriff's sales, and in 1886 it was sold at auction by Alvin Rochereau of Paris, France. He had acquired it as a result of a succession suit emanating from the death of J. R. Bougère, who owned the house from 1857 until 1869 when his heirs sold it. A floor plan attached to an act by J. Fahey on March 22, 1886, shows the original room arrangement with six rooms, a back, circular, interior stair, and a covered way leading to three service rooms. At this time, three doors and three windows punctuated the façade, which included an open side-gallery where the Classic-style entrance now appears.

2017

Faubourg Castanedo. This double-galleried, three-bay, frame house with hip-roof, Greek Revival entrance, and full-length openings on both levels has twentieth-century double galleries. Architectural analysis suggests that although the house has both late-nineteenth-century and twentieth-century building elements, it may have been originally a Greek Revival house built for Jean René Bougère after his purchase from William F. Goldthwaite of most of the square (September 16, 1857, A. Ducatel). Bougère's estate was not settled for many years, but this house stood on this lot on September 24, 1873, when his widow sold the property to her daughter Hermance, Widow Auguste Candide Avenec, as recorded by J. Fahey. Hermance Bougère sold it at auction on December 26, 1874, to Alfred Jacquet who owned it until July 2, 1886, when he sold it to the American Homestead as recorded by the notary, M. T. Ducros. The homestead sold it that year for $1,000, a surprisingly low figure, for the land alone measured 43 feet in front by 157 feet in depth.

2216

Faubourg Gueno. The Victorian, galleried cottage was built around 1892 for Leopold L. Trepagnier. The architectural design features a gallery returning around the side of the house, a hip-roof with slight cant, and lacy millwork. Slender turned colonettes, along with pierced-work door and window cresting, are typical of this period. Trepagnier bought the lot in 1892 for $850, and his family retained the house until 1921, when it was sold to the Mutual Building and Homestead for $2,450. The 1975 photograph illustrates the rural setting of the house, framed by nandina and aspidistra, and evokes the turn-of-the-century atmosphere and once-existant charm of Faubourg Gueno.

2418–20

Lotz Creole Cottage. Leonard Lotz bought this lot in 1850 from Mme Madeleine Gueno, Widow J. J. Buss. Mme Buss was a daughter of Mme Pierre Gueno, née Felicité Loubie, who had subdivided the Faubourg Gueno in 1835. Lotz, a carpenter from Darmstadt, Germany, built this house and continued to live in it until his death in 1907. Descendants maintained the house until 1978. This galleried creole cottage, detailed in the Classic style with a gable-sided kitchen building behind the main house, was probably built soon after the 1850 property acquisition. Such cottages are rare today; most of them are set back on the lot and have suffered wraparound front additions. The gable-sided service building, once detached, has been joined to the main house. The interior retains the fine millwork, including the stairway, that Lotz installed.

LAHARPE

2403

Faubourg Gueno. This tripedimented, late-Victorian, bayed cottage with ell has decorative exterior features of fleur-de-lis and icicle-patterned vergeboard, as well as pierced work and spindle friezes. Attractive details include heavy cornices above narrow, elongated stained-glass windows and double doors. The ell affords the owner privacy and use of floor space that is superior to the shotgun room arrangements. The center-ridge roof tiles signal a final touch of Victorian plumage to this attractive home, marred by the new gallery rail, awnings, cement steps, and chain-link fence. The Robinson Atlas of 1883 indicates a corner building at this location, perhaps this house. The entire square had only four structures at that time.

2439

Faubourg Gueno. A frame, late-Victorian, three-bay cottage with side ell has a front gallery supported by turned columns and a spindle course. Moorish-influenced millwork adds an exotic note. The cottage is five rooms deep with a long hall, behind which is a recessed side gallery. The original gas-electric chandeliers are in place, and the floors are cypress. The interior remains much as it appeared at the time of its 1890s construction, with original plaster, porcelain doorknobs, and wrought-iron locks.

2455

Lotz Cottage. Here, a three-bay, late-Victorian cottage in excellent condition exhibits fancy jigsaw work and double front gables in the 1890s style. Icicle vergeboard, a sunburst in one gable, a frieze-band with spindles and pierced-work spandrels with finials, and tripartite window-door surrounds were selected from White's Millwork Catalog. The combination, however, reflects individual preference. This house, like 2439 Laharpe, has a side ell; but here it is from an early creole cottage set back on the lot, to which an 1890s addition was attached in the front, and the creole cottage was redecorated. The arrangement is often found in houses of Faubourg Gueno. Leonard Lotz, a German immigrant who lived at 2418 Laharpe from the mid–nineteenth century, bought this lot too and built the underlying creole cottage as rental property. The wraparound and redecoration took place in the 1890s judging from the double front gables, projecting portico, fancy tripartite opening surrounds, and lacy pierced-work frieze and spandrels.

2544

Dantagnan Shotgun. The 2500 block of Laharpe reveals a cluster of almost identical, shotgun double houses with a variety of decorative brackets and cornice crestings. Many rear service structures remain, as do the wide, horizontal-board, cypress fences. The house at 2544 is an unusual, two-bay, shotgun cottage, which was raised sometime after its construction date. The present second level has segmental-arched, full-length openings, crowned by cap-molded lintels as façade articulation, along with drop-siding, quoins, and overhang with brackets. In 1891 Miss Marie Rosella Thierry inherited this lot and many others from her father, Jacques Henri Thierry. She sold them on May 7, 1892, as recorded by J. F. Meunier, to Dominique Dantagnan. Dantagnan was probably the builder of the house.

2626–28

Faubourg Gueno. This plain, double, frame creole cottage without dormers probably was built during the 1860s. At that time, Madeleine Gueno, Widow James Joseph Buss, was selling many lots in this area from her father's plantation. The corrugated tin roof is not original but is in keeping with the simplicity of this cottage; only wooden box steps and a slate roof would be required to bring the dwelling back to its 1860s purity.

LAPEYROUSE

1738

1714–16, 1726, 1738. At the corner of Lapeyrouse and N. Roman, the last building on the even side of the block in the Castanedo division is a traditional, two-story, corner store-house at **1738**. Designed with a Classic-style cornice with dentils, it has batten shutters on the first level and louvered shutters on the second. The store entrance is angled and recessed below a deep overhang supported by turned columns. Architectural analysis indicates that this is a pre–Civil War construction. At **1714–16** Lapeyrouse, a frame shotgun with a bracketed overhang has segmental-arched openings with decorative architraves of fluting, bull's-eye, and pierced work. It is in the style of the 1890s. The house at **1726** was built as a two-level, two-bay house, which was very popular in the late nineteenth century. It has since been altered but could easily be returned to its original appearance.

1816, 1820–22

1816, 1820–22, 1824. A variety of double and single, frame, Victorian shotgun houses enhance the street scene along Lapeyrouse in the Castanedo division. Both sides of the block are partially paved with brick sidewalks. **1816** Lapeyrouse is a two-story, three-bay, late-Victorian townhouse with a deep overhang at the second level, supported by steamboat brackets and ornamented with a fleur-de-lis vergeboard and front gable. The entrance has been moved to the center, although the original door was retained. The segmental-arched openings have cap-molded lintels. The house was probably built sometime in the 1890s, when many lots of the Castanedo division were partitioned from the large holdings of investors. The family of Jacob Hussy owned the house at the turn of the century. The four-bay shotgun at **1820–22** and the two-bay at **1824** are harmonious in style with 1816, although they differ in scale and were also built in the 1890s.

1936–38

1908, 1918–20, 1936–38. A frame creole cottage with built-in overhang has been altered at **1908** Lapeyrouse. In contrast, at **1918–20** stands a double, frame, shotgun house with a bracketed overhang and a wide gable covered with shingles. This simple late-Victorian shotgun was designed in the style of the 1890s and has a relatively restrained decoration. The brick sidewalk remains, a street improvement dating from after the T. P. Sourd 1860 ownership of the block. The house at 1918–20 probably was built following the 1883 sale of lots here by Jean Ferrand. Heavy foliage creates a rural atmosphere at the corner location of **1936–38** Lapeyrouse. This 1850s-style creole cottage was built with French doors within the gabled sides. Batten shutters can be seen on the attic windows. L. Bringier made a plan of "fifteen lots of ground in Faubourg Castanedo to be sold at auction," dated July 12, 1836. Many purchases were of large blocks, so that by 1860 Mme T. P. Sourd owned six lots in the square, including this one. She sold the corner and other property on the block to Jean Ferrand, the son-in-law of Paul Cheval, f.m.c., in 1875. Jean Marie Latour purchased the property at 1936–38 with 70 feet fronting on Lapeyrouse and a 125-foot depth on Johnson in 1883 as recorded by notary E. A. Peyroux.

2001

Ethiopian Theater (2001) 2004–06. Bean's Variety Store at **2001** Lapeyrouse is a four-bay, front-gabled, frame shotgun with bracketed overhang, altered into a corner store-house. Behind, and now attached, is the Ethiopian Theater housed in a brick, one-level, hip-roof building, which has four segmental-arched openings. The arches are splayed with three courses of bricks, and the openings are equidistant. Well-proportioned, the original use of the structure is unknown. The Ethiopian Theater is a nonprofit, educational, charitable, and literary organization promoting the dramatic arts. Continuing the tradition of the creole cottage in the Castanedo Division is **2004–06**. The tall dormers of this cottage reflect its 1850s building date. It has a well-proportioned canted roofline with overhang. Unfortunately, the attractive house is covered with asbestos siding. Belle E. Aubert, f.w.c., purchased two lots here on April 1, 1847, for $100 from François Sallières, according to the act before J. Agaisse, notary. She sold the two lots with "buildings and improvements" for $300 to Paulin E. Fleitas on May 22, 1866 (S. Magner). Fleitas also sold both properties but for an increase to $650 on May 9, 1870, to J. B. Jourdain (A. E. Bienvenu). In 1879, the creole cottage was sold to Widow Celestine Olivard for $850, at which time the adjacent lot was sold separately.

LAPEYROUSE

2105–07

Faubourg Gueno. The mid-nineteenth-century, Classic-style, double creole cottage at **2101–03** Lapeyrouse has retained its side-gabled roof with cant. The roofline is further distinguished by the slate covering and central chimney. The building at **2105–07** exemplifies a transitional phase between the creole cottage and the later, double shotgun house. It is four bays wide and three rooms deep and features a rusticated wood façade in the Italianate manner. The present step enclosures need plastering, and the aluminum screen doors obscure handsome doors and transoms with oval lights. The house was built soon after 1873, when Peter and Leon Jochum bought three lots from George Frank for $600 each. The two brothers retained the lots until Peter Jochum sold his share, along with buildings and improvements, to his brother on November 8, 1881 (COB 115/841).

2127–29

Faubourg Gueno. This house is not indicated on Robinson's Atlas of 1883. Though similar to 2107, it was built after 1887 for Philip Plapp, who had owned the property since 1872. On February 23, 1887, Plapp mortgaged his lot to finance the building of this house, as recorded before F. Zengel, notary. The house is a five-bay, frame, shotgun variation with a side-gallery entrance on one side and a handsome door and transom. The roofline is hipped and marked by three chimneys. The French doors and the alternating, double-hung windows are unusual façade treatments for this type of house. Its appearance would suggest an earlier building date than that indicated by title research.

2217

Union Baptist Theological Seminary (2217). The cornerstone indicates that builder J. H. Rolfs constructed this two-level, frame, five-bay building in 1891. The hip-roof structure with front portico is reminiscent of Eastern Seaboard prototypes. The paneled pillars and double doors reflect the style of the 1890s. The gallery across the rear elevation, with box columns and simple railings, is more reflective of New Orleans traditions and building styles. Two large, pedimented dormers have simple bracketed decoration and are eclectic in style.

2622

Faubourg Gueno. This galleried creole cottage has undergone a number of alterations since it was sold for unpaid taxes in the name of Joseph E. Blouin to George Nightheart in 1899 (COB 174/165). Blouin was able to redeem the property, and his relatives still retained it in 1949. The present dormer, gallery, columns, and steps were probably added by the Clement Bergeron family within the last thirty years. Mr. Bergeron's wife was Poleski Blouin. The cottage dated from the 1860s when the Orleans Railroad Company subdivided the square.

2632

Viavant House. This fine galleried house is a superior example of the enlarged creole cottage, a house-type peculiar to Faubourgs Tremé and Gueno between N. Claiborne and N. Broad. Four-bay width, gabled sides, and double dormers are the traditional vocabulary, here enlarged to a full two-story building with service wing extending from the rear. Built in the late-Classic style, the house dates from 1872. Originally part of the old Gueno plantation, the property here was acquired by the Orleans Railroad Company in the 1860s. In 1872 Augustin Viavant, Sr., who had acquired three vacant lots here, sold them to Henry Viavant for $1,500. Viavant built this house immediately, taking out a loan with the New Orleans Credit Finance Association, which allowed him a finished house for $6,728. It remained in the Viavant family until January 12, 1886. The house is located in the portion of Faubourg Gueno that followed the shores of Bayou Gentilly and is one of the few included in this inventory on the "Lake-side" of N. Broad Street.

MARAIS

1012–14

Fleitas Cottage. This beautifully proportioned, dormered creole cottage retains many characteristics of its 1830s building date. There are flush, casement door frames, small dormers with roundheaded windows, and gabled ends with brick fire extensions. The deep cornice is composed of five rows of fancy brickwork, including sawtooth patterns and the traditional dentil. Like the earliest urban houses in Faubourg Tremé, this one is set quite low, just off the banquette. Fortunately, the herringbone-patterned brick sidewalk remains to complete the nineteenth-century atmosphere. The charming house is similar to 1020–22 Tremé. The site was vacant until the City Corporation sold an *L*-shaped lot fronting on both Ursulines and Marais to Félix de Armas in 1826 (August 12, H. Lavergne). After an 1830 auction of the de Armas property, a section of the original land, along with some Ursulines Street frontage, went to Basile Beauregard. The act of sale was passed on December 31, 1830, before A. Mazureau; the price was $800. Beauregard retained his Ursulines Street frontage (see 1322 Ursulines) but sold the 15 feet fronting Marais to J. M. Fleitas on October 29, 1836 (T. Seghers). Son of Domingo Fleitas, one of the important Spanish colonials, he inherited several properties such as 2275 Bayou Road and was the owner by this time of many purchases, including 2510 Dumaine. Fleitas added this small lot to other Marais Street property that he had bought from the Company of the Architects of the Eighth District at a sheriff's sale that same month. It was he who built this house for rental use and held it until 1872, at which time he sold to Edward Lehmann for $2,250. Across the street, the odd side of the 1000 block of Marais was part of the Alexandre Duhamel de Bellecourt holdings in the 1820s. Ursulines Street was not cut through here until 1826. The block features a row of six, late-Victorian, frame, shotgun houses of varying styles and a two-story, corner store-house with cast-iron balcony at the second level. The door frames of the store-house have been lowered and the doors altered, spoiling the façade proportions of the traditional building.

1122

Santos Houses. 1118–20, 1122. The house at **1122** Marais Street stands on property that faced Bayou Road in 1807 when Claude Tremé sold it to Marcely Cornu. The Bayou Road frontage extended 210 feet deep into the area of the future Marais Street. Cornu may have developed a *maison de maître* complex along Bayou Road. On January 29, 1829, the estate of his widow, Arthémise Cantrelle, sold to Jeanne Clary a lot of 30 feet fronting on Bayou Road by 210 feet along newly established Marais Street (F. de Armas). The heirs of Pierre Amy first subdivided the Marais Street frontage of the property in 1834; a plan attached to the act of sale to J. J. Montfort, f.m.c., on January 23, 1832, showed the lots offered at a January 17 auction (L. Fernand). Beginning in 1834, Montfort developed some of his property in partnership with Nelson Fouché, f.m.c.; however, he sold these two lots to the Soulié brothers, f.p.c., on October 22, 1835, before the notary T. Seghers. The Soulié brothers sold the lots in 1848 to Bernard de Santos, who built the two-story, gable-sided, dormered creole house at 1122 Marais, selling it along with "six other lots and seven slaves" to Lucien Constant Adam for $18,600 on November 21, 1851, as recorded by A. Ducatel. Santos also built **1118–20**, a four-bay, hip-roof creole cottage, at this same time. This house remains, as does its neighbor, greatly altered from its original late 1840s appearance. Research has revealed the intricacies of real estate dealings and speculation in the Faubourg Tremé. When Joachim Courcelle died in 1868, Lucien Adam turned the property at 1122 over to the Courcelle estate because, he declared before the notary S. Magner, the property that he held in his own name was actually the property of Courcelle (February 12, 1886). As the administrator of the estate, Bernard Soulié sold the two houses to Jean Numa Avegno at an auction held on February 15, 1866. At that time, **1122** Marais Street was described as "a two-story, wooden house, covered with slates, having an entry and two rooms on each floor, a two-story wooden kitchen, covered with slates, containing 2 rooms on each floor, paved yard, hydrant, etc. numbered 254 Marais." Avegno completed the purchase of 1122 Marais before S. Magner on February 19, 1866, for $3,725. The once-attractive home is disfigured today by the removal of the balcony, which once had either a wrought-iron railing or simple, square, wooden balusters, and the alteration of the fenestration and entrance. All millwork and surrounds have been removed from the façade, but the dormer above the overhang is an indication of the former Classic style of the front elevation.

1126

Gardes House. The frame, gable-sided house at 1126 was built with attached service wings by Hilaire Courcelle, builder, for Alphonse Gardes between November of 1848 and June of 1849. Gardes bought the lot from investors Bernard and Albin Soulié, f.p.c., who had sold the adjacent lots to Bernard de Santos. Gardes paid $600 for the lot in 1848; he sold it with buildings and improvements to Hilaire Courcelle for $2,600 on June 16, 1849, before A. Ducatel. Since the Courcelles were builders, it is likely that Gardes had them build the house and sold it to them in lieu of payment. Courcelle died in 1852 and his wife, Manette Alpuente, died just one year later. Her succession sold the house at auction on March 3, 1853, to Marie Mathilde Drouet, Widow Louis Bourgeois, for $2,500 (March 15, O. de Armas). Josephine Toledano, widow of Jean Louis Drouet, acquired the house from her relatives and donated it in 1855 to her granddaughter, Louisa Bourgeois, in her marriage contract to Thomas Taquino (January 12, A. E. Bienvenu). An unsightly dormer has ruined the roof and alteration of all doors and windows further spoils a house that could be restored to its fine 1849 appearance.

1105

Delahaye House. The three-bay, single, frame shotgun house at 1105 Marais replaced part of the earlier Alexandre Duhamel de Bellecourt *maison principale*, which was constructed soon after 1809 when Duhamel bought 52 feet fronting Bayou Road by 540 feet on Marais from Claude Tremé. The present house features a Greek Key recessed entrance and jigsaw decorative millwork, probably added later. The old Duhamel house stood until after 1842, but the exact date of the present house is not known. Buildings are not mentioned in an 1865 auction of the lot by Widow Henry Germain, née Alexandrine Lakanal of Paris, who was the daughter of the president of the Collège d'Orléans. Thus the house may have been built for the purchaser, Emile Antoine Delahaye, who received title to the property for $950 on February 13, 1873, before the notary, C. T. Soniat. His heirs owned the house until 1881.

1109

Bienvenu Cottage. Here, an 1830s creole cottage has been altered and raised. Presently it features a deep gallery with late-Victorian millwork, full-length openings, and an attached service wing. There are a number of unusual features. The deep gallery, superimposed across the front in the manner of Garden District houses, is rare on creole cottages, yet frequently seen on shotgun doubles. The gallery angles slightly and does not square with the cottage. Bull's-eye decoration and paired, turned columns at each corner represent late-Victorian modifications. Pierre Dupeux subdivided the Duhamel de Bellecourt land after his acquisition in 1825, selling this lot to Francisco Tío at a sheriff's sale in 1833. Tío sold the lot with creole cottage to Mme Alexandre Emile Bienvenu on October 17, 1835, for $3,200, according to O. de Armas. The Bienvenu family held the cottage as rental property until 1884 when Mme Bienvenu's four children sold it to André Doriocourt, Jr., for $1,750 (April 10, P. E. L. Théard). Doriocourt, who was responsible for building several houses in the area at this time, may have raised the house and added the service wing, gallery, and late-Victorian millwork.

1115

Duhamel de Bellecourt Property. The three-bay, frame, late-Victorian shotgun in the style of the 1890s has a front-gabled roof with an overhang supported by brackets and cornice decoration. Full-length, segmental-arched openings with molded cornices are topped by pierced-work decoration. The porch railing of turned balusters complements the drop-siding of the façade. The house is set back slightly, retaining its small, wrought-iron fence, marked "Hinderer's Iron Fence Works." Recently restored, the house has been painted in two colors to emphasize the rusticated effect of the drop-siding, which was a traditional stylistic device at the turn of the century. A bathroom has been added on the side. This property, as well as its neighbors, was once part of the A. Duhamel de Bellecourt holdings acquired by him from Claude Tremé in 1809. The Duhamel family retained its land until 1825, when Pierre Dupeux purchased and subdivided it. Subsequently he sold the Duhamel *maison principale* to Antoine de Villiers Guesnon.

1123–25

Murphy House. This spacious, frame creole cottage is a fine example of the enlarged version of that house-type designed with Classic-style detailing. The property was acquired in the 1830s by the Company of the Architects of the Eighth District of New Orleans, which sold the undeveloped land to Robert and William Murphy on December 27, 1839 (Tureaud). William E. Murphy, a lawyer, built a house on the site and resided there. After buying his brother Robert's interest in the property, he probably demolished the house and built this one in 1850. He continued his residency there until 1889, when the house was listed as old number 253. Murphy was married to Citye Rose Alvarez by whom he had two daughters who lived in France and inherited Bayou Road property also owned by their father.

1135, 1139

Morand Habitation. This property was developed by Jacques Tinchant, f.m.c., after his 1834 acquisition. He held his improved property for two years before selling to free woman of color Marie Glapion for $3,000. The Glapion family owned the property for thirty-six years during which there was a family partition. After the 1872 sale by Clara P. Glapion to William H. Offenstadt, the present two-level townhouse at **1135** was built on the site of an earlier house. The present house does not appear on the 1883 Robinson Atlas. Built just beyond the banquette, with a cast-iron balcony at the second level and a recessed entrance, the house, if stripped of its present awning, concrete steps, and new siding would be improved greatly. A single, hip-roof, three-bay shotgun house at **1139** Marais incorporates a bracketed overhang. Removal of the metal awning would reveal an interesting, Classic-style shotgun with brackets and cornice decoration added to a simple 1850s-style building. This house also postdates 1883.

1143

Thomas Cottage. This lot was carved from the Bayou Road property that Claude Tremé sold to Alexandre Duhamel de Bellecourt prior to the sale to the city in 1810. Thus the development of this lot begins with the present 1400–04 Bayou Road (Governor Nicholls) or the original 52-by-540-foot Duhamel land. Soon after 1831, when Arnold Myers sold the lots to Louis A. Neel for $1,675 (March 18, C. Pollock), Neel built a house fronting on Bayou Road. Elie Norbert Henry purchased it for the substantial sum of $6,500 on March 15, 1836. When the estate of P. F. Thomas sold the Bayou Road house to Etiènne and Baptiste Perez (May 30, 1866, S. Magner), the lot's depth had been reduced many times and was then recorded as 83 feet on Marais. It was probably Dr. Pierre Frederick Thomas who built 1143 Marais as rental property behind his other brick rental unit facing Bayou Road. His ownership spanned thirty years. This particularly intriguing creole cottage has a number of features that make it outstanding. It is an unusual type, similar to 1125 and 1127 St. Philip, having three bays in the Greek Revival style and a single, front dormer. Such French and Spanish vernacular creole houses reflect American influences in the Greek Key entrance surrounds and plain lintels above double-hung or full-length windows. The fire extension above the gable on the left indicates one brick side; a weatherboarded gable on the right may cover a brick-between-posts construction. It is possible that this was once part of a pair of identical houses. The façade is plaster over bricks or lathes. A detached outbuilding to the rear may predate the main house. Such house-types are relatively rare and most date from the 1850s, although they appear in both type and style to reflect elements of the 1830s.

1218–20

Montreuil Property. The frame, double shotgun with front gable has decorative shingles and a bracketed overhang. Note the fancy jigsaw window and door architraves with hoodmolds on segmental-arched openings. The original shutters for the doors are paneled below with louvers above. The gabled front with apron overhang suggests an 1890s building date; the structure is not illustrated on the 1883 Robinson Atlas. In 1803 Claude Tremé sold Charles Montreuil a lot facing Bayou Road and extending back half of the present Marais frontage of the square. Montreuil, f.m.c., fought with distinction in the Battle of New Orleans and was the owner of several properties in Faubourg Tremé. The adjacent segment of Marais to Esplanade was purchased from Claude Tremé in 1805 by Narcisse Gastier. That block remained vacant throughout the nineteenth century with the exception of a mansion facing Esplanade.

1221

Thibodeaux House (1221), 1215. The lot on which the 1889 house at **1221** stands emanates from the Isnard-Plauché *habitation* on the right side of Bayou Road (Charles Zimpel map, 1834). As early as 1847, there was a "brick-between-posts house with a wooden kitchen" on this lot described as 46 feet on Plauché Street (Marais) and 138 feet in depth. The house was valued at $1,450 in the Plauché succession of 1847 (COB 42/444). By 1857 the Coquet brothers and sisters had bought the house and "another lot in the square" for the high price of $9,500 (April 9, A. Dreyfous). The Coquets sold the early house without the adjacent lot for just $2,925 to Esteban del Nodal (November 15, 1866, A. D. Doriocourt). The del Nodals kept the property for twenty years, selling it to Benjamin Thibodeaux for the low price of $730 on October 31, 1889, before C. G. Andry. By that time the old house had been demolished, and Benjamin Thibodeaux contracted with Samuel B. Allison, contractor and builder, to construct "a one-story frame dwelling house with a two-story back building attached . . . in strict conformity with the plans, elevations, and sections and the specifications which have been made by Paul Andry, architect," (November 23, 1889,

C. G. Andry). The cost of the building was $2,750, and the house was to be ready by March 1, 1890. This is a very important building contract, since such documents are rare for late-Victorian houses, cottages, or shotguns. It serves along with surveys and title analyses as an indicator for dating similar houses in the area. This kind of galleried cottage was quite popular, especially between N. Claiborne and N. Broad, most notably in the Pontalba division and Faubourg Gueno. The gabled front with shingles, hexagonal side bay, gallery with projecting portions, recessed entrance, and stained-glass windows are all characteristic of such cottages. It is also notable that the house was designed by an architect; Paul Andry is associated with a number of fine buildings in the central business district as well as major mansions along St. Charles Avenue. The three-bay, late-Victorian shotgun next door at **1215** Marais crowds the banquette and was built onto the front of a small creole cottage in the rear of the lot. That small, frame building could have been part of the 1840s Plauché complex. The present house postdates 1883 and has an unusual hip-roof incorporating a bracketed overhang and full-length, segmental-arched façade openings. Paint and side-yard landscaping would greatly improve its appearance.

1225–27, 1231

Cousin Cottages. This pair of creole cottages was built by the Cousin family between 1828 and 1843. Térence Cousin built **1231** Marais and his cousin François, **1225–27**; both sold their houses in 1843. A handsome, detached, common-wall kitchen runs along the common property line between the two houses. These once-similar, gable-sided, brick, parapeted creole cottages remain today outstanding examples of their 1830s type and style. 1231 was built as a single dwelling, according to the Robinson Atlas of 1883, thus accounting for the single entrance and three short, double-hung windows. 1225–27 Marais appears to have always been a double creole cottage. It has lost its double dormers at the front elevation. Both houses were originally of plaster over bricks. 1225–27 has an original *abat-vent* under which an overhang with rafter ends has been attached. The brick cornice with moldings and dentils can still be seen under the rafters. In spite of exterior alterations that have been applied to 1231, it has survived in a manner in keeping with its building date. The property had been part of the small François B. Languille *habitation* on the right side of Bayou Road. Languille sold the *habitation* to Widow Jean Louis Isnard in 1816. She married J. B. Plauché, and the property became part of the Jean Baptiste Balthazar Plauché holdings. The then Madame Plauché sold these lots at an auction on December 1, 1828, along with others subdivided by Louis Pilié. Térence Cousin bought the site of 1231, and François bought the property at 1225. The act before O. de Armas, December 9, 1828, refers to the "newly opened" Plauché Street (later Marais). The houses that they then constructed detered the extension of Barracks Street so that it dead-ends here and recommences at N. Prieur Street. François Cousin sold 1225 Marais to Felicité Brulé, f.w.c., widow of George Deslond, for $3,400 before A. Ducatel on June 21, 1843. She made $700 selling the house to Louis F. Drouet the following year. In 1855 Josephine Toledano, Widow Drouet, gave the house along with 1126 Marais to her grauddaughter as part of her dowry in the marriage contract between Louisa Bourgeois and Thomas Taquino. It was valued at $4,400 when acquired by Constant Cambas at a sheriff's sale on July 23, 1873 (6DC#4,649). Cambas may have removed the original dormer, adding the early-twentieth-century version seen now. Térence Cousin sold 1231 Marais to Adolphe Dupré on May 6, 1843, before Pierre Lacoste, the act describing the land with "the buildings on said lot of ground . . . erected by the said Térence Cousin." Dupré kept the house until 1871, selling it for $5,300 to Charles Andry (E. Grima, March 23).

1239–41

Plauché Property. 1239–41. Another double creole cottage with semi-incorporated overhang sits on land that was part of the Isnard-Plauché *habitation*. The simple cottage without dormers at **1239–41** dates from the 1840s. Present façade decorations, including surrounds with bull's-eye motifs and narrow weatherboards, were added to the earlier cottage, as were the more recent cement steps. The modern, two-level, brick apartment house adjacent at 1235 Marais destroys the street symmetry and nineteenth-century scale. When these twentieth-century architectural interruptions thoughtlessly appear, they spell doom and degradation to authentic, desirable, urban neighborhoods even though they may temporarily raise the surrounding property values and appraisals.

1438–40, 1436

Mager Property. The early history of this land extends from an 1801 sale by Claude Tremé to Pierre Barran. Jean Mager subsequently acquired the property comprising the block; it remained undeveloped at his death. His sister and heir, Agathe Mager Collard, sold the area, and it was subdivided in the 1840s. At **1436** Marais is a five-bay, center-hall, frame cottage with gabled sides and built-in overhang. A wide central entrance with recessed door leads to a hall with two rooms on each side. The entrance steps, which are not original, and the present porch piers spoil the effect of this late-

Classic-style house, dating from perhaps the late 1860s. The similarity of building types and styles among 1476 Marais, the Maspereau house, and this house at 1436 would indicate that the brackets and verge at 1436 were added. Next door at **1438–40**, a four-bay, frame, double house with four, full-length segmental-arched openings, hip-roof, and bracketed overhang postdates 1883. Note the herringbone-patterned sidewalk. The corner location makes possible a convenient, third apartment entrance along Kerlerec Street.

1425–27

Fortin House. The Jean-Baptiste Plauché *habitation*, although very narrow as it fronted the right side of Bayou Road, had fields that stretched from the 1200 to the 1500 blocks of Marais, incorporating also the land that is presently Esplanade Avenue. Many handsome houses such as 1425–27 Marais replaced Mme Plauché's gardens. This four-bay, galleried, frame house is a late-Classic-style double shotgun. The façade rustication and four full-length openings have simple Classic surrounds. The deep box cornice has dentil molding and a tripartite parapet above the nonoriginal gallery supports. The porch has been covered with concrete, and central steps now cut through the foundation course. The chain wall should be restored and five box columns set beneath the architrave. Stylistic analysis suggests the house could date from the 1860s or the 1870s. It is a pretentious example of the galleried shotgun style. Robinson's Atlas of 1883 indicates a similar house once stood adjacent downriver. Mme Charles Fortin, who owned this property from 1860 until 1885 along with her residence at 1439 Marais, probably built the house. She also had the double houses at 1425–27 and 1429–31 built as rental units.

1439

Fortin Residence. This handsome, galleried, Italianate residence was built for Mme Charles Fortin during her twenty-five-year ownership between 1860 and 1885. An earlier creole cottage was sold by the city to F. Romagosa in 1858, its right side yard having been used for the opening of Kerlerec Street. That building is seen in plan book 48, folio 69 and had been owned by Adolphe Charbonnet as rental property until the city purchased it for the Kerlerec extension. Mme Fortin paid Dr. Martin Moll $2500 on August 14, 1860, before notary Grima for the earlier cottage situated on this part of the old Plauché *habitation*. Her new home, the present 1439 Marais, may have incorporated portions of the old cottage. The house is quite large, its gabled side containing an attic above the dormered level. The Greek Key entrance with oval sidelights and transom, as well as the paired cornice brackets and parapet on the entablature suggest an 1860s building date. The decorative parapets atop the dormers were added. The five-bay arrangement with wide entrance to one side of the front elevation is relatively unusual; in most such cases the fifth opening is an addition to an earlier creole cottage. The house is brick up to the point of the gabled ends, which are weatherboarded. There are central chimneys front and rear and one side chimney. Widow Fortin lived in the house until her death in 1883, and in 1885 an inventory of her holdings valued the house at $6,500. She also owned five other lots in the area (August 11, 1885, O. Villere). Her heirs, E. and G. Fortin, sold the house soon after the inventory to Widow Martial LeBoeuf for $5,500.

1466–68, 1476

Trosclair and Maspereau Houses. In this second 1400 block at **1466–68** is a five-bay cottage with a Classic-style side entrance leading to a recessed door with fanlights, behind which is a small entrance hall backed by a recessed side gallery. The Classic-style entrance here would indicate that the brackets of the overhang and the sawed-work cornice cresting on the full-length windows were added after the house was built. The single house, now used as a double, dates from the 1860s, as do most five-bay houses with entrances to one side of the façade. Lucien Trosclair purchased this and several other lots in 1860 for $1200 from Seraphim Maspereau, who later built neighboring 1476 Marais. Trosclair sold the 65-by-102-foot property to L. Baguie, an accountant, for $7,000 before notary E. G. Gottschalk on August 27, 1867. This sale included the extant house on 50 feet of the 65-foot parcel. Leopold Baguie owned and lived in the house from 1867 until 1872. In 1872 it was sold, after an intervening sale, to Widow Charles Courcelle, who lived there until 1876. Two nonresidents, Widow Adolphe Reggio and Hortaire Reggio of St. Bernard Parish, owned the property from 1876 until 1891. Seraphim Maspereau, the builder of 1317–19 Columbus and an owner of 1321 Columbus, built **1476** Marais, a dormered villa in the Classic-style, late in 1860. At his death in 1878, the tinsmith owned a dozen lots in the immediate neighborhood. He resided at a variety of addresses: on Esplanade in the 1850s, St. Claude in the 1860s, and in this cottage at 1476 Marais in the 1870s. Maspereau had acquired the "unimproved" property in 1860 from the estate of Madame Agathe Collard, Jean Mager's sister. An 1838 archival drawing of 26 lots (plan book 91, folio 29) shows Mager's extensive holdings in the area between Plauché (Marais) and St. Claude, Ste Julie (Esplanade), and St. Bernard. He owned all but two lots. Kerlerec and Columbus

MARAIS

Street did not extend past St. Claude at that time. Stephen Escoffier acquired this house for his home from Maspereau's estate in 1878. There, he and his family remained until 1917. 1476 Marais has been maintained as an owner's residence throughout the years, and the selling price reflects excellent maintenance.

1501–03

Maspereau House. Title research on 1321 Columbus, in the same square as 1501–03 Marais, shows that this lot was included in Seraphim Maspereau's holdings in 1856. There is a strong indication that this cottage was built as an investment by him in the 1850s or 1860s. However, an earlier construction date is suggested by the original arched openings in the dormers, the row of four 3-quarter-length side openings, the gracefully canted roof, and the handsome, detached one-story kitchen. Note the pair of shuttered full-length openings on the gabled side with panels below and louvers above. The Greek Key surround on the far-right entrance suggests that this house may have had other Greek Revival details on the interior. Stephen Escoffier owned the house by April 27, 1881, when, before James Fahey, he sold it to W. A. Bienvenu for $2,200. Bienvenu sold the house to Pierre Barthe in 1882, and the house was included in Barthe's succession (CDC number 3, 157, December 8, 1890). The lot is situated at the intersection of the Claude Tremé and Bernard Marigny holdings. Marigny owned the frontage along St. Bernard extending back almost to Columbus, where his property line met that of Claude Tremé.

N. MIRO

315–25

Samuel Moore Claim. An unusual and attractive row of three, common-wall, dogtrot creole cottages are features of this block. Though built with common roofs, each has decorative details of different styles. **315–17** has segmental-arched doors and original ovoid-light panel doors. **319–21** has Greek Key surrounds, and **323–25** has Classic-style details.

823

Dorgenois Property. The gabled ends, fine proportions, and unusual, scalloped vergeboard are indications of the early date of this once handsome, raised, galleried house with a center hall. Unfortunate façade mutilations have obscured its character. The house sits on part of the Dorgenois land, which Lebreton Dorgenois left to his children after his death in 1819. The house could date from any time after 1840.

927

Dorgenois Division. This five-bay, frame, late-Victorian-period, American cottage is a late version of the center-hall house plan with 1890s detailing. The front gable with apron serves as a bracketed overhang and is typical of most shotgun houses, both with or without hall plan. While three-bay and four-bay late-Victorian houses abound in New Orleans, five-bay houses remain rare. Several have been noted in the area between Canal and St. Bernard. Some are single-family, center-hall houses; others are double houses comprised of a three-bay, side-hall apartment on one side and a smaller two-bay shotgun on the other.

1120

Macarty Property. This early, two-bay, galleried shotgun in the Classic style has a high hip-roof and side overhang that suggest an 1850s building date. It was among the many holdings of Drausin Macarty, f.m.c., and his wife, Louise Courcelle. The Macarty family lost the house after a lawsuit was brought against Louise Macarty by Jean Alvarez Latorre in 1879. Then, William Williams acquired the house for just $470. The Williams family retained ownership until 1958. The building could have been built by Macarty or earlier owners, free colored *entrepreneurs* Julien Colvis and Joseph Dumas (COB 109/917). The land emanated from the Dorgenois estate, via Antonio Mendez.

Dorville Complex. Alterations to the façade openings have obscured the character and spoiled the classicism of this galleried, center-hall cottage. Title research and the gallery incorporating the side-gabled roof indicate a mid-nineteenth-century building date. This tract of land belonged to Alexander Milne at the time of his death in 1838 and was subdivided by executors of his estate in the 1840s. Money from this sale was to be used for the support of Milne's philanthropies, according to his will. Joseph Soniat-Dufossat sold the vacant lot to J. B. Auvignac

1117

N. MIRO

Dorville in 1855 for $400. Dorville built a house facing Governor Nicholls, and in 1866 sold it for $3,300 to Louise Pauline Gondran. The original lot size was 135 feet of front by 234 feet. This house, facing N. Miro, was the back portion of the Governor Nicholls complex. The lots designated as A and B continued to be sold with description oriented toward Governor Nicholls until after 1876. The Robinson Atlas of 1883 showed single ownership of the block along N. Miro with a house set back on the lot deeper than it appears today. This may indicate that the house was moved forward and may possibly explain the gallery alterations and the lengthening of the box columns.

1300

Caboche Cottage. This turn-of-the-century, frame cottage with gallery and a large bay forming part of the façade has a suburban flavor. Plain Doric columns supporting an undecorated cornice and traditional weatherboarding lend a dignified aspect to the home. The simple decoration includes the gabled front with shingled surface, pierced-work cornice, and turned wooden balusters of the porch railing. The cottage sits on a large corner lot with an iron fence from Hinderer's Iron Fence Works. Clusters of large camphor trees, crepe myrtles, cedars, oleanders, boxwood, banana trees, and native vines are planted in the garden. A. D. Doriocourt acquired the property via the Milne estate in the 1840s. His heirs kept four lots along N. Miro until 1866, selling them to Pierre Gerard on August 29 (A. Doriocourt). Emile Caboche, who bought 51 feet on N. Miro by 100 feet along Barracks from his relative Félicie Caboche, widow of Pierre Nouvet, in 1905 for $800, probably built the present 1300 N. Miro.

1301–03

Milne Estate. A three-bay, two-level, frame house with cast-iron balcony has a side hall with a recessed entrance. The segmental-arched doorway is in the Italianate tradition, yet the cap-molded lintels are Classic in style. The drop-siding and quoins suggest the 1880s, although the lintels, entrance, and cast-iron balcony were utilized throughout the 1860s. Thus, the house has details from several periods. The building did not appear on the Robinson Atlas of 1883, and title research indicates that it could have been built in 1894 for Emile Vergnes, who sold it three years later to F. J. Garcia for $2,100. The land was part of the Milne estate in the 1840s. Joseph Chalon, a prominent lawyer and landowner behind the city, was the plaintiff in a lawsuit against Joseph Hoey in 1851 in which Rosalie Euphémie Seveignes acquired this lot and the adjoining one at a sheriff's sale on July 23, 1851. She sold both lots on April 12, 1853, before the notary A. Doriocourt, to André Burtin.

1422–24, 1426–28

Chambers Houses. These two houses occupy the back portion of land that was once included in 2139 Esplanade Avenue. The property, in 1822, was owned by Paul Cheval, f.m.c. On his 1834 map, Zimpel attributed the *habitation* to Pierre Darby, f.m.c. The farm fronted on Bayou Road and ran on a line in a downriver direction almost to Columbus Street. When Esplanade reached this point in the 1850s, the *habitation* was subdivided. Soon after, 2139 Esplanade was built for William Chambers. It is possible that the 1920s owner, Jovite Cau, subdivided again, and these present two houses were constructed, thereby demolishing what appeared on an 1883 map as a creole cottage set on the banquette. The twin houses at **1422** and **1426** N. Miro enjoy the stylistic characteristics of early-twentieth-century, two-level doubles, which are found throughout the New Orleans and Carrollton areas. These two examples are well maintained and have shallow, front gardens behind neat iron fences.

1454

Roy House (1439–41) 1454. A dormered, four-bay, creole cottage with gabled sides was built at **1439–41** on the Pierre Darby *habitation*. Modern additions of aluminum window louvers and the broken quarry tiles covering the porch are inappropriate. In 1862 Dominique Dumaine sold the present lot to Pierre Roy, a builder. In partnership with Henry Menage, Roy built this house, which was sold by his heirs after thirty years of ownership, along with three other lots, to Henry Turner. A corner creole cottage is marked on the 1883 Robinson Atlas and is situated back from N. Miro in this square. An 1892 auction notice recorded by J. Divigneaud on February 3 described it as "a neat, double, frame cottage, one story and attic, containing on each side five rooms, rear hall, cistern, shed, privy, etc." In the second 1400 block, **1454**, a late-Victorian shotgun, has a gallery supported by turned millwork and decorated with quoins, drop-siding, and window hoods. It is a charming example of its type. The millwork was probably ordered from one of several millwork factories that produced ready-to-order building materials. The land on which this double shotgun stands was once the small farm of M. Zardais, whose property was one-half *arpent* facing Bayou Road extending a few feet from the Columbus Street corner.

1458

Philippe House. François C. Philippe built this six-bay, galleried, front-gabled house as rental property, owning it from 1884 until 1926. He had bought the vacant lot along with four others from Robert Madison Flautt. The posts on brick piers and casement windows are alterations of the original construction, perhaps made when Philippe's daughter inherited the property in 1926. The two 1400 blocks of N. Miro on both sides of the street were part of the eighteenth-century Hubert concession. Then in the nineteenth-century, they were the property of Pierre Darby and M. Zardais, both f.m.c.

1486

Bourquin Villa. Double entrance doors with etched-glass panels lead to the central hall of this gable-sided, villa-type cottage with its Classic-style detailing. A segmental arch over the transom is crowned by a dentiled cornice. Behind the deep gallery supported by box columns is a façade of narrow, nonoriginal weatherboards. A flushboard or rusticated façade would be more appropriate. The house may have been built soon after 1860, when the city and M. Ponchélu sold nine lots to Edouard Bourquin. One year later, Bourquin sold his nine lots with this house to William Faivre, f.m.c., for a price of $4,500 (March 4, 1861, T. J. Beck). Hélène Ida Jarreau sold the property to Mary Suzannah Walker in 1865 for only $300 less, indicating that this real estate substantially retained its value after the Civil War. The corner was the tip edge of the Castanedo *habitation*.

1467

Bachelier House. This raised frame house has a large, Second Empire dormer and Eastlake-style millwork. The six-bay house with a recessed and arched entrance includes a mixture of projecting gables, dormers, bays, and chimneys. The lot on which it is situated once faced Columbus Street and was developed while still a part of the Tala *habitation*, according to Zimpel's map of 1834. An auction notice attached to an act by A. Dreyfous, September 27, 1865, read: "Succession Tranquile Bachelier to Joseph Le Blanc: Together with the buildings no. 268 on Columbus and improvements thereon, consisting of two, small frame houses, built in the interior of the said ground, and having each two rooms, front and back galleries, closet, cistern, well, privy, stable oven, chicken house, a large fruit, flower, and vegetable garden, $1,600." Sometime between 1865 and 1883, this present house was built facing N. Miro, probably by Adèle L. Galieque, Widow Tranquille Bachelier.

1562–64

Faubourg Castanedo. In the Robinson Atlas of 1883, there was a large house of this configuration standing on the river corner of Columbus, facing N. Miro. This house may have been moved to its present location and raised on high piers, providing a raised basement. The six-bay, frame house has a high, front-gabled roof with shingles and a scalloped verge, apron, sunburst-patterned brackets, and turned bosses. Two, open side galleries lend evidence to an 1880s dating, as do the façade details of drop-siding, quoins, and segmental surrounds on the full-length windows. This entire section of Faubourg Castanedo was developed in the late 1800s.

1555

Faubourg Castanedo. Situated on a large lot, this frame house with its two-level gallery has undergone massive remodeling. Once, it had three bays; now it has two. A portion of a cornice seen at the end of the roof was perhaps across the façade. A Greek Key entrance and beveled-glass doors are interesting amalgams of early and late architectural details. The gallery is supported by paneled box columns, and the second-level railing is of cast-iron. Since the entire square was essentially undeveloped in 1883, this house postdates that period, unless it is a rebuilding of a back building to a larger house that faced Laharpe.

2129

2221

2536–38, 2540

2100, 2200, 2500 Blocks. This house at **2129** Onzaga was built in the 1890s on a square that contained "a cow stable, a house of 2 rooms with gallery and 2 closets, cisterns, and wells." The property was in the succession of Julien Maury, November 12, 1866 (E. Gueno) and was sold to Thomas Saix for $3,770. The square was a part of the old Gueno plantation and *briqueterie*, which Pierre Gueno had bought in 1803 from Suzanna Caüe, Widow Peyroux. From 1890 the house changed owners almost every two years until the 1940s. The two-bay, frame construction, shotgun house with front-gabled roof and apron has segmental arches over the openings with cap-molded lintels and pierced-work cresting. These features, along with the brackets supporting the overhang, the drop-siding, and quoins, all reinforce the 1890s date for this house. The updated, two-bay, frame shotgun at **2217** may have been built soon after 1875. That year Catherine Antoine bought this lot from Eugène Lefevre; in 1890, she sold it with the house for $350. The price reflected the modest character of houses in the Faubourg Gueno. Late in the nineteenth century, **2221** Onzaga was built in a similar style—two-bay, frame construction with a hip-roof. The St. Boniface Convent was directly across Onzaga and used an entire square. Shotgun cottages at **2536–38** and **2540–42** were built of frame construction with hip-roofs, dormers, drop-siding, and quoins, indicating a turn-of-the-century date. Also typical of the late-Victorian period are cap-molded lintels with scalloped borders and scroll-shaped brackets supporting the overhang of the roof. The plan of the six-bay, hip-roof, double at **2544–46** Onzaga is, in effect, two, single shotguns with a common wall. This is an unusual example of the six-bay shotgun since most have gable-fronted roofs. The cap-molded lintels are topped by simple pediments; the original doors have applied, carved panels. The house was built soon after 1906 on the rear of a large portion of ground on which the Duncan Kennedy, Jr., master-house once stood, at the corner of N. Broad and Onzaga.

ORLEANS

1821

French Hospital. The property on which the French Hospital (Peter Claver Hall) stands was subdivided in 1832 by the Griffon heirs (Jean Marie Griffon, Mlle Marie Thomas Suzanne Griffon, and Mlle Marie Françoise Odile Griffon). A plan made at the time shows the Griffon house on Bayou Road but no buildings on this square (J. Pilié, March 15, 1832, plan book 55, folio 1). Oliver Blineau acquired the entire square bound by Orleans, N. Roman, N. Derbigny, and St. Ann in two separate purchases, one from the Griffon heirs and one from the Corporation of the City on the same date (May 14, 1832, L. T. Caire). Blineau held the entire property until 1859, when he donated a lot running through its center to La Société Française de Bienfaisance et d'Assistance Mutuelle de la Nouvelle Orléans. This lot had frontage of 124 feet on both St. Ann and Orleans streets. Blineau was the president of the group at this time, and his donation was "to give witness to the price that he attached to its success and future prosperity." The Société was organized in 1839 and incorporated in 1843 as "a society for fraternal, benevolent, and charitable purposes." Its first hospital had been established in 1844 on Bayou Road near N. Robertson in a central-hall, gable-sided, double-galleried house. The French Society had purchased the land for $300, and a French visitor to New Orleans contributed 30,000 bricks to build the early infirmary known as the Asile de la Société Française. Preserved in the acts of O. Drouet, June 15, 1860, is a building contract between "Joseph Jouet, *entrepreneur*, and Oliver Blineau, president of the French Society for construction of a new asylum, a brick building of multiple stories, roofed with slates for $29,500." Nine pages of specifications are attached to the act. Another contract, never fulfilled, was recorded by the same notary on March 29, 1860, between Alexander Sampson, Jacques Pustiene (*entrepreneur*), and Oliver Blineau to build a new asylum for $24,850. Two years later Blineau donated two additional lots, one on each side, to the Société (O. Drouet, May 3, 1861). Each lot fronted 25 feet on Orleans Street and 25 feet on St. Ann and was bound by the asylum on one side and by more property of Oliver Blineau on the other. Each lot contained dependencies, and each was valued at $2,000. The Société's property now fronted 174 feet on Orleans and St. Ann. In 1881 the Société acquired the rest of the block in four separate acts from four separate owners. According to the Robinson Atlas of 1883, the building was a modified *T*-shape facing St. Ann Street, but early in the twentieth century an annex was built, making the building resemble an *H*. Construction began in 1914; in 1917 the address was changed from St. Ann to Orleans, and the entrance placed on Orleans Street. The three-story earlier building is a late example of the Greek Revival style of architecture. Two-story-high pilasters above and a central projecting block below articulate the façade into three segments. Rustication and arched openings at the ground level and small dormers above the entablature

ORLEANS

recall the French tradition in New Orleans architecture. The roof is encircled by a parapet interrupted by a low pediment above the original St. Ann Street entrance. The two-story, twentieth-century addition continues the original architectural style. The French Benevolent and Mutual Aid Association of New Orleans, referred to commonly as the French Asylum, operated a hospital here until 1949. In 1951 at a meeting conducted in French, the association decided to sell the block, which measured 297½ feet on Orleans and St. Ann by 149 feet, for $82,500. The purchasers of the French Asylum were the Knights of Peter Claver (A. P. Tureaud, April 21, 1951), who used the buildings as their national headquarters. The Knights of Peter Claver is a Catholic fraternal organization for blacks, "a society for fraternal, benevolent and charitable purposes," having 116 councils and 10,000 members in sixteen states. The future of this historic landmark is presently uncertain. The organization has abandoned the building for a modern structure at 1825 Orleans adjacent to the old building.

2501

2000, 2100, 2400, 2500, 2600 Blocks. What is now Orleans Street was in 1820 a waterway called the Girod Canal. The banks of the canal had a variety of brick and frame creole cottages and early, two-bay shotguns. Some examples of the latter remain in rows in the 2000 block at **2007–09**, **2011**, and **2013**. A cluster of nineteenth-century frame, rental units exists in the 2100 block. At **2131** is a two-bay shotgun with hip-roof; **2133** is a contrasting two-bay, gable-sided creole cottage; at the corner of Galvez stands an early store-house. The **2400** block illustrates the pattern of two-bay frame shotguns with seven remaining; there are also three in the 2500 block at **2509**, **2513**, and **2515**. At **2501**, a frame, four-bay, hip-roof, two-room, corner cottage represents a strange New Orleans house-type. It continues the creole traditions but adds a lowered hip-roof attachment containing one or two rooms to its rear. Of very modest detail, these houses were most often doubles, with the doors placed on the outer edge and the windows in the middle of the façade. This building probably dates from the 1860s; here windows have been shortened. The 2600 block of Orleans preserves its nineteenth-century appearance more than others of that street. At **2600–02** is a mid-nineteenth-century, corner creole cottage of four rooms with a beak-roof, and at **2626–28** is a smaller version, just one-room deep. Continuing on the downtown side, at **2633–35** and **2637–39** are two more of similar type and date. Contrasting at **2623** is a very small, two-bay shotgun, a lone remnant of a once-common house-type.

N. PRIEUR

927

Pontalba Division. This mid-nineteenth-century example of the two-story creole house at **927–29** N. Prieur was designed just one room deep on the interior, but with deep front and rear galleries (originally) on the exterior. The house has four bays and is gable-sided.

1021–23

Pontalba Division. 1019, 1021–23. This area has a number of three-bay, late-Victorian cottages with ells and galleries. **1021–23** N. Prieur, a frame cottage, has turned columns resting on new brick bases. The house has retained the façade features of segmental-arched openings with pierced-work window hoods and a shingled pediment bordered with a fleur-de-lis verge, popular features of the 1880–1890 period. The original fence erected by Hinderer's Iron Fence Works still stands on the lot. At **1019** N. Prieur, the earlier, three-bay, frame cottage with Classical detailing has a hip-roof, gallery, and a hexagonal bay to the rear. The box columns have been altered at the base by the addition of brick piers, which along with porch alterations have marred the front elevation. Architectural features of note are the flush-framed siding on the façade, the cast-iron railing on the gallery, and the original cast-iron fence. Plantings of mature sweet olive trees increase the charm of this cottage.

1133

Pontalba Division. The pair of once-identical, frame, double shotguns at **1121–23** and **1125–27** N. Prieur have hip-roofs, segmental-arched openings, and applied brackets supporting the roof overhang. They date from the late-Victorian period. Unfortunate alterations to 1121–23 have spoiled the character of this house. A turn-of-the-century, five-bay cottage with center hall, **1133** N. Prieur has a shingled front gable with a deep apron overhang. The house is located in the former Pontalba division, and could be vastly improved by replacing its wooden porch landing and low turned baluster railing.

N. PRIEUR

1224–26

Brugier Cottage. This dormered creole cottage has a masonry front with gabled ends of frame construction. The doors have been lowered, altering the original façade balance; lintels and sills of the windows, as well as the dormer millwork, retain their Classic decoration. In 1843 this lot in the Duchamp estate was part of another parcel of land fronting N. Prieur Street, in which the syndic of the creditors of Camille Suppo de Valetti sold 60 feet on Barracks by 120 feet on Prieur to Antoinette Chotard, wife of Philippe Brugier, for $250 (December 28, 1843, F. Percy). The Brugier family built this house, and it remained in the family until after 1880. Then on September 22, Emile Angaud, a family connection, sold the house to Marie Josephine Lotz, wife of Philippe Brugier, in an estate sale for $396, according to the act recorded by notary O. Villere.

1228–30

Duchamp Division. This raised creole cottage with double dormers has a façade with five bays. The narrow central entrance, with a Greek Key surround, was probably the alley or dogtrot between the two sides. The undecorated doors and small dormers are traditional, early creole building features. The chimney's location at the roof ridge is unusual. The present overhang brackets and steps postdate this 1840s type; the latter replace two sets of box steps. This cottage was standing on land that once had been part of the Duchamp plantation when Eugène Mioton bought the house after a sheriff's sale to settle a lawsuit between P. T. Commagère and Jean Montane. The house, which had been advertised in local papers on December 5, 1865, sold for $1,825. Mioton immediately resold the property to Odile Bazanac, Widow Théophile Perrault. A subsequent owner, Jean Baptiste Henry, left it to the Little Sisters of the Poor, who then sold it in 1889 for $500 to Marie Descans, Widow Pierre Duplaa.

1434

1420, 1422, 1434, 1438, 1442. This group of five shotgun houses was once intact and identical—Classic-style, three-bay, frame houses with galleries across the front. The façade details of each included an entrance with dentiled cornice, full-length windows with cap-molded lintels topped by pediments, and a box cornice with dentiled molding. The gallery roof was supported by four, square columns on each house; **1420** now has the closest version to the original box columns. The floor plan was three rooms deep with an unattached service building to the rear. On the interior may be found typical 1850 features, such as double parlors divided by sliding doors with Greek Key surrounds and mantels decorated with pilasters. The houses have been remodeled, thus losing their character of repetitious symmetry. **1442** N. Prieur complements the Classical detailing so evident on the block. It was built in the 1850s as a traditional, creole, corner store-house with hip-roof and a gable in the rear. Louis Bringier bought the land in the 1400 block of N. Prieur, square 987, in 1836 from Widow Castanedo (T. Seghers; September 8, act missing). Bringier built five houses on these lots, probably between 1850 and 1860. He held them until 1866, when they were sold at a sheriff's sale to settle a lawsuit with the Citizens Bank (number 18078, recorded in book 3, folio 370, Sixth District Court). Louis Colomb purchased them and sold them to Benjamin Tureaud on June 20, 1868 (B. Trist). In 1868 Tureaud sold the houses to H. C. Millaudon, who in turn sold them in 1875 to Louise Eysalenne, Widow François Pierre Duconge.

1419–21

Wogan House (1425), 1419–21. Pictured is a frame, double creole cottage with four bays. The kitchen was originally the one-story, frame building across the rear of the lot. The façade was designed with French doors and cap-molded lintels of the 1840 period; later additions of millwork brackets were placed beneath the canted roof overhang. **1425** N. Prieur was once a handsome, two-story frame building, a fine example of the five-bay, two-story house with side gables, and a central-hall plan. The façade has been obscured by the addition of a stuccoed gallery, but the rear elevation has retained the original box columns, thus indicating the former Classic appearance of the front. This is one of the outstanding historic houses in the Tremé area, and it merits restoration. The land on which it stands was originally the part of the Castanedo estate sold to Louis Bringier in the 1830s. The estate of Michel Doradou Bringier, having acquired twelve lots, sold the property in 1868 to Mlle M. S. Walker. Stylistic analysis indicates that the house was standing at that time. On November 16, 1870, Charles Nicholas Wogan purchased it from his relative Léonce Nicholas Olivier, an interim owner. Three generations of the Wogan family lived here well into the twentieth century. Marie Adeline Augustin, widow of Charles N. Wogan, inherited the house in 1919. Her son Charles N. Wogan, Jr., a sugar broker, lived here with his family, which included Daniel S. Wogan and Caroline Wogan Durieux, a renowned painter and printmaker. At that time 1425 N. Prieur was an elegant house without the superimposed façade.

1439–41

1400 Block. These properties were an 1834 Louis Bringier acquisition from Widow Castanedo. Bringier did not develop them before his death, and his heirs sold the lots separately at auction on July 10, 1869. On October 11, 1869, before notary W. J. Castell, the lot at **1439–41** sold to L. N. Olivier, who built the present, double shotgun in the Classic style and immediately sold it to L. B. Breton on July 23, 1870, for $3,500. It is very similar in style to the four cottages across the street at numbers **1420**, **1422**, **1434**, and **1438**. Features worth noting include a deep box cornice with dentil molding and frieze, window and door hoods with cap molding and dentils, and entrances flanked by pilasters. **1435–37** is a creole cottage similar to its neighbor at **1439–41**, and, like that house, quite retardate in style since it dates after 1869. Although it has recently been given a twentieth-century façade, **1433** was built in the creole cottage style of the 1840s or 1850s; it has a gallery across the front and is set back from the street.

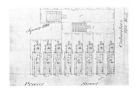

1443–1477

Second 1400 Block. An 1879 surveyor's report (May 17, O. Morel) showed that **1477** N. Prieur was one of a row of eight identical, frame, shotgun houses with open side galleries and attached kitchens. The survey was made for a sale of this house and others in the second 1400 block by the owner, Jules LeBlanc of Cienfuegos, Cuba. Alcide LeBlanc, brother of Jules, had obtained fifteen undeveloped lots of the Duchamp plantation at an 1857 sheriff's sale on July 15 as a result of a suit between Widow J. F. H. de St. Gême and Joseph Bruneau (5th District Court, #11,736 or COB 75/221). Alcide LeBlanc probably built the row of houses, since he sold the fifteen lots in this square to his brother Jules in 1862 for $24,000. Jules LeBlanc sold the house at 1477 in 1882 to Augustin Gambois for $1,150.

1505–07

Bruneau Cottage. The Duchamp succession sold this lot along with seven others, "together with circumstances and dependencies," to R. Rousseau on May 26, 1841, as recorded by the notary Lucien Hermann. The properties constituted the entire square bound by N. Prieur, Columbus, Laharpe, and N. Johnson. Rousseau, a lawyer who lived at 71 Bayou Road, sold the same seven lots to Joseph Bruneau on November 12, 1847, according to the act recorded by Félix Percy, notary. Joseph Bruneau owned and built a large number of houses in this area, but he made 1505–07 his *maison de maître* soon after 1847. Bruneau, a feed-store owner and drayman, lived on Prieur near Esplanade from 1849 until 1852, according to city directory references. In 1861 he transferred the house and lots to his wife, and she in turn sold them along with the remaining lots to Louis Ducros in 1878. The property stayed intact until 1890 when Joseph Numa Charbonnet, who had bought the large tract in 1883, sold small parcels of the land, like this lot at 1505–07, to J. P. Kearney, as recorded by notary C. Andry on July 28, 1890. This frame *maison de maître* was built with dormers, round-headed lights, and intersecting muntins. The gallery is supported by traditional box columns, and the openings on the façade are framed by familiar, cap-molded hoods. The original French doors and transoms with muntins, arranged in an early pattern, add distinction to the façade, but the later addition of drop-siding and cement steps has altered its original appearance.

1568

Beaulieu Cottage. This house retains its original batten shutters, French doors, strap hinges, slate roof, and gabled sides; the two doors and windows have flush opening surrounds and there is simplicity of detail. The creole cottage is rural in flavor, being set back deeply on its lot in the second 1500 block. James Mooney sold fourteen lots of the Castanedo estate in 1836 to Jean Donau. The block, according to the act before L. T. Caire on May 4, 1836, had been laid out by Louis Bringier on April 28, 1833. In 1848 Donau sold eight of these lots to Louis Marcos Tío, f.m.c. When Tío sold the property in 1854, the eight lots were partitioned;

and L. Beaulieu purchased one where 1568 N. Prieur now stands. The present house was probably built years before by Tío, for it represents the style prevalent in the 1840s. The first documented description of the house did not appear until 1864, when L. Beaulieu sold it to Mme Elizabeth Jourdain at an auction on November 9 (O. Drouet). The act described the cottage as being "a frame house, #29, of four rooms, double kitchen, well, cistern, fruit trees, etc." John Currau, who owned other houses in this area, purchased this one from Mme Jourdain in 1877 at a sheriff's sale. Currau's daughter, Marie Louise Chapotel, acquired it on December 10, 1890.

229, 231

Soulié Rowhouses. These two, important, three-story, masonry, Greek Revival-style rowhouses with cast-iron lintels and dentiled cornices are missing some of their balconies of cast- and wrought-iron; the first levels have been mutilated. Handsome, three-story service wings with wooden side galleries extend along Iberville and Bienville toward Basin. The houses are the remnants of a group of four rowhouses built around 1834 by Norbert Soulié, *bâtisseur* (builder). Soulié had acquired the land from the city on May 22, 1819 (M. de Armas). The city directories for 1834 and 1837 list Bernard Soulié, Norbert's relative and business associate, at 377 Rampart, the old address for one of the houses. In 1850 Bernard Soulié is identified as a free man of color who, like Norbert and Albin, lived in Paris and was an active real estate *entrepreneur* in Faubourg Tremé. In 1852 Soulié sold three of the houses: lot 4 at 231 N. Rampart to Mme George Fosdick; lot 3 at 229 N. Rampart to Henry Hopkins; and lot 2, now demolished, to Charles H. Daret. The buildings on lots 3 and 4 were bought as owner-residences; the other, as an investment. A similar row of houses at 1301–03–05 Governor Nicholls Street cost only $3,200 in comparison to $6,500 paid for those on N. Rampart. The Governor Nicholls Street row has retained its residential character, albeit shabbily, while the N. Rampart Street properties are now a defaced reminder of the street's former residential character. A building contract dated 1847 documents three other rowhouses in the block, built by Joshua Peebles for George A. Holt, with Morris Hurley to supervise construction. After being used primarily as owners' residences, the three houses were brought under the single ownership of Mrs. B. Salony on June 8, 1885 (Meunier). In 1892 the three lots with houses were evaluated at $25,000. As late as 1883, this entire block was lined with large rowhouses, with each corner the site of a side-bayed townhouse with gardens. 229 and 231 N. Rampart are important as the only remaining major rowhouses in the Commons segment of N. Rampart Street. The N. Basin Street elevation reveals the handsome three-story service wings attached to the rear of the houses.

Doebele Cottage (1009–11), 1015–17. The double, frame, Victorian camelback at **1009–11** has retained two original, oval-paneled doors with matching transoms and two double-hung windows with pediments. The overhang is supported by brackets and accented by cast-iron ventilators and a cornice marked by small brackets; the façade is further distinguished by drop-siding. A side gallery on the second level of the camelback is partially enclosed. An early creole cottage on the site was owned by the family of Adelaide Delhomme (de l'Homme) and Widow Arsène Delhomme, later Mme Fleurian de Bellemarré. In the April 10, 1860, succession of Widow Bellemarré, her daughter Cecile Fleurian de Bellemarré, wife of Flavious LeBesque, inherited the property (2DC#16,525). Mme LeBesque then sold it to Severin Doebele on February 24, 1876, for $1,725 (A. E. Bienvenu). Doebele either demolished or rebuilt the old house; his estate partitioned the property in 1899. Anna Marie Doebele, Mrs. M. Funk, acquired this house, selling it to Mrs. Charles E. Montardin on April 30, 1902 (C. J. Théard). At **1015–17** N. Rampart, the frame, Victorian, double shotgun with hip-roof has a distinguished façade of four French doors and brackets supporting a paneled overhang. Wooden lintels have an applied crest of a flattened, simplified, Greek Revival anthemion in the style of the 1880s.

1035, 1037

Berquier-Chiapella House. (1037). The land here on N. Rampart Street from the site of 1037 to the corner of Ursulines was part of a lot that the city sold to Pierre Paul Roffignol de Grammont in 1819, before M. de Armas. The property was established as a *maison principale* and complex by 1833, when the Antoine Abat estate was auctioned. Notary Carlisle Pollock's acts of February 8, 1833, describe, "une maison principale batié en briques couverte en tuiles une autre bâtisse contenant chambres domestiques, cuisine et chambre repassé, une office, cave, hangard, etc." valued at $10,300. The early complex was sold to David Oliver. In 1848 Mlle Eugènie Berquier purchased the subdivided site of 1037 N. Rampart Street (27 feet on N. Rampart by 90 feet) from owner M. Elliot. The act of sale mentioned "land and building for $1,900, land which Elliot had purchased from the sale of the property of Widow Pigneguy" (April 16, 1863, S. Magner). A year later, Mlle Berquier contracted with builder John Gastel to construct the extant three-bay creole cottage, which replaced an earlier house. The building contract before Achille Chiapella is dated August 25, 1849. The earlier house on the site, probably built by Antoine Abat, is shown partially in a drawing in plan book 40, folio 11, to the right of the illustration. The old kitchen was still standing in 1849, since the building contract provided that a story be added to the existing kitchen. The contract, recorded in French, is translated here: "Jean Gastel, *entrepreneur* for Mlle Eugènie Berquier; to build on a lot 27 feet Rampart between Ursulines and St. Philip by 90 feet, a house on dais of bricks, slated, lathed on exterior, plastered inside, façade of bricks and the rest, brick between posts to height of 3 feet only; to raise to two stories the kitchen which is presently existing on the lot; the second story similar to the first, finished in the same manner; to pave the yard with bricks . . . house to measure 45 feet by 21 feet; height of 12 feet; gables 12 feet high, three rooms downstairs with gallery on side of 6 feet wide by the whole length of house; end closed in manner of a *cabinet* in third room; a stairway to reach the *mansard* [attic]: room of 15 feet by 21 feet, height of 9½ feet, with wooden balcony 3 feet wide that runs the length of the room, three doors on the street, two of which are with balustrades turned or united; these openings 3½ feet wide by 9½ feet, with double frame inside; two interior doors and door in third room to go into yard; each room to have door giving into gallery; the room in rear to have casement windows onto yard; the *cabinet* will have door communicating with rear room and two windows onto the court-yard and one onto the yard; the room in *mansard* to have two doors onto balcony, with two dormer windows, one onto the street, and one onto the yard, proportioned to the size of the roof. Stairway of three steps and pilasters on the street and one also of three steps, but simple on yard. All wood to be cypress, floor raised 2½ feet from banquette; beams projecting on front 4 feet and on rear 1 foot to form *abat-vent.*, façade in lake bricks; two chimneys; one simple, one of two fires; all lathed and plastered in two coats; two ventilators of iron on façade; woodwork of fireplaces to be pilasters with cornice and plinth and mantelpiece returns in pretty taste. The doors on the walk framed, 2 inches thick; the other doors barred and 1¼ inches thick; the interior doors paneled; plinths of rooms and gallery 12 inches high with moldings; gallery held by three pilasters with moldings; yard between house and kitchen divided in two; fence with door inside and outside, three coats white paint; doors and windows exterior Paris green; mantel-pieces black and varnished; before each foyer a plaque of marble. Kitchen: raised one floor, re-covered in slate, rooms should be in same proportions with same openings as on first floor. Wooden balcony on second story across façade of kitchen; also stairway outside to lead to rooms above. Yard to be paved in bricks; also a dais in bricks to hold a tank. Building finished and keys delivered in 2½ months from this day; also, a laundry shed in the yard; to cost $1,700: $400 when house covered, floors down; $400 when house finished, kitchen raised, keys delivered; $500 fifteen days after delivery. If house not finished in time, Gastel to pay rent of $1 per day." Retaining full ownership of the house and grounds until 1863, Mlle Berquier sold it on April 16 of that year to notary Achille Chiapella (S. Magner). The act of sale stipulated that Mlle Berquier would have usufruct of the house. Chiapella lived at Morales and Goodchildren (Marais and St. Claude) in 1846, when he married Marie Louise Pollock, and later on Esplanade Avenue. Then on September 27, 1867, Chiapella sold this house back to Eugènie Berquier for $2,000 (S. Magner). The act of sale noted that Mlle Berquier could not write and would make her mark. Marie Louise Pollock, Chiapella's wife, witnessed the sale and gave up her own rights to the property.

40/11 (1035)

Pierre Roup House. An archival drawing executed by Pueyo and Cosnier for an auction (plan book 40, folio 11) illustrates the appearance of this cottage on April 3, 1845. The house was advertised in the local news-papers: "That good brick house situated in Rampart Street between Ursulines and St. Philip designated by No. 311, divided into four *appartements* with gallery in the rear, terrace roof, marble mantels, chimneys in parlors, a brick kitchen of four *appartements* roofed with shingles, with a large washing shed, and a privy, divided in two, well and yard paved with brick, etc. The house is insured to the 15th of May next. Said house is built on a lot measuring 32 feet front on Rampart Street by 128 feet, 9 inches in depth." This important house was probably built soon after 1816 and before 1823. Benoit Milbrouck sold the property to Pierre Roup on November 29, 1816 (M. de Armas). Roup sold the lot with a masonry-fronted house, as shown in the archival elevation, to Mark Lafitte on August 28, 1823. Lafitte sold the house to a well-to-do free woman of color, Fanchonette Robert, as investment property. She lived at 630 Royal. Mme Robert left this house at 1035 Rampart in equal parts to Armand Richard Clague, f.m.c., and to Mme Elizabeth Dawson. Clague, the half-brother of the well-known landscape painter, bought out Mme Dawson on February 13, 1860 (F. de Armas). He used the property as rental investment, since he lived with his family in the Lower Garden District. Upon his death in 1879, the house was sold to E. Hernandez (April 21, A. E. Bienvenu). The 1820s cottage has been altered through succeeding generations but retains one brick parapet gable, which is now covered with weatherboard.

1101–03

Dupaquier House. This handsome 2½-story, masonry, Italianate store-house is complimented by a service wing with gallery and detached stable. The gallery re-turning around the corner is supported by slender cast-iron colonettes with cresting at the second level. The deep, bracketed cornice above the attic frieze and the segmental-arched openings with masonry hoodmolds are Italianate hallmarks. The recessed entrance has paneled storm doors and black-and-white marble, combined with granite, steps. The interior retains some original moldings and plaster, with a ceiling medallion in the foyer. Wrought-iron gates

---

opening to the side yard are initialed "DB." The sidewalk is paved with fine, Belgian flagstone. This square was developed with four, set-back, rural-type creole cottage com-plexes according to a plan by Bourgerol dated 1840, annexed to act 175, October 27, 1840, by C. Foulon, notary. All of these have been demolished except one urban-style creole cottage at 1111–13 St. Claude, which may be an adaptation. The plan of the existing Italianate house is illustrated in a sketch by D'Hémécourt, May 30, 1879, an-nexed to act 140 of J. Cuvillier of that year, and was built then according to a building contract dated April 3, 1879 (MOB 176/138–40): "G. A. D'Hémécourt, architect, for laying roof for Dr. A. Dupaguier, north corner Rampart at Ursulines." D'Hémécourt was the architect and supervised construction, contracting out for roofers, coppersmith, sla-ter, plumbing (all recorded in MOB 176/138–141): "J. A. Branden, slater; J. H. Chapman, coppersmith, $460; Louis S. Paultier, glazer, $800; John McNally, contractor for wood-work, $4,200; M. H. Appligan, plumber, $748."

1111–13

Kitchen

Bourg Cottage. The frame creole cottage with four French doors at 1111–13 has been renovated several times since its construction between 1810 and 1828. Jean Marie Pierre Bourg bought the lot from the city, July 24, 1810 (M. de Armas), selling it with buildings and improvements for $2,200 to Jules Pucheu in 1828. In 1831 Mayor Denis Prieur bought the house from Pucheu for $3,700 and kept it until 1853. A. Dorio-court described the house in the 1853 Prieur sale to Benjamin William Hebrard for $6,000: "with house containing four rooms, two *cabinets*, glazed gallery; two-story brick kitchen with eight rooms, privy, shed, oven, waterworks, flower garden with two entries. . . . Three lines of omnibuses run in front of the property every ten minutes." Prieur is never listed at the house in the city directory. Beneath the present weather-boards, and despite several alterations during the Prieur ownership, the brick-between-posts construction, dat-ing between 1810 and 1828, probably remains. The larger, eight-room, brick, two-story kitchen may be glimpsed on the rear property line, detached beyond the garden. It retains brick parapets, original slate roof, and ridgepole. Casement openings have splayed brick lintels, and there is a gallery at both levels supported by narrow box columns with caps. The mention of waterworks in 1853 suggests the possibility of a garden fountain; there remains today evidence of a parterred garden. The modern brick apartment house at 1115, adjacent to this early complex, is intrusive in style and proportion. It replaces a set-back creole cottage. The street today is lined with granite curbing and brick herring-bone-patterned sidewalks.

1201–1209

Milbrouck-Degas-LeBlanc Properties. The Benoit Mil-brouck *maison de maître* stood amidst orange trees and parterred gardens on this block of N. Rampart. Milbrouck had acquired the property from Bertrand Casteres, "Captain in the American Navy," on Octo-ber 14, 1820 (Marc Lafitte). The Milbroucks lived here in their suburban home from 1820 until 1832. Widow Milbrouck, Louise Roulet, sold her garden area, 68 feet on Rampart by 46 feet on Bayou Road (Governor Nicholls), for $3,600 to J. B. Sauvinet, a well-known émigré and real estate speculator. The act stipulated "together with buildings," which were probably outbuildings of the Milbrouck complex (June 19, 1832, L. T. Caire). Mme Milbrouck, two years after her sale to Sauvinet, sold her home to Michel Musson. This investment-purchase was made to celebrate the birth of the later-famous artist, Edgar Degas. Michel Musson purchased the property for Laurent P. A. H. Degas, his banker-cousin who lived in Naples, in behalf of his newborn son, Hilaire Germain Edgar Degas. The property was bought "together with the house and other buildings found there" for $2,374 on December 23, 1834 (A. Ma-zureau). That early house, which had "two rooms and rear gallery with two *cabinets*, a brick outbuilding, etc," remained in the ownership of the artist until 1866, when Michel Musson, acting for "Hilaire Germain Edgar Degas of Paris," sold it to Jules LeBlanc for $2,130. Degas' signature is seen on this act of February 7, 1866 (A. Boudousquie). Soon after 1866 Jules LeBlanc included the Degas property in his redevelopment of the block. In 1866 LeBlanc also purchased the corner portion of the Milbrouck property, which Sauvinet had owned. LeBlanc is responsible for the construction of the fine masonry row in the late-Italianate style at **1201**, **1205**, and **1209** N. Rampart. He lived in Cienfuegos, Cuba, in 1879 when he sold the rowhouses separately. L. Fuget purchased **1205** N. Rampart on May 20, 1879 (O.Morel) for $4,900; and 1209, on the same day, sold to Edmond Dubois for $3,750. The two-story townhouses and store-house are distinguished by cast-iron pillars on the commercial segment, marble steps, two original cypress en-trances with segmental-arched panels, and one segment with fine, cast-iron galleries and balconies.

1225

Tharpe-Sontheimer-Laudaumiey Funeral Home. The funeral home at 1225 N. Rampart is a joining of two of the houses that Jules LeBlanc built in the block between 1871 and 1879; they remain beneath this City Beautiful-style adaptation of the original LeBlanc Italianate-style townhouses. A plan by J. A. D'Hémécourt dated April 1, 1867, and preserved in the acts of E. Eude, April 11, 1867, illustrates that on that date Blaise Pradel had a fine urban-style, 1½-story creole cottage replete with two-story detached "kitchen, bath house, chicken house, and cistern house." On this site, LeBlanc demolished the main house and was responsible for an entire block of Italianate town and row housing by 1879 between Bayou Road and Barracks.

N. ROBERTSON

820, 822, 824

Roach Cottages. These three Greek Revival creole cottages stand on lots that were part of a larger parcel of the City Commons on which Louis Dansac had built a *maison de maître* soon after 1833, when he bought a larger lot from his relative Armand Dansac for $400. Three years later in 1836, Dansac sold a house on a lot 55 feet on N. Robertson by 120 feet to Pierre Evariste Wiltz for $3,000 (May 3, F. de Armas). Wiltz sold the early house to Ann Cavanaugh Roach at auction, October 29, 1836, for $3,600. Either Mme Roach built the present houses after demolishing the earlier; or **824**, a four-bay, weatherboarded, creole cottage, may be the earlier house in the garden of which she built one or two, three-bay, creole cottages. Mme Roach remained in one of the houses where, "James Roach, paver, undertaker," was listed in 1846. She sold another in 1845 to Adrian Blanchard (December 1, 1845, E. Barnett). The two single cottages in the Greek Revival style retain evidence of their construction dates and are worthy of careful study. **820** N. Robertson has a Greek Key entrance with dentiled cornice, leading to a recessed door. The façade was originally rusticated. **822** has a canted, gabled roof, and the entrance leads to a side gallery. An iron balcony remains above the side gallery. The present front jigsaw brackets are not original.

823–25

Buisson Cottage. Marie Elizabeth Guillotte, wife separate in property from her husband, Frederick Buisson, sold this house to Widow Joseph Castanedo for rental use in 1842. When Widow Castanedo's estate sold the house to Auguste Dudoussat, on March 5, 1862, H. Pedesclaux preserved the auction notice: "A brick house with an attic, having four rooms, gallery, closet, and a pantry under the staircase leading to the attic which is divided into two large rooms on the ground floor and two above; another two-story frame building adjoining the above, equally divided into four rooms; paved yard, alleyways, two hydrants, shed, cistern, privy.... The above-described premises divided into two tenements and rented at $51 per month." It is a fine, double-dormered, masonry creole cottage with arched dormers, four French doors, and cornice with sawtooth and dentil molding; the round heads and small proportions of the dormers suggest a building date of the 1830s. A two-level service building is detached across the rear of the lot.

827–29

Cerresolles Cottage. A two-story, double-dormered, frame house has combined an old creole cottage with post–Civil War, Second Empire-style alterations. There is a narrow, two-story, detached, frame kitchen in the back. This house is an interesting example of alteration of the creole cottage type, enlarged and adapted to the style of the 1870s to 1890s. The creole cottage was on the lot in 1853, when M. Cerresolles, f.m.c., son of Eulalie Rouvant, f.w.c., sold it to Prosper Macarty, f.m.c., for $2,000 (June 13, 1853, A. Boudousquie). Macarty kept the house until 1870, when he sold it for $2,500 to Joseph Alcindor. In 1881 Alcindor sold it to Félix Fageret for $1,200. The Fageret family kept the house until after 1930, when it was valued at $3,000 in the partition of the Fageret estate. The original antebellum house had probably fallen into disrepair before 1881, when Fageret purchased it. The present appearance suggests that Fageret retained the original creole cottage, adding the mansard roof suggestive of the 1880s, along with Victorian details; the result is whimsical and highly original.

N. ROBERTSON

923–25

923–25, 931–33. The property at 923–25 N. Robertson was one of the many in which Joseph Dolliole, free colored builder, realtor, and developer, was involved. Emilie Piron purchased the lot from Dolliole in 1839 and agreed to have Dolliole construct "a frame house having four rooms, closed gallery and a two-story kitchen with four rooms, for $3,600" (July 2, 1839, F.Grima). The house was demolished, but the kitchen building remains, built of brick with a double-arched center section. It exemplifies the French manner of having a more architecturally sophisticated building facing the courtyard rather than the street façade of the house. A building contract before O. de Armas (April 18, 1849) indicates that Mlle Emilie Piron contracted with Pierre Théobald Olivier, free colored *entrepreneur*, to build a house for $2,200 in the adjacent lot (917–19 Robertson). The succession of Emilie Piron sold the two lots, two houses, and one other lot to Philomène de Santos in 1860 (September 20, 1860, C. V. Foulon). At **931–33** N. Robertson a frame, two-story residence was once a double, two-story kitchen, which served the house previously standing at the corner of St. Philip and N. Robertson.

1018–20

Macarty Cottage. The masonry-fronted, dormered creole cottage with gabled ends covered with wooden siding, has a large, two-story, frame, service building detached to the rear of the lot. No decoration has been added to this late-1840s cottage. Title research indicates that the present building was built for Drausin Barthélémy Macarty, f.m.c., soon after his 1847 purchase from Widow Louis Peyre Ferry (November 18, T. Guyol). Macarty sold the house to Joseph Freyd in 1855 (January 22, A. E. Bienvenu). The First Municipality had sold the lot to Thomas Soublet, f.m.c., in 1837 (March 27, F. de Armas). In 1889, when I. Wright turned the house over to his wife, it was referred to as a "double tenement," numbered 224 and 226 Robertson. The present doors, porches, and railings are unfortunate alterations to a good, early cottage.

1022

76/44

Paty Cottage. This masonry-fronted creole cottage has wood covering on one side with plaster below; weatherboards cover the right side. An archival drawing by J. N. de Pouilly, dated January 15, 1850, plan book 76, folio 44, shows the extant house as it appeared in the mid-nineteenth century. The fine, two-story kitchen remains detached across the rear of the lot. The brick added to the façade, the replacement of windows with aluminum frames, and the addition of a platform porch are unfortunate alterations. This fine 1830s cottage with well-proportioned dormers and graceful canted roof could be returned to its original appearance with a minimum of façade renovation. Title research indicates that Leon Paty, f.m.c., built this house in 1838, selling it the next year (January 5, P. Lacoste) to Charles Delery. Paty had bought the lot at an auction resulting from the suit, *Municipality No. 1 v. J. F. Perrault and Pierre Crocker, f.m.c.*

44/84

Chevillon Cottage. This four-bay, frame creole cottage probably was built to have a lathed and plastered façade, as indicated in an 1854 drawing in plan book 44, folio 84, by C. A. de Armas. A plastered brick façade can be distinguished from a lathed and plastered front usually by the wood enframement at the outer edges of the latter. The cottage retains its roof flare at the eaves and central chimneys. The house could date from the early 1840s. The lot was one that Claude Tremé sold from his *habitation* prior to 1810. Pouponne Decoudreaux, f.w.c., purchased 30 feet on Bayou Road by three *arpents*, left side (540 feet), from him in an act before Pierre Pedesclaux on December 6, 1806. In 1821 Bazile Demazillière, f.m.c., acquired this deep lot, bound on one side by land of Widow Blaise Cenas and on the other by land of Jean Foucher, f.m.c. Demazillière entered into a contract (November 26, 1821, M. de Armas) with Antoinette Françoise Dubreuil, f.w.c., his future wife, selling her the lot for $1,000. "The vendor promises to build in four months a house of *colombage* covered with slates measuring 26½ feet by 24 feet divided into four rooms with double chimney in the two front rooms, a gallery front and rear with a room and one cave beneath. In the court a kitchen, 20 feet by 12 feet with chimneys, also privies. . . . The vendor reserves the right to rent the house when it is finished." This 1821 house faced Bayou Road, at the present 1614 Governor Nicholls and was demolished. In 1832 Demazillière and his wife added enough property to their early purchase to square off three lots fronting N. Robertson, or about 80 feet on N. Robertson by 90 feet deep. Demazillière sold two lots to Antoine and Jean Pierre Chevillon in 1835 (July 11, F. de Armas), who had a partition in 1847. J. P. Chevillon retained this lot, on which he built this house. It is possible of course that the brothers had already built two creole cottages before the partition between 1835 and 1847. Antoine Chevillon kept the adjacent lot and built an identical creole cottage, which has been demolished.

1418

Lieutaud Townhouse. A one-time three-bay townhouse, with a recessed pilastered entrance in the Greek Revival style and gabled sides, stands on half of Paul Lieutaud's lot number 29 (see 1420 N. Robertson). Lieutaud sold this property with buildings in 1848 for $1,700 to Elijah Ensign of New Albany, Indiana. From 1849 to 1853, Jean Louis Hastier, f.m.c., owned and lived there. Then in 1853, the property passed to Irene Vidal. Directory research revealed this as the home of Judge Charles Leaumont of the Fifth District Court from 1866 to 1877. The property then went to Dimitry Agapitas, whose family held it until 1896. It has been poorly altered in this century, but façade restoration by analogy is possible and some decorative millwork remains for correct installation.

1420

Lieutaud Cottage. A Greek Revival, gable-sided house stands upon one-half of a lot originally purchased by Alexander Milne in 1800 from Claude Tremé. Designated number 29 in an 1836 plan by Bringier, the lot was divided and developed by Paul Lieutaud, after he acquired it from Milne's estate in 1844. Lieutaud occupied the extant house from 1844 to 1846, when he sold it to Mme Samuel Johnson for $2,500. From 1865 to 1868, Fanny Risso, Orleans Street dry goods store proprietor, owned and lived in the house. In 1868 auctioneer Thomas P. McDavitt paid $2,800 for the 1½-story cottage with three openings and a gallery supported by boxed columns. His family remained there until 1882. The house has been repeatedly altered so that its 1846 appearance is difficult to distinguish. The Greek Revival detailing may be an 1850s renovation. The dormer is a twentieth-century mutilation, as are the box column alterations.

1421–1433

Milne Property. The three-bay, two-level, frame Victorian townhouses at 1421, 1425, and 1433 have deep overhangs at the second level. The profile is one of multi-levels and multi-planes. Although balconies have been removed at the second level and cornices from one house, handsome entrances with pilasters, segmental arches, and decorative spandrels leading to recessed doors remain. These houses are reflective of the Esplanade-style influence on side streets. Such houses on Esplanade date from the 1870s and continued in popularity into the 1890s. This group dates from after 1883. Herringbone-patterned brick sidewalks should be retained.

1435–37, 1439. The four-bay, frame double shotgun at 1435–37 has a hip-roof and bracketed overhang. The brackets and dentil motifs, as well as the pedimented cornice on this house, are identical to those at 1439 N. Robertson. 1435–37, built after 1883, is later than its neighbor. 1439 is a three-bay, single, frame shotgun with hip-roof and deep overhang supported by steamboat brackets. Observe the small brackets between the house façade and the overhang in the Italianate manner. Curiously, there is also a dentil motif crossing the overhang in front. The house probably dates from the 1870s. The entrance door is original, a handsome example illustrated in the Robert's catalog. It is recessed behind a decorative Greek Key surround topped by a dentiled cornice. The two full-length windows have pedimented cornices. This early shotgun has an interesting combination of decorative motifs, and it is difficult to ascertain which parts have been added to the original structure.

1449

1449, 1461–63. In the second 1400 block of N. Robertson, both sides of the street on the old Duchamp property are lined with shotgun cottages and camelbacks. The creole cottage at 1461–63 predates 1883. In 1849 builder William C. Lee constructed a one-story frame house on this block for Jacques Delille for just $900—perhaps this house (December 18, A. Chiapella). 1449 is the only two-story building on the block; it is a three-bay, two-level, double-galleried house, which has a combination of Classic and Italianate features and appears on Robinson's Atlas of 1883. The appearance of the dormer and the bracketed and dentiled cornice suggests an 1860s building date. This part of the Alexander Milne property was sold to A. Rasch on December 10, 1836 (C. Pollock).

1477

Christian Mission Baptist Church. This unusual building in the Greek Revival style was built in 1884, after La Société Bienfaisance Mutuelle, represented by Emile Dousseau and Charles Charbonnet, acquired the property in 1879 from François Ricca for $250 (May 29, 1879, O. de Armas). In 1884 a permit was issued to "Emile Dousseau for a one-story frame house with a shingle roof; builder, Louis Rousseau; amount $200; on Robertson Street between Columbus and Kerlerec." Used as a jazz hall, the building is historically important for its association with the development of jazz. It has been mutilated by a senseless modernization after this photograph was taken.

1535–37

1539–41

1508, 1531, 1535, 1539. The four-bay, frame shotgun with hip-roof and bracketed overhang at 1508–10 N. Robertson is three rooms deep. The two full-length openings have the original doors with vertically set oval panels above and square panels below. Two double-hung windows set in segmental-arched openings and drop-siding complete the façade details of this 1880s-style house on the Milne estate. Across the street at 1531–33 and 1535–37 are two, small, frame shotgun doubles with overhangs and hip-roofs; the main body of each side is two rooms deep, with a central service wing to the rear suggestive of an 1850s building date. 1539–41, a four-bay, frame, double shotgun with bracketed overhang, is accented by gables with sawed work, shingles, and louvered ventilators. Four full-length, segmental-arched openings exhibit fancy architraves, having tripartite cornices with sawed-work cresting. A herringbone-patterned brick sidewalk remains on this part of the former Duchamp estate.

1545

Guerlain Division 1545, 1547–49. The two-bay, single, creole cottage pictured has gabled sides and a semi-incorporated overhang. The estate of Pierre de la Ronde sold a large section of unimproved lots, part of an old briqueterie belonging first to Pierre Marigny and subsequently to Widow Guerlain. Paul Pandely purchased this de la Ronde property on May 24, 1827, before F. de Armas. By May 11, 1839, when the syndic of Paul Pandely sold this lot and three others for $1,560 to Sévérin Latorre, f.m.c., improvements had been made. A row of similar creole cottages was built to be used as rental property. However, by the time Pierre Duhart of France, who owned the four lots from 1853 to 1855, sold them to François Lacroix, the price was just $715 for the whole, suggesting vacant lots. François Lacroix, f.m.c., was a prominent real estate investor who lived in Faubourg Marigny. If this building was not extant in 1839, it is likely that he constructed it soon after his June 26, 1855, purchase of this and three other lots (P. Courdain.) Lacroix's succession sold the houses on January 26, 1877, before C. Morel. The four-bay, frame, double shotgun with hip-roof and bracketed overhang at 1547–49 still has its full-length openings with drop-siding and quoins. It probably dates from the 1880s.

201

Public Market. Property including the site of the market at 201 N. Rocheblave was claimed by Samuel Moore and his partners, as well as by Baroness de Pontalba. However, in 1853 the contested property was partitioned and this corner lot assigned to the Baroness. In 1870, Lacestière V. Labarre bought a lot, "72-foot front on Iberville by 134 feet on Rocheblave," for $915. Labarre was married to Mlle Dorgenois. He sold the lot to T. J. Raymond in 1889 by private signature. In 1892 the city of New Orleans agreed to purchase the lot and have Raymond build a market, with the right to collect stall fees for thirty years. A July 12, 1892, contract for the market included specifications by Harrod and Andry, Architects, and was recorded in the archives of J. D. Taylor. In 1949 the city sold the market to Harry Katz and Joseph Daum for $22,000.

1000 Block

Fleitas Division. On this block were built six, late-Victorian, frame, double shotgun cottages, which enhance the street scene with their continuous but slightly varied façades. One cottage has a gallery with turned columns and a spindle course of turned and cut-out millwork decoration. Bricked and stuccoed sections of the lower half of the columns and the porch spoil the excellent proportions. The other shotgun cottages are designed with overhanging roofs supported by brackets and stoops. They have peaked gables with scalloped vergeboards as decoration. The brick sidewalks are pleasant nineteenth-century street expressions. Curbing and improved paving would add to this neighborhood.

1118–20

Fleitas Division. This frame creole cottage has gabled ends, dormers with pediments and pilasters as decoration, and simple door and window surrounds. The building resembles many other creole cottages in this area, which were built throughout the 1840s period. N. Rocheblave was originally part of Widow Fleitas' long striplike plantation in the early nineteenth century.

1113–15, 1117–19

Coquet Division. This pair of identical, frame, two-level, four-bay houses dates from the late nineteenth century. Both have balconies of fancy millwork supported by brackets, which are repeated under the roof overhang. Roundheaded transoms over the doors are echoed by roundheaded windows and shutters. At the roofline is a peaked gable covered with shingles. The original porches on both houses have been removed, and most of the shutters are missing from 1113–15. Tarpaper siding has marred the side of the house at 1113–15. These houses may be dated in the 1880s. Characteristic of this time period, they probably both had quoins and drop-siding on the façade. On the side of N. Rocheblave, the property emanates from the lands owned by B. Coquet.

1474

1470, 1474. Two well-kept, single, frame, bayed cottages at **1470** and **1474** N. Rocheblave remain in excellent condition, reflective of their building date during the last two decades of the nineteenth century. The cottages are atypical for New Orleans, unlike the familiar creole cottage, shotgun, or two-story townhouse. By their paucity they gain in importance. Projecting bays, recessed gables, ells, side-bays, and multiple rooflines characterize them and recall those described and illustrated in the books written by the landscape architect, Andrew Jackson Downing, and built throughout the country in the 1840s and 1850s. Each picturesque cottage has window and door surrounds of fluted pilasters with bull's-eyes. The gallery, supported by turned columns and a spindle course, creates the effect of an arcade. The gables on the roof, which are covered with shingles, have windows with pointed arches, suggesting the Gothic Revival. This land was originally part of the Gueno tract. Although the Widow Gueno subdivided it in the 1830s, it was not until the late nineteenth century that urban development of the small lots was accomplished.

1435–37

Gueno Properties. This square once was included in the large Gueno *habitation*, although little evidence of this early development has remained. **1435–37** is a corner creole cottage with a pitched and slightly canted roof with overhang and an attached shed in the rear; the complex was probably built soon after the Civil War. The old brick sidewalks have remained intact along one side. The two-bay, single shotgun at **1439** N. Rocheblave was built of frame construction with an ell to the rear; this house may be dated in the late-Victorian period. The later addition of a porch has detracted from the original proportions. The traditional cottage has a façade designed with cap-molded window and door hoods and brackets supporting the roof overhang. The wrought-iron fence is marked "Schultz," with the number 206 on the gate. The cottage at **1445** was also designed with an ell to the rear. Other features of this late-nineteenth-century house include a recessed front entrance leading to a hall, behind which was originally a side gallery, as well as a gable-fronted roof, a gallery supported by turned columns, and a spindle course. The house has its original screens with an interesting arrangement of muntins. The wrought-iron fence is marked "Hinderer's Iron Fence Works." The houses at **1451–53** and **1455–57** N. Rocheblave are identical shotguns of frame construction, designed with gable-fronted roofs, overhang supported by brackets, roundheaded door and window openings, dropped siding, and quoins. The doors and windows are framed by a molding of pierced-work designs, brackets, and bull's-eye crowned by tripartite cornices. Drop pendills and a scallop-bordered vergeboard complete the decorative features of these cottages. Architectural details are typical of buildings constructed in the last two decades of the nineteenth century. Porches were added in recent years. Another late-Victorian-period, three-bay cottage with an ell to the rear is located at **1461**. This raised cottage was designed with a gable-fronted roof and a gallery supported by turned columns and a spindle course of pierced panels. Peach and mimosa trees planted in the side yard of the cottage add charm, as does a wrought-iron fence. The steps to the porch are later additions. Despite its 1890s building date, the cap-molded lintels lend a classical feeling to this house. At **1469–71**, a double shotgun cottage was built in the late nineteenth century. This cottage features a gable-fronted roof and segmental-arched openings around the windows and doors. The porch is not original to the house.

1568–70

1509–11

1509–11, 1526–28, 1545, 1568–70. The 1500 block of N. Rocheblave still exhibits an inventory of modest frame creole cottages with and without dormers. These cottages, built in the 1860s as rental units in the Faubourg Gueno, are retardate in style, adhering to earlier building practices. At **1509–11** door frames with Greek Key surrounds distinguish the façade. The saddle-bag, two-bay, creole cottage with a pitched and canted roof at **1526–28** N. Rocheblave was built in 1866 for Martin Halbritter, a large property owner, who had purchased five lots at auction from the estate of Eliza Ross, the widow of Isaac Taylor, f.m.c., for $2,025 (May 29, 1866, J. Cuvillier). Within three months he had built this modest house, for when he sold the five lots, it was recorded: "with the buildings which were put up on the same (5 lots) by the present vendor since he made the purchase thereof." The purchaser was Mlle Celestine Soniat-Dufossat, whose family retained the house until 1871 when the lots were sold separately. Across the street at **1545** N. Rocheblave, a two-bay, single, frame creole cottage with a pitched and canted roof has Classic-style cornices above the two openings; these are obscured by metal awnings. An 1860s creole cottage in the style of the 1850s at **1568–70** now has an apron roof set beneath the earlier canted overhang to provide a covering for the new gallery. The door frames have been lowered, thus spoiling the proportions.

1617–19

Faubourg Gueno. Pierre Soulé bought this entire square, incorporating the odd side of the 1600 block of N. Rocheblave, from Widow Gueno. He developed a suburban garden with a large central fountain surrounded by flowers. The house at 1617–19 may be one of the few 1850s galleried cottages remaining in this faubourg. Without a nineteenth-century drawing or a conference with the owner, it is difficult to determine absolute changes in this cottage; however, it may have been originally ungalleried, lower to the ground, with a detached kitchen. The front edge of the gabled roof seems to have been sliced away and a new gallery and roof added.

N. ROCHEBLAVE

1725

1700 Block. The even side of this block is characterized by four, modest, late-Victorian, frame shotgun houses with front-gabled roofs, overhangs supported by brackets, and slightly varying window and door millwork. This rhythm of repetitive forms and patterns has created street unity. Original paneled doors characterize **1744** and **1750** N. Rocheblave. Across the street at **1725** stands the "Chinese Palace," an unusual landmark in Faubourg Gueno. The structure is a narrow bungalow, partly frame and partly stucco, with calligraphic applied designs in the pediment of the gabled-front and repeated under the side casement windows. An outbuilding in the rear has buttresslike, dragon-head supports.

N. ROMAN

222

St. James Methodist Episcopal Church. This church was incorporated on October 6, 1848, by private signature. It purchased this property on April 18, 1879, "for the usage of the Parson of the Congregation of this Corporation known as St. James Chapel." The sale was executed before notary W. J. Castell, after Michael Gilmore's family sold a cottage known as number 35 N. Roman at auction for $700. The land was part of that inherited by the heirs of General Lafayette which, in 1841, was sold to entrepreneur John Hagan. Another giant on the New Orleans real estate scene, Paul Tulane, purchased the land that same year and held it for several years. A series of four more sales transpired before the 1879 acquisition by the church. In 1903 the church was reorganized, and architects Diboll and Owen were hired for this building's renovation.

1016

Pascall Cottage. This masonry-fronted, three-bay, single creole cottage has Italianate detailing; a recessed entrance with a pedimented surround is balanced by elongated windows framed by pedimented cornices. The service wing extends from the rear, featuring an attractive gallery supported by box columns. Léonville Augustin Pascall bought this property in three purchases between 1849 and 1853 (COB 49/51; 55/577; 61/369). Pascall built the house during his ownership, which extended until 1885. Taxes were paid from the year 1869, which suggests that the building may date from that time. Among the owners of the property in the 1840s were Louis Barthélémy Rey, f.m.c., and Charles Ghaudurier, f.m.c. The lot was part of the succession of Andrew Oelze in 1849 and was part of the Charles Griffon estate, subdivided in 1832.

1027

Jaeger House (1027), 1025. A major structure on the Forstall section of the Pontalba division, the illustrated house was built for Charles Jaeger, who owned the lot between 1854 and 1860. This lot and most of the land in the division were acquired from the Pontalbas by Manuel Julien Lizardi, a creditor of Forstall. While living in London in 1847, Lizardi had Placide and Edmond Forstall arrange an auction of lots. Later, Jaeger bought the lot at 1027 N. Roman from its interim owners, F. B. Faures and J. Fallandry. Houses like this one with gabled sides and second-level galleries on the front and rear elevations appeared in the creole suburbs in the late 1840s. The design was essentially a two-story extension of the creole cottage. This handsome example was built with a double-pitched roof that is visible from the gabled ends. Batten shutters and French doors are traditional, but the turned balusters of the gallery railing postdate the construction of the house. A portion of **1025** may be seen to the left of the photograph. This frame building was once used as an auditorium and is associated with the development of jazz. Double dormers are framed by bull's-eye surrounds; stepped gables and a false front complete the façade detailing. One window on each side of the entrance is missing its decoration.

N. ROMAN

1207–09

1217–19

44/1

28/15

Colsson Cottages (1207–19). The appearance of the double cottage at **1207–09** N. Roman is indicated by two archival drawings dated 1838 and 1848 when there were dormers on both rear and front elevations (plan book 44, folio 1, plan book 28, folio 5). Baroness de Pontalba sold ten lots in this square, including this lot and those at 1211–13 and 1217–19, to Pierre Henri Colsson, after a public auction on December 28, 1836. Colsson, a speculator and officer for the Building Company of the Eighth District, paid $7,000 for the large property (F. Grima, January 12, 1837). Colsson immediately built the masonry-fronted creole cottage at 1207–09. It remains one of the earliest extant houses in the Pontalba division. A new, hip-roof shed in 1848 replaced the 1838 pitched roof lean-to shown in the archival drawing. Although the house has lost its dormers, chimneys, and attractive shutters and screens now obscure the original doors, its general appearance, including the masonry façade band, remains. The double-dormered, frame creole cottage with gabled ends at **1211–13** was built for Colsson in 1837. Two of the doors of the façade have Classic-style surrounds. In the late nineteenth century, drop-siding and brackets were added to update the building. A two-story service wing in the rear of the lot is connected by a passageway to the main house. Another Colsson creole cottage of 1837 stands at **1217–19** N. Roman. Described in an 1866 document as "a very comfortable house with attic No. 222 Roman, brick between posts containing four rooms, a shed, privies, cistern, etc." Although the house has a side gallery and entrance with Greek Key surround, Colsson built it as a simple, unadorned, two-bay creole cottage. The two dormers and the deep box entablature postdate the original design. This house remained in the Lalmant family from 1866 to 1905.

1311

Cheval Division. This 1840s, two-story, four-bay house in the creole tradition was built with double galleries across the façade. The present millwork on the galleries dates from the late nineteenth century. The house plan was just one room deep with gabled ends extending to incorporate the gallery. This property belonged to Pierre Crocker, f.m.c., in 1834. Originally it was a portion of the ten by three *arpents*, which Madame Paul Moreau sold to Almonester y Rojas in 1780; later Joseph Cultia acquired it, followed by Antoine Ramis and Paul Cheval, f.m.c., through whom Crocker bought it after subdivision of a larger portion of ground.

1426

Duchamp Division. This is a rural-type, galleried creole cottage in the Duchamp division. The original box columns of the early-Classic-style gallery have been removed, and a room has been added to enclose half the gallery. Dating from the late 1840s or early 1850s, it is an important example of a small, set-back *maison de maître*.

1435–37

1427, 1435–37. The twentieth-century addition at 1427 N. Roman is a disguising wraparound of an 1840s, three-bay creole cottage. An interesting feature of this house is the side gallery. **1435–37** is a creole cottage, with a fifth opening serving as the entrance to a side gallery. There are only a few examples of this type of five-bay cottage in Faubourg Tremé. The house with its masonry façade, basically frame construction, French doors, and pedimented dormers was a type built in this section of the former Duchamp estate; the side entrance was probably added. In 1869, this house, retardate in style, was constructed for André D. Doriocourt, who had purchased three lots from Clementine Volant Labarre, Widow Ovid Guerin, in that same year.

N. ROMAN

1468–70

96/29 (1468–70)

1468–70, 1476. The double, four-bay creole cottage at **1468–70** was illustrated in an archival drawing by F. N. Tourné dated 1864 (plan book 96, folio 29). It was then auctioned as old number 277 Roman with its two-room detached kitchen, which still remains. Either the doors and windows were reversed in later alterations to the house, or they were drawn incorrectly by the draftsman, F. N. Tourné. Built on land belonging to the Duchamp estate, the cottage may be dated from the late 1840s. Another creole-type house is exhibited on the block at **1476**. This is a frame, two-bay single, often called a maisonette. It also may be dated in the late 1840 period.

1518

Rabi Cottage (1518), 1508. The house pictured was designed as a narrow, single-dormered creole cottage with a masonry front, canted gables, and wooden sides. The brackets and front door are not original. Jean Rabi, f.m.c., following Widow Duchamp's auction, purchased two lots for $100 on March 19, 1842 (L. Herman). He built **1518** N. Roman, selling to Beaugé Lafargue, after an ownership of twenty-seven years (June 21, 1869, C. Martinez). This creole cottage with its unusual proportions elicits one's attention.

ST. ANN

Pumping Station. The City Pumping Station stands at St. Ann and Marais on land that, in the eighteenth century, bordered the Charles de Morand plantation and the City Commons. In 1831 the Parish Prison was built on this site and remained standing until it was demolished in 1895. A contract between the Sewerage and Water Board and W. M. Wren, New Orleans contractor, is dated June, 1906. This building and the attractive octagonal structure at 2435 Palmyra were constructed at that time in the Spanish Revival style.

1504–1522

Architects' Company Cottages. In this block stand five outstanding, detached creole cottages dating from the 1830s when the area was developed. The entire block had been part of the City Commons, which was subdivided and auctioned in 1829. Although the cottages at **1504–06** and **1508–10** St. Ann have had Victorian alterations, their configuration and dormer style indicate their early building date. There is a possibility that the Company of the Architects of the Eighth District, which owned 120 feet fronting on St. Ann and Orleans (September 15, 1834, H. Pedesclaux), was involved in their construction. **1512–16** is a creole cottage with a detached, two-story, wooden kitchen built soon after the 1831 acquisition of the lot by Etiènne Vallière, f.m.c. He purchased the lot, extending to Orleans (Basin) Street, from François Leonard on August 10,1831, for $405 (C. Janin). When Vallière died in 1850, his sister, widow of Edmond Labat, f.m.c., inherited the cottage. Upon her death in 1859, her children became heirs to the property. The Labat heirs did not auction it until June 29, 1867, at which time notary A. E. Bienvenu described "a handsome house, lighted with gas, No. 258, with sliding doors on each side, and having ten rooms, four of which are in the attic. A two-story kitchen of four rooms, paved yard, two hydrants, privies, etc. The whole covered in slate and divided into two tenements, and rented at $80 per month." Pierre Rey bought this house for $6,300 and subsequently sold it in 1889 for only $1,950. The site of **1518–20** St. Ann was among the lots acquired by the Company of the Architects in 1834, and it was sold to Samuel Chapman in 1835. By 1839 (November 20, W. Y. Lewis, acts destroyed), Pierre Gabriel Bertrand sold the lot with this new house to Summerville Campbell, f.w.c. She was sued by Pierre Bourg and lost the property at the resultant sheriff's sale, where Joseph Joubert acquired it. In 1862 Joubert sold to Robert Smith Upshur for $3,150. This masonry-fronted creole cottage has frame sides and a two-story detached kitchen. The cottage at **1522–24** was sold to George Pollock on December 30, 1839 (T. Turead), by the Company of the Architects of the Eighth District. The act specified "a new, brick house with four rooms, cellars, *cabinets*, gallery, brick kitchen, latrines, well, cistern, and gravelled courtyard." In 1847 George Pollock sold 1522–24 and contiguous Orleans Street property to Céleste Dessales, f.w.c., for $6,020; she sold it two years later to Angelo Lanata. In 1867 Lanata sold to Pierre Pereuilhet, who died the next year. His heirs auctioned the property to Barthélémy Reboul for $5,875 (April 29, 1868, A. Ducatel). At this time 1522–24 St. Ann was described as "a brick house, Nos. 66 and 68, with alleyway on each side; said house having six rooms, two being in the attics, two closets, closed gallery used as a dining room, two-

ST. ANN

story brick kitchen of four rooms, two cisterns, two hydrants, paved yard, privy, etc. The whole divided into two tenements, and sold subject to a lease, well-secured at $65 per month, ending March 31, 1870." From the difference between the two auction notices, it is apparent that alterations were made between 1839 and 1868 to this masonry-fronted creole cottage with sawtooth-bordered cornice; the rooms in the attic were added, and the gallery was enclosed. The detached, two-story kitchen remains.

5/11

Kitchen

1505–07

1527–29

Gobet and Larochette Cottage. Once part of the City Commons, this property was auctioned to the free colored cabinetmaker, Dutreuil Barjon, in 1829. He sold two years later to Oliver Blineau, a prominent investor in the area. In 1833 Blineau sold to builders Henry Gobet and Antoine Larochette two lots totalling 120 feet on St. Ann by 120 feet on N. Villere for $3,000. Gobet and Larochette built several creole cottages, with kitchen buildings, facing St. Ann. 1505–07 was auctioned in 1841 at Larochette's death, at which time the lot measured 30 feet on St. Ann by 80 feet deep. Sophie Philippe, who lived nearby at old number 158 St. Philip, was the purchaser. The next record of this lot appears in an 1855 tax sale, when Emile Bonnaffon bought it for taxes owed by his deceased father, S. Bonnaffon. In attachments to this act, Emile's two sisters and brother swear that their father owned this lot long before 1860, but the act of acquisition is yet to be uncovered. The frame creole cottage has an extraordinary, detached, two-story service building, painted the original deep terra-cotta color. There are central, arched openings at each level flanked by French doors with strap hinges and at the outside, windows with original shutters. The building is of brick covered with plaster, part of the 1830s complex built by Gobet and Larochette. It extended toward N. Robertson Street as part of a common-wall kitchen row behind the creole cottages facing St. Ann. A part of the kitchen row, along with its creole cottages, was demolished in the twentieth century. In plan book 5, folio 11, an auction drawing by G. Strehler, dated June, 1873, illustrates a similar service building. This drawing would serve as restoration aid.

City Commons. This block was subdivided in 1829, with several creole cottages being built in the 1830s. The masonry-fronted creole cottage has weatherboarded side gables with built-in overhangs. These features, as well as the Greek Key entrance and low rectangular ventilator, suggest an 1830s building date. The lowering of the door and window on one side and the addition of late-Victorian jigsaw work spoil the original Greek Revival façade of this building, which is probably of brick-between-posts construction.

34/46 (1601–03)

1607–09, 1611–13

1611–13

Bertrand Property. These properties, part of the City Commons, were sold to Jean Marie Fernández by the Corporation of the City in 1829. Marie Bassert, Widow Pierre René Bertrand, bought the group of lots at a sheriff's sale on September 25, 1834, and immediately built two or three of these creole cottages. When she sold the present **1613–15** St. Ann to Alexander Hugh McConnick on September 22, 1835, it was described as situated on a lot 34 feet on St. Ann by 117 feet in depth, "a new house, brick between posts, divided into four *appartements* [meaning main rooms], two *cabinets*, and one gallery [rear]. Each of the openings of said main rooms with *impostes* [transoms], a ceiling height of 12 feet, one of the *cabinets* has a stairway which leads to the attic, composed of four livable rooms, with plastered ceiling, and four *cabinets de décharge* [storage rooms], with a wood kitchen of four rooms not quite finished." The price was $3,200. The house is shown in plan book 34, folio 46, dated 1835, the time of the sale to McConnick. In 1845 McConnick sold the house to Madame Joseph Aristide Baquié for $2,600; and it was described as a "dwelling house containing eight rooms, kitchen with ironing room, two privies, cistern, etc." 1613–15 remains today a fine creole cottage, the brick-between-posts construction hidden as usual by weatherboards on the sides and a plastered façade. The detached kitchen with pitched roof still exists. Mme Bertrand built another house on the large property toward the N. Robertson Street corner, which she sold to Ann Cavanaugh, Mme James Roach, for $5,800 in 1836 (September 22, J. Cuvillier). This is the present **1607–09** St. Ann, a dog-trot, brick creole cottage, old numbers 275 and 277 St. Ann, described as "two, one-story and attick [sic] brick dwellings" in an 1886 sale by Joseph LeBlanc's heirs to Peter Lepari. The house retains its two-story brick kitchen in very bad condition across the back of the lot. The corner creole cottage store-house at **1601–03** also stands on part of the parcel once owned by Mme Bertrand. The house was there as early as 1835 when Bourgérol made an elevation of Mme Bertrand's property for a sale and was acquired by Mme Roach in 1836 on a lot 59 feet by 117 feet for $5,800. The complex was illustrated in plan book 34, folio 46, dated 1835, and in an unsigned and undated drawing in plan book 98, folio 53. Mme Roach sold 1601–03 and 1607–09 in 1845 to Fred Zambelli, whose family kept it almost one hundred years, from 1845 until 1923. The façade has a twentieth-century alteration of brick facing and shortened openings, but a balcony added after 1835 to the side gable on the N. Robertson Street side remains, as does a one-story detached kitchen.

1712–16

Guirot Cottage. This land was sold by Claude and Julie Tremé to the city in 1810; later, in 1839, the city auctioned it to the public. The Company of Architects of the Eighth District bought this lot in March and sold it with this house, as stipulated in the J. Cuvillier act of July 15, 1839. Antoine Joseph Guirot was the purchaser for $3,400. He held the property until his death in 1871. The double creole cottage is built close to the ground, about 26 feet wide with a medium height, and has a gable-sided roof with built-in overhang. It is in excellent condition, retaining appropriate, if not original, louvered-paneled shutters for the four façade openings and original pilastered double dormers. The chimneys are gone, and a modern roof has replaced the original one.

1718–20

Architects' Company Property. These houses were situated on land that the Tremés sold to the city in 1810 and that was later in the 1839 auction to the Company of the Architects of the Eighth District. On July 15, 1839, the company sold the lot and building that they constructed at **1718–20** St. Ann for $3,400, along with the vacant lot next door at 1722–24 for $920, to Augustin Liautaud, f.m.c. When Liautaud died in 1846, Philippe Alvarez, as his universal heir, inherited the property, which he sold four months later, along with another, to Rose Denise Plantey, f.w.c., for $3,000. Rose Plantey probably built the house at **1722–24** St. Ann soon after this acquisition. In her will, recorded by notary A. Ducatel, February 11, 1879, she stated that she was about seventy-five years old, had never married, and named her four children, surnamed Liautaud, as heirs. To Barthélémy Adolphe and Joseph Armand, she gave the house at old number 310–12 St. Ann (1718–20). To Joseph Numa and Geneviève Céci, she gave the house next door at number

1722–24

314–16 St. Ann (1722–24). She also owned a lot on Orleans in this square that served as a garden and two lots in the 2200 block of St. Ann that she ordered sold to fulfill other bequests, including $500 to each of her five grandchildren. In 1898 Pierre St. Raymond bought the house at 1718–20; in 1905 he acquired 1722–24 St. Ann. Both properties were owned by successive heirs until Albert St. Raymond inherited them in 1938. This block of St. Ann became a cul-de-sac when a ramp from the Claiborne overpass cut the street off from its route to Bayou St. John. Nevertheless, if restored, this block with its varieties of creole cottages could provide the city with a picturesque street rather than a neglected dead end.

94/46

Architects' Company House. The city acquired this land by purchase from Claude Tremé in 1810. In 1839 the First Municipality sold four lots in this square to the Company of Architects of the Eighth District. Laurent Cordier was one of the architects for the company; and a building contract before J. Cuvillier, September 16, 1839, notes that he built seven houses in the square bound by St. Ann, N. Claiborne, Dumaine and N. Derbigny, of which 1719–21 St. Ann is one. One year later the company sold this new house to James Hopkins for $4,175. The description of the building read: "The house . . . which . . . faces St. Ann, is built of bricks with a main floor and *mansard* above, divided into four rooms, a glassed gallery, two rooms in the *mansard* [attic], *cabinet, cave,* and office, with a two-story kitchen having four rooms with fireplaces, built in the courtyard which is graveled." In 1849 James Hopkins lost the house at a sheriff's sale to Charles W. Hopkins, whose heirs sold on December 10, 1858, to Drausin Barthélémy Macarty, f.m.c., (E. G. Gottschalk). This sale description read: "One-story brick house No. 326" for $3,150. Plan

1719–21

book 94, folio 46 (an unsigned, undated drawing) illustrates the appearance of this brick creole cottage, which has had its façade openings insensitively shortened.

1835–1841

Griffon-Hagan Lands. This block is situated partially on the land of the Charles Griffon heirs and partially on land subdivided as Faubourg Hagan in 1841. Originally, the block was developed as a series of brick-fronted, two-bay and four-bay creole cottages and maisonettes, probably dating from the 1830s and 1840s prior to the building of the French Hospital across the street. A pair of turn-of-the-century double shotguns at **1839–41** and **1835–37** continues the height and overall scale created by the creole cottage row. A herringbone-patterned brick banquette is granite-edged. The repetition of rectangles, fenestrations, overhangs, and façading results in an abstract rhythmic scheme. The entire block offers an opportunity for simple restorations.

2426, 2428–30

Dorgenois Division. The early-nineteenth-century lands of Domingo Fleitas, Lebreton Dorgenois, and Alexander Milne converged on this block of St. Ann. Parts of the present square were developed after the sales of the properties in the 1850s. These single and double shotguns at **2426** and **2428–30** were probably built in the 1890s, judging from the architectural details. The plan of the houses provides an excellent solution to the division of the land into narrow lots. The herringbone-patterned sidewalk curbed with granite and the latticework were traditional building materials that brought charm to New Orleans street scenes even before these houses were built.

2439–41

2437, 2439–41. Creole cottages with high gabled roofs appear in Faubourg Tremé in the late 1850s. A gamut of millwork treatments, from simple to ornate, was applied to them in the 1890s. These neighborhoods were initially established for speculative rental property. Houses were placed directly on the banquette. Kitchen and service buildings bordered property lines, and court areas were paved as outdoor spaces. Within the last thirty years, as the neighborhood declined, the proportions of these frame and brick creole cottages have been insensitively altered. Shortened windows and doors, the installation of picture windows, and projecting air-conditioners have marred the façades or rooflines. All these changes can be seen at **2439–41** St. Ann, which was once a four-room, double house with attic, rear *cabinets* within a gallery, and detached service buildings. Although presently a corner restaurant, it could be restored with the retention of its commercial activity and improve the neighborhood. The early, two-bay shotgun at **2437** St. Ann could also be reclaimed with a minimum of exterior restoration. Frame creole cottages along N. Rochéblave behind 2439 St. Ann need only paint to enhance their architectural features.

ST. CLAUDE

1014–16

Laurent-Roux Cottage (1014–16), 1006–1028. The lot for the cottage illustrated was sold to the city in 1810. On June 12, 1819, it was purchased by Jean Laboreaud for $600 plus ground rent, before notary Michel de Armas. The same year, Laboreaud sold part of the lot, 30 feet on St. Claude by 60 feet, to Jacques Laurent for $325 and 6% ground rent. There, Laurent built **1014–16,** selling it on August 30, 1821, to Anne Barron for $925. Mlle Barron, f.w.c. from Kingston, Jamaica, did not live in the house, but at the corner of St. Philip and Tremé. At the time of purchase, she was unmarried and fifty years old with one living child, Paul Roux, aged 24. He was married to Eulalie Fauchier, f.w.c., and they had one daughter, Marie Josephine. On March 12, 1839, Paul Roux acquired the property from the succession of his mother. When he died, the land with building and improvements was sold at public auction on July 1, 1851. His widow reacquired it for $1,000 and retained it for thirty years, selling on December 1, 1883 to André Doriocourt for $950. The house, probably brick-between-posts beneath weatherboard, is important not only as an early house built between 1819 and 1821, but because it remained in the same family from 1821 until 1883. This early creole cottage is surrounded by 1840s-style, frame double creole cottages at **1006–08, 1010–12, 1018–20,** and **1026–28,** the façades of which might be restored to reflect a street scene as it appeared in 1850.

1017

Chevallon House (1017), 1023. The illustrated, two-story, plastered brick, Greek Revival townhouse was planned with creole features, including its façade proportions. Townhouses in the American sector are usually taller and narrower, an extension of English and Eastern Seaboard prototypes, unlike the wider, lower proportions of this creole townhouse with its typical batten shutters on the lower-level and second-level casement openings. Other architectural features are gabled ends, cornice with dentils, cast-iron balcony with lyre motif, chimney on the gabled ends, and Greek Key entrance. The house probably dates from the 1840s, built perhaps for Antoine Chevallon, who left it to his daughter, Mme Joseph Salvant. Auctioneer Grimault described the house in 1878 as a "two-story brick house, No. 251, having on the ground floor, hall, parlor, and dining room with sliding doors; two rooms and a dressing closet in the upper story, with balcony on the street; two-story kitchen of four rooms, paved yard, cistern, shed, etc." The house was sold at this auction by Joseph Salvant, Jr., et al to H. Rousselin on July 15, 1878, before J. F. Meunier. **1023** St. Claude, a three-bay, Greek Revival, dormered creole cottage, has a Greek Key entrance that leads to a side hall. Tall, frame, gabled sides and three French doors articulate a house probably built in the 1840s.

1108–10, 1112

Buisson-Dupeux Cottages. These fine, common-wall, brick creole cottages were built between 1840 and 1847 for Pierre Dupeux after his purchase of the lots with partner Frederick Buisson from the estate of Michel Meffre-Rouzan. The sites had been part of an earlier complex with rental houses and a *maison de maître*, facing St. Claude, built for Meffre-Rouzan after his purchase of this and adjacent lots from the city on September 28, 1819. The early complex sold to Buisson and Dupeux in 1839 from Rouzan's estate for $14,000. It is seen in a plan in the notarial book of C. V. Foulon, October 27, 1840, and is described in an act before Foulon on July 27, 1839. One lot had a "house of three *apartements*" and was built of brick-between-posts construction with *galerie* and *cabinet*. This lot measured 60 feet facing Ursulines between N. Rampart and St. Claude with 172 feet along St. Claude. The lot corresponding to 1131 Ursulines had *une petite maison et d'autres bâtisses*, now demolished, set back on the lot, 60 feet facing Ursulines by 152 feet in depth. The existing common-wall creole cottages at **1108–10** and **1112** St. Claude are a rare type for any New Orleans neighborhood. Both façades originally had scored plaster to resemble stone, sawtooth-bordered cornices beneath the *abat-vent*, parapet gables, and batten shutters, as seen in the photograph of 1108–10. 1112 St. Claude has had alteration of the fenestration, mutilating the façade.

1200, 1300 Blocks. Claude Tremé had established Rue St. Claude between Chemin du Bayou and Ste Julie in 1799. There was, of course, no Barracks Street then, but Tremé sold lots on St. Claude in the present square 109 to Charles Duval in 1805, Chalinette Duval, f.w.c., in 1807, Marianne Capuchin in 1804, Henriette Rousseve, f.w.c., in 1803, Nanette Enoul, f.w.c., in 1805, and Marie J. Willamane, f.w.c., in 1807. Charles Meunier, f.m.c., purchased about 60 feet on St. Claude by 150 feet from Claude Tremé in 1801 (July 21, P. Pedesclaux). When Barracks Street was extended between Rampart and St. Claude into Faubourg Tremé after 1819, the city acquired at least 30 feet of Meunier's St. Claude street frontage. This left him with frontage on the new Barracks Street; and he built a new house, 1124–26 Barracks, which his estate sold in 1834. The house was rebuilt by owner F. Roy in 1836. The house plan illustrated by Tanesse in 1816 on St. Claude in the middle of the block between Chemin du Bayou and Ste Julie was the home of Charles Meunier, which had to be demolished about 1823, the year that the city negotiated with Meunier to buy and sell portions of his land.

1220–1230

1224–26

Bruneau Shotguns. These three-bay shotguns have hip-roofs, recessed side galleries, and built-in overhangs with new brackets. **1220–22** and **1224–26** originally had detached, two-story kitchen buildings that have been joined to the main houses creating camelbacks. Documents date the appearance of shotguns with recessed side galleries as early as the 1840s and show them to be more common in Faubourg Tremé than in any part of the city. Research indicates that this house-type continued to be built by investors until the early twentieth century. D'Hémécourt illustrates the development of the camelback house plan in a drawing dated May 19, 1879 (O. Morel). The houses have one chimney to the side of the front rooms, double central chimneys between the second and third rooms, and a four-opening chimney off-center to the rear. Brackets were added later to these mid-nineteenth-century, Classic-style shotguns. Title research verifies the structural analysis of a mid-nineteenth-century building date for 1220–22,

1224–26, and **1230.** Joseph Bruneau, who owned other properties in the vicinity, bought 72 feet along St. Claude by 180 feet in 1847 for $2,500. He sold the same property on August 15, 1851, including a small lot in the same square behind it, for $13,600 to Alcide LeBlanc with these three cottages (A. Mazureau). LeBlanc and his brother Jules owned most of the square by the 1850s, and they built along N. Rampart and Barracks. They retained these houses as well as 1114 Barracks until about 1879, when they sold 1226 St. Claude to A. M. Nicks for just $1,500.

1234–36

Meunier Property. Comparison of this corner cottage with the 1848 archival drawing of creole cottages situated in the middle of the block indicates that it dates from before 1848 and remains today similar to those illustrated in the archival drawing, plan book 106, folio 45. The old-fashioned *abat-vent* with iron bearers and the simplicity of the façade are two indications of an early date. The cottage was probably built of brick-between-posts construction in the early 1830s. The present two-story kitchen behind the house is in keeping with that date, but either the roofline has been altered or the second story added. The doors of the façade have recently been lowered.

1219–21

Chabert Property. This 1850s-style, two-story, four-bay, frame, double creole house is built at the banquette with balcony above and gabled ends; one original paneled door remains. The 1200 block of St. Claude was laid out by Tremé in 1799. He sold this lot to Bazile and Théodore Chabert on June 12, 1799, before Pierre Pedesclaux. In 1805 the Chabert family sold the vacant lot, bound on one side "by Mme Lesassier and on the other by the heirs of Gabriel du Mertraux," to Laurent Montinard for $350. The house with large garden indicated on the Jacques Tanesse map of 1816 probably belonged to Gabriel du Mertraux. Laurent Montinard built a creole cottage somewhere on the lot, which he sold on February 1, 1821, to Marcelite Hazeur, f.w.c., on a lot 60 feet on St. Claude by 190 feet "bound by Mr. George, Mr. Lambert, and Mr. Mager." The Pierre Lambert family in 1848 added the lot at 1219–21 St. Claude to their large holdings with *maison de maître* in the square. The Lambert heirs sold two lots here to Hugh Dowling at the estate auction on February 20, 1849, for $3,000. Dowling may have built the present four-bay, two-story, gable-sided, double house with iron balcony, selling it on the present single lot to J. O. Cassard in 1858. The façade could easily be restored to its period appearance by using archival drawings of similar houses.

1300–06

Penot Cottages. This property was owned by Claude Tremé, who sold part of it in 1804 to Nanette Enoul and another portion in 1807 to Marie J. Willamane, both f.w.c. The double-dormered cottages at 1302–04–06 St. Claude have a common wall and were originally planned to have four units of three rooms each, plus a large attic room. Gracefully curved gables with parapets may be seen at two elevations due to the corner location. Straight lintels with flush opening frames, shutters at the rear elevation, full-length batten shutters at the rear elevation, masonry steps, full-length batten shutters, and the eight intact dormers are outstanding. The entire complex, as seen in the 1973 photograph, is a sophisticated reflection of its building type and style. A contract recorded by notary E. Barnett on June 17, 1847, indicates that the complex was built by James Stevenson, builder, with architect Henry Möllhausen for Henry Penot. The 1847 contract describes "two, one-story, brick houses with two-story kitchen buildings situated at the corner of St. Claude and Barracks and costing $5,000." When Pierre Cougot sold the property to Henry Larquié in 1855, the auction notice described the houses as brick "divided into four tenements, each composed of three rooms on the ground floor and a large room in the attic; two, two-story buildings in the yard of four rooms each, privies, waterworks, paved yard, etc. (March 26, 1860, A. Ducatel)."

1308

Tremé Subdivision. The outstanding, two-bay, brick creole cottage at 1308 features brick parapet gables and a fine, small, roundheaded dormer. The façade is enframed with an outline of plasterwork, continuing a Spanish colonial tradition. The side elevation retains its original batten shutters. Across the rear of the lot is a one-story wooden kitchen. Stylistic analysis suggests that the house dates from the early 1830s.

1318

85/11

Tremé Subdivision, 1314–16, 1318. The three-bay, frame creole cottage at **1318** stands on land which Claude Tremé sold to Henriette Rousséve, f.w.c., in 1803. The present cottage is perhaps the second structure on the site and probably dates from the 1840s, when three-bay creole cottages were built in great numbers in Faubourg Tremé. The photographs provides an excellent example of how detached kitchens were in later years attached to the main house by filling in the garden area, here with a chimneyed room. The adjacent 1314–16 St. Claude, a four-bay, double-dormered creole cottage, was demolished in 1975. It probably corresponded to the building contract between George L'Hôte and August Huard dated September 4, 1848 L. T. Caire, which described a one-story house *en madrier de bout entre poteaux* to cost $2,100. Plan book 85, folio 11 illustrates the house as it appeared in an 1866 drawing by P. C. Boudousquie.

1311

44A/50

Dumée-Brasco Cottage. Research on this house extends back to 1845, when the executor of Jean Mager's estate delivered to Scholastique Dumée, f.w.c., her legacy of La Petite Maison on St. Claude, previously occupied by Mme Collard, Mager's sister. Scholastique received the bequest in grateful recognition of deeds rendered to Mager during his final illness. When Mme Dumée sold the property at auction in 1859, it was described as "buildings and improvements together with a two-story-and-attic house containing seven rooms, a two-story kitchen, and four rooms and another building; cistern, well, privy, etc." (June 15, O. de Armas). The early cottage is illustrated in plan book 44A, folio 50, in a drawing by Tourné and de L'Isle for this 1859 sale. At that time the house passed to Marie Rachel Fitz, f.w.c., who had nine children by Pierre André Destrac Cazenave, commission merchant. In 1875 Cazenave was listed in the city directory as an accountant living on St. Claude with his son, a carpenter. After an eight-year interim ownership by the New Orleans Canal and Banking Company, John Trisconi, saloon keeper and Milneburg Hotel proprietor, purchased the house in 1873. When Trisconi died, his inventory revealed the same early Dumée house with "room, parlor, dining room, two bedrooms, and kitchen valued with furnishings at $5,000" (COB 190/372). The house was purchased by Anthony B. Brasco, who probably filled the original garden area with the present, five-bay, center-hall, raised villa. It appears that the original Scholastique Dumée cottage remains attached to this twentieth-century addition.

1442

Perrault Cottage. Mme and M. Appolinaire Perrault, f.p.c., purchased a vacant lot measuring 33 feet on St. Claude by 94 feet at the auction of eleven lots belonging to L'Etoile Polaire, paying $4,650 in 1852. The act described the lodge as *du rite ancien libre et accepté Ecossais*. In 1859 Mme Perrault purchased an adjoining lot with buildings and improvements from Louis Mestier for $1,200. This house was built by the Perraults in the 1850s and remains an excellent example of a three-bay creole cottage. A canted roof contains a built-in overhang. Although the rough stucco is a disfiguring, twentieth-century alteration, it probably covers a smooth plastered façade. The sides are covered with weatherboard, a traditional treatment. An 1879 auction notice described "the improvements consisting of a fine, family, brick residence, having a lower floor, three rooms, bathrooms, dining room, kitchen range, three rooms in the attic with four *cabinets*, cellar, brick yard, cistern, hydrant, garden, etc. The property possesses all the advantages to render it agreeable, is situated in close proximity to the cars, churches, markets, schools. It is built of first class materials and is in perfect repair" (December 1, 1879, M. V. Dejan). There is a contract for the repair of the house in 1881. Octave Montagnet and Besnard, builders and contractors, contracted with Dorcas Helen Marshall, wife of James Fahey, for $500 worth of work (May 23, M. V. Dejan).

1454–58

Commagère Cottage. This six-bay cottage was first designed with the traditional American plan of central hall with two rooms on each side. A sixth façade opening is a narrow, Classic-style entrance that led to a recessed side gallery, not included in the main roof and possibly a later addition. The house with its deep-gabled sides was probably built in the 1860s. Part of the Maspereau-Commagère holdings, the house was built for Pierre Théophile Commagère after 1858 and sold by his estate in 1889. In 1829 there was an earlier *maison de maître* on this site that measured "143' on Columbus and 62' on St. Claude bounded by L'Etoile Polaire and Widow Similien's holdings," when on February 20, Joseph Vigneaud sold the house and grounds with two slaves to Widow Armand Guilbert, Saturnin Bruneau, and Louis Rocheford (L. T. Caire). Vigneaud had purchased the property from Jean Pinaud at an auction on April 21, 1821 (H. Lavergne). When the succession of Widow Guilbert sold her land on January 18, 1833, this lot with buildings and improvements had been subdivided and measured "30 feet St. Claude by 80 feet Columbus by 78 feet property Jean Louis Bruneau by 30 feet property Julien Rauzeau, cost $1,275." In 1833 Jeanette Robin, Widow Jean Castelin, f.w.c., rejoined the two lots, buying the corner piece from J. L. Bruneau, f.m.c., and Joseph Brunel. The house burned after the 1974 photograph was taken and is now demolished.

1429–31, 1433–35

Maspereau Cottages. Seraphim Maspereau, tinsmith, built both the double, dormered creole cottage with two-story, detached kitchen bulding at **1429–31** and its twin at the corner, **1433–35**. He owned the two lots and a posterior one from 1849 until 1877 and built the cottages soon after purchasing them. The containing lots came to Maspereau from his business associate, Bernard Nautre, who had acquired the land from Madame Collard, Jean Mager's sister. Originally, it was part of the large tract belonging to Madame George Boyd, Widow Honoré Guerlain. Maspereau sold the property in 1877 to his daughter Seraphine Maspereau, divorced wife of Ernest D'Aquin. She, in turn, sold the house at 1429–31 St. Claude to Fernand de Ranie in 1880. It remained rental property throughout the years. The tall, narrow dormers of the two identical cottages have peaiments with squared lights. The high-gabled roofs have a deep cant, affording ample attic space for rooms.

1447

Perrault Cottage. This three-bay, plastered brick, single creole cottage with dormer, gabled sides, and hallway features a sophisticated doorway with oval sidelights and a transom recessed behind a handsome Greek Key entrance leading to a side gallery. The double-hung windows and oval, cast-iron ventilators indicate that there was no porch, although the original steps faced front. The overhang here now is built into the gable. A rough façade surface beneath the overhang replaces a string course or row of dentils. The well-proportioned and original dormer remains, but the original twelve window lights have been changed to four. 1447 St. Claude is a good example of the tenacious popularity of creole cottages throughout the development of Faubourgs Tremé and Marigny. This one dates from around 1870, when a clerk named Octave Perrault acquired the containing lot and probably built the house. In 1866 B. L. Millaudon bought the lot plus three adjoining ones from L. A. Poincy, president of the flour inspectors board. The purchase included a two-story frame building at the corner of St. Claude and Kerlerec where Millaudon lived. When Millaudon sold the lot at 1447 to Madame Amedée Ducatel for $1,000 in 1868, the transaction mentioned no buildings. On March 18, 1870, Mme Ducatel sold this lot of ground to Perrault for $1,050 (A. Ducatel).

1449–51

Pessou *Maison de Maître*. Immediately to the right of the 1870s creole cottage at 1447 St. Claude is an earlier one, from the 1820s. Alphonse Pessou, gunsmith, must have built this set-back creole cottage after he acquired the property from Louis Honoré Guerlain in 1824. City directories show Alphonse and V. Pessou at the St. Claude address from 1834 through 1875. Henry Collin bought the cottage for $1,500 from the Pessou estate and sold it for $1,100 to Widow Justine Trudeau in 1879. George Trudeau, probably the son of the widow, occupied the cottage, which was held by his widow until 1894. The rural setting of this cottage, set back from the banquette, still includes a brick center walk and remnants of a parterred garden. Many of the recessed cottages have lost their garden space to wraparound front additions, making the few remaining ones rare and desirable.

ST. LOUIS

1534

Friebault House. Joseph Friebault acquired this property, which was originally part of the City Commons, from Wilhelmina Pauschen and Paul Lacroix for $1,025 in 1846. Two years later, on October 19, 1848, Friebault sold "the brick house of two stories, the kitchen also of brick, two stories, and other buildings," which the act stipulated that he had built, to Pierre Lazare for $6,000 (C. V. Foulon). It remained in the Lazare family for thirty years. Lazare's heir, Emile Edward Lazare, sold it at auction to Edward Whitmore in 1876 for $1,975. This rather large building with stepped gabled ends, once incorporating chimneys, has been altered. It was built as a four-bay house facing St. Louis Street, with entrances on St. Louis and N. Robertson, and is one of the very few houses remaining in the area associated with Storyville.

ST. PETER

1429–31

Fire Station. This mid-nineteenth-century, 2½-story, masonry, double townhouse can be viewed from all angles. Located on a triangle where N. Villere meets St. Peter and Orleans, it has particularly fine, stepped, gabled ends and a two-story brick kitchen. In 1847 the property without buildings was leased by P. B. Fauvre and G. E. Demburent with the stipulation that any buildings and improvements would belong to the owner of the property, P. Billiard, when the lease expired. In 1848 the lease was transferred to Pierre Brunet with the same stipulation. The house was apparently built for Joseph Eysallenne between 1849 and 1859. His widow sold it to François Ducongé when they married in 1859. The Ducongé family kept the house until 1881, when it was sold to Jean Baptiste Rossi at the low price of $2,500. The city of New Orleans acquired this historic property, and under the leadership of Winston Lill in Mayor Moon Landrieu's office, plans were made in 1976 to save the buildings and adapt them for use as a fire station. Pio Lyons, architect for the renovation, returned the three-bay, masonry, double creole houses to their 1850s appearance. This is one of the finest examples of adaptive reuse by a municipality. The appended building for the fire engines in no way detracts from the architectural integrity of these structures.

2550

General Laundry. The unusual building in the 2500 block of St. Peter was built for the General Laundry by architects Jones, Roessle, Olschner, and Weiner in 1929. It represents one of the few Art Deco-style buildings in New Orleans and was placed on the National Register in 1975. Decorative features are glazed tile motifs in blue, green, yellow, terra-cotta, and deep rose; pilasters with green tile caps having palmettes, leaves, and yellow corn; and a tile parapet with alternating chevron and sunflower designs, beneath which is a band pierced with ventilation windows framed with an egg-and-dart motif of deep rose-colored tiles. Above the pilaster-framed windows are green tile crests with palmettes and anthemion-type motifs. The foundation course is tiled in an abstract pattern up to the window sills. Entrances are framed with fluted tiles and dentiled lintels. The entire entrance areas are banded by terra-cotta tiles and display green doors, yellow engaged columns with blue tile caps, and a deep glass transom of muntins forming an abstract star design.

ST. PHILIP

1127

Dolliole Cottages, 1125, 1127. The Dolliole family, f.p.c., were builders, carpenters, and *entrepreneurs.* Purchasers of the large lot that included **1125, 1127,** and the now-demolished 1129 St. Philip were Pierre Dolliole, J. L. Dolliole, and Norbert Fortier. The Dollioles bought 120 feet by 120 feet on St. Philip from the City of New Orleans Corporation for $670 in 1816 (July 18, M. de Armas), which were numbered lots 30 and 31 on the Jacques Tanesse survey of that year. Two members of the family partnership sold the property to the third, Jean Louis Dolliole, in 1821 (July 18, C. Pollock); and he built three houses, 1125, 1127, and 1129. His own home was on Bayou Road between N. Robertson and N. Villere. He sold the fine, three-bay, single creole cottage at 1127 St. Philip to Louis Henry in 1857 for $1,900. It features one bricked, gabled end; a brick façade; and a frame, recessed, open gallery on the N. Rampart street side. The entrance surround is a reversed Greek Key molding, and the original windows are almost full-length. The lotus swirl, wooden brackets and window-door cornices were added at the turn of the century. This potentially lovely house at 1127 has sold at least fifteen times in the past 150 years, bringing the highest sale price of $9,700 in 1970. Another outstanding three-bay cottage at 1125 St. Philip has a brick

ST. PHILIP

front, one frame side, and one brick side with a fire-extension parapet. It was part of the Dolliole property, built at the same time as 1127 with the same floor plan and materials. The 1971 mural on the masonry wall of the St. Claude side of 1127 depicts the exodus of black citizens of the Tremé area when the city administration, in the 1960s, began demolition for a cultural center. This mural is one of several by Bruce Brice; another, with a jazz theme, was painted on the N. Rampart Street side of 1139 St. Philip; and a third, at 1205 St. Philip.

1139

Bouland-Montet Property. The unusual, two-story, three-bay, masonry, Greek Revival townhouse exhibits a gabled back end and front hip-roof with high parapet and cast-iron balcony covering the banquette. The recessed entrance is framed with pilasters and a simple wooden cornice; its paneled reveals are retained, and the granite steps are original. A second St. Claude Street entrance indicates an original double occupancy. Presently attached to the building is a late-nineteenth-century ell or frame wing, which creates an interesting courtyard fronting St. Philip. The side wall toward N. Rampart on this wing is a stepped gable of masonry with two chimneys. On this wall is one of three murals by native New Orleanian Bruce Brice. Painted in 1971, its bright colors and primitive style depict the history of black residents of the Tremé area. By 1819 the property on which this house stands had been bought by the City of New Orleans Corporation from the Durge Land Corporation. M. Sabouveau purchased the lot from the city for $1,000, and "a house situated at the corner of St. Philip and St. Claude" is mentioned in the succession of Mme Eléonore Sabouveau (November 28, 1825, C. de Armas). Marie Elizabeth Bouland bought the early house from the Sabouveau estate in 1825 for $1,200. It was sold in her own estate to her son, Thomas Soublet, f.m.c. (August 2, 1849, L. T. Caire). Plasterer Soublet ultimately married Virginie Labastérie, his common-law wife and the mother of his five children. She owned a residence at N. Derbigny and Hospital (presently Governor Nicholls Street, formerly Bayou Road) and another piece of property on N. Miro between Dumaine and St. Ann. Soublet lived at St. Ann in 1849 "on a lot of ground 60 feet by 91 feet . . . with a house . . . of brick between posts and . . . stables." He may have moved to 1139 St. Philip; but by July 9, 1855, he had sold it to Pierre Montet (A. Dreyfous) for $1,654. The Montet family probably built the extant house after demolishing the earlier structure. The Montets are listed in the 1855 and 1857 directories at St. Claude and St. Philip. Pierre Montet presented the house to his daughter, Madame Guenador, in a settlement on April 6, 1858 (L. Magner). Fourteen years later Mme Guenador sold the property to John Rey for $7,700; within seven years Rey sold to Joseph Trépagnier.

1209–11

2/3

1201, 1205, 1209–11 St. The City Corporation auctioned lots in the 1200 block of St. Philip, odd side, in 1826 after the closing of the Collège d'Orléans and the subsequent division of the square. The property at **1201** has a corner hip-roof and a gabled side near the adjacent two-story townhouse. Commercial use for corner buildings is a traditional adaptation. Here the structure has been bricked over, the doors and windows altered, and the foundation proportions destroyed. **1205** St. Philip is one of the few remaining examples of the creole adaptation of the London townhouse and may date from the 1850s. Archival drawings indicate that in Faubourg Tremé and the City Commons there were once many more examples of the 2½-story creole townhouse with dormers and gabled sides. At 1205, the present dormer with paired windows is not original but is enhanced by the "rainbow" mural painted by Bruce Brice. The narrow door to the right may have led originally to a side gallery or rear entrance, which would suggest a strong French architectural trait. The present service wing appended to the rear of the house replaces a detached kitchen. The original house was frame and was plastered over in 1974 when the three, second-level openings were lengthened and batten shutters added. These alterations represent an improvement over the pre-1970 appearance of the house. Victoire Gallaud, f.w.c., divorced wife of Thomas Urquhart, bought this portion of the Collège d'Orléans property from the City Corporation in 1826 and kept it until her death in 1850. Her daughter, Victoire Urquhart, sold for the low auction price of $610 to George Bauer on December 2, 1850 (T. Guyol). It is possible that Bauer built this simple, three-bay house because of his sale of a house on this site the following year for $2,500 to John Berg. At **1209–11** there stood, until its 1978 demolition, a double, frame creole cottage with gabled ends. Like many fine creole cottages, dating from the 1830s and 1840s in this area, alterations throughout the years obscured the original appearance. Interior chimneys were removed, and shingles covered the gabled ends that should have been of weatherboards. Short casement openings on the front, along with paneled shutters and wooden back steps, are shown in an archival drawing, plan book 2, folio 3, dating from 1872, by Strehler. The drawing could illustrate 1209–11 or its previously demolished neighbor, which stood at 1213–15. The drawing indicates a dormered house with curvilinear muntins suitable for the 1830s. The lot of 1209–11 was sold by the City Corporation on August 1, 1826, to Jean Baptist Patron, having been part of the Tremé sale to the city in 1810 (then part of the Collège d'Orléans property). The house was built soon after 1830 by speculators J. Colvis and Joseph Dumas, f.m.c., who bought the lot on September 18, 1830, from Antoine Benjamin, f.m.c., for $750. In the act of partition between Colvis and Dumas in 1836, there was described on this 40-by-120-foot lot a "frame house, brick kitchen and other improvements" appraised at $4,500 (January 26, T. Guyol). Plan book 86, folio 39 shows a plan without elevation of this house, dated February 16, 1869, in a drawing by A. de Armas made for the sale by Mathilda Colvis (Mme Pierre Sicard of Paris) to Mme Andrinette James of St. Charles Parish (March 20, E. Bouny). The plan shows the house with four rooms, two *cabinets* at each end of a gallery, kitchen, two cisterns, well, privy, trees, and hydrant. Pierre Villarceaux Macarty bought the house in 1877; and his heir, Isadore Albin Macarty of Bordeaux, France, sold to his sister, Julie Josepha Macarty, wife of Paul Claude Fernand Dupuy, also of Bordeaux, "Rue de l'Eglise St. Seuvin No. 7," before notary Casterja of Bordeaux (see 1223 St. Philip). In this sale, the house was described as "constructed of boards, plastered inside, having four rooms, two *cabinets* with gallery, having two kitchens and two rooms in the rear of the courtyard" (COB 112/365, April 1, 1880).

1223–25, 1227, 1229

Dolliole Properties. Jean Louis Dolliole, f.m.c., acquired a substantial portion of the Collège d'Orléans property after it was auctioned in the 1820s. The lot at **1223–25** was bought from interim owner Victoire Wiltz, f.w.c., by Rosette Dolliole, f.w.c., (July 3, 1827, C. de Armas). The 50-foot lot fronting St. Philip was described as "part of the *emplacement* known under the name of Collège d'Orléans, bound on one side by lot 5, belonging to Jean Louis Dolliole, and lot 7 in the rear belonging to Laurent Alpuente." Rosette Dolliole sold the property to Joseph Dolliole for $800 in 1834. He probably built the fine house at 1223–25 soon afterward, since it was inventoried with his 1868 estate as a $4,000 value (December 16, J. Cuvillier). His widow, Josepha Rodríguez, sold the house to Mme Augustin Gourde in 1869 for $4,600 (March 13, J. Cuvillier). Subsequent owners included Isadore Barthélémy Albin Macarty "of Bordeaux, France, temporarily residing in this city," according to the act of O. Villere, October 15, 1881. Macarty bought the house from Jean Numa Avegno for $2,000. This double creole cottage has two dormers with arched lights, but recent rebricking and lowering of openings have spoiled the façade. Plans by J. A. D'Hémécourt, dated May 10, 1854, show *cabinets* to the rear containing two stairways. The standard four rooms plus rear *cabinet* gallery were complemented across the rear courtyard by a detached, side-gabled kitchen with four rooms and rear gallery. A privy was placed at the back property line. The lot containing **1227** St. Philip was part of the 50-foot purchase of Joseph Dolliole, who subdivided the property, creating two lots. He probably built this narrow, two-bay house and sold it to Mme A. C. Tallaire, née Zélime Alphonsine Chopard, for $2,700 in 1854. Mme Tallaire occupied the house following her marriage to Lucien Lafossé, from 1855 until 1878. She sold it, at a loss, to George Edward Hess for $900. The house was resold in the 1937 succession of Mrs. Victoria G. Videau, for just $500, to Melvin W. Mathes. This rare, two-bay, dormered creole cottage has a brick façade now covered with weatherboard, and brick sides with fire extensions. Batten shutters, hardware, and a small kitchen building appear to be original. The overhang replaces an original *abat-vent*. A side chimney behind the roof remains. At **1229** St. Philip is an unusual and picturesque adaptation of a creole cottage as a church. The church front with two small windows and recessed entrance has been applied to a frame creole cottage with gabled sides. The plaque denotes the founding of Calvary Spiritual Church, incorporated May 12 1942, Reverend Louis A. Reimeno, Pastor. The land containing the frame creole cottage behind the church belonged to the Lambert family in 1856. It was built, probably in the 1830s, when adjacent houses of similar type were constructed by the Dolliole family.

1319–21

1311–13, 1315–17, 1319–21. The even side of the 1300 block of St. Philip has been demolished by the city of New Orleans. Building contracts as early as 1827 show creole cottages being built on this block. Property owners included Pierre Baron Boisfontaine in 1827 and Marie Françoise Montamat, f.w.c., in 1832. Plan book 45, folio 46 shows a large, double creole cottage that stood on this block of St. Philip. This house-type predominated on this block of the square, which is now a cultural park area. Across the street at **1311–13**, a late-Victorian, double shotgun has an older, two-story, frame kitchen to the rear of the lot, dating from an 1830s complex. The façade of the shotgun exhibits fine zigzag pierced work with cresting on the cornices. Multiple patterns on the vergeboard and brackets with applied work and bosses complete the decoration. The double, frame, Victorian shotgun at **1315–17**, with segmental-arched openings and original screens, replaces part of still another earlier complex; behind is a gable-sided frame kitchen remaining from the earlier house. **1319–21** St. Philip is an early-twentieth-century, double cottage showing Neoclassic Revival decoration. The arched windows with stained glass, three Ionic columns, and double doors create the twentieth-century variation to the typical cottage theme. The original cast-iron fence has adjunctive thistle caps.

1526–28

Ceresolle House. 1526–28 and **1532** St. Philip emanate from an acquisition from François Boquille, f.m.c., August 18, 1829 (F. de Armas), from a sale of the City Commons. He sold the 60-by-120-foot lot at the corner of St. Philip and N. Robertson to Charles Gérard in 1834 (see 1532 St. Philip). 1526–28 St. Philip remained an empty lot next to a coal and wood shop at 1532 St. Philip until after 1867 when it was described as vacant, in a sale from Pierre Pereuilhet to Victor Louis Ceresolle (April 26, A. Ducatel). Stylistic analysis would indicate that Ceresolle built this house before selling the property to François Jonville in 1876 for $1,800 before notary A. Dreyfous. Jonville was a grocer listed in the 1880 city directory at 151 N. Robertson nearby, and in 1881 and 1882 at 275 St. Ann. Ceresolle is not listed in any New Orleans city directory between 1867 and 1876, when he owned this property. However, he probably built the fine, late-Classic-style, double house soon after 1867. Even the unfortunate new door and window panels used to shorten the original tall openings cannot disguise the sophisticated scale of the plastered façade. The doorway cornices with dentils above the tall pilasters coordinate the façade overhang, which is a box cornice having dentils and modillions.

1532

Gérard House. The frame, double-dormered cottage with gabled ends at 1532 St. Philip is used as a corner store-house. An altered façade and shortened side windows cannot obscure the fine quality found here. It was built for Charles Gérard, who bought this lot and the adjoining one from François Boquille, f.m.c., in 1834 (April 26, L. T. Caire). An 1856 archival drawing, plan book 7, folio 23, by Persac, shows a coal and wood shop on this site. Gérard sold 1532 St. Philip to L. Picheloup of Vendôme, France, for $3,500 on April 7, 1859. In 1867 Pierre Pereuilhet, who also owned the stable at 1523–25 Dumaine, sold this building to C. J. Crovetto for $1,900. A newspaper ad described Pereuilhet's property at the time of the sale (April 26, 1867, A. Ducatel): "This lot and two others forming the corner of St. Philip designated as No. 1, 2, and 3, according to the plan now at the auction house . . . together with a house of several rooms, gallery, *hangar* [shed], etc." Crovetto kept the property until 1879, when he sold it to John Toussaint for $2,050. Toussaint sold it to Eugène Chrétien in 1881 for $2,325 (August 23, O. de Armas).

1509–11

1501–03, 1505–07, 1509–11. This fine trio of dormered, weatherboarded creole cottages with gabled sides and detached rear kitchens evidences the most typical house-type of Faubourg Tremé. Two of these three buildings have been rehabilitated by recent painting, but the French doors have been altered and tall dormers blanked by plywood boards. Proportions of the casement doors and their muntins and transoms indicate that the three were built in the late 1840s. Applied jigsaw brackets were added later. The cottage at **1501–03**, though mutilated, appears interesting with its half-hip, half-gabled roof, a customary treatment for a corner cottage. The row sold on July 16, 1877, at a sheriff's sale as a result of a suit between David Dufraicheau and Louis Valles (COB 109/147). Dufraicheau acquired the properties, keeping them until 1892 when he sold them for $4,000 to Louis Valles (February 5, J. F. Meunier).

1523–25, 1519–21

Chaigneau Cottage (1519–21). This cottage is similar in appearance to its neighbors at **1523–25** and **1533** and dates from about the same time, but research indicates a different title history. Madeleine Chaigneau, f.w.c., had the fine cottage built during her ownership from 1835 to 1862. On January 24, 1862, in an act before F. Percy, she sold it to Jean Agut for $3,300. John Raquet Clay, f.m.c., held a mortgage on Agut's purchase; and in 1868 he bought the house from the Agut succession, selling it to David Dufraicheau the same year for $3,400. The Genois family purchased it in 1870, retaining it for thirteen years until 1883. The roundheaded dormer lights and flaired gabled ends of this house and its neighbor are significant indications of an 1830s building date. **1523–25** appears today as a five-bay, frame creole cottage with gabled sides, two dormers, and bracketed overhang. Doors and windows have been lowered and the façade refaced, altering the proportions of a normal, four-bay creole cottage. It was built in the 1830s by one of the three owners holding title during that decade. In 1830 the City Corporation sold the lot, then measuring 86 feet on St. Philip, to Manis Jacob, who bought many lots in Faubourg Tremé. Jacob sold it in 1834 to Pierre Rodolphe Colsson, an officer of the Company of the Architects of the Eighth District, who turned the property over to the company that same year. Two years later, in 1836, the company sold the lot to Myrtile Courcelle, f.m.c., a builder who probably constructed the cottage for the company or for profit soon after his purchase. On March 20, 1840, Courcelle sold this house to Drausin B. Macarty, f.m.c. Three years later Henry Raphael Denis, living on Esplanade, bought it as rental property. C. L. J. Villiers built the creole cottage at **1533** St. Philip (not illustrated) for investment, after buying the lot from Pierre Commagère on March 25, 1845, before A. Mazureau. The Villiers lived nearby on St. Philip between Tremé and St. Claude in 1846. The house was sold by Villiers for $4,000 to Josephine Toledano, Widow Jean Louis Drouet (May 4, 1848, O. Drouet). Mme Drouet was living in the house in 1849 and is known to have died there in 1866. Her succession sold the house to Claire Conand, Widow Théodore Tureaud, for $5,455 on August 7, 1866 (A. E. Bienvenu). Mme Drouet also owned property at 1126 Marais, which she gave to her granddaughter as a dowry.

1600–02

Dumas Cottage. A fine creole cottage at the corner of N. Robertson dates from the 1850s, although dormer proportions with arched lights and the roofline with cant suggest an earlier date. The masonry façade in the Classic style has had Victorian brackets added, and the modern, double cement steps and platform spoil the front elevation. Wide boards cover the N. Robertson Street side, and an attic opening in the side gable has full-length shuttered doors leading to a balcony. An altered, two-story kitchen remains beyond a patio. Pierre Bernonville, f.m.c., purchased the lot, part of the City Commons, from the City Corporation in 1829 (September 28, F. de Armas). In 1843 Bernonville sold it to investors Julien Colvis and Joseph Dumas, f.m.c. The house was built after 1849, during Dumas' ownership. He sold this rental house to Drausin Barthélémy Macarty, f.m.c., for the high price of $4,800 in 1860 (July 25, J. Lisbony); Macarty left the house to his widow, Anne Louise Courcelle.

1612

Macarty Properties, 1604–1620. The type and style of the three-bay, dormered, creole cottage at **1612** indicate that it was built after the 1846 acquisition of lots by the Drausin Barthélémy Macarty family, f.p.c., at a sheriff's sale on October 28 (5DC#34). Macarty, who owned many rental properties in the area, acquired the site when Widow Quessaire and her two minor children lost it at a sheriff's sale. Macarty built this house, leaving it to his widow, Louise Courcelle. It was sold to Mme Camille Latorre at a sheriff's sale in a suit between the Macarty heirs and Jean Alvarez Latorre of Paris, France, on December 13, 1879, for $2,667. Included in the purchase were five lots (four facing St. Philip and one facing N. Robertson), buildings, and improvements (COB 111/981). The side-galleried cottage, with pediments and paneled cornices added in a late-nineteenth-century renovation, was restored in the 1970s. The house stood alone on the five lots until 1881. When Mme Latorre sold this house and land on March 1, 1880, she specified that the carriage gate "belongs to the vendor who will have it removed to her property" (J. F. Meunier). In 1881 she sold another 30 feet of the side yard for $460. Plan book 1, folio 11 (not illustrated) includes adjoining property in a drawing by Seghers and de L'Isle, April 2, 1878. At that time, the land on which **1608–10** and **1604–06** now stand was the side garden of the creole cottage. During the 1890s, a pair of double, Victorian cottages was built on the property. Applied garlands on their brackets and overhangs are typical of their period, although cement steps replace the original wooden box ones. At **1618–20** is a hip-roof, frame, double shotgun with simple unbracketed overhang. The only decorative features of this cottage are two, original, front doors as illustrated in the Robert & Company catalog of the 1850s.

1609–11

Boisdoré House. In 1830 Félix de Armas received from the city the half-square between N. Robertson and N. Claiborne, facing St. Philip, in exchange for a right-of-way on N. Robertson Street. De Armas sold the lot at 1609–11 St. Philip the same year, and it remained undeveloped until 1836 when Calis Cobet, f.m.c., sold the $900 lot to Marguerite Boisdoré, f.w.c., who contracted with builder Myrtile Courcelle, f.m.c., to construct this house. In the April 28, 1836, act of sale before A. Mazureau, there was a note: "M. B. paid with two notes order of M. Courcelle payable in 12 months." On March 15, 1837, Mme Boisdoré sold the new house to speculator-partners J. Dumas and Julien Colvis, f.m.c., for $3,194.31, with a bill for $800 due Courcelle. This four-bay, double creole cottage retains features of the 1830s in the roundheaded dormer lights (now filled in), the canted roof, and superb proportions of the roof, doors, windows, and foundation height. Built at the banquette, this house and its neighbors could be restored with a minimum of face-lifting techniques.

1826–28

Griffon Division, 1813, 1819, 1826–28. The rural appearance of the frame creole cottage at **1826–28** is achieved by the gallery and the recessed location of the house. Features include the gabled ends with built-in gallery and simple Classic cornice. The Doric columns are not original and should be replaced with full-length box columns extending to the porch level. The low iron fence across the front of the property postdates the mid-nineteenth-century cottage. The Griffon heirs subdivided in 1832, selling three lots, each 31 feet by 124 feet, to Louis Dubreuil, f.m.c., and Evariste Wiltz in separate sales in 1832 and 1835. This partnership probably built the house, selling it on a 93-foot lot for $1,000 on March 8, 1836 (G. Legardeur). Four subsequent sales of the property with improvements took place before February 3, 1842, when the syndic of the creditors of Pierre Joseph Gregoire sold it with buildings at auction for $1,670 to Alexandre Marrionneau. Marrionneau subdivided this property as early as 1843, as shown by his sale to J. B. Oternod (April 29, A. Chiapella). Many houses built in the decades preceding the Civil War were moved at a later date to other locations on the same lot. The Robinson Atlas of 1883 suggests that this occurred with 1826–28 St. Philip. The odd side of the 1800 block was also once a part of the Griffon estate. It is enhanced by a variety of creole cottages and Victorian double and single shotguns, all constructed on a similar scale. **1819** is a typical example of erroneous modernizing of an otherwise fine, two-bay, creole cottage. Here, and at **1813**, pseudobrick façades and aluminum picture windows totally destroy the integrity of these mid-nineteenth-century cottages.

1838

1/21

Forstall Division. This traditional, frame, corner storehouse has attractive proportions and features a gallery at the second level on two sides and a roof gabled on one side and hipped at the corner. Plan book 1, folio 21, an 1865 drawing by Castaing and Selles, architects, suggests that the structure may have been cut down from a four-bay, hip-roof, creole corner storehouse with gallery on four sides and a covered walkway. Situated in the Forstall division, which was subdivided by Manuel Julien de Lizardi in 1847, the storehouse at 1838 St. Philip was built between 1847 and 1850 by Hugh Dowling, who had bought the lot from Lizardi. Dowling sold the new store-house to George Tagnoni for $1,030 on February 25, 1869 (A. E. Bienvenu).

1920

Forstall Division. Centered on its lot and set back slightly from its iron fence, this two-bay, frame, galleried shotgun at 1920 St. Philip has full-length, segmental-arched openings with fancy cornices among its attractive assets. Lacy, pierced-work and openwork decorations are combined with spindles to achieve spandrels, bosses, and a frieze below a cornice of double rows of scalloped jigsaw work. The inset gable in the front of the hip-roof suggests an 1890s building date and exhibits attractive vergeboard scallops and applied-work decoration of the period. The recessed side opening into the lean-to kitchen wing adds to the whimsical aura of this well-kept shotgun.

1923

Rectory, St. Peter Claver Church. This commodious Edwardian house is in dramatic contrast to the small shotguns and creole cottages that line St. Philip Street. Its location, adjacent to the Gothic-style church, is propitious, since it affords a transition in scale from the small houses to the large church. Edmond Forstall owned this land in the 1840s and subdivided the square into lots. This house is an early-twentieth-century addition to the street.

1921

St. Peter Claver Church (St. Anne). The *Daily-Pica-yune*, July 20, 1852, reported: "The new Catholic Church of St. Anne, Mr. T. E. Giraud, architect, built on ground donated by the Abbé Lefranc, on St. Philip between Roman and Prieur, was ready for opening on the festival of St. Anne. It is 90 feet by 46 feet, 32 feet high in the nave, 21 feet in the aisles, of the early-thirteenth-century English style, with fresco ceilings. The tower and spire, detached from the main building, rise from the centre front 105 feet." St. Anne's Church was built on land formerly belonging to Edmond Forstall, who subdivided it. Originally the Catholic congregation was both white and black, with segregation being practiced within the church. Marriage and baptismal records date from 1856. The records were kept in three separate lists, designated: *blanc* (white), *couleur libre* (free Negro), and *esclave* (slave). Reorganized in 1920, the white members of the congregation moved to a location on Ursulines and N. Galvez, keeping the name of St. Anne's Church. The church on St. Philip was given to the Josephite Fathers for the founding of an all-Negro church to be renamed St. Peter Claver, after the Spanish Jesuit missionary whose work among Negroes in Colombia in the sixteenth century caused him to become the patron saint of many black Catholics. At the time of the reorganization, a school from kindergarten through the eighth grade was founded and still continues on the site. Although there have been few major alterations, the exterior brick has been stuccoed and the interior renovated with the unfortunate removal of some original features.

2014

Bouchard-Costanza House. One of the finest Italianate houses in the Pontalba division is the former residence of Mr. and Mrs. Joseph Costanza at 2014 St. Philip Street. This Italianate, two-story townhouse on a lot 30 feet by 120 feet has a deeply rusticated wooden façade with a handsomely detailed Italianate entrance with deep reveals and a heavy box cornice with brackets and dentils. Ornate entrance brackets have been removed since the 1972 photograph. Batten shutters on the lower level contrast with the extreme sophistication of the other façade features. The double, etched-glass front doors, sidelights, and transoms with original hardware are protected by heavy, double, cypress storm doors with hand-carved decorative panels in the baroque style. These were originally painted in the *faux-bois* manner to imitate oak. The second-level balcony has a cast-iron railing of the "Widow's Mite" motif. The stairhall with original medallions and molding opens to handsome double parlors having hand-carved wooden moldings, dividing screen, and window cornices. Original light fixtures of gas with electric arms added and white marble mantels are features here and in the dining room to the rear. Four upstairs bedrooms have marble mantels with original cast-iron gratings and covers. An ample service wing extending to the rear retains original batten shutters and hardware. Acquiring the lot from Louis Frigère for $737, M. and Mme Adolphe Bouchard had the house built in the 1850s (April 15, 1857, A. Ducatel). Widow Bouchard, Agnes Boyer, sold the house at the estate auction on November 8, 1867 (E. Barnett) to Emile Couder for $7,500, "together with improvements consisting of a two-story frame dwelling, No. 308 St. Philip." Within a year, Josephine Abat, Widow J. B. Victor Déjan, bought the house for $5,500. The Déjan family and eventually Victor Déjan's son Michael V. Déjan kept the house until 1890, when he sold it to Mme Judith Blardone. Oral history reports that Victor Déjan was a Yankee colonel stationed in New Orleans during the Civil War; he so enjoyed the city that he remained here. In 1907 Charles G. Deffurge acquired the house from the Blardone estate, selling it in the same year to Mrs. Felice Costanza, whose son Joseph grew up in the house and lived there with his own family until 1975.

Gurlie Division. There was an early complex at **2024** on this part of the Pontalba-Gurlie division in April of 1843, when Joseph Alcinor sold the lot and buildings to Victoire Picon, wife of Armand Dreux, before notary L. L. Turgeau. Mlle Josephine Courieux and Mme F. Berthier sold remnants of the early complex to Joseph E. Rimbolt for $900 on January 31, 1865 (COB 89/46). The Rimbolts probably built the present house in the still-popular Greek Revival style soon after 1865. They kept the house until Rimbolt's death in 1911, after which E. J. Soudain acquired it for $1,600 from the French Market Homestead on January 12, 1912. The two-level, frame, Greek Revival house with a two-room depth features a wood-paneled door with molding in the baroque manner around each panel.

2017

Gurlie Division. This unusual cottage exhibits one of the more decorative late-Victorian façades in the Tremé area. It features protruding and hexagonal wings, deep overhanging gable, and a profusion of varied jigsaw decoration. The property was part of the Nicolas Gurlie *habitation*, subdivided in 1831. When Gregorio Curto bought two of the lots on September 9, 1846, there were earlier buildings on them. They remained in his family until 1872, when his widow sold them separately. This house was probably built in the 1890s in the yard of the earlier complex (January 9, 1890, M. T. Ducros). Owners during that decade were Simeone M. Fucich and Mrs. Joseph Dellande, who bought from Widow Curto, later Mrs. Eugenie Grandjean (COB 139/412). Alice Tujague, Widow Etiènne Arnoulh, sold the house for $2,900 to the Liberty Homestead on March 6, 1936 (COB 484/605).

2204

Cauvain House. Here is one of the very important, early, masonry shotguns in the Greek Revival style. The Greek Key entrance leads to the side gallery, which was formerly open. The front has a cornice with band and dentils. The property is one of many on St. Philip associated with investor D. B. Macarty, f.m.c., who sold the lot to Manuel Cauvain for $425 in 1855 (December 7, J. Lisbony). Cauvain built the house at 2204 and sold it with a slave to Florville Foy, before A. Ducatel, April 2, 1862, for $3,300. Foy, the same week, sold the house and slave to Mlle Marie Françoise Thomas Johnson for $3,500. Numerous sales over the last 115 years reveal some low prices for this fine property, such as $800 in 1890 and $500 in 1935; however, in 1962 it was valued at $8,500.

N. TONTI

823

Fleitas Habitation. This galleried house may be recognized as villa style with a presently altered center hall and mutilated gallery. Mme Louisa Rinardo lost this house at a sheriff's sale just two years after it was built as her residence in 1872. Julius Socha purchased it in 1874 for $2,000. Between 1876 and 1909, it was the property of Ernest Landry and was subsequently used as the Tonti Social and Athletic Club and the Palace Social Club.

101/14

1124

Gérard House. This Classic-style, double-galleried, frame, side-hall house with Greek Key entrance surround was built by the owner, Hubert Gérard, in 1860. The façade includes paneled pillars with Corinthian caps on the upper story, where there are three full-length windows. The gallery latticework has been added, but an original cast-iron railing remains. The ground floor has been altered by modern replacements and the removal of the gallery floor. An auction drawing, executed by J. F. Bauer and dated 1883, illustrates the appearance of the structure at that time, when the pillars extended the full two levels. The handsome house dates from mid–nineteenth century, after this area was subdivided by Alexander Milne's estate. Milne was the curator for Marie Michel, alias Noyen, f.w.c., who owned the land in 1829. James Powell, Milne's agent, purchased the land at auction that year on December 1, according to the act of L. T. Caire. Milne bought the land from Powell the following June for $1,000. The 1829 land description read: "300 feet on Bayou Road, other side by Catin Marc, f.w.c." Catin Marc owned the land, which became the Bernard Coquet property. The Milne land was subdivided in 1844, and this lot was unimproved until Hubert Gérard purchased it in 1859 from Jean Dorville. Gérard, a builder, constructed and owned the house until 1862, when he sold to Mlle Ann Heation for $11,500. The property is described as "a large, two-story, frame dwelling with outbuildings, well-ordered grounds, known as No. 12 N. Tonti Street. The remainder of the said portion of ground is vacant." Members of the Heation family named Samuels continued in ownership until 1884.

1125

Lafon Home of the Holy Family. Thomy Lafon, f.m.c., purchased this property from B. B. Beauregard on July 23, 1836, as recorded by notary H. Pedesclaux. Beauregard had purchased the entire tract, "two *arpents* front on Bayou Road, bound above by Fleitas and below by Marie Michel, f.w.c., on June 26, 1836," from the estate of Bernard Coquet (C. Pollock, act missing). In the 1820s the land had belonged to Catin Marc, f.w.c. Lafon sold two lots to Auguste Le Blanc for $300 in 1845, but he repurchased them undeveloped in 1850 for $500. In the early 1860s he built this asylum, formally turning the "two lots, circumstances, and dependencies over to the L'Association pour L'Assistance des Orphelins de Couleur de la Louisiane." The land and buildings were valued at $1,400 (October 31, 1866, R. J. Ker). In 1876 the Société de la Sainte Famille, which was formed in 1847 to care for "old and infirm colored women," took over the asylum. During a reincorporation in 1880, the Society of the Holy Family listed the following as new objectives: "to educate the young colored children both in boarding and day school; to keep asylum for destitute young colored orphans; to support in asylums poor old colored people." The society sold this building in 1976 to the Odyssey Institute, a nonprofit organization based in New Jersey. It is ironic that the president of the society at the 1976 sale was Mother Rose de Lima Hazeur, S.S.F. The Hazeur family had appeared as free people of color in Faubourg Tremé in 1798 before the establishment of the suburb, when Rose Hazeur (Mme Prosper) purchased land from Claude Tremé. The authors feel it unfortunate that the Sisters and their elderly patients have left their neighborhood. Indeed, the names of the residents of the area throughout the twentieth century reflect the history of the faubourg's free people of color, since these families settled here in the eighteenth and nineteenth centuries.

1231

Coquet Division, 1221, 1231. The Italianate-style villa with raised basement at **1221** N. Tonti was built with a central entrance and gabled ends. The enclosed front gallery once featured simple wooden pillars supporting a deep cornice with dentils and parapets. Although altered, the house still retains its handsome beveled-glass door with transom and sidelights, as well as a large oak tree in the front yard. The filled-in gallery, piers, and tiled, front steps are unfortunate additions. The house is illustrated on the Robinson Atlas for 1883, shown set back on the lot. At **1231** N. Tonti, a two-level, three-bay, side-hall house with box columns at the first-level balcony and overhang above is a late Victorian interpretation of the townhouse. Above a traditional first-level gallery is a balcony, and at the roofline, a deep box cornice supported by steamboat brackets. Stylistically popular from the 1870s through the 1890s on Esplanade Avenue, examples of this house style may also be seen in many upriver New Orleans neighborhoods.

1623

Faubourg Gueno. The large, gable-sided, frame house at 1623 has been altered over the years so that its present architectural style is mixed. The central entrance is not original; the house was probably built with four openings across the front with a built-in gallery. The present apron overhang of the gallery is an addition, as are the steps and the rail. Despite these obvious changes, this spacious, rural-style cottage built in the 1860s, continues the traditional creole cottage ambience of the area from N. Broad to N. Rampart.

1637

Faubourg Gueno. The predominantly, early-twentieth-century residence may incorporate elements of an earlier house. It has ample front and side porches lined with Doric columns supporting an incorporated apron overhang. These characteristics and the large, triple, window dormer are typical of the City Beautiful style. Many examples may be seen in the area between Canal, Tulane, S. Broad, and Carrollton. This house is contained on a spacious corner lot planted with yew and azaleas.

1020–22

Aliquot-Charles House, (1020–22), 1018. The fine, brick, double creole cottage with parapet gabled ends and dormers with arched lights reflects the style of building in the 1830s. It recalls the Sauvinet house located at 1809 Dauphine Street in the Marigny section. In a recent renovation, a fine, saw-toothed, dentiled cornice was uncovered. The flush or slightly recessed window and door frames are typical features of the 1830s, as are box steps. The two central windows were lengthened and appropriate batten shutters added during the renovation. All paint was removed from the exterior, which is a modern interpretation; in the eighteenth and nineteenth centuries, houses of local brick were always painted or plastered. The land on which this house stands was subdivided in 1829, purchased by Casimir Alpuente, and sold by him, undeveloped, to Jean Dagorret in 1832. A year later, it was resold, still undeveloped, by owner Joseph Forneris, f.m.c., to Mlle Marie Jeanne Aliquot. Mlle Aliquot, the financial founder of the Society of the Holy Family, was a white Frenchwoman, who chose to accomplish charitable acts through this order of black nuns. She built this house, selling it in 1834 to Joseph Charles, f.m.c. A mortgage, dated August 22, 1839 (T. Seghers), lists Charles as owner, and describes "a house and a kitchen in brick and other dependencies." He left the property to his wife, Josephine, according to the act recorded by A. Mazureau on January 30, 1846. Each sale included a second property until 1878, when owner Louis Mathé sold to P. LeBlanc. At that time, the two-bay, Victorian shotgun at **1018** probably was built on the side garden of 1020–22. Set back from the banquette behind an iron fence, 1018 illustrates the New Orleans trait of utilizing street frontage to the maximum.

1026–28

Thielin Cottage. This frame, creole cottage without dormers or decorative detail was built on the grounds of an early *maison de maître* that faced Ursulines and extended back to Tremé. The early house, which no longer exists, was built for Charles Raymond soon after the 1826 division of the Collège d'Orléans property. In 1833 Raymond sold the house to "Rita Lougard, widow of Charles Viavant, f.w.c.," for $3,000 (August 1, F. de Armas). When she sold it in 1840 to Isaac Legassie, who resided there four years, it was described as a house on a lot of 50 feet facing Ursulines and 80 feet in depth on Tremé, indicating that the present 1026–28 was at that time an empty garden area. Widow Viavant, having moved to France, signed this act by private signature in the Basses-Pyrénées. The John Thielin family owned the corner Ursulines Street house from 1846 until 1877. Thus, this modest cottage could date from any point in the Thielin ownership when they decided to build rental property behind their residence. Stylistically, 1026–28 fits well into either the 1840s or 1850s.

1015–1027

1000 Block. The 1000 block, odd side, of Tremé Street exhibits a variety of nineteenth-century building types and styles. It contains a row of frame shotguns and frame creole cottages in sturdy condition, as well as a gable-sided townhouse. Most of the structures have had additions of Victorian woodwork brackets and window hoods. These buildings contribute to the nineteenth-century aesthetics of the street scene. **1015** Tremé was probably built in the 1850s as a three-bay creole cottage. The attached shed and Italianate decorations postdate its construction. The house at **1019** was built on land owned from 1833 to 1895 by the family of Julia and Aimée Hardy, f.w.c. This continuous single ownership makes the dating of the actual construction difficult. When Julia Hardy, widow of Vincent André, sold the house on April 6, 1895, the property was described as "30 feet on St. Philip by 120 feet on Tremé . . . a double tenement and other small buildings and occupied as a bakery." Thus the house may have been built in the 1840s, as is suggested by its gabled ends and Greek Revival decoration, and then renovated with Italianate decoration in the 1870s. **1023** and **1025–27** are late-nineteenth-century shotguns built on the grounds of 1019 Treme after the Hardy-André succession sale.

1110–12

Collège d'Orléans Property, 1110–12, 1114–16. The house pictured is situated on the old Collège d'Orléans property, that is, the portion that was sold to Pierre Crocker, f.m.c., in 1826. Crocker sold a lot at Tremé and Ursulines Street to Caroline Palao, f.w.c., for $250 in March of 1827. She built on that lot "a brick-between-posts building having two rooms, two *cabinets*, and one gallery and other appurtenances, constructed at her orders and expense," according to the May 25, 1830, act before T. Seghers. This act also recorded the sale of this new house to Caroline Vela, a free colored minor, for $436. After the prolongation of Tremé Street in 1836, Mlle Vela sold to François Gignac, f.m.c. The act before L. T. Caire, January 18, described "30 feet on Tremé and 34 feet on ground reserved by the city for the prolongation of Tremé." The extant frame-covered, four-bay, two-story, and gable-sided creole house was sold along with a lot 60 feet on Tremé by a 50-foot depth to Auguste Guerin in 1838, for $3,000. Guerin sold in one year for the same price to Mlle Marie Noël Cordier, f.w.c.; and she, in turn, sold on October 16, 1840, to Auguste O'Duhigg, as recorded by A. Ducatel. This act described the house as *la maison à étage, cuisines, constructions, et dependences*. Subsequent speculative owners of the house include Joseph Sauvinet and his brother Jean Baptiste and, in 1853, Séraphim Masereau. This house is a good example of a type built almost exclusively in Faubourgs Tremé and Marigny. It recalls the style of the houses at 1920 Dauphine and 1218 Ursulines. At **1114–16** a small creole cottage, with built-in overhang, may well date from the 1830s like its neighbor at **1110–12** Tremé. The building may have been one of the service buildings to the latter, or it may have been constructed sometimes during the 1840s. Stylistic repetition is common in creole cottages. François Gignac, f.m.c., owned both properties, 1110–12 in the 1830s and 1114–16 in the 1840s. He sold the former in 1836 when the property measured 60 feet on Tremé by 50 feet in depth. It was not until 1842 that the lot measurement of 1110 Tremé was reduced to 30 feet by 50 feet, and 1853 when Gignac is mentioned as being the owner of the creole cottage at 1114–16 Tremé. The original batten shutters used on this building illustrate the importance of simple details to the overall appearance of the cottage.

1119

Guigou Cottage. The rare, three-bay masonry-fronted creole cottage was built without dormers. The entrance has a Greek Key molding and two short double-hung windows. Such houses, designed with Greek Revival-style interiors, usually were built during the 1840s. They are highly esteemed for their proportions and floor plan. Mme J. B. Guigou (formerly Mme Benjamin Mercier, née Marie Fratel) inherited half of a Bayou Road *habitation* from her uncle, François Camus, and the other half from her aunt in 1844. Camus owned a substantial amount of property in Faubourg Tremé, and his *maison de maître* faced Bayou Road (Governor Nicholls) in this square. He had bought the land January 29, 1829 (F. de Armas), from the widow of Marcely Cornu for $1,150, after an auction held December 26, 1828. The lot fronted on Bayou Road, "35' Bayou Road by 210' on Tremé." Camus immediately contracted with François Boisdoré to build a house and outbuildings for $4,000 on Bayou Road (Governor Nicholls) near where Tremé was later cut through. Camus died about the time the house was finished. The October 21, 1829, inventory of Camus' possessions recorded by J. Arnaud described the property as "35 feet on Bayou Road bound on the left by the property of Widow Galatos 120 feet, then it opens 25 feet to the property of Madame Rolland where it has a second depth of 90 feet where it has a width of 60 feet; a *maison principale* and a stable which have just been built." By 1864 Mme Guigou's husband, Jean Baptiste, of Angers, France, had built seven houses on various lots created from his wife's inherited property, presumably including this one at 1119 Tremé. In 1864 the children from his wife's first marriage forced Guigou to sell the properties to them. 1119 Tremé could date from any time between 1844, when Mme Guigou inherited the entire Camus property, and 1864, when her husband sold it to her children. Though dating from mid-century, the woodwork, hardware, and perhaps brick-between-posts construction of this Greek Revival cottage bespeak an earlier period.

1226

Soulié Cottage (1226), 1222–24. The city acquired the site of this house when land was purchased for the prolongment of Tremé (Liberty). The municipality bought 69 feet on Bayou Road by 263 feet in depth along the future Tremé from Denis René Beranger on July 6, 1836, as recorded by F. de Armas. There were buildings and other improvements on this land, which sold for the high price of $10,000. The present, urban, style, double creole cottage of brick construction was built as an investment for Albin and Bernard Soulié, f.m.c., who bought this lot and an adjacent one after the city extended Tremé Street and subdivided the property facing it (March 21, 1837, F. de Armas). The Soulié family retained ownership until 1885, when it was purchased by a family of investors, the Lafferanderies. Beginning with Jean Marie Lafferanderie, that family held title to the house well into the twentieth century. The brick creole cottage has retained its gabled ends with fire extensions on both sides but may have lost its dormers and chimneys in a reroofing. The façade drastically needs restoration. Although sandwiched between two late-Victorian houses, it could emerge as an excellent example of an early, brick creole cottage. A double, frame shotgun house was built around the turn of the century at **1222–24** Tremé with the typical gabled front and apron overhang supported by brackets. The five full-length openings are framed by pierced-work cornices. The attached side gallery was added to the house as a solution popularly employed in this area to shotguns without halls.

1221

1221–23, 1225–27, 1231–33. The two-story, masonry-fronted, five-bay house at **1221–23** Tremé was built in the Greek Revival style as a multiple-family dwelling, probably soon after 1857, when Achille Tardie, owner of an Esplanade lumberyard, bought its containing lots. The house has side galleries at the first level beyond the entrances and second-level façade galleries with cast-iron railings and overhang cresting. Although Tardie acquired buildings with his purchase,

1225

21/20

archival research has indicated that they were part of a vanished complex of common-wall creole cottages illustrated in an 1841 drawing by Gaux (plan book 21, folio 20). Tardie lived in the townhouse at 1221–23 only until 1860. It then passed into the hands of several investors: Armand, Duchenne, D'Aquin, and Lafferanderie. The Lafferanderie family held the property, along with numerous other holdings in the area until 1956, at which time it was brought by Dr. Anita Crozat. The cottage at **1225–27**, to the right of the townhouse, with an unadorned canted overhang, was once a segment of a common-wall creole cottage (plan book 21, folio 20). Athalie Drouillard, f.w.c., evidently built 1225–27 and **1231–33** after acquiring the lots in a sale from the First Municipality in 1841. Mme Drouillard's houses occupied over 105 feet of frontage on Tremé; they included a triplex, frame creole cottage approximating the present site of 1221–23 and a quadruplex, corner creole cottage incorporating the present houses at 1225–27 and 1231–33. Once a common-wall quadruplex, the house was split, leaving a double creole cottage now 1225–27. The present corner property at 1231–33 has been raised, filled-in, and mutilated; the detached, two-story kitchen survives behind it, as seen in the 1841 archival drawing by Gaux. Mme Drouillard sold both sets of houses in the summer of 1841, but she reappears in the title between 1853 and 1857.

1300, 1306

Collard Properties, 1300, 1306, 1312. Jean Mager left much Faubourg Tremé property to his sister, Mme J. B. Collard, who lived in France. Her sons, J. B. and A. T. Collard, also lived in France and received this Tremé Street property in their mother's succession in 1859. The same year they sold two lots, perhaps with the extant house at **1306**, to M. Edmund Soniat-Dufossat for $4,500. Dufossat subdivided the lots in 1860 and sold the corner at **1300** Tremé to John Clark for $1,700, as recorded by A. Doriocourt on May 15. Clark probably built the corner house after 1860, selling it in 1881 for $2,125 (November 21, A. J. Lewis). The side-hall townhouse, recently renovated, has original Classic-style decorative elements, such as Greek Key entrance, second-level cast-iron gallery, and Classic cornice. **1306** Tremé, another side-hall, galleried townhouse, has been drastically altered. The side gables here suggest that the house may date from the Collard ownership before 1859. The handsome Italianate entablature could have been added to an earlier Classic-style structure. The second-level, front gallery has been filled in, and an ill-proportioned side octagonal bay added. Unfortunate and incorrect brick facing at the first level has been superimposed on the façade. **1312** postdates 1883, but it is compatible in scale with its earlier neighbors and remains an intact, late-Victorian townhouse.

URSULINES

1118–20

Levasseur Cottage. When Firmin Levasseur bought this property on March 31, 1848, at the sheriff's sale of the estate of Widow Pigneguy, the property included "a good kitchen consisting of five rooms, together with the privies attached to said lot. Said kitchen being partly built of solid bricks, and partly of bricks between posts." Widow Pigneguy's house faced N. Rampart, extending 120 feet on Ursulines, and the kitchen belonged to her house. Seven months later, on October 28, 1848 (A. Ducatel), Firmin Levasseur sold 30 feet of the Pigneguy property with a brick, gable-sided creole cottage to Nelson Maritche for $1,700. The act of sale described "a house of which one slope of the roof gives onto the neighboring property belonging to the said Sieur Levasseur, at the top of which, to the height of said roof, is placed a gutter to receive the rainwater; it is expressly agreed, by those present, that the things will stay just as they are, in so far as the said house will not be destroyed either by a major force, nor by the will of the said Sieur Maritche." After twenty years, Maritche sold the creole cottage to Marguerite Guillard, Widow F. Escoffier, for $2,200 in an act before O. Drouet on February 17, 1868. A close look at this property reveals the original 1848, brick, gable-sided creole cottage. However, things did not stay as they were; a subsequent owner has added a two-story front to this cottage and tacked on a 1930s-style, stucco, double-level porch.

1122–24

Fleitas Cottage. Siding, millwork, and overhang decoration have been added to this outstanding creole cottage, probably built in the 1820s. Barthélémy Fleitas purchased this lot, with a variety of earlier buildings, from Baptiste Bazile Beauregard on December 24, 1824, for $1,825 before notary C. de Armas. Beauregard and a previous owner, Julien Domingon, both owned larger portions of the square with a *maison de maître* built on the property. Fleitas, however, removed the service buildings and had this creole cottage constructed soon after his 1824 purchase. When Marie Dorothée Cucullu, Widow Barthélémy Fleitas, sold the house on March 17, 1876 (J. Mossy), it was numbered 164 and 164½ Ursulines Street. Since this 1974 photograph, a wooden porch has been replaced by a concrete one. Neither porch represents an original arrangement; the cottage once had wooden steps either at all four openings or at the outer two. The banquette also has been widened, thus putting this slightly set-back creole cottage directly on the sidewalk.

1130–32

Levasseur Properties. Among the properties owned by the Claude Levasseur family for fifty years were these two houses at **1126** and **1130–32** Ursulines. Monsieur Levasseur purchased 120 feet on Ursulines from 1126 to the corner, numbered 1040 St. Claude in 1822. The previous owner had been H. J. Domingon, who purchased two 160-foot lots, one from the city and one from Joshua Veasey in 1816 and 1819 (November 18, 1816, M. de Armas; June 20, 1819, John Lynd). Claude Levasseur built two handsome houses on his lots. One of them, the extant house at 1130–32 Ursulines, was described in 1860 when there was a partition among the Levasseur heirs. Térence Firmin Levasseur acquired "house, brick between posts, five rooms, of which four rooms are with fireplaces, gallery, two-story brick kitchen of six rooms with fireplaces, cistern, waterworks, etc." The described house was probably built soon after Levasseur's 1822 acquisition of the property. As seen today, 1130–32 has a masonry front and fifth opening in the Greek Revival style added later as an entrance to a side gallery. The brick-between-posts sides are covered with weatherboard. The large two-story kitchen remains across the back of the lot. Térence Levasseur kept his family home only six years, selling it to Widow A. Lanusse on April 13, 1866, before P. Larèsche. The two-bay, masonry house standing at 1126 Ursulines is an attractive part of the street scene with two French doors and a half-hip-roof. It stands on a 22½-foot lot. The retaining wall toward N. Rampart Street with its chimneys may have served as a two-story kitchen for the 1820s complex. Whether 1126 Ursulines was part of the kitchen belonging to the elder Levasseur or is a reconstruction using old bricks is not known. There is also an old masonry building spanning the property lines of 1126 and 1130–32, part of the former Levasseur property. Three shotguns facing St. Claude have replaced the other Levasseur cottage and gardens.

1135–37

75/1

Rouzan Property, 1135–37, 1139–41. These properties were part of the *maison de maître* complex of Michael Meffre-Rouzan, who owned them between 1819 and 1840, after purchasing them from the city on September 28, 1819, as indicated in the title for 1112 St. Claude. At the St. Claude corner, **1139–41**, a masonry creole cottage with hip-roof and gabled fire-extension side was built between 1840 and 1849. On June 23, 1849, an archival drawing was made by A. Castaing to advertise the sale of the house (plan book 75, folio 1). The drawing, although damaged, reveals an *abatvent* completely surrounding both street roof elevations, as well as a banquette covering, supported by posts. The cottage has four, full-length, casement doors opening onto Ursulines and St. Claude; two double-hung windows remain in their original placement. **1135–37**, with which this house presently shares a common wall, was also built in the 1840s for F. Buisson and P. Dupeaux. They bought the lot from the Rouzan estate in 1840. Both houses have been reroofed, thus altering their original configuration.

1200

Abadie Store-House. This 1200 block of Ursulines Street marks the beginning of the property line of the Collège d'Orléans. In 1826 when the college failed and the property reverted back to city ownership, Félix Pinson, architect, acquired 150 feet fronting on Ursulines by 110 feet facing St. Claude. As early as 1827 there was a brick house near this site, facing St. Claude at 1027–29, now demolished. Pinson sold the corner lot to Bazile Raphael Crocker, f.m.c., in 1829. Crocker then sold the lot to F. Lambola (October 7, 1830, L. T. Caire). By July 21, 1856, when the heirs of Juan Marcos sold this lot to Demosthenes Charles Azaretto for $3,500 (O. de

Armas), there were "two houses, one at the corner and a two-story brick house facing Ursulines." The corner house was demolished, probably soon after November 10, 1856, when Azaretto sold his property to Bertrand Abadie, before J. Cuvillier. Abadie built the extant, two-level store-house, which was described in the 1883 sale to Jules Benezech as "having a large room used as a grocery, three bedrooms, a little building of bricks facing St. Claude, another two-story building of wood, a courtyard, etc." Painting and improved sign placement would restore this four-bay façade.

1201–17

Morand Plantation. Toward the end of the century, such galleried shotguns replaced earlier creole cottages. Their scale and repetition create a pleasant addition to the street scene. Some were constructed of flatboat boards set vertically on a sill, covered with weatherboards. Others were of traditional frame construction. The price of these cottages, with similar proportions and numbers and sizes of rooms depended upon the quantity of jigsaw work with which the box-like houses were embellished.

1208

Collège d'Orléans Property. This two-story brick house on the property of the former Collège d'Orléans may well be a portion of the original college building designed by Gurlie and Guillot in 1814. Sold to Félix Pinson and Evariste Blanc, the property was described in 1827 as a "lot with two houses, one at the corner, and one two-story brick house fronting Ursulines Street." On September 18, 1829, Pinson sold the entire property, measuring 150 feet on Ursulines by 120 feet on St. Claude, to Basile Rafael Crocker, f.m.c. (L. T. Caire). Crocker sold both the corner property and this two-story house at 1208 to Francisco Lambola the following year, and in 1832 they were purchased by Juan Marcos for $3,600. Marcos and his wife, Dame Carmelite Arambureo, retained the property for twenty-four years, after which she sold them before N. Vigné on July 12, 1856. Demosthenes Charles Azaretto bought the two houses, selling 1208 Ursulines in 1865 to Pierre Casse. It was described in the act recorded by J. Cuvillier on August 10, 1865, as: "One lot of ground 28 feet front on Ursulines by 48 feet depth. A two-story brick house à étage, No. 176 having three rooms for domestics, an iron balcony over the street on the side, water works, latrines, etc." This house, if it indeed is the one extant in 1826, has been altered through the years. The present fence, rear buildings, and the house itself are of architectural and historical importance; and the house is among the few two-story buildings dating from the 1820s in Faubourg Tremé. Most of the original college buildings were demolished for the extension of Ursulines Street.

1218

Lavigne House. Here stands an early, two-story, gable-sided creole house—a rare house-type. Such urban examples are built flush with the banquette, often having balconies or galleries at the second level, front and rear. The house, one room deep, has a rear gallery that has been enclosed. It was described in the 1848 succession sale of Edouard Lavigne to A. Desjardin, when it brought $1,850, as "the wood house with two stories and all the dependencies," In fact, the house appears to date from 1830, when it may have been one of a number of "buildings not yet finished," which Bazile Raphael Crocker, f.m.c., sold to Christian Roselius for $1,500. The lot was part of the Collège d'Orléans complex, which was purchased by Félix Pinson and Evariste Blanc in 1826 after the college closed. Pinson sold the "establishment known formerly as the Collège d'Orléans" to Crocker in 1829. One year later, Crocker made his sale to Roselius, in which the act stipulated that "the vendor promises to furnish the doors, and glass for doors and windows, a quantity of prepared planks . . . all the moldings necessary for the double mantlepieces and the fastenings for shutters, a quantity of bricks, and finally, about fifty cypress laths 15 feet long, 7 inches wide and ¾ inch thick, all wood of good quality and well made" (November 25, 1830, L. T. Caire). Crocker contracted with Clemire Joseph Orso and Louis Coussy to finish the buildings.

1223

1221

Demonceaux House (1223), 1221. These two residences illustrate the continuing preference for the side-gallery version of the shotgun in this neighborhood. The hip-roof shotgun at **1223** is detailed in the Classic style, with the narrow, pilastered entrance peculiar to the creole suburbs. The brackets were probably added along with the drop-siding in the late nineteenth century. All other indications are that the house dates from the mid–nineteenth century. The same floor plan is utilized at **1221** in a once-identical twin that has been remodeled in the style of the 1890s with façade and roof alterations. 1223 Ursulines was built for Pierre Derrys Demonceaux, whose family owned the lot from 1833 until 1882. The lot had been acquired by Pierre R. Colsson, president of the Architects Company, who also had bought part of the Pontalba division in 1827, a year after the city subdivided the square of the Collège d'Orléans grounds. When Colsson sold much of the block to Pierre Courotte for $2,500 in 1829, there were buildings and improvements (June 9, F. de Armas). Courotte made a profit, selling these same old buildings and improvements to Demonceaux for $4,000 in 1833. The old buildings were demolished probably about 1860, but Demonceaux kept a lot 50 feet on Ursulines, building this Classic-style house at 1223. The Demonceaux heirs sold it to Marie Queyron, widow of Charles Vignaud, for $1,200 in 1882 (May 22, O. Drouet).

1314

Collège d'Orléans Property, 1304–06, 1314. When the Collège d'Orléans failed in 1826, a subsequent sale of property was held by the city on August 12, and Felix de Armas bought lots on Ursulines by 172 feet for $300 (H. Lavergne). Without making improvements, de Armas sold his land within a few days to Baptiste Hardy and Isabelle Dupart, f.p.c. This property included the sites of 1304–06 and 1314. Paul Cheval, Isabelle Dupart's son, acted on her behalf in these sales. Roman Otero owned the property at **1304–06** and the corner of Ursulines and Marais in 1836. The present four-bay, shotgun double at 1304–06 represents at least the second structure on the site. At **1314** Ursulines, a turn-of-the-century, two-bay shotgun replaced a "brick-between post-house roofed in slate with eight rooms, a two-story kitchen, and other edifices in the court," which the heirs of Paul Cheval sold on October 29, 1850, for $3,200 before notary P. C. Cuvellier.

1318–20

Biamonti Cottage (1318–20), 1322. A close look at the side of the illustrated residence reveals that a set-back creole cottage has been changed by the additions to the façade of a Second Empire-style tower and front gabled room. A building contract for the cottage, notarized by C. Pollock on May 21, 1836, states that Jean Labernadie built the house for Joseph Biamonti, who had bought the lot earlier that year from Raphael Roth. The house was to be "27-foot front on Ursulines by 40-foot depth, divided into eight rooms, four rooms, and two *cabinets* below and two little rooms in the attic, with a gallery across the rear; openings comprise twelve doors, four on the façade, four for communication, two on the gallery and two for *cabinets*. Four windows, one to each *cabinet*, and one to each room giving onto the roof, conforming to the plan; cost $2,200." The Biamonti heirs sold the house to Louis Reichman for $4,300 on May 28, 1867, before E. G. Gottschalk. The alterations to the house were probably made about 1890. The property at **1322** emanates from a portion of the Collège d'Orléans, sold by the city to Felix de Armas in 1826. On December 31, 1830, Bazile Beauregard received title to this lot as part of a larger parcel, bound on the right 172 feet by land of Isabelle Dupart, f.w.c., and on the left 161 feet by land of Ramon Otero. Beauregard bought the property at a December 11, 1830, auction of De Armas holdings for $800. When he sold it to Gaspard Romain seven years later, there was a creole cottage on the site. Romain kept his property for fifty-three years; his heirs sold it for $1,300 in 1890. Purchaser of the early house was Dr. Oscar Lanng, who replaced the creole cottage with this single, frame shotgun with hip-roof. The three-bay house exhibits a recessed front door and panel reveals. Date palms in the courtyard and sweet olive trees across the front of the lot are a nostalgic note.

1330–32

Dupeaux Cottages. 1326 is a single, three-bay, frame shotgun with hip-roof and brackets supporting an overhang. The entrance leads into a recessed side gallery. **1330–32** Ursulines, a double shotgun identical in detail to its neighbor, is a four-bay version of the local, shotgun house-type. These houses with restrained decoration postdate 1883, replaced a corner creole cottage that faced Marais Street, and were probably the property of B. Dupeaux. Ursulines Street was not cut through until Dupeaux gave the land to the city for its extension. Housed in the Louisiana State Museum in the American Documents, Book 4084, 1823–1835, states: "Aug. 11, 1827. The undersigned respectfully represents to you that he is the owner of a certain lot of ground situated between St. Philippe and Marais streets and the Bayou Road; that for public benefit he is disposed to dedicate Ursulines street upon said property, which would lengthen it by about 300 feet, providing the Corporation immediately lay sidewalks and curbings upon both sides of said portion of street, [re straightening Marais St. per surveyors plan—opposes it]. B. Dupeaux. The undersigned intends to have several houses built upon Marais Street immediately."

1313

44/72

Fernández Cottage. The archival drawing in plan book 44, folio 72 shows this three-bay creole cottage as it appeared in 1870. Comparison with the extant house illustrates how a cottage like this one, dating from the 1830s, was changed through the years. The house today has segmental-arched, full-length openings, a bracketed overhang, and a façade with wooden siding. The archival drawing reveals that the façade originally was lathed and plastered and had a Greek Key entrance and two, square-headed, full-length, casement windows. The plan shows an entrance leading to the side hall of a four-room house. A delicate, wrought-iron balcony in the side gable looked over a garden enclosed behind a high, handsome fence with wood-paneled base. The detached kitchen was originally a two-level building with pitched roof along the side of the lot. Title research terminated when the house was sold by Marie Tessier, Widow Philocles Fernández, to her five children in an 1878 succession sale (May 20, W. H. Seymour), when it was old number 201. It was resold immediately to Chrétièn Geiser for $1,100.

1317–19

Brulé Cottage. This once-fine creole cottage with double dormers probably dates from 1826–1828, about the same period as its neighbor at 1313 Governor Nicholls. Segmental-arched dormer lights with fluted pilasters and four full-length casement openings are clues to the early building date. The present doors, drop-siding, molded cornices, and overhang with brackets postdate the construction of 1317–19 Ursulines. When the Collège d'Orléans was sold in blocks, Florville Brulé, f.m.c., and François Meilleur purchased this lot in 1826. When Brulé sold out to Meilleur on December 15, 1828 (F. de Armas), the description was "a lot 30 feet on Ursulines by 111 feet in depth, together with the house of brick between posts, not yet finished, plus materials." The price for Brulé's half-interest was $950. Here is a typical example of a business partnership between races in Faubourg Tremé. By August 10, 1830, Oscar Fortier, f.m.c., had bought the lot and the brick-between-posts house, selling it to Innocente Montegut, Widow Galatos, for $2,000. The Amedée Galatos succession sold the property at a public auction on February 14, 1846 (T. Guyol).

1428, 1432–34

1400 Block. The only remaining early building in this block of Ursulines today is a three-bay, frame, single shotgun with hip-roof at **1428**. The Greek Key entrance leading to a recessed side gallery backed by a *cabinet* and a high hip-roof suggest that this house could date from the 1860s, with a new roof and weatherboarding added. It is shown on the Robinson Atlas of 1883. The four-bay, double shotgun at **1432–34**, although similar in type and configuration to 1428, is a much later house, postdating 1883. Economy Hall, well known because of its association with the development of New Orleans jazz, once stood adjacent to 1428 Ursulines at 1424–26. Louis Armstrong was among the musicians who performed there, and the structure was a landmark until demolished as a result of damage suffered in a 1964 hurricane. Many benevolent societies in the mid–nineteenth century were organized to aid their members in financial and social matters. The Société Economier et d'Assistance Mutuelle built Economy Hall as a meeting place in 1856. The building contract between William Belley and the Société was recorded on September, 1856, by J. Lisbony. Representing the Société were A. Delpeuch, A. J. Cheveau, Joseph Abeilard, Adolphe Angelain, and François Boisdoré. According to the contract, Belley was obliged to demolish an old building on the lot and use the materials.

1431–33

Passebon Cottage. This outstanding plastered-brick, creole cottage was built in 1843 by Pierre Passebon, the builder of a row of masonry cottages in the 1300 block of Esplanade. According to testimony before notary Félix Percy, November 25, 1843, Passebon sold the corner lot with the new house, which he had built and paid for, to Marie Glapion, f.w.c., for $2,900. Passebon had acquired the empty lot from André Billaud in July of 1843 for $500 before notary Percy. Earlier owners of the land were several free persons of color, including Celestin Populus and Joseph François Valentin. The Glapion family held the house and lot until 1857, when on May 7, before notary J. Lisbony, it was sold for $3,000 to Charles St. Martin. St. Martin used the house as rental property. Subsequent owners were Charles Genois and Claire Bourgeau. Architectural features of 1431–33 include a *cabinet* to the rear, cornice with sawtooth and dentil molding, narrow delicate double dormers, and flush opening frames. One gable end has a quarter-moon ventilation opening, apparently with the original strap-hinged covers.

1526–28

Soublet-Fortier House. J. F. Perrault, f.m.c., bought two lots on which the present house at 1526–28 Ursulines stands, purchasing one from builder J. L. Dolliole, f.m.c., in 1832 and another from A. B. Courcelle in 1836. He resold to Thomas Soublet, f.m.c., for $1,250 in 1836. Soublet built a creole cottage the same year, selling it to Fifi Poupon, f.w.c., for $3,000 on July 27, 1836 (T. Seghers). Mme Poupon kept it only a year, selling to L. A. Morin, f.m.c. (October 21, 1837, L. T. Caire). Morin turned over the creole cottage in 1839 for $3,250 to Rosella and Henriette Fortier, who retained the oft-traded property until 1901. The Fortier sisters, probably in the 1850s, incorporated the early Soublet creole cottage into the present, six-bay, double house. There are open side galleries behind each Classic-style entrance, which were added to the four-bay creole cottage. Behind the screens early French doors and transoms remain. The hip-roof is pierced by the original chimneys.

1511

Tureaud House. This Classic-style, galleried, center-hall, side-gabled cottage is an important building in Faubourg Tremé. The central entrance has Greek Key molding with a Classic-style lintel. A stuccoed front contrasts with wooden side gables. The gallery cornice has dentils and paired brackets. Full-length façade openings, dormers with arched lights, side gables, and *cabinet* galleries are creole characteristics. A late-nineteenth-century garden planted with sweet olive, lantana, crepe myrtle, and poinsettias adds charm. Widow Thérèse Conand bought the lot in 1845 from Lucien Soulié (June 9, T. Guyol) and in 1849 presented it to her daughter Catherine Claire Conand, when she married Théodore Tureaud. The house was built soon afterward and was the Tureaud family home until 1891, when Mme Tureaud left it to her children and grandchildren. These heirs sold it to John Klorer in 1891 for $1,315 on March 2, before Paul Conand. Théodore Tureaud was a Frenchman who had come to New Orleans in 1814; between 1823 and 1842 he lived on Bayou Road between Tremé and St. Claude. His mother-in-law, Mme Conand, lived at 179 Customhouse, which is the present 1300 block of Iberville. The early history of the property reveals ownership, from 1837 until 1845 by three prominent free persons of color, Appolinaire Perrault and Bernard and Albin Soulié.

1519–21

Sauvinet Property. The five-bay, double camelback is an unusual version of the late-Victorian, two-family dwelling, dating perhaps from the 1880s. There are two entrances, one of which leads to a side gallery on the N. Villere side of the house. Pierced-work cornices, brackets and verge, drop-siding, quoins, and cast-iron ventilators are typical decorations of this period. The steps and landings are architecturally incompatible with the house style.

1523

Sauvinet Cottage. This is a three-bay, frame creole cottage with dormer in the early-Classic style. The lot was part of the holdings of Valery Robert Avart, whose syndic sold it to Manis Jacob on January 31, 1824, before Félix de Armas. J. L. Dolliole, f.m.c., owned part of the lot in 1832 but sold it to A. B. Courcelle. Joseph Sauvinet joined three small parcels on Ursulines by 1837, having bought from Manis Jacob and A. B. Courcelle. Sauvinet built this house in the early 1840s, and his family sold it to Carlos Menendez on November 4, 1873, as recorded by notary J. L. Laresche. The Menendez family retained the fine cottage for almost a century. In 1957 Dr. Anthony Menendez and other heirs inherited it from the succession of Marie Menendez.

1527

Ladreyère-Cheron House. This house was originally a two-bay, galleried townhouse as shown in an illustration in plan book 2, folio 14, dated 1872, executed when the Celina Clermont succession sold to Henriette Blache for $3,500. The alteration of the house into a three-bay townhouse occurred sometime after 1872. The house was built in 1847, when Caroline Périn, f.w.c., sold an earlier creole cottage to Cyprien Courbé Ladreyère for $800. Ladreyère constructed this two-story house, selling it to Pierre André Destrac Cazenave for $4,000. The house was described in an 1898 sale as "a fine, two-story residence, rented at $16 per month. It is near the Canal and Claiborne cars, and the Dumaine Street line passes in front. Close proximity to churches, markets, schools, and other conveniences. Residence having two rooms, hall, and gallery on lower floor; two rooms, *cabinet*, and side gallery on upper floor; rear building with three rooms, gallery privies, cistern, etc. known as 1527 Ursulines." On May 21, 1928, tutor Henry Ries sold the house to his charge, Herbert Cheron, who has lived there ever since (W. M. Gurley).

2/14

Soulié-Tureaud Cottage. The double-dormered, creole corner store-house at 1529–33 is of brick construction, with a recent wooden layer over the exterior. Batten shutters retain their original hardware. The door and window surrounds are narrow strips of cypress set flush with the brick, indications of an early building date. The angle of the gabled ends and fine proportions of the dormers with arched lights further suggest an 1830s construction. In 1837 Achille Barthélémy

1529–33

Courcelle sold this lot to Bernard Soulié, f.m.c., the prominent investor-builder whose offices were located on N. Rampart Street. Lucien Soulié, brother of Bernard, sold the lot, with the new house he had built about 1838, to Claire Conand, Widow Théodore Tureaud (June 9, 1845, T. Guyol). She and her heirs kept the house until March 2, 1891, when her succession sold it to Emile Cheron, who lived next door (P. A. Conand).

1605–07

1600 Block. The Bayou Road *habitations* in this block from which Ursulines was formed were subdivided by their respective owners in the early 1830s. **1605–07** Ursulines, a creole cottage with weatherboards, has small roundheaded dormers, suggestive of an 1830 to 1840 building date. Five frame, late-Victorian cottages with a variety of jigsaw work and rooflines replace other cottages. A two-level, plastered structure was formerly the kitchen building of a creole cottage at **1604–06**. The hip-roof and proportions suggest an 1830s building date and remind one of the kitchen at 1505–07 St. Ann. Fenestration alteration and a new balcony with a center stair disguise the true nature of an early creole outbuilding. The houses at each end of the block have been mutilated. The Claiborne expressway dead-ends here; it could be an attractive tree-lined cul-de-sac.

1726

Griffon Division. This fine, single-dormered, two-bay, creole cottage has an excellent, galleried, two-story service wing. It was built soon after 1859, when Hippolyte Griffon sold the lot to Louis Mathé for $600. When Mathé's widow, Evelina Davis, died a half-century later, the house at old number 270 Ursulines was her residence. It was valued at $3,000 on February 23, 1903, when her estate sold it to Alice Celine Boubède, wife of Leon L. Paty (J. F. Meunier).

1723

Griffon Division. The three-bay, Greek Revival creole cottage at 1723 Ursulines has been drastically modernized. The front gallery, brick façade, arrangement of openings, and front-gabled roof were added in the 1930s. The cottage retains gabled sides, the first clue to its original appearance. It was built on the land of the old Griffon *habitation*, subdivided in the 1830s.

1800

Piernas Store-House. The two-story, gable-sided structure set back on the lot is part of an early, corner creole cottage complex built for Antoine Crispin Piernas in the late 1830s. Piernas combined two lots after two purchases, buying 23 feet on Ursulines by 60 feet on N. Derbigny in 1836 from Daniel Montesquieu, f.m.c., and 15 feet on Ursulines by 60 feet depth from Vincent Gonzalez in 1838. Piernas sold the house and outbuildings to Joseph Chevalier for $1,400 (May 10, 1860, J. Lisbony). The creole cottage at the banquette was reroofed and Victorianized with a front gable, segmental arches, brackets, drop-siding, and quoins by L. C. Huet and his wife, Marie Lagrange, in 1889. In the same year, they sold the building, referred to as a "grocery store and contents," to Pauline Clairin, Widow John Puissegur. At that time the real estate was valued at $1,600 and the grocery store at $250.

1818

Duberalle Cottage. The present siding, steps, and City Beautiful-style columns make the dating of this dormered, creole cottage with built-in gallery difficult to see. Title research indicates, however, that the cottage was built in the 1850s. Théodule Duberalle's family lost it at a sheriff's sale to A. Pignatel in 1858 for just $600. The act of sale indicates that there were buildings and improvements; just seven months later, Pignatel sold the house to J. A. Delery fo $1,600. The cottage was probably raised and remodeled by the Emile Bonnaffon family, who owned it from 1903 through the 1940s.

1834

Pontalba Division. Plan book 2, folio 8 shows this very early, three-bay shotgun with side gallery as it appeared in 1859, when the plan and elevation were made by C. A. de Armas for a sheriff's sale. The house was built soon after Ursulines Street was cut through here, at about mid–nineteenth century. Removal of the entrance transom and batten window shutters has spoiled the picturesque effect; the cement landing is too massive for the scale of the house.

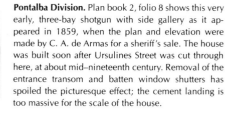

2/8

1803

Griffon Division. 1803, 1817, 1821. A three-bay, frame, creole cottage pictured has one front dormer, gabled sides, and a two-story, frame, three-bay galleried service wing extending from the middle portion of its rear. The cottage was designed in the Greek Revival style with late-nineteenth-century millwork additions. It stands on a corner lot with herringbone-patterned brick sidewalks on the N. Derbigny Street side. The house was built soon after 1858 for Joseph Azemar, f.m.c., who bought the vacant lot for $700 from Mlle Louise Arsène Vitry, f.w.c., at auction before A. Doriocourt on March 31, 1858. The property had been part of the Griffon tract, but this portion of Ursulines was not cut through until the late 1840s. The city had originally bought this lot for the Ursulines

Street projection. When Azemar sold on June 6, 1865, to François Surmely before A. Boudousquie, the cottage was described as "a frame house with three rooms and *cabinets* and entrance and room in the attic. Also a kitchen, etc." The lot then measured 42 feet on Ursulines by 83 feet on N. Derbigny, and the complex sold for $3,975. At **1817** Ursulines is a four-bay, two-story, 1870s, frame house with a two-story, detached, service wing running across the rear of the lot. The balcony at the second level is presently railed with wrought iron. A deep overhang with dentils is supported by brackets. **1821** is a three-bay, frame, creole cottage with gabled ends and a two-story ell to the rear on N. Roman. There is also a detached service building across the rear. The house now has a large, Second Empire-style dormer, possibly dating from the last quarter of the century, as do the decorative vergeboard, brackets and pierced-work cornices. The handsome recessed entrance has a cut-glass oval transom.

1933–35

1910–12, 1922–24, 1933–35, 1934–36. This Victorian double, two-story house at **1933–35** Ursulines illustrates the continued preference in New Orleans for the box-shaped, symmetrical house. The double front gables, central dormer with paired windows, and repetitive spindle work are rhythmic motifs superimposed on the basic structure. It was probably built between 1880 and 1889 by George Lanaux. Joseph Dumas sold four lots, including this site, to Dorcino Landry for $5,200 on July 31, 1860 (E. Laresche), the high price indicating that there were rental houses on the four lots. Landry made $2,000 seven years later in 1867, selling the same property of four lots to Jules Lemaire for $7,250. In an 1879 sheriff's sale, Lemarie lost the property at public auction to Isabelle Chery Rigaud, Widow Edouard de Phelps. Mme de Phelps, who lived in Paris, sold the property to George Lanaux. Lanaux redeveloped the property and built the present double house, selling it on April 18, 1889, to John Morris for $4,900 (A. Hero, Jr.). Across the street at **1910–12** Ursulines is a 1920s-style, frame cottage set behind a wrought-iron fence. This pleasant house is an unusual example of the southern country house of the turn of the century, not often found in the city. Two frame shotgun doubles at **1922–24** and **1934–36** have minimal decoration, including segmental-arched openings and drop-siding.

2014–16

44/36

Gurlie Division. This four-bay, galleried, frame creole cottage with gabled ends was built on the Gurlie division, subdivided in the 1830s. The late-Victorian window frames contrast with a simple gallery having Greek Revival-style pillars supporting an undecorated cornice. The original wooden floor to the gallery has been cemented. An archival drawing by C. A. de Armas in plan book 44, folio 36 illustrates this galleried creole cottage in 1855. The cottage then appeared at the banquette and was flanked by a split cypress fence and several outbuildings within the garden area. The façade of the house was either rusticated wood or plaster, and all four casement openings had transoms and batten shutters. Later, 2014–16 was probably raised and moved slightly back into the garden behind an iron picket fence. Box columns similar to those seen in the 1855 drawing remain, as does a central chimney.

2007

Gurlie Division, 2007, 2037. Rustication on the façade, along with the heavy cornice with brackets and dentils, suggests an 1860s building date for this gable-sided house in the late-Classic style at **2007**. The spindle work and turned columns were added in the late nineteenth century; the gallery rail is new. The recessed entrance originally opened onto a side gallery, as is common with Classic-style houses of the 1860s. Chimneys are placed on exterior walls in the original part of the unusual, gable-sided house. Title research substantiates the architectural analysis. The house was built for Mme Emeline Doremus after 1851 (October 29, A. Chiapella), when she purchased the lot from Alexandre Emile Bienvenu. After her death, about 1867, her son August Boyd Doremus and her daughter Eleanora Maria sold their share of the new house to their sister, Osmane Maria, Mme Casanovas, who in turn sold in 1869 to Mme Caroline Hoffman Oulif for $1,300. The frame, Greek Revival cottage at 2037 Ursulines has a handsome, central, recessed entrance with pilasters and dentiled cornice and paneled storm doors. The door has sidelights and an oval transom. Two dormers with pilasters match the entrance. There is a service wing extending to the rear of the N. Johnson Street side.

2100

St. Joseph's Academy. Three Sisters of St. Joseph from Bourg, France, were sent by the Catholic Church in France to Louisiana in 1854 to work in the field of Catholic education. Their first school was in Bay St. Louis, Mississippi, but in 1857 they came to New Orleans at the request of Archbishop Blanc. Their first local location was a building on N. Galvez that they purchased; the school opened in 1858. Soon after, they established a boarding school on N. Galvez at St. Philip. At this time, a small chapel was built. In the yellow fever and cholera epidemic of 1867, the Sisters bought two houses on St. Philip, one of which was used as a community room and the other as a school for boys. Also, a small house on N. Johnson was purchased for the free school, which they had opened in 1858. Five buildings enhance this square and complete a comprehensive expansion program, which lasted from 1889 to 1960. The first building constructed by the Sisters which remains is the chapel. Located on the corner of Ursulines and N. Galvez, it was completed in 1887 and designed in the Gothic style by J. Freret, architect. Between 1964 and 1977 the chapel was used as the library for the Bell Junior High School. The Academy Building was erected by the Sisters of St. Joseph in 1904–1906, and was designed by Owen and Diboll, architects. The Diamond Jubilee Memorial Building on N. Galvez, behind the chapel, was erected to celebrate the seventy-fifth year since the founding of the order in New Orleans. This building was completed November 30, 1931, and designed by Diboll and Owen; the contractor was H. Pratt Farnsworth. St. Ambrose Hall was built for the Sisters in 1937, with Allison Owen as architect and Lionel F. Favret as contractor. All of this property was sold by the Sisters of St. Joseph to the Orleans Parish School Board in 1960. The order then moved to new buildings at 1200 Mirabeau Avenue. In 1964, the school board erected an addition to the buildings that became Andrew J. Bell Junior High School. This addition was designed by George Leake, architect. The contractor was C. B. Spencer Company, Inc.

St. Ann Grotto, 2101. According to the *WPA Louisiana Guide*, the "National Shrine of St. Ann is a composite shrine incorporating the features of Lourdes, Calvary, and the Scala Sancta with a shrine to St. Ann, all combined in a miniature cave of pink artificial rock." The Holy See established the Archconfraternity of St. Ann in New Orleans in 1926 and established the St. Ann National Shrine soon afterward.

2117

Pontalba Division, 2117, 2139. This raised, villa-style house in the photograph was built about 1858 for Charles Zenon Derbigny. In the eighteenth century, the property had been part of Almonester's holdings and was known in the nineteenth century as the second Pontalba division. Madame de Pontalba sold this square to Charles Z. Derbigny in 1837 (January 12, F. Grima). Derbigny sold eight lots, "with buildings built by the vendor since his acquisition," to Alcée Jacques Villere in 1859 for $4,500. In 1863 the house was involved in a partition and described as a "one-story frame house having five large rooms and two small rooms, a hall in the center, the outbuildings having six rooms, the whole covered with slate together with a shed in the yard, etc." Mme A. J. Villere, who was Delphine Odile Fleitas, sold the house to Mlle Marinace Castanedo on March 22, 1866, before S. Magner for $8,000. The present columns and other decorative details postdate the Classic-style house. It was raised; and the present columns, dormer, weatherboards, and cement gallery and steps are a result of this alteration. At **2139**, a two-story three-bay, late-Victorian, frame house has a medallion cornice decoration at the second-level gallery. The gallery supports, which are not original, ruin the effect of this sturdy house, situated on a large corner lot with brick sidewalk on the N. Galvez side.

2212

Dorgenois Division, 2212, 2220. Modern awnings, a brick-veneered façade, and fenestration changes have ruined this once-fine house at **2212**, which was probably built in the early 1850s in the old Lebreton-Dorgenois tract. There are indications that the gabled side has been re-covered, after removal of a portion of the house. At **2220** is a three-bay, late-1860s-style shotgun with a front gallery and Italianate double-bracketed and dentiled cornice below a parapet. Fluted Doric-type columns, cast-iron railing, and an entrance, framed by Classic-style pilasters, complete the composition.

2226–28

Valeton House. This late-Classic-style, four-bay shotgun with hexagonal bay has had late-Victorian decoration added. The façade has the original decorative parapet, bracketed and dentiled cornice in the Italianate manner, and iron gallery railing. The spindle work and pierced-work colonettes, spandrels, and bands are not original; but they add to the variety of decorative elements on the gallery as does the latticework boxing on the step sides. The present double-step railing of cast iron is a twentieth-century addition. The house was built between 1859 and 1868 for Henri Valeton from Nice, France. Valeton bought several lots from the McDonogh estate for $385 each, in 1859 (March 28, E. G. Gottschalk). When he sold this one to Alfred Broutin in 1868 for $1,600, the house stood on it (September 5, E. Eude). The property had been part of the Lebreton-Dorgenois holdings, which F. J. Lebreton Dorgenois had bought from Antonio Ramis in 1807 (September 24, P. Pedesclaux). After Dorgenois' death in 1814, it was inherited by Mme Joseph Labarre, the former Estelle Dorgenois. She sold a half-interest in her inheritance to L. W. Oakey, and they subdivided in 1844, when John McDonogh bought this square (November 2, P. P. Labarre).

2539

2539, 2637. This nineteenth-century, center-hall house at **2539** is located in the former Bernard Coquet tract. It recalls similar houses at 1511 and 2117 Ursulines. Gabled sides, small dormers, dentiled cornice, and wide columned gallery are all reflections of the Classic style. The present Doric columns and the narrow façade weatherboards, as well as the Queen Anne-style steps, are twentieth-century renovations. The five-bay, center-hall, late-Victorian house at **2637** was raised to create a New Orleans basement.

2640–44

Faubourg St. John. The Robinson Atlas of 1883 indicates that this entire square was undeveloped at that date. This six-bay, double shotgun probably was built in the 1890s. It has outside entrances leading to recessed side galleries. There is a shingled front gable, and a deep, slanted apron covers a gallery. This shotgun variation is a relatively rare type. It often has a recessed side gallery opening to an ell wing on both sides. The Queen Anne-type steps were added.

N. VILLERE

819

City Commons. This two-level, two-bay, frame house has a wooden gallery at the second level that returns around one side of the building. The house was built two rooms deep but has been doubled in size by the addition of another connecting wing. It was built for Félix Martin Alva after he bought property from Jean Théophile Cavelier, f.m.c., for $210 on December 1, 1835, as recorded by Félix de Armas. The house was held by the Alva family until March 18, 1860, when the Alva succession sold it at auction to Marie Elizabeth Dabdeuil, f.w.c., widow of St. Fort Aubrey. The act was passed on May 1, 1860, before notary F. Percy. Widow Aubrey held the house until 1862, when she sold it to Oscar Robin for $1,500. The property was originally a part of the City Commons, subdivided and sold at public auction on August 17, 1829.

825–27

City Commons, 821–23, 825–27. This portion of the Commons was subdivided in 1826 in a survey by J. Pilié, and three lots were then sold by the City Corporation to cabinetmaker Pierre Dutreuil Barjon, f.m.c. This is the same land from which 1505–07 St. Ann emanated. Among the property's speculators after Barjon were Oliver Blineau, P. R. Colsson, and La Compagnie des Architects. The present creole cottage at **825–27** was built between 1834 and 1836 by architect Maurice Pizetta, a one-time partner of Félix Pinson. La Compagnie des Architects auctioned the house to Isidore Lombard on January 25, 1836 (H. Pedesclaux), with a notice of special payment to Pizetta, Joseph Laurent, and Germain Plessy, respectively. A succession of free persons of color, including Virginie Trinidad and Eulalie Mandeville and her heirs, owned the cottage from 1838 until 1858. **821–23** N. Villere is a late-nineteenth-century, double, frame, Victorian camelback with hip-roof, jigsaw work, and segmental-arched openings. It is a replacement of another creole cottage built by the above investors. Free persons of color represented by Pierre Macarty, son of Eulalie

Mandeville, sold both houses to Jacques Becker in 1858. The subsequent owners included George Mery, Bertrand Morotte. François Dupierres, Jean Bazax, and Prosper Darrieux, bringing French ownership into the twentieth century.

917, 919–21

Morand Plantation, 917, 919–21, 925. The side-hall townhouse at **917** N. Villere was built as one of the three identical houses for Prosper Ganel soon after the 1859 purchase of three lots from Charles Gérard. Two of the lots faced Dumaine and one fronted on N. Villere. The house is described in the 1868 Ganel auction as a "two-story frame house No. 193; having, on the ground floor, hall, double parlors with sliding door, dining room and pantry under the staircase, three rooms above, two *cabinets* and balcony on the street; a two-story frame building in the yard of six rooms, paved yard, cistern, waterworks, privy, etc. . . . slate-roofed." E. Arata bought it for $5,950 (see 1501 Dumaine). **919–21** is a two-level, four-bay, Greek Revival house, which is a probable match to an 1859 building contract made before Edward Barnett, notary, on April 20, 1859. Elijah Cox, architect and builder for Marcelin Esmard, was to construct "a double, two-story dwelling of two tenements with kitchens and privies. Cost $4,700." **925** N. Villere is another three-bay townhouse, doubtless dating from the 1850s like its two neighbors.

1110, 1114

1110, 1114, 1116–18. In the eighteenth century a plantation including the small lots at 1110, 1114, and 1116–18 N. Villere was owned successively by Charles Morand, Paul Moreau, and Claude Tremé. From the early nineteenth century, they belonged to a succession of illustrious owners such as J. J. Isnard, Simon Meilleur, and Sylvain Peyroux. In 1808 the land had been part of a small *habitation* fronting 60 feet on Bayou Road and 540 feet along N. Villere, which Claude Tremé had sold to Pierre Guenon. Simon Meilleur demolished the early *maison principale* after his 1828 purchase, built the extant house at 1415 Bayou Road (Governor Nicholls), and sold the entire tract in 1836. Sylvain Peyroux, a heavy real estate investor throughout the city, had surveyor L. Surgi subdivide the remaining land into lots in 1839. Pierre Passebon bought these three lots in 1843, the act indicating that two notes were made to the order of Athalie Drouillàrd, Passebon's *placée* (July 5, F. Percy). The three creole cottages at **1110**, **1114**, and **1116–18** were probably built by Passebon before 1845; Mlle Drouillard acquired full ownership of 1110 in 1853. The pair of two-bay creole cottage at 1110 and 1114 have no dormers. The gabled ends are covered with wooden siding. 1110 has had a complete new façade added during the late Victorian period including enlargement of doors, decorative jigsaw surrounds, applied-work brackets, drop-siding, and quoins. At 1116–18 is a disguised, frame creole cottage with detached kitchen. The original gabled sides are still visible. The house may originally have been placed at the banquette, and was subsequently moved in order to attach the front building.

1222

Morand Plantation, 1222, 1236, 1240. A three-bay, single, frame camelback shotgun at **1222** was designed with two short windows, a recessed front entrance, and a low hip-roof. The architraves of the façade openings have fluting, bull's-eye, brackets, and cap-molded lintels with applied scallops. Two similar, small, three-bay, camelback, frame houses with hip-roofs at **1236** and **1240** were built with pilastered entrances leading to recessed side galleries. The type and proportion of the entrance surrounds on each house indicate the cottages may have been built in the 1860s. Perhaps the camelbacks were added as well as the Victorian verge decoration and brackets.

1231–33

1215, 1225–27, 1231–33. Illustrated is a handsome example of an unusual house-type. The six-bay, frame house with gabled sides and dormers was built as a double, using a combination of traditional creole building vocabulary with American decorative details. These American elements include the appearance of two narrow entrances in the middle of the façade, joined by a single Greek Key surround. 1436–38 N. Villere is another example of this rare type. Both of these houses were built in the 1880s. In 1868 this property, as yet undeveloped, belonged to speculator D. C. Azaretto. Azaretto sold it at a sheriff's sale on July 28, 1874, to investor C. E. Luther, who resold it immediately to the widow of the prominent architect-surveyor Louis Surgi. Mme Surgi paid $1,100 for her property, which contained some old kitchens and outbuildings from the earliest Dauphin complex and a warehouse used as the Pelican Brewery in 1883. Mme Surgi sold the brewery

building in 1886, along with a larger piece of land fronting on both N. Robertson and N. Villere, for $2,250 to Mme J. M. Sabalot, who built the present house. Mme Sabalot was residing in her new home by 1887, according to the city directory, when the home was numbered 293 Villere. Upon her death in 1892, an inventory of her property revealed ownership of 285, 287, and 289 Villere, as well as other lots in the square. The row of late-Victorian frame shotguns, both single and double, one-story and camelback, starting at **1215** through **1225–27** N. Villere forms an interesting unit adding to the overall street scene. All structures postdate the late 1880s. According to the Robinson Atlas of 1883, a brewery once occupied this N. Villere Street site also.

1253–55

Jane Milne Cottage. This fine, brick creole cottage is one of four that were built for Nancy and Jane Milne, f.w.c., by architect Claude Gurlie in November of 1840, according to a stipulation in the will of Alexander Milne, which read as follows: "after stipulating freedom to be given to his said two slaves as a compensation for their services and the great care they had taken of him in his old age and infirmities: first, a lot of ground, situated near his later residence, in the rear of this city, [bound by] Esplanade, Robertson, Villere and the contemplated projection of Quartier [Barracks] forming the corner of Esplanade and Villere; second, two brick houses of the cost of two thousand dollars each, and two other brick houses of the cost of three thousand dollars each, to be delivered together with the said lot, unto them the said Nancy and Jane, in full property to be had, held and owned by them in common as their proper estate; and third, the household furniture contained in his residence at the time of his decease, together with an allowance of three dollars per diem for their common support, from the day of his death to the period of the delivery of the aforesaid legacies and bequest . . . [building contract passed by this notary] between the said dative executor and Claude Gurlie, Master Builder, on the seventeenth of November 1840" (May 21, 1841, C. Pollock). Two of these houses faced Esplanade (see Volume V, *New Orleans Architecture*, page 80). The house at **1253–55** N. Villere was sold to Jane by Nancy Milne's estate in 1858 and was retained until 1875 by her. Then, before notary T. Buisson, Jane Milne, Widow Gustave Auguste Dauphin, f.w.c., sold it to John McIntosh Crawford for $1,050. This architect-designed, brick creole cottage with gabled parapets and central chimneys typifies the Classic style of the 1840s. The façade was originally plastered, and the dormers would have had the traditional pilasters and perhaps roundheaded lights. The four full-length openings were altered, and a fifth pilastered entrance leading to a recessed side gallery was added. A cast-iron gallery remains at the side second level, indicating that the property once included a garden site.

1436

De George House. This double house was built for Eugènie Montet, the wife of Antoine de George. She bought the lot for $700 from Frank Landfried on March 22, 1882, as recorded by notary O. Drouet. Since the house is not shown on the Robinson Atlas of 1883, it was built soon after. Dame Montet sold the house on March 2, 1914. Like 1231–33 N. Villere, this fine house exhibits both American and creole characteristics. The façade features, including two narrow, central entrances with segmental arches, wooden rustication, and a similar treatment of the large dormers, help to date the house. The built-in overhang has handsome brackets doubled at each end and interspersed with small brackets serving as dentils. This urban house is built very low to the ground at the banquette.

1419

Milne Estate. The site of this cottage was part of the Alexander Milne estate, which sold to Jean Adolphe Blanc on June 3, 1844, as recorded by notary Carlisle Pollock. By 1861 Blanc had sold the lot, which then contained a creole cottage complex, to Gustave Ducros for $2,700. The present house, however, was not built until after 1880. Thalie Guillotte, Widow Joseph Omer Ramos, bought the empty lot from Wentzel Zimmerman in 1879, leaving it to her daughter Josephine, Widow Auguste Huard. In 1884 Widow Huard's estate left the property to her son and daughters: Auguste, Thalie, and Blanche. The present house was built for these heirs, as documented by an auction notice in 1886 describing the property, when they sold it for $3,600. The auction notice presented in an act before P. A. Conand on May 11, described "an elegant, comfortable, and newly constructed one-story, frame, slated cottage, retired from the street, and containing front gallery, hall on the side, parlor, dining room, and four large bedrooms, and *cabinet*, comfortable bathrooms supplied with water from extra large cistern, pantry, kitchen, detached from main building, cellar, coalroom, privies, parterre on the side, alley way, bricked yard, etc." Louis Arnaud Pepin bought the house, selling it in 1892 for $3,500 to John Rousset with the following description: "The improvements consist of the charming raised cottage, retired from the street, nearly new, and in perfect order and condition, known by the municipal number 317 Villere, about 100 feet from Esplanade Avenue, and contains front gallery, side hall, parlor, dining room, three bedrooms, bathroom, kitchen, gas throughout, shed, privies, cistern, etc.; yard paved all with flagstone."

1423

Milne Estate. This three-bay, frame Classic-style camelback shotgun was built with a hip-roof and simple overhang, a recessed front entrance flanked by Classical pilasters with square capitals, and two full-length windows crowned by cap-molded lintels. A two-story service wing attached to the rear now creates a camelback, although this service area and kitchen were probably separate when the house was built, possibly in the 1860s.

1433

Clay House. (1433), 1435–37. The galleried, Classic-style cottage pictured features a bracketed cornice with parapet and a handsome pilastered entrance with dentiled cornice. Four box columns once had a wooden balustrade between them. Pierre Rillieux, builder, erected this house for Cecilia Clay, f.w.c., in 1855 for $1,100. The specifications of the building contract described this rare, galleried, two-room-deep hip-roof house: "The main building . . . 24 feet by 31 feet including two galleries . . . shall have two rooms in front with fireplace in each. The back gallery will be 10 feet and have a *cabinet* in each end . . . 7½ feet wide . . . the front gallery 6 feet wide with wooden balusters and cornice. . . . The building will rest on brick pillars . . . 24 inches above the banquet [*sic*] . . . all interior lathed and plastered three coats and hard finished . . . four dormer windows . . . all outside wall of weatherboarding except front . . . [which is to be] plastered three coats . . . all floors yellow pine, mill-dressed, tongued and grooved planks . . . two stairs . . . at front and back. . . . All doors and windows shall have sashes except two *cabinet* doors and garret windows. . . . All the woodwork painted as usual on the inside and outside, one coat of . . . yellow paint, and the balance two coats of white lead and oil or such other plain colors as may be chosen. The outside doors and windows . . . green. The kitchen shall be 20 feet by 10 feet divided in two rooms with a fireplace in each . . . built with flatboat planks and a whitewashed outside and inside; the doors and windows painted. A double privy shall be built with the same materials as the kitchen. All the buildings to be covered with shingles. There shall be tin gutters to the back part of the house conducting water to the cistern; said cistern shall be furnished by the proprietor. All materials . . . supplied by builders. . . . All the work . . . to be finished in three months from this date not including bad weather." Achille Tardy bought this house at a sheriff's sale on June 13, 1856, as the result of a suit between Paul Lieutaud and Cecilia Clay; selling it to Catherine McCarthy, Widow William Collerton, for just $2,300 three months later in an act before T. Guyol, September 24, 1856. When Mme Collerton died in 1884, this house was her residence, numbered 325 Villere. The four-bay frame creole cottage with gabled sides and built-in overhang at **1435–37** features two full-length openings

and two double-hung windows. The brick herringbone-patterned sidewalk still remains. The house was probably built in the late 1840s or 1850s when much of the Milne estate was built on.

1500–02

1500–02, 1522. This well-kept corner store-house at **1500–02** began as a creole cottage set back from the corner of Columbus and once was embellished with a front garden. The gabled sides and the central chimney remain and are incorporated into the present unit. The extension to the banquette of Columbus is an 1890s addition to an 1850s creole cottage. At **1522** a late-Victorian, frame shotgun, with two full-length front windows and front-gabled roof with apron, is being used as a church. A fancy gallery returns around the side of the house. The roof is supported by turned columns, above which is decorative sawed work with spindles, arranged in an unusual manner. Segmental-arched openings with the most decorative surrounds available in Robert's catalog have tripartite cornices with sawed-work cresting, bull's-eye, and fluting.

Guerlain Division, 1501–15. This row of four modest, early, frame creole cottages with built-in overhangs and gabled ends comprises an attractive grouping. The double houses, situated on the banquette, are notable in their simplicity; Victorian brackets and wooden lintels were added to the corner cottage in the 1890s. The row was probably built sometime after 1860 by Victor Morano after he purchased this first lot from François Pouget of Bordeaux, France, on June 6, 1860, as recorded by notary E. Bouny. The land in the eighteenth century was owned by Charles Morand and sold by his heirs to Paul Moreau, whose grandaughter Julie married Claude Tremé on March 21, 1793. Tremé sold a large portion of this property to Alexander Milne in 1800. Creole cottages, ranging in municipal numbers from **1501** to **1515**, begin at the corner of Columbus Street and run to the property line (now the middle of the block), which separated the Morand concession from the eighteenth-century holdings of the Marigny family. The property line is clearly marked on the Zimpel Survey of 1834 and separated Milne's holdings from those of Widow Honoré Guerlain. The frame creole cottages at **1527–29** and **1531–33** N. Villere are similar to four others on this block; however, the Greek Key surrounds on the openings of 1527–29 and 1531–33 are refinements not found on the others. The scallop-bordered overhangs were added later. The succession of Emile Dussuau gave incomplete information in the conveyance book records; therefore, an early title listing has not been found. Nevertheless, the two cottages stylistically seem to have been built in the 1860s.

NOTES

INTRODUCTION

1. Sidney K. Eastwood, "The Pintado Papers," *New Orleans Genesis*, vol. 3 (March, 1964), p. 139.
2. The street is called "Hospital" in "Atlas of the City of New Orleans, Louisiana," Elisha Robinson (New York, 1883).

Chapter I/**EARLY SETTLEMENT**

1. Marcel Giraud, *Histoire de la Louisiane française* (4 vols.; Paris, 1953–74); vol. 2: *Années de Transition, 1715–1717* (1958), pp. 80–81.
2. André Penicaut, *Fleur de Lys and Calumet: Being the Penicaut Narrative*, trans. and ed. Richebourg Gaillard McWilliams (Baton Rouge, 1953), pp. 203–204.
3. Marcel Giraud, *Histoire de la Louisiane française* (4 vols.; Paris, 1953–74). Translation of material pertaining to Hubert by Ghislaine Pleasanton, archivist, L.H.C.(A.).
4. "Plan de la Nouvelle Orléans, 1798," Carlos Trudeau. Map delineates the Hubert tract with measurements; L.S.M.
5. Penicaut, *Fleur de Lys*, pp. 210–11.
6. *Ibid.*, Chap. 22; see also Mobile Baptismal Records, May 18, 1718. When Hubert's child was baptized, his wife was listed as Lesteri.
7. Marc de Villiers, *Histoire de la Fondation de la Nouvelle Orléans* (Paris, 1917), p. 47.
8. Penicaut, *Fleur de Lys*, Chap. 22.
9. Giraud, *Année de Transition*; see Pleasanton translation, F.O.C. files, vol. 6, 1978.
10. Dunbar Rowland, *Mississippi Provincial Archives* (Jackson, Miss., 1917), p. 236.
11. "Figurativo de las diligencias mandadas por decreto del día," Carlos Trudeau, c. 1789; copy by M. Hardie, city engineer (March 5, 1912), City Engineer's Office, New Orleans.
12. Marcel Giraud, *Histoire de la Louisiane française* (4 vols.; Paris, 1953–74); vol. 1: *Le Regne de Louis XIV, 1698–1715* (1953).
13. Black Books, 1738, L.H.C.(L.). Joachim de Gauvrit's first daughter, Catherine, married Jean Baptiste Destrehan in New Orleans; Marie Elizabeth, Gauvrit's child by his second wife, married Joseph Mathurin Pellerin and lived on Bayou St. John. After his death she married Etiènne Bauré de Monléon.
14. "Carte Particulière du Fleuve St. Louis . . . ," Ayer Collection, Newberry Library, Chicago.
15. "Plan de l'Habitation de M. de Pontalba . . . ," Plan book 15, folio 1, N.O.N.A.
16. Black Books, October 13, 1731, L.H.C.(L.).
17. "Plan de la Nouvelle Orléans, 1798," Carlos Trudeau.
18. Black Books, 1753, L.H.C.(L.).
19. Map with annotations in private collection of Samuel Wilson, Jr.
20. Black Books, 1738, L.H.C.(L.).
21. Sale of land, Michel Brosset to Etiènne de Benac, March 26, 1738. Superior Council records, translated by Ghislaine Pleasanton, L.H.C.(A.).
22. "Plan of New Orleans Capitol City of Louisiana," Dumont de Montigny, Collection Guerre-Etat Major, Paris.
23. Black Books, 1735, L.H.C.(L.).
24. *Ibid.*, 1747; Duhomel was probably Louis Charles Duhomel, whose wife was Catherine Chauvin de la Frenière, daughter of Nicolas de la Frenière.
25. *Ibid.*, July 14, 1728.
26. Amos Stoddard, *Sketches, Historical and Descriptive of Louisiana* (Philadelphia, 1812), p. 152.
27. "Paul Alliot's Reflections," in J. A. Robertson (ed.), *Louisiana Under the Rule of Spain* (Cleveland, 1911), vol. 1, p. 97; Minter Wood, "Life in New Orleans in the Spanish Period," *L.H.Q.*, vol. 22 (July, 1939), pp. 642–709.

Chapter II/**MORAND**

1. Louisiana Census, 1727, L.H.C.(A.).
2. Morand estate sale, Records of the Cabildo, February 1, 1772, L.H.C.(A.).
3. Letters from Morand to directors of the Company of the Indies, June 1, 1724 (C13A, p. 187), Archives Nationales, Paris. Translated by Samuel Wilson, Jr.
4. *Ibid.*, May 22, 1745 (C13A, pp. 189–93).
5. *Ibid.*, December 16, 1726 (C13A, p. 194).
6. *Ibid.*, December 14, 1728 (#28, p. 179).
7. Superior Council Records (C13A, p. 82), Archives Nationales, Paris. Translated by Samuel Wilson, Jr.
8. Black Books, September 15, 1736, L.H.C.(L.).
9. Marriage contract, 1745, *L.H.Q.*, vol. 8 (July, 1925), p. 416.
10. Sale of plantation by Charlotte Bossua Duval to Charles de Morand [*sic*], 1729. Superior Council Records. Translation by Ghislaine Pleasanton, L.H.C.(A.).
11. Black Books, 1754, L.H.C.(L.).
12. "Plan de la Nouvelle Orléans, 1798," Carlos Trudeau, L.S.M.
13. Heloise Cruzat, "French Colonial Procedure in Louisiana for the Appointment of Tutors to Minors," *L.H.Q.*, vol. 8 (April, 1925), pp. 218–20.
14. Will of Sieur Latil, Black Books, November 10, 1762.
15. Lease of plantation by Morand estate to Chateaubeaudeau et al., April 27, 1765, Superior Council Records, L.H.C.(A.).
16. Bill of sale for cotton shipped to France from Morand plantation, Black Books, 1768, L.H.C.(L.).
17. Sieur Latil v. Sieur de Valière, May 7, 1765, Black Books, L.H.C.(L.).
18. *Ibid.*
19. Documents Relating to the Morand Estate, August 30, 1771–October 19, 1772; "Inventory of the Morand estate, May 2, 1765," Records of the Cabildo. Translated by Ghislaine Pleasanton, L.H.C.(A.).
20. *Ibid.* This inventory was made specifically to note repairs to be made on the estate, therefore accentuating the damages; however, it provides the layout of the plantation.
21. *Ibid.* Iron hinges, locks, and keys were rare and expensive; many were imported from France. They are meticulously listed every time in period inventories.
22. *Ibid.* The wall covering is not specified in this document, but the fact that bricks are uncovered in a few places implies a protective covering of some sort.
23. *Ibid.* The French word *cour* has too often been translated in modern times by the Spanish word *patio*, even when it meant service court as in this document.
24. *Ibid. Bricté* or *briquete* has also degenerated into *briquette* and in translation, "small bricks between posts," but actually the word *briquete* means bricked, which is not to be confused with *briquetage*, meaning a covering of bricks.
25. *Ibid. Colombage* consists of a heavy wood framework of squared timbers, morticed, tenoned, and pegged together, each section of a wall being assembled on the ground before being erected as a unit. (This dovecote was probably covered with wide boards). Definition by historian Samuel Wilson, Jr.
26. *Ibid.* Upright stakes are often specifically noted, implying that other methods are used; for example, "stakes into the ground" in the same document.
27. *Ibid.* These cabins, together with the moat and the hospital mentioned in this document, correspond to the information given in the Dumont plan (c. 1730), which places them in the vicinity of Bayou Road.
28. *Ibid.* The cabins on the right side of Bayou Road are indicated on Dumont's plan, c. 1732.
29. *Ibid.* The number of unfenced *arpents* is not specified here.
30. *Ibid.* The French word *fossoirs*, meaning hoes, may have been misspelled here.

31. *Ibid.* *Casa alta* has the same meaning as *maison a étage* (raised house).

32. Inventory of Morand property, October 19, 1772. Records of the Cabildo, L.H.C.(A.).

33. *Ibid.*

34. Sale of land, Widow Julie Prevotier Moreau to Andrés Almonester y Rojas, September 7, 1780; Leonard de Mazange, notary, N.O.N.A.

35. Sale of land, Latil to Almonester, October 3, 1780; L. Mazange, notary, N.O.N.A. "I Alexander Latil sell to Andrés Almonester y Rojas two *arpents* of land which they call *Sipriera* located on the *Camino del Bayou San Juan* and behind the lands of the buyer (Almonester) which he has from Madame Moró, lined on the side of the cypress swamps with lands of the free Negress *Martina.* I sell it for 200 *pesos.* Said land or *Sipriera* I have had for more than twenty years; I bought it at the public auction which was made of goods of Don Vincente Doberville [*sic*], *Gobernador* of this province in June of 1757."

36. Sale of land, Chalon to de la Chaise, October 2, 1781; L. Mazange, notary, N.O.N.A.

37. Sale of land, de la Chaise to Cultia, April 22, 1782; L. Mazange, notary, N.O.N.A.

Chapter III/**TREMÉ**

1. Marriage license of Don Claudio Tremé and Julie Moró, March 21, 1793. Records of the Cabildo, L.H.C.(A.). Translated by Dr. Daniel Wogan, Tulane University.

2. *Claudio Tremé v. Claudio Chavot,* July 2, 1785, Black Books, L.H.C.(L.).

3. Black Book, March 1, 1787, L.H.C.(L.).

4. *Don Claudio Tremé & Co. v. Delery Desilet,* March 1, 1787, Black Books, L.H.C.(L.).

5. Index cards under heading, Tremé, L.H.C.(L.).

6. Criminal proceedings instituted against Don Claudio Tremé for having shot a Negro of possession of Don Bernoudy, December 21, 1787, L.H.C.(A.).

7. *Don Claudio Tremé v. Nicolas Cayeux,* September 9, 1791, Black Books, L.H.C.(L.).

8. Index cards under heading, Tremé, L.H.C.(L.).

9. *Ibid.*

10. Survey of Tremé lands, March 17, 1810, Michel de Armas, notary, N.O.N.A.

11. Lot no. 26 on plan attached to act of Pierre Pedesclaux, notary, March 17, 1810, N.O.N.A.

12. Sale of land, C. Tremé to City of New Orleans, March 17, 1810, Michel de Armas, notary, N.O.N.A.

13. *Ibid.*

14. Inventory of the property of Claude Tremé, May 10, 1828, L.H.C.(L.).

15. *American State Papers,* vol. 3(L832–61) 266, no. 482, H.N.O.C.

16. Inventory of property of Claude Tremé, May 10, 1828, L.H.C.(L.).

Victoire, a Creole mulatress aged about 40 yrs, $600;

Françoise, a Creole Negro woman (a cook) being asthmatic, aged 45 yrs, $400;

Eulalie, a Creole mulatto woman, aged 35 yrs, a hawker, with her child Genie aged seven yrs, $800;

Thérèze, a Creole mulatress aged about 18 yrs, with her two children named Marthe aged 2 yrs, and Marie Louise aged one month, valued together at $800;

Marie, a Creole Negro woman, washer and hawker, aged 35 years, and her child Justine, a mulatto girl aged four years, $900;

Claire, a Creole washer and cook mulatto wench aged 38 yrs and her two children, Honoré of two years and a half, and Caroline of one month and a half, $800;

Lafille, a Creole Negro woman aged 40 yrs, afflicted with epilepsy, $400;

Marthe, a Creole Negro woman aged about 34 yrs and her child Athenais aged about four years, $750;

Sarah, an American Negro woman aged about 40 yrs, $500;

Marguerite, an African Negro woman aged about 40 yrs, $300;

Pepita, daughter of Lalie, a Creole mulatress aged about 15 yrs, $500;

Hypolite alias Balaillon, son of Lalie, a Creole Negro boy, aged about 14 yrs, $500;

Louise, daughter of Marthe, a Creole Negro girl aged 12 yrs, $500;

Celestine, daughter of Claire, a Creole Negro girl aged 12 yrs, $450;

Augustin, son of Claire, a Creole Negro boy aged 15 yrs, $500;

Pierre, son of Claire, a mulatto boy aged 16 yrs, $500;

Joe, son of Lafille, a Negro boy aged fifteen yrs, $500;

Pierre, son of Lafille, a mulatto man aged 18 yrs, $600;

Marie Thérèze, a Creole mulatress aged 18 yrs, daughter of Lafille, and her two children Marselin of 2 yrs, and the other newly born, $900;

Antoine, a Creole griff aged about 30 yrs, a good brick-maker and moulder, $950;

Petit Joseph, a Creole Negro man aged about 31 yrs, $950;

Pierre, Creole Negro man, aged 31 yrs, $950;

Joseph, a Creole mulatto man, aged 38 yrs, $800;

Facile, a Creole mulatto man, aged 50 yrs, a carpenter and good workman, $600;

Tony, an American Negro man aged 28 yrs, $900;

Bob, a Creole Negro man aged 32 yrs, a cart driver, $800;

Louis, a Creole Negro man, aged 50 yrs, a gardener, $600;

Valentin, an African Negro man aged 25 yrs, $700;

Candio, an African Negro man aged 80 yrs, for memorandum (not valued);

Ned, an American Negro man aged forty yrs, $450;

Lefille, an African Negro man aged 60 yrs afflicted with a hernia, $200;

Adams, an American Negro man aged 45 yrs, $500;

Peter, an American Negro man aged 57 yrs, a moulder, $600;

Petit Louis, a Creole griff aged 25 yrs, $950.

17. Plan of New Orleans and vicinity, August 11, 1811, Jacques Tanesse, city surveyor, City Engineer's Office, New Orleans.

18. Collège d'Orléans.

19. 1208 Ursulines Street is probably a remnant of the Collège d'Orléans incorporated into a dwelling.

20. Mainlevée to Dlle Jeanne Marie Aliquot, January 6, 1836, #1039, J. Seghers, notary, N.O.N.A.

21. B. Norman, "New Orleans and Its Environs" (1845).

22. See files of St. Augustine's Church, F.O.C. files, vol. 6.

Chapter IV/**PLANTATION TO FAUBOUG**

1. "Plan of the subdivision . . . Commons and Faubourg Tremé," June 20, 1812, Jacques Tanesse, N.O.N.A.

2. "A Plan of the Environs of New Orleans, Six Miles in Circumference, 1803," Boqueta de Woiserie, H.N.O.C.; "Plan de la Nouvelle Orléans," Jacques Tanesse, H.N.O.C.; "Map of New Orleans and Vicinity, 1834," Charles Zimpel, H.N.O.C.; "Plan au prolongement projeté de la rue de l'Esplanade jusqu'au Bayou St. Jean, April 26, 1822," Joseph Pilié, City Engineers Office.

3. Sale of land, see title, 1502 Governor Nicholls Street; see also inventory of J. L. Dolliole, February 11, 1861, F.O.C. files, vol. 6 (1978).

4. Sale of land, Tremé to Milne, September 24, 1798, Pierre Pedesclaux, notary, N.O.N.A.

5. Sidney Eastwood, "The Pintado Papers," *New Orleans Genesis,* vol. 3 (March, 1964), pp. 137–87.

6. Succession of Alexander Milne, June 3, 1844, C. Pollock, notary, N.O.N.A.

7. Sale of land, Charles Ducoudreaux to Philippe Pijeaux, July 16, 1816, Philippe Pedesclaux, notary, N.O.N.A.

8. Sale of land, P. Pijeaux to J. Garside, auction notice preserved in the acts of H. Lavergne, notary, December 30, 1826, N.O.N.A.

9. J. Saul listed in 1849 directory at 826 St. Charles.

10. Sale of land, E. Soniat to S. Jaudon and J. Saul, July 31, 1831, Adolphe Mazureau, notary, N.O.N.A.

11. Sale of land, J. Saul to Victor Seré, May 22, 1855, Adolphe Mazureau, notary, N.O.N.A.

12. Sale of land, Tremé to Rocheblave, March 8, 1802, P. Pedesclaux, notary, N.O.N.A.

13. See title, 1324 Kerlerec, F.O.C. files, vol. 6 (1978).

14. Plan of property belonging to G. Pavie, plan attached, January 10, 1814, Marc Lafitte, notary, N.O.N.A.; see also *New Orleans Architecture: Esplanade Ridge,* vol. 5, p. 54.

15. Sale of land, Emile Sainet to Prosper Foy, March 12, 1817, Narcisse Broutin, notary, N.O.N.A.

16. Sale of land, Manuel Andry to Louis Honoré Guerlain, February 8, 1823, Michel de Armas, notary, N.O.N.A.

17. Sale of land, Almonester to Chalon, January–July, 1781, L. Mazange, notary, N.O.N.A.

18. Sale of land, Chalon to Chesse, April 22, 1782, L. Mazange, notary, N.O.N.A.; also sale of land, Chalon to Cultia, March 14, 1785, Rafael Pérdomo, notary, N.O.N.A.

19. Sale of land, Cultia to Ramis, December 20, 1786, Fernando Rodríguez, notary, N.O.N.A.

20. Sale of land, Suarez to Cabaret, January 11, 1796, Pierre Pedesclaux, notary, N.O.N.A.

21. See acts of G. LeGardeur, notary, February 5, 1835, N.O.N.A.

Chapter V/PEDESCLAUX–DUCHAMP

1. Sale of land, Claude Tremé to Juan Lugar, February 27, 28, March 1, 1800, Pierre Pedesclaux, notary, N.O.N.A.; see also Pintado Papers, 1800, L.H.C.(L.).

2. Sidney Eastwood, "The Pintado Papers," book 2, p. 90; also *New Orleans Genesis*, vol. 3 (March, 1964), pp. 137–87.

3. Jack D. L. Holmes. *Honor and Fidelity: The Louisiana Infantry Regiment and Louisiana Militia Companies, 1766–1821* (Birmingham, Ala., 1965), "Juan Lugar Service Sheet, December 31, 1797,"; also see Baton Rouge, Minutes of the Cabildo, book 4088, 1800, N.O.P.L.

4. Sheriff's sale to settle *Pintat v. Pedesclaux*, *Le Courier de la Louisiane*, June 23, 1809, p. 3, col. 4.

5. "Memoirs," in the private collection of Fenella Castanedo Farrington.

6. *F. M. Galés v. Heirs of Pedesclaux*, G. W. Morgan, Sheriff, Bureau of Comptrollers of Alienation, folio 39, N.O.N.A.

7. Oral history source, Miss Adèle Pourcine, descendant of Pedesclaux-Duchamp family, New Orleans, Louisiana. One of the St. Martinville Duchamp houses now belongs to the city after many years of use as a Federal Post Office. The second house is a plantation belonging to Miss Chapuis.

8. Duchamp, public auction of property, June 7, 1839; see Lucien Hermann, notary, May 24, 1841.

9. *Ibid.*

10. *Ibid.*

11. Auction of Duchamp property, May 2, 1848, advertised in undated and unnamed newspaper, found in the acts of Lucien Hermann, notary, June 28, 1848, N.O.N.A.

12. See acts of Lucien Hermann, notary, June 24, 1848, N.O.N.A.

Chapter VI/RAMIS–CASTANEDO

1. Proof of purity of blood, Black Books, January 24, 1788, L.H.C.(L.).

2. Sale of land, Castanedo to Ramis, March 6, 1800, Pierre Pedesclaux, notary, N.O.N.A.

3. "Plan de la Nouvelle Orléans," 1798, Carlos Trudeau, L.S.M.

4. General Index: "Juan Arnoul from Pedro de Parc, 1775," N.O.N.A.

5. Castanedo inventory, May 4, 1819; see Hughes Pedesclaux, notary, May 29, 1832, N.O.N.A.

Chapter VII/PEYROUX–CHEVAL

1. "Figurativo de las diligencias mandadas por decreto del dia, 1756," Carlos Trudeau. (Trudeau's earliest known map found in Louisiana dated from 1789. He died in 1814.)

2. Sale of land, Latil to Almonester, October 3, 1780, L. Mazange, notary, N.O.N.A.

3. See acts of P. Pedesclaux, notary, October 22, 1800, N.O.N.A.

4. Sale of land, Girod to Henry, August 28, 1833, L. Ferrand, notary, N.O.N.A.

5. Plan book 47A, folio 46, N.O.N.A. Plan shows house plan with attached newspaper auction advertisement.

6. See acts of Pierre Pedesclaux, notary, October 22, 1800; mulatto Gabriel, alias Dick, owned this land which was bound by the Castanedo II tract; also see an 1819 retrospective map by Pintado illustrated in the "Early Settlement" of this volume.

7. "Figurativo de las diligencias mandadas por decreto del dia, c. 1789," Carlos Trudeau.

8. *Ibid.*

9. See Pierre Pedesclaux, notary, July 1, 1800: Widow Peyroux attests that she inherited this land from her husband, who bought it from "Juan Arnould fifteen years ago."

10. Records of the Cabildo, January 31, 1781, L.H.C.(A.).

11. Sale of land, Widow Peyroux to Pedro Dulcido Barran, July 1, 1800, Pierre Pedesclaux, notary, N.O.N.A.

12. Barthélémy Lafon, Contract Record Book, English translation, Samuel Wilson, Jr. H.N.O.C.:

Between us the undersigned Bmi Lafon architect in the city of New Orleans and Narcisse Broutin public writer agent for Jh. Zeringue, are agreed

That I Bmi. Lafon oblige myself to construct for the said Jh. Zeringue a house on the site of his property, situated on the road of Bayou St. John, conforming to plans below No. 1,2,3. To Wit:

A ground floor composed of six brick columns, a simple brick chimney in the center, a chimney at each corner of the house in back, then nine wood posts to support the house, the whole should only serve to support the house, not being there to close in the interval 2nd.

A floor composed of a gallery in front of eight feet outwork, two rooms of eighteen feet by twenty outwork with a double chimney in the middle, a gallery behind thirteen feet wide with two closets at each end of thirteen foot outwork, and a chimney in each corner.

The foundation shall be nine by nine, that of the gallery eight by eight, the joists in the galleries in front, five by six, those of the middle four by eight, those of the back five by six, the posts and gaiters of the house four by five, the wall plates five by eight, the whole covered in paper. The ceilings above will be in boards planed and whitewashed below but not above, those of the two rooms will also be of whitewashed board on both sides and planed, those of the galleries will be square jointed and whitewashed on one side, the chimney will not be wainscotted, the bars of the galleries will be straight and square.

The house will be brick outside of the posts and plaster on both sides, the outside doors will be two barred, swinging doors, the inside doors A,B,C, will be paneled, it will have four doors and six glass windows. To wit four openings in each room and one in each closet, all the above mentioned woodwork being on the contractor's account.

The whole finished and ended under expert inspection deliverable in June for the sum and price of two thousand five hundred piasters.

And I Narcisse Broutin oblige myself to pay the sum of two thousand five hundred piasters for the building of the above mentioned as follows. One thousand piasters cash, one thousand in the course of work, and five hundred at the completion of the building. It is understood that Mr. Lafon will not take from my land the earth which he needs for masonry, and that, if the house is not finished by the 30 June, he will pay the interest of 10% of the received charge.

Done in duplicate New Orleans the 13 January 1806.

I the undersigned declare to have received from Mr. Lafon, as legal representative of Sir Jph. Zeringue, the above mentioned house to be paid and satisfied.

New Orleans 2 June 1807
Narcisse Broutin

Chapter VIII/DUPARC–GUENO

1. Louisiana Census, 1727, L.H.C.(L.).

2. Black Books, February 16, 1729, L.H.C.(L.).

3. Heloise Cruzat, "Records of the Superior Council of Louisiana, XXV: Supplemental Index No. 2; September 4, 1734–January 14, 1736," *L.H.Q.*, vol. 8 (January, 1925), p. 135.

4. Manuscript dated August 26, 1769, L.H.C.(A.).

5. Will of Pierre Delisle Duparc, September 17, 1775, J. B. Garic, notary, N.O.N.A.

6. "Plan de Verification d'Arpentages Commencées en 1796 par ordres du Gouverneur General le Baron de Carondelet, et continués par ordre du Gouverneur Daniel Gayoso De Lemos jusques au 4 Decembre 1798," City Engineer's Office, New Orleans.

7. See sale of land, Widow Peyroux to Manuel Ximenes, May 22, 1801, P. Pedesclaux, notary, Act 39, N.O.N.A.

8. *Ibid.*

9. Sale of land, Peyroux to P. Barran: "I, Pierre Barran sell to Pedro Guesnon of this area 1½ *arpents* situated on the Road to the Bayou leading from this city on the right and 3 *arpents* depth backed by land of Simon Favre and on the other by lands of the buyer, these belong to me from having bought a major portion from Doña Suzanna Caüe, Widow Peyroux, July 1, 1800. 1500 *pesos*." May 23 and June 15, 1803, acts of P. Pedesclaux, notary. Note that the Spanish wrote the name "Barran," although he himself signed "Baran"; he was identified as a free mulatto in some acts, N.O.N.A.

10. Sale of land, Carlos Montreuil to Pierre Gueno, July 27, 1803, P. Pedesclaux, notary, N.O.N.A.

11. See sale of land, De Verges to de Kernion, July 18, 1806, Narcisse Broutin, notary, N.O.N.A.

12. *Ibid.*

13. Sale of land, Huchet de Kernion to P. Gueno, September 25, 1815, P. Pedesclaux, notary, N.O.N.A.

14. Plan of New Orleans, 1814, L. Hirt, H.N.O.C.

15. See acts of M. Barnett, notary, August 24, 1836, N.O.N.A.

16. See title 2607 of Laharpe, F.O.C. files, vol. 6, (1978).

Chapter IX/**LEBRETON –GRIFFON HABITATION**

1. "Plan de l'Habitation de M. de Pontalba sur le Chemin de St. Jean destruite pour être vendu in divers lots, le neuf de janvier, 1812," plan book 15, folio 1, N.O.N.A.

2. Laura L. Porteous, "Index to the Spanish Judicial Records of Louisiana," *L.H.Q.*, Vol. 10 (October, 1927), p. 611.

3. "Plan de la Nouvelle Orléans, 1798," Carlos Trudeau, L.S.M.; also "Figurativo de las diligencias mandadas por decreto del día," c. 1789, Carlos Trudeau, City Engineers Office.

4. See acts of L. T. Caire, notary, May 14, 1832, N.O.N.A.

5. See donation of land, Vincent d'Auberville to Louis de Morand, represented by Alexandre Latil, April 29, 1765, Jean Baptiste Garic, notary, N.O.N.A.

6. Sale of land, Louis de Morand, represented by Alexandre Latil to Marie Corbin, Widow Voisin, November 13, 1776, Jean Baptiste Garic, notary, N.O.N.A.

7. Sale of land, Griffon to Derneville, April 19, 1800, Pierre Pedesclaux, notary; act contains survey by Carlos Trudeau, N.O.N.A.

8. See act of L. T. Caire, May 14, 1832: "Charles Griffon . . . left for his heirs five children from his second marriage, to wit: M. Jean Marie Griffon, Dlles. Marie Thomas Suzanne Griffon, Marie Françoise Odile Griffon, Marie Henriette Palmire Griffon, wife of M. Thomas Barrett, and Hugues Marie Deneville Griffon," N.O.N.A.

Chapter X/**PONTALBA –FORSTALL AND GURLIE**

1. See lawsuit, *Kenton v. Pontalba*, Louisiana State Supreme Court, January 31, 1838; enclosed is "Copie du Plan et Figure de la Terre au Dominic [sic], fils de jeu Sr. C. Morand relevé et limité le 13 avril, 1765, Olivier de Vezin," F.O.C. files, vol. 6 (1978).

2. Sale of land, LeBreton to Dame Petit de Coulange, Widow d'Auberville, May 30, 1757, Chantalou, notary, reported in act of L. T. Caire, notary, May 14, 1832, N.O.N.A.

3. Act of sale, Widow d'Auberville to Latil, J. B. Garic, notary, August 24, 1758, N.O.N.A.; see also plan enclosed in suit, *Kenton v. Pontalba*.

4. Lease of land, Latil to LeBlanc, October 31, 1771, J. B. Garic, notary, N.O.N.A.

5. Sale of land, Latil to Anna Corbin, Widow Voisin, September 13, 1776, J. B. Garic, notary; see also November 21, 1776, "a *habitation* for the price of 1200 pesos, located in the area known as Bayou St. Jean and bound by land of Pablo Moreau and land of the black man named Luis Lanuit [sic]."

6. Contract of marriage, Micaela Almonester de la Ronde to Joseph Xavier Celestin de Pontaba, 1811, N.O.N.A.

7. "Plan de l'Habitation de M. de Pontalba sur le Chemin de Bayou St. Jean, le douze janvier, 1812," plan book 15, folio 1, N.O.N.A.

8. Auction notice, sale of Pontalba *habitation*, February 27, 1812, *Louisiana Courier*, p. 3, col. 5.

9. Mortgage of land by D. J. Forstall, August 7, 1826, H. Lavergne, notary, N.O.N.A.

10. Sale of land, P. and E. Forstall to I. Lizardi, August 10, 1843, C. Boudousquie, notary. The plantation below the city was "2 *arpents* front on the river by 120 *arpents* deep, with a *briqueteries*, building, dependencies, barts, horses, mules, animals, etc. as well as slaves," N.O.N.A.

11. Mortgage of land by Louis Gurlie, October 27, 1834, Theodore Seghers, notary, N.O.N.A.

12. Samuel Wilson, Jr., "Almonester—Philanthropist and Builder in New Orleans," in *The Spanish in the Mississippi Valley*, ed. J. F. McDermott (Urbana, 1965), p. 188.

13. *Ibid.*

14. Lease of land, *Moniteur de la Louisiane*, April 17, 1808, p. 3, col. 17.

15. Leonard Huber and Samuel Wilson, Jr., *The St. Louis Cemeteries of New Orleans* (New Orleans, 1963), p. 28.

Chapter XI/**DORGENOIS–MENDEZ**

1. Sale of land, Joseph Cultia to Antonio Ramis, December 3, 1786, Fernando Rodriguez, notary, N.O.N.A.

2. Sale of land, Martin Palao to A. Mendez, August 1, 1825, Pierre Pedesclaux, notary, N.O.N.A.

3. Auction notice; see undated advertisement for sale of property to settle suit of *S. W. Oakey v. Estelle D'Orgenoy*, wife of J. N. Volant Labarre, in acts of P. P. Labarre, November 2, 1844, N.O.N.A.

Chapter XII/**MILNE GARDENS, COQUET AND FLEITAS**

1. Milne estate sale, C. Pollock, notary, January 3, 1844, N.O.N.A.

2. Sale of land, Latil to Lanuitte, December 23, 1774, J. B. Garic, notary, N.O.N.A.

3. Sale of land, Lanuitte to Martina, April 8, 1777, J. B. Garic, p. 156: "I, San Luis, alias Lanuitte, free Negro of this city, sell to free Negress Martina, two *arpents* land front on the Road to Bayou St. John by the depth it can have, bound on one side by the Chevalier and on the other by land of seller, which lands belong to me from having bought them from Alexandre Latil on December 23, 1774." Also see December 16, 1777, J. B. Garic, p. 487: "I, San Luis, alias Lanuitte, free Negro of this city, sell to John Bautiste and Marguerite, married free Negroes, a land composed of two *arpents* front with all the depth it can have bound on one side by lands of Widow Voisin, and on the other by land of the free Negress Martina."

4. See Milne estate sale.

5. Sale of land, Beauregard to Lafon, October 31, 1866, R. J. Ker, notary, N.O.N.A.

6. Sister Mary Frances Borgia Hart, "Violets in the King's Garden" (New Orleans, 1976), pp. 7, 8.

7. Sale of land, Dufour to City, October 12, 1836, F. de Armas, notary, N.O.N.A.

8. Fleitas estate inventory, see title, 2275 Bayou Road, F.O.C. files, vol. 6.

9. Sale of land, Widow Peyroux to Suarez, July 19, 1796, Pierre Pedesclaux, notary, N.O.N.A.; see title, 2510 Dumaine, F.O.C. files, vol. 6.

10. Sale of land, Gabourdet to Dorgenois, January 14, 1807, Pierre Pedesclaux, notary, N.O.N.A.

11. Auction notice, D'Orgenois *habitation*, *Louisiana Courier*, March 22, 1816, p. 3, col. 4.

12. Sale of land, Dorgenois to Cauchoix, February 24, 1819, Narcisse Broutin, notary, N.O.N.A.

13. Sale of land, Fleitas to Coquet, July 30, 1828, C. Janin, notary, N.O.N.A.

14. Partition of Coquet land, December 16, 1836, J. Cuvillier, notary, N.O.N.A.

Chapter XIII/**BLANC–VIDAL–CLARK**

1. "Map of New Orleans, 1723," Ayer Collection, Newberry Library, Chicago. The Langlois concession is defined as "Habitation with buildings and outbuildings of Sr. Langlois."

2. Estate inventory, Black Book, L.H.C.(L.). Provanché and his widow had no property on Bayou Road when her estate inventory was taken by the Superior Council in the 1750s. They had no children, but they owned a plantation on the Mississippi River when Provanché died.

3. Superior Council Records, 1729, L.H.C.(A.). François Duval left at least one daughter and a widow, Charlotte Bossua, who was married a second time to Renaud d'Hautrive. (Their home is indicated on the Dumont map, 1730, across the bayou as that of "Sieur de Rive.")

4. Pintado Papers, L.H.C.(L.). Inscribed on the survey is "original limits of the Concession of M. Lebreton and the Concession of Bayou St. John halfway between the Carondelet Canal and Bayou Road."

5. Black Book, 1720s, L.H.C.(L.); also research of Ghislaine Pleasanton, L.H.C.(A.).

6. Stephen Langlois was the son of Louis Langlois and Marie Louise Girardy; he married Pélagie Loraine's mother, her first marriage.

7. Marriage, Madeleine Brasilier to Enrique Desprez, December 4, 1770, *L.H.Q.*, vol. 6 (October, 1923), p. 536.

8. Will of Magdalena Brasilier, December 13, 1773, Andrés Almonester y Rojas, notary, N.O.N.A.

9. Sale of land, Brasilier to Chalon, October 15, 1774, J. B. Garic, notary, N.O.N.A.

10. Sale of land, Chalon to Almonester y Rojas, May 7, 1781, L. Mazange, notary, N.O.N.A. "We sell to Andrés Almonester y Rojas a *habitation* that belongs to us for having acquired it from Andrés Jung, after an auction [Remate] of the land, before the present buyer with the rest of the *habitation* [that part bought from Magdalena Brasilier, widow of Despres before notary J. B. Garic October 15, 1774]. It is situated in the Parish which they call the Bridge of the Bayou San Juan, one half league distant from New Orleans, composed of 16 *arpents* of land front and 22 *arpents* depth with various buildings built of wood and brick, bound on one side by the Camino Real [Bayou Road or the name by which it was called after the turn at the old Indian Market or Halle Bretonne] and bound on the other side with *Tierras Realinguas.* We also sell three Negroes . . . twenty-four head of cattle, one horse, three wagons and all the pigs and other animals which we bought. $6000 *pesos.*"

11. Sale of land, Almonester to Blanc, January 2, 1793, and February 8, 1798, François Broutin, notary, N.O.N.A.

12. Sale of land, Blanc to Vidal, January 30, 1800, Pierre Pedesclaux, notary, N.O.N.A. "Six *arpents* fronting on the Camino Real bound on one side with lands of Josef Suarez and on the other with lands of Don Luis Antonio Blanc."

13. Sale of land, Vidal to Clark, July 24, 1804, Pierre Pedesclaux, notary, N.O.N.A.: "on the right side of the Camino Real leaving from the city for the Gran Bayou, land composed of 4 *arpents* front bound on the city side with the Puente de las Lavadoras and Pequeño Bayou of the deceased Don Gabriel Peyroux, and by the other part of land belonging to the free Negress Fanchon Montreuil, and through the depth with Camino Gentilly and Pequeño Bayou and with the lands of Pedro Gueno, which before belonged to Don Manuel Ximenes, and with lands of the Deverges ladies which in diverse portions I bought from Josef Suarez, Fanchon Montreuil, Don Pedro Juzan and his wife and Doña Marie Suzanna Caüe, widow of Peyroux, before notary Don Carlos Ximines, December 10, 1798, January 26, 1799 and before this notary [Pedesclaux] May 19 and July 3, 1801 as drawn by Carlos Trudeau."

14. Royal land grant to Vidal. Preserved in the notarial acts of H. D. Gordon, 1826, relative to the sale of lands by Evariste Blanc to the city:

"Don Nicolas Maria Vidal, *Teniente Gobernador, Auditor de Guerra, actual Gobernador politico interimo de esta Provincia de Louisiana y Florida del Queste* . . . is asking that as possessor of a part of a *habitation* along the *Camino que de esta ciudad va al gran Bayou titulado San Juan* [Road to the Bayou] situated on the left, which land he bought from Don Louis Antonio Blanc, and since it does not have the corresponding depth, he desires for this motive, from the precise line to his domestic uses and of the part necessary for his cattle, and since these lands are vacant and *realengas* those that are found behind the said *habitation* and of Louis Blanc are now conceded to said Señor [Vidal] the expressed lands bound on one side by the *habitation* of Josef Suarez on the other side with the Gran Bayou San Juan and on the part behind with the Canal named Carondelet, and the land is free for his possession and ownership, all with respect of a survey by Don Carlos Trudeau . . . having been assured me that the related lands are found abandoned and vacant, it serves me to order to avoid delays, a certified copy of said information to be presented. The land contains in its area of a trapezoid 130 *arpents* square enclosed by the above mentioned boundaries . . . given in New Orleans April 16, 1800.

15. *New Orleans Architecture: The Esplanade Ridge*, vol. 5, p. 151 (1977).

16. Sale of land, Vidal to Clark, July 24, 1804, Pierre Pedesclaux, notary, N.O.N.A.

17. Sale of land, Blanc to Clark, January 25, 1805, and February 7, 1806, François Broutin, notary, N.O.N.A.: "six *arpents* fronting Bayou Road with the depth it is able to have, joining on one side the lands of the seller [Blanc] and on the other the lands of the acquirer" [the Vidal tracts bought by Clark] for $5,000.

18. See Zimpel survey depicting Blanc's complex.

19. Survey of Suburb St. Jean, June 9, 1809, vol. 58, p. 245, Pierre Pedesclaux, notary, N.O.N.A.

20. Sale of land, Clark to Lecesne, June 15, 1809, Pierre Pedesclaux, notary, N.O.N.A.

21. *New Orleans Architecture: The Esplanade Ridge*, vol. 5, p. 151.

22. Plan book 21, folio 18, by A. J. Bourgerol also shows one of the early houses between N. Dorgenois and N. Broad.

23. Sale of land, Clark Estate, represented by Richard Relf to Evariste Blanc, October 2, 1813, by private signature, John Lynd, notary,

N.O.N.A. Blanc, living on Bayou St. John (in his father's house, 924 Moss) purchased "135 square *arpents*, next to the Chemin du Canal Carondelet, to the lands of M. E. Cauchoix, to the Grande Rue on Broad and la Rue Bellechasse of Faubourg St. Jean to the lands of Mme Veuve Hersey and those of the acquirer, E. Blanc."

24. Sale of land, Evariste Blanc to City Corporation, September 26, 1834, Felix de Armas, notary, N.O.N.A.

Chapter XIV/**CITY COMMONS**

1. Mary Louise Christovich, et al, *New Orleans Architecture: The Esplanade Ridge*, vol. 5 (Gretna, 1977), pp. 5–9.

2. *Heirs of Lafayette v. Mme Pontalba, heirs of C. Griffon, heirs of Lebreton D'Orgenois, et al.*, United States Circuit Court, Eastern District of Louisiana, filed March 26, 1852.

3. "Philip Pittman's Map," c. 1765, Ann Arbor, William L. Clements Library.

4. *Inventory of Government Property, 1766*, by Foucault, L.H.C.(L.).

5. Samuel Wilson, Jr., "Almonester—Philanthropist and Builder in New Orleans," in *The Spanish in the Mississippi Valley*, ed. J. F. McDermott (Urbana, 1965), pp. 192–196.

6. Sale of land, Andrés Almonester to Maurice Conway, book 7, act 500, Pierre Pedesclaux, notary, N.O.N.A.

7. Sale of land, Joseph Chalon to Andrés Almonester, May 17, 1781, Leonard Mazange, notary, N.O.N.A.

8. Samuel Wilson, Jr., "Almonester—Philanthropist and Builder."

9. Leonard Huber, *Our Lady of Guadalupe Church*, (New Orleans, 1976).

10. *Carondelet Canal, Times-Picayune*, April 3, 1921, sec. 4, p. 1, col. 1.

11. "Survey of the Right of Way of the Canal Carondelet," 1925 copy, Frank H. Wadill, Walker and Avery, Inc., 920 Carondelet Bldg., New Orleans.

12. *New Orleans Republican*, January 24, 1873, p. 1, col. 3.

13. David Lee Sterling, ed. *New Orleans, 1801. An Account by John Pintard, L.H.Q.*, vol. 34 (July, 1951).

14. Request for land grant, Francisco Bermudez, July 14, 1797, Records of the Spanish Cabildo, Cabildo Book 4, L.H.C.(A.).

15. *Ibid.*

16. *American State Papers* (public lands), claim no. 87, (1832–1861).

17. Book 40, records of New Orleans City Council, N.O.P.L.

18. Subdivision, auction and sale of Bermudez tract, L. T. Caire, notary, March 8, 1830, and April 14, 1829, N.O.N.A.

19. Acts of sale, July 18, 1823, May 14, 1825, June 16, 1827, August 27, 1827, G. R. Stringer, notary; January 23, 1832, February 29, 1832, March 13, 1832, L. T. Caire, notary, N.O.N.A.

20. W.C.C. Claiborne, *Official Letter Books*, Dunbar Rowland, ed., 6 vols. (Jackson, 1921).

21. "Parish Prison" (ms., 1975, Tulane University Library). Copies at F.O.C. files, vol. 6, L.H.C. and H.N.O.C.

22. Contract between the city and James Lilly, November 8, 1850, J. Cuvillier, notary, N.O.N.A.

23. Acts of Narcisse Broutin, notary, vol. 6, folio 705, N.O.N.A.

24. Henry Kmen, "The Roots of Jazz and the Dance in Place Congo: A Re-appraisal," *Yearbook for Inter-American Musical Research*, vol. 8 (1972), pp. 5–16.

25. *Ibid.*

26. *Ibid.*

27. New Orleans *Daily Picayune*, April 21, 1879, p. 9.

28. Building contract, Perseverance Lodge and Correjolles & Chaigneau, builders, March 11, 1830, M.O.B., N.O.N.A.

29. See architectural files, Samuel Wilson, Jr.; also F.O.C. files, vol. 6, L.H.C. and H.N.O.C.

30. Leonard Huber, et al, *New Orleans Architecture: The Cemeteries*, vol. 3 (Gretna, 1974), pp. 135–37.

31. Al Rose and Edmond Souchon, *New Orleans Jazz* (Baton Rouge, 1967), p. 129.

32. *Ibid.*

33. Phil Johnson, "Good Time Town," *The Past As Prelude*, ed. Hodding Carter (Tulane University, 1968), p. 245.

34. *Ibid.*, p. 241.

35. *Ibid.*

36. James Wesley Stewart, *Faubourg Tremé*, forthcoming.

37. Johnson, "Good Time Town."

38. Al Rose, *Storyville, New Orleans* (Tuscaloosa, Ala., 1974), p. 96.

39. *Ibid.*

40. *Ibid.*

41. Rose, *New Orleans Jazz*, p. 44.

42. Rose, *Storyville*, pp. 96, 169.

43. Letter in the collection of Alicia Heard, great-granddaughter of Moody.

Chapter XV/**LAFAYETTE–HAGAN AND MOORE**

1. Kathryn Abbey, "Land Ventures of General Lafayette in the Territory of Orleans and the State of Louisiana," *L.H.Q.*, vol. 16 (July, 1953).

2. *Ibid.*

3. The *Times-Picayune—New Orleans States*, Sunday, March 18, 1851.

4. Sale of land, Blineau to La Société Française, May 14, 1832, L. T. Caire, notary, N.O.N.A.

5. Sale of land, Blineau to La Société Française, May 3, 1861, O. Drouet, notary, N.O.N.A.

6. Sale of land, French Society to Knights of Peter Claver, April 21, 1951, A. P. Tureaud, notary, N.O.N.A.

7. Sale of land, Ramis to Dorgenois, July 16, 1805, Pierre Pedesclaux: this referred to 1¼ by 4 *arpents* that Ramis bought from Joseph Cultia on December 3, 1786, before F. Rodríguez; on January 28, 1806, Ramis sold Dorgenois ¾ by 4 *arpents* before Pierre Pedesclaux; see Pierre Pedesclaux act 58, June 6th–December, 1807, for confirmation, N.O.N.A.

8. Sale of land, Fleitas to Kenton, May 19, 1835, T. Seghers, notary, N.O.N.A.

9. Commission from king of Spain to C. Guadioli, May 20, 1801; see N. Broutin, notary, June 5, 1805, for Carlos Guadioli sale to Fleitas.

10. See Frank H. Wadill, civil engineer, "Survey of Right of Way of the Carondelet Canal . . . ," 1923.

11. "Plan de la Nouvelle Orléans," retrospective map, 1798, Carlos Trudeau, L.H.C.(A.).

12. American State Papers (public lands), J. B. Macarty Claim, November 24, 1806, nos. 103, 194 (1832–1861).

13. Confirmation of Macarty claim is evidenced in *Pontalba v. Copeland*, January, 1848, Supreme Court, State of Louisiana.

14. *Heirs of Lafayette v. Mme Pontalba et al*, May 10, 1853, Northeast Circuit Court, Louisiana.

Chapter XVI/**THE ROLE OF THE FREE PEOPLE OF COLOR IN FAUBOURG TREMÉ**

1. Census, 1726.

2. Sale of land, Dauberville estate to Latil, August 24, 1728, J. B. Garic, notary, N.O.N.A.

3. Sale of land, Lanuitte to Martina, April 8, 1777, p. 156, J. B. Garic, notary, N.O.N.A.; sale of land, Lanuitte to Juan Bautista, December 16, 1777, J. B. Garic, notary, N.O.N.A.

4. Pintado Papers, L.H.C.(L.).

5. Plan of the canals to rear of city, June 17, 1825, Joseph Pilié, City Engineers Office.

6. Will of Francisca Montreuille (Françoise Montreuil), 1801 book of Narcisse Broutin, notary, N.O.N.A.; Pintado Papers, 1800, L.H.C.(L.).

7. Sale of land, Montreuil to Magnemassa, p. 414 of the acts of P. Pedesclaux, 1802, N.O.N.A.

8. Will Books, N.O.P.L.

9. Jack D. L. Holmes, *Honor and Fidelity* (Birmingham, Ala., 1965), p. 250.

10. See act of sale, Tremé to City, March 17, 1810, Michel de Armas, N.O.N.A.

11. Sale of land, Carlos Montreuil to Pierre Gueno, July 27, 1803, P. Pedesclaux, notary, N.O.N.A.

12. Will Books, 1825, N.O.P.L.

13. See acts of Pierre Pedesclaux, notary, October 22, 1800: "mulatto Gabriel, alias Dédé (Bique)," N.O.N.A.

14. Will Books, 1814, N.O.P.L.

15. Marriage Records, St. Louis Cathedral, October 20, 1812, no. 166, Mallorquin witnesses; see also, no. 146, April, 1814, Ursuline Convent Museum.

16. Will Books, 1814, N.O.P.L.

17. Funeral Books, St. Louis Cathedral, May 11, 1841, no. 338, Ursuline Convent Museum.

18. Marriage Books, St. Louis Cathedral, October 1818, no. 246.

19. *Ibid.*, October, 1816, no. 207.

20. *Ibid.*, March, 1801, no. 66.

21. Sale of land, Widow Peyroux to Pedro Barran, July 1, 1800, P. Pedesclaux, notary, N.O.N.A.

22. Sidney Eastwood, "Pintado Papers," *New Orleans Genesis*, vol. 3 (March, 1964), p. 139.

23. Marriage Books, St. Louis Cathedral, June 1807, no. 118.

24. Holmes, *Honor and Fidelity*, p. 103.

25. Mary Louise Christovich, *et al.*, *New Orleans Architecture*, vol. 5, p. 86.

26. Rodolphe Lucien Desdunes, *Our People and Our History* (Baton Rouge, 1973), p. 77.

27. Annie Lea West-Stahl, "The Free Negro in Ante-Bellum Louisiana," *Louisiana Historical Quarterly*, vol. 25 (April, 1942), p. 373.

28. "Spanish Judicial Records, August 3, 1781," *Louisiana Historical Quarterly*, vol. 17 (January, 1934), pp. 203–204.

29. Marcel Giraud, *A History of French Louisiana: The Reign of Louis XIV, 1698–1715* (Baton Rouge, 1974), vol. 1, p. 189.

30. Desdunes, *Our People*, p. 86.

31. Will Books, 1830, N.O.P.L.

32. Superior Council Records, November 28, 1727, trans., *Louisiana Historical Quarterly*, vol. 4 (April, July, October, 1921), pp. 236, 355, 503.

33. Superior Council Records, January 28, 1737, trans., *Louisiana Historical Quarterly*, vol. 8 (October, 1925), p. 696.

34. Superior Council Records, July 12, 1737, trans., *Louisiana Historical Quarterly*, vol. 9 (April, 1926), p. 303.

35. Superior Council Records, December 1, 1745. L.H.C.(A.).

36. Superior Council Records, trans., *Louisiana Historical Quarterly*, vol. 1 (July, 1917), pp. 108–110.

37. Spanish Judicial Records, 1783, trans., *Louisiana Historical Quarterly*, vol. 22 (April, 1939), pp. 592–93.

38. Spanish Judicial Records, September 23, 1784, trans., *Louisiana Historical Quarterly*, vol. 24 (October, 1941), pp. 1274–75.

39. Will of Marguerite, March 1, 1770, J. B. Garic, notary, N.O.N.A.; see also *Louisiana Historical Quarterly*, vol. 6 (April, 1923), p. 316.

40. Will Books, N.O.P.L.

41. City Council Records, March 19, 1806, N.O.P.L.

42. François Xavier Martin, *A General Digest of the Acts of the Legislature of the Late Territory of Orleans and of the State of Louisiana* (New Orleans, 1816), I; and Charles Gayarré, *History of Louisiana* (reprinted, New Orleans: Pelican Publishing Co., 1965), I, appendix.

43. Superior Council Records, August, 1743, trans., *Louisiana Historical Quarterly*, vol. 11 (October, 1928), p. 649.

44. Superior Council Records, April 8, 1747, trans., *Louisiana Historical Quarterly*, vol. 18 (January, 1935), pp. 168–69.

45. Spanish Judicial Records, September 7, 1781, trans., *Louisiana Historical Quarterly*, vol. 17 (January, 1934), pp. 213–19.

46. Marriage Books, St. Louis Cathedral, August 14, 1725.

47. Superior Council Records, November 16, 1769. L.H.C.(A.).

48. Sheriff's Register Books, 1841–1862, N.O.P.L.

49. Roland C. McConnell, *Negro Troops of Antebellum Louisiana* (Baton Rouge, 1968), p. 48.

50. H. E. Sterkx, *The Free Negro in Ante-Bellum Louisiana* (Cranbury, N. J., 1972), p. 63.

51. Successions, 1839, Emelie Guidry Armitage Passebon, N.O.P.L.

52. Manuscript Census, 1850, Microfilm, U.N.O., Earl K. Long Library.

53. Will Books, 1815, N.O.P.L.

54. City Council Records, April 16, 1822, N.O.P.L.

55. Marriage Books, St. Louis Cathedral, February, 1818, no. 227.

56. *Ibid.*, March, 1822, no. 309.

57. Manuscript Census, 1850, U.N.O., Earl K. Long Library.

58. *Ibid.*

59. *Ibid.*

60. Baptismal Books, St. Louis Cathedral, book 17, p. 103, no. 728.

61. Roulhac Toledano, *et al.*, *New Orleans Architecture*, vol. 4, p. 31.

62. Manuscript Census, 1850, U.N.O., Earl K. Long Library.

63. Will Books, March 30, 1821, N.O.P.L.

64. Marriage Books, St. Louis Cathedral, August, 1803.

65. *Ibid.*, 1805.

66. Christovich, *et al.*, *New Orleans Architecture*, vol. 5, pp. 61, 66, 103.

67. Desdunes, *Our People*, pp. 79, 80.

68. Marriage Books, St. Louis Cathedral, December 27, 1827.

69. Holmes, *Honor*, p. 169.

70. Marriage Books, St. Louis Cathedral, July, 1829.

71. Desdunes, *Our People*, p. 114.

72. *Ibid.*, pp. 114–20.

73. McConnell, *Negro Troops*, pp. 62–68.

74. Marriage Books, St. Louis Cathedral, December 1, 1798, and 1802.

75. Desdunes, *Our People*, p. 67.

76. Sterkx, *Negro Troops*, pp. 11–12.

77. Holmes, *Honor*, p. 17.

78. McConnell, *Negro Troops*, pp. 18–19.

79. *Ibid.*, pp. 24, 29.

80. George C. H. Kernion, "The Chevalier de Pradel," *Louisiana Historical Quarterly*, vol. 12 (April, 1929), pp. 238–54.

81. Jack D. L. Holmes, work forthcoming.

82. Spanish Judicial Records, March, 1783, trans., *Louisiana Historical Quarterly*, vol. 20 (July, 1937), pp. 841–64.

83. Andre Lafargue, "Pierre Clement de Laussat, Colonial Prefect and High Commissioner of France in Louisiana: His Memoirs, Proclamations and Orders," *Louisiana Historical Quarterly*, vol. 20 (January, 1937), pp. 175–77.

84. McConnell, *Negro Troops*, p. 84.

85. R. McC. B. Adams, "New Orleans and the War of 1812," *Louisiana Historical Quarterly*, vol. 16 (October, 1933), pp. 696–97.

86. *Ibid.*

87. McConnell, *Negro Troops*, p. 68.

88. *Ibid.*, p. 77.

89. Powell A. Casey, *Louisiana in the War of 1812* (Baton Rouge, 1963), pp. 76–77.

90. Mary F. Berry, "Negro Troops in Blue and Gray: The Louisiana Native Guards, 1861–63," *Louisiana History*, pp. 165–90.

91. Desdunes, *Our People*, p. 118.

92. West-Stahl, "Free Negro in Ante-Bellum Louisiana," *Louisiana Historical Quarterly*, vol. 25 (April, 1942), p. 315.

93. Jack D. L. Holmes, work forthcoming.

94. François-Xavier Martin, *A General Digest of the Acts of the Legislatures of the Late Territory of Orleans and the State of Louisiana* (3 vols.; New Orleans, 1816).

95. Barthélémy Lafon, Contract Record Book, English translation by Samuel Wilson, Jr., H.N.O.C.

96. Sister Audrey Marie Detiege, *Hentiette Delille, Free Woman of Color, Foundress of the Sisters of the Holy Family* (New Orleans, n.d.), pp. 14–20.

97. Desdunes, *Our People*, pp. 101–108.

98. Betty Porter, "History of Negro Education in Louisiana," *Louisiana Historical Quarterly*, vol. 25 (July, 1942), pp. 760–67.

99. Desdunes, *Our People, passim.*

100. Porter, "Negro Education," pp. 760–67.

101. John W. Blassingame, *Black New Orleans* (Chicago, 1973), pp. 49–77.

102. Desdunes, *Our People*, p. 133.

103. *Ibid.*, p. 73.

104. Blassingame, *Black New Orleans*, pp. 75–76.

105. Desdunes, *Our People*, p. 83n.

106. Marcus B. Christian, unpublished memoirs, Archives and Manuscript Department, U.N.O., Earl K. Long Library.

107. Blassingame, *Black New Orleans*, p. 77.

108. Desdunes, *Our People*, pp. 141–42.

109. Christian, unpublished memoirs, Archives and Manuscript Department, U.N.O., Earl K. Long Library.

110. Jack V. Buerkle and Danny Barker, *Bourbon Street Black* (New York, 1973), p 9.

111. Desdunes, *Our People*, pp. 29–30.

112. Buerkle and Barker, *Bourbon Street Black*, pp. 10–11.

113. Donald M. Marquis, *In Search of Buddy Bolden, First Man of Jazz* (Baton Rouge, 1977), pp. 89–91.

114. Al Rose and Edmond Souchon, *New Orleans Jazz: A Family Album* (Baton Rouge, 1967), p. 11.

115. *Ibid.*, pp. 10–11.

116. *Ibid.*, pp. 14–15.

117. *Ibid.*, p. 100.

118. *Ibid.*, p. 38.

119. *Ibid.*, p. 101.

120. *Ibid.*, p. 36.

121. *Ibid.*, p. 96.

122. Buerkle and Barker, *Bourbon Street Black*, p. 20.

123. Rose and Souchon, *New Orleans Jazz*, p. 220.

124. Desdunes, *Our People*, p. 10.

125. Charles B. Rousseve, *The Negro in New Orleans* (New Orleans, 1969), p. 9.

126. Manuscript Census, 1850.

127. Desdunes, *Our People*, p. 144.

128. Desdunes, *Our People*, p. xiv.

129. *Ibid.*

130. Rousseve, *The Negro*, p. 8.

PHOTOGRAPH CREDITS

Chap. XIV: figs. 11, 24; Bayou Road: 1418, 1903–09, 1137; Bienville: 1912–16; N. Broad: 800, 930, 1700–02; Canal: 2331, 2547; N. Claiborne: 800, 1234–40, 1245, 1480, 1506; Columbus: 1126, 1130, 1139; N. Derbigny: 925; N. Dorgenois: 1504; Dumaine: 1518–20; N. Johnson: 1240; Kerlerec: 1216, 1819–21, 2018–20; Laharpe: 1611, 2439, 2544; Lapeyrouse: 2217; Marais: 1105, 1466–68; Onzaga: 2129, 2221; Prieur: 927; N. Robertson: 1449, 1477, 1539; St. Ann: 1609–11–13–15; St. Claude: 1226; Ursulines: 1201–17; N. Villere: 917–21, 1423. **Marcus Fraser**.

Dumaine: 1604–06, 1612, 1617, 1628; Tremé: 1019–27, 1119; Ursulines: 1314; Villere: 1110, 1114, 1231–33. **Beatrice Pollock**.

Barracks: 1212, 1305–07; Bayou Road: 1624; N. Claiborne: 1417, 1423, 1427–29; Dumaine: 1509, 1514, 2518–20; N. Prieur: 1568; N. Robertson: 1018. **Poco Sloss**.

Chap. IV: fig. 9. **Ben C. Toledano**.

Chap. XIV: figs. 10A, 12, 27; Chap. XV: figs. 3, 6, 7; Bayou Road: 2275; Bienville: 2431; N. Broad: Pumping Station; Canal: 1800, 2335; N. Claiborne: 732, 1241–43, 1522; Conti: 1726–36; N. Galvez: 927; Kerlerec: 1324, 1917; Laharpe: 1722–26, 1915–25; N. Miro: 315–25; Onzaga: 2536–40; N. Rampart: 1225; N. Robertson: 1535; St. Ann: 2439; N. Tonti: 823, 1125; N. Villere: 1222. **Janet Urian**.

Bayou Road: 1315, 1326–28; Barracks: 1204, 1310–12; Dumaine: 1523–25, 1530. **Gypsy Van Antwerp**.

Chap. IV: figs. 10, 14; Chap. VIII: figs. 4, 5, 8; Barracks: 1124, view up; 2226, 2234–38, 2229; Bienville: 1803–05, 1838, 1912, 1936, 2226–34; Columbus: 1220, 2226, 2223–25; Conti: 1834, 2101–03; D'Abadie: 2815; N. Derbigny: 315–17; N. Dorgenois: 929, 1529, 1574, 1726, 2552; Dumaine: 1909, 1915–23, 1924; N. Galvez: 1455–57, 1465–67, 1561; Iberville: 2427; N. Johnson: 916, 1439, 1440, 1450, 2018–20; Kerlerec: 1201, 1214, 1336, 1418, 1422; Laharpe: 1729, 1833–35, 2403, 2626; Lapeyrouse: 2622; Marais: 1109, 1115, 1122, 1123–25, 1126, 1135, 1143, 1218–20, 1221, 1239; N. Miro: 1454–56, 1467; N. Prieur: 1023, 1133, 1434, 1443–47, 1505–07; N. Rampart: 1111; N. Robertson: 1022, 1119; N. Rocheblave: 1435, 1509, 1568, 1617–19; N. Roman: 1311, 1518; St. Ann: 1712–16, 1718–20, 1719–21, 1722–24, 2426; 2428–30; St. Claude: 1014–16, 1108–10, 1112, 1234–26, 1442, 1454–58 (now demolished), 1449–1451; Chinese Laundry on St. Peter St.; St. Philip: 1127, 1319–31, 1509–11, 1519–21, 1523–25, 1530–32, 1600, 1900, 1923; N. Tonti: 1623; Ursulines: 1122–24, 1130–32, 1200, 1218, 1330–32, 1317–19, 1326–28, 1519–21, 1523, 1527, 1533, 1723, 1726, 1800, 1818, Church on Ursulines, 2226–28; N. Villere: 1419, 1433, 1438–36, 1500–02. **Robin Von Breton**.

All other photographs by **Betsy Swanson**.

Chap. VIII: fig. 3. **Mercedes Whitecloud**.

BIBLIOGRAPHY

BOOKS, NEWSPAPERS, ARTICLES

Abbey, Kathryn T. "Land Ventures of General Lafayette in the Territory of Orleans and the State of Louisiana." *Louisiana Historical Quarterly*, Vol. 16 (July, 1933), 359–73.

"Abstracts of French and Spanish Documents Concerning the Early History of Louisiana." *Louisiana Historical Quarterly*, Vol. 1 (January 8, 1917), 103, 224.

American State Papers (Public Lands). Washington: Gales and Seaton, 1832–61.

Andreassen, John C. L. "Guide to the Depositories of Manuscript Collections in Louisiana." *Louisiana Historical Quarterly*, Vol. 24 (April, 1941), 317 (L. M. Gottschalk).

Arthur, Stanley Clisby, Huchet de Kernion, and George Campbell. *Old Families of Louisiana*. New Orleans: Harmanson, 1931.

Aucoin, Sidney. "The Political Career of Issac Johnson, The Orleans Navigation Company Case." *Louisiana Historical Quarterly*, Vol. 28 (July, 1945), 979.

Barker, Jacob. *Incidents in the Life of Jacob Barker, of New Orleans, Louisiana*. Washington, D.C.: n.p., 1855.

Barron, Bill. *The Vaudreuil Papers*. 1st ed. New Orleans: Polyanthos, 1975.

Baudier, Roger, K.S.G. *Annunciation Parish: A Century of Parish Activities*. New Orleans: Annunciation Parish Church, 1944–45.

Baudier, Roger. *The Catholic Church in Louisiana*. New Orleans: A. W. Hyatt Stationery Manufacturing Co., 1939.

Baudier, Roger, K.S.G. *Ste. Rose de Lima Church*. New Orleans: Archdiocese of New Orleans, 1949.

Beer, William. "Early Census Tables of Louisiana." Translated by Jay K. Ditchy. *Louisiana Historical Quarterly*, Vol. 13 (April, 1930), 205–29.

Bell, William C., comp. *Illustrated Catalogue of Mouldings, Architectural and Ornamental Woodwork*. New Orleans: Roberts and Co., 1880.

Benjamin, J. P., and T. Slidell. *Digest of the Reported Decisions of the Superior Court of the Late Territory of Orleans and of the Supreme Court of the State of Louisiana*. New Orleans: John T. Carter, 1834.

Berlin, Ira. *Slaves Without Masters: The Negro in the Antebellum South*. New York: Pantheon Books, 1974.

Berquin-Duvallon, *An Account of Louisiana*. Philadelphia: William Duane, 1803.

Berquin-Duvallon, "Observations of Berquin Duvallon on the Free People of Color in Louisiana in 1802." *Journal of Negro History*, Vol. 2 (April, 1917), 167–74.

Bezou, Henry C. *Metairie: A Tongue of Land to Pasture*. Gretna: Pelican Publishing Co., 1973.

Blassingame, John W. *Black New Orleans, 1860–1880*. Chicago: University of Chicago Press, 1973.

Borgia, Sister Mary Francis. *A History of the Congregation of the Sisters of the Holy Family of New Orleans*. B.A. thesis, Xavier University, 1931.

Borgia, Sister Mary Francis S.S.F. *Violets in the King's Garden: A History of the Sisters of the Holy Family of New Orleans*. New Orleans: Sister Mary F. Borgia Hart, 1976.

Brown, Wilbur S. *The Amphibious Campaign for West Florida and Louisiana, 1814–1815*. Birmingham, Alabama: University of Alabama Press, 1969.

Bruns, Mrs. Thomas Nelson Carter. *Louisiana Portraits*. New Orleans: Historical Activities Committee, The National Society of the Colonial Dames of America in the State of Louisiana, 1975.

Buckingham, James Silk. *The Slave States of America*. London: Fisher & Co., 1842.

Buerkle, Jack V. and Danny Barker. *Bourbon Street Black*. New York: Oxford University Press, 1973.

Burns, Francis P. "Book Review: Forgotten Frontiers." *Louisiana Historical Quarterly*, Vol. 15 (October, 1932), 712–14.

Burns, Francis P. "Charles M. Waterman, Mayor of New Orleans." *Louisiana Historical Quarterly*, Vol. 7 (July, 1924), 466–79.

Burns, Francis P. "The Graviers and Faubourg Ste Marie." *Louisiana Historical Quarterly*, Vol. 22 (April, 1939), 388.

Burns, Francis P. "Henry Clay Visits New Orleans." *Louisiana Historical Quarterly*, Vol. 27 (July, 1944), 717–82.

Burns, Francis P. "Lafayette Visits New Orleans." *Louisiana Historical Quarterly*, Vol. 29 (April, 1946), 296–304.

Burns, Francis P. "The Spanish Land Laws of Louisiana." *Louisiana Historical Quarterly*, Vol. 11 (October, 1928), 557–81.

Burns, Francis P. "West Florida and the Louisiana Purchase." *Louisiana Historical Quarterly*, Vol. 15 (July, 1932), 391–416.

Cable, George Washington. *The Creoles of Louisiana*. New York: Charles Scribner's Sons, 1884.

Carter, Clarence Edwin. *The Territorial Papers of the United States*, Vol. 9 (1805). Washington: U.S. Government Printing Office, 1951.

Carter, Hodding, ed. *The Past as Prelude: New Orleans, 1718–1968*. New Orleans: Pelican Publishing House and Tulane University, 1968.

Casey, Powell A. *Louisiana in the War of 1812*. Baton Rouge, Louisiana: Casey, 1963.

Castellanos, Henry. *New Orleans as It Was*. 2nd ed. New Orleans: L. Graham Co., 1905.

Caughey, John Walton. *Bernardo Galvez in Louisiana, 1776–1783*. Berkeley: University of California Press, 1934.

Census of New Orleans, 1805. Contained in the *New Orleans Directory*, 1805. Reprinted; New Orleans: Pelican Gallery, 1936.

Chambers, Henry. *A History of New Orleans*. Vol. 2. Chicago: American Publishing Co., 1925.

Chase, John. *Frenchmen Desire Goodchildren and Other Streets of New Orleans*. New Orleans: Robert F. Crager & Co., 1960.

Christian, Marcus. *The Battle of New Orleans; Negro Soldiers in the Battle of New Orleans*. New Orleans: The Battle of New Orleans 150th Anniversary Committee of Louisiana, 1965.

Claiborne, William Charles Cole. *Official Letter Books*. Edited by Dunbar Rowland, 6 vols., Jackson, Mississippi: Department of Archives and History, 1917. Vol. 5, pp. 346–47.

Cline, Isaac Monroe. *Storms, Floods, and Sunshine: Part 1, A Book of Memoirs; Part 2, Characteristics of Tropical Cyclones*. New Orleans: Pelican Publishing Co., 1945.

Cline, Rodney. *Pioneer Leaders and Early Institutions in Louisiana Education*. Baton Rouge: Claitor Books, 1969.

Cocke, Edward J. *Monumental New Orleans*. New Orleans: La Fayette Publishers, 1968.

Le Code Noir. Paris: Preault, Imprimeur Librairie, 1767.

Cohen, David, and Jack P. Greene, ed. *Neither Slave nor Free: The Freedmen of African Descent in the Slave Societies of the New World*. Baltimore: Johns Hopkins University Press, 1972.

Coleman, John P. "Historic Homes of New Orleans." *New Orleans States*, October 28, 1922–December 12, 1925.

Coleman, John P. "Historic Homes of New Orleans: The Picturesque Residence of the Tremés." *New Orleans States*, January 19, 1923, section 3, page 9.

Coleman, Will H. *Historical Sketch Book and Guide to New Orleans*. New Orleans: Will H. Coleman, 1884.

Collot, Victor. *A Journey to North America*. Translated by J. C. Bay. Paris, 1826.

Conrad, Glenn, and Allain Mathé, ed. *France and North America: Over Three Hundred Years of Dialogue*; Symposium of France American Studies, 1st, University of Southwest Louisiana, 1971. Lafayette: University of Southwest Louisiana, 1973.

Cruise, Boyd. *Louisiana Alphabet: Index to the Louisiana Historical Quarterly*. New Orleans: Plantation Bookshop, 1956.

Cruzat, Heloise, trans. "Concessions of Ste Catherine at the Natchez." *Louisiana Historical Quarterly*, Vol. 12 (January, 1919), 164–73.

Cruzat, Heloise H. "French Colonial Procedure in Louisiana for the Appointment of Tutors to Minors." *Louisiana Historical Quarterly*, Vol. 8 (April, 1925).

Cruzat, Heloise. "Wills of the French Colonial Period in Louisiana." *Louisiana Historical Quarterly*, Vol. 8 (July, 1925), 411–19.

Cruzat, Heloise, trans. "Records of the Superior Council of Louisiana." *Louisiana Historical Quarterly*, Vols. 3–22 (1920–39).

Cullison, William R. III. *Historic Mississippi Delta Architecture: Photographs from Tulane's Richard Koch Collection*. New Orleans: Louisiana Landmark Society, 1978.

Cunynghame, Sir Arthur Augustus T. *A Glimpse at the Great Western Republic, 1812–1842*. London: R. Bentley, 1851.

Curtis, Nathaniel Cortlandt. *New Orleans—Its Old Houses, Shops and Public Buildings*. Philadelphia: Lippincott, 1933.

Dabney, Thomas Ewing. *One Hundred Great Years: The Story of the Times Picayune from its founding to 1940*. Baton Rouge: Louisiana State University Press, 1944.

Damseaux, Emile de. *Voyage dans L'Amerique du Nord*. Paris: Hachette et Cie, 1878.

Dart, Albert Laplace, trans. "Ship Lists for Passengers Leaving France for Louisiana, 1718–24." *Louisiana Historical Quarterly*, Vol. 21 (October, 1938), 965–78.

Dart, Henry P., ed. "Decision Day in the Superior Council of Louisiana, March 5, 1746." *Louisiana Historical Quarterly*, Vol. 21 (October, 1938), 998–1020.

Dart, Henry P. "Family Meetings in French Period Louisiana." *Louisiana Historical Quarterly*, Vol. 3 (October, 1920), 543–47.

Dart, Henry P., trans. "First Law Regulating Land Grants in French Colonial Louisiana," *Louisiana Historical Quarterly*, Vol. 14 (July, 1931), 346.

Dart, Henry P. "Marriage Contracts of French Colonial Louisiana." *Louisiana Historical Quarterly*, Vol. 17 (April, 1934), 229–41.

David, Mother M., M.H.S. *Historical Summary of the Chapel of the Most Holy Sacrament Convent, 2321 Marais Street*. Lafayette, Louisiana: Sisters of the Most Holy Sacrament Motherhouse, 1971.

Davis, Jack. "New Orleans Art Deco Laundry Approaching Tragedy." *New Orleans States-Item*, March 13, 1974.

Davis, Jack. "An Art Deco Marvel Faces Demolition Peril." *New Orleans States-Item*, August 7, 1974.

De La Vergne, Pierre. "Early Economic Life in Louisiana." *Louisiana Historical Quarterly*, Vol. 26 (October, 1943), 915–36.

Delery, Simone de la Souchère. "Some French Soldiers Who Became Louisiana Educators." *Louisiana Historical Quarterly*, Vol. 31 (October, 1948), 853 (Collège d'Orléans).

Delery, Simone de la Souchère and Gladys Renshaw. *France d'Amerique*. Chicago: Otto F. Bond, 1932.

Desdunes, Rodolphe Lucien. *Our People and Our History*. Translated and edited by Sister Dorothea Olga McCants. Baton Rouge: Louisiana State University Press, 1973.

DeVoto, Bernard A. *Mark Twain's America, and Mark Twain at Work*. Boston: Houghton Mifflin & Co., 1967.

Dezert, G. Desdevises du. *La Louisiane a la Fin du 18e Siecle*. Paris: Edouard Champion and Emile Larose, 1914.

Digeste, General des Actes de Legislature du Territoire d' Orleans et de L'Etat de la Louisiana et des Ordonnances Du Gouverneur sous les Regimes Territoires. Vols. 1–3. New Orleans: Imprimerie Roche Frères, 1816.

Dunbar, Nelson and Alice. "People of Color in Louisiana." *Journal of Negro History*, Vol. 1 (1916), 361–76.

DuPratz, Le Page. *The History of Louisiana*. Edited by Joseph Tregle, Jr. Baton Rouge: Published for the Louisiana American Bicentennial Commission by Louisiana State University Press, 1975.

Eastwood, Sidney K. "The Pintado Papers." *New Orleans Genesis*, Vol. 3 (March, 1964), 137–87.

Evans, Harry H. "James Robb, Banker and Pioneer Railroad Builder of Ante-Bellum Louisiana." *Louisiana Historical Quarterly*, Vol. 23 (January, 1940), 213 (James A. Gasquet noted).

Everett, Donald Edward. "Emigrés and Militiamen: Free People of Color in New Orleans, 1803–1815." *Journal of Negro History*, Vol. 38 (1953), 377–402.

Fabre, E., surveyor. "The Rocheblaves of Colonial Louisiana." *Louisiana Historical Quarterly*, Vol. 18 (April, 1935), 332–45.

Faye, Stanley. "The Schism of 1805 in New Orleans, with Porée-Casa Calvo Letter." *Louisiana Historical Quarterly*. Vol. 22 (January, 1939), 98–125.

Federal Writers Project of the Works Progress Administration. *Louisiana, A Guide to the State*. New York: Hastings House, 1941.

Federal Writers Project of the Works Progress Administration. *New Orleans City Guide*. Boston: Houghton Mifflin Co., 1952.

Forner, Laura. "The Free People of Color in Louisiana and St. Domingo." *Journal of Social History*, Vol. 3 (1907), 406–30.

Fortier, Alcée. *History of Louisiana*. 4 vols. Paris: Goupil and Co.; New York: Manzi, Joyant and Co., 1904.

Fortier, Alcée. *Louisiana Studies: Literature, Customs of the Creoles*. New Orleans: F. F. Hansell & Brothers, 1894.

Frazier, E. Franklin. *The Free Negro Family: A Study of Family Origins Before the Civil War*. Nashville, Tenn.: Fisk University Press, 1932.

French, B. F. *History from the First Settlement of the Colony to O'Reilly's Departure in 1770*. Vol. 5 of *Historical Collections of Louisiana*. 1st series. New York: Lamport, Blakemans, and Law, 1853.

Gardner, J. M. *New Orleans Directory, Including Jefferson City, Gretna, Carrollton, Algiers, and McDonogh*. New Orleans: Gardner's, 1868.

Gayarré, Charles. *Creoles of History and Romance*. New Orleans: C. E. Hopkins, 1885.

Gayarré, Charles. *History of Louisiana*. 4 vols. Gretna, Louisiana: Pelican Publishing Co., 1965.

Genovese, Eugene D. *The Political Economy of Slavery: Studies in the Economy and Society of the Slave South*. New York: Vintage Books, 1967.

Genovese, Eugene D. *Roll, Jordan, Roll: The World the Slaves Made*. New York: Pantheon Books, 1972.

Giraud, Marcel. *Histoire de la Louisiane Française*. 4 vols. Paris: Presses Universitaires de France, 1953–74. Vol. 1: *Le Regne de Louis XIV, 1698–1715* (1953); Vol. 2: *Années de Transition, 1715–1717* (1958); Vol. 3: *L'Epoque de John Law, 1717–1720* (1966).

Giraud, Marcel. *A History of French Louisiana*. Translated by Joseph C. Lambert, with revisions and corrections by the author. Baton Rouge: Louisiana State University Press, 1974–. Vol. 1: *The Reign of Louis XIV, 1698–1715* (1974).

Gornay, P. F. de. "The Free Men of Color of Louisiana." *Lippincott's Monthly Magazine*, Vol. 53 (1894), 511–17.

Greiner, Meinrad, ed. *The Louisiana Digest: Laws of the Legislature of a General Nature, 1804–1841*. New Orleans: B. Levy, 1841.

Grima, Edgar. "The Notarial System of Louisiana." *Louisiana Historical Quarterly*, Vol. 10 (January, 1927), 76–81.

Guyol, Louise Hubert. "Grace King—A Southern Author in Her New Orleans Home." *Louisiana Historical Quarterly*, Vol. 6 (July, 1923), 365–77.

Hamilton, Thomas. *Men and Manners in North America*. 2nd American ed. Philadelphia: Carey, Lea, and Blanchard, 1833.

Harmon, Nolan B., Jr. *The Famous Case of Myra Clark Gaines*. Baton Rouge: Louisiana State University Press, 1946.

Heinrich, Pierre. *La Louisiane sous la Compagnie des Indes*. Paris: Guilmoto, n.d.

Hennick, Louis C., and E. H. Carlton. *The Streetcars of New Orleans, 1831–1965*. New Orleans: A. F. Laborde, 1965.

Higginbotham, Jay. *Fort Maurepas: The Birth of Louisiana*. Mobile, Alabama: Colonial Books, 1968.

Holmes, Jack D. L. *Honor and Fidelity: The Louisiana Infantry Regiment and Louisiana Militia Companies, 1766–1821*. Birmingham, Alabama: Jack D. L. Holmes, 1965.

Huber, Leonard. *Our Lady of Guadalupe Church*. New Orleans: The International Shrine of St. Jude, 150th anniversary ed., 1976.

Huber, Leonard, and Clarence Wagner. *The Great Mail: A Postal History of New Orleans*. State College, Pennsylvania: American Philatelic Society, 1949.

Hubert-Robert, Regine. *L'histoire Merveilleuse de la Louisiane Française*. New York: Edition de la Maison Française, 1941.

Humble, Sally Lacey. "The Ouachita Valley Expedition of DeSoto." *Louisiana Historical Quarterly*, Vol. 24 (July, 1942), 628 (Lafon map).

Jackson, Joy J. *New Orleans in the Gilded Age*. Baton Rouge: Louisiana State University Press, 1969.

Jaray, Gabriel-Louis. *L'empire Français de l'Amerique*. Paris: Armand Dolin, 1938.

Jewell, Edwin L., comp. *Jewell's Digest of the City Ordinances*. New Orleans: Jewell, 1882.

Kendall, John S. "Old New Orleans Houses and Some of the People Who Lived in Them." *Louisiana Historical Quarterly*, Vol. 20 (July, 1937), 794–819.

Kendall, John S. "The Strange Case of Myra Clark Gaines." *Louisiana Historical Quarterly*, Vol. 20 (January, 1937), 5–42.

King, Grace E. "Abstracts by William Price of State Papers Preserved in the Louisiana Historical Society with Notes." *Louisiana Historical Quarterly*, Vol. 1, Sec. 1 (January, 1917), 10.

King, Grace E. *Creole Families of New Orleans*. New York: Macmillan Co., 1921.

King, Grace E. *Madame Girard: Old French Teacher of New Orleans*. New Haven: Reprinted with permission from the *Yale Review*, 1922.

King, Grace E. *New Orleans—The Place and the People*. New York: Macmillan Co., 1915.

Kinnard, Lawrence, ed. *Spain in the Mississippi Valley, 1765–1794*. Vol. 2, Part 1. Washington, D.C.: Government Printing Office, 1946.

Kmen, Henry A. *Music in New Orleans: The Formative Years, 1791–1841*. Baton Rouge: Louisiana State University Press, 1966.

Kmen, Henry A. "The Roots of Jazz and the Dance in Place Congo: A Re-Appraisal." *Yearbook for Inter-American Musical Research*, vol. 8 (1972), 5–16.

Kniffen, Fred B. "Louisiana House Types." *Annals of the Association of American Geographers*, Vol. 26 (December, 1936), 179–93.

Latour, Arsène Lacarrière. *Historical Memoir of the War in West Florida and Louisiana in 1814–1815*. Translated by H. P. Nugent. Philadelphia, Pennsylvania: John Conrad, 1816.

Latrobe, Benjamin Henry Boneval. *Impressions Respecting New Orleans*. Introduction and editing by Samuel Wilson, Jr. New York: Columbia University Press, 1951.

Laussat, Pierre Clement de. *Memoirs of My Life*. Edited by Robert D. Bush; translated by Sister Agnes-Josephine Pastwa O.S.F. Historic New Orleans Collection Monograph Series. Baton Rouge and London: Louisiana State University Press, 1978.

LeBreton, Dagmar Renshaw. *Chahta-Ima: The Life of Adrien Rouquette*. Baton Rouge: Louisiana State University Press, 1947.

Ledet, Wilton P. "The History of the City of Carrollton-Land Grants." *Louisiana Historical Quarterly*, Vol. 21 (January, 1938), 229–81.

Lemann, Bernard. *Historic Sites Inventory*. New Orleans: Rader and Associates for the Regional Planning Commission, 1969.

Louisiana Historical Quarterly editorial staff. "Abstracts of Early French and Spanish Documents in the History of Louisiana." *Louisiana Historical Quarterly*, Vol. 1 (January, 1918), 224–25.

Louisiana Historical Quarterly editorial staff. "Almonester's Will." *Louisiana Historical Quarterly*, Vol. 6 (January, 1923), 21–34.

Louisiana Historical Quarterly editorial staff. "The History of Louisiana and Some of Its Leading Families." *Louisiana Historical Quarterly*, Vol. 1 (January 8, 1917), 95–98.

Louisiana Indians, 12,000 Years. New Orleans: Friends of the Cabildo, Louisiana State Museum, 1966.

Lugano, G., trans. "Records of the Superior Council of Louisiana." *Louisiana Historical Quarterly*, Vols. 23–26 (1940–43).

MacKay, Alex. *The Western World, Or Travels in the United States in 1846–47*. Philadelphia: Lea and Blanchard, 1849.

Marquis, Donald M. *In Search of Buddy Bolden*. Baton Rouge: Louisiana State University Press, 1978.

Martin, François Xavier. *The History of Louisiana*. New Orleans: James A. Gresham, 1882.

Margry, Pierre. *Decouverte et Etablissements des Français dans l'Ouest et dans Le Sud de L'Amerique Septentrionale*. Paris: Maisonneuve et Cie, 1879.

Matas, Rudolph. "An Evening with Gayarré." *Louisiana Historical Quarterly*, Vol. 33 (April, 1950), 269–93.

McDermott, John Francis. *The French in the Mississippi Valley*. Urbana: University of Illinois Press, 1965.

McDermott, John Francis. *The Spanish in the Mississippi Valley*. Urbana: University of Illinois Press, 1974.

Menn, Joseph K. *The Large Slaveowners of Louisiana*. New Orleans: Pelican Publishing Co., 1964.

Micelle, Jerry A. "From Law Court to Local Government: Metamorphosis of the Superior Council of French Louisiana." *Louisiana History*, Vol. 9 (Spring, 1968), 85–108.

Moehlenbock, Arthur Henry. "The German Drama on the New Orleans Stage." *Louisiana Historical Quarterly*, Vol. 26 (April, 1943), 373–79 (German Society of New Orleans).

Morazon, Ronald R. "Bicentennial Louisiana Almanac." *New Orleans Times-Picayune*, October 10, 24, November 28, December 5, 12, 16, 1976.

New Orleans and Southern Directory. New Orleans: Cohen Co., 1849–56.

New Orleans Bee, 1827–1923.

New Orleans City Directory. New Orleans: Polk Co., 1874–1900.

New Orleans Daily Crescent, 1848–69.

New Orleans Daily Delta, 1845–63.

New Orleans Daily Picayune, 1838–1914.

New Orleans Daily True Delta, 1849–66.

New Orleans Digest of Ordinances, Resolutions, Bylaws. New Orleans: Gaston Bruslé, 1836.

New Orleans Directory, 1832. New Orleans: Perey Co., 1832.

New Orleans Directory, 1832. New Orleans: Mygatt Co., 1832.

New Orleans Directory, 1841. New Orleans: Michel Co., 1841.

New Orleans Directory, 1842. New Orleans: Pitts and Clarke, 1842.

New Orleans Directory, 1857. New Orleans: Mygatt Co., 1857.

New Orleans Directory. New Orleans: Gardner Co., 1850–69.

New Orleans Directory. New Orleans: Edwards Co., 1870–73.

New Orleans Times-Democrat, 1881–1914.

New Orleans Times-Picayune, 1837–1978.

Norman, B. M. *New Orleans and Its Environs*. New Orleans: B. M. Norman; New York: D. Appleton and Co., 1845.

O'Conner, Stella. "The Charity Hospital of Louisiana at New Orleans: An Administrative and Financial History, 1736–1941." *Louisiana Historical Quarterly*, Vol. 31 (January, 1948), 21–39.

Olmstead, Frederick Law. *A Journey in the Seaboard Slave States*. New York: Mason Brothers, 1856.

O'Neill, Charles E., S.J. "Fine Arts and Literature of Nineteenth Century Louisiana Blacks." *Louisiana State Museum Conference on Louisiana's Black Heritage*, April 15–16, 1977.

Orleans Gazette and Commercial Register, 1804–22.

Orleans Parish School Board. *The New Orleans Book*. New Orleans: Searcy & Pfaff, 1919.

Padgett, James A. "Letters of James Brown to Henry Clay, 1804–35 Emigré Problems." *Louisiana Historical Quarterly*, Vol. 24 (October, 1941), 921–43.

Padgett, James A. "Some Documents Relating to the Batture Controversy in New Orleans (Deposition of Peter Dulcide Barran)." *Louisiana Historical Quarterly*, Vol. 23 (July, 1940), 679–732.

Patterson, Lindsay, comp. *International Library of Negro Life and History*. New York: New York Publishing Co., 1967.

Paxton, J. M. *The New Orleans Directory and Register*. New Orleans: Paxton, 1822.

Penicaut, André. *Fleur de Lys and Calumet: Being the Penicaut Narrative of French Adventure in Louisiana*. Edited and translated by Richebourg Gaillard McWilliams. Baton Rouge: Louisiana State University Press, 1953.

Perkins, A. E. *Who's Who in Colored Louisiana*. Baton Rouge, Louisiana: Perkins, 1930.

Pitot, Henry Clement. *James Pitot, 1761–1831: A Documentary Study*. New Orleans: Bocage Books, 1968.

Pittman, Philip. *The Present State of the European Settlements on the Mississippi*. London, 1770; reprinted, Cleveland: A. H. Clark, 1906.

Place Names of Jefferson Parish: What's In a Name? Metairie, Louisiana: Jefferson Parish Library, 1971.

Porteous, Laura L., trans. "Index to the Spanish Judicial Records of Louisiana." *Louisiana Historical Quarterly*, Vol. 16 (January, April, July, 1933), 151–69, 339–53, 515–34.

Porteous, Laura L. "Marriage Contracts of the Spanish Period in Louisiana." *Louisiana Historical Quarterly*, Vol. 9 (July, 1926), 385–97.

Price, Edith Dart, and Heloise H. Cruzat. "Inventory of the Estate of Jean Baptiste Prevost." *Louisiana Historical Quarterly*, Vol. 9 (July, 1926), 411–98.

Prichard, Walter. "Book Review: The Famous Case of Myra Clark Gaines, by Nolan B. Harmon, Jr." *Louisiana Historical Quarterly*, Vol. 30 (January, 1947), 338–42.

Prichard, Walter. "History of the Railroads of Louisiana." *Louisiana Historical Quarterly*, Vol. 30 (October, 1947), 1065–1325.

Reed, Merl E. *New Orleans and the Railroads—The Struggle for Commercial Empire, 1830–60*. Baton Rouge: Louisiana State University Press, 1966.

Reinders, Robert Clemens. "The Decline of the New Orleans Free Negro in the Decade Before the Civil War." *Journal of Mississippi History*, Vol. 24 (April, 1962), 88–98.

Reinders, Robert Clemens. "The Free Negro in New Orleans Economy, 1850–60." *Louisiana History*, Vol. 6 (Summer, 1965), 273–85.

Roberts, W. Adolphe. *Lake Pontchartrain*. The American Lake Series. Indianapolis: Bobbs-Merill, 1946.

Robertson, James A. *Louisiana Under the Rule of Spain, France, and the United States, 1785–1807*. Cleveland: Arthur H. Clark Co., 1911.

Robichaux, Albert, Jr., comp., trans., ed. *Louisiana Census and Militia Lists, 1770–1789*. Harvey, Louisiana: Robichaux, 1973.

Robin, C. C. *Voyages dans l'Interieur de la Louisiana*, Vol. 2. Paris: Librairie, F. Buisson, 1807.

Robin, C. C. *Voyage to Louisiana, 1803–1805*. Translated by Stuart O. Landry, Jr. New Orleans: Pelican Publishing Co., 1966.

Roncière, Charles de la. *Au Fil du Mississippi avec le Père Marquette*. Paris: Bloud et Gay, 1935.

Rose, Al. *Storyville, New Orleans*. Tuscaloosa: University of Alabama Press, 1974.

Rose, Al, and Edmond Souchon. *New Orleans Jazz—A Family Album*. Baton Rouge: Louisiana State University Press, 1967.

Roussel, Willis J. *Jottings of Louisiana: Illustrated Historical Sketch of the Most Illustrious Landmarks of New Orleans and the Only Remaining Buildings of Colonial Days*. New Orleans: Mendola, 1905.

Rousseve, Charles B. *The Negro in New Orleans*. New Orleans: Archives of Negro History, 1969.

Rowland, Dunbar, ed. *Official Letter Books of W. C. C. Claiborne, 1801–1816*. Jackson, Mississippi: State Department of Archives and History, 1917.

"St. Augustine-Surgi House." *New Orleans Times-Picayune*, April 10, 1949, pp. 10–12.

Samuel, Martha Ann Brett, and Ray Samuel. *The Great Days of the Garden District*. New Orleans: Parents' League of the Louise S. McGehee School, 1961.

Saucier, Roger. *Recent Geomorphic History of the Pontchartrain Basin*. Louisiana State University Studies, Coastal Studies Series, no. 9. Baton Rouge: Louisiana State University Press, 1963.

Schertz, Helen Pitkin. *Legends of Louisiana*. New Orleans: New Orleans Journal, 1922.

Seebold, Herman de B. *Old Louisiana Plantation Homes and Family Trees*. 2 vols. New Orleans: Pelican Publishing Co., 1944.

Segura, Pearl. "Sources of Spanish Records in Louisiana." *Proceedings of the Fourth Annual Genealogical Institute*. Baton Rouge: Louisiana State University Press, 1961.

"New Orleans and Bayou St. John in 1766." *Louisiana Historical Quarterly*,

Vol. 6 (January, 1923), 19–20.

Simon, Benedict. *The Southern Index, No. 1.* New Orleans: B. Simon, 1870.

Soard, L. *Soard's City Directory of New Orleans.* New Orleans: Soard's Directory Co., 1870–90.

Sparks, W. H. *The Memories of Fifty Years.* Philadelphia: Claxton, Remsen, and Haffelfinger, n.d.; Macon, Georgia: Burke and Co., 1870.

Stahl, Annie Lee West. "The Free Negro in Ante-Bellum Louisiana." *Louisiana Historical Quarterly,* Vol. 25 (April, 1942), 301–96.

Sterkx, H. E. *The Free Negro in Ante-Bellum Louisiana.* Cranbury, New Jersey: Associated University Presses, 1972.

Sterling, David Lee, ed. "New Orleans, 1801: An Account by John Pintard." *Louisiana Historical Quarterly,* Vol. 34 (July, 1951), 222–24.

Stewart, John Wesley. *Faubourg Tremé.* Forthcoming.

Stoddard, Major Amos. *Sketches, Historical and Descriptive of Louisiana.* Philadelphia: Matthew Carey, 1812.

Suarez, Matt. *This Old House.* New Orleans: Bicentennial Commission, 1976.

Surrey, Nancy Miller. *The Commerce of Louisiana During the French Regime, 1699–1763.* New York: Columbia University Press, 1916.

Surrey, Nancy Miller. "History of the Calendar of Documents in the Archives of Paris Relating to the Mississippi Valley." *Louisiana Historical Quarterly,* Vol. 7 (October, 1924), 551–63.

Surrey, N. Miller. "The Commerce of Louisiana During the French Regime, 1699–1763." *Columbia University Studies in History, Economics, and Public Law,* Vol. 7, no. 1 (1916).

Swanton, John R. "Indian Tribes of the Lower Mississippi Valley and the Adjacent Coast of the Gulf of Mexico." *Smithsonian Bulletin,* No. 43 (1911).

Tinker, Edward Larocque. *Creole City: Its Past and Its People.* New York: Longmans, Green, 1953.

Trotter, James M. *New Orleans: Musical and General Culture of Its Colored Citizens.* Boston, 1880. (William Ransom Hogan Jazz Archives, Tulane University Library.)

Vignaud, Henry. *Le Problème de Peuplement Initial de l'Amerique.* Paris: Au Siège de la Société, 1922.

Ville, Winston de. "Manuscript Sources in Louisiana for the History of the French in the Mississippi Valley." In *The French in the Mississippi Valley,* edited by John F. McDermott. Urbana: University of Illinois Press, 1965.

Villiers, Baron Marc de. *Histoire de la Fondation de la Nouvelle Orléans.* Paris: Imprimerie Nationale, 1917.

Waldo, Rudolph H. *Notarial Archives of Orleans Parish.* New Orleans: Orleans Parish Plan Book, Notarial Archives, 1946.

Warburg, Eugene. "Portraiture." *Virginia Historical Society Magazine,* Vol. 81 (January, 1918), 218–30.

Waring, George E., and George Washington Cable. *Social Statistics of Cities, History of and Present Condition of New Orleans.* 10th United States Census, Department of the Interior. Washington, D.C.: Government Printing Office, 1881. (Bound with *Commercial Social and Medical Statistics of New Orleans.*)

Warner, Charles. "New Orleans, Extra Illustrated." *Harper's New Monthly Magazine,* Vol. 74 (January, 1887), 186–206.

Warren, Harris G. "Book Review: Handbook for Translating Spanish Documents." *Louisiana Historical Quarterly,* Vol. 25 (January, 1942), 536.

West-Stahl, Annie L. "The Free Negro in Ante-Bellum Louisiana." *Louisiana Historical Quarterly,* Vol. 25 (1942), 301–96.

Whitney, Thomas M. *Whitney's New Orleans Directory and Mississippi Almanac.* New Orleans: Whitney's, 1811.

Whittington, G. P. "The Journal of Dr. John Sibley of Natchitoches, 1757–1837." *Louisiana Historical Quarterly,* Vol. 10 (October, 1927), 474–97.

Willey, Nathan. "Education of Colored Population of Louisiana." *Harper's New Monthly Magazine,* Vol. 33 (July, 1886), 244–50.

Williams, E. Russ, Jr. "Genealogical Research in Louisiana." *Proceedings of the Third Annual Genealogical Institute.* Baton Rouge: Louisiana State University Press, 1960.

Williams, William H. "The History of Carrollton Land Titles." *Louisiana Historical Quarterly,* Vol. 22 (January, 1939), 190–231.

Wilson, Samuel, Jr. "Almonester: Philanthropist and Builder in New Orleans." *The Spanish in the Mississippi Valley.* Edited by John F. McDermott. Urbana: University of Illinois Press, 1974.

Wilson, Samuel, Jr. *A Guide to the Early Architecture of New Orleans.* New Orleans: Wilson, 1964.

Wilson, Samuel, Jr. *New Orleans: The Vieux Carré Historic District Demonstration Study; Technical Supplement to Plan and Program.* New Orleans: Bureau of Governmental Research, 1968.

Wilson, Samuel, Jr., and Leonard V. Huber. *St. Louis Cemeteries of New Orleans.* New Orleans: St. Louis Cathedral, 1963.

Wilson, Theodore Brantner. *The Black Codes of the South.* Birmingham: University of Alabama Press, 1965.

Winston, James E., ed. "Faithful Picture of the Political Situation in New Orleans at the Close of the Last and Beginning of the Present Year, 1807." *Louisiana Historical Quarterly,* Vol. 2 (July, 1928), 359–433.

Winston, James E. "Free Negro in New Orleans, 1803–1860." *Louisiana Historical Quarterly,* Vol. 21 (October, 1938), 1075–85.

Wood, Minter. "Life in New Orleans in the Spanish Period." *Louisiana Historical Quarterly,* Vol. 22 (July, 1939), 642–709.

Woodson, Carter G. *Free Negro Heads of Families in the United States in 1830.* Washington, D.C.: Association for the Study of Negro Life and History, 1925.

Woodson, Carter G. *Free Negro Owners of Slaves in the United States in 1830.* New York: Negro University Press, 1968.

MAPS AND SURVEYS

"Atlas of the City of New Orleans, Louisiana." Elisha Robinson; New York, 1883.

"Carte Generale du Territoire d'Orléans . . ." Barthélémy Lafon, 1804.

"Carte Particulière du Fleuve St. Louis . . ." Ayer Collection, Newberry Library, Chicago.

Collection of Real Estate Maps. Real Estate Office, City Hall, New Orleans.

Dahlman-Junod Map and Survey Collection.

"Figurativo de las diligencias mandadas por decreto del dia." Carlos Trudeau, c. 1789. Copy of map by M. Hardie, city engineer (March 5, 1912), City Engineer's Office, New Orleans.

Lawyers Title Insurance Corporation, New Orleans. "New Orleans Savings Institute Plan Book." Allain d'Hemecourt, deputy city surveyor, 1875–1876.

Lawyers Title Insurance Corporation, New Orleans. "Plan Books." D. M. Brosman, city surveyor, c. 1886.

Lawyers Title Insurance Corporation, New Orleans. "Plan Book." Allain d'Hemecourt, city surveyor.

Lawyers Title Insurance Corporation, New Orleans. "Sketch Book." Louis Pilié, city surveyor, 1832.

"Map of New Orleans and Vicinity, 1834." Charles Zimpel; Historic New Orleans Collection.

"Map of the State of Louisiana . . ." John La Tourette, 1845, 1853.

"Map Showing Drainage to the Rear of the City of New Orleans." Joseph Pilié, 1825. City Engineers Office, New Orleans.

"Map Showing Land Ownership Between Bayou Road and Carondelet Canal and the Various Canals Projected Throughout the Colonial Period." City Engineers Office, New Orleans, c. 1812.

"Map Showing the Canals and Waterways Beyond the French Quarter for a Drainage Plan (title torn), 1818." Jacques Tanesse; E 11–3119, City Engineer's Office, New Orleans.

"Map Showing the Landing of the British Army, 1815." Major A. Lacarrière Latour, late principal engineer of 7th Military District, U.S. Army; Chalmette National Historical Park and Battlefield.

"New Orleans, Louisiana." New York: Sanborne Map and Publishing Co., 1876, 1896.

New Orleans Notarial Archives. "Plan Books." 150 vols.

"Outline of Index Maps of New Orleans." Historic New Orleans Collection, New Orleans, 1883.

Pintado Papers, 1800. Vincente Pintado and Carlos Trudeau; Louisiana Historical Center, Library.

"Plan au prolongement projeté de la rue de l'Esplanade jusqu'au Bayou St. Jean." April 26, 1822. Joseph Pilié; City Engineer's Office, New Orleans.

"Plan de deux lots de terre situés dans la première Municipalité." January–May, 1846. Act of J. Cuvillier, notary; New Orleans Notarial Archives.

"Plan de la Nouvelle Orléans, 1 mars 1753." Collection of Samuel Wilson, Jr., New Orleans.

"Plan de la Nouvelle Orléans, 1798." Carlos Trudeau.

"Plan de la Nouvelle Orléans, 1816." Jacques Tanesse; Historic New Orleans Collection, New Orleans.

"Plan de la Terre du Collège d'Orléans ayant une superficie de trente-sept terrains trois quarts, 20 mars, 1812." Jacques Tanesse; City Engineer's Office, New Orleans.

"Plan de la Ville et des Faubourgs incorporés de la Nouvelle Orleans, y compris les 600 verges de communes, et de la propriété acquiés par La Corporation de M. Claude Tremé, 20 juin, 1812." Jacques Tanesse, city surveyor. Copy of this plan hangs framed on the wall of the New Orleans Notarial Archives.

"Plan de l'Habitation de M. de Pontalba situeé sur on le chemin de St. Jean distruite pour être vendu en divers lots, 9 janvier, 1812." Plan book 15, folio 1; New Orleans Notarial Archives.

"Plan de Quinze Lots de Terre, Faubourg Tremé, janvier 1839." Louisiana Historical Center, New Orleans.

"Plan d'un Lot de Terre Située au Faubourg Tremé, 13 juin, 1836." Act of F. de Armas, notary; New Orleans Notarial Archives.

"Plan de Verifications d'Arpentages commencés en 1796 par Ordres du Gouverneur General le Baron de Carondelet, et continués par ordre du Gouverneur Daniel Gayoso De Lemos jusques au 4 Decembre 1798." City Engineer's Office, New Orleans.

"Plan of Fort St. Charles, April 27, 1821." Joseph Pilié, city surveyor; Plan book 100, folio 23; New Orleans Notarial Archives.

"Plan of New Orleans." Lt. Philip Pittman, c. 1765.

"Plan of New Orleans, 1798." Copy of the 1798 map by Joseph Pilié in 1838; also inscribed: "Habana 3 noviembre 1819, Pintado." Louisiana Historical Center, Accession number 9294, New Orleans.

"Plan of New Orleans, 1841." L. Hirt; Historic New Orleans Collection.

"Plan of New Orleans Capitol City of Louisiana." Dumont de Montigny; Ayer Collection, Newberry Library, Chicago, n.d., c. 1730; Collection Guerre-Etat Major, Vincennes, n.d., c. 1732.

"Plan of New Orleans Riverfront and Fort St. Charles, 1803." Boqueto de Woiserie; Historic New Orleans Collection.

"Plan of the City of New Orleans and the Adjacent Plantations." Compiled in accordance with an Ordinance of the Illustrious Ministry and Royal Charter, December, 1798. Carlos Trudeau; Cabildo, Louisiana State Museum, New Orleans.

"Plan of 249 Lots of Ground, Second Municipality, New Orleans, 1847." Louisiana Historical Center, New Orleans.

"Portion of a Map Illustrating Fort St. John and the Limits of the Concession of M. de Morand." Prepared by Carlos Trudeau in 1797, along with a lot survey prepared by Jacques Tanesse, 1810. City Engineer's Office, New Orleans.

Records of the City Council, 1770–1792: Survey showing the location of the Lepers' Colony on Bayou Road. Book 4083; Louisiana Historical Center, New Orleans.

"Survey of Right of Way of the Canal Carondelet from Rampart Street to Hagan Avenue, New Orleans, 23rd of November, 1923." Frank H. Waddill, consultant civil engineer.

MANUSCRIPTS AND RECORDS

Baptism Records, St. Louis Cathedral Archives.

Bill of Exception to the Evidence, Heirs of Lafayette vs. Mme Pontalba et al., Heirs of C. Griffon, Lebreton D'Orgenois. Northeast Circuit Court, Louisiana; Federal Courts Storage Center for Southwest Region, Fort Worth, Texas.

Bremensul, L., Jr. "Orleans Street Parish Prison." Student paper in Louisiana Architecture course; Samuel Wilson, Jr., Tulane University, December, 1975.

Campbell, Clara. "Political Life of Louisiana Negroes, 1865–1890." Master of Arts thesis, Tulane University, New Orleans, 1971.

Christian, Marcus. Papers. Earl K. Long Library, University of New Orleans.

De la Harpe, Bernard. Historical Journal of the Establishment of the French in Louisiana. Works Progress Administration Writer's Project, 1940.

Documents of the City Council of New Orleans, Book 4084. Louisiana Historical Center, New Orleans.

"The Environs of New Orleans." From scrapbook of articles of New Orleans Daily Crescent, 1866, no. 22 and no. 92. Special Collections Division, Tulane University Library.

Everett, Donald Edward. "Legislation Concerning Free People of Color in New Orleans, 1840–60." Master of Arts thesis, Tulane University, New Orleans, 1949.

Everett, Donald Edward. "The Free Persons of Color in New Orleans, 1803–1865." Dissertation for Doctor of Philosophy degree, Tulane University, New Orleans, 1952.

Funeral Books, St. Louis Cathedral Archives.

Indenture Books: 1814, 1820, 1846. New Orleans Public Library, Louisiana Division.

Johnson, Clifton H. "Some Manuscript Sources in Louisiana Archival Repositories." Johnson Collection, Amistad Research Center, Dillard University, New Orleans.

Laussat, Pierre Clement de. Memoirs and Correspondence of Laussat, 1803–04 to Spanish Officials Relative to the Cession of Louisiana. Survey of Federal Archives in Louisiana, 1940 (typescript).

Lawson, Frederick Lee. "The Marine Hospital of McDonogh, 1838–1861." Manuscript, Special Collections Division, Tulane University Library.

Marriage Records, St. Louis Cathedral Archives.

McConnell, Roland C. "Louisiana's Black Military History, 1729–1866." Louisiana State Museum Conference on Louisiana's Black Heritage, April 15–16, 1977.

McDermott, Elizabeth. "Urban Renewal in the Tremé Area." Typescript, University of New Orleans.

McGowan, Emma. "Free People of Color in New Orleans, 1803–1860." Master of Arts thesis, Tulane University, 1939.

Meyer, Robert, Jr. "We Name Our Schools." Unpublished paper, Special Collections Division, Tulane University Library, n.d.

New Orleans City Engineers Records. City Hall, New Orleans.

New Orleans City Hall Real Estate Office Records.

New Orleans, Dillard University. Duboclet-Grandjean Papers.

New Orleans Mayor's Office. Register of Free Colored Persons Entitled to Remain in the State: 1840–1857, 1856–1859, 1859–1861, 1861–1864. Louisiana Division, New Orleans Public Library.

New Orleans Resolutions and Ordinances: July 24, 1805–February 21, 1806. Louisiana Division, New Orleans Public Library.

New Orleans Notarial Archives. Notaries consulted:

Almonester, Andrés	March 10, 1770–May 28, 1782
Andry, Charles G.	March 16, 1838–February 4, 1891
Barnett, Edward	March 16, 1838–November 1, 1872
Beck, Theodore A.	May 23, 1910–March 1, 1930
Bienvenu, Alexander E.	November 12, 1846–July 16, 1879
Boudousquie, Adolphe	March 19, 1850–December 22, 1866
Boudousquie, Charles	December 26, 1837–March 14, 1850
Bouny, Eusebe	May 5, 1857–November 12, 1896
Broutin, Narcisse	May 18, 1799–July 29, 1819
Bunel, Antoine	September 14, 1735–February 25, 1738
Castellanos, Henry C.	March 14, 1861–April 29, 1861
Cenas, Hilary B.	June 7, 1834–September 27, 1859
Chantalon, Augustin	Miscellaneous and Succession Books, 56840–67485
Chiapella, Archille	February 8, 1839–March 27, 1857
Christy, George W.	November 15, 1865–January 20, 1891
Christy, William	May 25, 1827–April 28, 1857
Commagère, Ernest	January 25, 1856–May 18, 1897
Conand, Paul A.	July 19, 1880–May 11, 1892
Cuvellier, Pierre C.	May 8, 1850–November 28, 1874
Cuvillier, Joseph	June 23, 1830–November 28, 1874
de Armas, Charles	February 25, 1833–January 18, 1836
de Armas, Christoval	September 14, 1815–December 16, 1829
de Armas, Felix, Sr.	August 18, 1823–October 4, 1839
de Armas, Felix, Jr.	July 28, 1858–January 30, 1862
de Armas, Michel	August 1, 1809–August 1, 1809
de Armas, Octave	June 26, 1828–August 25, 1889 (No Acts 1863–1864)
Doriocourt, André D., Jr.	November 21, 1884–November 23, 1891
Dreyfous, Abel	March 7, 1845–October 25, 1892
Dreyfous, Felix J.	December 16, 1881–September 7, 1946
Drouet, Onesiphore	May 11, 1844–November 26, 1879
Ducatel, Amedée	February 10, 1836–September 19, 1890 (No Acts in 1863–1865)
Ducatel, Oscar	June 24, 1868–March 19, 1889
Ducros, Joseph	October, 1739–November 10, 1766
Garic, Jean Baptiste	June 6, 1739–September 23, 1779
Grima, Alfred	April 16, 1867–June 25, 1870
Grima, Edgar	October 6, 1869–May 14, 1930
Grima, Felix	December 19, 1833–December 15, 1885 (Missing April 25, 1845–June 5, 1857)
Guyol, Thèodore	April 29, 1845–April 10, 1893 (No Records 1863–1866)
Henri, Nicolas	October 11, 1745–October 6, 1749
Hermann, Lucien	November 12, 1839–March 19, 1850
Janin, Charles	March 4, 1828–April 22, 1833
Ker, Robert J.	April 4, 1850–August 4, 1886
Kernion, Huchet de	July 8, 1766–February 20, 1769
Lafitte, Marc	May 16, 1810–May 13, 1826
LaMothe, Guillaume	October 23, 1766–February 18, 1769
Laresche, Paul E.	November 15, 1845–June 24, 1871 (No Records for June, 1862–August, 1865)
LeGardeur, Gustave, Sr.	April 26, 1833–August 3, 1837
LeGardeur, Gustave, Jr.	June 1, 1867–June 28, 1909
Morel, Christoval	August 14, 1868–March 17, 1884
Morel, Octave	October 26, 1864–October 26, 1894
Mossy, Jules	February 20, 1833–June 3, 1881
Pedesclaux, Felix	March 28, 1828–May 3, 1830
Pedesclaux, Hugues	December 29, 1829–March 17, 1862
Pedesclaux, Philippe	August 26, 1816–July 10, 1826
Pedesclaux, Pierre	March 15, 1788–April 20, 1816
Pollock, Carlile	April 4, 1814–April 1, 1845
Queyrouze, J. Maxime	June 14, 1897–April 8, 1933
Rossard, Michel	March 21, 1735–April 8, 1735
Salmon, Gatien	September 26, 1739–October 24, 1739
Seghers, Theodore	March 1, 1828–May 28, 1846
Stringer, Charles	November 17, 1858–June 30, 1876
Stringer, Greenbury R.	March 24, 1843–September 7, 1849
Theard, Paul E.	May 9, 1853–June 20, 1890

Obituary Files. New Orleans Public Library, Louisiana Division.

Orleans Parish Conveyance Office Books. Civil District Court Building.

Orleans Parish Mortgage Office Books. Civil District Court Building.

Orleans Parish Assessment Records. Civil District Court Building.

Orleans Parish Will Books. Civil District Court Building and New Orleans Public Library.

Proceedings of the City Council of New Orleans. City Archives, New Orleans Public Library.

Puckett, Erastus P. "The Free Negro in New Orleans to 1860." Master of Arts thesis, Tulane University, New Orleans, 1907.

Records of Building Permits, 1883–1887. City Archives Department, New Orleans Public Library.

Records of the New Orleans City Council, 1770–1792: Book 4083. Louisiana Historical Center, New Orleans.

Records of the New Orleans City Council, 1794–1803: Book 4087. Louisiana Historical Center, New Orleans.

Records of the New Orleans City Council, 1815–1822: Book 4089. Louisiana Historical Center, New Orleans.

Richardson, Joe M. FSY. "The American Missionary Association and Black Education in Louisiana, 1862–1878." *Louisiana State Museum Conference on Louisiana's Black Heritage*, April 15–16, 1977.

Rowland, Dunbar. *Mississippi Provincial Archives*. Jackson, Miss., 1917.

St. Louis Cathedral Archives. Cemetery Records, New Orleans.

Stahl, Annie Lee. "The Free Negro in Antebellum Louisiana." Master of Arts thesis, Louisiana State University, Baton Rouge, 1934.

Transit Rider's Digest, 1950–1978. New Orleans Public Service.

United States Census of New Orleans, Louisiana, 1850. Microfilm Collection, University of New Orleans.

Walker, John E., surveyor. Personal Notes and Files. Cotton Exchange Building, New Orleans.

Weber, Stella. "History of Charitable Donations in New Orleans." Master of Social Work thesis, Tulane University, 1935. Tulane University Library, Special Collections Division.

Works Progress Administration. *Historic American Building Survey*. Richard Koch, district officer, New Orleans, 1933–34.

Works Progress Administration. Translation of the *Despatches of the Spanish Governors of Louisiana, 1775–1792*. Unpublished, Louisiana Historical Center, New Orleans, 1940.

Works Progress Administration. Translation of the *Records of the Superior Council Proceedings*. Black Books, Document Nos. 148, 2018, 2329, Boxes 26, 53, 57. Louisiana Historical Center, New Orleans. (Cited in notes as Black Books.)

INDEX

INDEX

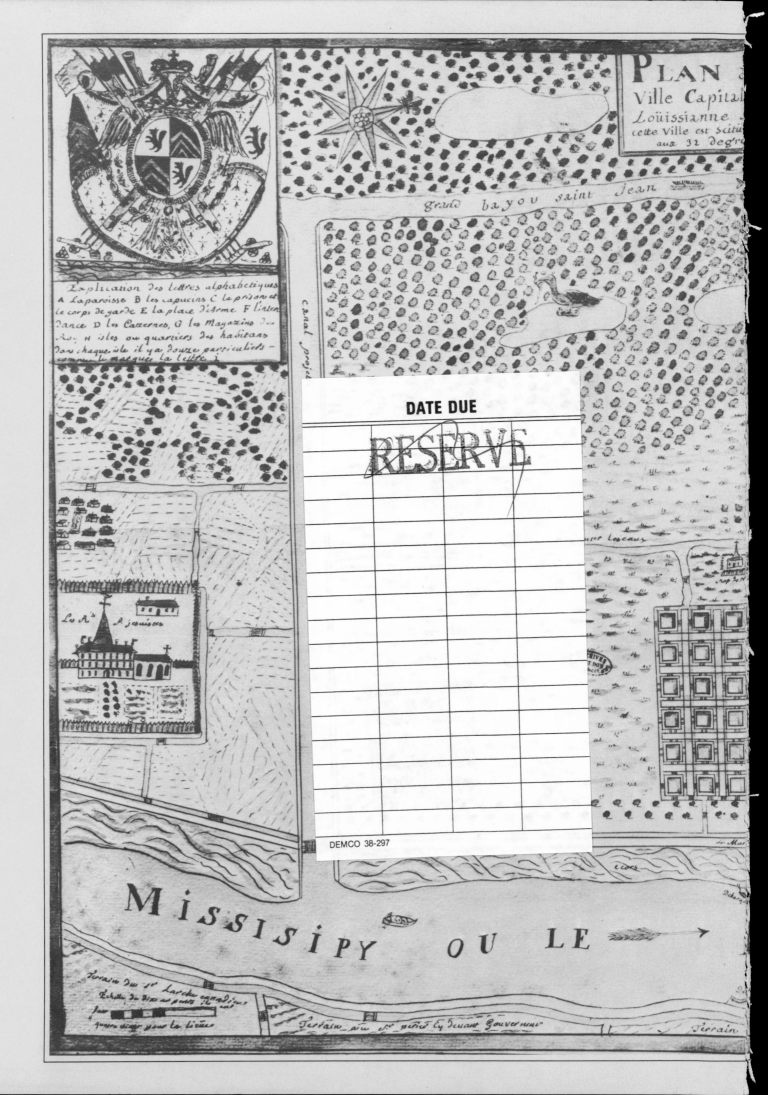